THE YALE PAPERS
ANTISEMITISM IN COMPARATIVE PERSPECTIVE

THE YALE PAPERS

ANTISEMITISM IN COMPARATIVE PERSPECTIVE

Charles Asher Small
Editor

ISGAP © 2015

INSTITUTE FOR THE STUDY OF GLOBAL ANTISEMITISM AND POLICY

Honorary President
Professor Elie Wiesel

Executive Director
Charles Asher Small

Co-Chairs of the International Academic Board of Advisors
Professor Irwin Cotler
Professor Alan Dershowitz

Chair of ISGAP Asia
Jesse Friedlander

Director of ISGAP, Israel
Mala Tabory

Director of ISGAP, Italy
Robert Hassan

Co-Directors of ISGAP, France
Glen Feder
Gunther Jikeli

Director of ISGAP, Canada
Michelle Whiteman

Director of ISGAP, Chile
Oscar Kleinkopf

ISGAP
165 East 56th Street, 2nd Floor
New York, New York 10022
Phone: 212-230-1840
Fax: 212-230-1842
www.isgap.org

The opinions expressed in this work are those of the author(s) and do not necessarily reflect the views of the Institute for the Study of Global Antisemitism and Policy, its officers, or the members of its boards.

Cover design and layout by AETS
Cover image by Kengphotographer / Shutterstock

ISBN 978 1 515057 79 6

In memory of Robert Wistrich (ז"ל)

An eminent and respected scholar who dedicated his life to illuminating the origins, history, and contemporary manifestations of antisemitism.

In memory of Berthe Kayitesi

Through her brilliant writing and speaking, Berthe was a bright light that illuminated the memory of the innocents murdered during the Rwandan genocide. She also had a profound understanding of the significance of the Holocaust and the dangers posed by contemporary antisemitism and the demonization of Israel, both for the Jewish people and for humanity as a whole. She was a true intellectual and a loving mother, daughter, sister, and friend.

Table of Contents

Introduction 1
    Charles Asher Small

SEMINAR SERIES 2005-2006

Anti-Israel Sentiment Predicts Antisemitism in Europe 5
    Edward H. Kaplan and Charles A. Small

The Road to an Internationally Accepted Definition of Antisemitism 19
    Dina Porat

SEMINAR SERIES 2006-2007

Hitler's Legacy: Islamic Antisemitism in the Middle East 33
    Matthias Küntzel

Continuities, Discontinuities, and Contingencies: Anti-Alienism,
Antisemitism, and Anti-Zionism in Twentieth-Century South Africa 43
    Milton Shain

WORKING PAPERS 2007

Anti-Zionism and Antisemitism: Cosmopolitan Reflections 57
    David Hirsh

This Green and Pleasant Land: Britain and the Jews 175
    Shalom Lappin

SEMINAR SERIES 2007-2008

Never Again? When Holocaust Memory Becomes Empty Rhetoric,
a Diplomatic Tool, and a Weapon against Israel 201
    Walter Reich

Leo Strauss as a Jewish Thinker 215
    Steven Smith

The Academic and Public Debate over the Meaning of the
"New Antisemitism" 225
    Roni Stauber

SEMINAR SERIES 2008-2009

Western Culture, the Holocaust, and the Persistence of Antisemitism 237
   Catherine Chatterley

Demonizing Israel: Political and Religious Consequences among Israelis 255
   Yossi Klein Halevi

Uncivil Society: Ideology, the Durban Strategy, and Antisemitism 263
   Gerald Steinberg

CONFERENCE ON THE PSYCHOLOGICAL IMPACT OF THE THREAT OF CONTEMPORARY GENOCIDAL ANTISEMITISM 2009

Victims of Success: How Envious Antisemitism Foments Genocidal
Intent and Undermines Moral Outrage 287
   Peter Glick

Why Well-Intentioned Westerners Fail to Grasp the Dangers Associated
with Islamic Antisemitism: Some Arguments Considered 299
   Neil Kressel

Trauma in Disguise: The Effects of Antisemitism 329
   Hadar Lubin

Mixed Emotional Needs of Israeli-Jews as a Potential Source of
Ambivalence in their Response to the Iranian Challenge 337
   Nurit Shnabel and John F. Dovidio

WORKING PAPERS 2009

Global Antisemitism: Assault on Human Rights 347
   Irwin Cotler

The Principles and Practice of Iran's Post-Revolutionary Foreign Policy 363
   Brandon Friedman

Missing from the Map: Feminist Theory and the Omission of Jewish
Women 379
   Jennifer Roskies

WILLIAM PRUSOFF HONORARY LECTURE 2009

1948 as Jihad 397
   Benny Morris

SEMINAR SERIES 2009-2010

Jews in China: Legends, History, and New Perspectives 407
   Pan Guang

Our World of Contradictions: Antisemitism, Anti-Tutsi-ism, and
Never Again 415
   Berthe Kayitesi

Two Steps Forward, One Step Back: Diplomatic Progress in Combating
Antisemitism 427
   Michael Whine

WORKINGS PAPERS 2010

Memetics and the Viral Spread of Antisemitism through
"Coded Images" in Political Cartoons 435
   Yaakov Kirschen

From Sayyid Qutb to Hamas: The Middle East Conflict and the
Islamization of Antisemitism 457
   Bassam Tibi

WILLIAM PRUSOFF HONORARY LECTURE 2010

Israel, Jordan, and Palestine: One State, Two States, or Three? 485
   Asher Susser

SEMINAR SERIES 2010-2011

A "Paradise of Parasites": Hannah Arendt, Antisemitism, and the
Legacies of Empire... 497
   Dorian Bell

"I Don't Know Why They Hate Us—I Don't Think We Did Anything
Bad to Hurt Them" 513
   Nora Gold

Introduction

Charles Asher Small*

Antisemitism is a highly complex and, at times, perplexing form of hatred. It spans history and has infected many societies, religious and philosophical movements, and even civilizations. In the aftermath of the Holocaust, some contend that antisemitism illustrates the limitations of humanity itself. Manifestations of antisemitism emerge in numerous ideologically-based narratives and in the constructed identities of belonging and otherness such as race and ethnicity, nationalisms, and anti-nationalisms. The investigation of antisemitism has a long and impressive intellectual and research history. It remains a topic of ongoing political importance and scholarly engagement. However, when it comes to the formal study of antisemitism, especially in its contemporary manifestations, such as extreme anti-Israel practice and sentiment and the growth of Islamist antisemitism in the West and the Middle East, there is an unwillingness within the academy to address the topic in accordance with its traditions of serious and unfettered intellectual inquiry. In fact, some might argue that, in this politically correct, postmodern moment, the academy in general has actually been guilty of antisemitism as a result of its refusal to engage with these important issues in an open and honest manner and its attempts to silence those who seek to challenge the new status quo. In other words, the academy itself has become a purveyor of antisemitism in contemporary society.

In 2004, the Institute for the Study of Global Antisemitism and Policy (ISGAP) was established with the aim of promoting the interdisciplinary study of antisemitism—with a focus on the contemporary context—and publishing high-caliber academic research in this area. ISGAP's mission encompasses the study of such subjects as the changing historical phases of antisemitism, regional variations, and how hatred of the Jewish people relates to other forms of hate. From the outset, the aims and objectives of ISGAP have been supported by scholars from many disciplines and countries and by a group of dedicated philanthropists initially led by the great humanitarian William (Bill) Prusoff.

ISGAP is committed to countering efforts to sweep antisemitism under the carpet by providing scholarly research, academic programming, curriculum development, and publications of unassailable quality. It is also the only interdisciplinary research organization that is seeking to confront and combat antisemitism within academia on a practical and ideological level. ISGAP aims to ensure that future generations of

---

* Founder and Executive Director of the Institute for the Study of Global Antisemitism and Policy (ISGAP); Koret Distinguished Fellow, Hoover Institution, Stanford University.

scholars and professionals are both aware of the destructive nature of antisemitism and determined to eradicate it from academia and society in general.

It is against this backdrop that ISGAP approached Yale University with a view to establishing an academic research center focusing on the interdisciplinary study of antisemitism. After determining that such a center would meet all its administrative, financial, and academic requirements, the university inaugurated the Yale Initiative for the Interdisciplinary Study of Antisemitism (YIISA) in 2006. It was the first center of its kind to be based at a North American university. ISGAP's Board of Trustees supported and funded all of YIISA's activities, co-sponsoring its seminar series and various other events and paying the salaries of its staff, including a full-time program coordinator, graduate and post-doctoral research fellows, visiting research scholars and professors, and undergraduate interns.

YIISA offered a successful graduate and post-graduate fellowship program and implemented a robust programming agenda. During its initial five-year mandate, YIISA hosted well over a hundred lectures by leading scholars from around the world in the framework of a high-level interdisciplinary seminar series entitled "Antisemitism in Comparative Perspective." It also organized three major international conferences, including the largest-ever academic gathering on the study antisemitism in August 2010, entitled "Global Antisemitism: A Crisis of Modernity."[1] In addition, it hosted special events, symposiums, and other gatherings at Yale University in New Haven and in New York, Washington, London, and Berlin. Throughout this period, YIISA fellows produced almost fifty papers, a significant portion of which were included in peer-review journals, published eight books and eight working papers, and participated in numerous academic conferences, policy forums, and other important gatherings. All this made YIISA one of the most active and productive academic entities at Yale University during its all-too-brief existence, which ended when the university decided not to renew its mandate for reasons that have never been properly substantiated. In fact, for the first time at Yale University, an academic review committee headed by Ian Shapiro not only closed a vibrant research center but did so while classifying its report as confidential and refusing to share it with any staff, faculty, or philanthropists associated with the center.[2]

Despite this minor setback, ISGAP has continued to flourish as an independent academic institute that works closely with leading scholars and top tier universities in the United States and around the world. Among its various activities, ISGAP currently runs academic seminar series at Harvard University, McGill University, Stanford University's Hoover Institution, and Columbia University Law School. As

---

[1] In 2013, a leading academic publisher published a selection of the papers presented at this conference. See Charles A. Small, ed., *Global Antisemitism: A Crisis of Modernity* (Leiden: Martinus Nijhoff Publishers, 2013). ISGAP subsequently published an even larger selection of papers in a five-volume collection reflecting the interdisciplinary nature of the conference as well as the diverse nature of the subject of antisemitism in general.

[2] Alan M. Dershowitz, "Yale's Distressing Decision to Shut Down Its 'Initiative for the Interdisciplinary Study of Anti-Semitism,'" Gatestone Institute, June 14, 2011, available at: http://gatestoneinstitute.org/2200/yale-anti-semitism; Charles A. Small, "Introduction," in *Global Antisemitism: A Crisis of Modernity*, ed. Charles A. Small (New York: ISGAP, 2013). At the present time, ISGAP is involved in research on the BDS movement that also touches on these issues.

part of its international efforts, moreover, ISGAP has established seminar series at Rome's Sapienza University (2013), at the Sorbonne University and the Centre National de la Recherche Scientifique (CNRS) in Paris (2014), and at the University of Chile in Santiago (2015), with more still in the pipeline.

ISGAP's publishing program is gaining momentum and currently includes online publications, self-published books and papers, and co-publications with leading international academic publishers. Two collections of papers from the above-mentioned seminar series—one in English and one in French—will be published in the coming months. Plans are also in place to launch a journal and a book series dealing with different aspects of antisemitism. Finally, a searchable database of conference papers, seminar papers, working papers and other materials will soon be available on ISGAP's website.

In the 1950s and 1960s, many prominent Jewish scholars who had found refuge in the United States began to study the Holocaust, antisemitism, and related matters for the first time. Scholars such as Theodor Adorno, Max Horkheimer, and Hannah Arendt analyzed antisemitism and its cultural and ideological roots and manifestations from an interdisciplinary perspective.[3] These intellectual pioneers received funding and support from Jewish communal organizations and philanthropists, and their efforts succeeded in placing these crucial issues on the "academic map."

However, the current atmosphere at many universities in the United States and other countries poses a challenge to scholars who wish to engage freely and openly in the study of antisemitism and its contemporary manifestations. To counteract this trend, ISGAP seeks to provide a safe academic environment in which they can carry out high-caliber interdisciplinary research, test their findings and ideas, and benefit from the constructive criticism of their colleagues. In this way, both the study of antisemitism and the careers of those who engage in it are sure to be advanced.

In line with the above, ISGAP's next major project is a curriculum development program to train university professors, which was inaugurated at Hertford College, Oxford University, in July 2015. Under the guidance of leading international scholars, participants will develop a course syllabus and curriculum for the interdisciplinary study of antisemitism, which they will put into practice at their home universities after they have completed the program by teaching courses for credit. This is just one of the ways in which ISGAP is encouraging and supporting the study of antisemitism within academia.

As mentioned above, ISGAP and YIISA hosted a high-level interdisciplinary seminar series at Yale University between 2006 and 2011. This seminar series, which was entitled "Antisemitism in Comparative Perspective," explored the issue of antisemitism from a wide range of perspectives. The present volume—*The Yale Papers: Antisemitism in Comparative Perspective*—presents a selection of the papers presented at these seminars, as well as several other working papers, conference papers, and lectures commissioned by or submitted to YIISA by eminent scholars and researchers from around the world. In addition to providing a fascinating overview and scholarly analysis of some of the many facets of historical and contemporary anti-

---

[3] For an examination of Hannah Arendt's views on racism and antisemitism, see Dorian Bell's contribution, "A 'Paradise of Parasites': Hannah Arendt, Antisemitism, and the Legacies of Empire," in this volume.

semitism around the globe, this volume stands as a solid and incontrovertible testament to the abundant—and, above all, productive—academic activity that characterized YIISA's truncated tenure at Yale University.

Like the seminars on which they are based, the papers in this volume cover a wide range of perspectives. Among those taking a regional approach are the paper by Edward Kaplan and Charles Small on the correlation between anti-Israel sentiment and antisemitism in Europe, Milton Shain's paper on anti-alienism and antisemitism in contemporary South Africa, Shalom Lappin's paper on Britain and the Jews, Nora Gold's paper on the antisemitic experiences of Jewish girls in Canada, Pan Guang's paper on the Jews in China, and Asher Susser's paper on the potential contours of a future peace settlement involving Israel, Jordan and Palestine. Several papers in this category examine the history, contemporary manifestations, and/or impact of Islamic antisemitism in the Middle East and Iran, including those by Benny Morris, Bassam Tibi, Matthias Küntzel, Neil Kressel, and Brandon Friedman.

Papers taking a more conceptual approach include those by Dina Porat on the path to a universal definition of antisemitism, Jennifer Roskies's paper on the omission of Jewish women from feminist theory, Yaakov Kirschen's paper on antisemitism in political cartoons, and Dorian Bell's paper on the connections between racialist imperialism and antisemitism. This category also includes Steven Smith's paper on Leo Strauss, as well as several papers on the psychology and psychological impact of antisemitism, such as Peter Glick's paper on the envious roots of antisemitism, Hadar Lubin's paper on its traumatic effects, and the paper by Nurit Shnabel and John Dovidio on the emotional needs provoked by antisemitism among Israeli Jews, especially in regard to their response to the threat posed by Iran.

The third approach focuses on manifestations of contemporary antisemitism and the efforts to combat them, in particular the ever-growing phenomenon of virulent anti-Zionism, which is often referred to as the "new antisemitism." Papers in this category include David Hirsh's long and detailed examination of anti-Zionism and antisemitism, Roni Stauber's paper on the academic and public debate on the "new antisemitism," Yossi Klein Halevi's paper on the effects of Israel's demonization on Israelis, Gerald Steinberg's paper on the role of NGOs in promoting anti-Zionism and antisemitism, Michael Whine's paper on diplomatic efforts to combat antisemitism, and Irwin Cotler's paper on the various contemporary manifestations of contemporary antisemitism, including the biased use of human rights to attack Israel. Finally, several papers look at the same issues from the perspective of the use and abuse of Holocaust memory, including those by Catherine Chatterley, Walter Reich, and Berthe Kayitesi, who draws parallels with the Tutsi experience of genocide.

It is the hope of all those connected with ISGAP and YIISA that the papers in this volume will stimulate and inspire readers and lead them to understand and confront the changing realities of contemporary antisemitism and to develop policies and strategies to combat and defeat this and other destructive hatreds. With the publication of this volume, as well as all its other academic efforts, ISGAP continues to fight antisemitism on the battlefield of ideas.

Anti-Israel Sentiment Predicts Antisemitism in Europe*

Edward H. Kaplan and Charles A. Small**

I. INTRODUCTION

On April 22, 2005, the Executive Council of Britain's Association of University Teachers (AUT) voted to boycott two Israeli universities (Bar Ilan and Haifa). The boycott was advocated "as a contribution to the struggle to end Israel's occupation, colonization and system of apartheid,"[1] while the boycott's main proponent stated that this action would increase pressure on the "illegitimate state of Israel."[2] Similarly spirited statements include London Mayor Ken Livingstone's assertion that Israeli Prime Minister "Sharon continues to organise terror. More than three times as many Palestinians as Israelis have been killed in the present conflict."[3] Addressing suicide bombings in Israel, philosopher Ted Honderich wrote that "those Palestinians who have resorted to necessary killing have been right to try to free their people, and those who have killed themselves in the cause of their people have indeed sanctified themselves."[4]

Many Israeli and Jewish individuals and organizations have characterized statements such as these as antisemitic in effect if not intent, given that Israel is singled out in the face of silence over human rights violations committed elsewhere. There is indeed a long and sad history of antisemitism in Europe and elsewhere (Almog 1988; Martire and Clark 1982; Selznick and Steinberg 1969). Dating back to the study of Adorno et al. (1950), several scholars have conducted empirical (i.e., survey-based) studies to determine those factors that characterize persons who exhibit more (or less) prejudice against Jews (Anti-Defamation League 1998, 2002; Frindte, Wettig, and Wammetsberger 2005; Konig, Eisinga,

---

* The data for this study were provided by the Anti-Defamation League (ADL), and while we thank the ADL for sharing their data with us, the views expressed in this article are ours and do not represent the official positions or policies of the ADL. Edward H. Kaplan was supported by the Yale School of Management research fund. Previously published in *Journal of Conflict Resolution*, Vol. 50 No. 4, August 2006, pp. 548-561.

** Edward H. Kaplan, School of Management, Department of Epidemiology and Public Health, School of Medicine, Department of Chemical Engineering, Faculty of Engineering, Yale University. Charles A. Small, Institute for Social and Policy Studies, Yale University, Institute for the Study of Global Antisemitism and Policy.

[1] http://www.zionismontheweb.org/AUT/autres.htm.
[2] http://education.guardian.co.uk/higher/worldwide/story/0,9959,1466250,00.html.
[3] http://www.guardian.co.uk/comment/story/0,,1430132,00.html.
[4] http://chronicle.com/free/v50/i09/09b01201.htm.

and Scheepers 2000; Konig, Scheepers, and Falling 2001; Lutterman and Middleton 1970; Weil 1985). In reviewing this literature, Konig, Scheepers, and Falling (2001) identify religious (e.g., Christian worldview, fundamentalism), social-psychological (e.g., anomie, authoritarianism), and sociostructural (e.g., age, education, gender) variables as key correlates of antisemitism at the individual level. More recently, scholars have addressed the relationship between antisemitism and anti-Zionism (Frindte, Wettig, and Wammetsberger 2005; Wistrich 1990, 2004), but whether extreme criticism of Israel, as exemplified in the recent AUT boycott debate, is de facto antisemitic remains bitterly contested.[5]

Although motivated by strong anti-Israel sentiment such as that earlier described, our research question is not whether anti-Israel *statements* are antisemitic in either effect or intent. Rather, we ask whether individuals with strong anti-Israel views are more likely to harbor antisemitic attitudes than others. Certainly, Bayes's rule would suggest this to be true. Let p be the proportion of the population with antisemitic leanings, q be the fraction of those with antisemitic leanings who are anti-Israel, and r be the fraction of those not antisemitic who are anti-Israel. Then, the fraction of those with anti-Israel views who are also antisemitic, f, is given by

$$f = \frac{pq}{pq+(1-p)r} \qquad (1)$$

Presumably, those with antisemitic leanings would be more likely to espouse anti-Israel viewpoints than those who are not antisemitic (given that Israel presents itself as a Jewish state), implying that $q > r$, which in turn implies that the fraction of those with anti-Israel leanings who are antisemitic (f) exceeds the unconditional proportion of the population that is antisemitic (p).

Following the logic of equation (1), one can ask not only whether those with anti-Israel leanings are more likely to be antisemitic but also whether the *degree* of anti-Israel feeling differentially predicts the likelihood that one harbors antisemitic views. This framework does *not* require any assumption regarding causality, that is, whether antisemitism "causes" anti-Israel sentiment (or vice versa). Rather, our analysis focuses on information updating (as is common in Bayesian analyses). Worded differently, our research addresses the following scenario: when confronted by an individual espousing anti-Israel statements such as those cited in the opening of this article, what is the probability that the person issuing such statements is antisemitic? Working from a baseline assessment of the fraction of individuals in the relevant population who are antisemitic, the presentation of strong anti-Israel statements constitutes new information, which forces attention on the fraction of such individuals who are antisemitic. More generally, we seek the fractions of those with anti-Israel views of differing severity who also harbor antisemitic views (as opposed to arguing whether such anti-Israel views themselves are or are not inherently antisemitic).

The contribution of this article is that for ten European countries, we are able to answer our research questions empirically. We next describe our data source and method of analysis, after which we present our statistical findings. Not only

---

[5] http://www.engageonline.org.uk.

do we find that the extent of anti-Israel sentiment differentially predicts the likelihood of antisemitism among survey respondents, but the predictions are sharp. Those with extreme anti-Israel sentiment are roughly six times more likely to harbor antisemitic views than those who do not fault Israel on the measures studied, and among those respondents deeply critical of Israel, the fraction that harbors antisemitic views exceeds 50 percent. Furthermore, these results are robust even after controlling for numerous additional (and potentially confounding) factors both singularly and simultaneously.

II. DATA

The Anti-Defamation League commissioned First International Resources to develop a study of attitudes toward Jews, Israel, and the Palestinians (Anti-Defamation League 2004). In addition to survey items probing such attitudes, questions addressed the degree of respondents' social contacts with Jews and respondents' attitudes toward others (e.g., different religion, immigrants). Respondents were also asked to provide standard demographic information (e.g., age, gender, income etc.). The resulting survey was administered by Taylor Nelson Sofres via telephone, resulting in interviews with 500 citizens in each of ten countries for a total sample of 5,000 (actually 5,004). No information is available regarding those contacted who refused to participate in the study, which raises an obvious statistical question regarding nonresponse bias. However, given that the goal of our analysis is to examine the relationship between antisemitism and anti-Israel sentiment rather than to estimate the true prevalence of either, nonresponse becomes less of an issue. The situation is somewhat akin to epidemiological studies relating, say, the incidence of cancer to smoking behavior: there is no need for the proportion of smokers in such studies to mimic the true percentage in the population. As will be detailed below, the consistency of the relationship between antisemitism and anti-Israel sentiment across many different analyses makes it difficult to believe that the results obtained are somehow artifactual due to nonresponse bias.

1. The antisemitic index

Table 1 reports the eleven statements used in this study to measure antisemitism along with the number of respondents who agreed with each proposition. As in prior ADL surveys (Anti-Defamation League 1998, 2002), an antisemitic index was defined by counting the number of statements with which a respondent agreed.[6] Figure 1A reports the survivor distribution for this index, which is the fraction of all respondents with index scores exceeding x for x ranging from 0 through 11. Consistent with the prior ADL surveys, we say that a respondent harbors antisemitic views if he or she agrees with more than five of the eleven statements in Table 1, although we will show that our results are not particularly sensitive to this cutoff. From Figure 1A, the overall fraction of respondents harboring antisemitic views equals 14 percent.

---

[6] See the online companion to this article for inter-item correlations, reliability, and other diagnostics for the antisemitic and anti-Israel indices.

Table 1: Statements comprising the antisemitic index
with corresponding response frequency in agreement (of n = 5,004)

Statements	Response frequency
Jews don't care what happens to anyone but their own kind.	1,052
Jews are more willing than others to use shady practices to get what they want.	784
Jews are more loyal to Israel than to this country.	2,200
Jews have too much power in the business world.	1,309
Jews have lots of irritating faults.	545
Jews stick together more than other (citizens of respondent's country of residence).	2,942
Jews always like to be at the head of things.	1,150
Jews have too much power in international financial markets.	1,460
Jews have too much power in our country today.	500
Jewish business people are so shrewd that others don't have a fair chance to compete.	884
Jews are just as honest as other business people.	485[a]

a. Frequency of respondents that disagreed with this statement.

Figure 1: Survivor distributions reporting the fraction of survey respondents with index scores exceeding x for (a) the antisemitic index (x ranges from 0-11) and (b) the anti-Israel index (x ranges from 0-4)

A. Distribution of the antisemitism index

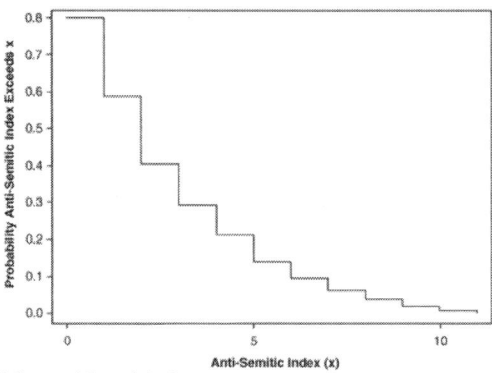

B. Distribution of the anti-Israel index

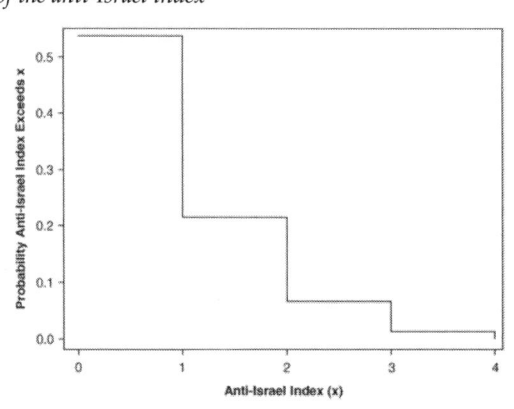

2. The anti-Israel index

Table 2 reports the four statements used in this study to ascertain anti-Israel sentiment and the number of respondents who agreed with each. Similar to the antisemitic index, we used the number of these statements agreed to by a respondent to define an anti-Israel index. The higher the value of this index, the stronger the anti-Israel sentiment expressed. Figure 1B reports the survivor distribution for the anti-Israel index. Just under half of all respondents report anti-Israel index scores of 0, indicating no measured anti-Israel sentiment, while only 1 percent of respondents agreed with all four of the anti-Israel statements considered.

Table 2: Statements comprising the anti-Israel index with corresponding response frequency in agreement (of n = 5,004)

Statement/Question	Response frequency
The Israeli treatment of the Palestinians is similar to South Africa's treatment of blacks during apartheid.	705[a]
Who do you think is more responsible for the past three years of violence in Israel, the West Bank and the Gaza Strip, the Israelis, or the Palestinians?	1,254[b]
In your opinion, during military activities inside the West Bank and Gaza Strip, do the Israeli Defense Forces intentionally target Palestinian civilians, or are civilian casualties an accidental outcome of Israel's military response?	1,765[c]
In your opinion, is there any justification for Palestinian suicide bombers that target Israeli civilians?	426[d]

a. Frequency of respondents that agree a lot with this statement.
b. Frequency of respondents stating Israelis.
c. Frequency of respondents stating that the Israeli Defense Forces intentionally target civilians.
d. Frequency of respondents stating yes.

III. Predicting Antisemitism from Anti-Israel Sentiment

To see whether anti-Israel sentiment is generally predictive of antisemitic views among the 5,000 respondents to our survey, we examined the survivor distribution of the antisemitic index for each of the five levels of the anti-Israel index. The results are shown in Figure 2A. The five curves are significantly different (log-rank $\chi^2 = 286$, $df = 4$, $p \approx 0$), confirming that measured antisemitism differs by the extent of anti-Israel sentiment. It is noteworthy that these five survivor curves *never cross*: for *any* value x of the antisemitic index, the fraction of respondents who agree with *more* than x antisemitic statements *strictly* increases with the value of the anti-Israel index. Figure 2B reports the fraction of respondents who agree with more than five of the eleven antisemitic statements for the different levels of the anti-Israel index. Recall that of all respondents, 14 percent harbor antisemitic views. Only 9 percent of those with anti-Israel index scores of 0 report harboring antisemitic views, but the fraction of respondents harboring antisemitic views grows to 12, 22, 35, and 56 percent for anti-Israel index values of 1 through 4, respectively.

Figure 2: (A) Survivor distributions reporting the fraction of survey respondents with index scores exceeding x for the antisemitic index (x ranges from 0-11), conditional on the anti-Israel index equaling, from bottom to top, 0 (solid bottom line), 1 (long-dashed line), 2 (short-dashed line), 3 (broken line), or 4 (solid top line); and (b) Fraction of respondents defined as harboring antisemitic views (antisemitic index scores exceeding 5) as a function of the anti-Israel index

A. Distribution of the antisemitic index (by anti-Israel index)

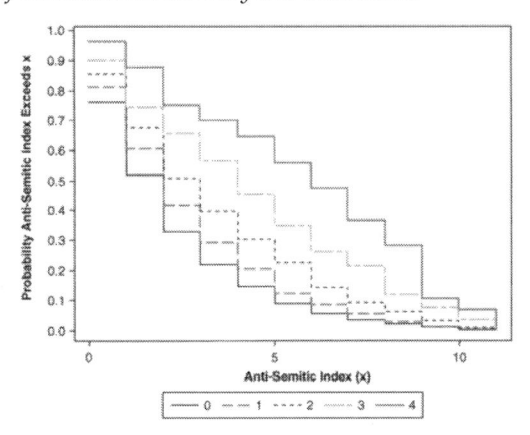

B.

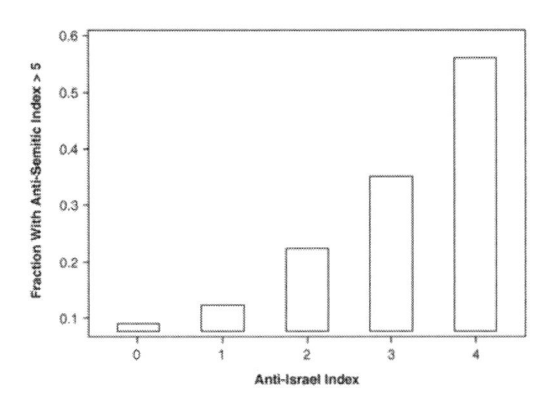

1. Third-factor interactions

As discussed earlier, presumably those with antisemitic views are more likely to oppose a Jewish state than others; therefore, the greater the extent of anti-Israel sentiment revealed, the higher the likelihood of associated antisemitism via Bayes's rule. However, it is also possible that the relationship observed between anti-Israel and antisemitic attitudes is the result of third-factor interactions. For example, those who are intolerant of others (e.g., different religion, different country of origin) might be more likely to express both antisemitic and anti-Israel sentiment as a result. Does the relationship displayed in Figure 2B survive when one controls for possible confounding factors?

Figure 3 explores such interactions by reporting the fraction of respondents harboring antisemitic views as a function of anti-Israel index levels while controlling for the levels of third factors. The most important observation from this graphical exploration is that the panels of Figure 3 repeat the basic pattern shown in Figure 2B for essentially all levels of all factors. Figure 3A shows that within each of the ten countries surveyed, the fraction of respondents harboring antisemitic views increases with the extent of anti-Israel sentiment measured. While there is considerable variation among these countries in measured anti-semitism overall—ranging from 8 percent in Denmark and the Netherlands to 22 percent in Spain—the association between anti-Israel and antisemitic leanings appears in each country. Figure 3B shows that for each of several different income levels (and including those who refused to divulge their income), the fraction of respondents harboring antisemitic views increases with the anti-Israel index. Figure 3C considers the interaction between antisemitism, anti-Israel sentiment, and religion. For Christian respondents and those who profess no religion, the fraction reporting antisemitic index values in excess of 5 strongly

Figure 3: Fraction of respondents harboring antisemitic views (antisemitic index scores exceeding 5) as a function of the anti-Israel index equaling 0 (solid black), 1 (forward slash), 2 (back slash), 3 (cross-hatch), and 4 (horizontal bar) controlling for (a) country of residence, (b) income, (c) religion, (d) attitudes toward illegal immigrants (see text), (e) frequency of contact with Jews (see text), and (f) fraction of respondents agreeing with specific antisemitic attitudes (see Table 1), as a function of the anti-Israel index equaling 0 (solid black), 1 (forward slash), 2 (back slash), 3 (cross-hatch), and 4 (horizontal bar)

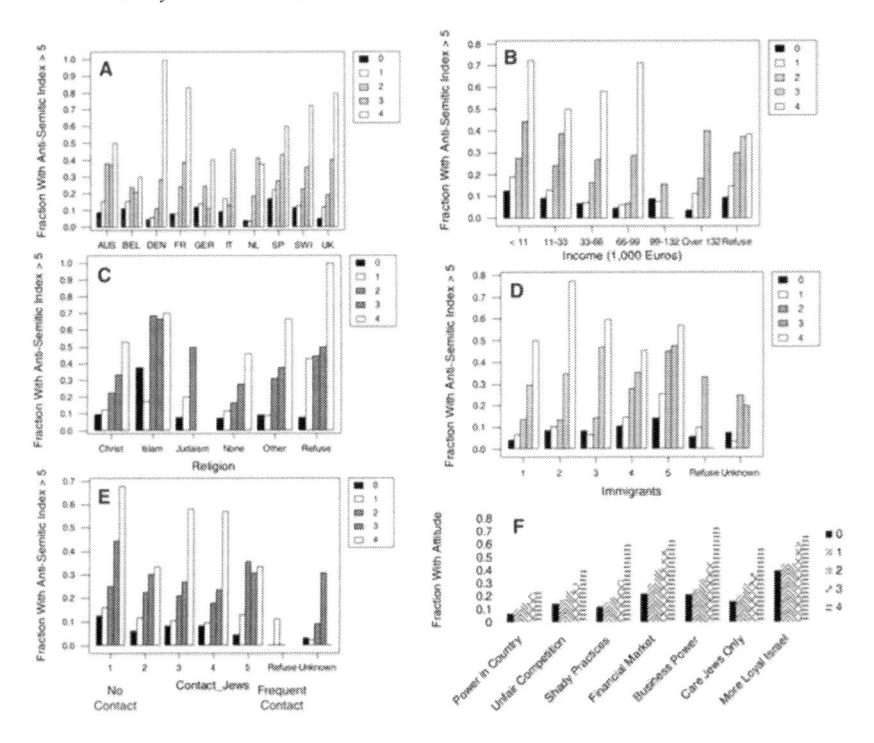

increases with reported anti-Israel sentiment. This is also true of those reporting "other" as their religious affiliation. Among Muslims, the reported level of anti-semitism jumps past 60 percent for those with anti-Israel index values of 2 or more; a similar rapid rise is seen among those refusing to state their religion. Even among Jewish respondents, one sees an increase in antisemitic responses as the anti-Israel index increases, but note that there are only 25 Jewish respondents (compared to 2,970 Christians, 1,547 reporting no religion, 92 Muslims, 295 reporting "other," and 75 who refused to state their religion). Among these 25 Jewish respondents, 13 scored 0 on the anti-Israel index (with one of these scoring over 5 on the antisemitic index), 10 scored 1 on the anti-Israel index (with 2 reporting antisemitic leanings), and 2 scored 2 on the anti-Israel index (with 1 reporting antisemitic leanings). When considering the statement "Illegal immigrants today are a burden on our economy because they take our jobs, housing and health care," Figure 3D repeats the same relation between antisemitism and the anti-Israel index for all attitudes toward illegal immigrants. Does the extent of contact respondents have with Jews matter? The survey asked respondents, "Approximately how often would you say that you come into contact with Jews either at work or in social occasions?" Figure 3E reports the by now familiar relationship between antisemitism and the anti-Israel index for different levels of contact. Finally, Figure 3F reports the fraction of respondents who agree with specific antisemitic canards (Table 1) as a function of the anti-Israel index. Whether the accusation is that "Jews have too much power in our country," "Jews are more willing than others to use shady practices to get what they want," or "Jews don't care what happens to anyone but their own kind," the fraction of respondents agreeing with these (and the rest of the) antisemitic stereotypes consistently increases as a function of the anti-Israel index.

2. Multifactor model

To further explore the association between the fraction of respondents harboring antisemitic views and the anti-Israel index, we fit a multiple logistic regression model to the survey data. Such a model enables estimation of the level of antisemitism as a function of the anti-Israel index while simultaneously controlling for possible confounding factors. The model also enables estimation of the independent effects (if any) of these same factors on the fraction of respondents harboring antisemitic views.

Several findings emerge from the results shown in Table 3.[7] First, even after controlling for respondents' country of residence, age, religion, income, gender, extent of contact with Jews, attitudes toward people of other races/religions, and attitudes toward illegal immigrants, the relationship between antisemitism and anti-Israel attitudes remains intact. The odds ratios of the fraction of respondents harboring antisemitic views for anti-Israel index scores greater than 0 (relative to those with an anti-Israel index of 0) equal 1.59, 3.28, 6.51, and 10.94 for anti-Israel index scores of 1 through 4, respectively. All of these scores are significantly

---

[7] A more complete table reporting estimated coefficients, standard errors, coefficient z-statistics and p-values, and overall goodness-of-fit tests appears in the online companion to this article.

different from unity (which would occur if anti-Israel index levels carried no information about antisemitism). The mitigating effects of the possible confounds considered are minor, as the equivalent odds ratios associated with the uncontrolled results of Figure 2B equal 1.43, 2.92, 5.45, and 12.94 for anti-Israel index scores of 1 through 4, a similar set of ratios with the same qualitative implications as the figures derived from the logistic model. Furthermore, of all the factors considered in this model, the anti-Israel index is by far the most important, as indicated by its chi-square of 196 at 4 degrees of freedom.

While simultaneously considering the factors shown in Table 3 did not meaningfully alter the relationship between antisemitism and anti-Israel attitudes in the data, these other factors all tested significant in their own right, as can be seen from their associated chi-square statistics in Table 3. The important relationships between these factors and antisemitism will now be summarized. First, the fraction of respondents harboring antisemitic views tends to increase with age. Second, relative to Christians, Muslim respondents are much more likely to harbor antisemitic views (odds ratio = 7.8). There was no statistically significant difference between the fraction of antisemitic responses obtained from Jews, other religions, or those reporting no religion as compared to Christians, although those who refused to identify their religion were more likely to harbor antisemitic views. Third, the fraction of antisemitic responses tended to decline as income increased. Fourth, women were much less likely than men to report antisemitic results. Fifth, the level of contact with Jews had no statistically significant relation to antisemitism, except that those who did not know how much contact they had with Jews were much less likely to harbor antisemitic views (odds ratio = 0.34 relative to those who reported no contact with Jews). Sixth, the less one feels in common with other races/religions, the more likely one is to exhibit antisemitism. Seventh, the less tolerant respondents were of illegal immigrants, the more likely they expressed antisemitism.

An important potential explanatory factor that is not included in the model shown is education. Unfortunately, the ADL survey did not provide a useful measure of the extent of respondents' education, asking instead, "At what age did you complete your full-time education?" There are two problems with this question. First, the respondents are asked for their age at completion of formal studies rather than the actual level of education attained. Second, the response options for this question are as follows: sixteen or younger, seventeen, eighteen, nineteen, twenty and older, don't know/not sure, and refused to answer. This range of ages is too narrow to assess meaningfully the amount of education received.

Finally, as a check on the sensitivity of our results to the specific cutoff employed in operationalizing antisemitism (antisemitic index values in excess of 5), we also explored ordered logistic models that estimate the probability a respondent reports *any* particular level of the antisemitic index (rather than only index values in excess of 5 or not). These more complex models did not lead to any important differences from the results described earlier, which is perhaps not surprising given what was shown earlier: conditional on the values of the anti-Israel index, the survivor distributions of the antisemitic index *never cross* (see Figure 2A), indicating strong explanatory power at *any* antisemitic index threshold and not just the ADL-inspired cutoff of 5.

Table 3: Multifactor logistic model predicting the probability a respondent reports an antisemitic index exceeding 5 from the anti-Israel index, controlling for country of residence, age, religion, income, gender, contact with Jews, commonality with other races/religions, and attitudes toward immigrants

Predictor	Odds Ratio	95% Confidence Interval Lower	Upper
Anti-Israel Index (Relative to 0)			
1	1.59	1.28	1.99
2	3.28	2.56	4.19
3	6.51	4.68	9.04
4	10.94	5.93	20.17
Country (Relative to NL)			
AUS	2.82	1.79	4.44
BEL	2.37	1.51	3.72
DEN	1.21	0.73	2.01
FR	2.30	1.43	3.70
GER	2.58	1.63	4.08
IT	2.11	1.31	3.38
SP	4.56	2.91	7.15
SWI	3.20	2.05	5.02
UK	1.45	0.90	2.34
Age (Relative to 18-24)			
25-34	1.10	0.73	1.66
35-44	1.25	0.85	1.84
45-54	1.62	1.10	2.39
55-64	2.03	1.37	3.01
Refuse	0.98	0.29	3.36
Unknown	2.62	1.77	3.87
Religion (Relative to Christianity)			
Islam	7.80	4.69	12.98
Judaism	1.84	0.58	5.84
None	0.97	0.79	1.20
Other	1.39	0.94	2.05
Refuse	2.88	1.52	5.47
Income (Relative to < 11k euros)			
11-33	0.75	0.58	0.98
33-66	0.56	0.41	0.77
66-99	0.43	0.26	0.69
99-132	0.65	0.30	1.40
Over 132	0.48	0.19	1.19
Refuse	0.72	0.56	0.94
Gender (Relative to male)			
Female	0.62	0.52	0.75
Contact with Jews (Relative to never any contact)			
Hardly ever	0.79	0.61	1.01
Once in while	0.77	0.59	1.00

Predictor	Odds Ratio	95% Confidence Interval Lower	Upper
Fairly often	0.76	0.52	1.12
Very often	0.97	0.62	1.51
Refuse	0.31	0.04	2.49
Unknown	0.34	0.21	0.54
Not Much in Common with Other Races/Religions? (Relative to disagree a lot)			
Disagree	1.20	0.92	1.56
Neither	1.25	0.92	1.72
Agree	2.33	1.80	3.02
Agree a lot	2.23	1.62	3.06
Refuse	2.00	0.68	5.94
Unknown	0.75	0.34	1.65
Immigrants Drain on Economy? (Relative to disagree a lot)			
Disagree	1.45	1.07	1.97
Neither	1.37	0.92	2.05
Agree	2.12	1.60	2.82
Agree a lot	3.82	2.85	5.12
Refuse	1.21	0.34	4.31
Unknown	1.15	0.55	2.40

Tests for Terms with > 1 Degree of Freedom

Term	Chi-Square	df	p
Anti-Israel	195.67	4	0.00
Country	75.22	9	0.00
Age	48.62	6	0.00
Religion	76.73	5	0.00
Income	19.73	6	0.00
Contact Jews	23.90	6	0.00
Common	60.41	6	0.00
Immigrants	97.50	6	0.00

IV. CONCLUSIONS

We began this article by noting that extreme anti-Israel sentiment has been interpreted by some as antisemitic in effect if not intent. It is therefore important to consider the competing motivations behind such sentiment. There are certainly critics of Israel on specific policy grounds, but there are also antisemitic individuals for whom attacks on Israel are manifestations of prejudice. Given this mix, what is one to think when presented with accusations such as "Israel is just like apartheid South Africa," "Israel is responsible for the violence in the Middle East," or "Israel deliberately targets Palestinian civilians"?

Our research directly addresses this issue. From a large survey of 5,000 citizens of ten European countries, we showed that the prevalence of those harboring (self-reported) antisemitic views consistently increases with respondents' degree of anti-Israel sentiment (see Figures 2 and 3 and Table 3), even after controlling for other factors. It is noteworthy that fewer than one-quarter of those with anti-Israel index scores of only 1 or 2 harbor antisemitic views (as defined by antisemitic index scores exceeding 5), which supports the contention that one certainly can be critical of Israeli policies without being antisemitic. However, among those with the most extreme anti-Israel sentiments in our survey (anti-Israel index scores of 4), 56 percent report antisemitic leanings. Based on this analysis, when an individual's criticism of Israel becomes sufficiently severe, it does become reasonable to ask whether such criticism is a mask for underlying antisemitism.

REFERENCES

Adorno, Theodor W., Else Frenkel-Brunswik, Daniel J. Levinson, and R. Nevitt Sanford. 1950. *The Authoritarian Personality*. New York: John Wiley.

Almog, Shmuel. 1988. *Antisemitism through the Ages*. Oxford, UK: Pergamon.

Anti-Defamation League. 1998. *Anti-Semitism and Prejudice in America*. New York: Anti-Defamation League. http://www.adl.org/antisemitism_survey/survey_main.asp.

———. 2002. *European Attitudes toward Jews: A Five Country Survey*. New York: Anti-Defamation League. http://www.adl.org/anti_semitism/EuropeanAttitudesPoll-10-02.pdf.

———. 2004. *Attitudes toward Jews, Israel and the Palestinian-Israeli Conflict in Ten European Countries*. New York: Anti-Defamation League. http://www.adl.org/antisemitism_survey/survey_ main.asp.

Frindte, Wolfgang, Susan Wettig, and Dorit Wammetsberger. 2005. "Old and New Anti-Semitic Attitudes in the Context of Authoritarianism and Social Dominance Orientation: Two Studies in Germany." *Peace and Conflict: Journal of Peace Psychology* 11(3): 239-66.

Konig, Ruben, Rob Eisinga, and Peer Scheepers. 2000. "Explaining the Relationship between Christian Religion and Anti-Semitism in the Netherlands." *Review of Religious Research* 41(3): 373-93.

Konig, Ruben, Peer Scheepers, and Albert Falling. 2001. "Research on Anti-semitism: A Review of Previous Findings and the Case of the Netherlands in the 1990s." In: *Ethnic Minorities and Inter-Ethnic Relations in Context: A Dutch Hungarian Comparison*, edited by Karen Phalet and Antal Orkény, 179-99. Aldershot, UK: Ashgate.

Lutterman, Kenneth G., and Russell Middleton. 1970. "Authoritarianism, Anomia, and Prejudice." *Social Forces* 48(4): 485-92.

Martire, Gregory, and Ruth Clark. 1982. *Anti-Semitism in the United States: A Study of Prejudice in the 1980s*. New York: Praeger.

Selznick, Gertrude J., and Stephen Steinberg. 1969. *The Tenacity of Prejudice: Anti-Semitism in Contemporary America*. New York: Harper & Row.

Weil, Frederick D. 1985. "The Variable Effects of Education on Liberal Attitudes: A Comparative-Historical Analysis of Anti-Semitism Using Public Opinion Survey Data." *American Sociological Review* 50(4): 458-74.

Wistrich, Robert S., ed. 1990. *Anti-Zionism and Antisemitism in the Contemporary World*. London: Macmillan.

———. 2004. "Anti-Zionism and Antisemitism." *Jewish Political Studies Review* 16(3-4): 27-31.

The Road to an Internationally Accepted Definition of Antisemitism

Dina Porat*

I. INTRODUCTION

On January 28, 2005, the Vienna-based European Union Monitoring Center on Racism and Xenophobia (EUMC) adopted a one-page "Working Definition of Antisemitism," which evolved as the result of consorted efforts of a large number of institutes and experts. These efforts lasted for about two years (2003-2004), during which many questions were raised regarding the appropriate principles and parameters to be used as guidelines. The main issue to be addressed here is the circumstances that necessitated such international efforts, given that a host of definitions of antisemitism had already come into being well before 2005, some of which could have perhaps been reused. A related issue concerns the term "new antisemitism," which has been used frequently since 2000. Is it really different enough to require a new definition, and in what ways is the new definition different from previous ones? This paper first presents some of the earlier definitions, and then describes and analyzes the circumstances leading to the adoption of the recent definition, as well as its subsequent contribution.

Before embarking on this analysis, two introductory remarks are appropriate. The first concerns the authors of the definitions. The term "anti-Semitism," coined in Germany in 1879 by Wilhelm Marr, the "patriarch of antisemitism," was redefined in various periods and in different ways, depending on the time, place, changing circumstances, and purpose of antisemitism. I would like to suggest that earlier definitions, from Marr to 2000, were mostly formulated by independent scholars and thinkers, often at the request of editors of encyclopedias and lexicons, while the new 2005 definition was formulated by academic and governmental teams, as a joint effort aimed at finding a wording acceptable to all participants. The second introductory remark concerns the difficulties associated with defining the term at all, since it encompasses a deep-seated emotional dimension as well as a conglomerate of centuries-old religious, political, and economic elements, not to mention the complications caused by the fact that the Jews are not the only Semites and by the rebirth of a Jewish political entity in the Land of Israel.

---

* Prof. Dina Porat heads the Stephen Roth Institute for the Study of Contemporary Antisemitism and Racism at Tel Aviv University.

II. Definitions Originating in Germany

The 1882 edition of the *Great Brockhaus Lexicon* contained a definition of "antisemite" that changed very little in subsequent editions, including those that appeared after World War II: "Anyone who hates Jews or opposes Judaism in general, and struggles against the character traits and the intentions of the Semites." This definition contains a number of components, among them an emotional one: hatred of Jews. The inclusion of an emotional component in a respected lexicon reflects the fact that this phenomenon existed in society as a permanent, or at least visible, fixture, to the extent that it was necessary to acknowledge its existence. In addition, this definition refers to hatred of the Jew as a person, rather than hatred of Judaism as a concept, mentioning only opposition to Judaism without further characterizing it. The second part of the definition refers to the antisemite as a person who fights the character traits and intentions of Semites.[1] This part of the definition, which was removed from post-World War II editions, creates a link between, and even conflates, Semites and Jews. This link is characteristic of the beginnings of racist theory during the second half of the 19th century. When Marr coined the term, he did not actually mean to refer to the Arab nations. He apparently chose it because of its ostensibly scientific ring,[2] and indeed it caught on and has been used worldwide ever since despite the problems that it created from the outset. It was only later that the Jews were differentiated from other Semitic peoples, especially the Arabs. Until then, the Jews of the definition were not merely Semites: they embodied and characterized Semitism, especially its alleged evil part.

Typical of racist theory is the identification of character traits among groups of people. According to this approach, they have certain permanent features that cannot be changed by education or environment. Therefore, racist theory is essentially anti-Christian in nature, since it does not recognize equality among peoples and the right of the individual to the mercy of God. In the case of the Jews, however, racist theory perpetuated the negative image created by the Church, which has been reaffirmed over the centuries and has become firmly embedded in society's consciousness.

Another key concept that appears in this definition, and which later became firmly embedded, is that the Semites (later identified as Jews) have certain intentions that antisemites seek to foil. The essence of these intentions is an ostensible desire to harm Christian society. It should be stressed that the *Brockhaus* definition was published about a decade prior to the publication of *The Protocols of the Elders of Zion*, which promoted the notion that the Jews were plotting to take over the world and were planning and organizing to realize their ambition.

Theodor Fritsch was one of the "founding fathers" of modern political antisemitism and served as a bridge between modern antisemitism and the Nazi Party. In 1887, he wrote a treatise entitled *Antisemitic Catechism*, which provided a set of "commandments" for antisemitism and appeared in dozens of editions throughout his long life.[3] His definition, too, was a clear one: "anti—to oppose, Semitism—the

---

[1] *Brockhaus Enzyklopädie*, Vol. I (Wiesbaden, 1966), pp. 585-6.

[2] Moshe Zimmermann, *Wilhelm Marr: The Patriarch of Antisemitism* (Jerusalem, 1982) (in Hebrew).

[3] Theodor Fritsch, *Antisemiten-Katechismus* (Leipzig, 1887).

essence of the Jewish race; anti-Semitism is therefore the struggle against Semitism." This is still a racist definition, because of the identification of the Jew as a Semite, and in essence it relates to the Jewish collective, defined as a race. The emphasis here is on the struggle against antisemitism that emerged in the years since Wilhelm Marr first coined the term.

The period that extended almost until the end of the 19th century was marked by substantial antisemitic activity. This activity, which took the form of political antisemitism, saw the emergence of political parties with antisemitic platforms or at least a central antisemitic plank. In most of the countries of Western and Central Europe, manifestos and petitions demanding a restriction of the Jews' civil rights were presented to parliament, accompanied by street demonstrations in the cities. Although the definition of antisemitism continued to be racist, the struggle became political in nature, and this was reflected in the terminology.

Fritsch's *Catechism* was still in effect as a basic text when the Nazi party came to power. During World War II, the party's leadership had to deal with the use of the term "antisemitism." On 17 May 1943, a German official sent a letter to a colleague referring to the meeting between the Grand Mufti of Jerusalem (Haj Amin al-Husseini) and Alfred Rosenberg, the Nazi party's chief ideologue, and the latter's promise to issue instructions to the press to refrain from using the term "antisemitism," which obviously blended Arabs and Jews together. In the letter itself, the word also appeared inside quotation marks, so as not to insult the Mufti, who was "a friend of the Germans," or to invite the accusation that the Germans were "throwing the Jews and the Arabs into the same pot."[4] Indeed, in 1944, the German Minister of Propaganda, Josef Goebbels, ordered the radio and the press to stop using the terms "Semitism" and "antisemitism," since they no longer suited the needs of the Third Reich, and to replace them with the words "Jew" or "Judaism" and "anti-Jewish" or "anti-Judaism." Rosenberg and Goebbels were not attempting to create another definition but to dismantle the existing one. They did away with the 19th century concept that Semitism was identical to Judaism. The first reason for this was Nazi Germany's categorical differentiation between Arabs and Jews due to its signing of various agreements with the Grand Mufti of Jerusalem, who made lengthy visits to Berlin and Rome. The Arabs, who were Semites and were now regarded as allies, could no longer be included in such a hostile or negative definition. The second reason was that the use of the terms Judaism and Jews created a clearer focus on those who were perceived in 1944—when the extermination was in full swing—to be the central and eternal enemies of Nazism. While this separation served the purposes of the Third Reich, the term "antisemitism" is still used in Germany today, sixty years after the defeat of the Nazis.

III. JEWISH SCHOLARS DEFINING ANTISEMITISM

In 1901, the first edition of the 12-volume *Jewish Encyclopedia* appeared in London and New York, the first work of this kind on such a scale to be published in Jewish history. It was compiled in the United States by more than 400 Jewish experts with

---

[4] Letter from Hans Hagemayer to Dr. Koepper, May 17, 1943, Doc. XCII-28, in Léon Poliakov and Josef Wulf, *Das Reich und die Juden* (Munich, 1978), p. 369.

the aim of educating the Jewish public and presenting the Jewish people and its wealth of culture to the world, especially in the United States. It is worth recalling that this period witnessed a mass immigration of Jews to the United States. Coming mainly from Eastern Europe, these Jews had not yet been absorbed into the country and were still seeking their place in it. This reality dictated the character of the encyclopedia to a certain extent, and it is reflected in the definition of antisemitism and the presentation of its history. For example, in the entry on the Dreyfus trial, which took place when the encyclopedia was being prepared, emphasis was placed on the religious origins of antisemitism and not on its secular-political ones, as if to say that antisemitism of this type could not develop in a modern country like the United States. Indeed, after the Dreyfus affair, there were signs of a decline in the intensity of the antisemitism that had manifested itself in Europe since 1870.

Nevertheless, the *Jewish Encyclopedia*'s definition of antisemitism, which was written by Gotthard Deutsch, a professor of Jewish history from Cincinnati, emphasized its racist—rather than religious—origins and focused on the racist characterization of the Jews, encompassing "greed, a special aptitude for money-making, aversion to hard work, clannishness and obtrusiveness, lack of social tact and especially of patriotism. Finally, the term is used to justify resentment for any crime or objectionable act committed by an individual Jew."[5] The definition implied that only a narrow-minded bigot steeped in prejudice would accuse the Jews of having these traits, and that Jews, both collectively and individually, were nothing like this in reality. This was an important message at the time, due to the arrival of large numbers of Jews in America. Many of them lived in poverty in the slum neighborhoods of large cities, where their customs and clothes drew attention and aroused suspicion. This had nothing to do with characteristics, said Jewish scholars, but rather with conditions and circumstances, which would change in the future. Indeed, other entries in the encyclopedia discussed the origins of the alleged collective characteristics of the Jewish people and expressed doubt as to whether Jews really had such traits, which might in fact be attributed solely to their living conditions. Various entries also discussed the positive features of the Jewish people, such as their high level of culture, amazing adaptability, and contribution to world civilization.

The entry on Theodor Herzl, the founder of political Zionism, follows the ideas of Leon Pinsker, who was among the first to define the situation of Jews in exile He considered antisemitism to be the outcome of exile and saw active Jewish nationalism as the solution, as described in his famous pamphlet *Auto-Emancipation*. Both Pinsker and Herzl offered a political solution that would go hand in hand with a spiritual and moral one. The First Zionist Congress took place only four years prior to publication of the *Encyclopedia*, and its impact, including Herzl's meteoric rise in the firmament of Jewish history, was evident in the entries.

It is possible, although there is no direct proof, that the 11th edition of the *Encyclopædia Britannica*, which was published in 1911, sought to criticize the tendency manifested in certain entries in the *Jewish Encyclopedia* to stress the religious element: "The Jews," wrote the author of the entry, Lucien Wolf, one of the most prominent members of the Anglo-Jewish community at the beginning of the 20th century,

---

[5] *The Jewish Encyclopedia*, Vol. I (New York/London, 1990), pp. 641-9.

"contend that anti-Semitism is a mere atavistic revival of the Jew-hatred of the Middle Ages." In other words, it had no place in the modern world of the new century, since atavism was a throwback to the emotions and phenomena of past generations. Wolf had little faith in the optimism of Jewish scholars, which derived from the decline of antisemitism in Europe from the last decade of the 19th century until the outbreak of World War I, nor in the continued stability of Britain, where he wrote his entry during the long reign of Queen Victoria. Thus, his criticism was directed at Jews both in the United States and in Britain. Religious prejudice, he believed, had indeed been reawakened by antisemitic incitement, but this prejudice was not the cause of antisemitism; it was, rather, racism, which had already played a part in various political struggles. He therefore urged the Jews living in the respectable refuge of Britain not to delude themselves, although they lived in an enlightened and democratic country. Instead, they should be aware of the true nature of antisemitism and the role it could play in the political struggles and tensions between various groups, even in tolerant countries.[6]

Other Jewish encyclopedias published during the 20th century, such as the *Encyclopedia Judaica*, first published in 1971, which included a lengthy entry written by historian Benjamin Eliav,[7] did not continue this line that places racism at center stage. Rather, they presented wide-ranging definitions of antisemitism, citing various sources—religious, economic, social, and racist—and even the animosity and the hatred that the term embodied. The definition of antisemitism in the *Encyclopedia of the Holocaust*, written by Yad Vashem historian Israel Gutman in the 1990s, adds a crucially important dimension: "Throughout the generations, concepts, fantasies and accusations have stuck to the term that portrayed a negative cognitive and emotional web, at times independent of Jewish society as it was fashioned and existed in reality."[8] This discrepancy between the real and the imagined, which forms the essence of antisemitism, and the use that has been made of it, will be discussed below.

IV. Non-Jewish Encyclopedias and Thinkers Following World War II

Two intellectual giants, Jean-Paul Sartre and Bertrand Russell, who referred to antisemitism during World War II and immediately after it, defined antisemitism and antisemites with disgust. Sartre described antisemitism as "blaming the presence of the Jews for all the disasters befalling the individual and the public, and making suggestions on what steps to take to improve the situation, from limiting their rights up to their deportation and annihilation." He categorically refused to view antisemitism as an opinion, which is a result of analysis, since the antisemite is "a person who fears, it is not the Jews that he fears, but rather himself, his conscious-

---

[6] *Encyclopædia Britannica*, Vol. I., 11th ed. (1911), pp. 134-45. Lucien Wolf, a prolific publicist, statesman, and historian, signed the entry as Vice-President of the Jewish Historical Society of England and as former president of the society.

[7] *Universal Jewish Encyclopedia* (New York, 1939-43 & 1948); *New Jewish Encyclopedia* (New York, 1962), pp. 17-8; *Encyclopedia Judaica*, Vol. II (Jerusalem, 1971), pp. 87-95.

[8] Israel Gutman, ed., *Encyclopedia of the Holocaust*, Vol. I (Yad Vashem/Sifriat Poalim, 1990), pp. 98-116 (in Hebrew).

ness, his liberty, his instincts, the need to admit responsibility for what he had done, his solitude, the changes that might affect him, society and the world ... in short anti-Semitism is the fear for the condition of man."[9] In *New Hopes for a Changing World*, Bertrand Russell put it even more succinctly: "Had Hitler been a brave man, he would not have been an antisemite."[10]

Encyclopedias published in the English-speaking world after 1945 also took up the question of defining antisemitism. The *Everyman's Encyclopedia*, published in Britain in 1949 and again in 1951 in New York, defines antisemites and antisemitism thus: "those who were opposed to the Jews in the second half of the 19th century. This hatred of the Jews, or antisemitism as it was called, was not the outcome of antipathy to their religion, but arose on account of their wealth and power which they were accumulating."[11] On the one hand, reference is made to an emotional dimension—hatred—but the description is written entirely in the past tense. This edition was published in the years immediately following World War II, after the overthrow of the Nazi regime, and contains the hope that antisemitism was indeed a thing of the past, that it too had been destroyed when the entire world had realized just how heavy a price Jews and non-Jews had paid for the hatred and persecution of minorities. On the other hand, the entry makes absolutely no mention of the Nazi regime, its antisemitism or its consequences, as if the events had never happened. It would appear that the reason for this was that these were the early years of the Cold War and that the previous enemy, Germany, had left the scene and been replaced by the Soviet Union.

Another example also provides proof of this frame of mind. About a year later, in 1952, Eleanor Roosevelt wrote a foreword to the first edition of Anne Frank's diary in English. She, too, makes no mention of the Jews, the Holocaust, or the Germans and does not even state that Anne was Jewish. Moreover, in the play, a muted and adapted version of the diary that opened on Broadway in 1955, the Germans were not shown at all, not even at the end.[12]

A no less striking aspect of the definition in *Everyman's Encyclopedia* is its reference to the rise of antisemitism as the result of the accumulation of wealth and power by the Jews, a fact with which the writer does not appear to disagree. On the contrary, it seems clear to him that the Jews had become so rich and powerful in the second half of the 19th century that they aroused resentment. Does this imply that the Jews actually brought antisemitism and its consequences upon themselves? Since property and power interest English-speaking countries more than religion or race, is there not a warning to non-Jewish readers implied in this definition? It should be borne in mind that the description appears in *Everyman's Encyclopedia*, which was intended for a mass readership. The *Hebrew Encyclopedia* (see below) states that,

---

[9] Jean-Paul Sartre, *Reflections sur la question juive*, trans. and comments Menachem Brinker (Tel Aviv, 1978), p. 31 (in Hebrew).

[10] Bertrand Russell, *New Hopes for a Changing World* (London, 1951), p. 109. Russell's analysis in this chapter is very much like Sartre's in his book.

[11] *Everyman's Encyclopedia*, 3rd ed., Vol. 7 (United Kingdom, 1949/New York, 1951), p. 373.

[12] Dina Porat, "A Forty-Year Struggle: Anne Frank's Diary and the Holocaust Deniers, 1958-1998," in *The Holocaust: The Unique and the Universal: Essays Presented in Honor of Yehuda Bauer* (Jerusalem, 2001), pp. 160-84 (in Hebrew).

"inherent in almost every hatred of a minority is a certain expression of strong powerful urges of possession and rule."

In the mid-1960s, there was a surprising turn of events. In 1966, the new edition of a leading English-language dictionary featured the following definition of antisemitism: "1. hostility toward Jews as a religious or racial minority group, often accompanied by social, economic and political discrimination." This was nothing new, but the definition continued as follows: "2. opposition to Zionism: sympathy with opponents of the State of Israel."[13] The time was just prior to the Six Day War, a period when the State of Israel was under increased threat, due to pressure exerted on the United Nations by the Soviet bloc, which supported the Arab states in their efforts to defeat the Jewish state, and the Third World. This coalition changed tactics following the Six Day War, when it sought to expel Israel from the United Nations and focused its efforts on boycotts and denunciation. It achieved some measure of success in this regard in 1975, when the UN General Assembly adopted a resolution equating Zionism with racism. When Merriam-Webster published its unambiguous definition of antisemitism as including opposition to Zionism and sympathy for those who opposed the State of Israel, it took a stand against the constant threat to Israel and its existence. It clearly implied that, just as the abrogation of the right of individual Jews to equality was defined as discrimination, the abrogation of the right of Israel to be an equal member of the international community also qualified as such. Prior to Israel's stunning victory in 1967 and the intensification of the Israel-Arab dispute, Israel was perceived in the Western world as a small democratic country that embodied the realization of the yearning of an ancient people for its homeland — a people that had not enjoyed fair treatment in the international arena and needed to be protected from its attackers and adversaries. The definition therefore rightly equated antisemitism to anti-Zionism and regarded both as discrimination.

Nevertheless, the dictionary did not give up its definitions of a Jew as "a person believed to drive a hard bargain" and the verb "to Jew" or "to Jew down," as driving a hard bargain, cheating by sharp business practice, or inducing a seller by haggling to lower his price, let alone its entries on the Jewbird (with its conspicuous beak) and the Jewbush (which has powerful emetic properties).[14] In fact, it could not give them up because they are a reflection of idioms and beliefs embedded in colloquial speech and popular culture.

V. Israeli Scholars Defining Antisemitism

The forefathers of Zionism, such as Herzl and Pinsker, had hoped that the creation of a Jewish state, or at least a form of Jewish emancipation, would normalize relations between Israel and Jewish communities abroad. They would cease to be part of a Diaspora with all its associated difficulties. Also, they hoped that a Jewish political entity would improve relations between the Jewish and the non-Jewish world and would be treated much as any other country. As a consequence, antisemitism, which originated in exile, would decline.

---

[13] *Webster's Third New International Dictionary* (1966), p. 96.
[14] *Webster's Third New International Dictionary* (1971), p. 1215.

About a decade after the establishment of the State of Israel, the fourth volume of the *Hebrew Encyclopedia* was published. It contained a comprehensive entry on antisemitism, the first part of which was written by the famous historian Ben-Zion Netanyahu. After the requisite discussion on the essence of the term, its meaning, and its history, Netanyahu added a new level to the subject, which was "hatred of the other, hatred of the alien, and hatred of the weak." He defined antisemitism as a kind of hatred of minorities that included all three of these hatreds "in a more forceful and consistent form than in any other form of hatred of minorities."[15] In essence, this is a Zionist definition and, like Zionism, it is optimistic. A state of being different, alien, and weak can be changed, and this can be done through the abolition of the Diaspora and the establishment of a Jewish state. Once the Jews had a state of their own, they would be like all other nations, and Jews who continued living outside the homeland, such as any Irishman or Italian living outside his home country, would be considered immigrants. They would no longer be foreigners whose status was different from that of other foreigners. As soon as this state became strong, those living outside it would draw personal strength and pride from the state, which would also support them wherever they were. The prophecy of the founding fathers of Zionism, as well as the hope of the state's founders and citizens, at least for the first twenty years after its establishment, was that Israel's existence would eliminate the elements that had given rise to antisemitism, regardless of time and place.

About a decade later, in 1969, Hebrew University historian Shmuel Ettinger attempted to revolutionize this concept. In an article entitled "The Roots of Antisemitism in Modern Times," he described antisemitism as a reflection of the stereotype of the Jew created over hundreds of years. According to Ettinger, the image had become an intrinsic part of Western culture—in sculpture, painting, sacred music, popular sayings, and various linguistic expressions—and would therefore never be uprooted but would continue feeding antisemitic sentiments in the future.[16] One might add that trying to erase these expressions would constitute an affront to a vast cultural legacy. In keeping with this view, for example, the Israel Philharmonic Orchestra plays passions and oratorios depicting cruel and bloodthirsty Jews in order to represent culture in its entirety.

In saying this, Ettinger essentially stated that Zionism would neither solve nor diminish the problem of antisemitism because there was no connection between them. The image of the Jew and the image of the State of Israel and its citizens existed separately. Today, we accordingly have the phenomenon of antisemitism without Jews, as found in Japan and Poland, which feeds on the existing representation of the Jew. The change introduced by Ettinger reflects the state of mind in post-1967 Israel. A society that considers itself stronger than in the past can afford openness, including self-criticism, and can face hopes that had proved an illusion. Zionism will not solve the problem of antisemitism, wrote Ettinger, and the existence of the State of Israel might even complicate matters for Jewish communities

---

[15] Ben-Zion Netanyahu, "Antisemitism," in *The Hebrew Encyclopedia*, Vol. IV (Jerusalem/Tel Aviv, 1959), pp. 493-508 at pp. 496-7 (in Hebrew).

[16] Shmuel Ettinger, "The Roots of Antisemitism in Modern Times," *Molad* 25 (1968), pp. 323-40 (in Hebrew).

around the globe. They will have to adopt a position on global affairs while being citizens of their own countries. Nevertheless, it is clear that the State of Israel has placed Jewish and Israeli reactions to antisemitism in an entirely different arena.

Two years later, Professor Jacob Tury and his students in the Department of Jewish History at Tel Aviv University continued Ettinger's analysis and arrived at the following definition: "Modern political antisemitism is the manipulation, used for political reasons, of emotions that have existed for a long time against an unrealistic image [about which Ettinger and later Gutman had written]. Antisemitism is not an ideology, as it is sometimes presented [as Sartre would agree], but rather 'a multi-faceted substitute' of ideology, and therefore it can serve the ideas of sundry circles." Tury recognized the central role of the unrealistic image but emphasized a differentiation that had not been made previously. On the one hand, there is the active antisemite who writes, publishes and signs petitions, desecrates cemeteries and torches synagogues, and strives to realize the political alliances and targets he has set for himself. On the other, there are large circles of people that hear of his acts or read what he writes and support him or vote for him. The activist is the one who manipulates public feelings in order to garner support for what he does. Antisemitism, here, is not an ideology but a tool employed by factions, groups, and political parties, even those diametrically opposed to each other, which can unite for this purpose despite their differences.[17] Tury's ideas also provide another explanation for *The Protocols of the Elders of Zion*. If the Jews are multi-faceted, including cosmopolitans and socialists, nationalist Zionists and converts to Christianity, secular scientists and the ultra-Orthodox, but nevertheless comprise one community, this suggests that they have some kind of sophisticated hidden master plan that determines how these roles are to be divided up among each part of the community so that the Jews are consolidated as a public. This danger must therefore be exposed, and the non-Jews must unite against it despite their differences.

In the summer of 1979, the so-called *Ma'ariv* trial, in which the Israeli newspaper was sued by two members of the British Parliament, was held in the Jerusalem District Court. Their work *Tell It Not in Gath*, which accused Israel of having acquired control over the world press through its connections with the Jewish communities, was described by the paper as "an antisemitic book written in Nazi propaganda style." Naturally, this called for a definition of antisemitism and an antisemite, and this author was called upon as an expert witness.[18] Being a student of Tury, I followed his line, adding the following points:

– The essence of antisemitism is the gulf between the image of the Jew as it was and still is constructed by the antisemite and the Jew's actual status and power. This is also true of the State of Israel, regarding its image and its true power and status. The wider the abyss, the stronger the antisemitism, and there is no greater proof of this than the pitiful state of the Jewish people on the eve of World War II, as opposed to the fanatical belief of the Nazi leadership in the Jews' omnipotent power.

---

[17] Jacob Tury, "The Debate on Rights for the Jews in the 18th and 19th Centuries," MA seminar, Department of Jewish History, Tel Aviv University, 1971.

[18] A copy of the trial minutes is located at the Stephen Roth Institute for the Study of Contemporary Antisemitism and Racism, Tel Aviv University.

- Legitimate criticism of individuals and countries is transformed into prejudice once it denounces their behavior as arising out of fixed, age-old characteristics and does not relate to the event itself, seeing it rather as a link in a chain of identical deeds. In 1986, renowned orientalist Bernard Lewis elaborated on this point in his book "Semites and Anti-Semites," claiming that it reflected the essence of Arab and Muslim antisemitism.[19]
- One does not have to read the writings of other antisemites in order to adopt their views. This worldview, filtered through the prism of *The Protocols* and centering on a belief in Jewish, and now Jewish-Israeli, power and machinations, is sufficient to create a state of mind, with accompanying expressions and conclusions, among those coming from completely different backgrounds, even among the highest levels of society.

VI. INTERNATIONAL INVOLVEMENT: 1990-2005

Can the above-mentioned series of definitions be reused to describe antisemitism in recent years? Although it includes most elements that comprise antisemitism and is useful as an analytic tool, it has not been reused for a number of reasons. First, each of these definitions reflects a certain culture and atmosphere at a certain point in history. In addition, the older definitions were more academic/theoretical in nature and were formulated by individuals, while the turbulent times, racism, and antisemitism of the 1990s and early 2000s require more practical definitions that can serve as a basis for international activity and legislation. Surprisingly enough, however, these turbulent years did not produce a new definition until 2005.

International bodies did not try to define antisemitism, not even following World War II, and in fact did not even mention it in treaties or agreements between 1945 and 1993, with one exception. Even racism was hardly mentioned in UN or European conventions and declarations, which instead used vague and general terms such as tolerance, equality, and the rights of minorities.[20] After World War II, all nations wished to start afresh and avoided pin-pointing culprits and victims, while the former allies did not wish to imply that their war effort was in any way motivated by Jewish demands. This situation did not change until the 1990s, despite the many changes that took place in the world during this long period.

The 1990s saw political and economic changes that are relevant to the issue of antisemitism. The first Gulf War of 1991 led to a rise in a wide range of antisemitic and anti-Israel expressions. The disintegration of the Soviet Union, the reunification of Germany, and the opening of the Far Eastern markets to international trade led to the privatization and globalization of world economy, much of which was blamed on Jewish magnates. The process of globalization also brought millions of immigrants and foreign workers from the poor southern hemisphere to the rich northern one, and some of them directed their frustration at failing to integrate into their host societies on the neighboring Jewish communities. Extreme right-wing elements

---

[19] Bernard Lewis, *Semites and Anti-Semites: An Inquiry into Conflict and Prejudice* (London, 1986), p. 242.
[20] Dina Porat, "The Evolution of Legislation against Racism and Antisemitism," in *Legislation in the Struggle Against Antisemitism* (World Jewish Congress/Roth Institute, 2006), pp. 5-10.

exploited the tensions between the newcomers and local society to further their goals, airing their anti-Jewish tendencies. Jews and Israel were blamed for being part of the policies of the United States, which became the world strongest and most hated power, especially in the eyes of Muslims and European leftists.

The Conference for Security and Cooperation in Europe (CSCE), which was replaced by the Organization for Security and Cooperation in Europe (OSCE) in 1994, was the first to report on the rise in antisemitism and to denounce it—without yet defining it—at its 1992 Copenhagen Conference. In 1993, in the wake of events in Rostok, Germany, where racist violence was combined with antisemitic outbursts, the European Parliament passed a resolution explicitly describing antisemitism for the first time since World War II, defining Holocaust denial as a form of racism, and calling upon EU member states to enact effective legislation to combat it.[21] Needless to say, before legislating one needs a definition. Indeed, when the United Nations convened a large-scale conference on human rights in Vienna in June 1993, all delegations were approached in order to reach a resolution stating that antisemitism was a form of racism.[22] Such a resolution was formulated by the UN Commission on Human Rights in March 1994, and was pronounced an historic declaration, which was quite ironic for such an obvious decision. While antisemitism was placed on a par with xenophobia, racial discrimination, and discrimination against Muslims and Arabs (later referred to as Islamophobia), this was actually the first time that it had been acknowledged by an international body as a wrong that had to be rectified. Also during this period, the European Commission against Racism and Intolerance (ECRI) was formed and started its work.

As immigrant-related problems increased and the impact of the 1993 conference proved to be limited, the European Union declared 1997 the "European Year against Racism." This endeavor similarly bore little fruit, and international efforts began to focus on the September 2001 UN World Conference against Racism in Durban, South Africa. As the conference drew near, it became evident that no definition of racism acceptable to all could be reached, and since antisemitism had been classified as a form of racism in 1994, it remained undefined once again. The only achievement of the conference in the area of definitions was a stronger emphasis on the term Islamophobia, as Arab countries claimed that antisemitism in the 21st century was actually hatred of Arabs by Jews and those who agreed with them. Moreover, the anti-globalization movement, which was very active in Durban, classified Arab countries as part of the poor non-white southern hemisphere and Israel and the Jews as part of the rich white northern hemisphere, thus further complicating the possibility of reaching a widely accepted definition of antisemitism. With or without a definition, the conference descended into an anti-Israeli and antisemitic fiasco, losing sight of its original goals.[23]

---

[21] Stephen J. Roth, *The Legal Fight against Antisemitism: A Survey of Developments in 1993*, supplement to the *Israeli Yearbook on Human Rights*, Vol. 25 (1995), 136 pp.

[22] The author was a member of the Israeli Foreign Ministry delegation to the Vienna Conference, charged with persuading the delegations to enter such a statement in their final speeches.

[23] Dina Porat, "Durban: Another Attack on Israel and the Jewish People," *New Directions* 7 (September 2002), pp. 51-60.

After October 2000, which saw the outbreak of the Second Intifada, a fresh wave of antisemitic activity began to manifest itself, especially in Western Europe. This so-called "new antisemitism" joined the list of ancient, medieval (early and late), 19th century political, Nazi, and post-WWII forms of antisemitism. This new incarnation was characterized by four major changes:

- First, this marked the first time that the initiative, images, and coordination of activities in this area moved from the Christian world to the Muslim one. Christian motives were used for political purposes outside the Christian world, and among the millions of Muslim immigrants residing in the West, groups of radical Islamists financed by oil-money started accelerating violence and intensive propaganda.
- Second, and partly as a result of this first change, anti-Zionism increased. The debate on whether this is simply another from of antisemitism has been raging for several years now, especially among intellectuals. A related question is whether this development was a result of events in the Middle East, including the war in Iraq, or whether the Israeli-Palestinian conflict was just a smokescreen for rampant anti-Americanism, anti-globalization, and the frustration of immigrant populations in the West.
- The third change characterizing this new antisemitism relates to the nature of anti-Jewish violence, which has become more brutal and is largely directed at Jewish individuals in academic institutions and on the streets, rather than Jewish cemeteries and synagogues. In addition, the perpetrators of such violence are mostly young first or second generation Muslim immigrants rather than right-wing extremists.
- The fourth change relates to the shift from Soviet, Arab, and Third World government-led antisemitism to the rise of antisemitism in academic and media circles in Western society. This development has had a sobering effect on Jewish communities, which previously believed that they belonged to and shared the values of Western society.[24]

VII. THE NEW DEFINITION OF ANTISEMITISM OF JANUARY 2005

After 2002, which was an especially difficult year in terms of antisemitic violence and anti-Zionist activity, European governments and organizations began to worry that this violence might get out of hand and be directed not only against Jews but also against the state institutions. Due in part to pressure exercised by the US State Department, the European countries decided to take action. In June 2003, the OSCE convened a conference on antisemitism in Vienna that called for the preparation of practical tools to tackle the situation, including an appropriate definition of antisemitism.

The European Union Monitoring Center on Racism and Xenophobia (EUMC) tried to respond to the challenge, but its 2002-2003 report represented a retreat to various outdated definitions of antisemitism based on Nazi, racist, and Christian

---

[24] See the Roth Institute's *Antisemitism Worldwide* annuals and its website at http://www.antisemitism.tau.ac.il.

representations of the Jew. The EUMC's definition referred, inter alia, to the "deceitful, crooked, foreign, corrupt nature of the Jew, his power and influence, and relation to money," as well as the age-old calumny that the Jews were responsible for Christ's death. This was obviously not the EUMC's own image of the Jew but rather how it believed Jews were perceived in the antisemitic imagination, but this referral to earlier definitions evoked ugly memories and did little to dispel the myth that the Jews themselves are to blame for the fire they attract. In addition, it ignored all recent developments, focusing on "traditional antisemitism" rather than the "new antisemitism," and contributed nothing to the solution of existing problems.[25] Moreover, the EUMC's attempt to discuss the relationship between antisemitism and anti-Zionism was so evasive and complicated, that even the clear—if debatable—analysis of Brian Klug, the Oxford scholar cited in the report, was of no avail.

The next conference, which took place in Berlin in April 2004, proved to be a milestone. After forcefully condemning all manifestations of antisemitism (and all other acts of intolerance) and clearly stating (in language reminiscent of the 1966 *Encyclopædia Britannica* entry) that international developments or political issues can never justify antisemitism, the Berlin Declaration urged the 55 members states of the OSCE to find the tools needed to monitor and combat antisemitism, including an all-encompassing definition. Soon after the conference, the European Commission against Racism and Intolerance (ECRI) issued its General Policy Recommendation on the Fight against Antisemitism.[26] It is to the credit of the EUMC that, following the failure of Berlin, it embarked on a coordinated effort with the OSCE's Office for Democratic Institutions and Human Rights (ODIHR) to formulate a better definition. A large number of scholars and institutes responded to the challenge.[27] As a result, a new "Working Definition of Antisemitism" came into being. It is a working definition in the sense that it is short and that it presents itself as a practical tool rather than an academic or theoretical exercise. In many ways, it constitutes a much-needed breath of fresh air. It deviates from the older definitions but does not ignore them. For example, the very first line mentions "hatred," just like many definitions have done since the late 19th century. It does not deal with the image of the Jew but rather with the antisemitic activities. It does not mention Judaism, both because this is a hard concept to define and because it is ultimately irrelevant to the definition of antisemitism. It addresses the recent developments that have led to the rise of the "new antisemitism." It facilitates the monitoring of antisemitic acts and expressions,

---

[25] *Manifestations of Antisemitism in the EU 2002-2003* (Vienna: EUMC, 2004), pp. 12-14; Kenneth S. Stern, "Proposal for a Redefinition of Antisemitism," in *Antisemitism Worldwide 2003/4* (Tel Aviv: Roth Institute, 2005), pp. 18-25.

[26] For the Berlin Declaration, see the OSCE website, http://www.osce.org/documents/cio/31432. For the ECRI General Policy Recommendation No. 9 on the Fight against Antisemitism of June 25, 2004, see http://coe.int/ecri.

[27] The participants in the deliberations listed on p. 19 of the EUMC's *Antisemitism: Summary Overview of the Situation in the EU 2001-2005* are: the European Jewish Congress, the Community Security Trust (UK), the Consistoire of France, the Stephen Roth Institute of Tel Aviv University, the Berlin Anti-Semitism Task Force, the American Jewish Committee, the Blaustein Institute for the Advancements of Human Rights, the Anti-Defamation League, B'nai Brith International, the Tolerance Unit of ODIHR/OSCE, Prof. Yehuda Bauer (Academic Advisor to the International Task Force on the Holocaust), and others.

comparisons between countries, and international cooperation. Finally, it does not tiptoe around the relationship between antisemitism and anti-Zionism and calls a spade a spade.

The definition is a result of deliberations in many countries but formally speaking constitutes an obligation undertaken by the 25 EU member states. Indeed, a careful reading suggests that it is influenced more by the European historical experience, which includes centuries of antisemitism and the Holocaust, rather than the North American one. Europe is more inclined to impose limits on antisemitic expression, be they legal or practical, while the United States is still in thrall of the First Amendment. To use a figurative example, antisemitism is like a chain composed of three links, each one leading to the next: an idea, a word, and an action. The idea, which is embedded in the head of the conceiver, obviously cannot be punished. The word, which expresses the idea, is punishable in Europe. In the United States, the word goes unpunished, despite the fact that it instigates action, and only the action that follows the word can be prohibited.

The new definition was unofficially adopted by the participants of the OSCE's Conference on Anti-Semitism and on Other Forms of Intolerance in Cordoba in June 2005. Since then, there are modest signs that it is being put to practical use.[28] Will it lower the number of future antisemitic activities or mute antisemitic expressions? The year 2005 was better than 2004 in terms of antisemitic violence, but only close monitoring over a period of several years will be able to pin-point long-term tendencies. Will it change, even slightly, the deeply rooted image of the Jew or perceptions of Israel? This is barely conceivable, but the definition does constitute international recognition of the fact that antisemitism is a wrong that can and should be put right and offers a framework within which efforts may be enlisted to achieve this goal.

---

[28] In July 2005, a Lithuanian court relied on the new definition when ruling that the editor-in-chief of the Vilnius daily *Respublika* published material propagating "enmity" while writing about a Jewish global plot. At the Cordoba Conference, it was reported that US police forces were already being trained to use the definition.

Hitler's Legacy:
Islamic Antisemitism
in the Middle East*

Matthias Küntzel**

I. INTRODUCTION

Nobody has forgotten the horrors of recent Middle East wars, but who still remembers the hopes of the summer of 2005, when Israel, despite massive internal resistance, pulled all its troops and settlers out of Gaza? Back then, many people hoped that the Gaza Strip would develop into a model Palestinian region that could form the nucleus of a Palestinian state alongside Israel.

But what happened was the opposite. Almost immediately, this territory was transformed into an outpost in a war against Israel, as new ammunition dumps and arms factories sprang up everywhere.

It was the same story in Southern Lebanon. Following the withdrawal of the Israeli army in 2000, it was turned into a deployment area by Hezbollah, which installed over 12,000 rockets, supplied by Iran via Syria, near the Israeli border. The area was turned into a base for aggression, with a well-planned system of fortified positions and a network of tunnels, from which an attack was launched on Israeli troops on July 12, 2006.

In both Gaza and Lebanon, the possibility existed of a normalization of relations with Israel, which could well have led to an economic upturn. So why do Hezbollah and Hamas prioritize weapons and war rather than peace and welfare? Why are they spurred on in doing so by Iran, a country that has neither a territorial dispute with Israel nor a Palestinian refugee problem? This is the answer given by Hezbollah leader, Hassan Nasrallah: "Israel is a cancer in the region, and when a tumor is discovered it must be cut out."[1] And here is what Khaled Mashal, leader of Hamas, has said on the issue: "Before Israel dies, it must be humiliated and degraded. ... We will make them lose their eyesight, we will make them lose their brains."[2]

A final example of this kind of statement comes from Mohammad Hassan Rahimian, the representative of the Iranian Supreme Leader Ali Khamenei. On

---

* Translated from the German by Colin Meade.
** Technical College, Hamburg; Research Fellow at the Vidal Sassoon Institute, Hebrew University, Jerusalem.
[1] Josef Joffe, "Der Wahnsinn an der Macht," *Die Zeit*, July 20, 2006.
[2] MEMRI, Special Dispatch, February 7, 2006.

November 16, 2006, Rahimian declared that "the Jew is the most stubborn enemy of the believers. And the decisive war will decide the fate of humanity.... The reappearance of the twelfth Imam will usher in a war between Israel and the Shia."[3]

Many Western commentators ignore such pronouncements, because they are so outrageous. But were Hitler's speeches any less outrageous? Hitler sincerely believed his propaganda and attempted, in his own peculiar sense of the word, to "free" the world of the Jews by murdering them. Islamists, too, genuinely believe in their own hate-filled tirades. They celebrate suicide attacks on Jews as "acts of liberation."

The fact that people who are not Islamists participate in this jubilation reveals a second similarity with the Nazi era. I am referring here to the impact of antisemitic brainwashing techniques, which have been refined since the days of Josef Goebbels.

One of the instruments of this brainwashing is the Hezbollah satellite TV channel *Al-Manar*, which reaches millions of people in the Arab and Islamic worlds.

Its popularity is due to its countless video clips, which use exciting graphics and stirring music to promote suicide bombings and murder. Indeed, *Al-Manar* has turned *The Protocols of the Elders of Zion*—Hitler's textbook for the Holocaust—into a soap opera.

Episode by episode, the series peddles the fantasy of a Jewish world conspiracy. For example, it claims that the Jews unleashed both world wars, discovered chemical weapons, and destroyed Hiroshima and Nagasaki with nuclear bombs. In short, the Jews have brought nothing but death and destruction upon humanity. The most bloodthirsty scenes are broadcast into Muslim homes by *Al-Manar*. In one such scene, a Rabbi says to a young Jew: "we have received an order from above. We need the blood of a Christian child for the unleavened bread for the Pesach [Passover] feast." In the following shot, a terrified youngster is seized from the neighborhood. The camera then zooms in on the child for a close-up of his throat being cut. The blood spurts from the wound and pours into a metal basin.

Here mediaeval antisemitism is being drummed into the collective consciousness of normal Muslim families with a suggestive force comparable to that of infamous Nazi productions such as the film "Jud Süss." A child who has seen this scene of slaughter will be affected for the rest of his or her life. It will take generations to remove this mental poison from people's minds.

When the Hezbollah-provoked war with Israel broke out in the summer of 2006, this investment in mass antisemitism paid off. Think of the pictures of the dead civilians in Lebanon and young victims of Beit Hanoun, killed by a stray Israeli shell. When Israel's army is compelled to defend itself, the results are not pretty on either side. But what is decisive is the context in which these images are viewed. Where the emotional infrastructure of antisemitism has been built up by a steady stream of propaganda over many years, the "meaning" of such images is self-evident. By such means, an eliminatory hatred of Israel and the Jews has been fostered on a mass scale, including in people who have nothing to do with Hezbollah.

---

[3] ISNA, http://isna.ir/Main/NewsViews.aspx?ID=News-825902, November 16, 2006, cited in "Iran: Antijüdische Parolen und Kriegsdrohungen," *Iran-Forschung. Übersetzungen und Analysen aus Iranischen Medien*, Berlin, November 17, 2006.

The fact is that not a single Muslim or Jew would have been killed after 2005 if Hamas and Hezbollah had decided to pursue peace rather than war. Once again, Judeophobia has led to terrible suffering. Peace in the Middle East requires a struggle against this hate propaganda. But what is the reason for this hatred? Is it Zionism and Israeli policies? Or might it be that Judeophobia is an integral part of Islam? Why and how did antisemitism come to the region? These and other questions are addressed in this paper, which approaches the issue of Islamic antisemitism from an historical perspective. The following question is a good place to start. What were the relations between Jews and Muslims like in the Egypt of the 1920s?

II. ISLAMIC MODERNISM...

In the 1920s, the Jews of Egypt were not isolated or hated but an accepted and protected part of public life. They served as members of parliament, were employed at the royal palace, and occupied important positions in the economic and political spheres. The Egyptian population, too, was favorably inclined toward the Jews.

"It merits emphasis," reported a Viennese journalist, "that the Jewish shopkeeper and commission agent enjoy great popularity with the domestic population and are mostly considered to be very honest."[4] How was this possible in a country where Islam was the state religion?

Astonishingly, the century-long history of Islamic modernism is now forgotten. This phase began at the start of the 19th century, reaching full bloom between 1860 and 1930. In 1839, for example, the Ottoman Sultan decreed equality for Jews and Christians, and this equality was enshrined in law in 1856. This measure was motivated not only by pressure from the European colonial powers, but also by the desire of the Ottoman elite to draw closer to European civilization. Of course, the *dhimmi* status of the Jews meant that their situation did not improve everywhere and at once. Some Jewish communities in several Arab lands still suffered persecution. But, at least in the urban centers, Jews were permitted to become members of parliament or hold government posts and, after 1909, were recruited into the military.

In the 1920s, most of the Islamic elites no longer lived under sharia law. Kemal Atatürk's regime abolished it in Turkey in 1924. In 1925, Iran began to secularize under Reza Shah. In Egypt, sharia law only applied in the personal sphere, while the rest of the legal code was of European provenance. In this period, rather than the nation being a subunit of Islam, Islam was a subunit of the nation, in which Muslims, Christians, and Jews enjoyed equal rights.

The Zionist movement was likewise accepted with an open mind. For example, the editor of the Egyptian daily *al-Ahram* wrote: "The Zionists are necessary for this region. The money they will bring in, their intelligence and the diligence which is one of their characteristics will, without doubt, bring new life to the country."[5] In the same vein, former Egyptian minister Ahmed Zaki wrote in 1922 that: "The victory of

---

[4] Abd Al-Fattah Muhammad El-Awaisi, *The Muslim Brothers and the Palestine Question 1928-1947* (London/New York: Tauris Academic Studies, 1998), p. 68.

[5] Stefan Wild, "Zum Selbstverständnis palästinensisch-arabischer Nationalität," in *Die Palästina-Frage 1917-1948*, ed. Helmut Mejcher (Paderborn, 1993), p. 79.

the Zionist idea is the turning point for the fulfillment of an ideal which is so dear to me, the revival of the Orient." Thus, in 1926, the Egyptian government extended a cordial welcome to a delegation of Jewish teachers from the British mandate territory. Even in 1933, the Egyptian government allowed 1,000 new Jewish immigrants to land in Port Said on their way to Palestine.[6] No wonder, therefore, that the German Nazi Party's Egyptian section was in despair in 1933. "The level of education of the broad masses is not advanced enough for the understanding of race theory," declared a spokesman for the Cairo Nazis in 1933. "An understanding of the Jewish threat has not yet been awakened here."[7]

To summarize, thirty years after the founding of the Zionist movement and twenty years before the creation of the State of Israel, relations between Jews and Muslims in Egypt, Turkey, and Iran were better than ever before.

III. ... AND ISLAMIST REACTION

To Islamic traditionalists, the advance of Islamic modernism was an outrage. Their resistance laid the groundwork for what is nowadays commonly described as the "Islamist" movement, that is to say, a movement combining Islamic fundamentalism with *jihad* in the sense of permanent holy war. It was from the outset both antimodern and anti-Jewish. Its three leading protagonists were Amin el-Husseini, appointed Grand Mufti of Jerusalem in 1921, the Syrian Sheikh Izz ad-Din al-Qassam, killed in 1934 by British soldiers, and the charismatic Hassan al-Banna, who founded the Egyptian Muslim Brotherhood in 1928.[8]

Their common teacher was Rashid Rida, a religious scholar heavily influenced by the Saudi Wahhabites. Rida's three prominent students followed their master in demanding a return to sharia law and traditional Islam, so as to drive Western civilization from Palestine and the Arab world before going on to defeat it throughout the world. Their Judeophobia was a declaration of war on the invasion of the world of Islam by liberal ideas. Nowhere was the impact of this invasion so divisive as in Palestine. As the Mufti complained to a conference of religious teachers: "They [i.e., the Jews] have also spread here their customs and usages that are opposed to our religion and to our whole way of life. Above all, our youth is being morally shattered. The Jewish girls who run around in shorts demoralize our youth by their mere presence."[9] For el-Husseini, "Jerusalem" was the focal point of the "rebirth of Islam" in its pure version, and Palestine was the centre from which the struggle against modernity and the Jews was to start. For the time being, however, the anti-Jewish pogroms organized by the Mufti in Palestine in the 1920s found no echo in the rest of the Arab world.

---

[6] See El-Awaisi, *Muslim Brothers*, p. 22ff.

[7] Gudrun Krämer, *Minderheit, Millet, Nation? Die Juden in Ägypten 1914-1952* (Wiesbaden, 1982), p. 278.

[8] "He hates Western civilization with undisguised passion," reported American journalist David W. Nussbaum after having visited the Mufti in 1946, "and except when he fled to Germany, had always given it a wide berth." Cited in Joseph B. Schechtman, *The Mufti and the Fuehrer* (New York: Thomas Yoseloff, 1965), p. 289.

[9] Uri M. Kupferschmidt, *The Supreme Muslim Council: Islam under the British Mandate for Palestine* (Leiden: E.J. Brill, 1987), p. 250.

To summarize, while the conflict between Zionism and anti-Zionism appeared on the surface to be about land, it actually concealed within it a far larger conflict regarding the question of how to relate to modernity. While the modernizers as a rule sought compromise with the Zionists, the Islamists denounced any attempt to reach an understanding with the Jews as treachery.

Until mid-1937, the balance of forces between the two currents was more or less in equilibrium. But from that point onward the picture began to change, as Nazi Germany threw its weight behind the Islamists.

IV. ISLAMISM AND NATIONAL SOCIALISM

From the time of the 1936 Berlin Olympics, the village of Zeesen, located to the south of Berlin, was home to what at that time was the world's most powerful short-wave radio transmitter. Between April 1939 and April 1945, Radio Zeesen reached out to the illiterate Muslim masses through daily Arabic programs, which were also broadcast in Persian and Turkish. At this time, listening to the radio in the Arab world took place primarily in public squares or bazaars and coffee houses. No other station was more popular than Zeesen's Nazi radio service, which skillfully mingled antisemitic propaganda with quotations from the Koran and Arabic music. The Second World War allies were presented as lackeys of the Jews, and the idea of the "United Jewish Nations" was drummed into the audience. At the same time, the Jews were attacked as the worst enemies of Islam. "The Jew since the time of Mohammed has never been a friend of the Muslim, the Jew is the enemy and it pleases Allah to kill him."[10]

After 1941, Zeesen's Arabic programs were directed by the Grand Mufti of Jerusalem, who had emigrated to Berlin. No less important than this technical innovation was the fact that the Mufti invented a new form of Judeophobia by recasting it in an Islamic mould.

The Mufti wanted to "unite all the Arab lands in a common hatred of the British and Jews," as he wrote in a letter to Adolf Hitler. But European antisemitism had proved an ineffective tool in the Arab world. This was because the European fantasy of the Jewish world conspiracy was totally foreign to the original Islamic view of the Jews. Only in the story of Christ did the Jews appear as a deadly and powerful force that allegedly went so far as to kill God's only son. Islam was quite a different story. Here it was not the Jews who murdered the Prophet, but the Prophet who murdered the Jews in Medina. As a result, the characteristic features of Christian antisemitism did not develop in the Muslim world. There were no fears of Jewish domination and no charges of diabolic evil. Instead, the Jews were treated with contempt or condescending tolerance. This cultural inheritance made the idea that the Jews of all people could represent a permanent danger to the Muslims and the world seem absurd.

The Mufti therefore seized on the only instrument that really moved the Arab masses: Islam. He was the first to translate Christian antisemitism into Islamic

---

[10] Seth Arsenian, "Wartime Propaganda in the Middle East," *The Middle East Journal* 2(4) (1948), p. 421; Robert Melka, *The Axis and the Arab Middle East 1930-1945* (University of Minnesota, 1966), p. 47ff; Heinz Tillmann, *Deutschlands Araberpolitik im Zweiten Weltkrieg* (East Berlin, 1965), p. 83ff.

language, thus creating an "Islamic antisemitism." His first major manifesto bore the title "Islam-Judaism. Appeal of the Grand Mufti to the Islamic World in the Year 1937." This 31-page pamphlet reached the entire Arab world, and there are indications that Nazi agents helped draft it. The following short passage is illustrative of its content:

> The struggle between the Jews and Islam began when Muhammad fled from Mecca to Medina.... The Jewish methods were, even in those days, the same as now. As always, their weapon was slander.... They said that Muhammad was a swindler ... they began to ask Muhammad senseless and insoluble questions ... and they endeavored to destroy the Muslims.... If the Jews could betray Muhammad in this way, how will they betray Muslims today?

What we have here is a new, popularized form of Judeophobia based on the oriental folk tale tradition that moves constantly back and forth between the 7th and 20th centuries.

Classical Islamic literature had as a rule treated Muhammad's clash with the Jews of Medina as a minor episode in the Prophet's life. The anti-Jewish passages in the Quran and *hadith* had lain dormant or were considered of little significance during previous centuries.

These elements were now invested with new life and vigor. The Mufti began to ascribe a truly cosmic significance to the allegedly hostile attitude of the Jewish tribes of Medina to the Prophet. He picked out the occasional outbursts of hatred found in the Quran and *hadith* and drummed them relentlessly into the minds of Muslims at every available opportunity—including via Zeesen's Arabic short-wave radio station.

To summarize, in 1937, Germany began to disseminate a form of Islamic antisemitism that fused together the traditional Islamic view that the Jews were inferior with the European notion that they were deviously powerful. In other words, the Jews were being derided as "pigs" and "apes" while simultaneously being demonized as the puppet masters of world politics. This specific form of antisemitism was broadcast to the Islamic world on Radio Zeesen. At the same time, Nazi Germany was heavily subsidizing the Egyptian Muslim Brotherhood and promoting its anti-Jewish agitation. There could no longer be any talk of a balance between Islamic modernizers and Islamists.

Radio Zeesen ceased operation in April 1945. But it was only after that date that its message of hate really began to reverberate in the Arab world.

V. THE SECOND DIVISION OF THE WORLD

After May 8, 1945, National Socialism was banned throughout almost the entire the world. In the Arab world, however, Nazi ideology continued to reverberate. In her report on the 1961 trial of Adolf Eichmann, Hannah Arendt discussed the reactions to the trial in the Arab media:

> [N]ewspapers in Damascus and Beirut, in Cairo and Jordan did not hide their sympathy for Eichmann or their regret that he "had not finished the job"; a broadcast from Cairo on the day the trial opened even injected a slightly anti-German note into its comments, complaining that there was not "a single incident

in which one German plane flew over one Jewish settlement and dropped one bomb on it throughout the last war."[11]

During this period, a twofold division took place in the world. The division in the political and economic sphere is well known as the Cold War. The second split—which was obscured by the Cold War—concerned the acceptance and continuing influence of National Socialist ideas. The fault line was already apparent by 1946 and had much to do with the period's most influential Arab politician, the former Grand Mufti of Jerusalem, and Western opportunism.

In 1946, el-Husseini was wanted on war crimes charges by several countries, including the United Kingdom and the United States. Between 1941 and 1945, he directed the Muslim SS divisions from Berlin and was personally responsible for the fact that thousands of Jewish children, who might otherwise have survived, perished in the gas chambers. All of this was known in 1946. Nonetheless, the United Kingdom and the United States chose to drop the criminal prosecution of el-Husseini in order to avoid spoiling their relations with the Arab world. France, in whose custody el-Husseini was being held, deliberately let him get away. The years of Nazi Arabic language propaganda had made the Mufti by far the best-known political figure in the Arab and Islamic world.[12] But the 1946 de facto amnesty granted by the Western powers enhanced his prestige even more. The Arabs saw in this impunity, wrote Simon Wiesenthal in 1946, "not only a weakness of the Europeans, but also absolution for past and future occurrences. A man who is enemy no. 1 of a powerful empire—and this empire cannot fend him off—seems to the Arabs to be a suitable leader."[13] But the biggest cheerleaders for the Mufti were the Muslim Brothers, who at that time could mobilize a million people in Egypt alone.[14] It was they, indeed, who had organized the Mufti's return and who from the outset defended his Nazi activities from any criticism.

The two opposing views of the Holocaust collided in November 1947 in the General Assembly of the United Nations. On one side were those who considered the Shoah a tragedy and therefore argued for a partition of Palestine and the founding of two Palestinian states: an Arab Muslim state and a Jewish state. On the other side were those who opposed a two-state solution in principle and whose most influential representative was none other than Amin el-Husseini, yet again playing the role of spokesman for the Palestinian Arabs. In el-Husseini's view, the Arabs "should jointly attack the Jews and destroy them as soon as the British forces have withdrawn [from the Palestinian Mandate territory]."[15] The Muslim Brotherhood likewise interpreted the UN Resolution from the standpoint of its antisemitic worldview. Hassan al-Banna, the Brotherhood's leader, "considered the whole United Nations intervention to be an international plot, carried out by the Americans, the

---

[11] Hannah Arendt, *Eichmann in Jerusalem* (Middlesex: Penguin, 1965), p. 13.

[12] Matthias Küntzel, *Jihad and Jew-Hatred: Islamism, Nazism and the Roots of 9/11* (New York: Telos Press, 2007), p. 46.

[13] Simon Wiesenthal, *Grossmufti—Grossagent der Achse* (Salzburg: Ried-Verlag, 1947), p. 2.

[14] See Richard P. Mitchell, *The Society of the Muslim Brothers* (London: Oxford University Press, 1969), p. 328.

[15] Nicholas Bethell, *Das Palästina-Dreieck* (Frankfurt am Main, 1979), p. 381.

British, and the Russians under the influence of Zionism."[16] So, as in 1946 with the triumphant return of the Mufti, in 1947 the reality of the Holocaust was denied a second time.

But there was yet a third viewpoint to be found in the Arab world in 1947. Particularly in Palestine, there were many Arabs who were not interested in the Holocaust for its own sake but were nevertheless in favor of partition because they knew "that the fight against partition was futile because the Arabs had no arms and the Jews had the support of the United States and Britain." Or because they were among the "tens of thousands of laborers who advanced the Jewish economy, especially by working in the citrus groves."[17] "Many Palestinian Arabs thus not only refrained from fighting themselves, but also did their best to prevent foreigners and locals from carrying out military actions," writes Hillel Cohen, the first scholar to investigate the movement of so-called Arab "collaborators." "Avoidance of war and even agreement with the Jews were, in their view, best for the Palestinian Arab nation."[18]

This group included the Arab leaders who sympathized with the partition plan, albeit only in private, since they were afraid to openly contradict the Mufti and Muslim Brotherhood. Among them was Abdullah, Emir of Transjordan, Sidqi Pasha, Prime Minister of Egypt, Abd al-Rahman Azzam, head of the Arab League, and Muzahim al-Pashashi, former Prime Minister of Iraq, who argued: "Eventually there would have to be an acceptance of the Jewish state's existence, but for now it was politically impossible to acknowledge this publicly." To do so, he said, would "cause a revolt in Iraq."[19] So the cowardice of the Arab leaders and the cynicism of the West, which let the Mufti escape, paved the way for one of the most fateful watersheds of the 20th century: the Arab military assault on Israel in 1948.

In 1952, the defeat of the Arab armies in this conflict brought to power yet another former associate of the Nazis, Gamal Abdel Nasser. Nasser had *The Protocols of the Elders of Zion* disseminated throughout the Arab world and in 1964 was still assuring the *Deutsche Nationalzeitung* that "the lie about the 6 million murdered Jews is not taken seriously by anyone."

After Nasser's military campaign against Israel also failed miserably during the Six-Day War of 1967, the Arab world's hatred of the Jews was once again radicalized in an Islamist direction. Nasser's anti-Jewish propaganda was still accompanied by a fondness for life's pleasures. Now antisemitism was mixed with the Islamists' hatred of sensuality and joy in life and popularized as religious resistance against all "corrupters of the world." Now it was "discovered" that not only was everything Jewish evil but everything evil was Jewish.

Thus, the most important manifesto of Islamist antisemitism, the essay "Our Struggle with the Jews" by Sayyid Qutb, millions of copies of which have been distributed throughout the Islamic world with Saudi Arabian help, declares, with allusions to Karl Marx, Sigmund Freud, and Emile Durkheim, that the Jews are

---

[16] El-Awaisi, *Muslim Brothers*, p. 195.

[17] Hillel Cohen, *Army of Shadows: Palestinian Collaboration With Zionism, 1917-1948* (Berkeley: University of California Press, 2008), p. 236.

[18] Ibid., p. 231.

[19] Cited in Bruse Maddy-Weitzman, *The Crystallization of the Arab State System 1945-1954* (New York: Syracuse University Press, 1993), p. 80.

responsible for the worldwide moral and sexual decline: "behind the doctrine of atheistic materialism was a Jew; behind the doctrine of animalistic sexuality was a Jew; and behind the destruction of the family and the shattering of sacred relationships in society was a Jew."[20] Palestine was declared sacred Islamic territory (*Dar al-Islam*), where Jews should not be allowed to govern even a single village, and Israel's destruction a religious duty. The first victims of the Islamist turn were the Muslims themselves. The "struggle against depravity" implies the suppression of one's own sensual needs, and the return to "sacred relationship in society" means the archaic subjugation of women.

With the Iranian Revolution of 1979, Islamism gained its first great victory. Three years later, Hezbollah, under the influence of Khomeini, began to systematically use human beings as bombs. The hatred of Jews was now greater than the fear of death. Whenever the possibility of a peaceful solution appeared on the horizon, it would be drowned in the blood of suicidal mass murders. The first major series of suicide bombings began in Palestine in 1993, at precisely the moment when the Oslo peace process was under way. It was resumed in October 2000 after Israel withdrew from Lebanon and had made its most far-reaching concessions yet to the Palestinian side at Camp David.[21] It was the same logic that dictated that in 2005 Israel's withdrawal from Gaza would be met by a hail of rockets.

VI. Conclusion

So what overall conclusions can we draw from this historical survey?

First, as regards the Islamic world, history shows that how any Muslim defines his or her relationship to Israel and the Jews is a strictly personal decision. The Mufti made a deliberate choice to torpedo any solution through dialogue, and Hamas too has made a deliberate choice to want to destroy Israel. There is nothing inevitable about such decisions.

Second, as regards Europe, we can see how catastrophic the consequences of European appeasement of Islamism have been and remain today.

Amin el-Husseini was installed and promoted by European powers. In 1921, it was the British who appointed him Mufti against the will of the majority of Palestinians. It was the Germans who paid for his services between 1937 and 1945. And it was the French who let him flee to Egypt in 1946, so enabling him to resume his activities. Despite this co-responsibility for the situation, Europe's politicians and media continue to refuse to recognize the existence of the Islamist antisemitism of Hezbollah and Hamas. But if this fact is ignored, the scale of Islamist terror becomes the new measure of Israel's guilt. The principle is as follows: the more barbarous anti-Jewish terrorism becomes, the more guilty Israel is. However, those who make Israel the scapegoat for Islamist violence are not only dancing to the Islamists' tune

---

[20] Qutb's text was written in 1950, but could not gain acceptance in the period of Nasser's bloody suppression of the Muslim Brotherhood, to which Qutb himself fell victim by hanging. See Ronald L. Nettler, "Past Trials and Present Tribulations: A Muslim Fundamentalist Speaks on the Jews," in *Antisemitism in the Contemporary World*, ed. Michael Curtis (London, 1986), p. 99ff.

[21] Joseph Croitoru, *Der Märtyrer als Waffe* (Wien, 2003), p. 130 and p. 165ff.

but are also subscribing to the latest version of the old European antisemitic trope that the Jews are behind everything bad, even when they are themselves the victims. The absence of clarity is thus the beginning of complicity.

Finally, as regards antisemitism itself, the historical record gives the lie to the assumption that Islamic antisemitism is caused by Zionism or Israeli policy. In fact, it is not the escalation of the Middle East conflict that gives rise to antisemitism; rather, it is antisemitism that gives rise to the escalation of the Middle East conflict—again and again.

This antisemitism cannot be mitigated by anything the Jews do or by any conciliatory step that the Israeli government might take. Those who have fallen prey to the demonizing delusions of antisemitism are bound to find their prejudices confirmed by whatever the Israeli government does or does not do.

Let me therefore conclude with an appeal by a Muslim, the scholar of Islam Bassam Tibi: "only when the public takes an appropriate stand against the antisemitic dimension of Islamism, will it be possible to say that they have truly understood the lessons of the Holocaust."[22]

---

[22] Bassam Tibi, "Der importierte Hass. Antisemitismus ist in der arabischen Welt weit verbreitet," *Die Zeit*, February 6, 2003.

Continuities, Discontinuities, and Contingencies: Anti-Alienism, Antisemitism, and Anti-Zionism in Twentieth-Century South Africa

Milton Shain*

I. INTRODUCTION

For many years, scholars have commented on the continuities, discontinuities, and contingencies of antisemitism through the ages: pagan and early Christian antisemitism, medieval and modern antisemitism, modern antisemitism and Nazism, and, more recently, antisemitism and anti-Zionism.[1] While these debates are general in their focus, it is apparent that continuities, discontinuities, and contingencies are also discernible within national polities. The South African case in the twentieth century is illustrative. It demonstrates continuities between anti-alienism at the turn of the century, the "Jewish Question" in the 1930s and early 1940s, and anti-Zionism during the latter part of the century.

II. ANTI-ALIENISM

By the early twentieth century a widespread anti-Jewish stereotype had evolved against the backdrop of a large influx of Eastern European Jews—mainly from Lithuania—beginning at the time minerals were discovered in the late nineteenth century. The newcomers attracted substantial hostile attention: in the interior as itinerant peddlers, in particular in the southern Cape Colony as traders in the ostrich feather industry; on the diamond fields as fortune-seekers associated with illicit diamond dealing; in the mining town of Johannesburg on the Witwatersrand as "Peruvians," associated with the seamier side of the city's life, including the illicit

---

* Director, Isaac and Jessie Kaplan Centre for Jewish Studies and Research, University of Cape Town. I wish to thank Richard Mendelsohn and Millie Pimstone for their valuable comments.

[1] See, for example, Marcel Simon, *Verus Israel. A Study of the Relations between Christians and Jews in the Roman Empire AD 135-425* (London: Littman Library of Jewish Civilization, 1996); Gavin Langmuir, *Towards a Definition of Antisemitism* (Berkeley and Los Angeles: University of California Press, 1990); and Robert Wistrich, "Anti-Zionism as an Expression of Antisemitism in Recent Years," in *Present Day Antisemitism*, ed. Yehuda Bauer (Jerusalem: Hebrew University of Jerusalem, Vidal Sassoon Center for the Study of Antisemitism, 1988), pp. 175-87. For an examination of the connections between antisemitism and Nazism, see Shulamit Volkov, *Germans, Jews, and Antisemites. Trials in Emancipation* (New York: Cambridge University Press, 2006), pp. 67-90.

liquor trade and prostitution, and as mine magnates or cosmopolitan financiers on the Witwatersrand, bent on dominating the country.[2]

The image of the manipulative and dishonest Jew that evolved by the early twentieth century must be seen in the context of urbanization and modernization. For the alienated and landless Boers—those constituting the incipient "poor white" problem—the Jewish store was, at least for some observers, a symbol of greed and dishonesty. Instead of being appreciated for his services, the itinerant Jewish trader and the small shopkeeper were blamed for corrupting a rustic world of innocence and harmony. In the urban centers, antipathy was driven by competing merchants— the established English-speaking mercantile class—who considered Jewish trading patterns repugnant.[3]

Far more sinister than the trader was the image of the Jew as part of a network of international finance, a trope well known at this time in Europe. The notion of the cosmopolitan financier found fertile soil in South Africa, where mining magnates or "Randlords," among whom Jews were disproportionately represented, were such a prominent feature of society. It made little difference that these Jewish financiers had largely assimilated and were Jews in name only. Their presence was particularly highlighted in England by the pro-Boers at the time of the Anglo-Boer War (1899-1902). Letters to the press and cartoon caricatures of corpulent and Semitic-looking financiers adorning the pages of *The Owl* and the *South African Review* reveal that these ideas percolated into South Africa.[4]

The conspiratorial view of international finance was most clearly enunciated by J.A. Hobson, the *Manchester Guardian*'s correspondent in Johannesburg. His sentiments were succinctly captured in his book, *The War in South Africa*, which postulated the war being fought in the interests of a "small group of international financiers, chiefly German in origin and Jewish in race."[5] These ideas were consolidated after the war, this time in connection with the controversial importation of Chinese labor to replace the dwindling reserves of African labor in the mines. Increasingly the alien plutocrats or "Hebrew Goldbugs" were portrayed as responsible for the scheme, while poems and satirical compositions alluded to a Jewish-Chinese takeover of Johannesburg.[6]

It was in this climate that "Hoggenheimer"—a quintessential Jewish parvenu based on a stage character[7]—became a household name and a visible component of the anti-Jewish stereotype, complementing the "Peruvian" image. In the eyes of the antisemite, it was the dishonesty of the "Peruvian" that enabled him to achieve plutocratic prominence. Hoggenheimer, allegedly the *eminence grise* of South Africa, merely symbolized on a higher plane the machinations of the Jewish peddler and of the illicit diamond and liquor dealers.

---

[2] See Milton Shain, *The Roots of Antisemitism in South Africa* (Charlottesville and London: University Press of Virginia and Witwatersrand University Press, 1994).

[3] See, for example, comment in *The Owl*, January 23, 1897.

[4] See Shain, *Roots of Antisemitism*, ch. 3, *passim*.

[5] J.A. Hobson, *The War in South Africa. Its Causes and Effects* (London: Nisbet, 1900), p. 189.

[6] See Shain, *Roots of Antisemitism*, ch. 3, *passim*.

[7] "The Girl from Kays," by Owen Hall was first performed in London before coming to South Africa in 1903. See Shain, *Roots of Antisemitism*, pp. 62-63.

During the First World War, the anti-Jewish stereotype was embellished with the Jew being identified as military "shirker" and—after the Russian Revolution—as a subversive Bolshevik. Thus a "Russian-Jewish" conspiracy was the way leading newspapers depicted the heady days of March 1922, the so-called Rand Revolt.[8] By the mid-1920s, newspapers began to question the potential for Eastern European Jews to integrate into South African society. "Unassimilability" became the new catchword, an idea influenced directly by nativist ideas from the United States as well as by a new domestic segregationist discourse in which race and culture were conflated.[9]

The anti-Jewish stereotype was thus intimately bound up with the local stresses and upheavals engendered by South Africa's "mineral revolution." For many categories of the social spectrum—the impoverished farmer, the unemployed worker, the competing merchant, the frustrated businessman, and the fearful worker—the stereotype served as a psychological cushion. It was a universal scapegoat in an age of turmoil. Most importantly, the Jew appeared to be the beneficiary of transformation and change. On the principal of *cui bono* (who benefits), it was presumed that the Jew, seemingly at home in the city, was the *eminence grise*.

III. ANTISEMITISM: THE "JEWISH QUESTION," 1930-1948

Given the evolution of the anti-Jewish stereotype, it was no surprise that the full spectrum of the English and Afrikaans press welcomed the Quota Act of 1930, which set out to curtail Eastern European Jewish immigration.[10] The Act heralded, in Todd Endelman's terms, the transformation of "private" into "public" or programmatic antisemitism. That is to say, antisemitism moved from relatively benign cultural and literary stereotyping to the public arena, with demands for political action.[11] This was driven by the South African Christian National Socialist Movement—better known as the Greyshirts—under the leadership of Louis T. Weichardt. At its peak, the movement had 2,000 members, and its success inspired a number of similar organizations to mushroom across the country. Although inspired by Nazi forms and racist or *volkisch* discourse, the substantive message of South Africa's fascist movements related to the South African experience: Jews had fomented the Anglo-Boer War, inspired blacks against white civilization, controlled the press, exploited Afrikaners, dominated society, and so forth. Against the backdrop of drought, depression, and rapidly increasing black economic competition, the Jew was an ideal

---

[8] See Shain, *Roots of Antisemitism*, ch. 5.

[9] See Saul Dubow, "Race, Civilization and Culture: The Elaboration of Segregationist Discourse in the Inter-war years," in *The Politics of Race, Class and Nationalism in Twentieth Century South Africa*, ed. Shula Marks and Stanley Trapido (London and New York: Longman, 1987), pp. 71-94.

[10] See the *East London Daily Dispatch*, February 3, 1930; *Die Burger*, January 30, 1930; *Sunday Times*, February 2, 1930; *The Cape*, February 7, 1930; *The Daily Representative*, February 10, 1930; *Ons Vaderland*, February 1, 1930; and *Cape Argus*, February 8, 1930.

[11] Todd M. Endelman, "Comparative Perspectives on Modern Anti-Semitism in the West," in *History and Hate. The Dimensions of Anti-Semitism*, ed. David Berger (Philadelphia: The Jewish Publication Society, 1986), pp. 95-114.

scapegoat.[12] Indeed, a variation of the notorious *Protocols of the Elders of Zion* appeared in 1934, leading to a libel action against *inter alia* Johannes von Moltke, the Eastern Province leader of the South African Christian/Gentile National Socialist Movement (the Greyshirts) breakaway group.[13]

Anti-Jewish ideas rapidly permeated the mainstream of Afrikaner nationalism, exacerbated by the influx of German-Jewish refugees in the wake of Hitler's ascent to power. The groundswell of anti-Jewish feeling prompted demands for the ending of Jewish immigration. These developments galvanized the ruling United Party to introduce stiffer educational and financial requirements for purposes of immigration. These were to take effect on November 1, 1936 and resulted in an interim increase in German-Jewish immigration. By the end of October, well-attended meetings led by a group of Stellenbosch University professors protested against the arrival of the *Stuttgart* carrying some 537 German-Jewish immigrants.[14] Fringe sentiment was gradually integrated into the core of the political program of the opposition Purified National Party, which—at least in some quarters—was calling for special action against recent Jewish arrivals, including restrictions on property rights and on access to the professions. These arguments were predicated upon Jewish "unassimilability" and fears of Jewish power and domination. In an obvious response to flourishing antisemitism, coupled with a private Bill introduced by future Prime Minister D.F. Malan to restrict Jewish immigration and stiffen naturalization laws, the United Party introduced an Aliens Act in 1937 designed to restrict Jewish immigration—particularly from Germany—without mentioning Jews by name. Immigrants were to be permitted entry by a Selection Board on the grounds of good character and the likelihood of assimilation into the European population.

The Act failed to satisfy the Purified Nationalists. For them any Jewish immigration was unacceptable, and the "Jewish Question" was now a central plank in their political platform. Malan, under pressure from the far-right Greyshirts, focused increasingly on the Jew as an explanation for the Afrikaners' political misfortunes. It was Hendrik Verwoerd, however, who stood at the vanguard of anti-Jewish agitation. In a major editorial in *Die Transvaler*, the newspaper he edited, he summarized the whole corpus of antisemitic discourse: Jewish domination in business and the professions, the unassimilability of Jews, Jewish alienation from the Afrikaners, questionable Jewish commercial morality, and the use of money by Jews to influence government through the English-language press.[15] Obviously, the "Jewish Question" was no longer the concern solely of fringe fascist groups: it was now firmly entrenched within mainstream white politics.

Malan's Purified Nationalists predictably stressed the "Jewish Problem" in the 1938 general election campaign. Party propaganda was underpinned by an insistence on the prospect of Jewish domination. The election year also saw the emergence

---

[12] See Patrick J. Furlong, *Between Crown and Swastika* (Johannesburg: Witwatersrand University Press, 1991), p. 13.

[13] Ibid., pp. 44-45. For an account of the trial, see Hadassah Ben-Itto, *The Lie That Wouldn't Die* (London: Vallentine Mitchell, 2005).

[14] Edna Bradlow, "Immigration into the Union, 1910-1948. Policies and Attitudes" (PhD diss., University of Cape Town, 1978), p. 266.

[15] *Die Transvaler*, October 1, 1937.

of a new paramilitary authoritarian movement, the *Ossewabrandwag* (OB). Born out of the centenary celebrations of the Great Trek, the *Ossewabrandwag* attacked so-called "British-Jewish-Masonic" imperialism and capitalism, "British Jewish" democracy, "Jewish money-power," and "Jewish disloyalty."[16] But it was also the association of Jews with communism that concerned some detractors. A leading Afrikaner Nationalist and inveterate antisemite, Eric Louw, attacked international Jewish communism together with liberalism, which he saw as a cover for communist ends.[17] This association of Jews with international communism had also been evident in the Greyshirt propaganda, which identified the Jews as an "Oosters Semitiese ras" (Eastern Semitic race) and as a menace or peril to Afrikaners.[18]

The rhetoric of protest and opposition was thus riddled with racist assumptions and antisemitic generalizations. Jews were aliens, disloyal, and bent on exploitation or subversion. Hostility was driven largely by Afrikaner intellectuals, some of whom had studied in Germany. Like their European counterparts on the Right, Afrikaner nationalists were opposed to liberalism, Marxism, and laissez-faire capitalism. The last, associated with British imperialism, was exemplified in Hoggenheimer, who was "English-speaking, imperialist, and clearly Jewish."[19] Nationalist sentiment, in other words, sharpened perceptions of the Jew as a quintessential alien. For the far-right Afrikaner, he symbolized all that was foreign and oppressive. Moreover, as English speakers for the most part, Jews were political enemies. They certainly helped to consolidate an all-embracing Afrikaner identity, understood in terms of cultural unity, national roots, and opposition to the foreigner. In this way, antisemitism helped in some way to cover or paper over class divisions and antagonisms within Afrikaner society. The Afrikaner's inferior status in society and his poverty could be explained in racial or national terms. By employing this discourse of race to exclude and denigrate Jews, the Afrikaner was in turn elevated. Consequently, it is no coincidence that antisemitism continued to suffuse specifically right-wing Afrikaner political discourse and programs—this despite the upturn in the economy from the mid-1930s. And it is also no coincidence that the "Jewish Question" was tied to internecine Afrikaner struggles, employed according to prevailing needs and power games.[20]

Antisemitism was given further impetus following the South African parliament's decision to support the Commonwealth war effort to resist Germany in 1939. A powerful antiwar movement was orchestrated by the OB in which the appeal of fascism and with it the rhetoric of antisemitism was strong. A range of major National

---

[16] Gideon Shimoni, *Jews and Zionism. The South African Experience 1910-1967* (Cape Town: Oxford University Press, 1980), p. 130.

[17] *Hansard*, February 24, 1939.

[18] A. Van Deventer, "Afrikaner Nationalist Politics and Anti-Communism, 1937-1945" (PhD diss., University of Stellenbosch, 1991), p. 273.

[19] T. Dunbar Moodie, *The Rise of Afrikanerdom. Power, Apartheid, and the Afrikaner Civil Religion* (Berkeley, Los Angeles and London: University of California Press, 1975).

[20] Van Deventer, "Afrikaner Nationalist Politics," p. 283. Of course, Afrikaner nationalism was not monolithic. For a microcosmic look at internecine struggles within Afrikaner nationalism at this time in the "Mecca of Afrikanerdom," see Joanne Louise Duffy, "Afrikaner Unity, the National Party, and the Afrikaner Nationalist Radical Right in Stellenbosch, 1934-1938" (PhD diss., Oxford University, 2001).

Party publications issued in the early 1940s demonstrated the formative influence of Mussolini and Hitler or the exclusive nature of an insurgent Afrikaner nationalism in which the Jew had no place.[21] Certainly the OB saw the Jews as a specific racial grouping in South Africa.[22] However, the struggle against Hitler gradually eroded the warm reception accorded to Nazi and fascist ideas. By 1942, mainstream National Party leaders, including Malan, Verwoerd, and Strijdom, "were unequivocally rejecting National Socialism as an alien import into South Africa, and endorsing parliamentary democracy."[23] Nonetheless, as late as 1944, an investigation into antisemitism demonstrated a wide-ranging hostility toward Jews.[24]

The 1930s had clearly witnessed a sea change in the nature and character of antisemitism, unquestionably related to specific traumas in the 1930s: the intensification of "poor whiteism" following the impact upon South Africa of the world depression, the emergence of Nazism in Europe, and—most importantly—the rise of an illiberal, anti-modernist, and exclusivist strain within Afrikaner nationalism. That is why "public" antisemitism in South African was an essentially, but not exclusively, Afrikaner phenomenon and why it appealed across the whole spectrum of Afrikaner nationalist opinion.

IV. ANTI-ZIONISM

The "Jewish Question" rapidly disappeared after the war. The Greyshirts and the far-right New Order disbanded, and the ban on Jewish membership of the Transvaal National Party was lifted in 1951.[25] A new Afrikaner bourgeoisie—well-educated, confident, and more optimistic than its forebears—enjoyed the economic fruits of racist exploitation and political power. They developed very rapidly a respect for enterprise and material success. The very scaffolding that had underpinned the Afrikaners' sense of inferiority was thus removed as they began to experience power and social mobility. Within a decade of coming to power a broad Afrikaner middle class had appeared.[26] The sense of competition with and fear of the Jew dissipated. A postwar consumerist culture meant the erosion of rural values and a newfound respect for the city. No longer was it an alien and inhospitable place. Most significantly, however, the impetus of exclusivist Afrikaner nationalism waned. English speakers, including Jews, were necessary for the apartheid project. As whites, they were to have a rightful and welcome place. In the postwar South African world, color was the cardinal divide and the greatest source of Afrikaner fear. Antisemitism was relegated to occasional uttering on the part of the far right, including instances of Holocaust denial in the 1970s.[27]

---

[21] Shain, *Roots of Antisemitism*, p. 148.
[22] See Van Deventer, "Afrikaner Nationalist Politics," p. 277.
[23] Hermann Giliomee, *The Afrikaners. Biography of a People* (Cape Town: Tafelberg, 2003), p. 444.
[24] See Albrecht Hagemann, "Antisemitism in South Africa During World War II: A Documentation," in *Simon Wiesenthal Center Annual*, vol. 4 (New York, 1987).
[25] The National Party was organized along federal lines with each party maintaining an autonomous structure.
[26] Giliomee, *The Afrikaners*, p. 490.
[27] Milton Shain, "South Africa," in *The World Reacts to the Holocaust*, ed. David Wyman (Baltimore: Johns Hopkins University Press, 1996), pp. 670-89.

At this time, however, a new source of hostility began to emerge around the question of Zionism, driven essentially, but not exclusively, by the minority Muslim population.[28] In apartheid South Africa, the views of this community were largely unknown to the whites, including Jews.[29] Jews certainly were unaware that common episodes and events were viewed in distinctive and predictably different ways. From the earliest days of the Mandate, for example, Muslims took a very different view to Jews.[30] For them, the Israeli War of Independence was a catastrophe (*Nakba*),[31] exacerbated by further Israeli victories against Arab forces, culminating in the Six Day War.[32] In short, South African Muslims shared in the humiliation of their Muslim "brothers and sisters." Jews, on the other hand, unquestioningly empathized with the Jewish state, fully supported till recent times by the "white" owned and Eurocentric media.

Although "Zionism" was a term of opprobrium and Israel was seen to be an aggressor state,[33] the Muslim communal leadership was largely quiescent until at least the late 1960s. They were increasingly challenged by a younger generation of Muslims, galvanized by the charged political atmosphere of the 1970s. Inspired by new radical teachings and the 1976 African student uprising in Soweto, and buttressed by Khomeinism and the international Muslim struggle against imperialism, this generation read the writings of Abdul-A'la Mawdudi (1903-1979) and Sayyid Qutb (1906-1966).[34] For them, secularism, the West, and deviant Arab regimes

---

[28] The 553,585 largely Sunni Muslims in South Africa (1.4 percent of the total population according to the 1996 Census) are essentially a part of the Colored and Indian population. They are the descendents of political prisoners brought to the Cape by the Dutch rulers from the Indonesian islands in the seventeenth century, ex-slaves, nineteenth century Indian immigrants, and the offspring of black/white relationships. See Ebrahim Moosa, "Islam in South Africa," in *Living Faiths in South Africa*, ed. Martin Prozesky and John de Gruchy (Cape Town: David Philip, 1995), pp. 129-54.

[29] Interaction in apartheid South Africa took place only in the labor and economic spheres; in the social context the racial divide was virtually absolute. Relationships, moreover, were based on a master-servant or employer-employee categories inherent in the apartheid framework.

[30] As early as 1925, *Muslim Outlook* criticized Jewish capitalists forcing Arab peasants off the land. See, for Example, *Muslim Outlook*, April 18, 1925.

[31] Muslims protested outside Cape Town against the "occupation of Palestine by the Zionists." See Muhammed Haron "The Muslim News (1960-1986): Expression of an Islamic Identity in South Africa," in *Muslim Identity and Social Change in Sub-Saharan Africa*, ed. Louis Brenner (London: Hurst & Company, 1993), p. 222.

[32] An article entitled "Barbarity of the Jews," which appeared in *Muslim News* on July 14, 1967, stated that: "1948 and 1967 show that despite centuries of wandering in Europe they [the Jews] have not lost their barbaric tendencies which previously incurred the wrath of God." See also *Muslim News*, July 28, 1967.

[33] See, for example, *Muslim News*, July 28, 1967; and Abdulkader Tayob, *Islamic Resurgence in South Africa. The Muslim Youth Movement* (Cape Town: University of Cape Town Press, 1998), p. 85. For further details, see Margo Bastos, "Muslim Anti-Zionism and Antisemitism since the Second World War, with special reference to 'Muslim News/Views'" (MA diss., University of Cape Town, 2002).

[34] See Tayob, *Islamic Resurgence*, ch. 3, *passim*; and Desmond Charles Rice, "Islamic Fundamentalism as a Major Religiopolitical Movement and its Impact on South Africa" (MA diss., University of Cape Town, 1987), pp. 438-52. The writings of Mawdudi and Qutb were serialized in the *Islamic Mission*, a newsletter started by the Claremont Muslim Youth Association.

were all targeted. A fortnightly newspaper, *Muslim News* (later renamed *Muslim Views*), and other Muslim publications increasingly vilified Zionist "intrusion" and commented on "The Tragedy of Palestine."[35] Muslims were warned about "Zionist designs" and were familiarized with the *Protocols of the Elders of Zion*.[36] The equating of Zionism with racism at the United Nations in 1976 was hailed as a victory for the Palestinian Liberation Organization (PLO) and a defeat for the United States and Israel.[37] For a community, characterized by one commentator as "Zionophobes," this was an inspiring moment.[38]

By the late 1970s, a Palestinian Islamic Solidarity Committee had been established in Durban,[39] and the Muslim Youth Movement (MYM) had embarked on a thorough training schedule, including study programs, special camps, and manuals, all linked intricately with international Islamic resurgent literature and tapes. Zionism, secularism, capitalism, and communism were all identified as threats.[40] Impetus was added by the success of the Iranian Revolution in 1979. The writings of Ali Shari'ati (1933-1977) and the Ayatollah Khomeini were now included in MYM reading lists. In 1980, the radical group Qibla was founded. Patently inspired by the overthrow of the Shah in Iran and palpably informed by global perspectives on the potential for challenging the South African state from a Muslim perspective, it spoke of an "Islamic Revolution in South Africa."

Muslim demonstrations against Israel and Zionism on the campuses of the University of Cape Town and the University of the Witwatersrand at the time of the 1982 Sabra and Shatilla massacres in Lebanon[41] revealed an intensification of Muslim anti-Zionism and a new determination for action among the younger generation. The growth of radical Islam was especially evident in the objection of some Muslims to being part of the broad-based anti-apartheid coalition, the United Democratic Front (UDF), which was founded in 1983. They were concerned that the UDF included non-Muslims, communists, "amoral" secularists, and Zionists[42] and that it would lead to a dilution of Muslim identity. Of particular concern was the Zionist question. By the 1980s, "progressive" South Africans shared a powerful mood of anti-colonialism, embroiled in a third-world *Weltanschauung*. Within this framework the illegitimacy of Zionism was an important component, especially given the fact that South Africa had close ties with the Jewish state. This mindset was capitalized upon by Qibla, which identified Zionism as the "citadel" of imperialism. For some observers, Jewish and Zionist manipulation was even responsible for apartheid.[43] Efforts by Jews—including charitable deeds—in the anti-apartheid struggle were questioned.

---

[35] *Muslim News*, August, 23, 1963. See also, for example, *Muslim News*, May 22, 1964.
[36] *Muslim News*, April 10, 1971.
[37] *Muslim News*, November 28, 1975.
[38] Ibraheem Mousa, interview in Tzippi Hoffman and Alan Fischer, *The Jews in South Africa. What Future?* (Cape Town: Jonathan Ball, 1988), p. 173.
[39] Haron, "Muslim News," p. 223.
[40] Tayob, *Islamic Resurgence*, p. 140.
[41] See *Varsity. Official Student Newspaper of the University of Cape Town* 41(9) (1982).
[42] These "Zionists" would have been progressive Jews, such as those belonging to Jews for Justice in Cape Town, an anti-apartheid grouping of Jews that supported the Zionist idea.
[43] Ebrahim Rasool, interview in Hoffman and Fischer, *The Jews in South Africa*, passim.

By the late 1980s, Muslims were increasingly visible in anti-apartheid protest marches. But once the ban on illegal organizations had been lifted by President F.W. De Klerk in 1990, they also focused on Bosnia, Kashmir, and "Palestine."[44] The embassies of the United States and Israel were regular targets of anger, and Israel's links to the United States were always noted. Muslims equated the struggle for liberation in South Africa with the Palestinian struggle: both were revolutions against colonial settler states dominated by the United States.[45] The "arch-enemy of Islam" and the "root cause" of problems in the Middle East was Israel. "The Zionists, through their servants, the Americans, have manipulated the situation in the Middle East to such an extent that they have succeeded in leaving the Middle East totally defenseless," explained *Muslim Views*.[46] Hostility gained apace after the Gulf War of 1991, evident in on-going conflict between Jewish and Muslim students at the University of Cape Town and the University of the Witwatersrand, and in solidarity meetings for Bosnian Muslims at which American and Israeli flags were burned.[47]

A visit in May 1994 by Yasser Arafat kept the Middle East firmly in focus. Speaking in a mosque in Johannesburg, the Palestinian leader called on South African Muslims to join the struggle to liberate Jerusalem. "Jihad will continue … you have to fight and start the jihad to liberate Jerusalem, your sacred shrine."[48] One year later on *al Quds* day, placards were displayed outside the Israeli embassy in Cape Town reading "Kill a Jew and Kill an Israeli" and "Jewish Blood."[49] Not surprisingly, the assassination of Israeli Prime Minister Yitzhak Rabin in 1996 was reported by *Muslim Views*—in the terminology of Hezbollah—as "a miracle from God."[50] By then, the Israeli-Palestinian conflict was undoubtedly the central concern of Muslims in South Africa. The Jewish state was a focus of evil and a conspiratorial center, rooted in the Zionist movement. Such sentiments were articulated at an international Muslim conference entitled "Creating a New Civilization of Islam," held in Pretoria in April 1996. Speakers referred to Jews as "a powerful economic force" and blamed Zionists for "all evils in society."[51]

This was the context within which "People Against Gangsterism and Crime" (PAGAD), a Qibla-inspired vigilante movement, emerged.[52] Building upon mount-

---

[44] Esack, *Qur'an, Liberation and Pluralism: An Islamic Perspective of Interreligious Solidarity Against Oppression* (Oxford: One, 1997), p. 224.

[45] *Muslim Views*, April 1990.

[46] Ibid.

[47] See Allie A. Dubb and Milton Shain, "South Africa" in *American Jewish Year Book*, eds. David Singer and Ruth Seldin (Philadelphia: The American Jewish Committee, 1994), p. 375.

[48] Milton Shain, "South Africa" in *American Jewish Year Book*, eds. David Singer and Ruth Seldin (Philadelphia: The American Jewish Committee, 1996), p. 357.

[49] "South Africa," *Antisemitism World Report 1996* (London: Institute for Jewish Policy Research and American Jewish Committee, 1996), p. 311.

[50] *Muslim Views*, May 1996.

[51] "South Africa," *Antisemitism World Report 1997* (London: Institute for Jewish Policy Research and American Jewish Committee, 1997) p. 356.

[52] According to Farid Esack, several militant elements within Qibla formed the core of PAGAD. See Farid Esack, "Pagad and Islamic Radicalism: Taking on the State?," *Indicator SA* 13(14) (1996), p. 9. See also, Anneli Botha, "Pagad: A Case Study of Radical Islam in South Africa," *Terrorism Monitor* 3(17) (2005), http://www.jamestown.org.

ing despair as law and order broke down in the aftermath of apartheid's demise and the loosening of the police state, and activated by a prior history of gangsterism in the "townships," PAGAD appeared to provide solutions. Against a background of unemployment and poverty, Muslims joined regular marches to the homes of known drug dealers. Islam was the only solution! When voices were raised against PAGAD's activities, these were blamed on "global conspiracy." And when a document, "The Threat of Fundamentalist Islam," was released by the ruling African National Congress (ANC), Fu'ad Rahman, a foreign journalist and one-time anti-apartheid activist based in Cape Town, responded in the columns of *Muslim Views* that the document was a product of "the Israeli intelligence network known as Mossad." The ANC government, he claimed, "is heavily influenced and controlled by Zionists"—an idea that would hardly have had traction in South Africa. Mossad, continued Rahman, "working hand in glove with the CIA (American intelligence), due to their extensive surveillance on Muslims here, knew about PAGAD before PAGAD knew about PAGAD."[53]

Rachman's conspiratorial outlook knew no bounds, reflecting an increasingly paranoid cast of mind: South Africa's moral collapse was linked to the (apostate) Jewish mining magnate Harry Oppenheimer, the "South African equivalent to the American moneymonger known as Rockefeller [sic] who due to his wealth and 'owning' America, dictates American policy." Oppenheimer was accused of being a Zionist, manipulating US President Bill Clinton, and defining his anti-Islamic policies. "This is why America (used and under control by the Zionist conspiracy) has ousted the popularly voted in FIS-government in Algeria and replaced it with a puppet yes-boss dictator," noted Rachman. In his view, South Africa was also being manipulated by "Zionists" whom, he alleged, in addition to controlling the Johannesburg Stock Exchange, had "infiltrated major ANC-government structures with so-called white liberals sitting in key positions." The Oppenheimer family, he maintained, "dictates global economy trends due to the wealth of all South Africans they have usurped.... He [Oppenheimer] is also linked to a major Zionist structure, conspiring to dictate world policy due to owning the world's wealth." Rachman even blamed the demise of the National Party that relinquished power in 1994 on the "Zionists" and ensured readers that the Zionists would similarly make the ANC incapable of governing. This would ensure "greater money control on the wealth of the nation." Muslims were not only informed of the evil machinations of Oppenheimer and his "Zionist" cohorts but knew that all those opposed to PAGAD were under the influence of "Zionists."[54]

Muslim attention on events in the Middle East was again evident after a bomb blast at a mosque in the small town of Rustenburg in January 1997. Members of the community suggested that Israel's Mossad intelligence agency was behind the bombing. A vociferous march on the Israeli embassy was led by Qibla, culminating in the by now ritual Israeli flag burning. A similar march took place in Johannes-

---

[53] *Muslim Views*, March 1997.
[54] *Muslim Views*, March 1997. See also "How the media manipulates the truth about terrorism," *Muslim Views*, April 1997, for evidence of conspiracy theories explaining how the West demonizes Islam. Similarly "Israel's attack on Christianity," *Muslim Views*, August 1997, in which the Western media are accused of helping to establish Zionism.

burg, organized by the Islamic Unity Convention (IUC), which had been founded in 1994 by Achmat Cassiem, an anti-apartheid activist who had spent a number of spells in jail, including Robben Island, as a political prisoner. This Islamist movement claimed to be a union of 200 groups.[55]

The hostile anti-Zionist mood was exacerbated by the breakdown in the Israeli-Palestinian Oslo peace process. In this atmosphere, even an invitation to the New National Party mayor of the Cape Metropolitan Council, the Reverend William Bantom, to attend an international mayoral conference in Israel in May 1998, led to fierce debate and heavy pressure on the mayor from Muslim organizations (supported by the ANC provincial caucus) not to accept.[56] In the context of such tensions, it was quite predictable that the Israeli Jubilee celebrations in Cape Town were marred by Muslim protestors, led by Qibla. "One Zionist, one bullet" and "Viva Hezbollah and Hamas" were chanted by about 70 protestors outside the Jubilee venue where placards equating Zionism with apartheid were held aloft.[57]

The mood was further inflamed when the South African government refused to issue a visa to Sheik Ahmed Yassin, spiritual leader of Hamas.[58] A telephone interview from Kuwait with Yassin was broadcast on a Cape Town Muslim radio station and relayed live to a public meeting in Gatesville, a predominantly Muslim suburb in Cape Town. Yassin denounced all Zionists as terrorists. Qibla protested against the government's decision to deny Yassin a visa outside the gates of parliament. Once again an Israeli flag was burned, while other flags were hurled into the street for protestors to "clean their shoes." Marchers chanted slogans such as "Death to Israel" and "One Zionist, one bullet," the latter echoing the well-known refrain of the Pan Africanist Congress, "One settler, one bullet."

The by now well-organized Muslim community continued to explain its views on Zionism in terms of conspiracy theories, built upon notions of a "New World Order" and the scapegoating of Muslims.[59] Zionists were at the core of global problems, again evident in the Second Intifada when calls were made on the South African government to cut ties with Israel.[60] Widespread demonstrations accompanied the new uprising[61] and laid the foundations for further radicalization. Anger reached its apogee just before and during the United Nations World Conference against Racism, Racial Discrimination, Xenophobia, and Related Intolerances (WCAR) in Durban in August 2001. Aided by what was palpably huge international support, the occasion turned into an extension of the Arab-Israeli conflict and an opportunity to portray Israel and the Zionist ideology as evil incarnate. Durban became a "byword for racism and anti-Semitism," in the words of Irwin Cotler, the

---

[55] See Esack, "Pagad and Islamic Radicalism."

[56] Milton Shain, "South Africa," in *American Jewish Year Book*, eds. David Singer and Ruth Seldin (Philadelphia: The American Jewish Committee, 1999), p. 413.

[57] Ibid.

[58] Minister of Justice Dullah Omar and Minister of Provincial and Constitutional Affairs Valli Moosa met with Hamas spiritual leader Sheik Ahmed Yassin while in Saudi Arabia in April 1998.

[59] *Muslim Views*, August 1998.

[60] *The Citizen*, October 14, 2000.

[61] *Business Day*, October 16, 2000.

former Minister of Justice and Attorney General of Canada, who attended the conference.[62]

Given the temper of the times, it is not surprising that many Muslims, following the September 11 attacks on the World Trade Center in New York and on the Pentagon, took conspiratorial ideas further. Zionist connections with the United States were invariably identified.[63] To be sure, what was in essence a political conflict over disputed territory was for many turning into a cosmological struggle, informed by a conspiracist cast of mind.[64] This was well captured in an interview conducted in September 2004 with a young Cape Town sheikh, Mogamat Colby, studying at the al-Azhar Institute in Cairo. The sheikh referred to the *Protocols of the Elders of Zion* and noted that Jews controlled the "economic systems in the world … all our land, all the means of the radio stations, the newspapers, the televisions—they are controlling all these things—and this is how they have full control over the whole world."[65]

V. CONTINUITIES, DISCONTINUITIES, AND CONTINGENCIES

By examining particular moments of hostility toward Jews through the twentieth century, it becomes apparent that the purveyors of hate changed caste over time. Anti-alienism—or hostility toward the Eastern European Jewish immigrants—emanated essentially from the white English-speaking merchant class and from Afrikaner farmers; the "Jewish Question" in the 1930s and early 1940s—built upon classic anti-Jewish motifs—was very much the concern of the (white) Afrikaner Right; and hostility toward Zionism emanates largely, but not exclusively, from the Muslim community, which by and large falls within the "non-White" category of the old apartheid order. The English-speaking community never bought into the "Jewish Question" and antisemitism among the Afrikaners effectively disappeared once the National Party gained political success in 1948.

In each of the phases of hostility, it is apparent that perceptions of the Jew were informed at least in part by ideas and intellectual traditions from beyond South Africa. This is hardly surprising. The period of anti-alienism was an age of increasing literacy, improved communications, and large population migrations, specifically between Britain and South Africa. The penetration of European ideas—including the deeply-rooted anti-Jewish stereotype—was inevitable, and a vaguely racial definition of "Jewishness" ensured that those traits traditionally associated with Jews would be ascribed to their co-religionists in South Africa.

The impact of European ideas was particularly apparent in the 1930s. The Radical Right manifestly shared many fascist ideas, evident in the "shirtist" movements, the OB, and the New Order, and in the penetration into South Africa of the *Protocols*

---

[62] *National Post* (Canada), September 12, 2006.

[63] *Muslim Views*, September 2001.

[64] Only a few days after the Durban conference—perhaps even inspired by the conference—Sheik Mogamat Gamaldien of Cape Town wrote a letter "The Golden Calf of Judaism" to the *Cape Argus* in which he quoted with approbation the *Protocols*. He reminded readers that the *Protocols* had been banned under the apartheid regime—a form of endorsement presumably—and that they clearly provided an explanation for Zionist and Israeli actions (*Cape Argus*, September 6, 2001).

[65] "Voice of the Cape" Radio Interview, September 10, 2004.

of the Elders of Zion. Local antisemites were well connected to a nexus of international antisemitism, demonstrable in the *Protocols* trial in Grahamstown in 1934.[66] One of those charged, von Moltke, claimed he was inspired by Hitler's "revolution" but even more influenced by Hamilton Hamish Beamish, a well-known Irish-born antisemite, who had found his way to the Cape Colony as a member of the Ceylon Mounted Infantry during the Boer War before returning to England (via Rhodesia), where he founded the antisemitic *Britons*.[67] Von Moltke was acquainted with Beamish's writings, and the Irishman gave supporting testimony at the trial.[68]

Muslim anti-Zionism also displayed features of the conspiratorial cast of mind, and it too was influenced by ideas from abroad. Intricate Muslim international networks shared ideas of hatred and fantasy, including Holocaust denial.[69] The success of the Jewish state, despite its pariah status for many, had to be explained. The groundwork was well laid in a global literature that demonized Jews, Israel, and the United States. All this connected smoothly to the *Protocols*, facilitated by the Internet with its hate-filled sites, including a South African site that links swiftly to international sites.[70]

As important as the impact of ideas from outside on the domestic discourse about Jews and Zionism were the specific contingencies within which these ideas operated and resonated: anti-alienism during the upheavals of the "mineral revolution" and the demonstrable power of mining capital; antisemitism during the 1930s and early 1940s during a period of heightened Afrikaner ethnonationalism; and anti-Zionism in a highly charged and hospitable political milieu at a time of radical transition.[71] Although Muslims identified with the notion of *Nakba* at the time of the Israeli War of Independence, and although they shared in the humiliation of Arab defeats at the

---

[66] See Milton Shain, "Humpty Dumpty Was Pushed: Anti-Jewish Conspiracies and the South African Experience" (Seventeenth Jacob Gitlin Memorial Lecture, Cape Town, 2005) p. 10ff.

[67] Beamish founded the Judaic Publishing Company, renamed Britons Publishing Company in 1922, which was noted for its antisemitic propaganda. In 1920, he published *The Jews' Who's Who*, allegedly exposing Jewish financial and political interests. See Gisela Lebzelter, *Political Anti-Semitism in England 1918-1939* (London: The Macmillan Press, 1978), p. 2 and pp. 22-23.

[68] See Beamish's evidence in Mark Lazarus, *The Challenge* (Port Elizabeth: The Mercantile Press, 1935) pp. 77-97.

[69] Holocaust denial became the subject of on-going legal dispute between the South African Jewish Board of Deputies and Radio 786, a Muslim radio station. Following the opening of the Cape Town Holocaust Centre in 1999, a series of articles in *Muslim Views* raised questions about the nature of the Holocaust and directed readers to classic denial literatures, including Arthur Butz's *The Hoax of the Twentieth Century*. See Milton Shain, "Humpty Dumpty Was Pushed," p. 20 ff.

[70] See, for example, http://www.islam.co.za.

[71] Of course this paranoia, as Peter Pulzer reminds us, is persuasive—be it "against Jews or Freemasons, Jesuits or Trotskyites"—because it has "some relation to ascertainable fact and to a hard core of genuine evidence. The charges against the chosen villain may be embellished by the most lurid fantasy, vast invalid conclusions may be drawn from trivial or isolated facts— but if there were *no* Jewish international bankers, if the Masons were *not* a secret society, if there had been *no* Communist sympathizers in the United States Foreign Service, the myths about them would lose their point." See Peter Pulzer, *The Rise of Political Antisemitism in Germany and Austria*, rev. ed. (London: Peter Halban Publishers, 1988), pp. 14-15.

hands of Israeli forces, it was only from the 1970s that a younger generation, operating in a different political milieu, began to find explanations for their condition in radical Islamist literature. South African Muslims increasingly viewed the plight of fellow Muslims in the world through a South African template, fed by radical Islamist thought from abroad. The Israeli-Palestinian conflict and American "machinations" in the Middle East in particular informed a sense of common victimhood, exacerbated by a second-class status in apartheid South Africa.

Notwithstanding the importance of contingent factors, the rhetoric and motifs of hostility toward Jews during the twentieth century had much in common. The target—Jew or Zionist—was identified as responsible for the evils of the day: at the turn of the century for undermining standards and for nefariously manipulating society; in the 1930s and early 1940s for threatening to dominate and to control society; and in the late twentieth century for malevolently orchestrating global affairs and oppressing Palestinians in a quest for domination. In this sense, radical Muslims in South Africa shared much with Hobson and with the Afrikaner Radical Right of the interwar years. Like the Hobsonians and the "Shirtists," they evolved fantasies to cope with and understand their world. In the case of Muslims, the added experience of living under a centrally controlled, authoritarian, and manipulative apartheid regime exacerbated beliefs in conspiracy and intrigue.

It is tempting to note that Hobson's Boer War, von Moltke's *Protocols of the Elders of Zion*, and Rachman's conspiracies each have a bearing on what Daniel Pipes refers to as the great "radical utopian ideologies" of our century—that is to say Leninism, fascism and Islamism. Each of these ideologies, argues Pipes, harnesses ideas of world domination. They are each informed by a "world conspiracy ideology," an attempt to dominate the world.[72] And yet, ironically, each of these ideologies sees others—and more specifically the Jew—as conspiring to challenge them and plotting to dominate the world. In short, we have what psychologists commonly refer to as projection. Thus, Hobson's understanding of imperialism captivated Lenin, who refined the idea of "monopoly capitalism" and its threat as a part of the communist worldview; the *Protocols* in turn informed Hitler and Nazism and served—in the classic phrase of Norman Cohn—as a "warrant for genocide"; and Islamists understand their struggle in apocalyptic terms that relate directly to the *Protocols*. Israel or the Jewish state serves as the locus of their fantasy. Hobson and the radical-left of the 1900s and the Afrikaner Radical Right of the 1930s had no such tangible and available target. The historical hand has moved on. But the "hidden hand" of the Jew remains.

---

[72] Daniel Pipes, *Conspiracy. How the Paranoid Style Flourishes and Where It Comes From* (New York: Simon & Schuster, 1999), p. 21.

Anti-Zionism and Antisemitism: Cosmopolitan Reflections

David Hirsh*

INTRODUCTION

1. The research question

Most accounts that understand antisemitism to be a pressing or increasing phenomenon in contemporary Europe rely on the premise that this is connected to a rise in anti-Zionism. Theorists of a 'new antisemitism' often understand anti-Zionism to be a new form of appearance of an underlying antisemitism. On the other side, sceptics understand antiracist anti-Zionism to be entirely distinct from antisemitism and they often understand efforts to bring the two phenomena together as a political discourse intended to delegitimize criticism of Israeli policy. The project of this work is to investigate the relationship between antisemitism and anti-Zionism, since understanding this central relationship is an important part of understanding contemporary antisemitism.

The hypothesis that this work takes seriously is the suggestion that, if an anti-Zionist world view becomes widespread, then one likely outcome is the emergence of openly antisemitic movements. The proposition is not that anti-Zionism is motivated by antisemitism; rather that anti-Zionism, which does not start as antisemitism, normalizes hostility to Israel and then to Jews. It is this hostility to Israel and then to Jews, a hostility which gains some of its strength from justified anger with Israeli human rights abuses, that is on the verge of becoming something that many people now find understandable, even respectable. It is moving into the mainstream.

An understanding of the rhetoric and practice of antiracist anti-Zionism as a form of appearance of a timeless antisemitism tends to focus attention on motivation. Frank Furedi makes the same observation:

> Bret Stephens of the Wall Street Journal is one of those who argue that many critics of Israel are motivated by an antisemitic impulse. However, he acknowledges that it is difficult to demonstrate, convincingly, that someone is antisemitic.

---

* David Hirsh is a lecturer in sociology at Goldsmiths, University of London. He has been centrally involved in the anti-boycott campaign within the British academic trade unions and is the founding editor of the Engage website (http://www.engageonline.org.uk), an anti-boycott campaign and an antiracist campaign against antisemitism. This positioning facilitates participant observation and action research by a key actor in these debates.

'[There] aren't many anti-Semites today who will actually come out with it and say "I hate Jews",' he notes. Therefore, 'spotting an anti-Semite requires forensic skills, interpretive wits, and moral judgement.' (Furedi 2007)

But even with such skills, wits and judgment, we cannot know what goes on inside the minds of social actors – neither the conscious mind nor the unconscious. All we can do is relate seriously to what people say, not to what we think they might mean or to what we think may be their true underlying motivation. This approach does not seek to denounce anti-Zionists as antisemitic, but it does sound a warning. If some people are treating Israel as though it were demonic, if they are singling out the Jewish state for unique hostility and if they are denouncing 'Zionists' as Nazis or racists or identifying them with apartheid, then in doing so they may be playing with the fire of antisemitism. The danger is that antiracist anti-Zionism is creating commonsense discourses that construct antisemitism as thinkable and possible. There are some people who are prepared to experiment openly with antisemitic ways of expressing themselves and are nonetheless accepted as legitimate by some antiracist organizations and individuals (Hirsh 2006i; Hirsh 2007).[1] At the moment, this form of antisemitism is generally played out at the level of discourse and politics, not on the streets. And those who wish for antisemitism to remain unthinkable are often faced with a charge of interfering with freedom of thought. What is more to the point, however, is the struggle over which notions become hegemonic or commonsense and which remain marginal. Because there is a relationship between discourse and violence, there remains a possibility that discursive antisemitism may manifest itself in more concrete political movements and that these may constitute an increased physical threat to 'Zionists', especially Jews and Jewish communities, around the world.

Some who theorize the connection between anti-Zionism and antisemitism (e.g. Matas 2005, Foxman 2004), argue that anti-Zionism is necessarily antisemitic on the basis that it denies national self-determination to Jews while recognizing a right of national self-determination for all other nations. Most writers who investigate the relationship between antisemitism and anti-Zionism, however, understand the relationship in more fluid and complex ways. Some argue there is often a level of 'enthusiasm' present in criticism of Israel which is not apparent in criticism of other similarly serious human rights abusing states and that this can only be explained by factors external to the critique. For instance, Abram de Swaan (2004: 1), maintains that this over-enthusiasm functions as

> a vent for righteous indignation that brings some relief from the still-burning shame of the memory of the Shoah, it employs facile equations reducing the Jewish State to the last bastion of colonialism and thereby conceals the true issues underlying this conflict.

Moishe Postone (2006) understands this 'singling out' of Israel to be a result of a particular kind of rupture in anti-hegemonic social movements, a shift from a positive politics of social transformation to a negative politics of resistance.

---

[1] I will argue, for example, that the jazz musician and activist Gilad Atzmon is a case in point.

Antisemitism can appear to be anti-hegemonic. This is the reason why a century ago August Bebel, the German Social Democratic leader, characterized it as the socialism of ools. Given its subsequent development, it could also have been called the anti-imperialism of fools. As a fetishized form of oppositional consciousness, it is particularly dangerous because it appears to be anti-hegemonic, the expression of a movement of the little people against an intangible, global form of domination. It is as a fetishized, profoundly reactionary form of anti-capitalism that I would like to begin discussing the recent surge of modern antisemitism in the Arab world. It is a serious mistake to view this surge of antisemitism only as a response to the United States and Israel. This empiricist reduction would be akin to explaining Nazi antisemitism simply as a reaction to the Treaty of Versailles. While American and Israeli policies have doubtlessly contributed to the rise of this new wave of antisemitism, the United States and Israel occupy subject positions in the ideology that go far beyond their actual empirical roles. Those positions, I would argue, must also be understood with reference to the massive historical transformations since the early 1970s, to the transition from Fordism to post-Fordism.

The central relationship between anti-Zionism and antisemitism may be thought of either as one of cause (underlying antisemitism motivates a disproportionate response to Israel) or as one of effect (a disproportionate response to Israel leads to antisemitic ways of thinking or to antisemitic exclusions of 'Zionists'). Postone points to the willingness of antiracist anti-Zionists to pursue political alliances with antisemitic movements and to turn a blind eye to the more open antisemitism of some mainstream Arab and Islamic forms of anti-Zionism.

2. *The outline of the paper*

In this working paper[2] of the Yale Initiative for the Interdisciplinary Study of Antisemitism (YIISA), I am interested in pursuing this more fluid line of thought. What follows will be a qualitative analysis of anti-Zionist discourse that suggests ways we might think through the relationship between hostility to Israel and antisemitism and thus help untangle this particular knot. Discourses of anti-Zionism appear in a number of different forms: academic writing, political speeches and essays, campaigning literature, public debates, newspaper columns and reports, letters pages, blogs and websites. It is a disparate and fragmented discourse. Some of the important actors straddle the political and academic spheres, and academic study tends also to constitute political intervention. This throws up complex methodological issues.

The scholarly study of contemporary antisemitism is a particularly contested field. First, there is a tendency for the distinction between primary and secondary research material to be blurred. An academic treatise is also, in Foucauldian terms, a 'monument' to an episteme and can function as a political intervention (Foucault 1982). It may itself be understood as an example of discursive antisemitism or an

---

[2] This is a working paper rather than a book or a journal article. It is intended to outline my arguments and to provide an extended and detailed analysis of a large amount of significant and relevant material analysis in the public domain. This will facilitate theoretical discussion and will also allow researchers access to a large amount of relevant material.

example of a spurious charge of antisemitism made to delegitimize criticism of Israel. Second, the official institutional framework also constitutes part of the terrain on which political struggles are conducted by, amongst others, academics. For example, the Report of the All-Party Parliamentary Inquiry into Antisemitism (2006) was not only a report but also an attempt, in which academic scholars were participants, to institutionalize as official a particular view of antisemitism. The legitimacy of this official framework was angrily rejected by scholars holding opposing views. The European Union Working Definition of Antisemitism[3] is similarly contested by scholars in the field, some of whom have been actively involved in the work of drafting the definition. The boundaries of the primary material I am addressing are porous and include scholarly, political, institutional and popular texts.

The outline of the paper as a whole runs as follows. In Part I, I will build a conceptual framework for thinking through the relationship between hostility to Israel and antisemitism. I do not accept the view of antisemitism as an ahistorical, ever-present phenomenon that throws up different manifestations of fundamentally the same disease in different times and places. At the same time, I am cautious about the claim that there is something radically new about the 'new antisemitism', and I am acutely aware that within the general rubric of anti-Zionism there are different streams and traditions. This text accordingly contextualizes the antiracist anti-Zionist movement alongside other anti-Zionisms and remains cognisant of the possibility that ideas and elements of rhetoric may move across the porous boundaries between different anti-Zionisms (Stalinist, Arab nationalist, jihadist, neo-Nazi, liberal and antiracist).

I develop a critique of what I see as a tendency in anti-Zionist writings towards 'explanatory flattening' – that is, to treat 'Zionism', at least in all important regards, as a homogenous phenomenon across time and across political divisions – for instance by treating the Israeli peace movement and the settler movement as manifestations of one singular Zionist project or by squeezing out the usual distinctions of sociological understanding between state and civil society or civilian and soldier. Another tendency in anti-Zionist discourse I address is its reliance on a methodological idealism that postulates an unusually direct relationship between the ideas of key Zionists and the actualization of those ideas in material reality. The existence of an allegedly racist state in the 21st century is held to be the result of an allegedly racist concept in the nineteenth century. The straight line narrated from concept to actuality does not take sufficient account of the material changes that occurred in Jewish life in the middle of the twentieth century and especially the Holocaust.

One of my own concerns is to understand the centrality of the Israel-Palestine conflict in contemporary left-wing and progressive thinking. I do not think that antisemitism provides an adequate explanation. Rather, I focus on the shift on the part of a significant section of the radical left from a social programme of working class self-liberation to a 'campist' view of the world, in which the central divide is between oppressed and oppressor nations. This view, which was characteristically labelled internationalist, raises anti-imperialism to an absolute principle. Amongst some on the left, anti-imperialism is no longer one value amongst a whole set – democracy,

---

[3] European Union, *EUMC Working Definition of Antisemitism*, http://fra.europa.eu/fra/material/pub/AS/AS-WorkingDefinition-draft.pdf, downloaded 8 November 2007.

equality, sexual and gender liberation, anti-totalitarianism, for example – but is the central value, prior to and above all others. If Israel is understood to be a key site of the imperialist system, this threatens to put 'Zionism' at the heart of all that is bad in the world. I am more inclined to look to this kind of political explanation rather than to a cultural antisemitism to explain the centrality of Palestine to much left-wing consciousness. The potentiality for a link between anti-Zionism and antisemitism is straightforward. Most people who are referred to by the designation 'Zionist' are Jews. Most Jews are in one political sense or another 'Zionists'. Most forms of antisemitism in history have allowed for 'exceptional' Jews. It is not a necessary attribute of antisemitism that it must target every Jew and so there could exist an antisemitism that exempts those Jews who do not identify as 'Zionist' from hostility. It is not, then, my contention that anti-Zionism or anti-Israeli over-enthusiasm is motivated by conscious or subconscious antisemitism. It is necessary to avoid the circularity of assuming antisemitism to be the cause of antisemitism.

My own methodological standpoint is cosmopolitan. I am aiming to use and to develop a framework for doing social theory that disrupts a methodologically nationalist tendency to view the division of the world into nations as being rather more fixed than it is. I also understand cosmopolitanism to be a materialist methodology, in the sense that, while it does aspire to radical social change, it retains a solid analytical connection to the world as it is. Robert Fine (2007) describes cosmopolitanism as 'a transformative as well as analytic project'. I have contended that cosmopolitanism

> ... is an argument for a way of fighting against totalitarianism that does not replicate that which it is fighting against. Yet it is a normative project that starts with an analysis of actual events and processes, not only with abstract principles or with utopian yearnings. (Hirsh 2005b: 378)

Fine (2007: xi) describes the appeal of cosmopolitanism as having to do with the idea that 'human beings can belong anywhere, humanity has shared predicaments and ... we find our community with others in exploring how these predicaments can be faced in common.'

Cosmopolitanism is therefore a universalistic methodology but one that seeks to avoid the emptiness of purely abstract, idealistic, or utopian universalisms. Such universalisms may be dangerous as well as empty, since they break human aspiration away from existing human conditions. It opens up a world where anything is thinkable and a world where it is easy to undervalue that which exists in favour of that which is in one's mind. To quote Fine again:

> Cosmopolitan social theory understands social relations through a universalistic conception of humanity and by means of universalistic analytical tools and methodological procedures. Its simple but by no means trivial claim is that, despite all our differences, humankind is effectively one and must be understood as such. (Fine 2007: xvii)

In the post-war era, Isaac Deutscher, for example, worked towards a cosmopolitan understanding of Israel and its relationships with Arabs and Palestinians. He understood the conflict as one in which there was both right and wrong on both sides of the ethnic or national divide. Israel was, in his view, a life-raft state, built under the severest emergency conditions imaginable by Jews who were pushed out of Europe. Deutscher insists that there could still have been outcomes other than seemingly endless conflict between Israelis and Palestinians. Deutscher's refusal simply to endorse the nationalism of one side or the other, coeval with the establishment of the State of Israel, contrasts with retrospective tendencies at a later time either to support the nationalism of the oppressed against the 'Zionism' of the oppressors or, alternatively, to support Israel against its 'Arab' neighbours.

One of the side-effects of relying on a binary opposition between the nationalism of the oppressed and that of the oppressor, a framework which is distinct from the cosmopolitan approach I am seeking to develop, is to construct the Palestinian nation itself as a single homogenous entity in its struggle for liberation. This approach lends itself to the charge of 'Orientalism' (Said 1978), in its inclination to downplay Palestinian agency and differences in favour of a unified narrative of unmediated oppression and resistance. The analytical task, as I see it, is to dispute the image of a simple dualism of oppressed and oppressor. My approach is to resolve the Israel-Palestine conflict into two analytically distinct elements: the Palestinian struggle for freedom and the Israeli struggle for survival. My argument is that an adequate analysis needs to recognize the reality and validity of both struggles, even if they become indistinguishable in practice.

In Part II, I move on from a conceptual discussion of the relationship between anti-Zionism and antisemitism to a discussion of how those concepts become actualized in public discourse. Here I present a number of case studies selected to illustrate how hostility to Israel and antisemitism have become knotted together in recent British debates. Antiracist anti-Zionists acknowledge that there is such a thing as antisemitism and that it is possible for antisemitism to appear on the left and within the Palestine solidarity movement. However, in any particular case in which the charge of antisemitism is made, when it relates to 'antiracist' criticism of Israel, they are prone to argue that, when examined on its merits, it turns out not to be a case of antisemitism at all; or that, when looked at alongside other more serious racist threats, it is insignificant; or that the antisemitism is exaggerated in order to smear critics of Israel.

I shall investigate a number of case studies of 'criticism of Israel' that lie within the disputed territory between criticism, demonization and antisemitism. I identify a phenomenon which I call the *Livingstone formulation*, after Ken Livingstone, the Mayor of London. He said: 'for far too long the accusation of antisemitism has been used against anyone who is critical of the policies of the Israeli government'. (Livingstone 2006) I have found that this response to a charge of antisemitism is a common one, yet it denies the crucial distinction between criticism and demonization and it subsumes both into the virtuous category of 'criticism'.

One case study concerns the role of the liberal media in the mainstreaming of those forms of anti-Zionism that touch on antisemitism. Through an analysis of *Comment is Free*, the website of the British liberal newspaper *The Guardian*, I discuss not only the effects of new technology in giving space to a wider range of unmediated opinions (some of which are arguably antisemitic) but also the role of the liberal press in normalizing debate in such a way as to give an entry to antisemitism that it does not give to other forms of racism.

The next section goes on to look at examples of rhetoric, themes and images that resonate with, or repeat themes from, older forms of antisemitism. These antisemitic themes may be split into two groups: blood libel, where Jews are accused of murdering children for their own pleasure or for the requirements of their religious observance, and global conspiracies to control the world, where Jews are accused of causing others to suffer in order that they can themselves benefit. In contemporary forms of anti-Zionist discourse, the former is mirrored, for example, in images and discourses that represent 'Zionists' as wantonly cruel killers of children. The latter is mirrored in scholarly theses concerning the capacity of the 'Israel lobby' to pervert US foreign policy from following its own national interest towards following the national interest of Israel. I argue that this thesis has had a major impact beyond the scholarly community and provides a vocabulary in which it is possible to articulate narratives of Jewish conspiracy in a form that does not appear to be antisemitic.

The trajectory of my case studies leads from the denial of particular manifestations of antisemitism if they take the form of criticism of Israel, towards an ever more diminished caution over expressions of antisemitism. In Part III, I turn to the campaigns for boycott, divestment and sanctions against Israel, with a particular focus on the proposal for an academic boycott. This section is a discussion of how the conceptual and discursive aspects of anti-Zionism combine in a movement for the concrete exclusion of Israelis, and of nobody else, from the cultural and economic life of humanity. There follows an account of what happened to the various campaigns in the UK to boycott Israel, a detailed exploration of the debate over the boycott of Israeli academic institutions and a discussion of the implications of the boycott campaign for our understanding of contemporary antisemitism. For example, the boycott campaign itself employed a version of the *Livingstone formulation* to protect itself against charges of antisemitism. It wanted to treat the exclusion of Israelis as though it was simply 'criticism of Israel'. 'Criticism of Israel cannot be construed as anti-Semitic,' declared a motion advanced by the campaign and passed by the 2007 UCU Congress. However, the boycott was not proposed for academics who work in other states held to be responsible for human rights abuses; it was only proposed against academics who work in Israel.

Such a policy would impact in a number of direct and indirect ways on Jews more than anybody else. I argue that the boycott campaign further encouraged an exaggerated hostility to Israel and licensed antisemitic ways of thinking. The material gathered in this paper shows concretely how this took place.

3. Methodological approaches to the study of antisemitism

One of the unusual aspects of the scholarly study of contemporary antisemitism is that the object of study includes ourselves. Everybody in these heated debates thinks that everybody else is guilty of making *ad hominem* arguments. Some scholars may expect this paper to fail to relate critically to what they say, but instead to accuse them of being antisemitic and thus to explain what they say. This paper makes every effort to relate to what people who are hostile to Israel *say* and *do*. It makes no claims about what they are or about how they are motivated. In *Homage to Catalonia* George Orwell has this to say on the *ad hominem* argument:

> ... so long as no argument is produced except a scream of 'Trotsky-Fascist!' the discussion cannot even begin. In such circumstances there can be no argument. What purpose is served by saying that men like Maxton are in Fascist pay? Only the purpose of making serious discussion impossible. It is as though in the middle of a chess tournament one competitor should suddenly begin screaming that the other is guilty of arson or bigamy. The point that is really at issue remains untouched. Libel settles nothing. (Orwell 2003)

Sometimes people prefix their statements with the phrase 'as a Jew'. This is also an *ad hominem* argument. They are inviting us to agree with them on the basis of their ethnic identity, not on the basis of evidence or argument. Jews too can make antisemitic claims, use antisemitic images, support antisemitic exclusions and play an important, if unwitting, part in preparing the ground for the future emergence of an antisemitic movement.

It is often claimed that people who warn of the danger of antisemitism are dishonest, particularly when the alleged antisemitism has a form that resembles criticism of Israel. It is said that those who seem to be concerned about antisemitism are really motivated by a wish to protect Israel from criticism of its human rights abuses, and so they 'cry antisemitism' or 'play the antisemitism card' in order to make such criticism appear to be illegitimate. This form of attack is also *ad hominem*. It refuses to take seriously what those concerned about antisemitism say. Instead it tells us what the cynic believes that the anti-antisemites really mean. The charge is that really they are concerned with defending the racist treatment of Palestinians and not with challenging the anti-Jewish racism that they themselves, it turns out, have either invented or provoked or, strangely, both. The campaign to boycott Israeli academia constitutes, in itself, one big *ad hominem* attack against Israeli scholars, who are to be excluded from the academic community not for what they write but for who they are (Pike 2007).

Nowhere in this paper is the claim made that all criticism of Israel is antisemitic; indeed, contrary to received wisdom, it is exceedingly unusual for any serious person to make such a claim. I do not think that this paper leaves itself open to the *ad hominem* attack that it treats all criticism of Israel as though it were antisemitic, even while it denies doing so. However, if we accept that it is possible for a text to take the form of criticism of Israel but also to be antisemitic in content, then we need to work through the distinction between criticism and demonization. We need to be aware of the possibility of demonization so that it can be avoided and so that criticism can be critical, strong, sharp and effective. Any literary or social critic knows that there is a distinction between demonization and criticism and that public debate over where and how the boundary is drawn is legitimate and important.

This paper is not centrally about Israel or Palestine; it is a paper about contemporary antisemitism, contemporary hostility to Israel and the relationship between the two. Antisemitism is not necessarily the worst thing in the world, it is not the original sin, apart from all other sins. Today, people who say antisemitic things are likely to have stumbled into antisemitic ways of thinking. They are unlikely to be wicked people. If I find that the demonization of Israel is common in the anti-Zionist literature and in the anti-Zionist movement, my intention is not to reverse the logic of demonization in order to demonize the demonizers. It is, rather, to work within a cosmopolitan framework that tries hard to avoid replicating that which it critiques.

In this paper, I pick up a few stones and find some traces of an antisemitic culture (or worse) underneath some of them. It does not follow that I see antisemitism under every stone.[4]

Antisemitism is not a timeless fact of human civilization. It exists within, not outside of, history and society. It is not a single monster across time and across the globe. Nor are manifestations of hostility to Jews isolated from other forms of racism and exclusion.

The struggles against Islamophobia, antisemitism and anti-Arab racism, the struggle against the occupation of the West Bank and the struggle against the project to smash the State of Israel – these are all potentially democratic struggles, and, although they are distinct, they can be understood in a cosmopolitan way as belonging to the same family.

In this work, antisemitism is written without a hyphen because there is no 'Semitism' that antisemitism is against. Antisemitism constructs 'the Jews' or 'the Zionists' who are to be hated or excluded. In this paper, antisemitism is taken to mean racism against Jews; it is not taken to mean racism against 'Semites' or people who speak Semitic languages or against anybody else. The term 'new antisemitism' is not my favourite, since there is no single authentic 'old' or classic antisemitism from which contemporary antisemitism is distinct. In the British Library, there is a book from 1921 entitled *The New Antisemitism* (1921), which debunks the *Protocols of the Elders of Zion*. This paper does, however, work with the hypothesis that a significant element of contemporary antisemitism is related to exaggerated hostility to Israel. I am not saying that anti-Zionism is a form of antisemitism but rather that there is a complex relationship between the two. This paper does not rely on a definitional identity of one with the other. It bases its case on an investigation of social reality, not on the meanings of words. Muslim, Islamist and jihadi antisemitism are important and relevant phenomena, but they are not the focus of this paper. They are relevant here only insomuch as they impact upon mainstream, left and liberal antisemitism in the UK.

This paper presents and analyzes a snapshot of contemporary events. It is not a historical study that traces the trajectory of anti-Zionist and antisemitic movements. While many of the case studies relate to ephemeral material, it is my contention that enduring threats are manifested through this ever-changing form of appearance. Much of the text is forgotten the day after it appears on the internet, but it is constantly regenerated with new articulations of opposition to 'Zionist' power, dishonesty and bloodlust.

There are a number of strange and particular difficulties that present themselves to the scholar studying antisemitism or to the activist opposing antisemitism. There is the repeated belittling, half-explicit, half-internalized allegation that one is being a touchy, paranoid, over-sensitive Jew – or that one will be thought of as such. There is

---

[4] I am aware that the objects of this study are global phenomena that manifest themselves differently in different places. While my own primary empirical focus is on the United Kingdom, it is necessary to avoid both British parochialism and abstract universalism in order to disentangle the global from the spatially and culturally particular. It is possible to come to conclusions both about the nature of global trends and about what may be specifically British factors that shape their local manifestations. However, this goes beyond the scope of this paper.

the fear that lifting up the stones to see what is underneath, prodding, investigating, labelling and opposing, encourages the growth of the nascent antisemitism that one finds. We may be advised to let sleeping dogs lie and not to make a fuss; others suffer more than Jews do: Jews are not poor, are not excluded, are not an underclass. Simply to write about antisemitism requires that we confront this quietism.

In developing this critique of the relation between anti-Zionism and antisemitism, my own approach is influenced by and draws upon the cosmopolitan and anti-totalitarian frameworks built by political activists and social theorists such as Hal Draper, Hannah Arendt, Isaac Deutscher, George Orwell and Robert Fine. All are radicals who refuse to accept the existing world as given, but whose analysis is firmly rooted within it and anchored to it; all are partisans of cosmopolitan projects that aim to find better, not worse, organizing principles than nationalism; all try to come to terms with the awful realities of radical projects whose solutions towered above the problems they were supposed to address in horror, cruelty and the negation of humanity; all are people who understand that we have much more to lose than our chains, but who still aim to break chains. All are human, not gurus or Gods; they change over time, they change their minds, they make mistakes, they get things wrong, they work things through.

Hannah Arendt struggled with the contradictions of Zionism and of fighting antisemitism 'as a Jew'; she rejected the intuitively attractive understanding of antisemitism as an ahistorical given. She was denounced as a traitor by conservative Jews and as a cold-warrior by conservative leftists. She devoted her intellect and energy to understanding how European civilization, and its emancipatory project, had thrown up the horrors, first of imperialism and then of totalitarianism. But she never stopped trying to understand; understanding, like friendship, was itself a crime against totalitarianism and punished severely. She thought the trial of the Nazi Adolf Eichmann in Jerusalem was a missed opportunity for the project of cosmopolitan law, but she insisted that Israel had every right to put him on trial. Robert Fine has struggled with the complexity of holding on both to the critique of the world as it exists and to the critique of the critique. If you drop the critique then you make your peace with endemic injustice; drop the critique of the critique and you recklessly, in spite of the repeated warnings of history, risk the horrors of totalitarianism. He has taken the Arendtian mission of understanding seriously in his critiques of democracy, apartheid, totalitarianism and antisemitism and in his reconceptualization of Marx's political philosophy and cosmopolitanism.

George Orwell stood for a left that valued internationalism, equality, respect, antiracism, anti-imperialism, anti-totalitarianism, democracy and secularism, yet he understood the danger of raising one of these values to an absolute at the expense of the all the others. He learned to shoot at Eton but went to shoot fascists in Spain; he learned to hate imperialism as a policeman in India, he fought against imperialism, but he also understood that some things were worse than British rule in India. Isaac Deutscher opposed Zionism when it was a political project, loved the State of Israel when it was founded, did not even consider the possibility of an anti-Zionism after the Holocaust, but never identified himself as a Zionist. If he was soft on Stalinism, he was not soft on Stalinist anti-Zionism. Hal Draper's interpretation of Marx was necessary to make explicit Marx's implacable opposition both to antisemitism and to totalitarianism. Draper's Marxism gave us a vision of the socialist movement as a democratic project, a project of self-liberation, a collectivity of free individuals – the exact opposite to what was generally accepted as Marxism in Hal Draper's time. Draper offered a socialist framework for understanding the Israel-Palestine conflict. He was not necessarily right, as it turned out, but he was a socialist. Many 'socialist' analyses of the conflict that are offered today are very far away from any conception of socialism with which he would have identified. Let me end with an example of how he addressed the issue in May 1948:

> To recognise the right of the Jews to self-determination, if it is not merely to be a pious obeisance to a formula, requires socialists also to recognize the right of the Jews to defend their choice of separate national existence against any and all reactionary attempts to deprive them of that right, whether by Arab feudal lords or UN imperialism. That is why we demanded recognition of Israel by the government, and why our British comrades particularly must demand similar action by the Labour government – as the concretization of the demand that the imperialists keep out. That is why we demand the lifting of the imperialist embargo on arms to the new Jewish state. The reunification of Palestine and of the two peoples in it can take place only through a struggle from below. The conditions for such a struggle are present as they were before partition – the class struggle within Jewish society, and the grinding exploitation of the Arab peasants by their lords and masters. While opposing any attempt by the Arab landlord regimes to overthrow the Jewish state and impose their reactionary sway on the whole land, it is the duty of real socialists in Israel to fight for a policy, programme and a government of the working people which can bring about such reunification instead of deepening the nationalist gulf. (Draper 1948)

I. Antisemitism and criticism of Israel: conceptual considerations

1. *The many headed hydra: an ahistorical model*

There is a commonsense intuitive view that interprets different manifestations of anti-Judaism as being forms of appearance of an ever-present underlying antisemitism. This view understands antisemitism as though it was like a many-headed sea monster. It is always lurking under the surface of the water, and it puts up different heads in different places and times. Antisemitism in this view is an ever-present fact of human history; the difference between a time or a place where it is visible and one where it is not is purely contingent. When one head of the monster is cut off it simply grows another, but it never dies.

Medieval Christian antisemitism was one such form of appearance of the underlying monster, one menacing head that became visible above the surface. This antisemitism demonized Jews as Christ-killers. It charged them with deicide and with regularly and ceremonially re-performing the crucifixion of Christ on innocent non-Jewish children (Julius 2006).

An early left wing form of antisemitism saw Jews as evil capitalists or as greedy money lenders. Some people who considered themselves to be on the left felt that campaigns against Jewish capital and Jewish bankers were legitimate and useful ways to introduce the masses to campaigns against capital and bankers in general.

Right-wing antisemitism has often portrayed Jews as embodying the Bolshevik threat. Jews corrupt the normal workings of society and nation by fighting for ideas such as socialism, human rights, equality and democracy, which work to undermine the cohesion and the natural functioning of social life.

Racist pseudo-scientific antisemitism emerged, which understood Jews as a biological infection to the social body. This head of the monster had no difficulty in holding that the Jewish infection worked both through Jewish capitalism and through Jewish Bolshevism. Both were means by which 'the Jews' polluted the human community.

Now, argue a number of theorists, we are seeing a 'new antisemitism' (Chesler 2003; Iganski and Kosmin 2003; Foxman 2004; Matas 2005; Phillips 2006; Rosenfeld 2006). Often, but by no means always, 'new antisemitism' is understood as a new form of appearance of the same old monster. Previous antisemitisms stressed the cosmopolitan nature of Jews. They stressed the abnormality of a people with secret international communal loyalties that threatened the 'normal' kinds of open loyalty that people have to their community, their nation or their class. But when Jews build a nation-state and 'normalize' their national allegiance, there arises a 'new antisemitism' that enables a shift of the embodiment of evil from the Jewish individual to the Jewish state. It is now the state that is accused of standing in the way of world peace, of being responsible for stirring up wars, of being uniquely racist or an apartheid state or dangerous in some other way. Anti-Zionism has a tendency to present the crimes and failings of the Jewish state as the whole and necessary truth of the Jewish state. This, it is argued by many 'new antisemitism' theorists, is analogous to the way that antisemitism presented the crimes and failings of particular Jews – the Bolshevism of Trotsky, the greed of the landlord Rachman, the capitalist exploitation of the Rothschilds – as the whole and necessary truth of all Jews in general.

One strength of this view, that these are all forms of appearance of the same underlying phenomenon, is that it is intuitively attractive. It has often felt to Jews that each new attack was nothing but a mere repetition of the old 'cancer', or a current mutation of the familiar 'virus', which was only ever in temporary remission.

Another strength of this view is that it can account for the fact that many of the themes and images of demonization are common to the different forms of antisemitism and are also frequently mirrored in contemporary anti-Zionist discourse.

One problem with the 'Hydra' explanation is that, while each form of anti-Judaism does draw on and replicate older forms, they are also hugely different phenomena. They arise and become widespread in radically different times and places. They have different manifestations, are employed by different social forces and make use of different narratives. The differences are actually as striking as the commonalities between the Spanish Inquisition, Christian antisemitism in nineteenth century Poland, socialist antisemitism in Germany at the time of August Bebel, right-wing antisemitic anti-Bolshevism, racist antisemitism, Nazi genocidal antisemitism, understated and gentlemanly English exclusion, contemporary anti-imperialist anti-Zionism and jihadi antisemitism.

The second problem for an ahistorical essentialist view of antisemitism is that there have been times and places where life has, in general, been good for Jews, where Jews have been able to function well as part of the wider community, where they have not been excluded from public life, education or the professions, where they have had freedom to worship and where other racisms have been more dangerous, immediate and threatening.

Contemporary Europe is in many ways one of those good times and places for Jews. Although the frequency of antisemitic attacks has been rising sharply in the last decade,[5] you are still more likely to be beaten up on the street, excluded from society, excluded from the economy, excluded from education or demonized in the media if you are black or Muslim, for example, than if you are Jewish.

The many headed sea-monster theory could lead us to react to current threats as though they were identical to previous threats. Some Jews mistakenly thought they could appease Nazism, deal with it and come to an accommodation with it, as they had, to an extent, been able to do with previous threats. But the Nazi threat was different. Now, some campaigners feel that they are facing an imminent genocidal onslaught of the kind that was faced in the 1940s.[6] But perhaps the current threat is not just a new manifestation of the previous one but is in fact a different set of phenomena, in a different society, at a different time, for different reasons.

Another problem with an essentialist and ahistorical theory of antisemitism is that, as Hannah Arendt argued, it undermines human agency and responsibility for antisemitism. It constructs antisemitism as an ever present structure that dominates human subjectivity:

> In view of the final catastrophe... the thesis of eternal antisemitism has become more dangerous than ever. Today it would absolve Jew-haters of crimes greater than anybody had ever believed possible. (Arendt 1975: 8)

Antisemitism understood as a timeless fact of human history is also likely to be thought of as undefeatable. This insight would have significance for the strategy adopted to respond to the 'new antisemitism' and in particular would shed light on who should be thought of as a racist enemy and who, on the other hand, should be thought of as being susceptible to argument, education and persuasion.

2. The tropes of anti-Zionism

I am using the term 'anti-Zionist' to denote a variegated set of movements that do not coalesce around criticism of Israeli policy or criticism of racist movements within Israel but rather around a common orientation to the existence or to the legitimacy of the State of Israel itself.

I do not argue that antiracist anti-Zionism and anti-Israeli over-enthusiasm are motivated by antisemitism. I am looking for more complex explanations of the outcomes of anti-Zionist thinking, and I maintain that to do this it is necessary to examine the central tropes of antiracist anti-Zionist discourse. It is by beginning to make sense of these discourses, what they claim, by what kind of methodologies they are produced and in what kind of political traditions they stand, that it is possible

---

[5] *Antisemitic Incidents Reports 2005*, Community Security Trust, London, http://www.the cst.org.uk/index.cfm?content=7&menu=7, downloaded 21 December 2006; *Antisemitic Incidents Reports 2006*, Community Security Trust, London, http://www.thecst.org.uk/docs/Incidents%5F Report%5F06.pdf, downloaded 15 February 2007.

[6] For example, Phyllis Chesler (2006): 'Just as Hitler was appeased until it was too late, so too has Ahmadinejad been appeased.'

to unravel some of the elements of the central relationship between these discourses and antisemitic ways of thinking that may be immanent within them. It may be asked why one should focus on anti-Zionism when most contemporary critics of Israel are not existential anti-Zionists. Yet criticism of Israel, of this or that thing that Israel does, is not the focus of this work. The focus of this work is antisemitism. So it is a hypothesis, at this stage, that anti-Zionist discourse is important in shaping not criticism of Israeli policy but those whose hostility to Israel constitutes something more threatening than criticism, something, indeed, that cannot be properly understood as criticism.

Hostility to the idea and practice of Israel comes from various sources – amongst which are liberal nationalism, Marxist anti-imperialism and democratic cosmopolitanism – and it is not the same as hostility to Jews. I am asking whether it can nevertheless throw up a politics and a set of practices that creates a commonsense notion of Israel as a unique evil in the world and thereby sets itself up for a fight with Jews – those Jews, at any rate, who do not define themselves as anti-Zionist. The antiracist variants of anti-Zionism constitute minority discourses and minority movements within the global set of anti-Zionist discourses and movements. They are conditioned by their location within this set of different discourses and movements, through the circulation of common elements of rhetoric, of commonsense assumptions and through explicit or tacit political alliances.[7]

Contemporary left-wing secular antiracist anti-Zionism cannot be understood solely as an intellectual or political critique of 'Zionism' but also needs to be understood as a broad and variegated movement that exists alongside a set of other anti-Zionist movements. Methodologically, therefore, it is necessary to look at the theory, the discourse and the claims of anti-Zionists, but it is also necessary to take into account the social reality of the ways in which these are actualized in the world. The movement is the site where the relationship between a set of shared conceptual meanings and understandings, on the one hand, and the real-world political and social actualization of those understandings and meanings, on the other, are played out.

This contemporary movement is distinct from late nineteenth and early twentieth century anti-Zionist movements. These were predominately Jewish movements that proposed responses to antisemitism other than Zionism, such as Bundism or revolutionary socialism.[8] Contemporary anti-Zionism often sees itself in these anti-Zionist traditions but actually exists in a radically different world, made different by the history of the twentieth century. It is largely the way that contemporary anti-Zionism relates to this different world that defines it as a movement. Opposition to

---

[7] An example of an alliance between antiracist anti-Zionism and Islamist anti-Zionism is the Respect party in the United Kingdom (now apparently splitting apart). An example of the kinds of compromises that are tempting is the adoption of the slogan 'We are all Hizbollah now!' by many in the summer of 2006 (Hirsh 2006b). Hizbollah is open about its own antisemitism.

[8] Miller (2007) focuses on the commonalities between non-Jewish anti-Zionism in Britain before 1948 and today; he foregrounds the similarities, 'in particular the common arguments that both current and past British anti-Zionists have used to demonize and delegitimize Zionism'. My argument here, in contrast, focuses on the differences between opposition to a political movement and opposition to a nation state.

Israel's existence tends to constitute a battle of ideas against an idea. Its first focus is on 'Zionism' as an ideology, and its relationship to real-world phenomena is often conditioned by its explanatory emphasis on ideology.

Post-1948 anti-Zionism is not a single movement but a collection of differing currents. There is a current of Middle Eastern anti-Zionism that was hostile to Jewish immigration into Palestine, to a Jewish presence there and to the foundation and the continued existence of the State of Israel. In the Middle East, there are both secular and Islamic anti-Zionist traditions. In the Soviet Union and the Eastern Bloc, there was a tradition of Stalinist anti-Zionism. Right-wing and neo-Nazi antisemitism is increasingly articulating its hostility to Jews in the form of anti-Zionist rhetoric (for example, David Irving and David Duke[9]). There is also a contemporary current of anti-Zionism that toys openly with antisemitic rhetoric but is hard to place in terms of the left/right scale and has connections with both (for example, Gilad Atzmon,[10] Paul Eisen and Israel Shamir).

In order to approach a clear analysis of this contemporary anti-Zionism, it is necessary to do more than look at the arguments and narratives that anti-Zionist theorists produce. It is also necessary to look at how they are realized in the practices of political movements and campaigns. In this arena ideas do not exist in isolation; they are part of a movement. And the anti-Zionist movement has unclear, porous and shifting boundaries. The debate exists at the intersection of a number of different and mutually hostile terrains: the left discourses of 'anti-imperialism' and post-colonial theory, the totalitarian discourses inspired by Nazism, jihadi fundamentalism and Stalinist communism, the nationalist discourses of Arab and Palestinian anti-colonialism, the Christian and Muslim religious discourses of antisemitism and Jewish communalist minority anti-Zionist movements. Concepts and commonsense notions developed within one kind of discourse tend to slip and slide, and metamorphose, into those of the other terrains.

I am interested in the emergent properties of these ideas, discourses and narratives when they are actualized in these living movements; when elements of rhetoric that are not formally antisemitic gain a life of their own; when they escape the control and supervision of the antiracists who formulate them and put them to work in political campaigns. The political work here is to win mainstream left and liberal milieus over to the internalization of various claims about Israel and 'Zionism' as commonsense and heartfelt truths.

If some elements of the broad anti-Zionist movement are self-consciously antisemitic, that is, racist against Jews, it is necessary to analyze the ways that those who think of themselves as antiracist relate ideologically to these other traditions and to look at how concepts function in the movements that take them up, how they migrate and develop in their exposure to the public sphere, and how that actuality relates back to the development of narrative and theory. I am not only interested in the truth or coherence of the ideas of anti-Zionism but also in the properties that emerge, sometimes unforeseen or unintended, through their use and propagation.

For example, anti-Zionist discourse often challenges the claim that Zionism is a form of nationalism. Nationalism is usually understood to contain racist potentiali-

---

[9] Duke (2004; 2004a).
[10] See Part II for a fuller discussion of Atzmon.

ties as well as elements that define a community of common responsibility. But Zionism is often understood to be essentially different from all other nationalisms – as nothing at all but a mode of exclusion. It is necessary to investigate the empirical truth of this claim as well as the coherence of the argument. But this will only uncover half of the story. The other half is to be understood by looking at the ways that the Zionism=Racism claim is actualized in the movement and in the world beyond. How does the anti-Zionist movement actually relate to 'Zionists', who are defined as racists? How does it license or encourage others to relate to 'Zionists'? How does it, in practice, define the group 'Zionists', who are to be treated as racists, and how do others define the term?

This is partly a question of how anti-Zionist theorists and activists understand their own political responsibilities. Michael Neumann, a philosophy professor at Trent University in Canada, is an extreme example of one who refuses to take political responsibility for the consequences of his anti-Zionism. He outlines his approach to the question in an email exchange with an antisemitic group (Jewish Tribal Review 2002). They ask him whether he thinks that their website is antisemitic. He replies:

> Um, yes, I do, but I don't get bent out of shape about it. I know you're site and it's brilliantly done. Maybe I should say that I'm not quite sure whether you guys are antisemitic in the 'bad' sense or not… [I]n this world, your material, and to a lesser extent mine, is a gift to neo-Nazis and racists of all sorts. Unlike most people in my political niche, this doesn't alarm me: there are far more serious problems to worry about… [O]f course you are not the least bit responsible for how others use your site.[11]

This discussion occurred five months after Neumann (2002) had published a piece entitled 'What is Antisemitism?' in which he argued that antisemitism is trivial compared to other racisms and that it is understandable that Israeli crimes result in a hatred of Jews in general. Here are some quotes from this piece by Neumann, which illustrate a wilful and showy refusal by somebody who considers himself to be an antiracist to take antisemitism seriously:

> Undoubtedly there is genuine antisemitism in the Arab world: the distribution of the Protocols of the Elders of Zion, the myths about stealing the blood of gentile babies. This is utterly inexcusable. So was your failure to answer Aunt Bee's last letter… The progress of Arab antisemitism fits nicely with the progress of Jewish encroachment and Jewish atrocities. This is not to excuse genuine antisemitism; it is to trivialize it… If Arab antisemitism persists after a peace agreement, we can all get together and cluck about it. But it still won't do Jews much actual harm… Israel has committed war crimes. It has implicated Jews generally in these crimes, and Jews generally have hastened to implicate themselves. This has provoked hatred against Jews. Why not? Some of this hatred is racist, some isn't, but who cares? Why should we pay any attention to this issue at all? (Neumann 2002)

---

[11] This email exchange is published by 'Jewish Tribal Review' against the wishes of Michael Neumann. I asked Neumann whether this exchange was a forgery: 'The material is not a forgery but I do not vouch for its reliability because I no longer have the original correspondence' (email, 5 July 2005).

The anti-Zionist movement has a tendency to flatten analytically important distinctions. For example, many believe the distinction between state and civil society in Israel to be entirely absent; indeed, some take this insight to such lengths that they do not define Israel as a state at all.[12] The idea of a unity of 'the people' with 'state' sets up a frame for doing criticism that tends to dissolve politically relevant distinctions. Anti-Zionism tends to fuse civil society with the state. It erodes the distinction between the people in their plurality and state policy. It erases the complexities of Israeli society and history. It is often also tempted to dissolve the distinction between civilian and soldier. 'Zionism' is typically presented in anti-Zionist discourse as a one-dimensional unity. There is a rejection of a methodology that is interested in development over time or in understanding the phenomenon in context or in understanding the complex and contradictory dynamics that are usually thought to characterize the development of a movement or state.

Distinctions between left and right, bigots and antiracists, one form or tradition of Zionism and another, settlers and non-settlers, occupied territories and Israel, Arab citizens and Arab non-citizens often become fuzzy. The distinction that remains clear, that dominates, is between Zionist and anti-Zionist; the significance of everything else is downplayed.

Anti-Zionists may respond to this charge by saying that it is not the anti-Zionists who blur distinctions but 'the Zionists'. It is Israel that has no separation between state and civil society; it is Israel that wants to annexe the West Bank; it is Israel that subordinates politics to the imperatives of 'security'; it is Israel that singles itself out in the world.

This is an illustration of the way that anti-Zionism tends to replicate in its critique the errors and crimes of 'Zionism'. 'Zionism' in this paper is often in inverted commas because it is not actual Zionism or the actual practices of Israel that the anti-Zionists replicate, but rather their own construction of 'Zionism', which bears little resemblance to the material reality of the State of Israel or Israeli society. Their 'Zionism' is a totalitarian movement that is equivalent to racism, Nazism or apartheid. Anti-Zionism tends to define itself against a notion of 'Zionism' that is largely constructed by its own discourses and narratives. The 'Zionism' that anti-Zionist discourses typically depict and denounce is more like a totalizing and timeless essence of evil than a historical set of changing and variegated beliefs and practices. It is presented as an unthinkable object that requires either unconditional rejection or belief, rather than as a social and political phenomenon. The term 'Zionism' is often used in such a way as to bring it closer to the language of evil than to the province of social scientific or historical understanding. 'Zionist' often hits out like an insult and carries such pejorative connotations that the reality behind it has ended up disappearing under layers of stigmatization. For example: 'The Zionists think that they are victims of Hitler, but they act like Hitler and behave worse than Genghis Khan', President Ahmadinejad quoted in Jerusalem Post (2006); 'Zionism is a form of racism', UN General Assembly Resolution 3379 (later rescinded); 'Zionists and their friends are desperate to silence the voices of and for Palestine', from an op-ed piece in the *Guardian* newspaper (Soueif 2006); '[Respect] is a Zionist-free party… if there

---

[12] See, for example, Image 5, a map of Lebanon on the Respect website, entitled 'Map of Israeli Terror'. The countries around Lebanon are named: Syria and 'Occupied Palestine'.

was any Zionism in the Respect Party they would be hunted down and kicked out. We have no time for Zionists', Yvonne Ridley, February 2006, Imperial College, London (Or-Bach 2006).

The demonization of 'Zionism' appears to be part of an anti-oppression politics, but it points in another direction: towards a totalitarian way of thinking whose language is that of conspiracy conducted by dark forces.[13] A solution is often conceived not in terms of peace and reconciliation but rather in terms of destroying or uprooting the evil, wherever it is to be found.[14]

Joseph Massad (2003) begins his analysis with the assertion that Zionism is a colonial movement that is 'constituted in ideology and practice by a religio-racial epistemology', adding that it is 'important also to analyze the racial dimension of Zionism in its current manifestation...'. He understands Zionism to be defined by its commitment to 'building a demographically exclusive Jewish state', which he understands alongside the European colonial ideology of white supremacy over colonized people. Already we can see that Massad's notion of Zionism is, for practical purposes, homogenous. It is one 'Jewish supremacist' movement, from the 1880s to the present day. There are no significant differences between Zionism in the 19th and in the 21st century; between left and right Zionism, between religious and secular Zionism, between Labour Zionism and the Zionism of the fundamentalist settlers. Massad writes as though there was a single Israeli culture with a single ideology and a single purpose: a homogenous body of Israeli Jews. All differences are flattened out by the dominating principle of 'Jewish supremacism'. This assumption of homogeneity underpins a methodology that takes incidents and quotations from particular people, places and times to stand for and to illustrate the true nature of all Zionists in all places and throughout history.[15]

---

[13] For example, Sue Blackwell, 'the boycott was defeated following a well-funded campaign by the Zionist lobby', http://www.sue.be/pal/academic/AUT.html, downloaded 15 February 2007. More examples are analyzed in Part II of this paper.

[14] For example, Hayim Bresheeth on the Oslo peace process: 'The Palestinians are not turkeys, and will not vote for Christmas, and the idea that they can be forced into the 16 ghettoes is ludicrous.' (Bresheeth 2004)

[15] For example, Massad tells that the leading Russian language daily in Israel published an article in January 2002 called 'How to force them to leave', suggesting that the Israeli government should use the threat of castration to encourage Arabs to leave the country (Relying on Galili 2002, which is a newspaper report translated into English from Hebrew of the original newspaper article in Russian). The assumption of Zionist unity means that one opinion piece in one newspaper can be understood to illustrate the nature of Zionism as a whole. The fact that the paper reportedly received no outraged feedback from its readership should not come as a surprise, Massad tells us, since the following month the Tourism Minister Benny Elon proposed that the entire Arab population should be expelled from Israel. Elon, a fundamentalist religious Jewish settler who is defined by his support for what he euphemistically calls 'transfer', according to the assumption of Zionist homogeneity, speaks for all 'Jewish supremacists', or Zionists. Shimon Peres, Ariel Sharon, Benny Elon, Theodor Herzl, Golda Meir and the Meretz party are all used in this piece to exemplify 'Jewish supremacism'. One piece in the Israeli newspaper *Ma'ariv* entitled 'The Jews who run Clinton's cabinet' demonstrates the 'major ideological convergence between anti-Semites and Jewish supremacists' (Massad 2003: 446).

David Duke, a right-wing, open antisemite also uses the term 'Jewish supremacism'. He uses the term to refer primarily to the world Jewish conspiracy, although his rhetoric takes both

While antiracist anti-Zionism often claims to rest on a 'historical materialist' methodological foundation, some of its central assumptions seem to rely more on a methodology that gives primacy to ideas in the shaping of social life than to one that focuses on material factors. Antiracist anti-Zionism has a complex relationship with the Nazi genocide of the Jews, yet it is often more comfortable looking at cultural constructions of the Holocaust than it is thinking about the material effect of the Holocaust itself.

Massad's methodology starts with 'Zionist' ideology and this task is much simplified by the assumption that, in all its essentials, 'Zionist' ideology is one coherent body of thought. This assumption, in turn, is justified by reference to two things in Massad's work. Firstly, Zionism is understood as part of the European colonial project. This expands the methodology of explanatory flattening globally and across five hundred years. The whole history of 'white' imperialism is understood as essentially one racist project. The Crusades, British rule in India, colonization of Australia, New Zealand, the United States, South Africa, the British Mandate in Palestine, US policy during the Cold War in South and Central America and East Asia, the wars against Saddam Hussein's regime in Iraq, Belgian rule in Congo: all are essentially the same. Particularity becomes insignificant next to the one explanatory element of European racist exploitation. And Israel is part of this wider project. Actual history, human agency and contingency constitute little but the way that the big project happens to have played itself out in different places and at different times.

The second justification for the assumption that 'Zionist' ideology is one coherent body of thought is that the 'Jewish supremacist' project is not a racist movement amongst Jews, in Massad's understanding, but rather it is presented as something global:

> [T]he only way these arguments acquire any purchase is in the context of an international, read Western, commitment to Jewish supremacy, wherein Jews are seen as white Europeans defending white European values and civilization against the primitive Arab hordes. (Massad 2003: 449)

'Zionists' and Israel constitute, therefore, for Massad, one central element of the larger Western imperialist project. Some nineteenth century 'socialists' constructed Jews as being a central element in the workings of international capitalism. Much

---

anti-Jewish and anti-Zionist forms. Duke (2004) also makes much use of the *Ma'ariv* article in his piece 'Want to know the truth about Jewish Supremacism in their own words?' on his website.

The *Ma'ariv* piece is a manifestation of the Zionist project of 'turning the Jew into the anti-Semite' (Massad 2003: 446), which was, Massad tells us, from the early days of the Haskala thinkers and Herzl himself, what Zionism aimed to do. An Israeli newspaper article, an assertion and a quote from Herzl's diary are employed to outline Zionist thinking on anti-semitism. In a footnote, Massad directs us to another of his papers for his analysis of 'Zionism's complicity with anti-Semitism and its use of anti-Semites as a model'. He then adds an incident where an Israeli officer said that there was something to be learnt about military technique from the methods employed by the Nazis to clear the Warsaw ghetto, as well as an assertion that it is Israeli practice to write numbers on the arms of thousands of Palestinians in detention camps, to reveal something more about the relationship between Zionism, antisemitism and Nazism.

contemporary anti-Zionism understands the Jewish state to play a pivotal role in global imperialism.

The second element that justifies the assumption of Zionist homogeneity is definitional. What various 'Zionists' have said and written is interpreted as coherent and unified agreement upon an essentially racist project. Zionism is defined by Massad as 'Jewish supremacism'; it is related to racist movements, to Nazi movements, to colonialist projects and to apartheid. The essential, necessary and unchangeable character of Israel is defined by etymology. Actuality is found to be a manifestation of this definitional necessity. One key way of defining the difference between anti-Zionism, in the sense that we are using it here, and criticism of Israeli policy is the anti-Zionist insistence that Israel is necessarily and unchangeably unique. 'Zionism' is Nazism but Israel is not like Germany; 'Zionism' carries out ethnic cleansing but Israel is not like Croatia or Serbia; 'Zionism' settles occupied land but Israel is not like China; 'Zionism' is a colonial settler project but Israel is not like Australia. For anti-Zionism Israel is the totalitarian movement, not a nation or a state. Its policy at any particular time is often understood to be a manifestation of its inner essence, derived definitionally.

This framework gives huge explanatory importance to ideas and ideology. The racist idea is held to create and define the necessarily racist state. The story is often told by anti-Zionists. It begins with Herzl and it picks out some racist quotes from his book; it moves on to Jabotinsky and to Ben Gurion, picking quotes and anecdotes, before it arrives in 1948 and the Nakba, as the actualization of the racist idea in the world. It goes on to 1967 and shows how the inherently expansionist and colonial character of the 'Zionist idea' is manifested by the taking and settling of territory.[16]

There is a joke from the 1920s: What is the definition of a Zionist? A Zionist is one Jew who gives money to a second Jew so that a third Jew can go to Palestine.

Contemporary anti-Zionist discourse is comfortable on the terrain of the narrative construction of the Holocaust but it is less comfortable with the Holocaust itself. The Holocaust is understood as the trauma that psychoanalytically pathologizes Israel, rendering it uniquely compromised (Rose 2005).[17] The Holocaust is understood as something that is used by the 'Zionists' to justify their racist actions and to make some money on the side (Finkelstein 2003); it is understood as an event that, if not authored by the Zionists themselves, was aided by them or in which they were tied by complicity (Brenner 1983; Allen 1987);[18] it is understood as a source of illegitimate Jewish power and Jewish moral authority.

---

[16] The withdrawal of settlers from Gaza, first held by the anti-Zionists to be impossible, then interpreted only as another manifestation of racist demographic necessity, is now understood as a means of further imprisoning and constricting and isolating the inhabitants of Gaza and facilitating a more barbaric form of occupation. The fault-line in Israeli politics at the time of the withdrawal, between the orange and the blue, was understood only to be illusory and, anyway, an insignificant spat between Jewish supremacists over how best to further the cause of the racist movement.

[17] For a critique of Jacqueline Rose by Shalom Lappin and for her response, see Issues 6 and 7 of *Democratiya*, at http://www.democratiya.com.

[18] For more on Jim Allen's *Perdition* and on the relationship between the anti-Zionist left and Holocaust denial, see Ezra (2007) and Rich (2007).

Gillian Rose wrote about a tendency in the 1990s to treat the Holocaust as something ineffable. She criticized Habermas's implication that the Holocaust should be thought about as though it was holy, as though it was outside of history:

> It is this reference to 'the ineffable' that I would dub 'Holocaust piety'... 'The ineffable' is invoked by a now wide-spread tradition of reflection on the Holocaust: by Adorno, by Holocaust theology, Christian and Jewish, more recently by Lyotard and now by Habermas. According to this view, 'Auschwitz' or 'the Holocaust' are emblems for the breakdown in divine and/or human history. The uniqueness of this break delegitimizes names and narratives as such, and hence all aesthetic or apprehensive representation (Lyotard). (Rose 1996)

Rose was right to warn against Holocaust piety and was also perhaps prescient in understanding that what would follow piety would be its opposite, Holocaust sacrilege. First Holocaust piety was misunderstood and misrepresented as a wilful self-interested and dishonest instrumentalism rather than as a healthy seriousness and respect taken too far. Then it became possible for antiracist anti-Zionists to allow themselves the frisson of committing sacrilege – in the cause of Palestine, naturally.[19]

The anti-Zionist movement understands itself to be in the tradition of pre-war opposition to the project of Zionism, but it has difficulty relating its tradition to the material, historical events of the twentieth century. What happened was that the perspectives of the European Jewish anti-Zionists were not only politically defeated by Nazism (not by 'Zionism') but most of the anti-Zionists were also killed by Nazis.[20] Jewish life and culture over large parts of Europe was removed. Certainly amongst the remnants, the attraction of Zionism, of the idea of Jewish national independence, was strong. But it would surely be incomplete to understand events as the actualization of an unbroken thread of ideas and to neglect the huge material transformation that gave an entirely new context to those ideas.

In the middle of the twentieth century, Israel was not imagined as a European colony. It is strained, to say the least, to believe that Jews in the refugee camps in Europe and in British Cyprus, recovering from starvation and from existences as non-humans, were thinking of themselves as standard bearers of 'the European idea'. The seamless insertion of the history of 'Zionism' into a schematic history of colonialism casts Jews as going to Palestine in order to get rich on the back of the people who lived there. Jews, who are said to embody some European idea of whiteness, also embodied a European idea of rats and cockroaches, which was held to constitute an existential threat to Europe. Massad mentions the effect of the

---

[19] Simonon (2006) tells the story of the political wrangles that occurred around the commemoration of the Holocaust in Belgium at the site of the deportation of Belgian Jews to Auschwitz in Mechelen: 'So, in September 2005, the new committee of experts published their conclusions. Their opinion on the museum [at the site of the deportations under Nazi occupation] was that it should be transformed into a more inclusive outlet, a memorial not just to the Holocaust but to all genocides and crimes against humanity. In other words, its Jewish specificity was inappropriate.'

[20] This fact, perhaps, sheds light on why many anti-Zionists go to such length to demonstrate the ideological 'similarity' of Nazism and Zionism. It is only in this way that it is possible to paint the Nazi defeat of pre-war anti-Zionism as a victory for 'the Zionists'.

Holocaust in transforming 'Zionism' but he does not analyze its significance.[21] He does not discuss what it was about the Holocaust and the establishment of the State of Israel that changed the terms of the debate so completely. He writes as though the debate remains fundamentally the same in spite of the fact that the social reality of Europe and its relationship with Jews had changed. It is difficult to imagine how it could have changed more radically. He also mentions the fact that Jews did not emigrate to Palestine en masse due to an ideological commitment to Zionism but due to their expulsion from European and Middle Eastern countries,[22] but he does not grasp the significance of this fact – that 'Zionism' was not only a construction of ideology but to a significant extent was the result of material circumstance.

Jews, Massad, rightly points out, did not go to Israel because they were convinced Zionists in the sense of the pre-Holocaust debates. They went to Israel because the world had changed, because they had nowhere else to go, because they were homeless and they wanted to find a home. Also, as Massad says, Jews arrived in Israel because they were expelled from a number of countries in the Middle East. Massad is not explicit about how this huge influx of refugee Jews was incorporated into the white Jewish supremacist colonialist project. But he believes that they were, quickly and completely.[23]

Left anti-Zionism is often adopted by people who consider themselves to be influenced by Marxist historical materialism, yet it operates with a methodology that tends to give an overwhelming explanatory importance to ideas. This methodology is selective. What it leaves out is as important as what it includes. For example the Holocaust; for example the ethnic cleansing of Jews from the rest of the Middle East in the 1950s and 1960s; for example the existence of the antiracist Israeli left and peace movement; for example Middle Eastern antisemitism; for example the influence of Nazism in the Middle East during the 1940s (Küntzel 2006).

Left anti-Zionism is often adopted by people who consider themselves to be anti-essentialist, yet it operates with a methodology that understands events as little more than the manifestations of Israel's racist, colonialist and totalitarian essences.

Left anti-Zionism is often adopted by people who consider themselves to be politically responsible, yet it operates in a world where, increasingly, antisemitism clothes itself in the rhetoric of anti-Zionism (e.g. Duke 2004; 2004a). It fails to see this context as significant, and it refuses to take reasonable care in its consciousness of

---

[21] He says: 'Jewish anti-Zionists continued to oppose Zionism's Jewish supremacist plans until 1948 when most of the support they had received over the decades dwindled against the reality of the Holocaust and the establishment of the Jewish supremacist state' (Massad 2003: 445).

[22] '[I]t is also important to remember that the majority of Jews who reside in Israel today, or at least who emigrated to Israel in the 1930s and 40s and 50s, did not come to Israel because of Zionist reasons. We have to remember that the larger segment of the Israeli Jewish population came to Israel as refugees after the war, and after 1948, from both Europe and the Arab countries, not because of the success of Zionism, but because they were refugees and had no other place to go.' (Whitehead 2002: 213).

[23] 'The Jewish side, and by that I mean both Israeli Jewish society and the Israeli government, are still as Zionist as they have always been, and committed to Jewish supremacy. Jewish supremacy is the basis of the Israeli state. This is exactly the crux of the matter.' (Massad in Whitehead 2002: 214)

the boundaries between the antisemitic demonization of Israel and the legitimate criticism of particular policies of the Israeli state. It operates as though the only kind of anti-Zionism that is significant is antiracist anti-Zionism. It often fails to take seriously the fact that much of the anti-Zionism around its own political universe is hostile to Jews, viscerally, religiously, implicitly or only *de facto*.

The anti-Stalinist left, particularly those sections that identified as Trotskyist, encountered huge difficulties in general when faced with a post-war world in which Trotsky's global revolutionary perspective had been entirely defeated. Neither of the two possibilities that Trotsky foresaw had happened: the 'degenerated workers' state' of the Soviet Union did not collapse, nor did the workers show signs of making a 'political revolution' against the 'bureaucracy'. In fact, the 'degenerated workers' state' came out of the war hugely strengthened, and it replicated itself across a significant section of the world. Capitalism showed itself again, also against all expectations, to be hugely dynamic, and its 'death throes' seemed to go on for a long time. The world seemed to find a third option that was neither socialism nor barbarism. Much of the anti-Stalinist left had great difficulty coming to terms with this new world, and much of it preferred to operate by denying that there was a new situation and a new stabilization. So the anti-Zionist denial about how the world had changed following the Second World War could be understood as only a part of a much wider failure to come to terms with a new situation.

Some on the Trotskyist left remained for decades in a state of frenzy, convinced that this was the moment of the final crisis of capitalism and of state 'socialism'. Others eventually over-embraced the new situation and became convinced that the Soviet Union, Eastern Europe and China were, after all, in spite of their evident failings, in some sense an advance on capitalism: they embraced one side of Trotsky's pre-war programme, 'defend the Soviet Union'. By this route, many on the Trotskyist left managed to downplay their opposition to the 'bureaucracy' in favour of defending the 'workers' states' against imperialism. In this way Marxist politics, for some, was radically transformed. It used to be a programme for the transformation of society from the dictatorship of the bourgeoisie into a democratic and free community of producers; yet many now saw their immediate task not as siding with the workers, or with the oppressed in general, but as siding with 'progressive' states against imperialist ones. Whereas classic internationalism was a programme of common struggle against capitalism, it now became a programme of taking sides in geopolitical power struggles.[24]

But the Soviet flag was not the first national flag that had been waved by some on the left. The first, perhaps, was the Tricolour of revolutionary France. France, and later Russia, were seen by some as universal nations, whose national interest coincided with the interest of humanity (or the working class) as a whole (Fine 2001).

How much easier to ally with some actually existing state than with a set of cosmopolitan politics? And later other options emerged, such as Cuba, Nicaragua and Venezuela. For some it did not matter that the leaders of the good 'progressive' nations wore military uniforms, had secret police forces and ruled tyrannically over

---

[24] One consequence of this was that very few Trotskyists later defended the right of Soviet Jews to leave the USSR, and very few spoke up for dissidents like Andrei Sakharov.

their own populations. What mattered was that there was some actually existing state to which they could attach their feelings of patriotism.

Interestingly, Israel, for some, in its early days, was seen as one of these good nations. The questions that Wheatcroft (2006), for example, asks about Israel, and the way that it is thought about in left and liberal circles in the United Kingdom, are more interesting than the tentative answers that he offers. He says that people on the left, and liberals, used to love Israel but have now reversed their position,[25] and he asks which is right? He is asking, in effect, whether Israel is a good nation or a bad nation, a progressive nation or a threat to progress. This methodologically nationalist framework for thinking is a break from the cosmopolitan tradition of the left, which aimed to unite people in all states against the social and political structures that divided them.

This phenomenon degenerated further for those who substituted victim nations for good nations. Good nations, that is, nations thought to have socialist or progressive regimes, were, some noticed, always opposed by imperialism. So some on the left began to support any regime that opposed imperialism. In this way, left-wing political currents arose that flew the flags of the countries that were opposed by the 'oppressor' nations, and some of them, in the name of anti-imperialism, even turned themselves into apologists for Saddam Hussein, Slobodan Milosevic, Mahmoud Ahmadinejad, Kim Jong-il and for the 'resistance movement' in Iraq.

Wheatcroft tells us that some people on the left in the 1950s had great illusory hopes in Israel as both a good nation and a victim nation and they began to wave its flag. It is sometimes these same people who have now swung round in disgust when it turns out that Israel is not a utopian beacon for mankind.[26] With all the passion of people who have been made fools of by history, and by the crumbling of their own adolescent illusions, sections of the left are now turning on Israel with a rage, a single-mindedness and an enthusiasm explainable more readily by feelings of betrayal than by looking at the actual nature of the conflict between Israel and Palestine.

Many on the contemporary left split the world into camps. In one camp is imperialism, in the other camp there are the oppressed. Those who adopt this campist

---

[25] 'There has, indeed, been a dramatic turn in opinion. It's very hard to recall the esteem and goodwill in which Israel once basked, not least on the broad liberal left, where there is now a received view that Israel has deserved this change in affections: that Israel and Zionism are vicious now, having been virtuous once. The view may be almost universal – but is it true?' Some pinned their hopes on Israel in the early days, as a new social democratic model and were inspired by the bold socialist experiment of the Kibbutz movement. This was mixed with a liberal 'philosemitism' and a feeling of 'horror and shame' about the Holocaust, he tells us. Yet this warmth was only achieved, he says, because the 'right-thinking liberal west closed its eyes at the time' to the 'wholesale expulsion of three-quarters of a million Palestinians in 1948'.

[26] Beller (2007) argues against an attitude that normalizes hostility between Israelis and Palestinians because they are at war, as follows: 'The "It is war!" argument is really a counsel of despair, and an admission of defeat for the higher values that Israel was meant to achieve. Jews are supposed to value human life above all, not just Jewish life, human life.' Kuper (2006) argues that it is legitimate to hold Israel to higher standards than other states on the basis that 'Israel sees itself as a state based "on the precepts of liberty, justice and peace taught by the Hebrew Prophets". In the words of Isaiah, "We are a light unto the nations."'

view tend not to support the oppressed but instead to support those who claim to speak for the oppressed and those who (sometimes forcibly) organize the oppressed. They are less concerned than they might be with the question of what kind of society those who speak for the oppressed propose to replace 'imperialism' with. The preponderance of this world view goes some way to explaining why there is so much visceral hatred of Israel on the left, while there is so little anger caused by much greater human rights abuses perpetrated by regimes that are not thought to be 'imperialist'.

The story goes that Israel is a creature of imperialism or a client state of the United States (putting to one side, for the moment, the story that says Israel controls global imperialism and the United States). John Rose, for example, relying on Noam Chomsky's argument that Israel became a 'strategic asset' in the securing of US access to Middle Eastern oil, argues that

> Israel could play its part in helping encase the region in a military structure, which would protect Western oil supplies.... Within just three years of its foundation, its ideologues were ready to tie Israel's survival to the predatory intentions of the 'Western powers'.... Radical nationalism was poised to sweep across the Middle East. Israel's statement of intent could hardly have been more prescient. Israel would indeed become the watchdog. (Rose 2004)

Whether Israel is represented as a part of the white project of colonialism or as America's 'strategic asset' in the Middle East, the amount of slippage required to transform Israel into an essentially imperialist entity is small. What makes Israel so demonic is an explosive mixture of racism, human rights abuses and imperialism. Some on the left are not enraged by, or motivated to act in solidarity against, much greater racism and human rights abuses committed by states that are not also 'imperialist'.

There are many disconnects between this world view and the actual world. One problem is that Israel would not have come into existence when it did without a shift in Soviet policy on the Middle East in the mid-1940s and Soviet bloc support for partition during 1947-1948. Israel's origins are bound up in early Cold War politics and growing US-USSR rivalry. Another problem is that Israel would have been killed at birth in the war of 1948 if it had not been armed by Stalin's Soviet Union against a British and American arms embargo.[27] Now perhaps the Soviet Union was

---

[27] An article in *Ha'aretz*, quoted in Hirsh (2006g), gives fascinating details of the military help that flowed from Czechoslovakia to the Jews in Palestine: 'The first arms deal with Czechoslovakia was signed in January 1948 – less than two months after the UN resolution creating Israel and four months before the state was actually established. Immediately after the Partition Plan was passed, Ben-Gurion began searching for sources to supply arms to the Israeli defense forces, but found that the legal sources in the United States and most European countries were closed off to the institutions of the Jewish state in formation. The only alternative seemed to be illegal arms acquisitions and an appeal to the Soviet bloc. ... As part of the deal signed in January, Czechoslovakia supplied some 50,000 rifles (that remained in use in the IDF for around 30 years), some 6,000 machine guns and around 90 million bullets. But the most important contracts were signed in late April and early May. They promised to supply 25 Messerschmidt fighter planes and arranged for the training – on Czech soil and in Czech military facilities – of Israeli pilots and technicians who would fly and maintain them. The

also imperialist, so it is after all true that Israel was helped into existence by 'imperialism'. Except that the Czechoslovakian weapons that were smuggled to the Jews in Palestine in 1948 were sent in the name of anti-imperialism by the 'Communists', who always denied that they were imperialists. In fact, they positioned themselves as part of the 'oppressed', who opposed global imperialism. Many of the 'anti-imperialists' of today who so despise Israel do not consider the old Soviet empire to have been an imperialist formation.

The leadership of the Jews fighting for a state in Palestine was nationalist, and nationalists tend to take help from wherever they can get it. Accepting help from the imperialist Soviet Union against the British Empire and in the face of an American arms embargo was unremarkable in the context of the history of nationalist struggles for independence. In the 1950s, the USSR reconstructed its Middle East policy when it realized that it could push its own imperialist ambitions in the Middle East more effectively by backing Arab nationalist regimes against Israel; and the United States gradually came to back Israel against the Soviet-backed Arab states. This was routine bloc politics of the Cold War. What is remarkable is the myth that is currently believed by many on the left, namely that Israel is not at all a nation state like any other but is in reality little more than a creation of, and a creature of, the United States. The assumption that some work under is that Israel was put there by Europe and America in order to facilitate the imperialist domination of the Middle East. Never mind the fact that the US-Israeli alliance, which began to develop in the early 1960s, was cemented only after the Six Day War in 1967. Never mind the fact that, when the United States wants to organize military adventures in the Middle East in the contemporary period, Israel is of no use to it, and it has to rely on Egypt, Turkey, Saudi Arabia, Kuwait and other regimes for air-bases.

Isaac Deutscher, who had lived his early political life in the Yiddish-speaking milieu of the Jewish left in Europe, before the Holocaust, wrote in 1954: 'I have, of course, long since abandoned my anti-Zionism, which was based on a confidence in the European labour movement, or, more broadly, in European society and civilization, which that society and civilization have not justified.' (Deutscher 1968: 111-112, written in 1954)

Deutscher dismisses anti-Zionism after the Holocaust without a second thought. It does not seem to have occurred to him that a new anti-Zionist movement might emerge to pump new content into his own political heritage. Yet Deutscher still did not identify himself as a Zionist. He was interested in coming to a non-nationalist, cosmopolitan analysis and politics. And in response to futile arguments over who started the conflict between Jews and Arabs, he tells the following story:

> A man once jumped from the top floor of a burning house in which many members of his family had already perished. He managed to save his life; but as he was falling he hit a person standing down below and broke that person's legs and arms. ... If both behaved rationally, they would not become enemies. ... But look

---

planes, which were disassembled and flown to Israel on large transport planes, after their reassembly played a very important role in halting the Egypt Army's advance south of Ashdod, at a place now called the Ad Halom Junction. The assistance to the air force continued to flow in during the second half of 1948 – when it consisted of 56 Spitfire fighter planes. These were flown to Israel, some of them by Israeli pilots.'

what happens when these people behave irrationally. The injured man blames the other for his misery and swears to make him pay for it. The other, afraid of the crippled man's revenge, insults him, kicks him, and beats him up whenever they meet. ... The bitter enmity, so fortuitous at first, hardens and comes to overshadow the whole existence of both men and to poison their minds. (Deutscher 1968: 136-137, from an interview in *New Left Review*, 23 June 1967)

If we understand the establishment of the State of Israel at least in part in the context of the huge events of the middle of the twentieth century, and if we understand that it has material causes as well as ideational ones, especially in the needs of a persecuted minority in both Europe and the Middle East, then we can see that anti-Zionism in 1929, for example, had a different meaning and content to the one that it has today. The debate now is about different issues. How can Israeli Jews and Palestinians forge a just peace? How can the racist currents within Israel and also within Palestine be defeated politically? How can the tragic history that brought Jews and Palestinians into such a bloody conflict be transcended in the future? But even now, Ghada Karmi (2007), for example, yearns 'to turn back the clock before there was a Jewish state and re-run history from there' (p. 265). She still wishes that the 'tormented, suspicious and neurotically self-absorbed community toughened by centuries of the need to survive' had never gone to Palestine (p. 120). But the terms of the debate, and what is at stake in the debate, have changed radically since the 1880s and the 1890s and the 1920s.

Norman Finkelstein quotes this very passage from Deutscher and, in his attempt to refute its relevance, exemplifies a number of defining features of left anti-Zionist discourse. He says that

> The Zionist denial of Palestinians' rights, culminating in their expulsion, hardly sprang from an unavoidable accident.... It resulted from the systematic and conscientious implementation, over many decades ... of a political ideology the goal of which was to create a demographically Jewish state in Palestine.... To claim that Zionist leaders acted irrationally in refusing to 'remove or assuage the grievance' of Palestinians, then, is effectively to say that Zionism is irrational: for, given that the Palestinians' chief grievance was the denial of their homeland, were Zionists to act 'rationally' and remove it, the raison d'être of Zionism and its fundamental historic achievement in 1948 would have been nullified.... To suggest that Zionists had no choice – or, as Deutscher puts it elsewhere, that the Jewish state was a 'historic necessity' – is to deny the Zionist movement's massive and, in many respects, impressive exertion of will, and the moral responsibility attending the exertion of this will, in one rather than another direction. (Finkelstein 2005: 11).

Here, Finkelstein relies on the assumption of Zionist homogeneity. While anti-Zionists often insist on rhetorically splitting 'the Zionist leadership' from the Jews who were persuaded, cajoled, fooled and forced into following, they also tend to insist on the homogeneity of Israelis and their total incorporation into the ideology of 'Jewish supremacism'. Here Finkelstein bestows his enemy, now collapsed into the phrase 'the Zionist Movement', with a satanic greatness, capable of a 'massive ... impressive exertion of will'. He cannot accept Deutscher's *ex post facto* explanation of Zionism's transformation from a utopian movement into a state (what other sort of explanation is there?). It can only be explained by the extraordinary (massive, impressive) 'will' of Zionism, since to accept that Israel's existence is somehow connected to the Holocaust and to the plight of oppressed Jews would be to muddy the explanatory dualisms upon which anti-Zionism relies: white/non-white; oppressor/oppressed; good nationalism/bad nationalism; colonizer/colonized.

Deutscher says that if both Israelis and Palestinians had behaved rationally then they would have not become enemies. Finkelstein here falls back onto an etymological rather than sociological explanation. He replies that the only way that Israel could have made peace with Palestine would have been to dissolve itself, since it was, by definition, incapable of living in peace. He says that the Palestinians' chief grievance was the denial of their homeland, and he then says that 'Zionists' could only remove this grievance by nullifying the 'raison d'être of Zionism'. Deutscher was trying to find a political orientation that could transcend both nationalisms. Finkelstein replies by saying that Israeli nationalism is definitionally racist, and so instead of looking for a political orientation that could move beyond nationalism he finds no other option than choosing to support one nationalism against the other. One of the nationalisms, in any case, is often represented by anti-Zionists as an *ersatz* nationalism, a totalitarian movement posing as a nationalism. The 'raison d'être' of Zionism would necessarily be removed, for Finkelstein, by a meaningful peace agreement. He goes on:

> It's equally fatuous to assert that Palestinians act irrationally when they 'blame' the Zionists 'for their misery' and not accept that they were 'the victim of circumstances over which neither of them had control.' It's only irrational if Zionists bore no responsibility for what happened. (Finkelstein 2005: 12)

Here he shifts the frame of the debate. Deutscher is arguing that the foundation of Israel can only be understood with reference to the events in Europe that preceded it. Finkelstein reads Deutscher as using 'the Holocaust' in order to justify the unjustifiable. And the only way Finkelstein can frame this claim is by totalizing it. Either 'the Zionists' were responsible (hyper-agents with a 'massive' and 'impressive' will) or they were innocent refugees (victims), in which case they would have behaved how innocent refugees 'ought' to behave. Finkelstein reads Deutscher as saying that 'Zionists' bore no responsibility for the hurt inflicted on Palestine. But what Deutscher seems to be trying to come to terms with is that it is understandable that Jewish refugees were taught to be frightened, angry and distrustful nationalists by their experience in Europe, and later in the Middle East, but that still other outcomes were possible. Events were not determined by the etymological essence of 'Zionism' but rather by twentieth century history and by political battles won and lost amongst Jews and amongst Palestinians.

Anti-Zionism, as well as some opponents of anti-Zionism (e.g. Chesler 2003; Phillips 2006), often construct the struggle over ideas in such a way as to compel one to choose between competing nationalisms. Supporters of each nationalism are tempted to tell the narratives of the Middle East so that we are forced to side with either Israel or with Palestine against the other. More cosmopolitan approaches attempt to break from this artificial binary, arguing that it is necessary to resist the simple choices we are offered and to go beyond a passive acceptance of the world as it exists. Such an approach would fight against the demonization of Israel and Jews, on the one hand, but would also reject alternatives and explanations that demonize

Muslims and Arabs, on the other. A more cosmopolitan approach is not incompatible with those enlightened Israeli and Palestinian nationalist approaches that assume national self-interest to consist first and foremost in building a political framework whereby both Israel and Palestine can be guaranteed national self-determination.

It is not only Israeli nationalist imaginings of homogeneity that are accepted by left anti-Zionism as a picture of reality but also Palestinian ones. The Palestinian population, Massad tells us, 'understood Zionism for what it was and resisted it from its inception in the late nineteenth century' (Massad 2003: 444). This view of the world as being divided into monolithic peoples, with single purposes and understandings, is recurrent in both Zionist and anti-Zionist writing. He repeats this claim in a debate with Benny Morris (Whitehead 2002: 213): 'From the Palestinian perspective, the nature of Zionism has always been clear.' He writes as though there was a single Palestinian perspective. But this perspective, it seems, is not always the one of the Palestinian leadership, which, during the Oslo process, Massad tells us, accepted 'in many ways, the Zionist version, both of Jewish and Palestinian histories, and succumbed to it.' (Whitehead 2002: 213) He writes, that is, as if there was only one Zionist version of history. 'The people' have always understood everything clearly; the leadership was corrupted and bought off by the enemies of the people.

He also says that he is in favour of the 'continuing resistance of Palestinians in Israel and the occupied territories to all the civil and military institutions that uphold Jewish supremacy' (Massad 2003: 450). The apparently straightforward statement of solidarity also hides and glosses over the centrally important political distinctions in Palestine. Does Massad understand the suicide bombing of buses, restaurants and nightclubs to constitute 'resistance' to institutions that uphold 'Jewish supremacy'? Does he understand Hamas and Hezbollah, with their clearly antisemitic rhetoric, to be a part of that 'resistance'? Palestine is presented as a monolithic anti-colonialist nationalist struggle, although held back by corrupt leaders. It is presented as though there were no politics in Palestine, no differences of attitude amongst Palestinians to the presence of Jews and to the presence of Israel in the Middle East. There is only the authentic resistance of the Palestinian people and the pro-Zionist collaboration of their leaders. Later, Massad (2006) threw his political weight behind the openly antisemitic Hamas movement and he characterized the secular nationalist tradition of the Fatah leadership in Palestine as being a 'collaborationist' one, subservient to Israeli interest. Since the Hamas coup in Gaza against the Palestinian presidency, it is becoming more common in the United Kingdom, both on the far left but also in mainstream liberal opinion, to understand Hamas as the single authentic voice of Palestine – and Fatah, therefore, as a pro-imperialist gang of Quislings.[28]

Massad says that if Jews were to give up their 'Jewish supremacist' ideology and allow Palestinians the 'right of return', then any threat to Jews would disappear (Massad 2003: 449). Terrorist threats to Jews, as well as antisemitism in the Middle East, and across the world, is thought of by many anti-Zionists as being a (legiti-

---

[28] 'The stunning military victory by the Palestinian Hamas movement over the rival Fatah organisation in the Gaza Strip last week was a strike against imperialism in the Middle East.' (Assaf 2007); 'We should hope – that may be all we can now do – that moderate Islamist movements manage to navigate these turbulent times, in spite of European attempts to prevent Islamism, which is clearly now the dominant regional current, from reshaping Middle Eastern societies.' (Crooke 2007)

mate? understandable? predictable?) response to Zionism. In this paradigm, 'Zionism' is responsible for the increase in antisemitism; antisemites are in this way absolved of responsibility, as well as human agency. Anti-Jewish racism is understood by anti-Zionists as being a profoundly different sort of racism to other racisms. Other racisms are not normally analyzed by antiracists in terms of what it is that the victims of those racisms are doing to make people hate them.[29]

The assumption of Palestinian homogeneity is based on a romantic picture of the Palestinian national movement. Yet in truth Palestinian nationalism has always been greatly influenced by the requirements of pan-Arab nationalist narratives and, more recently, of the global Islamist movement. And these narratives undergo further degradation and simplification before they become part of left common sense in Britain. They become further removed from an achievable conception of Palestinian national interest. Questions concerning a conflict of interest between Palestinian nationalism and Arab nationalism or Islamism are regarded with suspicion. One of the tropes of anti-Zionism is a refusal to take seriously the conflicting interests of Palestinians and Arab states and an unwillingness to allow oneself to be moved by the history of exploitation, repression, killing, moving on and instrumentalization of Palestinians by Arab regimes.

It is understood in anti-Zionist circles that great suspicion should fall on anyone who asks questions about the treatment of Palestinians in Arab states. Anyone who asks how it is that Palestinians in those states have not been allowed to integrate into society but have been kept separate and rightless as refugees is suspected of preparing a 'Zionist' denial that may hold Arab regimes or Arab nationalism at least partly responsible for the misery of Palestinians. While anger with (American-backed) Arab regimes may be appropriate in anti-Zionist circles, it is never allowed to disrupt the central truth, which is that Palestinians and Arabs in general are the victims of Israel and America, and of nobody else. When Palestinians have been victimized by other Arabs, it often turns out that imperialism was the moving force behind that victimization, either through Zionist machinations or American-backed puppets or as a result of the legacy of European colonialism. Hostility to Israel is such a deeply ingrained commonsense for many on the left that they often forget to ask what function anti-Zionism plays for the Arab ruling elites.

There are more questions that are widely understood to be forbidden in the anti-Zionist universe, which are excluded from the narrative. We have already touched on the ways in which certain kinds of narrative of the Holocaust are suspect if they seem to be mobilized towards an effort to justify Israeli crimes or to construct 'Zionism' as some kind of a Jewish liberation movement. If Holocaust narratives disrupt the simple Israelis-as-oppressors, Palestinians-as-oppressed binary, then they become not quite respectable in the anti-Zionist imagination. It is respectable to talk about how the Holocaust is abused by Israel as a discourse of legitimation.[30] It is

---

[29] Compare with this statement from the right-wing antisemite, Holocaust denier and anti-Zionist, David Irving: 'They [Jews] should ask themselves the question, "Why have they been so hated for 3000 years that there has been pogrom after pogrom in country after country?"' (Barkat 2006)

[30] Judith Butler in conversation with Jacqueline Rose, 22 September 2005, 'Holocaust Premises: Political Implications of the Traumatic Frame', Senate House, London.

respectable to understand Holocaust Memorial Day as an attack on British Muslims (Sacranie 2005).[31] But it is highly suspect in anti-Zionist circles to argue that it was the Holocaust that transformed the material condition of Europe such that 'Zionism' was transformed from a utopian minority idea amongst Jews into a majority one and, amidst the decline of Britain and the growing American-Soviet Cold War rivalry, into a nation state.

Another forbidden question is the one that asks how and why Jews were almost entirely pushed out of all the Middle Eastern states in the 1950s and 1960s. The forced movement of Palestinians from Israeli-held territory in 1948 is the original sin that forever renders Israel uniquely illegitimate. The forced movement of Jews from the whole of the Middle East to Israel, however, is often represented as a more or less free choice; it is explained as the result of 'Zionist' agents provocateurs manufacturing the antisemitism (or perhaps the justified anger with Israel?) that forced the Jews out of the great cosmopolitan cities of the Middle East, including Baghdad, Cairo, Beirut, Damascus and the rest. There is a right and justified anti-Zionist concern to disallow attempts to minimize or deny the suffering of Palestinians in 1948 and their subsequent partial exclusion from Israeli territory. Yet this concern can lead anti-Zionists to turn their eyes away from the wholesale expulsion of Jews from the Middle East as part of the Arab nationalist consolidation of ethnically defined Arab nation states.[32] Sometimes there are attempts to square the circle by portraying Jews who were pushed out of the Arab states as being really Arabs, who are, alongside other Arabs, victims of Ashkenazi or 'white' Jewish supremacism. In this narrative, the reality of the power divide in Israel between Jews of European and Middle Eastern descent is fitted into a binary world view that raises the power differences between 'white' imperialism and the rest of the world to an absolute and subsumes all other differences. Many Jews of Middle Eastern descent who live in Israel would be astonished to learn that some people in the West regard them as Arabs who are oppressed by 'white' Jews.

Although I have referred to the myth of Palestinian homogeneity as a romantic nationalism, it is actually, perhaps, more 'orientalist' (Said 1978) than it is benevolent. A respectful way to relate to Palestinians is not to pretend that they all think the same thing but to consider the plurality of different ways of thinking and different politics and different choices that are evident amongst Palestinians. The cosmopolitan project is precisely based on disrupting and challenging myths of national homogeneity (Hirsh 2003; Fine 2007) rather than giving them a left-wing stamp of authenticity.

---

[31] 'So we said that our common humanity called upon us to also recognize the crimes perpetrated against other people, and we called for the establishment of an EU genocide memorial day. Such a day would help dispel the – frankly racist – notion that some people are to be regarded as being more equal than others.' Sacranie went on to claim that 'Every year since the HMD [Holocaust Memorial Day] was inaugurated in 2001, the MCB [Muslim Council of Britain] has been subjected to intimidating smears of antisemitism in the press. We have been accused of wanting to "scrap" the HMD out of "hatred" of the Jewish people. This is hysterical nonsense.' (Sacranie 2005)

[32] There were a few Zionist agent provocateurs, and there were Zionists who wanted Jews from the Middle East to go to Israel, but it requires a willingness to stretch the facts hugely to give these factors such explanatory dominance. See, for example, Shiblak (2005) on how Jews were pushed out of Iraq and Hakakian (2004) on how Jews were pushed out of Iran.

Nothing is gained by infantilizing Palestinians. For example, there is a problem of antisemitism amongst Palestinians. Hamas, the most electorally popular party in Palestine, is explicitly founded on an Islamist version of the *Protocols of the Elders of Zion*. It is far from surprising that people who live under the occupation of an overwhelmingly Jewish army may be susceptible to antisemitism. But to naturalize that antisemitism by treating it as though it was entirely unmediated by human agency or by political choices looks rather orientalist. Most Arabs are not under occupation, yet antisemitism in predominately Arab or Muslim countries is also excused or underplayed. It is underplayed either by pretending that it is nothing but an epiphenomenon of the conflict and has no life or emergent properties independent of it or by pretending that antisemitism is a European colonialist invention and import into the Middle East and, therefore, that people in the Middle East bear no responsibility for it and are incapable of being authentically antisemitic. Other patronizing defences are attempted, for example that Arabic is too simple a language to cope with the (complex) distinction between Israeli and Jew, so that, when people express hatred for Jews, it is only because they are not capable of the clarity required to express their hatred of Israelis.[33]

Anti-Zionism tends to treat Palestine as one entity with a simple unifying narrative. It is common to hear anti-Zionists declare that the conflict is actually simple in spite of dishonest 'Zionist' attempts to introduce obfuscating complexity. Campaigns of boycott, disinvestment and sanctions against Israel are inspired by a fundamentally nationalist view of the world. They treat Israel and Palestine as single entities that must be either supported or punished. They thereby seek to make the cosmopolitan project of relating to differences within those nations, and commonalities between groups in both nations, impossible. Attempts to make alliances between democrats, antiracists and peace-seekers within each nation and against the racists and those who seek all out victory in both nations, are disrupted by good-nation/bad-nation nationalist world views.

3. A simple picture of oppressed and oppressors

Since before it formally existed, Israel has been engaged in two wars with its neighbours. One is a just war, waged by Palestinian Arabs for freedom, which became a struggle for Palestinian national independence; the other is a genocidal war that aims to end, or at least subjugate, Jewish life in the Middle East. It is my argument that a cosmopolitan framework should insist on the reality of this distinction and it should challenge those who recognize the reality of only one or other of these two separate wars.

However, in the summer of 2006, when Israeli tanks were stalking through the crowded streets of Gaza, when Katyusha rockets were slamming into a deserted Haifa, when Israeli F16s were blowing up buildings in the suburbs of Beirut and when Israeli soldiers were being held in underground dungeons waiting for their own beheading to be broadcast on al-Jazeera, the distinction seemed entirely notional.

Many people believe the war for Palestinian independence is a pretend war that functions only to give a liberational facade to the real war of annihilation; many

---

[33] I have heard this defence made by a British academic in a debate about antisemitism.

others believe the war of annihilation is an Israeli propaganda invention that functions only to allow Israel to thwart the just demands of the Palestinians – an invocation of the Holocaust as a blank cheque.

An interesting feature of social reality is that if enough people believe something to be true, and act as though it is true, then it may indeed become the truth. So if Israelis believe they are only ever fighting a war of survival, then they will use tactics and strategies that are appropriate to the war they believe themselves to be fighting. If Palestinians, meanwhile, come to believe that they can win their freedom only by destroying Israel, then they may come to think of Hamas, Hezbollah, al-Qaeda and the Iranian regime as their allies.

The way out is for cosmopolitan voices and political movements to insist on the reality of both wars and to separate them conceptually; to stand clearly for a Palestinian victory in the fight for freedom and equally clearly for an Israeli victory in the fight against annihilation.

There is a left 'common sense' in the United Kingdom that sees only one struggle going on – a war of the oppressed against the oppressors. This way of thinking denies that there is a substantial project to annihilate Israel and it insists that this is in any case not an immediate prospect because Israel is so heavily armed. But there really is a set of serious global political movements that aim to kill or subjugate the Jews of Israel. Such a movement rules in Iran and was elected into office in Palestine, it occupies southern Lebanon, it took power in Gaza, it has a foothold in Iraq and it has significant popular support across the Middle East and further afield.

If some people on the left are relying on Israel's military superiority to guarantee its survival, then they must, logically, if they are in favour of its survival, also be in favour of Israel's allies, particularly the United States, helping to maintain Israeli military superiority. But it seems more likely that an atmosphere is building on parts of the British left that would lead many to respond to the annihilation of Israel by saying: 'This second genocide of the Jews is genuinely tragic, but really, they have only themselves to blame.' Israeli Jews would be making a mistake if they relied on the solidarity of the British left to protect them from those who say they would like to slaughter them.

Meanwhile, the left in Israel is unable to insist on the reality of the just struggle for Palestinian independence. Much of the Israeli left was convinced in 2000 that Palestine had rejected at least a partial victory in its war for statehood in favour of the hope for victory in the war for Israeli annihilation. But there are still those in Israel and Palestine who have not given up on the project of separating the two wars.

The collapse of the peace process convinced many Palestinians that the war for independence could never be won and that their only option was to back the jihadi Islamist movements against the Jews. Yet Palestinian nationalism, the movement for Palestinian independence, has not yet been entirely defeated by the jihadi Islamists.

Even if events march on, and cosmopolitan perspectives continue to be defeated, it is still the job of the left to represent conceptually – even if it is unable to do so materially – a different possible direction. The wars of annihilation can only end in ever-deepening horror; the struggle for peace and freedom can end in peace and freedom.

It is as necessary to keep challenging those who think that the only real war is an Israeli war of survival as it is to challenge those who think that the only real war is against the Israeli oppressor. The cosmopolitan left needs to think differently, and it has to create a different reality. It is on the side of the Palestinian struggle for independence and it is on the side of the Israeli struggle against the jihadists (not to mention the Palestinian, Iranian, Syrian, Egyptian and Lebanese struggle against the jihadists, as well as the trade union, socialist, democratic, lesbian and gay, feminist and secular struggles against them).

But that is absurd, cries one camp: the jihadists are currently dictating the Palestinian struggle, and it is no longer a struggle for Palestinian independence. Hasn't it become one struggle? Hasn't it always been one struggle, Jews against Arabs? 'We offered them peace and they chose war – then they started raining missiles down on our heads.'

And the other side insists: 'Barak's offer during the Oslo peace process was to set Palestinian oppression in stone for ever, it was not an offer of Palestinian liberty. He offered slavery, not freedom. You talk about the annihilation of Israel, but it is Palestine that is prevented from existing – Israel assuredly exists. It has destroyed the project of Palestinian liberation.'

Is it a war of annihilation or a war of liberation? Both wars are real, even if only in our minds. But human beings have the capacity to make some impact on the world, to work for change, according to what is in our minds, and that is the cosmopolitan project in Israel and in Palestine.

II. Antisemitism and criticism of Israel

Part I looked at the context of anti-Zionist thought and movements, in general, and at the assumptions, methodology and tropes of antiracist anti-Zionism, in particular. It critically engaged with the central concepts of this movement and looked at how some currents of the left find themselves in a position where a politics of demonization appears to be a natural left-wing response to the Israel-Palestine conflict. Part II moves on from a conceptual discussion to an empirical analysis of a number of actualizations of those concepts in public discourse. The case studies are chosen because they illustrate particular tendencies that shed light on the actualization of anti-Zionism in a form that is related directly to antisemitism. Part III then looks at boycott campaigns, which aim to transform conceptual and discursive texts into concrete exclusions of human beings.

1. Denying antisemitism: 'Intensified criticism' of Israel and the Zionist manufacture of the antisemitism charge

Steven Beller (2007: 223), relying on Tony Judt and Antony Lerman as authorities, states that 'the claims of a sudden, horrendous burgeoning of antisemitism in Europe are incorrect.' Antony Lerman (2007) articulates the position as follows:

> Pro-Israel and Zionist groups have interpreted intensified criticism of Israel and anti-Zionism as the expression of a 'new antisemitism'. The [Independent Jewish Voices] initiative leans towards the view that this charge is far too often used in an attempt to stifle strong criticism of Israeli policies.

Part II presents an extensive survey and analysis of a number of key examples of what Lerman refers to as 'intensified' or 'strong' criticism of Israel. These examples are not narratives of straightforward antisemitism but they do raise questions about what kinds of intensification of criticism we are seeing. They are selected because they exemplify particular kinds of intensification; they are examples of discourse that take the form of exaggerated hostility to Israel. The analysis aims to explore whether and how those case studies mirror antisemitic discourse, rhetoric, images, texts or tropes. The majority of these case studies relate to public social and political actors in predominately British public life, and nearly all of the contested narratives have already been discussed in the public sphere.

Underpinning Lerman's formulation of the problem are two assumptions; first, that those who are concerned with antisemitism related to hostility to Israel are 'pro-Israel' or 'Zionist' and, second, that the articulation of this concern often constitutes a dishonest but collective attempt to 'stifle strong criticism of Israeli policies'. In other words, the debate over contemporary antisemitism is congruent with the debate over how strongly Israel should be criticized for its abuses of human rights. If you are very strongly critical of Israeli human rights abuses then you will also believe that concern about a 'new antisemitism' is misplaced because this concern blunts and 'stifles' deserved criticism.

If, on the other hand, you are worried about 'new antisemitism', then you will also be 'pro-Israel' or 'Zionist' and therefore, it is thought, reluctant to criticize or recognize Israeli human rights abuses.

These are strange underpinnings for a discussion of the danger of racism against Jews. Firstly, because they assume that criticism is something purely quantitative. How strongly critical are you of Israel on a scale of one to ten? But criticism contains both qualitative and quantitative components. The nature of a criticism is as important as its intensity. The Hamas Covenant (Hamas 1988) articulates a strong critique of Israel, but it is also antisemitic. Moreover, the Hamas critique of Israeli human rights abuses, given its own politics and practice, is unconvincing. At the time of the invasion of Jenin by Israeli forces in 2002, there was much 'strong' and 'intense' criticism; people screamed that there was a massacre and a genocide and a Holocaust being perpetrated by Israel. Such overblown claims that Israel was killing for the sake of killing and that Israel was just like the Nazis allowed the Sharon government to plead, in good faith, not guilty. Criticism was strong and intense but it lacked truth and political clarity. It was ineffective not because it was 'strong' or 'intense' but because of its quality. And one aspect of its quality was that it relied upon and reproduced a view of Israel (and the Jews who do not sufficiently distance themselves from it) as being uniquely evil in the world.[34]

---

[34] For an account of some of the things that Israeli forces actually did during the invasion, see (Yeheskeli 2002): 'Difficult? No way. You must be kidding. I wanted to destroy everything. I begged the officers, over the radio, to let me knock it all down; from top to bottom. To level everything. It's not as if I wanted to kill. Just the houses. We didn't harm those who came out of the houses we had started to demolish, waving white flags. We screwed just those who wanted to fight. ... No one refused an order to knock down a house. No such thing. When I was told to bring down a house, I took the opportunity to bring down some more houses; not because I wanted to – but because when you are asked to demolish a house, some other houses usually

Antisemitic opposition to Israel does not constitute 'strong' or 'intense' criticism of Israeli human rights abuses. On the contrary, such criticism harms those who fight for peace and against racism; it does damage to the Palestinian struggle for independence, freedom and democracy. It is the quality of intensification of criticism rather than the intensification itself that is crucial to the discussion of the relationship between hostility to Israel and antisemitism. Howard Jacobson (2007) puts it like this:

> Critical – as though those who accuse Israel of every known crime against humanity, of being more Nazi than the Nazis, more fascist than the fascists, more apartheid than apartheid South Africa, are simply exercising measured argument and fine discrimination.
>
> I know a bit about being critical. It's my job. Being 'critical' is when you say that such-and-such a book works here but doesn't work there, good plot, bad characterization, enjoyed some parts, hated others. What being critical is not, is saying this is the most evil and odious book ever written, worse than all other evil and odious books, should never have been published in the first place, was in fact published in flagrant defiance of international law, must be banned, and in the meantime should not under any circumstances be read. For that we need another word than critical.

One wonders whether the fatwa calling for the execution of Salman Rushdie could be considered to be literary criticism.

So there follows a discussion of a number of contested cases. They are not necessarily examples of antisemitic criticism of Israel – such examples are easy to find, for example in the official ideology of Hamas, Hezbollah and the current Iranian presidency, and they pose no analytic ambiguity. Rather, the examples that follow are examples of what Lerman refers to as 'intensification' of criticism. The particular forms that intensification takes are more relevant than the degrees of intensification.

A. The Mayor of London: deny antisemitism, cry Israel

In September 2006, the report of the British Parliamentary Inquiry into Antisemitism was published. Norman Finkelstein (2006) responded to this publication with a piece on his website in which he alleges that the parliamentary report was published as a response to the Israel-Hezbollah war in order to deflect attention from Israel's

---

obscure it, so there is no other way. I would have to do it even if I didn't want to. They just stood in the way. If I had to erase a house, come hell or high water – I would do it. And believe me, we demolished too little. The whole camp was littered with detonation charges. What actually saved the lives of the Palestinians themselves, because if they had returned to their homes, they would blow up. ... For three days, I just destroyed and destroyed. The whole area. Any house that they fired from came down. And to knock it down, I tore down some more. They were warned by loudspeaker to get out of the house before I come, but I gave no one a chance. I didn't wait. I didn't give one blow, and wait for them to come out. I would just ram the house with full power, to bring it down as fast as possible. I wanted to get to the other houses. To get as many as possible. Others may have restrained themselves, or so they say. Who are they kidding? Anyone who was there, and saw our soldiers in the houses, would understand they were in a death trap. I thought about saving them. I didn't give a damn about the Palestinians, but I didn't just ruin with no reason. It was all under orders.'

'murderous destruction of Lebanon'.[35] It is difficult to see how this claim could be true, since the report was being planned, written and researched before the war began; if true, it must rely on the premise that an all-party committee of British MPs was acting pre-emptively to protect Israel from criticism of a war that had not yet started.[36] Finkelstein is articulating the claim that the issue of antisemitism is raised dishonestly in order to delegitimize Israeli human rights abuses. This thought is communicated by four expressive words that constitute the title of his piece: 'Kill Arabs, Cry Antisemitism'. This charge is frequently made by anyone who is accused of failing to be careful about antisemitism, and its very invocation is itself almost inevitably an indication of a failure to take antisemitism seriously.

I will refer to the claim that people are accused of antisemitism in order to delegitimize their criticisms of Israeli human rights abuses as the *Livingstone formulation*, since, in the story that follows, the Mayor of London employed it most effectively. The *Livingstone formulation* often expresses a reversal of the truth. Ken Livingstone accuses the Board of Deputies of British Jews of 'crying antisemitism' as a response to his own criticism of Israel, but in reality he himself 'cried Israel' in response to criticism of his own, albeit trivial, late-night antisemitic insults – and his perhaps less trivial refusal to acknowledge them or to apologize for them. His insults were entirely unconnected to Israel or to its human rights abuses. The interesting thing about Ken Livingstone's brushes with antisemitism is that they apparently do him no damage, either in terms of popular support or in terms of the support of the antiracist left.

Oliver Finegold, a journalist for the *Evening Standard*, approached the Mayor as he left a party, late at night, at City Hall, on 8 February 2005.

Finegold: Mr Livingstone, *Evening Standard*. How did tonight go?[37]

Livingstone: How awful for you. Have you thought of having treatment?

Finegold tries again.

Finegold: How did tonight go?

Livingstone: Have you thought of having treatment?

Finegold tries a third time:

---

[35] '[P]redictably, just after Israel faced another image problem due to its murderous destruction of Lebanon, a British all-party parliamentary group led by notorious Israel-firster Denis MacShane MP (Labor) released yet another report alleging a resurgence of antisemitism.' (Finkelstein 2006)

[36] Later in this piece, Finkelstein sneeringly wonders whether Israel could organize a 'Berlin airlift' of gefilte fish to Jewish students. This is his response to a recommendation in the parliamentary report that Jewish students ought not to be excluded from events due to the lack of kosher food. The piece is illustrated by a picture of a can of gefilte fish attached to a parachute.

[37] This transcript comes from the website of the *Evening Standard*, 'Who said what when Ken clashed with reporter', 11 February 2005, http://www.thisislondon.co.uk/news/article-16539119-details/Who+said+what+when+Ken+clashed+with+reporter/article.do;jsessionid=NjT NFgBNyY7yGVy6SxGyvCpgV321w3WPyvhfh29jJXGNB0TxpTLT!-749300803!-1407319224!7001 !-1, downloaded 24 February 2007.

Finegold: Was it a good party? What does it mean for you?

Livingstone: What did you do before? Were you a German war criminal?

Finegold: No, I'm Jewish, I wasn't a German war criminal and I'm actually quite offended by that. So, how did tonight go?

At this point the Mayor understands that Finegold is Jewish and that he finds being compared to a 'German war criminal' offensive. And he has a tape recorder running. So how does Livingstone react? He thinks he is onto something clever, so he clarifies his point:

Livingstone: Arr right, well you might be [Jewish], but actually you are just like a concentration camp guard, you are just doing it because you are paid to, aren't you?

Finegold is hanging around outside City Hall trying to get a comment from the Mayor because it is his job. This, according to Livingstone, is 'just like' someone who participated in the Nazi genocide of Jews during the Second World War. The Mayor thinks that being a journalist for the *Evening Standard* is 'bad' in an analogous way as taking part in genocide is 'bad' – and both are done by people who are only doing their jobs.[38]

Finegold: Great, I have you on record for that. So, how was tonight?

Livingstone: It's nothing to do with you because your paper is a load of scumbags and reactionary bigots.

Maybe Ken is drunk? He later denied it. Ken Livingstone has, in his time, dealt with all the newspapers, owned by all kinds of 'scumbags and reactionary bigots'. He has worked for the *Evening Standard* and he has worked for the notorious left-baiting Murdoch tabloid, *The Sun*.

Finegold: I'm a journalist and I'm doing my job. I'm only asking for a comment.

Livingstone: Well, work for a paper that doesn't have a record of supporting fascism.

So Livingstone goes home and the story breaks the next day.[39] Why does he not just apologize? 'Sorry I was a bit drunk, I was tired, it was late, I was fed up with being chased around by reporters, and I said some silly things.' This would have solved the problem. But Livingstone decided not to apologize.

What if it had been a black journalist? 'What did you do before, were you a plantation owner?' 'No, I'm black, I wasn't a plantation owner, and I'm quite offended by that.' 'Well you might be black but actually you're just like a plantation owner.'

After Livingstone has had two weeks to think about it, he insists (Livingstone 2005) that his responses to Finegold were appropriate. He says the *Evening Standard*, as well as *Associated Press*, which owns it, have treated him badly in the past and that

---

[38] For a full discussion of Zygmunt Bauman's sociological analysis of the relationship between instrumental rationality and the decision to commit a crime against humanity in *Modernity and the Holocaust*, see Hirsh (2003) chapter 2.

[39] It is not broken by Finegold because he feels insulted but by someone else who heard the conversation.

they have now overstated this story in order to damage him politically. He points out that in July 1992 (13 years ago) there was a party at the *Daily Mail* where people dressed up in Nazi uniforms as fancy dress and *Associated Press* has not apologized for that. He says that the *Daily Mail* campaigned to bar Jews from entering Britain before 1905 (100 years ago). And the *Daily Mail* supported the British Union of Fascists in the 1930s (70 years ago). He says that in 1933 (72 years ago), the owner of the *Daily Mail* supported Hitler. In 1938 and 1940, the *Daily Mail* articulated antisemitic policies. And in 2001, a parliamentary sketch in the *Daily Mail* referred to someone in antisemitic language.

I, says Ken Livingstone, am much less antisemitic than the *Daily Mail* and *Associated Press*, as though that was an appropriate standard for the antiracist left. I, says Ken, have always fought racism and antisemitism. 'I', says Ken 'regard the positive contribution of the Jewish people to human civilisation as unexcelled'. 'The public' says Ken, 'understand that what is being attempted is a frame up orchestrated by racist sections of the press against someone with a long record of fighting against racism'. But he adds: 'Over the last two weeks my main concern has been that many Jewish Londoners have been disturbed by this whipped-up row.' Not by Ken's own behaviour. And then:

> I do believe that abdicating responsibility for one's actions by the excuse that 'I am only doing my job' is the thin end of the immoral wedge that at its other extreme leads to the crimes and horrors of Auschwitz, Rwanda and Bosnia. (Livingstone 2005)

Livingstone reacted to criticism by publishing an article in *The Guardian* under the title 'This is about Israel, not antisemitism' (Livingstone 2005a), in which he sought to change the topic of discussion by insisting that the problem is not antisemitism but Israel's human rights abuses. This represents a reversal of the now standard anti-Zionist claim that Jews 'cry antisemitism' in order to delegitimize those who criticize Israel.[40] The *Livingstone formulation*:

> For far too long the accusation of antisemitism has been used against anyone who is critical of the policies of the Israeli government, as I have been. (Livingstone 2006)

Here, Livingstone was 'crying Israel' in order to delegitimize those who were concerned about his antisemitic remark. He followed this up with an argument that normalized Palestinian suicide bombing against Israeli civilians. He had unreservedly condemned the suicide attacks on the London transport system on 7 July 2005,[41] but he found suicide attacks on the Israeli transport system to raise more complex

---

[40] E.g. Norman Finkelstein (2005): 'the book's real purpose will now come into focus: Israel's horrendous human rights record in the Occupied Territories and the misuse of antisemitism to delegitimize criticism of it.'

E.g. David Duke (2004a): 'It is perfectly acceptable to criticize any nation on the earth for its errors and wrongs, but lo and behold, don't you dare criticize Israel; for if you do that, you will be accused of the most abominable sin in the modern world, the unforgivable sin of antisemitism!'

[41] Livingstone (2005b): 'This was a cowardly attack. It was an indiscriminate attempt to slaughter, irrespective of any considerations for age, for class, for religion, or whatever.'

moral and political issues. 'Palestinians don't have jet fighters,' he said at his press conference two weeks later, 'they only have their bodies to use as weapons. In that unfair balance, that's what people use' (quoted in Lappin 2006).[42]

The Finegold incident, the 'crying Israel' as a response to an accusation of antisemitism and the equivocation over the campaign to kill Israeli civilians were followed by a sustained campaign by Livingstone to host and promote the Muslim cleric Yusef al-Qaradawi as a progressive religious figure and a leading Islamic moderate. It should be remembered that in the 1980s Ken Livingstone was widely recognized as a leading figure in municipal rainbow alliance politics, the movement that the political right shrilly and apocryphally denounced as 'political correctness gone mad'.

Now, Livingstone was hosting Qaradawi, a man who supported the indiscriminate killing of Israeli civilians in the name of Muslim anti-Zionism. Participation in 'martyr operations' in Palestine, he had claimed, 'is one of the most praised acts of worship'. He also taught that 'apostates' from Islam ought to be killed; that a 'Muslim husband is to order his wife to wear hijab'; that a man may admonish his wife 'lightly with his hands'; and that the appropriate state punishment for homosexuality is death (Tatchell 2005).[43] When leader of the Greater London Council in the 1980s, it would have been

---

[42] Lappin (20006) analyzes these comments as follows: 'First, [Livingstone] treats ordinary Israelis as unique in excluding them from the status of non-combatants accorded to civilians in any other conflict. But if the obvious asymmetry between the Israeli army and Palestinian irregulars is the basis for this move, then why are British and American civilians exempt from being construed as legitimate targets of terror attacks launched by opponents of the occupation of Iraq and Afghanistan, where powerful armies battle militarily weak insurgency forces? In short, what basis is there for Livingstone's resolute condemnation of Islamist terror in London, which can be excused and understood on grounds similar to those invoked in the case of Palestinian suicide bombing? Passing over the fact that political expediency (more accurately, political survival) would prevent the Mayor from applying his views consistently, even if he chose to do so, the effect of his exceptionalist treatment of Israeli civilians is to reinforce the idea that it is not simply Israel's policies which are worthy of opposition, but its existence as a country that is intolerable. The behaviour of the Israeli government has deprived its people of any collective legitimacy. Hence they are understandable (and so, ultimately, acceptable) targets of violence.'

[43] City Hall published a glossy brochure to defend Livingstone's links with Qaradawi (Mayor of London 2005). The brochure defends Qaradawi against charges of antisemitism, quoting him as follows: 'we do not hold any enmity towards the Jews'. The brochure argues that 'In contrast to claims that he makes "no distinction between Jews and Israelis" ... and "uses sermons to call for Jews – not Israelis but specifically Jews – to be killed", ... Qaradawi has repeatedly emphasised that "we do not fight Israelis because they are Jews but because they took our land, killed our children and profaned our holy places".' But this defence is not convincing. Whether the Mayor of London's office's defence of Qaradawi was in good faith or not is unknown; it has not responded to Qaradawi's subsequent exegesis of classic antisemitic blood libel.

One method of responding to criticism of Qaradawi by the Mayor's brochure has been to attack MEMRI, the Middle East Media Research Institute, which has produced some of the translations of Qaradawi's views from the original Arabic. MEMRI is run out of Washington, DC by a former member of the Israeli security services, Yigal Carmon. Its translations are therefore easily ignorable as 'Zionist' or 'Mossad' propaganda. Whitaker (2002) argues that MEMRI's translations are highly selective and therefore unrepresentative. Yigal Carmon (2002) responds in *The Guardian*. *The Guardian* carries an email debate between the two in 2003 (Carmon and Whitaker 2003).

inconceivable that Livingstone would have hosted such a figure. In praising Mel Gibson's 'The Passion of the Christ' a year later, Qaradawi said:

> In this film there is an important positive aspect. The positive aspect lies in its exposing the Jews' crime of bringing Jesus to the crucifixion.... More than 30 years ago, the Vatican issued a document, exonerating the Jews of [spilling] the blood of Jesus. Not all Christians accepted this document. The Pope in the Vatican and the Catholics are the ones who exonerated them. They exonerated them under political pressure..., I say that the Jews of the 21st century adopt what the Jews of the first century did. They adopt what [their forefathers] did to Jesus, and so they bear responsibility for it, unless they renounce it, saying: This was a crime, and we ask Allah to absolve us of it. But they have not said this, and therefore, the Jews of today bear responsibility for the deeds of the Jews of yesterday. (Al Qaradawi 2006)

The London Assembly and the Culture Secretary called for Livingstone to apologize for the Finegold incident. Livingstone insisted that he 'stood by his remarks' (News.BBC.co.uk 2005).[44] Following Livingstone's refusal to apologize,[45] the Board of Deputies of British Jews referred the case to the Standards Board for England, a body set up in the wake of the 'sleaze' scandals in British public life in the 1990s. The Standards Board eventually ruled that Livingstone's 'treatment of the journalist [had been] unnecessarily insensitive and offensive' and, since it judged that this contravened the Code of Conduct for Standards in Public Life, it decided to suspend him from office for four weeks.

A few days after the judgment, Livingstone (2006) responded with a piece in *The Guardian* in which he portrayed himself as the victim of an undemocratic coup.[46] Who was behind the coup? Livingstone's attack shifted during the time of the judgment from *Associated Press* to the Board of Deputies for British Jews. The Board

---

Qaradawi's position on Jewish-Muslim dialogue is also clear enough: 'There is No Dialogue between Us and the Jews Except by the Sword and the Rifle'. Also: 'The iniquity of the Jews, as a community, is obvious and apparent. Let me explain: The West, I can say about some of them [i.e. Westerners] who are iniquitous, and others who are not iniquitous. And it is possible. But iniquity on the part of the Jews is great iniquity, grave iniquity, iniquity that is incomparable and overt. Therefore, when it was suggested to me that Jews would be participating in the dialogue in the upcoming interview, I rejected this. I said no, we should not conduct a dialogue with these [people] while their hands are stained with our blood.' (MEMRI 2004)

[44] Livingstone: 'If I could in anything I say relieve any pain anyone feels I would not hesitate to do it but it would require me to be a liar.... I could apologize but why should I say words I do not believe in my heart? ... Therefore I cannot. If that is something people find they cannot accept I am sorry but this is how I feel after nearly a quarter of a century of their behaviour and tactics.' (News.BBC.co.uk 2005)

[45] From the judgment of the Adjudication Panel of the Standards Board: '[The Mayor's] representative is quite right in saying, ... that matters should not have got as far as this: but it is the Mayor who must take responsibility for this. It was his comments that started the matter and thereafter his position seems to have become ever more entrenched.' See http://www.adjudicationpanel.co.uk/documents/notice_of_decision_ape_0317_revised_copy1.pdf.

[46] 'The fundamental issue,' he wrote, 'in this whole affair is not whether or not I was "insensitive", it is the principle that those whom the people elect should only be removed by the people or because they have broken the law.'

of Deputies, Livingstone argued at his press conference, was pursuing a vendetta against him because he is critical of the Israeli government.

There are a number of elements to his case against the Board of Deputies. First, they use a charge of antisemitism instrumentally. They do not really believe that Livingstone has done anything antisemitic nor that he has ever behaved in such a way that may have contributed to the propagation of an antisemitic way of thinking. They use the charge disingenuously in order to silence legitimate criticism of Israeli human rights abuses. This charge of 'crying antisemitism' is necessarily a charge of dishonesty and also of conspiracy. Conspiracy, because to believe otherwise would mean that all of the diverse political currents, campaigns, lobbies and writers who make accusations of antisemitism are being dishonest independently but in the same way.

Second, the Board of Deputies, by referring Livingstone to the Standards Committee, was responsible for the action that was taken by the Standards Committee.

The third element is that Livingstone's long history of hostility to Israel and to 'Zionism' could be reasonably understood as mere criticism. Worries connected to antisemitism are often raised in response to conspiracy theory, to the demonization of Israel, to those who claim that Israel is uniquely an apartheid or a Nazi state, essentially racist, not a nation but an outpost of imperialism. The *Livingstone formulation* conflates all of these possibilities into mere criticism.

Livingstone does more than 'criticize the policies of the Israeli government'. For decades, he has been part of a movement in the United Kingdom that sees Israel as a pariah state with a menacing and malign influence well beyond its borders. In the 1980s, Livingstone was associated with the Workers Revolutionary Party, an extreme anti-Zionist group, and was the editor of one of its front organizations, Labour Herald (Matgamna 2003).[47]

This exaggerated hostility to Israel is perhaps connected to the fact that Livingstone treats the antisemite Qaradawi as an honoured guest; and to the fact that Livingstone is content to employ low-level racist abuse against a Jewish journalist even when he has been told that the journalist finds this offensive; and to the fact that he chose to make a big issue out of this story rather than to back down pragmatically; and to the fact that he reacted with a critique of Ariel Sharon to claims that his own conduct had been offensive. His exaggerated hostility to Israel is connected to the fact that he opposes the suicide bombing of buses in London but equivocates about the suicide bombing of buses in Tel Aviv.

Livingstone appealed his suspension to the High Court and won. The judgment went out of its way to give an official stamp of authority to the *Livingstone formulation*. The High Court judged that Livingstone's subjective feeling of opposing antisemitism was sufficient basis for it to conclude that he has never 'been antisemitic' – and it could not 'sensibly' be suggested otherwise. The judgment says that Livingstone has 'not approved of some of the activities of the State of Israel' but 'that has

---

[47] 'Early in his career, Livingstone formed an alliance with a Trotskyist sect called the Workers Revolutionary Party. It's remembered now for having Vanessa and Corin Redgrave amongst its cultists, when it should be known as the nastiest organisation on the late 20th century Left. The WRP spied on Iraqi dissidents for Saddam Hussein and took money from Colonel Gaddafi.' (Nick Cohen 2007)

nothing to do with antisemitism.'[48] Livingstone's snide insults against Finegold had a connection to Israel or 'Zionism' only inside his own head.

B. *Comment is Free*: anti-Zionist rhetoric goes mainstream

Comment is Free (CiF) was a new initiative started by *The Guardian* newspaper in February 2006. It is a website that brings together the opinion pieces from the printed version of the paper with a large number of pieces written by newly recruited bloggers. Readers are free to post comments anonymously under any article on CiF, whether they were written by journalists employed by the paper or by bloggers who work without pay.[49] Bloggers are free to submit pieces of writing to the website at any time, and they will, in general, appear on the site some hours later.

CiF is interesting in that it allows an unprecedented freedom of expression in a *Guardian* left/liberal space. In the 1980s, many of us grew up politically in an environment where there was a strict unwritten code about what may or may not be legitimately said in any left/liberal space. In the summer of 2006, a wave of absolute freedom washed over political discourse in the United Kingdom. Racist, sexist and homophobic comments attached themselves to every article on the website that was in any way relevant to these issues. With the anonymity of the medium came a splitting of text from author. Pure text was laid down, line after line, attached to the work of *Guardian* journalists and CiF bloggers. Where it came from and what it represented were unanswerable questions. Who was responsible for it? What was the responsibility of *The Guardian* and the CiF editors? Were these commenters to be thought of as 'authentic' *Guardian* readers or were they 'trolls' from outside, coming in mischievously to muddy the debate and to pollute the space?

The editors struggled to keep up with the commenters who were breaking their rules. The high volume of material on CiF means that it would be a huge task to monitor everything in advance. The editors were reluctant to monitor everything in advance because this would have radically changed the ambitiously open character of the new project.

But more interesting than those commenters who clearly break the boundaries of open sexism, racism and homophobia are those who take care to remain within the formal boundaries and thereby protect themselves with the principle of free speech. Let me present just a couple of examples from the summer of 2006 of the kind of comments that were attaching to Jewish or 'Zionist' journalists and bloggers on CiF. It should be remembered that there is nothing unique about these examples. This kind of comment would inevitably attach itself to all such articles.

Jonathan Freedland (2006) posted a piece on the arrest of Lord Levy in July 2006. He argued that the scandal of loans-for-peerages went to the heart of New Labour's relationships with corporate power and that Levy would not (and should not) be the

---

[48] '12. The Assembly resolution recognized the role played by the appellant in opposing racism and antisemitism. It could not sensibly be suggested that he is or ever has been anti-Semitic. He has not approved of some of the activities of the State of Israel and has made his views about that clear. But that has nothing to do with antisemitism.' See http://www.adjudicationpanel.co.uk/documents/livingstone_v_the_adjudication_panel_2006.pdf.

[49] The bloggers are paid £75 for an article only if it is chosen to appear in the 'Editors Picks' section of the website or if it is commissioned by the editor.

fall-guy or scapegoat for this political problem. Freedland referred to the danger of an antisemitic undercurrent lurking around this story: 'In the routine descriptions of him as a "flamboyant north London businessman" many in Britain's Jewish community have long detected old-fashioned prejudice.' Traditional English antisemitism is gentle and unspoken. It operates through a nudge here and a wink there. So Freedland mentioned it, but it was not the central point of his piece. I will look at just a few responses.

The first is a commenter[50] by the name of 'Rodi', who, at 03:23 UK time, offers a Jewish conspiracy story. He links Freedland, who is Jewish, with Levy, who is Jewish, by means of 'Israel lobby' rhetoric.

> Is it really a 'lazy scapegoating'? I do not think so. Let us not forget that Jonathan Freedland was a strong supporter of the war (and of Bush-Blair narratives for its justification) on Iraq until it began to go even worse. He has then tried to distance himself. So I myself will be a little suspicious of what he writes on a subject as this, Lord Levy's dealings with Blair and the British government at such a critical time. I sense that there is another side of the story, which will hopefully emerge, even partially. All the records of Lord Levy need a very careful study. The question: is there a strong 'Israel lobby' in Britain as well and Lord Levy, a prominent agent of it? The recently published excellent paper on the US Israel lobby by two American professors may provide an example: http://www.lrb.co.uk/v28/n06/mear01_.html.

'Rodi' is wrong about Freedland being a supporter of the war and a supporter of Bush and Blair's arguments for the war. In fact, Freedland was, from the beginning, an outspoken opponent of the war. 'Rodi' uses the respectable language of the 'Israel lobby' rather than the discredited language of Jewish conspiracy. He or she explicitly relies on Mearsheimer and Walt (2006a) for legitimation and authority. 'Rodi' impatiently awaits the emergence of the evidence that will link Lord Levy and his financial dealings to Freedland, the ideological scribbler for the 'lobby'.

'Ancientpistol' pops up at 04:35: 'I'm with Rodi on this'. 'ForeverPalestine' adds his or her analysis:

> Britains Jewish community, when they arent peddling open prejudice against Muslims or supporting zionist facism, are apt to see 'long detected old-fashioned prejudice' in any comment about someone who happens to be jewish which isnt ars* kissing of the highest order.

'MayorWatch' then weighs in with a misreading of Freedland, saying

> Sorry Jonathan but it's all a bit too easy to hurl claims of 'old-fashioned prejudice' just because a Nu Labour acolyte is in a spot of bother.

But Freedland is not trying to 'use' a charge of antisemitism to protect Blair, he is trying to prevent a cloud of antisemitism from helping to rescue Blair. Then more from 'ForeverPalestine':

> ... find an extreme anti-Muslim writer/commentator and they will invariably be either jewish or a strong supporter of Israel.

---

[50] Some of these comments were later deleted by the CiF editorial staff. The text of the comments were recorded in Hirsh (2006h).

And up pops a new character by the name of 'Enlight', recommending that we read more about 'Lord Schmooze'. Enlight has spotted another tentacle underpinning the British war effort:

> I would also like to see an investigation into the activities of another Jew, Lord Goldsmith and how he legalised the war on iraq thereby allowing our troops to die for Israel.

'Ruthe' also likes conspiracy theory, but a version not linked to Jews (yet). Ruthe believes that the separation of powers between the Metropolitan Police and the Government is nothing but a charade:

> I think the dramatic arrest of Lord Levy was the ultimate manipulation to stop the Select Committee starting their investigation again.

But no, conspiracy theory always seems to link to 'the Jews' eventually. It only takes 'Ruthe' another 12 minutes to come up with this:

> I can't really understand how somebody who is Jewish could be a special envoy for the Middle East. How could he show partiality?

'Tox06' represents another classic element of antisemitic rhetoric. Those Jews are so touchy, aren't they?

> I really dislike the knee-jerk suggestion that all this is motivated by mere anti-semitism.[51]

Nobody suggested that 'all this' is motivated by antisemitism, certainly not Freedland. 'Beslam' then decides that it is important that we know what Levy's middle name is: 'Michael Abraham Levy', not Lord Levy. 'Precon' wants to make something else clear, that those at the heart of the Guinness insider dealing scandal in the 1980s,

> weren't the scapegoats but the leading lights.... Most but not all were Jewish but if you look at Federal Court records for the 1980's the majority of people caught & prosecuted for this type of Financial crime were Jewish.

Thirteen minutes later, 'Precon' comes back with a quote from Tam Dalyell, a believer in the dangerous effects of Jewish advisors around Tony Blair (Brown and Hastings 2003). 'Downsman' introduces another 'corrupt' rich New Labour Jewish Lord into the discussion, Lord Sainsbury (except, ironically, Lord Sainsbury is not Jewish):

> There is a separate conflict issue about his business affairs and his science portfolio, but this has nothing to do with his ethnicity. We need some clear thinking here otherwise the antisemitism label gets easily slapped over all discussions of any prominent person who happens to be jewish.

---

[51] Seymour (2006): 'Apparently, the biggest criticism being leveled against the Jews is that you cannot criticize the Jews. Or, more exactly, you cannot criticize Israel because in so doing, Jews think that you are criticizing them and, as we all know, you cannot criticize Jews. Of course, not so heavily concealed in this argument is a wealth of antisemitic imagery and assumptions.'

'Enlight' then brings to our attention two more murderers:

> What about the Jewish Albright when she said that the death of half a million Iraqi children was a price worth paying (sanctions on Iraq). As for the mass murderer Kissinger....

'Antiscensorship':

> I suppose Jonathan Freedland is also Jewish... Spare me your pathetic attempts at sarcasm. its just a matter of public record that organized Jewry are extremely influential in banking, the law, media and in politics. This is not a matter for debate its a demonstrable fact. Your lame attempts at playing the anti semitism card will fail. Its always the way with Zionists. They attempt to play the anto semitism card like an old man who forgets he has told the same war story a thousand times already.

What can be said about this collection of text? This is a collection of edited highlights of comments from people with different ideas and making different points. Not all are antisemitic and not all are making the same points. I am interested in the shape of the swirling discussion as a whole, not in making a case against any particular commenter. I am interested particularly in the character of a swirl that is created by the mixing of entrenched anti-Zionist commonsense with a little open antisemitism.

One point is interesting in relation to the Levy story in particular. This is perfect material for an allegation of 'classic' or 'old' (or 'real') antisemitism. It is a story of somebody who in his public persona is thought of as a nouveau-riche and tasteless Jew (with the title 'Lord'!) who is accused of playing the middleman for the powerful, selling off peerages. It is fascinating, then, that many of the commenters used the language and the images of the 'new antisemitism' – even though the story has nothing to do with criticism of Israel or Zionism. Nowadays, even the gauche, tasteless, middleman Jew apparently caught with his hand in the till is denounced as a 'Zionist'. In fact, after a long and detailed police investigation, no charges were brought against the entirely innocent Levy – or against anybody else.

It seems reasonable to assume that most of these commenters think of themselves as being liberal or on the left, whatever that might mean to them. The comment thread is a *Guardian* space, not a fascist BNP space or a jihadi Islamist space or a right-wing conservative *Daily Telegraph* space.

Nearly all of the antisemitic commenters misread Jonathan Freedland's piece. Jonathan Freedland has, as anyone who reads *The Guardian* knows, a long record of opposing the policies of Israeli governments towards the Palestinians, as well as the policies of George Bush and Tony Blair regarding the war in Iraq. It is difficult to escape the conclusion that some of the commenters got this wrong because they believed that Freedland was ethnically, rather than politically, neocon.

Without knowledge of who these commenters are it is difficult to know what kind of strands of opinion this represents. And so we are faced simply with text, which represents nothing but itself and which was to be found all over the most important and influential left/liberal webspace in the United Kingdom in 2006.[52]

---

[52] There is scope for further qualitative and quantitative investigation of *Comment is Free*, its blogs and its commenters. It would be interesting to know whether the bigotry that appears

Much of the worrying material is material about whose legitimacy there is no consensus. Some observers will understand talk, for example about 'Zionist' influence of Hollywood and the news agenda, about 'Zionist' responsibility for starting the Iraq war and about the relationship between 'Zionism' and Nazism, as being a legitimate side of a legitimate debate. Others will argue that it is precisely these kinds of positions, which use respectable terminology but propagate antisemitic notions, that are the most threatening to the health of public discourse. At any rate, these are the kinds of ideas that cannot be simply deleted by the editors, because there is no broad agreement amongst *Guardian* readers as to their illegitimacy.

When a Jew who does not identify as an anti-Zionist writes a piece on *Comment is Free*, on any topic, they tend to attract comments challenging them to denounce Israeli human rights abuses. This mirrors the test that many leftist Jews have experienced in wider left and liberal circles. What's your position on Israel? Jews are not considered acceptable in some sections of the left and the labour movement until they have answered this question to the satisfaction of the anti-Zionists.[53]

When Nick Cohen (who is actually significantly less Jewish than his name) writes on any topic, his piece is littered by comments such as this:

> I've noticed you avoid commenting on international issues when the situation presents difficulties for your point of view. Well, Cohen, will you condemn Israel, or are you completely morally bankrupt?

Here is a comment from Nick Cohen's column in the week that I happen to be writing this passage, in which he defends Salman Rushdie. 'JusticeIsMine' writes:

> Cohen just can't help yourself can you? The first chance to attack Muslims, you are there like a randy terrier trying to hump our leg. This is all about ISRAEL isn't it Nick? I bet you can't wait for the next terrorist event so you and your mates can start ranting and raving again. Don't worry I'm sure the CIA and Mossad will come up with lots for you to rail against over the next year, in time for the US election.[54] (Cohen 2007)

When Norman Geras writes on cricket (2006) he is denounced for not having written about Israeli brutality.[55] And whenever Maureen Lipman wrote anything in the summer of 2006, she was denounced as a racist. When she wrote a piece about buying a white dress, someone responded, 'Given her views I'm surprised she didn't

---

against women and feminist writers was of equal intensity and volume to the bigotry against Jewish and 'Zionist' writers, and against Muslim writers and against Palestinian writers and supporters of Palestinian rights, and against gay and lesbian writers.

[53] The NATFHE conference of 2006 tried to apply this test to Israeli scholars as a condition of being accepted as part of the academic community. The international trade union website, LabourStart, was denounced by Sue Blackwell as not being a genuine part of the labour movement because it contained 'Zionists'. Sue Blackwell (2005b): 'I thought this was a bonafide trade union website supporting workers' struggles. However, it emerges that Eric Lee, who runs the site, is a supporter of the "Engage" anti-boycott site. Until a few years ago he actually ran LabourStart from Israel and even had a link to the IDF homepage!'

[54] The CiF editorial staff have since removed this comment but have left references to it by other commenters (6 November 2007)

[55] The CiF editorial staff have since removed a number of these comments.

have a spare brown shirt to put on.' (Lipman 2006)[56] When she writes about dogs (Lipman 2006a),[57] someone responds, 'Maureen's "conscience" is concerned about dogs, but is perfectly clear when it comes to those of the "wrong" race.' When she writes about showbiz, someone comments 'It's amazing that all the chaos, suffering and violence in the Middle East seems to have gone unnoticed by Maureen.'

This abuse followed an accusation that was made against Lipman, according to which she made a racist comment. She was having a discussion on a TV current affairs programme with Michael Portillo, Diane Abbott and Andrew Neil at the time of the beginning of the Israel-Hezbollah war of the summer of 2006. Portillo was talking about the fact that Hezbollah and Hamas are jihadi Islamist organizations of the same kind that were responsible for suicide bombing around the world. Abbott then raised the question of proportionality, arguing that the Israeli response to the attack on its soldiers could be seen as being disproportional. Maureen Lipman replied:

> What's proportion got to do with it, though, Diane? It's not about proportion, is it? I mean human life is not cheap to the Israelis, and human life on the other side is quite cheap...

It appears from the context of the discussion that by 'the other side' Lipman meant Hezbollah, Hamas, and the other jihadi Islamist organizations. CAABU, the Council for the Advancement of Arab-British Understanding complained to the BBC that this was a racist comment, because it understood Lipman to have meant that 'Arabs, whether Palestinians or Lebanese, do not value human life as much as anyone else.' (CAABU 2006)

Lipman had gone on to clarify what she meant: '... and human life on the other side is quite cheap because they strap bombs to people and send them to blow themselves up'. She seems to have been arguing that Israelis value life more than those who 'strap bombs to people and send them to blow themselves up' – that is, the jihadi Islamist terrorist organizations. It is they who send out suicide bombers, not Arabs, Palestinians, Lebanese or Muslims in general.

Whether Lipman was right or wrong to claim that Israelis value human life more than jihadi Islamists is a question that might be discussed. But it seems clear that, while one may agree or disagree, it is a misreading to claim that it is in fact a racist comment.

2. Antisemitic themes mirrored in anti-Zionist text

In section 1, I looked at the Ken Livingstone's claim that he is accused of antisemitism only because he criticizes Israel and at what appears to be a proliferation and normalization of anti-Zionist and antisemitic bigotry on *The Guardian* website. Both of these seem to represent a mainstreaming of the most demonizing anti-Zionist discourses combined with a denial that there was a problem; indeed more than a denial: a counter allegation against those who suggested that antisemitic ways of thinking were detectable coming from left and liberal sources. Section 2 presents

---

[56] The CiF editorial staff have since removed this comment.
[57] The CiF editorial staff have since removed this comment.

more examples of Lerman's 'intensified criticism', more examples of the mainstreaming of absolute anti-Zionism and of antisemitism, and examples that mirror the themes and rhetoric of older anti-Jewish movements. Two themes that re-occur in discourses that demonize Jews, over the centuries and across the globe, are the blood libel and the charge of Jewish conspiracy. Section 2 of Part II analyzes case studies of anti-Zionist text and discourse that mirror themes from (a) the blood libel and (b) conspiracy theory.

A. Blood libel

Image 1 (see bibliography for a list of numbered images) shows a wholesome Jaffa orange, cut in half, out of which blood is dripping. The slogan reads: 'Boycott Israeli Goods: Don't squeeze a Jaffa, crush the occupation'. The combination of Jews, food and non-Jewish blood creates a graphic, emotive and powerful image. If you eat the Jaffa oranges that the 'Zionists' are trying to sell you, you will metaphorically be drinking the blood of their victims.

How does such an image get produced? There are three possible explanations. The first is that the similarity with the old themes is purely coincidental. If this is the case, such coincidences seem to happen often. The second possible explanation for the 'blood orange' image is that the designer of the poster is an antisemite who is consciously drawing on antisemitic tradition. This is unlikely and is of course strenuously denied. Antiracist anti-Zionists who campaign for a boycott of Israel say quite clearly that they are not antisemites. They do not appear to be conscious Jew-haters and they are not knowingly drawing on older antisemitic themes.

The third possible explanation is that there is some sense in which antisemitic themes are deeply embedded in the culture and elements present themselves unconsciously to people looking for emotive images that can drive us to act against Israel. The mechanism of this cultural unconscious, how and why it works, how and why it is so often repeated, is one element of the relationship between hostility to Israel and antisemitism that requires further research and rigorous thinking-through. But many anti-Zionists are not prepared to think it through. Frequently the response to the observation that some of their imagery mirrors old antisemitic themes is disdainful denial followed by a counter-allegation of bad faith.

Ariel Sharon was caricatured eating a baby in *The Independent* newspaper on 27 January 2003 (Image 2). Dave Brown, the cartoonist, won the 'political cartoon of the year award' for this image. Perhaps this image of a corrupt, violent and bullying Jew eating an innocent child is only coincidentally analogous to classic blood libel imagery. 'Brown insisted he had never intended this meaning and that his cartoon was inspired by the Goya painting Saturn Devouring one of His Children.' (Byrne 2003)

Norman Finkelstein hosts an extensive gallery of cartoons on his website by the Brazilian artist 'Latuff'.[58] Latuff won second prize in Mahmoud Ahmadinejad's Tehran competition for cartoons that illustrate Holocaust denial. This, incidentally, is a clear example of the ways in which elements of rhetoric circulate around the

---

[58] See http://www.normanfinkelstein.com/article.php?pg=11&ar=176, downloaded 19 June 2007.

different anti-Zionist movements. Norman Finkelstein, who considers himself to be an antiracist and a scholar, hosts Latuff, who in turn is happy to compete in Ahmadinejad's Holocaust denial art festival. One image (Image 3) shows a swimming pool, the shape of the Gaza strip, filled with blood. The image shows Uncle Sam luxuriating in the blood, Ehud Olmert covered in the blood and using an Israeli flag as a towel, and a UN waiter bringing a drink of blood to the two swimmers. The world is pictured sitting in the sun, refusing to be concerned. There are a number of other images by Latuff, hosted by Finkelstein, that mirror themes of the blood libel. There is one that shows an innocent child who is either Lebanese, or who represents Lebanon itself, being doused in Israeli petrol (gasoline). Another shows an Israeli soldier washing the blood off his hands using an American tap. Another image shows Ariel Sharon with vampire fangs.

Sue Blackwell (2005), while campaigning for the exclusion of academics who work in Israel from British campuses, wrote that the 'sins of Bar-Ilan University and other Israeli universities are certainly as red as blood'. On being challenged about this image, she responded (2005b) with a piece entitled 'Bloody Ridiculous', writing 'OK chaps, I know you are desperate to pin the "antisemitic" label on me but just how low can you sink? Just carry on, you're doing a good job of digging yourselves deeper'.

The theme of Israel as a child-killing state is increasingly common. Any incident of an under-age Palestinian being killed during the conflict is liable to be understood and presented as a manifestation of Israel's essentially child-killing nature. The slippage from particular incidents to a generalized commonsense notion is a common characteristic of much anti-Zionist discourse. The particular truth is often essentialized as the necessary truth.

Blood libel always goes hand-in-hand with antisemitic conspiracy theory. If 'the Jews' kill children then certainly they conspire to hide the crime (Julius 2006). If Israel is based on child-killing and genocide, then certainly there must be a Zionist conspiracy or an Israel lobby that has the power to keep the fact out of the global media.

The most explicit and complete version of antisemitic conspiracy theory is the *Protocols of the Elders of Zion*, a late nineteenth century Russian forgery that purported to constitute a report of a meeting of the Jewish conspiracy in Prague. Contemporary echoes of the old theme of Jewish conspiracy take the form of an argument that there is a Zionist lobby with such huge global influence and power that it is able to send the United States of America to war in its interests and delegitimize any narrative of Israel and Palestine that it does not like as antisemitic. The *Protocols* and more contemporary charges of Zionist influence come together in the Hamas Covenant (1988), the founding document of the party that won the January 2006 election in Palestine and carried out a successful coup against the Palestinian presidency in Gaza. The Hamas Covenant explicitly plagiarizes from, and endorses, the original *Protocols* forgery and holds 'the Jews' responsible for all the revolutions, wars and imperialism of the modern era.

Ilan Pappe (2006) argues that Israeli forces are committing genocide in Gaza. The charge that Israel commits genocide, in Gaza or the West Bank, or in Lebanon, is a charge commonly made by anti-Zionists. At first sight, such a characterization would appear to be entirely counter-productive, since while Israeli forces are regularly responsible for serious human rights abuses, they can easily show themselves to be not guilty of genocide. When there is no genocide in Gaza why do anti-Zionists like Pappe continue to assert that there is? These repeated allegations have the effect of demonizing Israel, of implanting and reinforcing the notion that Israel is a unique evil. It simplifies: Israel is the 'oppressor', Palestine is the 'oppressed' and anything more complicated only serves to confuse this central issue.

The genocide charge is a particular kind of demonization. Genocide has a particular relevance to Israel, which was created three years after the end of the Holocaust. The contemporary claim that there is a genocide in Gaza is related to the claim that Israel uses the Holocaust instrumentally to justify its violence. The charge that Israel is like Nazi Germany functions to neutralize this alleged instrumentalization of the Holocaust. In order to neutralize the Holocaust in this way, it is necessary to normalize it and distort its reality.[59] So anti-Zionists often push a number of myths: (a) what happens in Gaza today is, in some sense, the same as the Holocaust, which is the point of naming it 'genocide'; (b) 'Zionists' collaborated with the Holocaust and so were partly responsible for it;[60] and (c) 'Zionism' is ideologically akin to Nazism.[61]

Pappe (2006) writes: 'Nothing apart from pressure in the form of sanctions, boycott and divestment will stop the murdering of innocent civilians in the Gaza Strip.' Perhaps his wish to advocate for this campaign is what has led him to make the over-blown claim of genocide; he does not use the term 'genocide' to describe events in 1948, which is his area of historical expertise. Yet his proposed remedy today does not seem to fit the alleged disease. If there was really genocide occurring in Gaza,

---

[59] For more on left versions of Holocaust denial, see Rich (2007) and Ezra (2007).

[60] See Korneyev (1977) for the classic Soviet version: 'Together with the Nazis, the Zionists bear responsibility for the destruction of Jews in 1941-1945 in Europe. The blood of millions of victims is on their hands and on their conscience.' Jim Allen's 1980s 'Trotskyist' version has his hero in *Perdition* making the following claims: 'The simple terrible truth is that the Jews of Hungary were murdered not just by the force of German arms, but by the calculated treachery of their own Jewish leaders' (p. 156); the Zionists worked 'hand in glove' with the Adolf Eichmann (p. 103); it was 'the Zionist knife in the Nazi fist' that had murdered the Jews (p. 156). The first remained in the final published version and the second and third were cut. They are taken from the version released by the Royal Court Theatre in 1987. Allen said in an interview that *Perdition* was 'the most lethal attack on Zionism ever written, because it touches on the heart of the most abiding myth of modern history, the Holocaust. Because it says quite plainly that privileged Jewish leaders collaborated in the extermination of their own kind in order to bring about a Zionist state, Israel, a state which is itself racist.' In 2007, the Scottish Palestine Solidarity Campaign held a reading of Allen's play and hosted Lenni Brenner, in order to use Holocaust Memorial Day to make their points about the connection between Zionism and Nazism.

[61] Mazin Qumsiyeh puts it like this on Mona Baker's website, http://www.monabaker.com/conflictfacts2.htm, in 'Ten Zionist Obfuscations': 'Zionism and Nazism were twins in their narrow nationalism and even collaborated against the public. The Zionists thus found no reason not to collaborate with the Nazis in the mid-thirties to rid Europe of its Jews.' For an extreme right-wing version of the claim, see Chiappalone (1997): 'Zionism and Nazism actually have a great deal in common. They are a desire for national identity, national socialism, "self-determination", and "freedom" from those who might be called "troublemakers". In fact, they are both philosophies of imagined racial superiority and purity, which have rationalized all of their actions in the name of some greater "good". And, they each conceal a deeper evil at their core.'

surely a more urgent, powerful and desperate response would be appropriate than carrying on the long, slow campaign for sanctions, boycott and divestment. Pappe finishes by exhorting the world 'not to allow the genocide of Gaza to continue'. He precedes this exhortation with the words: 'in the name of the holocaust memory'. The irony is that so long as Pappe employs this kind of political rhetoric, then it is unlikely indeed that it should communicate successfully with the majority of Israelis and Jews. But perhaps he is not writing for Israelis. Perhaps he has given up on building a peace movement and he has given up on Israelis as potential agents for progressive change: 'There is nothing we here in Israel can do against [the genocide in Gaza]', writes Pappe. Shortly after writing this piece, Pappe accepted a job at Exeter University in England.

B. Conspiracy theory

Conspiracy theory features in each of the four examples that we have looked at so far: the *Livingstone formulation*,[62] which holds that critics of Israel are silenced by a conspiracy to make mendacious accusations of antisemitism; Livingstone's view that the Board of Deputies is capable of fixing a desired result from a public investigation; the routinization of conspiracy theory on CiF; and conspiracy theory as the necessary twin of blood libel.

In March 2006, John Mearsheimer and Stephen Walt published a paper in two different forms. 'The Israel Lobby' (2006a) was published in the *London Review of Books* and 'The Israel lobby and US foreign policy' (2006b) was published as a Faculty Research Working Paper by Harvard University and the Kennedy School of Government. I do not offer here a detailed critique of the text of the paper, a straightforward task that was carried out more or less satisfactorily within a few weeks of its publication (Morris 2006; Herf and Markovits 2006; Dershowitz 2006).[63] Rather, I am interested in the way that the paper provided a language for the discussion of 'Zionist' conspiracy and the way in which this language was enthusiastically, quickly and widely adopted by many who found it natural to think within this framework.

Robert Fine (2006a) uses the concept of 'slippage' to examine the problem. The paper itself starts with something real and asks answerable questions. What is the

---

[62] Another example of the use of the *Livingstone formulation*: on the day that David Miliband was made Foreign Secretary, the BBC website ran a profile of him written by Paul Reynolds, World Affairs correspondent: 'David Miliband's Jewish background will be noted particularly in the Middle East. Israel will welcome this – but equally it allows him the freedom to criticize Israel, as he has done, without being accused of antisemitism.' (Reynolds 2007) The clear assumption here is that anyone who criticizes Israel should be afraid of being denounced as an antisemite and that that there is a hugely powerful 'Zionist' 'lobby' that is capable of intimidating a senior government minister into muting his legitimate criticism of Israel. When challenged, reports a commenter on Engage, who had received a reply from Reynolds to his complaint to the BBC, Reynolds referred to a piece by Anthony Julius and Alan Dershowitz (2007) that argued that the academic boycott of Israel was antisemitic, as an example. Reynolds thereby relies on the claim that 'criticism' is the same as a proposal to exclude Israeli academics from campuses, journals and conferences.

[63] Many more references are to be found on the Engage website, http://www.engageonline.org.uk/archives/index.php?id=17, collated by Jeff Weintraub.

nature and influence of various lobbying and campaigning organizations that relate to Israel and Jews in the United States, such as AIPAC (American Israel Public Affairs Committee), the ADL (Anti-Defamation League) and AJC (American Jewish Committee)? How do these different organizations operate, what do they want and what effect do they have? But even within the Mearsheimer and Walt paper itself, the focus on particular and differing organizations, and concrete questions, begins to slip into a conception of 'the lobby', which is discussed as though it was a hugely powerful, coherent, covert and therefore conspiratorial political agent. The particular claim made by Mearsheimer and Walt, which shows that they were discussing an extremely powerful and threatening world-straddling agent, is that the 'Israel lobby' was held to be responsible for ensuring that the United States went to war against Saddam Hussein's regime in Iraq. Robert Fine (2006a) writes:

> Their argument runs along the classic lines of conspiracy theory. There is the initial explanandum: the 'unwavering' material, diplomatic and military support the US grants to a foreign country, Israel. Two possible explanations for this policy are considered and rejected: one is the foreign country's strategic value to the US; the other is compelling moral imperatives to support this country's existence....
>
> Disposal of these two explanations paves the way for the Only True Explanation which explains why the US has been willing to sacrifice its own security to the interests of another state. It is the Lobby. They characterize it as the *de facto* agent for a foreign government. They maintain it makes Israel virtually immune to criticism in Washington. They say it quashes debate in the public sphere through the power of its money, its control of the media, its policing of academia and not least its exploitation of the charge of antisemitism against anyone who criticizes Israel's actions or the Lobby's own influence. They argue that, thanks to the Lobby, the US has come into line with Israeli positions rather than Israel come into line with US interests. The lobby, we are told, took on the President of the United States and triumphed. Sharon wrapped Bush 'round his little finger'. The demonic tail is wagging the gullible dog.
>
> Finally, this explanation is extended to explain all manner of other phenomena beyond the initial explanandum. The Lobby, we are told, was the critical factor behind the US decision to impose sanctions on Iran and Libya, to go war on Iraq and overthrow Saddam, and now to take on Israel's other enemies such as Syria and Iran. While the US does the fighting, dying and paying, they write, Israel is the beneficiary. The Lobby's influence increases the danger of terrorism, fuels Islamic radicalism, raises the spectre of further wars in Syria and Iran, makes impossible any resolution of Palestinian suffering, undercuts US prestige abroad and its efforts to limit nuclear proliferation, and erodes democracy within the US. All for Israel. What is needed is 'candid discussion of the Lobby's influence', a return to reality and the advancement once more of US interests.
>
> Slippage from criticism of American foreign policy to wild-eyed conspiracy theory punctuates this whole narrative.

At a public event organized by the *London Review of Books* in New York, John Mearsheimer said: 'The Israel lobby was one of the principal driving forces behind the Iraq War, and in its absence we probably would not have had a war.' (Stoll 2006) The accusation that a Jewish conspiracy pushes the world into unnecessary wars in the interest of the Jews is an old staple of antisemitic conspiracy theory. For example, Claire Hirshfield (1980) tells how some who opposed the Boer war blamed it on a Jewish diamond lobby manipulating the British Empire:

> If it could be demonstrated that the ... government had been tricked into war by the machinations of shady Jewish capitalists and that the public had been intentionally misled by omnipotent Jewish press lords, then sufficient pressure might indeed be generated to end what its opponents considered an immoral war. That the pursuit of this worthy aim involved an appeal to a base and discreditable prejudice seems to have little troubled the various socialists, radicals and labourites who utilized the shorthand of 'Jewish finance' as a convenient means of epitomizing the dark underside of British imperialism.'

Charles Lindbergh (1941) blamed unpatriotic Jewish power for trying to draw the United States into the Second World War against its own interests:

> I am not attacking either the Jewish or the British people. Both races, I admire. But I am saying that the leaders of both ... for reasons which are as understandable from their viewpoint as they are inadvisable from ours, for reasons which are not American, wish to involve us in the war.

Interestingly, Lindbergh also makes use of an early variant of the *Livingstone formulation* in the same speech:

> The terms 'fifth columnist,' 'traitor,' 'Nazi,' 'antisemitic' were thrown ceaselessly at any one who dared to suggest that it was not to the best interests of the United States to enter the war.

Conspiracy theories have been circulating on the internet ever since 11 September 2001, trying to blame 9/11 on 'Zionists', claiming that the Jews in the World Trade Centre were warned not to show up that day, claiming that Israeli agents had been seen celebrating in New Jersey as the twin towers collapsed. The Hamas Covenant (1988) explicitly blames Jews for every war and upheaval since the French and Russian revolutions. In a notorious speech to the Reichstag, Adolf Hitler held the Jews responsible for the First World War:

> In case the Jewish financiers ... succeed once more in hurling the peoples into a world war, the result will be ... the annihilation of the Jewish race in Europe.[64]

Other claims made in the Mearsheimer and Walt paper slipped into more explicit and less nuanced ones in a more political forum. Mearsheimer claimed that terrorist 'animus' against America was the result of US policy towards Israel, which itself is a result of the machinations of the 'lobby'. He added, employing his version of the *Livingstone formulation*, that this 'simply can't be discussed in the mainstream media.' (Stoll 2006)

The tendency for this kind of slippage to occur accelerated outside of the hands of the authors themselves and manifested itself in the uses people made of the paper. Anybody who wanted to talk about Jewish or Zionist power now had a Harvard and

---

[64] Adolf Hitler's announcement to the Reichstag in 1939, see http://www.nizkor.org/hweb/people/g/goebbels-joseph/goebbels-1948-excerpts-02.html.

Kennedy School stamp of respectability with which they could inoculate their own ideas against the spurious and disingenuous charges of antisemitism that would be sure to follow. The idea of disproportionate and dangerous Jewish power, and particularly its covert application in steering states towards war, was not new, but Mearsheimer and Walt offered a legitimate vocabulary with which to make these kinds of claims. And the offer was taken up enthusiastically by many people in the summer of the Israel-Hezbollah war that followed the publication of the 'Lobby' paper.

Philip Roth was one of the first to sense the paranoid zeitgeist that was on its way, under the surface of public discourse, in the first decade of the twenty-first century. *The Plot against America* (2005) was his counter-factual story of what might have happened in America during the early 1940s if Charles Lindbergh, an anti-semite and campaigner to keep the United States out of the war, had been elected president. It is a picture of a seemingly entirely normal world under the surface of which lies the menacing narrative of antisemitic conspiracy theory that holds Jews responsible for trying to drag America into the Second World War. The central characters in the novel feel the menace, while many others regard them as paranoid, backward-looking, tied to outdated notions of Jewish identity and unpatriotic.

Conspiracy theory in Britain existed before Mearsheimer and Walt. For example, in May 2003, respected Labour MP Tam Dalyell accused the Prime Minister Tony Blair of 'being unduly influenced by a cabal of Jewish advisers' (Brown and Hastings 2003).[65] Paul Foot (2003), well-known journalist and leading member of the Socialist Workers Party, leapt to Dalyell's defence: 'obviously he is wrong to complain about Jewish pressure on Blair and Bush when he means Zionist pressure'. Foot knew how to interpret an antisemitic statement as an anti-Zionist one. But after Mearsheimer and Walt came along, everybody knew how to do it and the specific terminology of the 'lobby' became ubiquitous in anti-Zionist discourse.

The theoretical journal of the supposedly antiracist Socialist Workers Party, *Socialist Review*, now writes things like this about the 2007 UCU decision to back the boycott campaign:

> A very powerful pro-Israel lobby has gone to work to denounce these decisions with the support of the pro-war 'left'. Meanwhile arch Zionist and Harvard lawyer Alan Dershowitz has threatened to 'devastate and bankrupt' any organisation which commits to a boycott of Israel. These figures want to block discussion of Israel's actions. We must defend the right of trade unions to democratically pass resolutions and hold political debates without being subjected to such threats. (Harman 2007)

A whole number of elements of conspiracy theory are here packed into one seemingly innocent paragraph: the use of the term 'pro-Israel lobby' to describe a single unvariegated and therefore dishonest conspiracy; its designation as 'very powerful'; the lobby's association with the 'pro-war' (pseudo) 'left', an allegation of the further dishonesty of pretending to be 'left' while not really being left, and the association of the 'pro-Israel lobby' with support for war; the reference to Alan Dershowitz, a name

---

[65] Dalyell had then employed the *Livingstone formulation*: 'The trouble is that anyone who dares criticize the Zionist operation is immediately labelled anti-Semitic.' (Marsden 2003)

universally recognized by decent people to connote pure evil or 'arch' Zionism; Dershowitz's threat to 'devastate and bankrupt' resonates with the menace and power of 'the lobby'; 'these figures', Dershowitz (the arch-Zionist and Harvard lawyer), the pro-war pseudo left and the pro-Israel lobby, the sum of all that is bad in the struggle against imperialism, want to block discussion of Israel's actions – a remarkable allegation, given that it is the boycotters who insist on discussing not 'Israel's actions' but instead the plan to exclude Israelis from British public life; next there is a substitution of the right to have debates for the right to support the exclusion of Israelis; then the right for trade unions to be free from criticism; then 'such threats', referring to one rather idle threat made by Alan Dershowitz is constructed as being something from which we must defend ourselves against the powerful, dishonest, pro-war, pseudo left lobby. Even after the elements that go to make up a paragraph like this are explained in detail, some people will look blankly and say, 'it all seems perfectly innocent to me'.

Richard Ingrams (2007), a columnist for *The Independent* newspaper, reviewed the book version of the Mearsheimer and Walt thesis when it was published in Britain in September 2007. Ingrams could not resist the temptation to make explicit that, in his reading of the 'lobby' thesis, it was covert Jewish influence and not only 'pro-Israel' lobbying that was decisive in sending the only superpower to war, not in its own interest, but in the interests of a foreign power:

> [Mearsheimer and Walt] demonstrate that the American invasion ... not only had the support of Israel but also that the overriding aim of those (mostly Jewish) neocons who were urging Bush to invade was to assist Israel.

Whereas Mearsheimer and Walt have repeatedly denied that their thesis has anything to do with Jews, arguing that many Jews do not support 'the lobby' and that many constituents of 'the lobby' are not Jewish, Ingrams interprets their book for a wider public in precisely the way that opponents of antisemitism had feared and predicted that it would be read and understood. In 2003, Ingrams (2003) wrote in *The Observer* newspaper that he had developed a practice when 'confronted by letters to the editor in support of the Israeli government to look at the signature to see if the writer has a Jewish name.' If so, he says, he tends not to read it. Ingrams, then, had a pre-existing opinion that British Jews had nothing of interest to say about Israel since their views would be explicable only by reference to their ethnicity and not to their experience, knowledge or judgment; the *ad hominem* argument *par excellence*. Inevitably, Richard Ingrams (2005) also makes use of the *Livingstone formulation*: 'The board [of Deputies of British Jews] ... thinks nothing of branding journalists as racists and antisemites if they write disrespectfully of Mr Sharon...'. Some may find that blaming Jews for the war in Iraq and finding it appropriate to leave letters to the editor written by people with Jewish sounding names unread are not precisely the same kinds of things as writing disrespectfully of Ariel Sharon. It is routine now that any accusation of antisemitism is responded to by demanding freedom of speech for criticism of Israel. Ingrams' writing exemplifies the process of slippage to which the Mearsheimer and Walt thesis lends itself. It again raises uncomfortable questions about the notion of political responsibility with which Mearsheimer and Walt operate. We should also note that it has become common and apparently normal for mainstream liberal 'antiracist' newspapers like *The Independ-*

ent, *The Observer* and *The Guardian* to give space to people like Richard Ingrams to opine on 'The Jewish Question'.

Another outrider for Mearsheimer and Walt is Anatol Lieven. The flagship morning radio news show of the BBC, *The Today Programme*, carried a report by its Washington correspondent, Justin Webb, which gave publicity to the Mearsheimer and Walt book on 10 October 2007. Webb said:

> Anatol Lieven of King's College, London, who worked recently in Washington was accused of antisemitism for doing little more, he says, than suggesting that America should put pressure on Israel to close the settlements.

> [Lieven's voice:] This accusation of antisemitism has no basis in evidence or rationality. It's not the kind of accusation which in any other circumstances would even be allowed to be printed. It is simply being used as a way of trying to terrify, to frighten, critics of Israel and of American support for Israel into silence. (Hirsh 2007a)

Webb accepts Lieven's account of what has happened, but he slips in the scare-phrases. 'Little more ... than', what, exactly, more? 'He says', but is it true? Did Webb check? Or did Webb simply accept the claim? 'Suggesting'? Did he really respectfully 'suggest'? But Webb does not know because he evidently did not check.

There may be people in the United States who would make an accusation of antisemitism against somebody simply for arguing for the dismantling the settlements. But here the apparent behaviour of one supporter of the settlements is held to illustrate the behaviour of the whole 'lobby'. So Lieven claims: 'This accusation of antisemitism has no basis in evidence or rationality.' He is not referring to this particular accusation but is now talking generally about the 'accusation of antisemitism'. The discourse has slipped from a particular but undefined and uncorroborated incident to a general claim. Lieven now claims: 'It's not the kind of accusation which in any other circumstances would even be allowed to be printed.' Moving into the passive, he does not specify who would normally disallow a charge of racism. But it is understood that he thinks that it is the 'lobby' that is in a position to legislate an exception to this rule: 'It is simply being used as a way of trying to terrify, to frighten, critics of Israel and of American support for Israel into silence.' So now we learn that such an accusation is not made in good faith; it is not a mistake. We learn now that such an accusation is part of a common plan and a secret plan. The verb 'trying' could not signify anything other than a concerted planned attempt to do something. To 'frighten'. To frighten 'critics of Israel' into silence.

Later in the same report we hear the following [beginning with the voice of Ralph Nader]:

> The Israeli puppeteer travels to Washington, the Israeli puppeteer meets with the puppet in the White House and then moves down Pennsylvania Avenue and meets with the puppets in Congress and then takes back billions of taxpayer dollars.

> [Back to the voice of Justin Webb:] Ralph Nader is a consumer rights advocate who has run for the presidency and makes the case against the Israel lobby with great gusto and in a manner that many Jewish Americans find deeply offensive. Mearsheimer and Walt also make the case that the Israel lobby is overly powerful but again, John Mearsheimer's language is careful and his point nuanced:

[The voice of John Mearsheimer:] We're not making the argument that this is a cabal or conspiracy. The American political system, as you know, has interest groups at its heart and interest group politics is what life is like in the American political system. And the Israel lobby is just like the National Rifle Association, the farm lobby, the American Association of Retired People and other lobbies. Small numbers of people who are deeply committed to a particular policy and are smart and energetic can influence policies in ways that are out of synch with what most people in the United States want.

Nader articulates conspiracy theory using the traditional antisemitic vocabulary of the 'puppeteer'. Webb describes this as making the 'case against the Israel lobby' with 'great gusto'. Webb tells us that Nader does it in a manner that many 'Jewish Americans find deeply offensive' but he does not explain why. He does not tell us whether the listeners, ordinary people who are not Jewish or American, should be offended. He does not tell us why this might be offensive. The politics of racism are reduced to the politics of trying not to give offence. Webb is operating with a notion that only Jews should be, or are, concerned about Nader's conspiracy theory. And then Webb goes on to say that Mearsheimer makes the same case as Nader – but that his 'language is careful and his point nuanced'. Webb has, perhaps, stumbled onto the exact truth here, but he seems not to understand the importance of the word 'also' in the sentence, 'Mearsheimer and Walt also make the case that the Israel lobby is overly powerful but again, John Mearsheimer's language is careful and his point nuanced….' The case is the same, it is heard as the same and it is used as authority for the same, but it is done more carefully and in a nuanced way. So we have a claim that Mearsheimer articulates a careful and nuanced version of the 'Jew as puppet master' narrative. And because it is 'careful' and 'nuanced' it is given airspace on BBC Radio 4.

i. Stephen Rose's use of the 'lobby' rhetoric

When Steven Rose, a leading proponent of the campaign for an academic boycott of Israel, appeared on Radio 4's *Today* programme (Hirsh 2006e) to comment on the report of the parliamentary inquiry into antisemitism (2006), he relied heavily on the concept of the 'lobby'. Rose admitted that there had been a rise in antisemitism but argued that this was primarily the result of the criminal actions of Israel in Palestine. The interviewer responded:

Interviewer: But that is Israel, that is the country, the government of Israel, it's not Jewish people.

Rose: That is precisely the point but the problem is always that the Israel lobby insists that Judaism and Zionism, Judaism and support of Israel, are identical and while they go on insisting that, and while they go on attacking those of us who actually oppose the policies of Israel as being antisemitic or being, in my case, a self-hating Jew, then they actually build this rod for their own backs…. (Hirsh 2006e)

Rose introduces the term 'Israel lobby' and claims that it is responsible for this false identity between Judaism and 'Zionism' (Rose translates 'Zionism' as 'support for Israel'). Here, Rose is broadening out the claim that antisemitism is the fault of Israel, into a claim that it is the fault of a global 'Israel lobby'. Immediately he conflates the multiplicity of campaigns and individuals who oppose his anti-Zionism and his boycotts into one shadowy and undefined term. The 'lobby', argues Rose, insists on this identity between 'Zionism' and Jews and it attacks those who 'oppose the policies of Israel' as being antisemitic or self-haters. This constitutes another shift: now it is not Rose's demonization and his boycotts that the 'lobby' wants to suppress with its trumped-up charge of antisemitism but actually criticism of Israeli policies.

Rose himself conflates 'Israel lobby' with 'Jews' by arguing that 'they' build a rod for their own backs. The 'lobby' builds the rod, but it is Jews in general ('their own backs') that get hit by it. So the 'lobby' has already become, in the way that Rose uses the term, a code word for Jews in general. Rose does not think it important to discuss who is doing the hitting with this rod that 'the lobby' has built for 'their own backs'. He is not interested in the responsibility of antisemites for antisemitism or in the responsibility of Jews and antiracists to oppose and confront the antisemites. Rose goes on:

> We've received death threats for actually daring to discuss the idea of a boycott of a racist university system within Israel itself. And so in fact the rise in anti-semitism is precisely because this equation of being Israeli and being Jewish. We don't say that but the Israelis do.

Rose is clearly implying here that it is 'the Israel lobby' that sends out death threats to him and his colleagues. And he is right. Because his understanding of the term 'lobby' includes everyone from AIPAC, the ADL, the AJC, Campus Watch and Melanie Phillips, to the UJS, the Board of Deputies and the All-party Parliamentary Committee, to Engage, Workers' Liberty, Jonathan Freedland, David Aaronovitch and Meretz USA, to loony late night green-ink letter-writers who send death threats. All those who stand against Rose's characterization of Israel as an apartheid state and illegitimate speak, in his imagination, with one voice, say one thing, adopt one tactic, have one politics. In other words, the 'lobby', in the way that Rose uses the term, is a global Jewish conspiracy. Nearly all newspapers, TV stations, websites, publishing houses and even Hollywood itself oppose his focus on Israel as a uniquely racist centre of global imperialism. And Rose cannot just be wrong; the fact that most people disagree with him needs to be explained, and it is explained with reference to the existence of a vast conspiracy.

ii. Robert Fisk, the United States of Israel and 'the lobby'

The Independent newspaper on 27 April 2006 carried a four-page piece by Robert Fisk (2006) headlined 'United States of Israel?' It was illustrated by a full-page, full-colour image of the Stars and Stripes with Stars of David replacing the usual stars (Image 4).

The piece profiles Stephen Walt as a hero who bravely stood up to the 'lobby' and its malicious and dishonest accusations of antisemitism.

The image used by *The Independent* of the Jewish Stars and Stripes says that Jews control America; these are Jewish symbols, not Israeli ones. The premise is that Jews are not patriotic Americans; Jews care more for their own narrow community than the wider national or human community. The same device of merging Jewish stars with the American flag has long been used by neo-Nazis, conspiracy theorists and jihadi Islamists.[66]

---

[66] Examples of antisemitic versions of the 'Stars of David & Stripes' can be found here: http://www.engageonline.org.uk/blog/article.php?id=653, downloaded 25 July 2007.

The Fisk article offers no evidence to back up the strong version of the thesis, the one that is illustrated by the flag, and there is little evidence to back up a weaker or more sophisticated version, namely that the 'Zionists' tricked or coerced the United States to spill the blood of its citizens in a war that was against its own interests. There is some overblown rhetoric about AIPAC, 'the agent of a foreign government [that] has a stranglehold on Congress – so much so that US policy towards Israel is not debated there'.[67] Fisk tells us that 'the lobby' monitors and condemns academics who are critical of Israel. Fisk repeats Mearsheimer and Walt's version of the *Livingstone formulation* (quoted from Mearsheimer and Walt 2006b), that 'anyone who criticizes Israel's actions or argues that pro-Israel groups have significant influence over US Middle East policy ... stands a good chance of being labelled an anti-Semite'.

Fisk does not give an example of anyone claiming that Mearsheimer and Walt are antisemites or are motivated by antisemitism. He quotes Alan Dershowitz as saying that 'the two scholars recycled accusations that "would be seized on by bigots to promote their antisemitic agendas"'. Fisk claims that Noam Chomsky is prevented by 'the lobby' from having a column in an American newspaper. He asserts that 'the lobby' prevented a repeated showing of a film that Fisk had made for Channel 4. He writes that an 'Israel support group' (unnamed, although apparently part of 'the lobby') insulted Fisk. He says that 'the lobby' prevented the showing of 'I am Rachel Corrie' in New York. 'The lobby' is presented as an unopposable, unstoppable force. It tells presidents and members of Congress what to do and what to say. Its tentacles reach into theatres, TV stations and newspapers. Americans would like to resist but are forced to act against their own interest by the 'lobby'. In the 1950s, the conspiracy theorists insisted that 'the Communists' controlled America; now 'the lobby' has replaced 'the Communists' as the hidden puppet master. Seymour (2007) argues that it is not a coincidence that a marked decline in UFO sightings has been matched by a marked increase in more 'realistic' conspiracy theories.

Fisk claims that the United States changed its policy towards Israel after 1967 'in response to lobbying by the American-Jewish community'. He does not consider the alternative possible explanation that Americans were concerned that Israel might be militarily defeated, and that this might not be a good thing. Neither does he consider an explanation in terms of US interest in the context of the Cold War. Events, politics, campaigns and disagreements are presented in the world view of the conspiracy theorist as being controlled by the vice-like grip of 'the Jews' (in some versions, the 'Zionists' or the 'lobby').

iii. Tony Judt: Jewish conspiracy and reasons for believing in it

On 12 October 2007, there was a conference at the University of Chicago on 'academic freedom' and in defence of Norman Finkelstein. The assumption of the conference was that academic freedom in general and Finkelstein in particular have come under

---

[67] Compare with this, from Charles Lindbergh, speaking against proposed US entry into the Second World War: 'As I have said, these war agitators comprise only a small minority of our people; but they control a tremendous influence. Against the determination of the American people to stay out of war, they have marshaled the power of their propaganda, their money, their patronage.' (Lindbergh 1941)

illegitimate and powerful attack by the Israel lobby. Tony Judt (2007) spoke the following words:[68]

> If you stand up here and say, as I am saying and someone else will probably say as well, that there is an Israel lobby, that there is ... there are a set of Jewish organizations, who do work, both in front of the scenes and behind the scenes, to prevent certain kinds of conversations, certain kinds of criticism and so on, you are coming very close to saying that there is a *de facto* conspiracy or if you like plot or collaboration to prevent public policy moving in a certain way or to push it in a certain way – and that sounds an awful lot like, you know, the *Protocols of the Elders of Zion* and the conspiratorial theory of the Zionist Occupational Government and so on – well if it sounds like it it's unfortunate, but that's just how it is. We cannot calibrate the truths that we're willing to speak, if we think they're true, according to the idiocies of people who happen to agree with us for their reasons.
>
> It may well be true – I know this because I have received an email from him – that David Duke thinks he has found allies in John Mearsheimer or Stephen Walt or myself. But I remind you what Arthur Koestler said in Carnegie Hall in 1948 when he was asked, 'Why do you criticize Stalin – don't you know that there are people in this country, Nixon and what were not yet called McCarthyites, who also are anti-Communist and who will use your anti-Communism to their advantage?' And Koestler's response was the response that I think we should keep in mind when we are faced with the charge that we are giving hostages to crazy antisemites or whatever, and that is you can't help other people agreeing with you for their reasons – you can't help it if idiots once every 24 hours with their stopped political clock are on the same time as you. You have to say what you know to be true and be willing to defend it on your grounds and then accept the fact that people in bad faith will accuse you of having defended it or aligned yourself with the others on their grounds – that's what freedom of speech means – it's very uncomfortable. It puts you in bed sometimes with the wrong people.

Judt's response to the charge that he and Mearsheimer and Walt provide a respectable vocabulary for the articulation of antisemitic conspiracy theory is a surprisingly candid and flat denial of political responsibility and an explicit refusal to 'calibrate' claims in such a way as to make them unhelpful to antisemites. There are a number of elements to this defence which are worthy of discussion.

First, Judt admits that he comes 'very close to saying that there is a *de facto* conspiracy or ... plot or collaboration' and that 'that sounds an awful lot like the *Protocols of the Elders of Zion* and the conspiratorial theory of the Zionist Occupational Government [ZOG] and so on'. He seems to imply that it is not just he who thinks so but that those who are on the panel with him think so too, including perhaps Tariq Ali, Noam Chomsky (participating via video), John Mearsheimer and Norman Finkelstein. He then says that antisemites 'happen to agree with us' (but for the wrong reasons) – they agree fundamentally on the claim that there is (something very close to) 'a *de facto* conspiracy or ... plot or collaboration ... that sounds an awful lot like' the *Protocols* or the ZOG. He admits for the third time that the anti-

---

[68] These words were transcribed from a sound file of his speech that was posted online (Judt 2007).

semitic conspiracy theorists say fundamentally the same things as he and his collaborators do (but for different reasons) when he says: 'you can't help it if idiots once every 24 hours with their stopped political clock are on the same time as you'.

Second, Judt makes an analogy with Koestler's criticisms of Stalin in 1948. Koestler thinks that the gulag exists and that one has a responsibility to say so, even if this appears to vindicate anti-Communists who also think that the gulag exists and who say so loudly. So Judt thinks that a *de facto* Jewish conspiracy exists and that he has a responsibility to say so even if antisemites, who also think that a Jewish conspiracy exists, are thereby apparently vindicated. The difference, however, is obvious. The gulag existed. A Jewish conspiracy of the kind that has sufficient covert muscle to send the world's only superpower to war against its own interests and expel critics of Israel from the American academy does not exist. Indeed, the McCarthyites were also conspiracy theorists who believed that America was falling under the spell of a Moscow plot that encompassed every liberal schoolteacher and every 'red' Hollywood actor. Koestler did not believe in the conspiracy, nor did he believe 'anything very close' nor a '*de facto* conspiracy' nor a 'plot' nor a 'collaboration'. Koestler was not like Judt. In fact, Judt's anti-Zionism (although not the rest of his world view) comes from the political tradition of those who did remain silent about the gulag on the grounds that to speak up would play into the hands of the imperialists. It is a political tradition that currently remains overwhelmingly silent about the crimes of any political movement or state that embraces anti-Zionist or anti-imperialist rhetoric. The left anti-Stalinists, Trotsky, Draper, Arendt, Koestler, Orwell and the others spoke out against the left commonsense of their day, namely that one should not criticize Stalin. Judt fails to speak out against the left commonsense of his day, which holds Israel, and the Jews who support it, to be both uniquely evil and uniquely powerful.

Third, Judt argues that the crucial factor distinguishing him from the antisemitic idiots is the reasoning behind the analysis. The analysis is fundamentally the same, but he believes in the existence of ('something that sounds an awful lot like') a '*de facto* conspiracy' because it exists, whereas David Duke believes in it because he is an antisemite. Duke's antisemitism has, on this one occasion, just by chance, led him to a true conclusion concerning the global threat of Jewish power and its responsibility for war. Judt's problem seems to be that he is unable – or unwilling – to show how what he believes is different from what the idiot antisemites believe. He is only able – or willing – to show that he has better reasons for believing it. While Duke (2004) believes that a global conspiracy based on the theory of 'Jewish supremacism' is responsible for all wars, Judt believes only that it is responsible for this war and that the antisemitic conspiracy theorists were wrong about the other wars.

Fourth, Judt says: 'You have to say what you know to be true and be willing to defend it on your grounds and then accept the fact that people in bad faith will accuse you of having defended it or aligned yourself with the others on their grounds. It puts you in bed sometimes with the wrong people.' Judt accuses his accusers of acting in bad faith: he relies on an *ad hominem* argument. In this way, he puts motivation at the centre of his defence. He is a good guy, he is on the left and he is motivated by the search for truth and justice (for the Palestinians). David Duke, who happens on this occasion to have stumbled onto the truth about the Israel lobby and its responsibility for war, has done so out of a malignant motivation. Those who ask why Judt and Duke have been discovered together in the bed of (*de facto*) Jewish conspiracy theory, claims Judt, do so in bad faith. The bad faith is that of the Israel lobby mendaciously playing the antisemitic card in order to delegitimize Judt's unmasking of the lobby by portraying it as similar to Duke's unmasking of the lobby.

My argument about the potential danger of Judt's conspiracy theory is not an *ad hominem* argument. It does not rely on an accusation of bad faith or malicious motivation. It does not accuse Judt of being secretly or unconsciously motivated by antisemitism. But it does point to the suggestion that Judt is insufficiently concerned about saying the same thing, using the same language and drawing on the same images as generations of antisemitic conspiracy theorists. Judt's response is 'it's unfortunate, but that's just how it is'. But it is not a coincidence that puts Judt in David Duke's political bed. He is there because Duke is saying the same as Judt and Judt refuses to 'calibrate' his claims such they become useless to Duke. If we are 'telling a truth' that puts us in bed with David Duke then perhaps it is reasonable to conclude that we are telling it wrong – or at least in an incomplete way. Judt does not find himself in this predicament because he is, like Duke, motivated by antisemitism. Judt is not motivated by antisemitism. But perhaps motivation is not the key here. The key is what Judt says and what he does, not what motivates him. The danger of licensing antisemitic claims and world views, of acting as midwife to an antisemitic movement, is not neutralized by the fact that Judt is an antiracist and a respected intellectual. Indeed, the fact that Judt is widely recognized as such exacerbates the danger.

3. *The diminishing caution over the expression of antisemitism*

So far, we have seen case studies illustrating the tendency to deny any particular manifestation of antisemitism that is related to hostility to Israel and case studies showing how the imagery and rhetoric of contemporary antiracist anti-Zionism tends to mirror older antisemitic imagery and rhetoric. We now move beyond denial and beyond the replication of antisemitic tropes to more explicit articulations of antisemitic claims that still make use of the language of anti-Zionism.

A. Jenny Tonge and control of the Western World

The Liberal Democrats are the centre party in UK politics, generally understood to be politically to the left of the Conservatives and to the right of Labour. Notwithstanding the complexities of such a characterization, they are a mainstream party in British political life and could not be understood as either an extreme left-wing or right-wing party. Jenny Tonge was fired as a Liberal Democrat spokesperson in January 2004 after having said that, if she had been a Palestinian, she would have considered becoming a suicide bomber.[69]

There are two senses in which these remarks are interesting. Firstly, they demonstrate an ignorance of conditions in Palestine, Palestinian politics and Palestinian paramilitary

---

[69] This is a sentiment that has been expressed by a number of other high profile people, for example Cherie Blair (News.BBC.co.uk 2002), who said: 'As long as young people feel they have no hope but to blow themselves up, we're never going to make progress, are we?' And Ken Livingstone, who said: 'Palestinians don't have jet fighters, they only have their bodies to use as weapons. In that unfair balance, that's what people use.' (Lappin 2006)

capability. Palestinians respond to the world in which they live in a whole number of different ways. Some respond politically, as nationalists, socialists or Islamists; some try to look after their communities, as doctors, teachers or leaders; some struggle to look after themselves and their families; some are involved in peace organizations and in groups that aim to bridge the divide; some argue for a boycott of Israel; and some engage in forms of armed resistance. It is not empirically true that Palestinians have no choice other than to blow themselves up near Israelis. The overwhelming majority of Palestinians find other ways to live and other ways to respond.

Yet Tonge's premise is that 'if she were Palestinian' then she would think differently from the way that she does, being British. It is difficult to escape the conclusion that at the bottom of such a sentiment is an 'orientalist' (Said 1978) othering of Palestinians. I am British, so I am a Member of Parliament, I think, I act politically, I speak. But if I were Palestinian then I would not think and reflect and act politically or ethically, but rather I would be driven by rage to the only course open to me, which would be suicide bombing. I would be forced to extinguish my life in a drama of anger and despair because no other form of expression would be open to me, if I was a Palestinian. But the truth is that most Palestinians do not act as though reading from the script of a twentieth century orientalist movie; they do not act the part of the irrational emotional anger-driven Arab, who has no choice and who cannot think beyond their fury. Tonge misrepresents, depoliticizes and essentializes Palestine.

Having been sacked from her job by the Liberal Democrat leadership, and then 'elevated' to the House of Lords by the nomination of the same leadership, Tonge said the following on 20 September 2006:

> The pro-Israeli lobby has got its grips on the Western World; its financial grips. I think they've probably got a certain grip on our party.[70]

It seems unlikely that Tonge's use of Mearsheimer and Walt's (2006a and 2006b) terminology is accidental. In Tonge's hands, the term 'lobby' slips and slides all the way back to antisemitic conspiracy theory. She is not describing a social phenomenon, a powerful lobbying organization or a well-funded political campaign, because the word 'grips' is incompatible with any of these possible interpretations. Something that has its grips on the Western world, no less, has gone beyond anything that an international relations professor might conceivably have been describing. How does the 'lobby' grip the Western world? Tonge is explicit: financially.

One kind of slippage to which the 'lobby' rhetoric lends itself is in implying that different campaigns with different aims and different politics are all, really, one. For Tonge, the term 'pro-Israel lobby' conflates all of the different campaigns into a strong enough centralized leadership to get a 'grip' not only on political parties but also on the whole of the 'Western world'. She is talking about a conspiracy with sufficient power to dominate on a global scale. Financial power. Another old antisemitic theme is the connection of Jews to money and finance. Tonge's language is not appropriate to describe a situation where 'pro-Israel' campaigns have won support; it is only appropriate to describe a situation where there is a huge financial conspiracy to corrupt and to lie.

---

[70] This part of her speech was broadcast on Radio 4's Today programme the morning after the remarks were made, and transcribed by Hirsh (2006a).

Jenny Tonge may be unaware of what the language that she uses means and the secondary meanings that it connotes. She is not a naïve newcomer to these debates. And she did not backtrack or apologize when the problem was pointed out to her. Instead she defiantly responded with her own version of the *Livingstone formulation*: 'I am sick of being accused of antisemitism when what I am doing is criticizing Israel and the state of Israel.' (http://www.inminds.co.uk 2007)

B. Chris Davies: Jews, oppressors, Auschwitz and apartheid

The meeting at which Tonge made her 'lobby' comments was organized by Chris Davies, who had been the leader of the Liberal Democrats in the European Parliament until some months earlier, when he had also been forced to resign. On returning home from a trip to Gaza, Davies expressed his anger and horror at conditions there on his website and in the press. One comment he made was:

> I visited Auschwitz last year and it is very difficult to understand why those whose history is one of such terrible oppression appear not to care that they have themselves become oppressors.[71]

This was a classic example of the 'Jews should know better' argument. The Jews 'appear not to care that they have themselves become oppressors'. He could only mean 'the Jews'. He is talking about 'those whose history is of such terrible oppression', who came to his mind when he visited Auschwitz. Jews used to be oppressed; now they are oppressors – and they don't even care (apparently).

This generalization, that the Jews have become oppressors, goes to the heart of the current of contemporary antisemitism that is connected to anger with Israel. Davies shifts focus from acts that he understands as oppressive to those people who he holds responsible for them and he calls them 'oppressors'. And then he adds that they (apparently) don't care, as though Jews speak with one voice (or care with a single conscience).

The overwhelming majority of the Jews who were at Auschwitz (where Davies visited as a tourist or perhaps as a VIP) left that place through the chimney. Many of them, one may assume, did not have time to sit down and ponder the lessons that they were supposed, by this Member of the European Parliament, to have been learning there.

What were the lessons being taught to at Auschwitz? What should 'the Jews' have learnt from the Shoah experience? It would seem that the lesson learned by many Jews is 'next time, have more tanks and fighter planes'. 'Have more powerful friends' perhaps, too. Many Jews learnt the central lesson that the twentieth century seemed to go to such lengths to teach so many people: 'If you don't have a nation state of your own, then you have no rights'. It is hardly a surprise or a sign of a moral deficiency if this lesson was taken on board. The corollary to this lesson is that 'if you don't look after "your own" then nobody else will look after you'. Many Israelis seem to be more attached to these lessons than to the 'Jews should know better than to oppress others' lesson that we might think they ought to have learnt.

---

[71] These words did appear on Chris Davies' website but do not appear there now (June 2007). They are cited in Hirsh (2006f).

It was, of course not just 'the Jews' who learnt this lesson in the twentieth century but many others too. The Ottoman and Austro-Hungarian empires taught people across Central and Eastern Europe, as well as across the Middle East, the same lesson. And so the fall of these two Empires in 1918 was followed by upsurges of ethnic nationalism and bloody struggles to carve out nation states in Czechoslovakia, Poland, Hungary, Romania, Bulgaria, Turkey and throughout the region. Following the Second World War, the big European empires faced nationalist opposition throughout Africa and Asia and were pushed out by people who also had learnt the lesson of the twentieth century: 'If you don't have a nation state of your own, then you have no rights'. Following the break-up of the Soviet empire in 1989, many more people learnt the lesson that history had taught them. And so in Croatia, Serbia, Latvia, Lithuania, Estonia and Czechoslovakia there were struggles for 'national' independence, often trampling on the rights of minorities who were held not to be part of the nation that was to be self-determined (Arendt 1975; Fine 2001).

Before Hitler came to power many Jews rejected this narrow politics of nationhood, 'national liberation' and 'self-determination'. Most Jews chose, either through political commitment or through inertia, not to go to Palestine to build a Jewish state. Zionism was an eccentric, utopian, minority project amongst Jews. It was only during the 1930s and 1940s, when the Nazi plan to sweep Europe clean of Jews came together, that nationalist politics really began to take hold amongst Jews. The European labour movement and the European left had been defeated, and the Jews who had put their faith in it were killed or were running for their lives. Jews from the great cosmopolitan cities of the Middle East were later pushed out of their homes by Arab nationalist regimes that had also been busy learning the 'gotta have a state' lesson. A million Russian Jews came in the 1990s after enduring decades of Soviet antisemitism, which had come packaged in the language of hostility to Zionist imperialism.

And of course many Palestinians have learnt the lesson of the twentieth century too: 'no state, no rights'. Without a state of their own, they have been treated appallingly both by Israel and by a number of Arab states. None of this is to support the politics of nationalism. But analysis begins with the world as it is, and this is a world structured by the fact that human rights, in the absence of a nation state to guarantee them, have often, under pressure, turned out to be worthless promises. So the cosmopolitan task, in Israel/Palestine and also further afield, is to find a politics that creates a different truth for the twenty-first century. (Hirsh 2003; Fine 2007)

Jews straggling out of Europe in the late 1940s can hardly be blamed if most of them did not set changing the world in a cosmopolitan direction as their immediate goal. Most of them wanted to feel safe, and many believed that the only way they could feel safe was in a state of their own. But Chris Davies divides the world into 'oppressed' peoples and 'oppressor' peoples. 'The oppressed' are the Jews who arrived in Israel after being pushed out of Europe, the Middle East and more recently the Soviet Union. 'The oppressors' are those Jews a few years or decades later, along with their children and grandchildren.

In truth, Chris Davies' confusion as to whether Jews are 'oppressed' or 'oppressors' is far from new. Jews have often been treated by parts of the left as either one or the other, good or bad, on 'our side' or on 'their side'. Jews have been much more comfortably understood by some only as victims or as global threat. Much analysis on the topic of Israel and Palestine deals with entirely abstract notions: evil 'Zionism' that stands for global imperialism and good Palestinian revolutionaries who represent the vanguard of the global *intifada*. For many commentators, Israel and Palestine, as well as Iraq, are not important or interesting in themselves but only inasmuch as they represent the good and evil of the global struggle. Darfur does not have this emblematic status; neither does Congo Hence the millions of deaths there are not big issues on the European and American left.

Jews do not all think the same thing. Some Jews learnt different political lessons from the Holocaust to other Jews. It was neither evil nor stupid to think, after the Holocaust, that Jews would have been in less trouble if they had a state and an army. It is the Israeli government that is responsible for Israeli policy, not 'the Jews' who used to be 'oppressed' and are now 'oppressors'.

Davies did resign as the leader of the Liberal Democrat group in the European Parliament. He was not sacked because he criticized Israel or because the 'Jewish lobby' forced him out. A constituent criticized him for comparing current Israeli policy to the Holocaust. He replied with a one-line email: 'Sounds like racism to me. I hope you enjoying wallowing in your own filth.'

She responded that this was a disgraceful way to reply to a constituent's email. Rather than apologize, he wrote back to her denouncing Israeli policy and the 'Jewish lobby'. When he was asked to comment by a local Jewish newspaper, he said that at the time he had received a number of abusive emails. He then offered to enter into a dialogue with his constituent on the condition that she first detail her own disagreements with Israeli policy.

Was this an example of the pro-Israel lobby forcing the resignation of a critic of Israeli human rights abuses by employing a dishonest charge of antisemitism? Let us analyze carefully how 'the lobby' achieved this. Firstly, *Jewish News* reported Chris Davies' comments, which he had already put on his own website. Then a number of people sent abusive emails to Davies. Then the *Jewish News* reader sent him an email criticizing him for comparing Israel's treatment of Palestinians in the West Bank with the Holocaust. In the meantime, I myself had written a piece on *The Guardian* website (CiF) criticizing Davies' use of the clichéd Jews-should-know-better argument (a re-working of which appears above). *Jewish News* went to the leadership of the Liberal Democrats for a comment, and Menzies Campbell, then the leader of the party, fired Chris Davies (by mutual agreement).

One free weekly newspaper, a number of angry people sending abusive emails, at least one more considered email writer and a sociology lecturer with access to *The Guardian*'s website. This constellation of mighty influence was predictably presented as a manifestation of the power of the global 'lobby' that smoothly moved into action to have this critic of Israel punished.

Chris Davies was not forced to resign because he criticized Israel, but he did say a number of things that one could argue made him an unsuitable person to hold the post of Liberal Democrat leader in the European Parliament. None of these things include criticizing Israeli policy, which is an entirely reasonable thing to do.

Firstly, he made use of two analogies that are routinely used not to shed light on the Israel-Palestine conflict but to demonize Israel and to foster a commonsense popular loathing of Israel. The Israel-Palestine conflict is a nasty and long-running dispute over (on a global scale) a small amount of territory, in which neither party is entirely right or wrong. The Israeli occupation of the West Bank relies on organized daily violence, repression and humiliation of Palestinians. But the occupation is not the result of an Israeli wish to dominate or of a particularly Israeli cruelty. It is the result of a long and violent dispute between Jews and Arabs, and Israelis and Palestinians, in which those who have argued for peace and reconciliation on both sides have usually been defeated politically. Many Palestinian responses to the occupation (and to the presence of Jews in Israel) have been murderous and self-defeating. But the idea that Israel is a Nazi state is absurd and offensive. There is not, and there never has been, a genocide of Palestinians; there are no Israeli gas-chambers, concentration camps or *Einsatzgruppen*; the total number of deaths on both sides throughout the conflict is analogous to the number of murders that the Nazi regime routinely committed every few minutes.[72]

The use of the apartheid analogy is designed to isolate Israel as South Africa previously had been, as an illegitimate state. This analogy is not designed to shed light on the conflict but to act as a short-cut to a boycott. The analogy could be used, honestly, to illuminate some aspects of the occupation, but when used politically it often functions as a method of demonizing rather than of explaining. Many other analogies are more appropriate, for example analogies with nationalist movements in the Balkans or in other fragments of the old empires. There is a serious situation in the West Bank, where Jewish settlers, backed by Israel, do live in a legally privileged relationship with Palestinians that does have some resemblance to apartheid. They do enjoy privileged legal rights, democratic rights, rights of movement, rights to resources, rights to water. But it is because the situation is not the same as in the former South Africa that most Israelis think that the Jewish settlers ought to go home to Israel. A peace between Israel and Palestine will not be forged in a unitary state (like the new South Africa). It is much more likely to require a two-state solution precisely because this is a struggle between two national communities, not a struggle against an apartheid system of racism.[73]

So Davies made use of two demonizing analogies. He also claimed that Jews had now become 'oppressors' and that they don't seem to care. This claim, that the Jews are oppressors, is particularly inflammatory in the context of the North West of

---

[72] When it is pointed out to anti-Zionists who use the Zionism-Nazi analogy that the analogy is not appropriate, they often respond with something like the following: 'The Gazans, you tell us, are not facing genocide. Indeed. We must really give Israel high marks for not killing all of them? They are facing starvation, in plain and simple English – food, medicines, electricity and fuel are being stopped at the border, not to mention students who cannot leave to study. So all that is not important, as long as there is no genocide? I cannot believe that you are comfortable with this.... Are you really comfortable with Israel's continued barbarities? If so, please tell us.' This was written by a well-known boycott supporter on the internal UCU activists list under the heading 'Not yet enough hell in Gaza'. As well as giving readers a small taste of the quality of the boycott debate within the union, it is also an example of a standard anti-Zionist form of argument. It concedes that the Nazi analogy is inappropriate but then insists that it can be inferred that the one who called it inappropriate therefore thinks that there is no problem in Gaza. Either Gaza is like the Warsaw Ghetto or it is like North London – there can be no middle position. Anti-Zionism often sets up spurious binary oppositions and insists that we choose one or the other. Notice that, in this case, it also presents a false picture of events (there is no starvation in Gaza), and, particularly since it is repeated again and again and with authority, many people accept that picture of events as true.

[73] See Strawson (2006) for an excellent legal analysis of the Zionism-apartheid analogy.

England, which he represents in the European Parliament, where the BNP (the neo-Nazi British National Party) is trying to organize the 'white' vote and the Islamists are trying to organize the 'Muslim' vote. To characterize Jews as oppressors in this context is not trivial. And then Davies insulted a constituent who criticized him by denouncing her as a racist (because he assumed she was a 'Zionist') and writing 'I hope you enjoying wallowing in your own filth.'

He denounced what he called the 'Jewish lobby', which, he claimed, has too much influence. He later said that he stood by this comment, but admitted that he did not understand the distinction between the claim that there is a 'Jewish lobby' and the claim that there is a 'pro-Israel' lobby. The Mearsheimer and Walt paper had only been published a few months earlier, and Davies had not yet learned the terminology he ought to have used to express his conspiracy theory while protecting himself from a charge of antisemitism.

Chris Davies is not an antisemite in the sense that it is unlikely that he was motivated by Jew-hatred, but he was guilty of negligence. Davies went out of his way to intervene in the Israel-Palestine conflict and took an extremist position that he fiercely defended. But he did not educate himself with any seriousness about the conflict, and he did not educate himself about the nature of contemporary antisemitism. When he was publicly challenged over the potentially antisemitic discourse that he seemed to be buying into through ignorance, he angrily refused to consider the possibility instead of stopping to think about it. It is unlikely that he is similarly careless, thoughtless or ignorant when it comes to anti-black racism or anti-Muslim racism. Liberals and politicians on the left do not make the same kind of mistakes when emailing their black or Asian constituents.

There is not a choice to be made about whether to oppose Islamophobia or anti-Jewish racism; it is possible and democratic to oppose both. If we fail to stand against both then we become partisans for the extreme end of one nationalism, or fundamentalism, or the other.

C. How antisemitism can become acceptable amongst antiracists

The two above-mentioned Liberal Democrat politicians, Tonge and Davies, seem to have stumbled into antisemitism without understanding the significance of what they were doing or saying. True, they refused to take the possibility of antisemitism seriously, even after the problems were pointed out to them, but they are not people who think of themselves as antisemites.

Gilad Atzmon does not think of himself as an antisemite either, but he is much more self-conscious and knowing when he plays with antisemitic formulations, ideas and rhetoric. The Socialist Workers Party and the Scottish Palestine Solidarity Campaign are not put off by Atzmon's use of antisemitic language, and they continue proudly to host him at their events. He is a former Israeli paratrooper, a well-known jazz saxophonist, a campaigner for Palestine and someone who is comfortable employing openly anti-Jewish rhetoric.

For example:

> I would suggest that perhaps we should face it once and for all: the Jews were responsible for the killing of Jesus who, by the way, was himself a Palestinian Jew. (Atzmon 2003)

And:

American Jewry makes any debate on whether the 'Protocols of the Elders of Zion' are an authentic document or rather a forgery irrelevant. American Jews (in fact Zionists) do control the world. (Atzmon 2003)

And:

To regard Hitler as the ultimate evil is nothing but surrendering to the Zio-centric discourse. To regard Hitler as the wickedest man and the Third Reich as the embodiment of evilness is to let Israel off the hook. To compare Olmert to Hitler is to provide Israel and Olmert with a metaphorical moral shield. It maintains Hitler at the lead and allows Olmert to stay in the tail.... Israel has already established a unique interpretation of the notion of wickedness that has managed to surpass any other evil. It is about time we internalise the fact that Israel and Zionism are the ultimate Evil with no comparison. ... Now is the time to stand up and say it, unlike the Nazis who had respect for other national movements including Zionism, Israel has zero respect for anyone including its next door neighbours. The Israeli behaviour should be realised as the ultimate vulgar biblical barbarism on the verge of cannibalism. Israel is nothing but evilness for the sake of evilness. It is wickedness with no comparison. (Atzmon 2006a)

In November 2006, Atzmon spoke and played music at an event in Edinburgh organized by the Scottish Palestine Solidarity Campaign, entitled Zionist Control. His argument (Atzmon 2006b) at that event was that the clean distinction that anti-Zionists make between 'Zionists' and Jews, anti-Zionism and antisemitism is largely fictional. He argued that Israel is a 'fascist state' supported by 'the vast majority of Jewish people around the world'. Anti-Zionist Jews in the Palestine solidarity movement, therefore, play a Jewish role there, as gatekeepers who try to control the Palestinian narrative:

As soon as anyone identifies the symptoms of Zionism with some fundamental or essential Jewish precepts a smear campaign is launched against that person. (Atzmon 2006b)

Atzmon fights for explicitly anti-Jewish politics within the Palestine solidarity movement, and in order to win it is necessary first for him to defeat the anti-Zionist Jews and their antiracist allies:

I would use this opportunity and appeal to our friends amongst the Jewish socialists and other Jewish solidarity groups. I would ask them to clear the stage willingly, and to re-join as ordinary human beings. The Palestinian solidarity movement is craving for a change. It needs open gates rather than gatekeepers. It yearns for an open and dynamic discourse. The Palestinians on the ground have realised it already. They democratically elected an alternative vision of their future.[74] (Atzmon 2006b)

Atzmon's central problem with the Jewish anti-Zionists is that they, even though they themselves treat Israel as though it was demonic, also oppose openly antisemitic

---

[74] Presumably the 'democratically elected ... alternative vision' that he refers to is the racist antisemitism of jihadi Islam as set out in the Hamas Covenant (1988).

expression in the Palestine solidarity movement. He particularly opposes those who do this 'as Jews'. Atzmon is trying to lead an antisemitic purge of the anti-Zionist movement that will ditch the formal antiracism to which many anti-Zionists still cling. In spite of opposition to Atzmon, in which anti-Zionist Jews are active,[75] the Socialist Workers Party and parts of the Palestine Solidarity Campaign[76] continue to treat Atzmon as an antiracist and as a legitimate member of the Palestine solidarity movement.

The week after the Edinburgh event, Atzmon spoke at a Respect Party event, advertised in *Socialist Worker*, entitled 'Jazz Racism and Resistance'. Socialist Worker (2006), the following week, brought us the news that Gilad Atzmon was to feature in 'one of the biggest cultural events Socialist Worker has put on for many a year.' The report went on: 'Gilad declared, "I will be playing at the Cultures of Resistance concert because I support the Socialist Worker appeal."'

Atzmon's writing regularly appears in *Counterpunch* (e.g. 2003a; 2006a), which thinks of itself as an antiracist journal. There are links to his writing on the PSC Gymru-Wales website,[77] *The Jerusalemites* website,[78] *Middle East Online*,[79] *Dissident Voice*[80] and many more 'respectable' Palestine solidarity publications.

Some Jewish and antiracist anti-Zionists have flirted with Holocaust denial by defending the appropriateness of comparisons between Israel and Nazi Germany. Some have routinely minimized antisemitism, often finding excuses for the rhetoric of Jewish conspiracy, Jewish domination of the media and Jewish power. Some have found excuses for movements that wish to wipe Israel off the map. Some have gone along with the 'truism' that people who talk about antisemitism do so dishonestly because they are part of a conspiracy to hide the crimes of 'Zionism'. Some have routinely fought for the commonsense notion that Israel is a uniquely serious human rights abuser. Atzmon shows how a charismatic leader could begin to harvest the antisemitic potential of these kinds of anti-Zionist staples into a concrete movement. There must be a possibility that antisemites may push the antiracist anti-Zionist leadership out of the way and take over the anti-Zionist movement. The antiracist anti-Zionists are ripe for take-over if they do not understand their own part in the

---

[75] The Jewish Socialist Group (2006) wrote an open letter in which it attempted to warn the Scottish Palestine Solidarity Campaign and the Socialist Workers Party what Atzmon was trying to do. Despite this, both of these organizations gave him a platform.

[76] At least one local PSC group, the Bucks and Berks branch, sent out Atzmon's Edinburgh speech to its membership, in its mailing of 27 November, with the following introduction: 'Gilad Atzmon argues that the Palestine solidarity movement should focus soley [sic] on the Palestinian cause and urges Jewish sympathizers to support the Palestinians for what they are rather than expecting them to fit into a Jewish worldview.' Bucks and Berks PSC, here, is adopting Atzmon's antisemitic language, for example 'Jewish worldview', relating to 'Jewish sympathisers' within the Palestine Solidarity Campaign.

[77] Palestine Solidarity Campaign Gymru-Wales, http://psccymru.org.uk/index.php?option=com_weblinks&catid=23&Itemid=49, downloaded 28 February 2007.

[78] Jerusalemites, http://www.jerusalemites.org/articles/english/2006/November/23.htm, downloaded 28 February 2007.

[79] Middle East Online, http://www.middle-east-online.com/english/?id=17604, downloaded 28 February 2007.

[80] Dissident Voice, http://www.dissidentvoice.org/Feb06/Atzmon07.htm, downloaded 28 February 2007.

creation of this new current and if they don't know how to respond politically. They are being victimized by antisemites and they do not know how to defend themselves effectively. Atzmon wrote the following to an anti-Zionist Jewish blogger who has for years been churning out pieces that demonize Israel as a uniquely racist state:

> You are now presented 'as being a manifestation of Jewish exclusivity or supremacy on a par with the State of Israel' on every left and pro Palestinian site around the world ... may I suggest that it is never too late, you can still join humanity. Chicken soup is not a political argument.

Atzmon is not satisfied with demonizing Israel. He also demands that anti-Zionist Jews cease to define themselves as Jews; only then may they be accepted into the human community and the Palestine solidarity movement.[81] And Atzmon's antisemitism is found acceptable by people who think of themselves as antiracists. Indeed, Atzmon was given space on the 'antiracist' *Guardian*'s website to denounce me as an 'ultra-Zionist', as a dishonest academic, as a 'Zionist ideologist', as someone who 'needs antisemitism'. 'Antisemitism (rather than anti-Israel political reaction) exists solely in the Zionist's mind', he assures us (Atzmon 2006c).

In November 2007, Atzmon was quoted as follows in the *Morning Star*, a newspaper which thinks of itself as antiracist:

> I know deep inside me that the Hebraic identity is the most radical version of the idea of Jewish supremacy, which is a curse for Palestine, a curse for Jews and a curse for the world. It is a major destructive force.... For an Israeli to humanise himself, he must de-zionise himself. In this way, self-hating can become a very productive power. It's the same sense of self-hating I find, too, in Jews who have given the most to humanity, like Christ, Spinoza or Marx. They bravely confronted their beast and, in doing so, they made sense to many millions. (Searle 2007)

III. CONCEPT AND DISCOURSE BECOME CONCRETE EXCLUSION: BOYCOTT

In Parts I and II, I have analyzed concepts and discourse. Part III turns to the actualization of concepts and discourse in the form of concrete exclusion. There is a campaign to exclude Israelis, and only Israelis, from universities, sports stadia, theatres, concert halls – from the cultural and economic life of the world.

1. A chronology of the campaign for a boycott of Israel

> In Medieval times, Christians were not allowed to enter a Jewish synagogue; they were not allowed to celebrate a holiday with Jews; they were not allowed to go as guests to Jewish banquets and anyone thus 'defiled by their impieties' was in turn to be shunned by Christians (to quote from a canonical collection). It would be wrong to have 'fellowship with God's enemies'. Medieval England was especially active in excluding or 'boycotting' Jews. For example, at the 1222 Canterbury Council, Archbishop Langton threatened with excommunication any Christians

---

[81] Atzmon is not a unique figure. He has a coterie of supporters, for example on the 'Peace Palestine' blog, http://www.peacepalestine.blogspot.com. Also, there are others in the Palestine solidarity movement who are increasingly comfortable with openly antisemitic rhetoric, such as Paul Eisen and Israel Shamir.

who had any familiar dealings with Jews or even sold them provisions. In his first pastoral circular following election as Bishop of Lincoln, Robert Grosseteste enjoined his archdeacons, 'as far as you are able, study to prevent the dwelling of Christians with Jews'. (Julius and Dershowitz 2007)

Boycotts against Jews and exclusions of Jews are not new. In 1904, there was a boycott of Jewish businesses in the city of Limerick in Ireland organized by the Catholic priest, the Rev. Father Creagh. Currently supporters of the campaign to boycott Israel are in the habit of marshalling the rhetoric of free speech. They portray those who are reluctant to discuss whether or not Israel is a unique evil, whether or not to exclude Israelis from our campuses, whether or not 'Zionists' control US foreign policy, as people who threaten free debate.[82] The *Limerick Leader* expressed similar sentiment regarding the campaign to boycott the Jews in 1904, in a piece entitled 'Hear all sides':

> In another column of our issue this evening we insert Mr. Davitt's letter to the *Freeman's Journal* on the subject of the Rev. Father Creagh's recent remarks on the Jewish community in Limerick. In giving the letter publicity we are not to be taken as adopting his views, our desire being merely to show all sides fair play.

The *Leader* is certainly not antisemitic, and it warns its readership that their opponents are in the habit of exaggerating any sniff of antisemitism in order to increase the campaign of vilification against the boycotters:

> It has come to our knowledge that the Jews for the past few days have been subjected to ill-treatment and assault while passing through our public thoroughfares. We regret that such has been the case. We are living in critical times when every advantage is taken by unscrupulous opponents to misinterpret our acts and the cause of our religion. In such a crisis it is not wise to give a handle to vilification. If the people do not want the Jews, then leave them severely alone. Above all

---

[82] For example, Jacqueline Rose (2007), in a letter to *The Guardian* also signed by eight others: 'The recent decision of the University and College Union congress was to organise a debate on whether an academic boycott of Israeli academic institutions would be an appropriate response to the occupation of Gaza and the West Bank. It was not a decision to inaugurate such a boycott. We are perplexed at the suggestion that there is something improper or undesirable about such a debate. The opponents of the boycott debate argue that a boycott is inimical to academic freedom, yet they are engaged in a campaign of vilification and intimidation in order to prevent a discussion of this issue. While defending academic freedom, therefore, they seem only too willing to make an assault on the freedom of speech. The UCU congress and its members have a right, and arguably a duty, to confront the ethical and political challenge represented by the repression in the occupied territories.' Note the classic slippage in the last sentence from a debate as to whether Israeli academics – and only Israeli academics – should be excluded from the academic community to a debate on how to 'confront the ... challenge represented by the repression in the occupied territories'; as though criticism of state policy and exclusion on the basis of nationality were the same thing. The accusation that opponents of the boycott are engaged in a campaign of 'vilification and intimidation' is Jacqueline Rose's version of the *Livingstone formulation*. The letter is also based on the false claim that Motion 30 at the 2007 UCU congress mandated a debate. In fact, it mandated UCU to campaign for an academic boycott and to treat the PACBI argument for a boycott as a 'call'. It did not mention the circularity of asking British academics to 'respond' to the PACBI 'call', which was itself a response to the call of Stephen and Hilary Rose to issue a 'call'.

things have no recourse to violence. Such a policy only shows weakness, if not foolish vindictiveness, and will never succeed in accomplishing that which is, or may be desired. (Both quotations from the *Limerick Leader*, Monday evening, 18 January 1904, quoted in Keogh and McCarthy 2005.)

Father Creagh was also quite 'prepared to admit that there are many [Jews] who are irreproachable'. His boycott was only aimed at those Jews who 'grind and oppress those who are unfortunate enough to get into their power' (Reverend Father Creagh, 8 February 1904, *Northern Whig*, Belfast, quoted in Keogh and McCarthy 2005). In these short passages we have represented a number of extremely contemporary themes: boycotters' reliance on the rhetoric of free speech; the Jews as exaggerating and manipulating antisemitism to vilify the boycotters; the fact that the boycott is not against all Jews; and the possibility of a test for good Jews who may be exempted from the boycott.

The Limerick boycott was organized at the height of the campaign against Jewish immigration into Britain, which culminated with the passing of the Aliens Act in 1905. The British Trades Union Congress supported this Act, which constituted a nationalized boycott of Jews, and many trades unions supported a boycott of Jewish members. There were also boycotts of Jewish businesses advocated by some who thought of themselves as being on the left as a stand against sweatshop labour and for trade union rates of pay (Cohen 2005).

A boycott of Jewish businesses was one of the tools in Hitler's armoury during the early days of Nazi rule in Germany, and it was followed by a campaign to exclude Jews from the professions, the universities and then from any public or cultural space, transport, entertainment, arts, film and theatre. The contemporary campaign for a boycott of Israeli academic institutions situates itself in the tradition of the boycott against South African apartheid. It is perhaps worth remembering that there is also a less heroic strand to the boycott tradition.

A few months after the final defeat of German Nazism, on 2 December 1945, the newly formed Arab League Council declared the beginning of the Arab boycott: 'Jewish products and manufactured goods shall be considered undesirable to the Arab countries.' All Arab 'institutions, organizations, merchants, commission agents and individuals' were called upon 'to refuse to deal in, distribute, or consume Zionist products or manufactured goods' (Bard 2007). The Arab boycott of Israel was supported by the Soviet Union, which invented contemporary left anti-imperialist anti-Zionism and used it as a cover for antisemitism (Crooke 2004).

In April 2002, Steven and Hilary Rose 'initiated'[83] the call for a moratorium on European research collaboration with Israel. Later, they participated in setting up BRICUP,[84] the British Campaign for the Universities of Palestine, and PACBI,[85] the

---

[83] Steven and Hilary Rose did 'initiate' the call for a moratorium on European research collaboration with Israel in April 2002, according to Steven Rose's own account in his profile on *The Guardian*'s website, *Comment is Free*, http://commentisfree.guardian.co.uk/steven_rose/profile.html, downloaded 14 February 2005. It was later that they portrayed themselves as answering a Palestinian call rather than themselves initiating action.

[84] BRICUP, British Campaign for the Universities of Palestine, http://www.bricup.org.uk.

[85] PACBI, Palestinian Campaign for the Cultural and Academic Boycott of Israel, http://www.pacbi.org.

Palestinian Campaign for the Academic and Cultural Boycott of Israel. It subsequently became an important element of their political rhetoric that they are not initiators of the boycott call but are, rather, responding passively to a call from within Palestine.

In May 2002, Mona Baker, an academic at UMIST,[86] fired two Israeli academics – Miriam Shlesinger from the board of her journal, *The Translator*, and Gideon Toury from the board of her journal, *Translation Studies Abstracts* – because of their institutional connections to Israeli universities. Both have long and distinguished records as campaigners for human rights and for peace in Israel and Palestine.[87]

In May 2003, Sue Blackwell proposed a motion (Woodward 2003) at AUT (Association of University Teachers) Council asking members to sever 'any academic links they may have with official Israeli institutions, including universities'. AUT Council discussed the motion and it was comfortably defeated.

In June 2003, Andrew Wilkie rejected[88] the application of an Israeli PhD student to study at Oxford University because he was Israeli and had therefore served in the armed forces.

In April 2005, Sue Blackwell came back to AUT Council with what she said[89] was a more sophisticated and tactical attempt to win a boycott. She proposed to boycott

---

[86] UMIST, University of Manchester Institute of Science and Technology, subsequently merged with Manchester University.

[87] Mona Baker's 'personal statement' is available on her website at http://www.mona baker.com/personalstatement.htm, downloaded 14 February 2007, together with links to the correspondence she had with the woman who had been her friend, Miriam Shlesinger, and her letter to Gideon Toury. She writes: 'In May 2002, following the sharp rise in the level of atrocities committed against the Palestinian population in the West Bank and Gaza, I decided to join the call to boycott Israeli academic institutions. The boycott was conceived along the same lines as the sanctions which ultimately led to the collapse of the apartheid regime in South Africa. The call was initiated by Professor Steven Rose (Physics, Open University) and Professor Hilary Rose (Bradford University). ... I first wrote to Miriam Shlesinger (Bar Ilan University, Israel) on 23 May explaining my decision and asking her to resign from the Editorial Board of *The Translator*. She refused. I also wrote to Gideon Toury (Tel Aviv University, Israel) on 8 June along the same lines, asking him to resign from the panel of Consulting Editors of *Translation Studies Abstracts*. He too refused. I removed them both from the boards of the respective journals.'

[88] 'Andrew Wilkie, the Nuffield professor of pathology and a fellow of Pembroke College, is under investigation after telling Amit Duvshani, a student at Tel Aviv university, that he and many other British academics were not prepared to take on Israelis because of the "gross human rights abuses" he claims that they inflict on Palestinians. Prof Wilkie made the comments after Mr Duvshani, 26, wrote to him requesting the opportunity to work in Prof Wilkie's laboratory towards a PhD thesis. Mr Duvshani, who is in the last months of a master's degree in molecular biology, included a CV detailing his academic and outside experience, including his mandatory three-year national service in the Israeli army.... In a reply sent by email on June 23, Prof Wilkie wrote: "Thank you for contacting me, but I don't think this would work. I have a huge problem with the way that the Israelis take the moral high ground from their appalling treatment in the Holocaust, and then inflict gross human rights abuses on the Palestinians because they [the Palestinians] wish to live in their own country. I am sure that you are perfectly nice at a personal level, but no way would I take on somebody who had served in the Israeli army. As you may be aware, I am not the only UK scientist with these views but I'm sure you will find another lab if you look around."' (Henry 2003)

[89] 'It's a tactical attempt to get it through,' admits Birmingham's Sue Blackwell, one of the motion's authors. 'We've got to be a bit more sophisticated. We are now better organised. One

three particular Israeli universities. She also said that she now had a 'clear call from Palestinians'. There was a truncated debate at Council that did not include speeches against the motion. AUT Council voted to boycott Bar-Ilan University, citing its links with Ariel College in the occupied West Bank.[90] It also voted to boycott Haifa University on the basis of allegations concerning academic freedom centring on the Teddy Katz case and on claims made by an anti-Zionist academic at Haifa University, Ilan Pappe.[91] Finally, AUT Council voted to 'refer back' proposals to boycott Hebrew University, Jerusalem, on the basis of a claim that the university was building a new dorm block on Palestinian land.[92]

About a hundred, mainly Jewish, academics resigned from AUT (see, for example, Lappin 2005). More might have resigned but for a group who formed the Engage network and website,[93] which argued that the vote could be reversed only if academics remained within the union (see Geras 2005 for the opposite case).

Jon Pike, a founder of Engage and a philosophy lecturer at the Open University, organized the required signatures of Council members to force the union to hold a Special Council to re-examine the issue of the boycotts. Debates were held up and down the country in AUT local associations. The boycotters did not win their position in any of these debates.

In May 2005, there was a five-hour debate at the Special Council meeting on the issue. This meeting was better attended than any routine council meeting and was connected to the opinions of members by the preceding debates. Special Council decided to rescind the boycotts and to set up a Special Commission to work out a policy. In April 2006, AUT's Special Commission, in part directly elected by union members, proposed a consistent and thought-through policy[94] that related to international 'greylisting' and boycotts. It was a policy that left open the possibility of boycotting universities but set forward a consistent procedure to be followed. Crucially, a university, it recommended, can only be boycotted if the academic union at that institution calls for it. AUT Council in 2006 adopted these recommendations as policy, but the policy fell shortly afterwards, when AUT merged with NATFHE, the National Association of Teachers in Further and Higher Education.[95]

---

of the reasons we didn't win last time was that there was no clear public call from Palestinians for the boycott. Now we have that, in writing.' (Curtis 2005)

[90] For a presentation of the case against Bar-Ilan University, see Avnery (2005). For a discussion of the issue and of Avnery's case, see Hirsh (2005).

[91] For a presentation of the case against Haifa University, see Zalman (2005). For Haifa University's response through its solicitor, Anthony Julius, see the Haifa University website at http://boycottnews.haifa.ac.il/html/html_eng/AUT.pdf, downloaded 14 February 2005.

[92] For the case against The Hebrew University, see Yamada (2004). For The Hebrew University's reply through its lawyer, Anthony Julius, see http://www.engageonline.org.uk/archives/index.php?id=46.

[93] See http://www.liberoblog.com (no longer operational) and later http://www.engageonline.org.uk. For more on the birth of Engage, see Hirsh (2005a).

[94] See Document, Association of University Teachers (2005), http://www.aut.org.uk/circulars/html/la7753.html, downloaded 14 February 2007.

[95] Jon Pike (2005; 2006b), who was a member of the Special Commission, discusses the issues underlying the debates around 'greylisting' policy and defines his distinction between boycott as solidarity and boycott as punishment, or voluntary and non-voluntary boycott.

At its last conference, three days before the merger, NATFHE voted for a motion at its conference to boycott those Israeli academics who do not 'publicly dissociate themselves' from 'Israel's apartheid policies'. The leadership of AUT and NATFHE responded by saying that this policy did not stand in the new union.

In May 2006, Richard Seaford of Exeter University refused to review a book for an Israeli journal saying: 'I have, along with many other British academics, signed the academic boycott of Israel, in the face of the brutal and illegal expansionism, and the slow-motion ethnic cleansing, being practised by your government.' (Halkin 2006)

In April 2007, the conference of the National Union of Journalists passed a motion that instructed its executive committee to:

> continue to support the work of the Palestine Solidarity Campaign including the organisation of boycotts of Israeli goods, similar to those boycotts in the struggle against apartheid South Africa.[96]

Following this decision of the NUJ conference, many journalists and institutions protested at the decision, often calling for a ballot of members, including the editor of *The Guardian*;[97] the Foreign Press Association;[98] *The Guardian* leader;[99] petitions of NUJ members at BBC News[100] and ITN;[101] Jon Snow, news anchor at Channel 4 news;[102] BBC London NUJ branch;[103] NUJ chapel at Reuters;[104] and NUJ Manchester branch.[105] What took the wind out of the sails of this campaign to reverse the boycott decision in NUJ, however, was the decision made at UCU (University and College Union) Congress in June.

In June 2007, the first congress of the new merged union voted to support the boycott campaign. It instructed the National Executive to:

- circulate the full text of the Palestinian boycott call to all branches/LAs for information and discussion;
- encourage members to consider the moral implications of existing and proposed links with Israeli academic institutions;
- organise a UK-wide campus tour for Palestinian academic/educational trade unionists;
- issue guidance to members on appropriate forms of action.

It also passed its version of the *Livingstone formulation*: 'criticism of Israel cannot be construed as anti-Semitic.' Congress affirmed this after a delegate had read out the following example of antisemitic 'criticism' of Israel during the debate, from Hassan Nasrallah, leader of Hezbollah:

---

[96] The text of NUJ motion is available on the Engage website at: http://www.engageonline.org.uk/blog/article.php?id=967.
[97] http://www.haaretz.com/hasen/spages/849987.html.
[98] http://www.fpa.org.il/?categoryId=14190.
[99] http://www.guardian.co.uk/leaders/story/0,,2061527,00.html.
[100] http://www.engageonline.org.uk/blog/article.php?id=985.
[101] http://www.engageonline.org.uk/blog/article.php?id=991.
[102] http://www.totallyjewish.com/news/national/?content_id=6186.
[103] http://stopnujboycott.blogspot.com/2007/05/london-branch-calls-for-ballot.html.
[104] http://www.engageonline.org.uk/fighting/article.php?id=39.
[105] http://www.engageonline.org.uk/fighting/article.php?id=40.

If we searched the entire world for a person more cowardly, despicable, weak and feeble in psyche, mind, ideology and religion, we would not find anyone like the Jew. Notice, I do not say the Israeli. (This quote comes originally from Saad-Ghorayeb 2002: 170.)

High profile Jewish supporters of the boycott campaign played an important role. Their repeated assurances that antisemitism was not a relevant issue succeeded in neutralizing it as a factor in the debate. From the *Independent Jewish Voices* initiative in February, to the BRICUP fringe meeting at Bournemouth, to the debate itself at UCU Congress, respectable and senior Jewish academics, intellectuals and political activists repeated again and again when considering the plan to boycott Israeli academia – and only Israeli academia – that antisemitism was relevant only insofar as it was a spurious charge that 'Zionists' or the 'pro-Israel lobby' would throw at 'critics of Israel'. The message was repeated by Jacqueline Rose, Jonathan Rosenhead, John Rose, Rosemary Bechler, Steven Rose, Hilary Rose, Michael Cushman, Haim Bresheeth, Ilan Pappe, Jews for Justice for Palestinians, Independent Jewish Voices, Brian Klug and Antony Lerman. Furthermore, this message was repeated by these people and groups not just on the basis that they thought it to be true, but on the basis that they speak 'as Jews'. When these well-respected and high-profile antiracist Jews reassure the British intelligentsia that there is not a contemporary threat of antisemitism, we should not be surprised that they are believed. Not all of the above individuals and organizations support boycotts. But they all argue that it is legitimate to have an on-going debate about whether Israelis should be excluded, and they all agree that allegations of antisemitism are wildly and dishonestly exaggerated. The role they played in helping to get UCU to support the boycott campaign was not to make the argument for a boycott: it was to help to neutralize the issue of antisemitism.

The slogan that 'criticism of Israel cannot be construed as antisemitism' should be reversed, because, in truth, antisemitism cannot be construed as criticism of Israeli actions or policies. Antisemitism is not critical, it is necessarily mendacious, cannot help Palestinians and demands no critical response from those against whom it is directed.

UNISON,[106] the biggest union in Britain before the merger of AMICUS and the T&G (Transport and General Workers Union) to form UNITE, decided to make its support for the boycott campaign clear on 20 June 2007: 'Conference believes that ending the occupation demands concerted and sustained pressure upon Israel

---

[106] In UNISON, the hunt to root out 'Zionism' began even before the vote to support the boycott campaign. LabourStart is an international trade union network and website that carries news and publishes calls for trade union solidarity and reports on activity. UNISON had asked Eric Lee, the editor of LabourStart, what it could do to help, so Eric asked for a donation of £2000. The international affairs committee agreed and the decision to ratify this went to the national executive. Eric Lee: 'A member of the executive said they had three questions for me: was it true that I was a Zionist?; does LabourStart censor Palestinian news?; and had I supported the Israeli invasion of Lebanon last year?' Mr Lee responded: 'It is no secret that I am a left-wing Zionist, as are many Israelis. LabourStart has links to Palestinian sites and they take many of our news items, and I took the same view of Lebanon as did Tony Blair and the Labour government. 'The [question of the] donation was then sent back to the first [international affairs] committee.' The issue of the donation went back to the executive a second time, 'but they decided it was too controversial so they turned it down. See http://www.thejc.com/home.aspx?ParentId=m11s18&SecId=18&AId=53345&ATypeId=1.

including an economic, cultural, academic and sporting boycott.' Tony Greenstein, an anti-Zionist activist who had been steadfastly making the same speeches for 30 years, that Zionism is racism, that the Zionists collaborated with the Nazis, that Israel must be dismantled, suddenly found himself being given a standing ovation by UNISON Conference for a speech in favour of the boycott. 'I was overwhelmed by the reaction of delegates,' he said.[107] The T&G section of UNITE also passed policy supporting the boycott campaign in July 2007.

2. A critical examination of the debate over an academic boycott of Israel

At the 2005 AUT conference where the decision was made (later to be reversed) to boycott Bar-Ilan and Haifa universities, the case for a boycott was made in a very straightforward way. Advocates of the boycott stood up and made emotional speeches about how difficult life is in Palestine under Israeli occupation. They pointed to ways in which the human rights abuses committed against Palestinians are legal under Israeli law, and they therefore declared that Israeli institutional racism constitutes apartheid. 'We know what to do with an apartheid state,' say the boycott advocates, 'we boycott it.' 'We are academics so we are therefore under an obligation to boycott Israeli colleagues as a gesture of solidarity with Palestine.'

The PACBI case for a boycott relies heavily on the analogy with apartheid South Africa. Emphasis is thus taken off the case for boycott itself, because the case for boycotting apartheid South Africa, including its academics, is taken as a given truth by the majority of the antiracist audience of the boycott campaign. So, once PACBI succeeds in characterizing Israel as an 'apartheid' state, support for the boycott follows automatically.[108]

A. The political test

One difficulty for the boycott campaign is how to respond to criticism that an academic boycott would exclude opponents of Israeli human rights abuses – Jewish, Christian or Muslim – who work at Israeli universities. One way of solving this problem is to offer a political test which, if the academic passes, would lead to immunity from the boycott.

The 2006 NATFHE motion offered such a test when it suggested that the union should backlist members who 'do not publicly dissociate themselves' from Israel's 'apartheid policies' (Pike 2006). The problem with this method is that the boycott campaign then lays itself open to criticism that it is undermining academic freedom with a 'McCarthyite test'. The boycott would be targeted against people who were not ready to sign up to the required beliefs in public and under threat. Steve Cohen (2006) argues as follows:

> Loyalty tests have a particular significance when forced on Jews. The significance is the assumption of collective responsibility, of collective guilt. Intrinsic to this is the requirement to grovel. Grovelling, the humiliation of Jews, is fundamental to all antisemitism....

---

[107] http://www.thejc.com/home.aspx?ParentId=m12s30&SecId=30&AId=53602&ATypeId=1.
[108] PACBI makes its case for a boycott, relying on the apartheid analogy, on its website in a 'Frequently Asked Questions' format, http://www.pacbi.org/faqs.htm, downloaded 14 February 2007. See Hirsh (2006) for a rebuttal.

What was important [under McCarthyism] was naming names – the degradation ceremony. Likewise the deep antisemitism behind the NATFHE resolution is not the boycott principle. It is the loyalty test on which it is based. It is the loyalty test more than anything else which exceptionalises Israel.... It may be that the loyalty test was clumsily added as a 'compromise' against a blanket boycott. So what? It doesn't make it any less antisemitic in its consequences.

The boycott campaign was always reluctant to say what kind of bureaucracy it was in favour of setting up to oversee exceptions on political grounds. In the steadfast absence of such a proposal, it is reasonable to assume that the idea was that the decent people who were implementing the boycott would simply know who should be made an exception to the exclusion. It seems unlikely that a boycott with a political test, therefore, would have been implemented against non-Jews or against anti-Zionist Jews at Israeli universities. The boundary might have been drawn in a particularly haphazard way, on a case-by-case basis.[109]

The political test would have functioned as a net with which to catch Israeli 'Zionists' and would have been based on the assumption that being a 'Zionist' is not compatible with being a decent, ethical academic. One logical extension, which the NATFHE motion allowed, although presumably through bad drafting more than through design, was the possibility of extending the campaign against 'Zionist' academics outside Israel. If the principle is established that we do not do business with Israeli Zionists, then some may be tempted to extend the reach of the boycott to 'Zionists' who happen to work outside of Israel. This prospect is less remote when we remember that there have been campaigns to 'no platform' 'Zionists', as though they were racists, from student unions; also when we remember that a boycott policy would not always be implemented by people as sophisticated as the antiracists who run the boycott campaign.

An academic who comes originally from Poland and who now lives and works in the United Kingdom said that the rhetoric of the boycotters reminded him of events in Poland in March 1968, the year following the beginning of the Israeli occupation. Under the cover of solidarity with Palestinians, and using the rhetoric of anti-Zionism, the Polish state had purged the Jewish intelligentsia. Jewish intellectuals were challenged to declare themselves anti-Zionist. Most of them refused, and many left the country. Poland lost a large number of its thinkers, teachers, writers, and researchers. For this individual at least, the current boycott proposals resonated strongly with echoes of older antisemitic campaigns.[110]

B. Institutional boycott

The political test thus tends to create more problems for the boycott campaign than it solves. Another way around the problem is therefore to sacrifice the 'exceptional Israelis', who would in any case be happy to make such a sacrifice, and to argue for an 'institutional boycott'.

This is an attempt to depersonalize the issue. It is an attempt to make it more difficult for opponents to characterize the boycott as a campaign against Israeli Jews

---

[109] The political test has echoes of the designation of the 'exceptional Jew' that was part and parcel of most antisemitic parties prior to the development of Nazism.

[110] Personal correspondence with the author, 13 May 2005 and 16 May 2005.

or as an exclusion from campuses, journals or conferences. It becomes a campaign against institutions and not against individuals. Israeli individuals will continue to be welcome members of the academic community so long as they do not appear in the name of their institutions, are not funded by their institutions and do not attempt to host events at their institutions.

In his rebuttal of this institutional turn, Jon Pike (2006a) makes two central points. Firstly, it is rare for academic institutions to produce research outputs: papers are written by individuals, presentations are made by individuals and conferences are attended by individuals. So, he argues, the reality of an institutional boycott would still be an exclusion of individuals. Further, in an argument reminiscent of one against the political test, he asks how the distinction between institutions and individuals will actually be made in practice:

> [The] covert boycott (a 'quiet stand' according to BRICUP) is, of course, denuded of a political message. But also, there is no mechanism of accountability for their actions. They claim that there is a difference between an institutional boycott and an individual boycott, and I think that there's no difference. But we won't be able to know whether or not there is an operable distinction, because the operation is now conducted in secret. We won't be able to know whether people engage in Wilkie type actions (without the incriminating email). And I guess, the boycotters who think it's OK to adopt an 'institutional' rather than an 'individual' boycott simply think we should trust them on that one. (Pike 2006a)

Sue Blackwell, an outspoken supporter of the boycott campaign has threatened to sue people involved in Engage for defamation, because they wrote that that she is an 'outspoken supporter of the campaign to exclude Israeli academics from UK campuses'. She responded:

> you know very well that while I am certainly an outspoken supporter of the campaign to boycott Israeli institutions, I have NEVER campaigned to 'exclude Israeli academics from UK campuses'.

Interestingly, she goes on to admit that such a campaign would, indeed, be illegal:

> Considering that such an action would be illegal (discrimination on the grounds of nationality) and that you are thereby accusing me of advocating a course of action which would be in breach of the law, I consider your remark defamatory.

Blackwell was referring to an email from Jon Pike that publicly drew analogies between a case of institutional discrimination at Birmingham University, where the closure of courses had impacted disproportionately on ethnic minority staff, and Blackwell's proposed 'institutional' boycott, which, he argued, would also act disproportionately against Israelis and Jews. So is it reasonable to describe Sue Blackwell as 'an outspoken supporter of the campaign to exclude Israeli academics from UK campuses' when she claims that she is only for a boycott of Israeli institutions, not for a boycott of any human beings?

Sue Blackwell has supported campaigns for exclusions of individual Israeli academics from global academia. Blackwell carries on her website[111] a number of

---

[111] http://www.sue.be/pal/academic/boycott.html.

articles about, and by, both Andrew Wilkie (Layfield 2003) and Mona Baker,[112] under the title 'Academic and cultural boycott of Israel, divestment etc.' It is already clear that Blackwell understands the actions of these two people, who did want exclude individual Israelis, one from his campus and the other from her journal, as being part of the general campaign that she supports. On another part of her website,[113] Blackwell outlines her tactical disagreement with Mona Baker as follows:

> I try to draw a distinction between institutions and individuals: the target is the Israeli government, not ordinary citizens. Of course it's a slippery distinction, as Mona Baker herself points out: in fact it's impossible to boycott an institution without in some way affecting the individuals who work for it. I take her point, but nonetheless I try not to target individuals as far as possible. So I draw the line in a different place from Mona; all the same I respect her right to draw her own line where her conscience tells her to, and I think the witch-hunt against her is disgusting.

Blackwell is very clear. The 'institutional boycott' does affect individuals, the distinction is 'slippery' and impossible to maintain clearly in the real world, and an 'institutional boycott' does exclude individual Israeli academics. Blackwell is also clear that she sees herself as being part of the same campaign as Mona Baker (i.e. the campaign to exclude Israeli individuals from UK campuses, journals and conferences) and that she supports Baker against the 'disgusting' 'witch-hunt' inspired by Baker's exclusion of individuals. Now Blackwell admits that the sacking of individuals because of their nationality 'would be illegal (discrimination on the grounds of nationality)'. At the time when Baker was sacking Israelis, she called the angry response to the discrimination a 'witch-hunt'. Blackwell says that she supports only an 'institutional' boycott. But when somebody sacks individuals because they are Israeli, she supports them.

Blackwell then goes on to explain that she believes that Baker's exclusion of Israeli individuals in any case only constitutes an 'institutional boycott':

> She is not boycotting all Israeli academics, let alone all Jewish academics; she is boycotting people who are employed by Israeli institutions, whatever their nationality, ethnicity or religion.

In 2005, Blackwell supported the AUT motion that proposed the exclusion of academics from global academia who worked at three Israeli institutions. 'Conscientious Israeli academics and intellectuals opposed to their state's colonial and racist policies' were to be recognized as exceptional and excused from the boycott – the political test is a weapon aimed at individuals, not at institutions. It is true that Blackwell is not for the exclusion of all Israeli academics – only the ones who work in Israel; and it is true that she is not for the exclusion of only Israeli academics – she says that she is for the exclusion of any academic who is connected to an Israeli institution. However, it is difficult to imagine a Palestinian or Arab academic, with an institutional affiliation to an Israeli university, being targeted by the boycott campaign in the United Kingdom. They may well be targeted by the boycotters in Palestine, as collaborators, but that is a different issue.

---

[112] http://www.monabaker.com/personalstatement.htm.
[113] http://www.sue.be/pal/FAQs.html.

In defending herself against the charge of promoting a policy that is racist in effect if not in intent, a policy that in reality would exclude Israeli Jewish academics vastly more than anybody else, she does not make a convincing case. This is where the discussion started – Blackwell has shown herself to understand full well the concept of unintended or institutional racism against black and other minority staff at her own university, but she rejects the same way of thinking if it involves the unintended or institutional exclusion of Israelis or Jews.

C. Academic freedom

The standard liberal argument against a boycott of Israeli academia is based on the principle that such a boycott would violate the norms of academic freedom. Blakemore et al. (2003) published a general articulation of this argument against scientific boycotts[114] in *Nature*, arguing that such a boycott would be illegitimate except for in the most extreme cases. Michael Yudkin (2007), one of the authors of the *Nature* article updated the argument in 2007, broadening it out to cover academic boycotts in general rather than just scientific boycotts, and also focusing it on the question of Israel in particular. He argues:

> The principle of the Universality of Science and Learning – that academics do not discriminate against colleagues on the basis of factors that are irrelevant to their academic work (such as race, religion, nationality, etc.) – is well established and almost universally respected. To boycott academics by reason of their country of residence breaches this principle and harms the interests of the academics concerned.

In this article, Yudkin goes beyond a straightforward defence of academic freedom to challenge a number of the arguments put forward by those who support an academic boycott of Israel.

Howard Jacobson (2007) tells that a supporter of the boycott campaign wrote to him denying that they threatened the academic freedom of Israelis. He was not in favour of gagging or silencing Israeli voices but merely of refusing to listen to them. Jacobson argues that refusing to listen, closing your ears, is not primarily an act of violence against the speaker but is in the first place an act of violence against oneself:

> To say you intend knowingly and purposefully and on principle 'not to listen' is to say you are waging a sort of war on your own faculties, because listening, if you are a reasoning person, is chief amongst the tools you reason with. Most of what Socrates did was listen. No longer to listen is no longer to engage in the dialogue of thought. Which disqualifies you as a scholar and a teacher, for what sort of example to his pupils is a teacher who covers truth's ears and buries it under stone. A university that will not listen does far more intellectual damage to itself than to the university it has stopped listening to. (Jacobson 2007)

Anthony Julius and Alan Dershowitz (2007) make the same point in a different way:

---

[114] Two prestigious scientific journals have recently opened 'debates' on whether to exclude Israelis. *New Scientist* did so with an editorial on 9 June 2007 entitled 'Should scientists boycott Israel?' and the *British Medical Journal* did so with pieces for and against the boycott in its 21 July 2007 issue.

freedom of expression must incorporate freedom of address. It is not sufficient for my freedom of expression for me simply to be free to speak. What matters to me is that people should also be free to hear me. There should at least be the possibility of dialogue. Boycotts put a barrier in front of the speaker. He can speak but he is prevented from communicating. When he addresses another, that other turns away.

The point here is that the harm of the academic boycott begins at home. The boycott intends to harm Israeli universities, and it may or may not, in the end, succeed in this aspiration. But it definitely and immediately harms the universities doing the boycotting or the universities in which the campaign for the exclusion of academic colleagues rages. In hosting the false claim that Israeli universities are not genuine universities and should be shunned, British universities face the danger that their own status as universities will be degraded.

When challenged about why Israeli academics are singled out for punishment while academics in other human rights abusing states are not, many boycotters respond that they would also support boycotts against the other states if somebody was to organize them and if the oppressed in those states were to call for it. It is true that if there were boycotts of academics in all states that abuse human rights as much as, or more than Israel, then the academic boycott would no longer be effectively antisemitic. It would, however, indicate the end of the academic project and the end of the university. The aspiration to international scholarly and scientific cooperation would be rendered vain.

Judith Butler (2006) argues that a liberal abstract notion of academic freedom is not sufficient to make sense of the boycott debate. While Palestinian academics and students may enjoy an abstract right to academic freedom, the material conditions necessary for the enjoyment of those rights do not exist under occupation, she argues:

> [S]tudents and faculty at institutions on the West Bank are regularly stopped at checkpoints and fail to get to class; they are often without fundamental material support for schooling, even lacking classrooms and basic supplies, and are subject to sudden closures that make the idea of a completed 'semester' almost unthinkable. Indeed, substantive notions of freedom of 'movement' and freedom of 'communication' are systematically undermined under such conditions.

Many who argue for an academic boycott of Israel say that it is hypocritical for Israelis to insist on their own right to academic freedom while their state denies such freedom to Palestinians. Or as Steven Rose put it in a debate at Goldsmiths College UCU on 27 September 2006, Israelis are hypocritical to 'squeal' about their own academic freedom while the occupation continues to deny freedom to Palestinians. It should be noted here that this way of thinking risks setting the precedent that academics should be held responsible, and punished, for the policies of the government or state in which they work. Yet Butler is right to argue that academic freedom is severely limited in the occupied territories, not by a denial of the abstract right, but by the occupation, which renders academic freedom materially extremely difficult to realize. This is true even if it is one-sided since the universities of Palestine were also founded under Israeli occupation and did not exist before the Israeli occupation. There is a problem of academic freedom in Palestine. It is possible to respond to this by arbitrarily and artificially removing the academic freedom of

Israelis, as punishment, in order to balance the situation, or in an effort to exert pressure on Israel to respect Palestinian freedom. Or it is possible to respond to this by campaigning against the occupation and against the material denials of academic freedom that come with it. Butler does not argue that abstract academic freedom may be trumped by other more important rights, but the opposite:

> I do not mean to say that we cannot invoke academic freedom in the abstract to show its absence in certain political conditions: we can and we must. But it makes no sense to value the doctrine in the abstract if we cannot call for its implementation.

Butler is not arguing that one should balance an absence of material freedom in Palestine by regarding academic freedom in Israel to be unimportant; she argues that the principle of abstract freedom must be strengthened and deepened, made material by creating the conditions for its implementation.[115]

This is an old theme in radical and Marxist thought and it is perhaps a central indicator of the most important schism in that tradition, the one which divides totalitarian thought and politics from the politics and philosophy of self-liberation. The totalitarian traditions fight for uncompromising critiques of abstract right; they hold law, democracy, freedom of speech and human rights to be worse than useless to the disempowered. Formal equality is, in these traditions, nothing but the form of rule of power. It hides illegitimate exploitation behind an ideology of fairness, behind the American dream. Men dominate women through the phallocentric notion of abstract equality; the bourgeoisie rules over the poor and exploited through the class-ridden hypocrisy of equality before the law; imperialist states legitimize their wars of interest with the cry of human rights. This is the really radical tradition; not only does it see bourgeois rights as being promised but denied to the majority; it sees bourgeois rights as the very form of rule of illegitimate power.

Marx himself was entirely explicit in his own critique of this vulgar and dangerous 'Marxism'. In *On the Jewish Question* (1994), he defended bourgeois rights – in this case the right to religious freedom for Jews – uncompromisingly against an argument that offered a much more 'radical' critique of society. Against Bruno Bauer, who argued that Jews did not need religious freedom but really needed to free themselves of their religion, Marx argued for a framework that takes rights seriously but is not satisfied with their purely abstract nature in society as it exists. Far from seeing rights as something unimportant or positively dangerous, Marx's position was that radicals should fight for rights and should fight to extend them beyond the purely abstract. His was a project of making rights real for all, not one of scoffing at those who 'squeal' about their rights.[116]

---

[115] Butler (2006) also makes this remarkable claim: 'many of the Israelis most vocal in their opposition to the Occupation, such as Ilan Pappe, were also those who were saying "boycott me!"' This claim is wrong in two ways. Firstly, it is not true to say that 'many' of the most vocal Israeli opponents of the Occupation support the boycott – in truth only a handful of vocal Israeli opponents of the Occupation support the boycott and the vast majority of vocal Israeli opponents of the Occupation oppose the boycott. Secondly, it is misleading to characterize Pappe as being an opponent of the Occupation since he does not distinguish between the Occupation and the rest of Israel; he believes it all to be illegitimately occupied territory.

[116] See Robert Fine (2006) who argues that those who read Marx himself as an antisemite are quite wrong.

The boycott campaign sees academic freedom in Israel and throughout the globe as being something that may be legitimately sacrificed for the greater good of ending the occupation; academic freedom, they argue, is part of the ideological armoury brought to bear against those who fight the occupation. I would argue the opposite. The concept of academic freedom is important in itself but it does not go far enough; a material conception of academic freedom is necessary to go beyond the critique of the boycott all the way to a fight for freedom in the West Bank. Academic freedom is not a principle that we should reject because sometimes it fails to deliver what it promises; rather, we should fight to hold it to its promise.

D. Damage to UCU

As the violence done to the principle of academic freedom is felt first in the boycotting university, so does antisemitism strike first there too. The boycott is not caused or motivated by an underlying antisemitism, but is itself a cause or a catalyst or a licence for antisemitism to emerge; it is also, in itself, an antisemitic policy. The boycott 'debate' launches the boycotters into a fight against the vast majority of Jews who oppose their campaign to exclude Israelis and who experience their campaign as an antisemitic attack. True, many boycotters are Jews, but not many Jews are boycotters. No matter how often and how loudly Jewish boycotters speak 'as Jews', no matter how hard they struggle to neutralize antisemitism as an issue in the 'debate', no matter how desperately they insist that the Jewish community is split on the issue, they do not succeed: the Jewish community is not really split and antisemitism is an issue in the 'debate'.

So the appearance of the campaign to exclude Israelis from our campuses brings with it a toxic atmosphere. People who oppose the boycott are portrayed as pro-imperialist, pro-Zionist, pro-apartheid, uncaring of Palestinian suffering, supporters of the occupation and users of the charge of antisemitism as a dishonest smoke screen. And most of the people thus accused are Jews. With the campaign to exclude Israelis comes a campaign to libel Jewish academics and Jewish union members, Jewish students too. Not all Israelis are to be excluded; not all Jews are to be libelled; not all those to be excluded are Jews; not all those who are libelled are Jews; but Nazism was an unusual and exceptional antisemitism insofar as it allowed no exceptions, no exceptional Jews, no good Jews.

The boycott campaign threatens the principle of the university as well as the principle of the trades union. It is not a coincidence that many of those who consider themselves to be on the left of the trade union movement are pushing this campaign against Israelis at a moment when trade unions have never been less able to deliver on their core business. UCU is supposed to fight for the pay and conditions of people who work in universities and colleges and for the principle of education in Britain. For those who have raised 'anti-imperialism' far above all other radical principles, the fact that the union is unable to win on bread-and-butter trade union issues is less important than the project of joining in the global struggle against imperialism alongside the 'resistance' in Iraq, Hamas and Hezbollah, Chavez, Castro and Ahmadinejad.

At the same Bournemouth conference that passed the motion to support the campaign for an academic boycott of Israel, another motion was passed that illustrates this point clearly. An amendment was proposed to add the following text to the motion opposing the war in Iraq:

> The various so-called resistance forces have regularly killed trade union, women's and LGBT activists. The 'resistance' groups – various types of Ba'athist-fascist and Islamist organisation – are unremittingly hostile to the new labour movement.

This text was removed and replaced with the following:

> The 650,000+ excess civilian deaths in Iraq since 2003 and the destruction of civil society, including the attacks on trade unionists, women and LGBT people, derive directly from the presence of occupying US and UK forces – practically, morally and legally under the Geneva Conventions.

A stark illustration of the importance of this political disagreement was provided by Hamas, which on 18 July 2007 looted and smashed up the Palestinian General Federation of Trade Unions office in Gaza and summoned trades unionists for 'interrogation'.[117]

UCU still represents university and college staff on national pay-scales and in national negotiations. This is an achievement that is under threat. The elite universities, the Russell Group, would like to break away from this framework, pay their elite staff better, and let the rest of the sector sink or change from being universities into being feeder schools for postgraduate study at research-active institutions. In 2006, university staff were involved in 'action short of a strike' in pursuit of a pay claim. This campaign ended inconclusively when unity began to crumble under pressure. The employers settled for a small increase in pay and the union came out of the action intact and with national bargaining still in place.

The context of the boycott 'debate' is a union where unity is crucial to the achievement of its core aims; a moment when trade union unity might mean the difference between a national education system and a completely marketized system; a moment when the very existence of a union that represents all college workers is under threat. This is the moment that the pro-boycott 'left' chooses to divide the union between those who know how to recognize the smell of anti-semitism and those who cannot recognize it or who refuse to sniff the air.

In 2005, when AUT had a policy of boycotting Haifa University and Bar-Ilan University, and there was a possibility of boycotting the Hebrew University of Jerusalem too, there were a number of serious legal threats to the union. Given that much of the pretext for these boycotts was false, AUT was in a position where it was spreading libel against globally respected academic institutions. Anthony Julius, who had successfully represented Deborah Lipstadt against Holocaust denier David Irving, represented both Haifa University and the Hebrew University. Julius wrote to AUT threatening legal action for defamation.[118] These kinds of threats, given the archaic legal framework governing defamation law in England, were threats that might have bankrupted the union. Some trade unionists argue that it is illegitimate

---

[117] http://www.engageonline.org.uk/blog/article.php?id=1271, downloaded 25 July 2007.
[118] The letter to Haifa is available here: http://boycottnews.haifa.ac.il/htmI/htmI_eng/AUT.pdf. The letter to The Hebrew University is available here: http://www.engageonline.org.uk/archives/index.php?id=46.

to threaten legal action in a trade union dispute, to run to the 'bourgeois' courts to settle a labour movement dispute; but it seems clear enough that trade unions have a legal duty not to push defamatory claims about entirely respectable universities, and those universities have every right to defend themselves by legal means.

Many UCU members have resigned from the union over its support for the boycott. Many, like Shalom Lappin, have done so openly and have given their reasons publicly.[119] It is likely that many others have simply stopped paying their dues, forgotten to renew their membership or decided not to join in the first place. In these ways, Jews and antiracists (people who oppose antisemitism) are being pushed out of UCU. Shalom Lappin is a serious left Zionist, a person whose adult life has been spent fighting for peace between Israel and Palestine, fighting for workers' rights through trade unions and fighting for political change through authentic social democratic politics. Lappin has had enough of standing in the dock within UCU and defending the right of our Israeli colleagues to be treated as human beings by us. Nobody else needs such a defence. He argues that the debate about whether to exclude Israelis is illegitimate – in the same way that a debate over whether or not the Holocaust happened is illegitimate, or a debate about whether women have souls. He refuses to legitimate such a debate by taking part or by remaining in a union where such a debate is raging.

The sections of the left that ceaselessly push the boycott debate, that respond to defeats by pushing it once more, that treat the campaign to boycott Israel as though it were the most important political task in the world, are risking the very future of the union.

E. Damage to Palestine

Palestine is in crisis. Hamas won a parliamentary election and carried out a successful coup against the Palestinian presidency in Gaza. The occupation is intensifying, the wall is being completed, the checkpoints are as numerous and humiliating as ever and the Israeli settlements are growing and multiplying.

In Britain, in 2007, the Palestine solidarity movement rebranded itself by building a new broad organization called the 'Enough Coalition'. Many legitimate civil society organizations have signed up to this coalition, such as the charity 'War on Want', the green pressure group 'Friends of the Earth', the Transport and General Workers Union and Amicus (now merged into UNITE) and the public service workers union, UNISON. The Enough Coalition calls itself 'a campaign for a just peace for all people in Israel and Palestine'[120] yet while presenting itself as a coalition against the occupation, it fails to affirm Israel's right to exist within the pre-1967 borders. Indeed it clearly implies, in its mission statement,[121] that the descendents of the 1948 refugees should be 'allowed home', a demand that, understood in an unproblematized way, is incompatible with a two-state solution to the conflict between Israel and Palestine.

---

[119] See http://normblog.typepad.com/normblog/2007/06/responding_to_t.html and http://normblog.typepad.com/normblog/2007/06/why_ive_resigne.html.

[120] http://www.enoughoccupation.org/?lid=13695.

[121] http://www.enoughoccupation.org/Mission%20Statement%2013810.twl.

Even after this rebranding exercise, even while riding the wave of the media discussion focused around the 40th anniversary of the occupation, even during the summer in which much of the trade union movement has backed a boycott of Israel, even when the situation in Palestine continues to be desperate, the Palestine solidarity movement was unable to build mass support for its showpiece demonstration on 9 June 2007. 'Enough' claim that there were 20,000 people there, while other estimates are as low as 2,000.[122] Even if there were as many as ten or twenty thousand present, this represents a failure to broaden the movement from the narrow activist core into a mass protest reminiscent of those against apartheid South Africa in the 1980s, which attracted hundreds of thousands of marchers.

One hypothesis is that 'ordinary people' who have sympathy with the plight of the Palestinians are still put off these demonstrations by the smell of antisemitism that swirls around them. A number of groups that speak 'as Jews' were there, hoping that their presence would demonstrate that at least some Jews should not be hated for their 'Zionism': Jewish Socialist Group, Jews Against Zionism, Jews for Boycotting Israeli Goods and Jews for Justice for Palestinians. Yet the usual sprinkling of antisemitic placards was also present. George Galloway, who says that Jews are foreigners in Jerusalem, called for a boycott of Israel from the platform. The leader of the antisemitic Hamas movement in Palestine, Ismail Haniyeh, spoke via video link to the rally and was received enthusiastically.

Within the trade unions, the boycott 'debate' is not between those who support Israel and those who support Palestine, nor is it between Jews and Muslims. It is in fact almost entirely a debate amongst people who say that they support freedom for Palestinians. Some boycotters allege that anti-boycotters are lying when they say they support a Palestinian state; some anti-boycotters notice that many of the boycotters support the military conquest of Israel by Hamas and Hezbollah, an eventuality that they doubt would result in any kind of freedom either for Palestinians or for Israelis. But the overwhelming majority of those on both sides of the 'debate' hopes for a just peace and for freedom for Palestinians. But the boycott campaign splits in half those who support a just peace and who want to oppose the occupation. Discussion of Palestine and Israel has been almost entirely displaced by the completely different discussion about whether Israelis should be excluded from the cultural and economic life of the planet. The Palestine Solidarity Campaign has, for the last five years at least, been a campaign for the boycott of Israel and for the delegitimization of Israel.

A political goal of the boycott campaign is to have its own definition of a 'friend of Palestine' adopted as left commonsense. It defines a friend of Palestine as somebody who supports a boycott of Israelis and an enemy of Palestine as somebody who opposes a boycott of Israelis. So a whole layer of people who think of themselves as friends of Palestine, who work towards an end of the occupation, who support the peace movements in Israel and in Palestine, who oppose racism in both Israel and Palestine – these people are treated by the boycott campaign as enemies of Palestinians. In this way, the boycott campaign splits and disables Palestine solidarity work in Britain. In this way, the boycott campaign damages Palestine.

---

[122] http://www.jpost.com/servlet/Satellite?cid=1181228582339&pagename=JPost%2FJPArticle%2FshowFull.

F. Inconsistency: why boycott only Israel when there are many more serious human rights abusers on the planet?

A question that is often the first one to occur to somebody when they learn that there is a campaign to boycott Israel, is 'Why Israel?' There is genocide going on in Darfur as I write, and it has killed hundreds of thousands of people, as well as causing the death of hundreds of thousands more of the millions who have been displaced. There is a dictatorship ruling Zimbabwe that fails to feed its population and has organized hundreds of thousands of house demolitions in the last few years. China has been running a bloody and repressive occupation of Tibet for decades, has moved millions of its own settlers into Tibet and has deported hundreds of thousands of Tibetans to the Laogai camps, the Chinese version of the Gulag. Russia is running an occupation of Chechnya that has resulted in the deaths of countless thousands of Chechens, particularly during its reconquest of Grozny, the capital city, in the mid 1990s. There are very many states in the world where there are ethnic or gendered exclusions from citizenship, or systems of two-class citizenship, or systems whereby many of the people who do the work are defined as non-citizens or guest-workers. There are very many states in the world that came into being following ethnic struggles over territory and the forced movement of populations. There are many states in the world that are still fighting over pieces of territory with their neighbours. There are many states in the world where there is no freedom of the press, no freedom of speech and no functioning legal system. There are many places where trade unions and political parties are illegal and repressed. There are many places where there is no democracy. So, why, in British trade unions and in the pages of *The Guardian* and *The Independent*, why on British campuses and in the British left intelligentsia, are there campaigns only to punish Israel? Norman Geras (2005a) notices that the boycotters and the blacklisters all assure us that this is not about blank prejudice. It's about human rights, racism and what have you, and Israel just happens to be the privileged exemplar. But when you ask for a principled reason that picks out Israel, and Israel exclusively, not only can the boycotters and blacklisters not give one satisfactory reason, they do not even converge on a common reason. Now it's supposedly because they were called upon by Palestinian organizations. Now it's because no one has yet brought a resolution to AUT on China, or Sudan, or Chechnya, or Iran, or Zimbabwe, or Iraq (in Saddam's day), or the US (since then). Or else Israel is not a special case, but it is a case, and it's good enough if it is a case and this just happens to be the case we are focusing on. Or it's because of illegal occupation, or because of UN resolutions. Or it's because of racism, like with apartheid (or, *sotto voce*, and sometimes not so *sotto voce*, like with Nazi Germany). But for want of decent reasons, the boycotters have something unfortunately as powerful, and this is a fixed hostility towards the State of Israel.

Richard Kuper (2006) finds a number of reasons to single out Israel for particular criticism, although it should be noted that we are more interested here in reasons for singling out Israel for unique punishment than for criticism. Anyone may be criticized on particular grounds, but if someone is to be the only one punished then this must be because they are the only one worthy of punishment. Kuper admits that 'other states in the Middle East, such as Saudi Arabia or Iraq under Saddam Hussein, have been far greater violators of human rights' but he goes on to offer four reasons why Israel is 'legitimately singled out'.

First, Israel should not be judged against other states in the world but 'in terms of its own founding principles'. So Kuper proposes that it is reasonable to judge Israel as a 'light unto nations' and as a democratic state. Theological debate is beyond my competency (and beyond Kuper's too, I suspect), but it seems to me extremely threatening to imply that Israel should deserve unique punishment if it is judged to have failed to be the most moral and the best behaved state in the world (a light unto nations). Similarly the idea that Israel should be punished if it fails to live up to the promise of democracy, while states that are not democratic should not be so punished, has little to recommend it.

This argument, in fact, is one that holds the crime of hypocrisy to be the greatest crime imaginable, worse than genocide. But anyway, does Kuper really imagine that the official narrative of Israeli nationalism is the only one to make rather overblown claims? Does he imagine that North Korea should be judged not against international human rights and humanitarian norms, but according to how it fails to be the socialist paradise on earth that it is constitutionally bound to be?

Second, Kuper suggests that Israel should be judged according to different criteria than other states because it has, within its territory, a number of sites that are of special significance to Christians, Jews and Muslims worldwide. The claim here seems to be that the presence of such sites means that Israel's record on human rights abuses should be judged differently to that of other states. But Kuper does not go on to discuss how this principle of holding states with religious sites to different human rights standards would impact on other states that are the home to religious sites, such as Saudi Arabia.

Third, Israel is singled out by the United States for a particularly strong alliance. But Kuper does not explain why this fact should cause people concerned about human rights abuses to be more concerned about Israeli human rights abuses. Presumably this argument boils down to a charge of hypocrisy, this time levelled against the United States.

Fourth, Israel claims to be not just a state for its citizens, says Kuper, but also a state for all Jews. It exaggerates the danger of antisemitism in order to encourage Jews to identify with Israel, and it implicitly makes a charge of disloyalty against Jews who are critical of some of its policies. Kuper inverts the real situation here. Israel is open to all Jews for historical reasons connected to its birth following a serious outbreak of antisemitism in Europe, following the expulsion of Jews from the states of the Middle East and following the long experience of Russian antisemitism. Israel has been a refuge from antisemitism; it is one of the rather sad myths of anti-Zionism that Israel benefits from, invents, exaggerates and provokes antisemitism in order to encourage Jewish immigration.

It is true that any individual has every right to be concerned about whatever particular cause happens to engage them. But a trade union has a duty not to act whimsically or arbitrarily but consistently. A trade union should be concerned with human rights abuses, and it should try to do something about human rights abuses. It should not be concerned with and try to punish only one small set of human rights abuses.

When you get pulled over to the side of the road for speeding, and you stand with the self-righteous police officer while he is writing out the ticket, and you watch the succession of other cars driving past at the same speed you were doing, you are likely to experience a feeling of injustice. It is not, in truth, unjust. You were breaking the law, and you have been caught. In the long run, most of the others will eventually be caught and punished too if they carry on driving at that speed. But the boycott of Israel is not like this. The boycott would punish speeders, but not speeders at random and not every speeder. The boycott would punish nearly all Jewish speeders. It would find reasons to be much more concerned to punish Jewish speeders than any others. Many reasons would be proposed, and none of them would appear to be antisemitic.

Many nineteenth century socialists opposed capitalism; some of them singled out 'Jewish capitalism' for particular attention. Many people oppose street crime; some single out black muggers for particular attention. Many people oppose religious bigotry; some single out Islam for particular attention. Even then, it is possible and perhaps necessary to have a reasoned discussion about the relationship between Jews and capitalism, about the relationship between black kids and street crime and about the relationship between homophobia and Islam. But it is also possible for these relationships to function at the heart of a racist commonsense – possible and likely.

G. Universities as particular targets of the boycott campaign

There are two strands to the argument about why academics in particular should be boycotted. One is that there should be a general boycott of Israel and that, as part of that, academics around the world should boycott Israeli academics. The other is that Israeli academic institutions are themselves guilty, or particularly guilty, of facilitating, turning a blind eye to, legitimating and providing personnel for Israeli human rights abuses. The boycott campaign continues to recycle a number of libels and half-truths about Israeli academia. These are effective with an audience that knows little about Israel and less about Israeli universities. Both Haifa University and the Hebrew University have about 20% Arab students as well as significant numbers of Arab faculty members. This is a rate of inclusion of minorities that would shame many elite British institutions. Another common misrepresentations is that 'Israeli academics as a community – with some brave exceptions – are at best silent and at worst open in their advocacy' (Rose 2006) of Israel's immoral and illegal acts. The truth is that the universities are spaces in Israel where conflict is pursued through words and ideas rather than guns and bombs. They are amongst the most antiracist spaces in Israel; spaces where ideas for peace are forged, taught and practised.

Some academics will indeed be right-wing; some may be profoundly reactionary. That is the nature of an open, democratic and free education system. It is a system that also guarantees a safe, tenured chair for the extreme anti-Zionist Ilan Pappe, even when he calls upon the world to boycott his own colleagues and his own institution.

There is a list of names of hundreds of Israeli academics,[123] hardly brave exceptions, who publicly support those of their students who refuse to serve in the Israeli army in the occupied territories. The Oslo peace process, destroyed by Israeli and Arab extremists, was forged by links between Israeli and Palestinian academics.

---

[123] http://www.seruv.org.il/UniversitySupportEng_Print.asp.

Certainly there are institutional and other connections between Israeli universities and the armed forces and the defence industries; this is standard throughout the world. In many states, universities are state-controlled institutions. In Israel, as in most democratic states, they are formally, and to a large extent actually, independent institutions.

One precedent that the boycott campaign seems to set is that academics (and musicians and artists and sportspeople) should be held responsible and should be punished by exclusion for the human rights abuses committed by their state. This kind of collective responsibility is not the usual attitude taken by left and liberal critics of state human rights abuses.

H. Antisemitism

The political culture in which the boycott 'debate' takes place is extremely poor, and political education is often lacking. The debate that takes place on the UCU activist email list is astonishing. One UCU colleague wrote: 'I have a big problem with this 'right to exist' business', as though Israeli sovereignty was an impertinence. Somebody else admits that the boycott 'could qualify as indirect race discrimination' but argues that this is necessary for the greater good. Another manufactures a difference between antisemitism and 'antisemitism', and pleads guilty to the second because he defines it as 'objecting to the policies of Israel'. Or: 'Why should Israel's legacy of horror and trauma be exploited to deprive the Palestinians [of] their homeland? Just how long can the history of antisemitism and the holocaust be used ... to exempt Israel?' One colleague wrote the following:

> What security is Israel entitled to? To non-hypocrites, the answer is obvious. The same security it gives Palestine, no more, no less. On its current record, then, Israel has no right to exist and it's people must be conquered, partially expelled and brutalised by Occupation. (21 September 2007)

Another wrote:

> The whole Israeli education system – from nursery to university – is embedded in the Israeli obsession with war as some sort of 'defence' against who knows what.... The minute I tried to probe the fears of the Israelis I met the conversation moved into something that I can only describe as a dreadful mix of possibly real and totally unreal anxieties about Europe in the past, Biblical history, contemporary Judaism, work, land and the American dream.... These conversations were a gush of insecure and often irrational stuff that I tried to understand. But I could not. (19 September 2007)

This colleague went on to write the following:

> But a one point we as a union are going to have to some eyeball to eyeball stuff with our counterparts in Israel and the message has to be got over that the occupation has to end ... if Israeli academics think otherwise then let them say so in the international press ... Lets tease them out! (23 September 2007)

Often a swirl of discourse can mix together different kinds of expression, from tacky rambling, to sharp criticism that merits serious responses, to clear antisemitism, to playground insults. When different voices allow what they say to coalesce into an indistinguishable swirl it is difficult to hear the whole as anything other than demon–

ization. The union has threatened anyone who publishes any of these emails with exclusion from the list. This protects the privacy of those who are employing language and arguments that lay the foundation for antisemitic ways of thinking. UCU has a policy against antisemitism to which members can appeal. But UCU says that 'criticism of Israel cannot be construed as antisemitic'. This formulation protects any statement that resembles or incorporates criticism of Israel, whether it is actually antisemitic or not. In this way antisemitism was neutralized as an issue before the debate began.

The threat of the boycott campaign is not abstract or theoretical. Antisemitic ways of thinking and expression are here now, in the unions, on campus, in the media and in the public sphere. The warnings of the parliamentary inquiry on antisemitism are minimized by those who make it their business to explain away and rationalize every claim of antisemitism (Bechler 2007). Concern about antisemitism, they say, is really a dishonest neo-con smoke-screen, intended to delegitimize criticism of Israeli human rights abuses. Stephen Walt and John Mearsheimer's book, the follow-up to the 2006 working papers, was published in September 2007. Their outriders are barking that anyone who does not want a debate about 'Zionist' responsibility for war is an opponent of free speech.

I. The defeat of the boycott campaign in UCU

On 28 September 2007, the campaign within UCU for the exclusion of academics who work in Israel from British academia floundered to what seems to have been an abrupt and final defeat. The union had sought legal advice on the question of the boycott, and at least two separate legal opinions were studied by the union's Strategy and Finance Committee. Neither opinion is so far wholly in the public domain. One was written by Lord Anthony Lester, a widely respected human rights lawyer who had been inspired to campaign for antiracism legislation in Britain during his time working in the civil rights movement in the American South in the early 1960s[124] and who had been influential in shaping the legislation that finally became law in the United Kingdom in the 1970s. UCU released[125] the following excerpts from the opinion:

> It would be beyond the Union's powers and unlawful for the Union, directly or indirectly to call for or to implement a boycott by the Union and its members of any kind of Israeli universities and other academic institutions; and that the use of Union funds directly or indirectly to further such a boycott would also be unlawful ... to ensure that the Union acts lawfully meetings should not be used to ascertain the level of support for such a boycott.

---

[124] Lord Lester (2006): 'My involvement with the campaign for effective equality laws began in the early 1960s, when I was in the USA studying at Harvard Law School. In 1961, I saw at first hand the entrenched racism in the Deep South during the period of civil rights activism. In 1964, I returned for Amnesty International to report on racial injustice in the American South during the "Long Hot Summer". When I returned, inspired by Dr Martin Luther King, I joined Dr David Pitt and others to found a civil rights organisation in Britain, the Campaign against Racial Discrimination (CARD).'

[125] Email from UCU to its members, 28 October 2007.

Paragraph 2.5 of the rules of UCU states the following one of the 'Aims and Objects' of the union to be:

> To oppose actively all forms of harassment, prejudice and unfair discrimination whether on the grounds of sex, race, ethnic or national origin, religion, colour, class, caring responsibilities, marital status, sexuality, disability, age, or other status or personal characteristic.[126]

Given the legal advice, the Strategy and Finance Committee had no choice but decisively to end the union's flirtation with a boycott of Israeli academia. To persist would have left the union vulnerable to lawsuits, presumably on the grounds of unfair discrimination in violation of the Aims and Objects of the union and/or in violation of the Race Relations Act (1976). Union trustees and members of the Strategy and Finance Committee, as well as National Executive Committee members, could have found themselves held personally liable if they had ignored clear legal advice. The Strategy and Finance Committee voted unanimously to end all consideration of the boycott proposal.

Within days, a petition was being circulated and was signed by the hard-core of the boycott campaign. The petition, entitled 'No gag on debate in UCU' opposed a 'deluge of media abuse and the threat of legal action' that the union had had to face since the passing of Motion 30. The petition cast the boycotters as victims of a campaign against free speech. 'We call on the UCU not to cave in to these outrageous legal threats of censorship.'[127] The UCU Left is the caucus in the union that, while it does not formally support the boycott, in fact provided the overwhelming majority of the activists for the campaign. Eventually, the six UCU Left members of the Strategy and Finance Committee had to step in to explain to their own people why it had been necessary to vote to end union backing for the boycott 'debate'. On 2 October 2007, the UCU circular to branches had made clear that this rhetoric about 'gagging' was inappropriate by quoting another passage from Lester's opinion:

> the Union and its members are fully entitled to exercise their right to freedom of expression, discussion and debate by considering the pros and cons of the proposed boycott, and, if so minded, to pass and publish resolutions criticizing the policies of the Israeli government and its supporters and expressing support for the rights of Palestinians, withdrawal by Israel from the occupied territories, and so on.[128]

On 8 October, the six UCU Left members of the Strategy and Finance Committee made it clear to their own supporters that the boycott was really over:

> The decision made on Friday 28th September by the Strategy and Finance Committee (SFC) was based on a discussion of the implications of the legal advice given by two QCs asked for separately by UCU and the Trustees. That advice was

---

[126] UCU Rules, http://www.ucu.org.uk/media/pdf/e/a/ucurules_jun07.pdf, downloaded 14 October 2007.

[127] Petition 'No gag on debate in UCU', http://www.petitiononline.com/nogagucu/petition.html.

[128] UCU circular to branches, 2 October 2007, http://www.engageonline.org.uk/blog/article.php?id=1443.

clear and unequivocal: that a boycott of Israeli academic institutions and a call for such a boycott would be unlawful and therefore expenditure of money to 'test support' for a boycott would also be unlawful. As has now become public knowledge through a letter to *The Guardian*, UCU's QC is recognised as a leading expert on equality and human rights legislation. It would have been highly irresponsible for us to ignore such authoritative and unusually robust advice and thereby place union funds in jeopardy.

There will still be those who are tempted to explain the defeat by reference to a capitulation to bourgeois or Zionist power. But they will find it difficult to insist that anti-discrimination law is a mode of state repression when many people still understand it as a victory hard won by generations of antiracist activists. It is easy to conceive of circumstances in which a union might decide to risk all in a fight against a law that was designed to make it weaker, but anti-discrimination law was designed to make unions stronger, and it was functioning in this case to make UCU stronger, by ending the divisive campaign that made the union inhospitable to the overwhelming majority of Jewish college and university workers. There is law in place that prohibits bodies like UCU from discriminating against Jews. There was a time when there was no legal prohibition on Jewish quotas and silent or explicit exclusions and boycotts of Jews by civil society organizations such as universities, golf-clubs and trade unions. The exclusion of Jews, it seems, is now no longer a private matter of choice for an organization; it is now illegal.

Those who were for a boycott of Israel were not for boycotting the academics in all states that abused human rights but only in Jewish states that abused human rights. It was a proposal that singled out the academics of one state for unique punishment.

There will be some people who supported the boycott campaign who will persist with their demonization and their rhetoric of powerful 'Israel lobbies'. They will claim that well-funded lobbies defeated them; they will claim that British law or British lawyers are part of the Israel lobby; they will claim that the leadership of UCU sold out the rank and file. In truth the real rank and file of the union was mobilizing. Hundreds of UCU members had rallied to the 'Campaign for a UCU ballot' within a week of it being set up.

Union members up and down the country were part of the Engage network to oppose the boycott campaign. A repeat of the AUT members' revolt of 2005 had been imminent, where the union was rescued from the grip of a small coterie of Israel-hating activists by open debate and by the insistence of ordinary union members on having their say. Some boycotters will persist even after their boycott has been widely recognized – morally, legally and politically – as a counterproductive and racist proposal. But the majority of UCU members might take this opportunity to rescue their union and to make it again into a union for all of its members.

3. Sporting and cultural boycott

In April 2006, West Ham United (a football club) had two Israeli players. When West Ham took their team for a few days' relaxation and training in the desert sun of Dubai, they sent their two Israelis off to Spain for a break (Adar 2006). Israeli citizens are not welcome in the United Arab Emirates. Bolton Wanderers left their Israeli player at home when they visited Dubai earlier in the season.[129] West Ham and Bolton quietly acquiesced to the racist policy of the United Arab Emirates without making a fuss.

Emirates Airlines have sponsored the new Arsenal stadium (The Emirates Stadium) in a £100m deal. Arsenal does allow Israelis to play football at the Emirates Stadium. But the Palestine Solidarity Campaign (PSC) launched a campaign against Arsenal because they also made a £350,000 advertising deal with the Israeli tourist board. Nobody opposed the lash-up between Arsenal and the United Arab Emirates, where women do not vote – and men's votes do not determine the government – and where significantly less than half of the population are deemed to be citizens of the state. The PSC urges us to contact Arsenal and to 'remind' them that Israel is a racist apartheid state (perhaps Arsenal had forgotten?). PSC also proposes to pressurize the Football Association's successful antiracist campaign, Kick It Out, to take a stand against this deal with the Israeli 'apartheid' state. The campaign to boycott South African sport focused on the fact that South African sport was 'racially' segregated. It argued that sports people from around the world should not play as normal with teams that were picked according to the principle of 'race' rather than talent. Israeli sport is not segregated because Israel is not an apartheid state.

In 2001, the UN organized a global conference against racism in Durban, with a parallel conference for non-governmental organizations (NGOs). The anti-Israel enthusiasts prevented both of these global conferences from doing anything useful about racism anywhere in the world. They did this by insisting that the greatest manifestation of racism in the world was 'Zionism'. They took over both of these conferences and used them to denounce Israel as racist and apartheid and to insist that everyone else also denounce Israel. One result was that nothing useful came out of either of these conferences on antiracism. Now the PSC risked destroying the successful Kick It Out Campaign in a similar way.

Footballer John Barnes, who knows what it is like to face 40,000 people making monkey noises at him because he is black, clearly did not think that Kick It Out should be derailed in this way. He visited Israel in March 2006 (Giver 2006) where he helped to launch Israel's version of the Kick It Out campaign against racism amongst football fans. Their slogan is 'Let's Kick Racism Out of Football'. This campaign has been successful in helping to transform British football from the state it was in when John Barnes was a young player; a campaign against racism amongst Israeli football fans is sorely needed. While those who are in favour of boycotting Israel would prefer antiracists not to campaign against racism in Israel, John Barnes appears to disagree. Barnes visited Israel only a week after the PSC began its effort to win the Kick It Out campaign to a boycott of Israeli 'apartheid'.

In July 2006, the European cricket cup took place in Scotland. This is far from being a professional and high-profile event. The only European country that plays cricket at the top level is England, which did not take part. This was an amateur event without

---

[129] There is nothing new about sports teams bowing to the racist policies of states that they visit. The English cricketing authorities tried to find a way of leaving Basil D'Olivera, who was classified as 'coloured' by the apartheid regime, at home when they were due to tour South Africa in 1970. In the end they were forced to cancel the tour rather than bow to the South African government who wanted to choose who could play cricket for England.

any great media coverage and without many spectators. The Scottish PSC launched a campaign against the Israeli cricket team's participation in the tournament:

> The Israeli cricket team is playing in Scotland on 3, 5, 6 July 2006 – help us STOP the game, Israel must not be allowed to enjoy their status as a 'normal' state, enjoying rest & recreation, while Lebanon burns and Palestine is imprisoned! Contact secretary@scottishpsc.org.uk.[130]

This campaign was successful in preventing Israel's matches from going ahead. The organizers announced that matches were cancelled due to 'public safety issues' (News.BBC.co.uk 2006).[131] After John Barnes, another high profile antiracist 'boycott breaker' was Roger Waters, former member of Pink Floyd and the man who wrote the iconic 1970s song 'The Wall'. Waters went to Israel to play a gig and while he was there, he took some time to campaign against the separation barrier being built by the Israelis on Palestinian land.[132] His gig had originally been planned to take place in a park in Tel Aviv but following pressure from the boycott campaign, Waters agreed to move the venue. The gig took place at Neve Shalom/Wahat al Salam, a village called 'Oasis of Peace' in English. This village was founded jointly by Jewish and Palestinian Arab peace campaigners to educate for peace and to live in a mixed community. Waters seems to have done a deal with the boycott campaigners that they were able to spin as a victory. But, in truth, Waters played in front of thousands of fans in the heart of pre-1967 Israel, just off the main highway that connects Jerusalem to Tel Aviv. He made his political opposition to Israeli policy clear but he rejected the boycott:

Waters articulated his position as follows:

> I have a lot of fans in Israel, many of whom are refuseniks. I would not rule out going to Israel because I disapprove of the foreign policy any more than I would refuse to play in the UK because I disapprove of Tony Blair's foreign policy. (McGreal 2006)

> I am happy to play to anybody who believes in peace. I don't discriminate between any of my fans, wherever they live. Being an Israeli does not disbar from being a human being. (McIntyre 2006)

---

[130] This quote is from the Scottish PSC website and is no longer online. See http://www.engageonline.org.uk/blog/article.php?id=548, downloaded 26 February 2006.

[131] Osama Saeed, of the Muslim Association of Britain, said of the decision to drop the match: 'This is fabulous news, though we would wish that the decision had been taken earlier by the organisers on the grounds of principle rather than practicality.'

However, Dr Kenneth Collins, from the Glasgow Jewish Representative Council, said: 'We have already had daubings on a synagogue in Glasgow and one in Edinburgh and we are very worried that threats to Israeli interests could spread to Jewish interests in the city. The Jewish community in Glasgow are not spokesmen for Israel. We have a natural sympathy with what happens there and many of us have relatives there and we are very concerned about how Israel is treated and how it's looked upon.' (News.BBC.co.uk 2006)

[132] Waters: 'The poverty inflicted by the wall has been devastating for Palestinians. It has kept children from their schools, the sick from proper medical care and continues to destroy the Palestinian economy. I fully support War on Want's campaign, and hope that as many people as possible sign the wall as a strong message to the UK government that immediate action is essential.' (WarOnWant.org 2006)

'I've seen pictures of [the wall], I've heard a lot about it but without being here you can't imagine how extraordinarily oppressive it is and how sad it is to see these people coming through these little holes,' he added. 'It's craziness.' (YnetNews.com 2006)

He sprayed the words 'No Thought Control' in huge red letters onto the wall.

It seems likely that one strategy we can expect more of from the Palestine Solidarity movement is to harass particular individuals who 'break the boycott' of Israel. We should expect people like Waters to be at the centre of campaigns designed to make others think that it is just not worth the hassle of going to Israel. The threat is of pickets of concerts and the branding of artists as 'Zionists' and 'apologists for apartheid'.

CONCLUSION

1. Is criticism of Israel antisemitic?

Sometimes criticism of Israel is antisemitic. For example, in the Hamas Covenant, which criticizes Israel for being a manifestation of a Jewish conspiracy, alongside the French and Russian revolutions and the First and Second World Wars. In this case, not only is criticism of Israel antisemitic, but so is the criticism of the French and Russian revolutions. Sometimes criticism of Hilary Clinton is misogynist, and sometimes it is not. Sometimes criticism of Zimbabwe is racist and sometimes it is not.

2. Is criticism of Israel necessarily antisemitic?

No, of course not, but who says that it is? There are very few Jewish communal spokespeople or Israeli politicians who are prepared to make such an evidently false claim. The contention that criticism of Israel is necessarily antisemitic nearly always functions as a straw-man argument. The difficult arguments for some over-enthusiastic critics of Israel to deal with are that criticism of Israel is often expressed using rhetoric or images that resonate with antisemitism; or that criticism often holds Israel to higher standards than other states, and for no morally or politically relevant reason; or that it often employs conspiracy theory; or that it uses demonizing analogies; or that it casts Jews as oppressors; or that criticism is made in such a way as to pick a fight with the vast majority of Jews; or that the word criticism is really being used to stand for discriminatory practices against Israelis or against Jews. These much more serious and realistic charges are too often brushed off by blithely employing the *Livingstone formulation*: 'for far too long the accusation of antisemitism has been used against anyone who is critical of the policies of the Israeli government.' (Livingstone 2006)

The *Livingstone formulation* does two things. First, it denies the distinction between criticism and demonization by subsuming both into the simple category of 'criticism'. This is dangerous because what we need is clarity about the distinction, not denial. Criticism of Israeli human rights abuses is not only legitimate, it is appropriate and important. But those who deny the distinction between criticism and demonization render themselves incapable of making serious and legitimate criticism. Apart from the direct damage done by demonization, these 'critics' also find that they have put themselves into a position where they are unable to do anything to help the cause of Palestinian independence, freedom or democracy; against their own intentions, they are actually more likely to harm than to help those causes. Precisely where the boundary between criticism and demonization lies is an open question for public discussion and debate.

Secondly, the *Livingstone formulation* does not simply accuse anyone concerned with contemporary antisemitism of being wrong but also accuses them of bad faith: 'the accusation of antisemitism *has been used* against anyone who is critical' [*my italics*]. Not an honest mistake then, but a secret, common plan to try to delegitimize criticism with an instrumental use of the charge of antisemitism. Crying wolf. Playing the antisemitism card. The *Livingstone formulation*, which as we have seen is becoming a standard response for those who seek, against the clear and mounting evidence, to deny that there is a problem of contemporary antisemitism, is both a straw-man argument and a charge of 'Zionist' conspiracy. It is itself an antisemitic claim. Its regular appearance is also, in itself, evidence that antisemitic ways of thinking are unexceptional in contemporary mainstream left and liberal discourse.

The Reverend Steven Sizer (2006), a leading supporter in the Church of England of the campaign for boycott, divestment and sanctions (BDS) against Israel, added a Christian twist when he articulated the *Livingstone formulation*. He wrote a letter to *The Independent* responding to an argument by the Chief Rabbi that the campaign for BDS was part of an emerging antisemitic culture in the United Kingdom. The Synod (parliament) of the Church, declared Sizer, would not be 'intimidated by those who like Chicken Little cry "antisemitism" whenever Israeli human rights abuses in the occupied territories are mentioned.' Sizer conflates the campaign for BDS with the 'mentioning' of human rights abuses. He goes on to ask 'Why has the Archbishop faced a torrent of criticism over [a vote to divest from Caterpillar]? Simple: the people in the shadows know that Caterpillar is only the first. "Let justice roll."' He confirms the suspicion of some opponents who argue that the campaign against Caterpillar is a wedge being used to open up the possibility of the complete isolation of Israel. And he strengthens the misgivings of others, who suspect that the use of terms like 'people in the shadows', with connotations of secret conspiracy, to describe opponents of BDS, is perhaps not coincidental.

3. Is anti-Zionism a form of antisemitism?

David Matas (2005) makes the argument that anti-Zionism is indeed a form of antisemitism:

> Zionism is the expression of the right to self-determination of the Jewish people. Anti-Zionism, by definition, denies and rejects this right by denying the right to a state for the Jewish people. Anti-Zionism is a form of racism. It is the specific denial to the Jewish people of a basic right to which all the peoples of the world are entitled.

This is an argument that employs a similar methodology to that which produces the vulgar anti-Zionist result 'Zionism=Racism'. Zionism is racism (by this definition) because it necessarily builds a state that defines belonging according to a prior notion of ethnicity; anti-Zionism is racism (by Matas' definition) because it denies the right of Jewish self-determination while defending self-determination for all other nations. By this methodology we can understand the world by looking carefully at the definitions of words. In contrast, this work has employed a methodology of understanding that starts with an investigation of the world as it exists; concepts, yes, but also discourse and their actualizations in social movements. In writing about both the Israel-Palestine conflict and contemporary antisemitism the concept of society is often absent. As we have seen, anti-Zionism, even in its most macho historical materialist forms, often affords huge explanatory weight to ideas. It appears reluctant to base its critique in an understanding of how society is actually functioning and changing, an understanding of how actual people relate to each other and to the social structures that they create and by which they are created. There is too much schematic thinking coming out of ideational frameworks that are only tenuously anchored to actual social processes, agents and structure. Anti-Zionism is not a form of racism. But it is a profoundly flawed, shallow and light-weight framework and world view. Antiracist anti-Zionism presents itself as the legitimate child of Jewish socialist opposition to Zionism in the first third of the twentieth century, but some suspect that its real father is Soviet antisemitism. I have presented some of the kinds of evidence that are necessary to pin down the complex relationship between anti-Zionism and antisemitism. A genealogy, a historical analysis, would also help.

4. Would an academic boycott of Israel be antisemitic?

Yes. It is an antisemitic policy because it aims to punish Israeli academics, the majority of whom are Jewish, according to different standards to academics in other states. If a North Korean mathematician wants to come to a conference in Britain, we will be happy to discuss mathematics with her; we will not demand that she repudiates her state's constitutional claim that North Korea is a socialist paradise on earth nor that she admits that she lives in one of the most repressive and inhumane states on earth. This is how it should be. Discuss calculus during the day; discuss politics over dinner; help her to defect, if she wants. But if an Israeli wants to come to the same conference, she won't be allowed. She won't be allowed to attend the conference, to have her journal articles considered for publication or to remain part of the global academic community unless she first passes some kind of test, such as repudiating her university or ritually 'criticizing' the 'apartheid' policies of her state. The North Korean will be allowed in, the Israeli will not. This is an antisemitic policy.

It is a long time since the principle was universally acknowledged in liberal society that racism does not depend on people acting out of malice or hatred; racism usually propagates itself in a more insidious and unconscious way. In Britain, the final official bastion for this conception of racism was the police force, and it was eventually conquered by the High Court Judge Sir William Macpherson when he reported on the public inquiry into the police handling of the investigation of the murder of Stephen Lawrence. The report said:

> 6.13 Lord Scarman accepted the existence of what he termed 'unwitting' or 'unconscious' racism. To those adjectives can be added a third, namely 'unintentional'. All three words are familiar in the context of any discussion in this field.

It is instructive to see the sophisticated and experienced antiracists of the boycott campaign turn their palms to the sky in the innocent manner of twentieth century

Police Federation representatives and plead that a practice can only be racist if it is motivated by racism. The boycott of Israeli academics is not motivated by antisemitism, but it is nevertheless antisemitic in effect. Any kind of impact assessment would demonstrate that it is a policy that would impact on Jews – both Israeli and not – much more heavily than anybody else. And there is no morally, politically or legally relevant reason that could mitigate or excuse this racist impact.

Another sense in which the boycott is antisemitic is because it is a campaign that spreads antisemitic ways of thinking, that sets itself up for a fight with Jews and that creates a toxic atmosphere of accusation and mistrust towards those Jews who oppose the campaign. Non-Jews who oppose the boycott campaign are also treated as though they were part of a Zionist conspiracy or Israel lobby and are thereby also subjected to antisemitic libel. This sense in which it is antisemitic is not necessary to any imaginable campaign to boycott Israel; it is simply true of the boycott campaign that exists. It relies on fostering an emotional internalization of Israel as being a unique evil on the planet, and it cannot avoid allowing that passion to also be directed against those Jews who do not define themselves as anti-Zionist and speak out in opposition to the boycott. It is only necessary to picture a scene in which an Israeli professor who has failed to repudiate her status as a faculty member of Haifa or Tel Aviv University or to denounce her country for being an apartheid state, is picketed by British trade unionists in order to prevent her from giving a seminar; it is only necessary to picture this scene to know that this is an antisemitic policy. Even if the picket was fronted by anti-Zionist Jews, it would still be an antisemitic policy. Picture the mundane organizational work that would be necessary to make the picket happen. Picture the ways in which Jewish union members (the ones who are not anti-Zionist and have not yet resigned from the union in disgust) would have to be marginalized in the local branch. Picture the Jewish students' societies holding a counter-picket; picture the anti-Zionist Jewish students asserting loudly the right of the union to prevent the Israeli professor from speaking by screaming 'criticism of Israel is not antisemitic'.

And the boycott is antisemitic in another sense – once again not a necessary sense, but necessary to the world in which we live. The scene imagined above resonates in Jewish memory because of its similarities to previous anti-Jewish boycotts. Jews were pushed out of Polish universities in 1968 in a purge that used the language of anti-imperialist anti-Zionism. Jews were pushed out of the universities of the Middle East in the 1950s and the 1960s, all except for the ones in Israel. There were measures in place to exclude Jews, including quotas, in many US universities until the second half of the twentieth century. Jews were discriminated against in Soviet universities and were stopped from studying certain subjects. Jews were picketed out of the universities in Germany following the coming to power of the Nazis. Jews were kept out of many of the universities of Europe until they forced their way in during the second half of the nineteenth century. The boycotters can berate me impatiently and in outraged tones for bringing up all these entirely irrelevant stories; they can accuse me of 'using' antisemitism to delegitimize their 'criticism'; they can accuse me of invoking a red herring or of throwing dust in the eyes. In my own union branch it was argued that the fact that 'Zionists' are so horrified by the boycott – the fact that it 'hits a nerve' – is evidence of its effectiveness. They can deny the analogies as much as they like, but many Jews will know that it is not right for Israelis to be excluded from universities while everyone else in the world is allowed in. And people who consider themselves antiracist should know it too.

5. Are people who support the boycott campaign antisemitic?

I am not a prosecutor, in the Soviet style, accusing people of the crime of antisemitism. I do not know what goes on inside people's heads. I am interested in antisemitism as a social phenomenon and as a macro phenomenon. I am interested in what people do and what they say, and particularly in what is done and said in society in general. I am interested in the emergent properties of anti-Zionism. I am interested in the unintended consequences of people's actions who are simply motivated by a wish to support the Palestinians.

I am interested in the following statistical correlation: Kaplan and Small (2006) found in their analysis of survey data that 'anti-Israel sentiment consistently predicts the probability that an individual is anti-Semitic, with the likelihood of measured anti-Semitism increasing with the extent of anti-Israel sentiment observed.'[133] So if we select Europeans who believe that Israel is an apartheid state and who believe that the Israeli forces deliberately target Palestinian civilians, and if we put them in a room, then that roomful of people would contain many more antisemites, defined independently, than a room of random Europeans. Anti-Zionists should be aware of the fact that people who believe what they believe about Israel are significantly more likely than average to also be antisemitic. This fact should make them consider carefully the possibility that what they say and do might exacerbate antisemitism. It is interesting, then, that, by using the *Livingstone formulation*, these antiracists very often refuse to be careful in that way. But Kaplan and Small cannot tell us that there is not a current of antiracist anti-Zionism that is immune from the antisemitism that they detect in the general sample of people who show 'anti-Israel sentiment', and they cannot tell us what causal mechanism or what ideational processes or what chains of meaning relate hostility to Israel and racism against Jews.

It is important to distinguish between the ideologically committed anti-Zionist core of the boycott campaign and the periphery of people who are attracted or seduced by its rhetoric. The core knows, thinks it knows, has a responsibility to know, something about Israel and Palestine, past and present. It has a responsibility to think seriously about the possibility of stirring up, licensing or legitimizing antisemitism. Many of the people who are tempted to support the boycott campaign do so for the best of reasons and with the best of intentions. They want to do something to help the desperate situation in Palestine and to do so in solidarity with the Palestinians. The boycott campaign offers them a simple and easy way of demonstrating their uncompromising hostility to the violence and racism of the occupation. And many of the people seduced by the rhetoric of the core campaigns do not know much about the conflict or about the history and tropes of antisemitism. This is the group that is likely to make up many of the trade union activists who would be

---

[133] Kaplan and Small (2006): 'based on a survey of 500 citizens in each of 10 European countries, the authors ask whether those individuals with extreme anti-Israel views are more likely to be anti-Semitic' and they control 'for numerous potentially confounding factors...'.

responsible for implementing a boycott on the ground, in the colleges. This fact should give us cause for concern.

6. Is the left antisemitic?

No, the left is not antisemitic. Some streams and traditions which think of themselves as being on the left are fighting for their belief that Israel is a unique evil to be adopted as mainstream commonsense. They are having some success in mainstreaming this view, and with it often come certain antisemitic ways of thinking. These ideas are appearing all over mainstream discourse and are no longer marginalized on the extreme left and the extreme right. Most of the speakers who opposed the boycott at the 2007 UCU conference identified themselves as being on the left. Most of them were defending what they believed to be an authentic left wing position. They argued for building solidarity with Palestinians and with the Israeli peace movement; for helping to facilitate links between Palestinian academics, Israeli academics and the outside world; for a strategy to oppose the occupation; they warned against antisemitism; they warned of the dangers to UCU and college workers' unity that were posed by the boycott campaign; and they warned of the damage that would be done to the cause of Palestinian statehood by support of the boycott. The debate was between left traditions; the right was not really represented at UCU conference at all – not the 'Zionist' right, not the British right, unless one includes the Islamist right, whose influence was certainly felt but which was not significantly represented in person. There have always been pro-totalitarians and antisemites on the left, but they have never constituted the left because they have always been opposed by anti-totalitarians and anti-antisemites. This is still the case.

7. Why has the boycott campaign been so successful in Britain in 2007?

This is a question that this research can only begin to answer tentatively. Two peculiarities of the British come immediately to mind. One is that, almost uniquely in Europe, Britain was not occupied by the Nazis, and the other is that Britain has a particular memory of colonialism and empire. According to the Anti-Defamation League (ADL) report on attitudes towards Jews (2007) in Europe:

> Respondents over the age of 45 are much more likely than other segments of the British population to 'strongly oppose' the efforts to boycott Israel.... Of the 15 percent of those surveyed who say that they 'strongly oppose' a boycott of Israel, 79 percent are over the age of 45.

One explanation of this differential in terms of age might be connected to memories of the Holocaust. The older half of the population grew up and were politically formed in the shadow of the Holocaust. The younger half, perhaps, regards it as something from history rather than something connected to their own lives. Perhaps they are also influenced by anti-Zionist and antisemitic efforts to play down the extent to which the Holocaust was something connected to antisemitism or Jews in particular, and to play up the 'use' of the Holocaust and antisemitism that is allegedly made by 'Zionists'. If this explanation is right then it indicates that there were strong taboos against antisemitism in the post-Holocaust world. It may be that those taboos are now less strong than they were in the twentieth century, and it might also be that contemporary antisemitism tends to by-pass those taboos rather than to challenge them directly. In any case, Britain was less immediately affected by the Holocaust than most of Europe; Jews were not taken off to Auschwitz from amongst other British people;[134] and British society has not been forced to face the legacy of its own collaboration with that process, as many European societies have. The British were never offered the opportunity to collaborate.

Josephs (2007) quotes Barry Camfield, deputy general-secretary of the Transport and General Workers half of UNITE as saying in his speech to conference that Britain had stood alone against Hitler and had liberated Jewish victims of the Holocaust. 'So we will not have the Israeli state telling us that the boycott is antisemitic,' he said.

Apart from the senses in which Britain did much less than it might have done to liberate Jews, this could only be a British sentiment. Britain, in Camfield's imagination, is not only not implicated and not guilty, it is actually the hero of the Holocaust, the St George that slew the antisemitic Nazi dragon. Here is yet another way in which the Holocaust is dragooned into service for the boycott campaign.

While the inhibitions created by the memory of the Holocaust may be less strong in Britain than elsewhere, the legacy of British colonialism is not. In the British debate, the sentiment that Britain is somehow responsible for Israeli human rights abuses because of its role in the period before and during 1948, as well as its contemporary role in the alliance with the United States, seems to be important. If there are feelings of national guilt nursed on the British left then they are more likely to be concerned with the British empire than with the Holocaust. So one tentative explanation for the leading role that Britain is currently playing in the boycott campaign may be that the inhibition on antisemitism is weaker in Britain while the guilt element, driven by an essentialized and historically uninformed anti-imperialism, may be stronger.

But anti-Zionism and the boycott campaign are also genuinely global movements. While they do manifest themselves differently in different places, the centrality of the internet to the production and circulation of these narratives gives the movement a tendency to by-pass national particularities. The English language press in Israel, instantly available online – *Ha'aretz*, *YnetNews*, the *Jerusalem Post* – provides much of the daily raw material around which political narratives are constructed. Events and political interventions tend to impact quickly around the world. The 2006 CUPE (Canadian Union of Public Employees) boycott decision was made during the same weekend as the NATFHE decision in Britain; Ronnie Kasrils' and Desmond Tutu's words are taken up everywhere from South Africa; Americans Mearsheimer and Walt had a huge and immediate impact on the rhetoric of British anti-Zionism; Matthias Küntzel and the anti-Deutsch left in Germany make their interesting interventions. More comparative studies and more historical studies are necessary to shed more light on the question 'Why Britain?' This study offers more of a snap-shot of contemporary British events than a historical analysis. It offers some enduring analysis of necessarily ephemeral case studies. It looks at how antisemitism manifests itself in mainstream discourse, but not how much or how differently in Britain to other places.

---

[134] A small number of Jews were deported from the Nazi-occupied Channel Islands.

As well as being an analysis of contemporary anti-Zionism and its relationship to contemporary antisemitism, this paper is also meant as a case study in cosmopolitan politics. It brings together a conceptual discussion of anti-Zionism with an empirical analysis of public discourse in the United Kingdom, mainly between 2004 and 2007, with the boycott campaign, which I have argued constitutes a material actualization of those conceptual and discursive realities. Most anti-Zionists, as well as the boycott campaign, think of themselves as being internationalist, and, etymologically, they are indeed more internationalist than they are cosmopolitan. They largely accept the methodologically nationalist narrative of the world as being divided into distinct nations. They largely see international politics as being about the relationships between these national state actors. Mearsheimer and Walt (2006a; 2006b), whose work fits into the realist tradition of international relations, operate with a surprisingly unproblematized notion of 'national interest'. Anti-Zionism in general succeeds less in furthering the cosmopolitan project of disrupting the conceptual tradition of methodological nationalism than it does in rejuvenating the realist tradition of international relations. Anti-Zionist thought and practice, as well as Zionist thought and practice, tend to rest on the principles of collective (national) responsibility and collective (national) punishment, rather than the difficult political work of disrupting nationalist realities.

Bibliography

Adar, Shaul (2006) 'Israelis left out of West Ham's trip to the Gulf', *The Guardian*, 11 April 2006, http://football.guardian.co.uk/News_Story/0,,1751257,00.html, downloaded 26 February 2007.

Al Qaradawi, Yousef (2006) 'Interview on Qatar TV', 26 August 2006, Excerpts translated by the Middle East Media Research Institute (MEMRI), http://www.memritv.org/Transcript.asp?P1=1249, downloaded 24 February 2007.

Allen, Jim (1987) *Perdition – A Play in Two Acts*, London: press release version, Royal Court Theatre, 13 January 1987.

—— (1987a) *Perdition – A Play in Two Acts*, London: Ithaca.

Amit, Zalman (2005) 'The collapse of academic freedom in Israel: Tantura, Teddy Katz and Haifa University', *Counterpunch*, 11 May 2005, Petrolia Ca., http://www.counterpunch.org/amit05112005.html, downloaded 14 February 2007.

Arendt, Hannah (1975) *The Origins of Totalitarianism*, San Diego: Harvest.

Assaf, Simon (2007) 'Hamas's victory in Gaza is a blow to Bush's plans', *Socialist Worker*, 23 June 2007, issue 2056, http://www.socialistworker.co.uk/art.php?id=12130, downloaded 14 August 2007.

Atzmon, Gilad (2003) 'On antisemitism', 20 December 2003, http://www.gilad.co.uk/html%20files/onanti.html, downloaded 28 February 2007.

—— (2003a) 'The most common mistakes of Israelis', *CounterPunch*, 28 August 2003, http://www.counterpunch.org/atzmon08282003.html, downloaded 28 February 2007.

—— (2006) 'A response to David Hirsh', *Comment is Free*, 12 December 2006, http://commentisfree.guardian.co.uk/gilad_atzmon/2006/12/gilad_atzmon_responds_to_david.html, downloaded 15 February 2007.

—— (2006a) 'Beyond Comparison', 12 August 2006, http://www.aljazeerah.info/Opinion%20editorials/2006%20Opinion%20Editorials/August/12%20o/Beyond%20Comparison%20By%20Gilad%20Atzmon.htm, downloaded 28 February 2007.

—— (2006b) 'What is to be done? Palestine solidarity in a time of massacres', *CounterPunch*, 22 November 2006, http://www.counterpunch.org/atzmon11222006.html, downloaded 28 February 2007.

—— (2006c) 'A response to David Hirsh', *Comment is Free*, 12 December 2006, http://commentisfree.guardian.co.uk/gilad_atzmon/2006/12/gilad_atzmon_responds_to_david.html, downloaded 25 July 2007.

Avnery, Uri (2005) 'You brought the boycott on yourselves', Tel Aviv, 2 April 2005, http://gush-shalom.org/biu.html, downloaded 14 February 2007.

Baker, Mona (2002) 'Personal Statement', http://www.monabaker.com/personalstatement.htm, downloaded 14 February 2007.

Bard, Mitchell (2007) 'The Arab Boycott', *Jewish Virtual Library*, http://www.jewishvirtuallibrary.org/jsource/History/Arab_boycott.html, downloaded 22 July 2007.

Barkat, Amiram (2006) 'David Irving: Jews should ask themselves why they are hated', *Ha'aretz*, http://www.haaretz.com/hasen/pages/ShArt.jhtml?itemNo=804622&contrassID=1&subContrassID=1, downloaded 24 July 2007.

Bauman, Zygmunt (1993) *Modernity and the Holocaust*, Cambridge: Polity.

Bechler, Rosemary (2007) 'A Commentary on the All-Party Parliamentary Inquiry into Antisemitism,' Faculty for Israeli-Palestinian Peace, March 2007, http://www.ffipp-uk.org/AS_All-party_sum_070317.doc, downloaded 21 June 2007.

Beller, Steven (2007) 'In Zion's hall of mirrors: a comment on neuer Antisemitsmus', *Patterns of Prejudice*, Vol. 41, No. 2, 2007.

Blackwell, Sue (2005) 'Bar-Ilan tries to woo AUT members', http://www.sue.be/pal/academic/Isaiah.html, downloaded 16 February 2007.

—— (2005a) 'Bloody ridiculous', http://www.sue.be/pal/academic/intro.html, downloaded 16 February 2007.

—— (2005b) 'Sites I no longer link to', http://www.sue.be/pal, downloaded 28 February 2007.

Blakemore, Colin, Richard Dawkins, Denis Noble and Michael Yudkin (2003) 'Is a Scientific Boycott Ever Justified?', *Nature* 421: 314.

Brenner, Lenni (1983) *Zionism in the Age of the Dictators – A Reappraisal*, London: Croom Helm.

Bresheeth, Haim (2004) 'Two states, too little, too late', *Al-Ahram Weekly*, Cairo, 11-17 March 2004, http://weekly.ahram.org.eg/2004/681/op61.htm, downloaded 15 February 2007.

Brown, Colin and Chris Hastings (2003) 'Fury as Dalyell attacks Blair's "Jewish Cabal"', *Daily Telegraph*, 4 May 2003, http://www.telegraph.co.uk/news/main.jhtml?xml=/news/2003/05/04/ndaly04.xml&sSheet=/portal/2003/05/04/ixportaltop.html, downloaded 29 June 2007.

Bunting, Madeleine (2006) 'The convenient myth that changed a set of ideas into western values', *The Guardian*, 10 April 2006, http://www.guardian.co.uk/commentisfree/story/0,,1750579,00.html, downloaded 25 February 2007.

Butler, Judith (2006) 'Israel/Palestine and the paradoxes of academic freedom', Faculty For Israeli-Palestinian Peace UK, http://www.ffipp-uk.org/foto_papers/butler_FOTO_revised.pdf, downloaded 20 July 2007.

Byrne, Ciar (2003) 'Independent cartoon cleared of antisemitism', *The Guardian*, 22 May 2003, http://www.guardian.co.uk/israel/Story/0,2763,961357,00.html, downloaded 16 February 2007.

CAABU (2006) 'CAABU condemns Maureen Lipman's comment on the BBC', 14 July 2006, http://www.caabu.org/index.asp?homepage=press&article=releases&detail=lipman_comments, downloaded 28 February 2007.

Carmon, Yigal (2002) 'Media organization rebuts accusations of selective journalism', *The Guardian*, 21 August 2002, http://www.guardian.co.uk/israel/comment/0,,778373,00.html, downloaded 24 February 2006.

Carmon, Yigal and Brian Whitaker (2003) 'Email debate: Yigal Carmon and Brian Whitaker', *The Guardian*, 28 January 2003, http://www.guardian.co.uk/israel/comment/0,,778373,00.html, downloaded 24 February 2007.

Chesler, Phyllis (2003) *The New Antisemitism*, San Francisco: Jossey-Bass.

—— (2006) 'Manifesto for Survival', *The Jewish Press*, 13 December 2006, New York.

Chiappalone, J.S. (1997) *The Kingdom of Zion: exposing the worldwide conspiracy of evil*, Malanda Australia: Annwn.

Cohen, Nick (2007) 'The unholy alliance that damns Rushdie', *The Guardian*, 24 June 2007, http://www.guardian.co.uk/commentisfree/story/0,,2110240,00.html, downloaded 25 June 2007.

—— (2007a) 'Racist Islamophobe Fascist Spy!', *London Evening Standard*, 12 December 2007, available online at http://www.nickcohen.net/?p=277, downloaded 12 December 2007.

Cohen, Steve (2005) *That's Funny You Don't Look Antisemitic*, London: Engage, http://www.engageonline.org.uk/ressources/funny, downloaded 22 July 2007.

Crooke, Alistair (2007) 'Our second biggest mistake in the Middle East', *London Review of Books*, Vol. 29, No. 13, 5 July 2007, http://www.lrb.co.uk/v29/n13/croo01_.html, downloaded 14 August 2007.

Crooke, Stan (2004) 'The Stalinist roots of left anti-Zionism', 24 February 2004, http://www.workersliberty.org/node/1748, downloaded 25 July 2007.

Curtis, Polly (2005) 'Boycott call resurfaces', *The Guardian*, 5 April 2005, http://education.guardian.co.uk/egweekly/story/0,,1451869,00.html, downloaded 14 February 2007.

De Swaan, Abram (2004) 'Les enthousiasmes anti-israéliens: la tragédie d'un processus aveugle', *L'Antilibéralisme*, No. 16-2004/4.

Dershowitz, Alan (2006) 'Debunking the Newest – and Oldest – Jewish Conspiracy: A Reply to the Mearsheimer-Walt "Working Paper"', Harvard Law School, April 2006, http://www.ksg.harvard.edu/research/working_papers/dershowitzreply.pdf, downloaded 29 June 2007.

Draper, Hal (1948) 'Hal Draper on Israel, 1948: War of independence or expansion', http://www.workersliberty.org/node/8911, downloaded 24 July 2007.

Duke, David (2004) 'Want to Know the Truth About Jewish Supremacism in their Own Words?', 30 November 2004, http://www.davidduke.com/index.php?p=129, downloaded 8 September 2005.

—— (2004a) 'What is antisemitism?', 24 March 2004, http://www.davidduke.com/date/2004/03, downloaded 24 February 2007.

Ezra, Michael (2007) 'The abuse of Holocaust memory: the far right, the far left and the Middle East', *Engage Journal*, Issue 4, http://www.engageonline.org.uk/journal/index.php?journal_id=14&article_id=58, downloaded 15 February 2007.

Fine, Robert (2001) *Political Investigations: Hegel, Marx, Arendt*, London: Routledge.

—— (2006) 'Karl Marx and the radical critique of antisemitism', *Engage Journal*, Issue 2, May 2006, http://www.engageonline.org.uk/journal/index.php?journal_id=10&article_id=33, downloaded 21 June 2007.

—— (2006a) 'The Lobby: Mearsheimer and Walt's conspiracy theory', 21 March 2006, http://www.engageonline.org.uk/blog/article.php?id=310, downloaded 29 June 2007.

—— (2007) *Cosmopolitanism*, London: Routledge.

Finkelstein, Norman G. (2003) *The Holocaust Industry: Reflections on the Exploitation of Jewish Suffering*, New York: Verso.

—— (2005) *Beyond Chutzpah: On the Misuse of Antisemitism and the Abuse of History*, New York: Verso.

—— (2006) 'Kill Jews, Cry Antisemitism', http://www.normanfinkelstein.com/article.php?pg=11&ar=516, downloaded 15 February 2007.

Fisk, Robert (2006) 'United States of Israel?', *The Independent*, 27 April 2006.

Foot, Paul (2003) 'Worse than Thatcher', *The Guardian*, 14 May 2003, http://www.guardian.co.uk/comment/story/0,3604,955312,00.html, downloaded 29 June 2007.

Foucault, Michel (1982) *Archaeology of Knowledge*, London: Pantheon.

Foxman, Abraham (2004) *Never Again? The threat of the new antisemitism*, New York: HarperCollins.

Freedland, Jonathan (2006) 'The net closes in', 12 July 2006, http://commentisfree.guardian.co.uk/jonathan_freedland/2006/07/post_219.html, downloaded 28 February 2007.

Furedi, Frank (2007), 'What's behind the new antisemitism', *Spiked*, 6 March 2007, http://www.spiked-online.com/index.php?/site/article/2919, downloaded 23 July 2007.

Galloway, George (2005) 'Statement on the London bombings by George Galloway on behalf of Respect', 7 July 2005, http://www.socialistworker.co.uk/article.php4?article_id=6929, downloaded 25 February 2007.

Geras, Norman (2005) 'AUT Update', http://normblog.typepad.com/normblog/2005/04/aut_update.html, downloaded 14 February 2007.

—— (2005a) 'The Selection of Israel', http://normblog.typepad.com/normblog/2005/06/the_selection_o.html, downloaded 22 July 2007.

—— (2006), 'Smells like team spirit', *Comment is Free*, 24 July 2006, http://commentisfree.guardian.co.uk/norman_geras/2006/07/feels_like_cricket_spirit.html, downloaded 28 February 2007.

Goldberg, David (2006) 'Israeli force can stop the rockets but for how long?', *Comment is Free*, 9 August 2006, http://www.guardian.co.uk/commentisfree/story/0,,1840130,00.html, downloaded 1 March 2007.

Goldberg, Jeffrey (2002) 'A Reporter At Large: In The Party Of God (Part I)', *The New Yorker*, 14 October 2002, http://www.jeffreygoldberg.net/articles/tny/a_reporter_at_large_in_the_par.php, downloaded 30 June 2007.

Griver, Simon (2006) 'Barnes helps antiracist fight', *Jewish Chronicle*, 9 March 2006.

Hakakian, Roya (2004) *Journey from the land of no*, New York: Crown.

Halkin, Talya (2006) 'Bar Ilan warns of "silent" boycott by UK academics', *Jerusalem Post*, Jerusalem, 21 May 2006, http://www.jpost.com/servlet/Satellite?pagename=JPost%2FJPArticle%2FShowFull&cid=1145961382324, downloaded 14 February 2007.

Hamas (1988) 'The Covenant of the Islamic Resistance movement (HAMAS) – Palestine' 18 August 1988, http://www.yale.edu/lawweb/avalon/mideast/hamas.htm, downloaded 15 June 2007.

Harman, Chris (2007), 'Building Solidarity with Palestine', *Socialist Review*, July/August 2007, http://www.socialistreview.org.uk/article.php?articlenumber=10027, downloaded 23 July 2007.

Henry, Julie (2003) 'Outrage as Oxford bans student for being Israeli', *The Daily Telegraph*, 28 June 2003, http://www.telegraph.co.uk/news/main.jhtml?xml=/news/2003/06/29/noxf29.xml&sSheet=/portal/2003/06/29/ixportal.html, downloaded 14 February 2007.

Herf, Jeffrey and Andrei Markovits (2006) 'Mearsheimer and Walt on the Zionist conspiracy', http://jeffweintraub.blogspot.com/2006/03/mearsheimer-walt-on-zionist-conspiracy.html, downloaded 29 June 2007.

Hirsh, David (2003) *Law against Genocide: Cosmopolitan Trials*, London: Glasshouse.

—— (2005) 'Ariel Sharon invites the boycotters to dance', 2 May 2005, http://www.engageonline.org.uk/archives/index.php?id=16, downloaded 14 February 2007.

—— (2005a) 'Against the "Academic Intifada"', *Dissent*, Fall 2005.
—— (2005b) 'Cosmopolitan Law: agency and narrative', in Michael Freeman (ed.), *Law and Sociology: Current Legal Issues 2005*, Vol. 8, 2006, Oxford: OUP.
—— (2006) 'The argument for the boycott – Pacbi', 9 September 2006, http://www.engageonline.org.uk/blog/article.php?id=643#, downloaded 14 February 2007.
—— (2006a) 'Jenny Tonge: 'The pro-Israel lobby has got its grips on the western world', 20 September 2006, http://www.engageonline.org.uk/blog/article.php?id=660, downloaded 15 February 2007.
—— (2006b) 'Divided in peace', *Times Higher Education Supplement*, 28 July 2006, available at http://www.engageonline.org.uk/blog/article.php?id=525, downloaded 10 December 2006.
—— (2006c) 'Open antisemitism is challenging "antiracist" anti-Zionism in the Palestine solidarity movement', 30 November 2006, http://www.engageonline.org.uk/blog/article.php?id=763, downloaded 21 December 2006.
—— (2006d) 'Livingstone and the ayatollahs', *Comment is Free*, 22 March 2006, http://commentisfree.guardian.co.uk/david_hirsh/2006/03/livingstone_employs_lowlevel_r.html, downloaded 24 February 2007.
—— (2006e) 'Say that again, Steven Rose?', 6 September 2006, http://www.engageonline.org.uk/blog/article.php?id=639, downloaded 26 February 2007.
—— (2006f) 'Jews do not all think the same', *Comment is Free*, 26 April 2006, http://commentisfree.guardian.co.uk/david_hirsh/2006/04/the_jews_should_know_better.html, downloaded 26 February 2007.
—— (2006g) 'Which camp are you in?', *Comment is Free*, 11 May 2006, http://commentisfree.guardian.co.uk/david_hirsh/2006/05/israel_and_imperialism.html, downloaded 26 February 2007.
—— (2006h), 'What Jewish conspiracy?', *Comment is Free*, 13 July 2006, http://commentisfree.guardian.co.uk/david_hirsh/2006/07/jonathan_freedland_lord_levy_a.html, downloaded 28 February 2007.
—— (2006i), 'Openly Embracing Prejudice', *Comment is Free*, 30 November 2006, http://commentisfree.guardian.co.uk/david_hirsh/2006/11/a_new_menacing_current_is_appe.html, downloaded 3 May 2007.
—— (2007), 'Palestine Solidarity Campaign almost unanimously rejects two motions against antisemitism', 12 March 2007, http://www.engageonline.org.uk/blog/article.php?id=918, downloaded 3 May 2007.
—— (2007a), 'Radio 4's Today Programme asks: "Does the Israel lobby have too much power on US foreign policy?"', 10 October 2007, http://www.engageonline.org.uk/blog/article.php?id=1468, downloaded 12 October 2007.
Hirshfield, Claire (1980) 'The Anglo-Boer War and the Issue of Jewish Culpability', *Journal of Contemporary History*, Vol. 15, No. 4 (Oct., 1980), pp. 619-631.
Iganski, Paul, and Barry Kosmin (eds.) (2003) *A New Antisemitism?* London: Profile.
Ingrams, Richard (2003) 'Amiel's animus', *The Observer*, 13 July 2003, http://observer.guardian.co.uk/comment/story/0,6903,997338,00.html, downloaded 21 September 2007.
—— (2005) 'A futile pursuit', *The Guardian*, 11 September 2005, http://politics.guardian.co.uk/backbench/comment/0,14158,1567455,00.html, downloaded 21 September 2007.

—— (2007) 'It's about time someone spoke out', *The Independent*, 8 September 2007, http://comment.independent.co.uk/commentators/article2941918.ece, downloaded 21 September 2007.

InMinds.co.uk (2007), 'Enough Occupation: 40th Anniversary of the Occupation of large parts of Palestine', 9 June 2007, http://www.inminds.co.uk/enough.occupation.9june.2007.php, downloaded 29 June 2007.

Jacobson, Howard (2007), 'Those who boycott Israeli universities are doing intellectual violence – to themselves', *The Independent*, 14 July 2007, http://comment.independent.co.uk/columnists_a_l/howard_jacobson/article2768274.ece, downloaded 20 July 2007.

Jaschik, Scott (2006) 'Fiasco at AAUP', 9 February 2006, http://insidehighered.com/news/2006/02/09/aaup, downloaded 1 March 2007.

Jerusalem Post (2006) 'Ahmadinejad: Israel acting like Hitler', 16 July 2006, http://www.jpost.com/servlet/Satellite?pagename=JPost%2FJPArticle%2FShowFull&cid=1150886014306, downloaded 10 December 2006.

Jewish Board of Deputies (1921) *The New Antisemitism: the official protests of the British and American Jews*, London: Press Committee of the Jewish Board of Deputies.

Jewish Socialist Group (2006) 'Open letter to Scottish Palestine Solidarity', http://www.jewishsocialist.org.uk/spscopenletter.htm, downloaded 28 February 2006.

Jewish Tribal Review (2002) 'Ethics, antisemitism, the Palestinian cause and Israel: an email exchanged with Michael Neumann, Jewish professor of Philosophy', http://www.jewishtribalreview.org/neumann2.htm, downloaded 15 February 2007.

Josephs, Bernard (2007) 'TGWU joins the campaign', *Jewish Chronicle*, 6 July 2007, http://www.thejc.com/home.aspx?ParentId=m11s18&AId=53699&ATypeId=1&secid=18, downloaded 27 July 2007.

Judt, Tony (2007) 'In defence of academic freedom', verbal presentation, University of Chicago, 12 October 2007, MP3 file available at http://chicago.indymedia.org/usermedia/audio/6/af_tony_judt.mp3, downloaded 23 October 2007.

Julius, Anthony and Alan Dershowitz (2007) 'The contemporary fight against antisemitism', *The Times*, 13 June 2007, http://www.timesonline.co.uk/tol/comment/columnists/guest_contributors/article1928865.ece, downloaded 30 June 2007.

Julius, Anthony (2006) 'On Blood Libels', *Engage Journal*, Issue 3, http://www.engageonline.org.uk/joumal/index.php?joumal_id=12&article_id=42, downloaded 8 November 2007.

Kamm, Oliver (2007) 'The Milibands, The Jews and Foreign Policy', 29 June 2007, http://oliverkamm.typepad.com/blog/2007/06/the-milibands-t.html, downloaded 29 June 2007.

Kaplan, Edward H. and Charles A. Small (2006) 'Anti-Israel sentiment predicts antisemitism in Europe', *Journal of Conflict Resolution*, Vol. 50, No. 4, August 2006, pp. 548-561.

Karmi, Ghada (2007) *Married to another man*, London: Pluto.

Keogh, Dermot and Andrew McCarthy (2005) *Limerick Boycott 1904: Antisemitism in Ireland*, Cork: Mercier Press.

Klug, Brian (2004) 'The Myth of the New Antisemitism', *The Nation*, 2 February 2004, http://www.thenation.com/doc/20040202/klug, downloaded 21 June 2007.

Klug, Tony (2006) 'A normal hatred?', *Prospect Magazine*, Issue 125, August 2006.

Korneyev, L. (1977) 'The Sinister Secrets of Zionism' (Part II), *Ogonyok*, No. 35.

Küntzel, Matthias (2006) 'Hitler's legacy: Islamic antisemitism in the Middle East', 30 November 2006, http://www.matthiaskuentzel.de/contents/hitlers-legacy-islamic-antisemitism-in-the-middle-east, downloaded 23 July 2007.

Kuper, Richard (2006) 'Singling out Israel', *Red Pepper*, January 2006, http://www.redpepper.org.uk/palestine137/x-jan06-Kuper.htm, downloaded 10 May 2005.

Lappin, Shalom (2005) 'Why I resigned from the AUT', 8 April 2005, http://normblog.typepad.com/normblog/2005/04/why_i_resigned_.html, downloaded 14 February 2007.

—— (2006) 'The rise of a new antisemitism in the UK', *Engage Journal*, Issue 1, January 2006, http://www.engageonline.org.uk/joumal/index.php?joumal_id=5&article_id=15, downloaded 24 February 2007.

Layfield, Luke (2003) 'Oxford "appalled" as professor inflames boycott row', *The Guardian*, 4 July 2003, http://education.guardian.co.uk/higher/news/story/0,9830,991751,00.html, downloaded 22 July.

Lerman, Antony (2007) 'Reflecting the reality of Jewish diversity', *Comment is Free*, 6 February 2007, http://commentisfree.guardian.co.uk/tony_lerman/2007/02/hold_jewish_voices_8.html, downloaded 10 May 2007.

Lester, Anthony (2006) 'Thirty Years On', republished under the title 'Who is Lord Lester?', 14 October 2007, http://www.engageonline.org.uk/blog/article.php?id=1476, downloaded 14 October 2007.

Lily, Galili (2002) 'Israeli-Russian journalist calls for castration as anti-terror step', *Ha'aretz*, http://www.haaretzdaily.com/hasen/pages/ShArt.jhtml?itemNo=118898&contrassID=2&subContrassID=1&sbSubContrassID=0&listSrc=Y, downloaded 8 September 2005.

Lindbergh, Charles (1941) Des Moines Speech, 11 September 1941, http://www.pbs.org/wgbh/amex/lindbergh/filmmore/reference/primary/desmoinesspeech.html, downloaded 25 June 2007.

Lipman, Maureen (2006) 'Picture it: woman and new white dress, locked in battle like muntjak and muskox', *Comment is Free*, 17 July 2006, http://www.guardian.co.uk/commentisfree/story/0,,1822275,00.html, downloaded 28 February 2007.

—— (2006a) 'As a confirmed dog lover I'm horrified by this slaughter of greyhounds. And as for the man who did it...', *Comment is Free*, 24 July 2006, http://www.guardian.co.uk/commentisfree/story/0,,1827453,00.html, downloaded 28 February 2007.

Livingstone, Ken (2005) 'The Mayor's Response to the London Assembly', 22 February 2005, http://www.london.gov.uk/mayor/mayor_letter_220205.jsp, downloaded 24 February 2007.

—— (2005a) 'This is about Israel, not antisemitism', *The Guardian*, 4 March 2005, http://politics.guardian.co.uk/gla/comment/0,,1430185,00.html, downloaded 24 February 2007.

—— (2005b) 'Mayor's Statement', 7 July 2005, http://www.london.gov.uk/mayor/mayor_statement_070705.jsp, downloaded 24 February 2007.

—— (2006) 'An attack on voters' rights', *The Guardian*, 1 March 2006, http://society.guardian.co.uk/localgovt/comment/0,,1720439,00.html, downloaded 24 February 2007.

Macintyre, Donald (2006) 'Palestinians urge Roger Waters to boycott Israel', *The Independent*, 9 March 2006, http://news.independent.co.uk/world/middle_east/article350103.ece, downloaded 26 February 2007.

Marsden, Chris (2003) 'Britain: Labour extends antiwar witch-hunt to Tam Dalyell', 22 May 2003, http://www.wsws.org/articles/2003/may2003/lab-m22.shtml, downloaded 24 February 2007.

Marx, Karl (1994) 'The Jewish Question', in *Early Political Writings*, Cambridge: Cambridge University Press.

Massad, Joseph (2003) 'The Ends of Zionism: Racism and the Palestinian Struggle', *Interventions*, Vol. 5(3), pp. 440-451.

—— (2006) 'Pinochet in Palestine', in *Al-Ahram Weekly*, 9-15 November 2006, Issue No. 819, http://weekly.ahram.org.eg/2006/819/op2.htm, downloaded 17 January 2007.

Matas, David (2005) *Aftershock: Anti-Zionism and Antisemitism*, Toronto: Dundurn.

Matgamna, Sean (2003) 'The last time we were heresy hunted', 23 July 2003, http://www.workersliberty.org/node/1115, downloaded 24 February 2007.

Mayor of London (2005) 'Why the Mayor of London will maintain dialogue with all faiths and communities', http://www.london.gov.uk/news/docs/qaradawi_dossier.pdf, downloaded 24 February 2007.

McGreal, Chris (2006) 'Palestinian plea to Floyd's Waters', *The Guardian*, 9 March 2006, http://arts.guardian.co.uk/news/story/0,,1726698,00.html, downloaded 26 February 2007.

Mearsheimer, John, and Stephen Walt (2006a) 'The Israel Lobby', *London Review of Books*, Vol. 28, No. 6, 23 March 2006, http://www.lrb.co.uk/v28/n06/mear01_.html, downloaded 26 February 2007.

—— (2006b) 'The Israel lobby and US foreign policy', Faculty Research Working Paper Series, Harvard University and John F Kennedy School of Government, Working Paper Number: RWP06-011, 13 March 2006, http://ksgnotes1.harvard.edu/Research/wpaper.nsf/rwp/RWP06-011, downloaded 26 February 2007.

MEMRI (2004) 'Special Dispatch Series – No. 753', 27 July 2004, http://memri.org/bin/articles.cgi?Page=subjects&Area=antisemitism&ID=SP75304, downloaded 24 February 2007.

Miller, Rory (2007) 'British anti-Zionism then and now', *Covenant*, Vol. 1, Issue 1, http://www.covenant.idc.ac.il/en/vol1/issue2/miller.html, downloaded 3 May 2007.

Morris, Benny (2006) 'The ignorance at the heart of an innuendo', *The New Republic*, post date 28 April 2006, issue date 8 May 2006, https://ssl.tnr.com/p/docsub.mhtml?i=20060508&s=morris050806, downloaded 29 June 2007.

Neumann, Michael (2002) 'What is Antisemitism?', *CounterPunch*, 4 June 2002, http://www.counterpunch.org/neumann0604.html, downloaded 8 September 2005.

News.BBC.co.uk (2002) 'PM's wife "sorry" in suicide bomb row', 18 June 2002, http://news.bbc.co.uk/2/hi/uk_news/politics/2051372.stm, downloaded 26 February 2007.

—— (2004) 'Tonge sacked over suicide comment', 23 January 2004, http://news.bbc.co.uk/2/hi/uk_news/politics/3421669.stm, downloaded 26 February 2007.

—— (2005) 'Mayor censored over Nazi jibe row', 14 February 2005, http://news.bbc.co.uk/1Zhi/england/london/4262833.stm, downloaded 24 February 2007.

―― (2006) 'Conflict affects sport and arts', http://news.bbc.co.uk/1/hi/scotland/glasgow_and_west/5238840.stm, downloaded 26 February 2007.

Or-Bach, Alon (2006) 'Respect is a "Zionist free" party – Yvonne Ridley', 17 February 2006, http://www.engageonline.org.uk/blog/article.php?id=253, downloaded 15 February 2007, from a report, no longer available, at http://www.felixonline.co.uk/v2/article.php?id=2923.

Orwell, George (2003), *Homage to Catalonia*, London: Penguin.

Pappe, Ilan (2006), 'Genocide in Gaza', 2 September 2006, http://electronicintifada.net/v2/article5656.shtml, downloaded 16 February 2007.

Phillips, Melanie (2006) *Londonistan*, London: Gibson Square.

Pike, Jon (2005) 'After the Boycott', 25 September 2005, http://www.engageonline.org.uk/blog/article.php?id=10, downloaded 29 June 2006.

―― (2006) 'Chuck out 198c', 9 May 2006, http://www.engageonline.org.uk/blog/article.php?id=410, downloaded 14 February 2007.

―― (2006a) 'The Myth of the Institutional Boycott', 13 February 2006, http://www.engageonline.org.uk/blog/article.php?id=231, downloaded 14 February 2006.

―― (2006b) 'Academic freedom and the limits of boycotts: some Kantian considerations', *Engage Journal*, Issue 1, January 2006, http://www.engageonline.org.uk/journal/index.php?journal_id=5&article_id=25, downloaded 29 June 2007.

―― (2007) Speech to the Engage meeting, 11 July 2007, http://www.engageonline.org.uk/blog/article.php?id=1261, downloaded 19 July 2007.

Postone, Moishe (2006) 'History and Helplessness: Mass Mobilization and Contemporary Forms of Anticapitalism', *Public Culture* 18: 1.

PSC Campaigns (2006) 'Campaign to stop Arsenal supporting Israeli apartheid', http://www.palestinecampaign.org/campaigns.asp?d=y&id=142, downloaded 26 February 2007.

Qumsiyeh, Mazin (no date) 'Ten Zionist Obfuscations', http://www.monabaker.com/conflictfacts2.htm, downloaded 16 February 2007.

Reynolds, Paul (2007) 'Profile: David Miliband', 29 June 2007, http://news.bbc.co.uk/2/hi/uk_news/politics/6248508.stm, downloaded 29 June 2007.

Rich, Dave (2007) 'The Left and the Holocaust', *Engage Journal*, Issue 4, http://www.engageonline.org.uk/journal/index.php?journal_id=14&article_id=55, downloaded 15 February 2007.

Rose, Gillian (1996) *Mourning Becomes the Law*, Cambridge: CUP.

Rose, Jacqueline (2005) *The Question of Zion*, Princeton: PUP.

―― (2007) 'Lets have more boycott debate', *The Guardian*, 15 June 2007, http://www.guardian.co.uk/letters/story/0,,2103659,00.html, downloaded 2 August 2007.

Rose, John (2004) *The Myths of Zionism*, London: Pluto.

Rose, Steven (2006) 'Let's boycott the universities' *Comment is Free*, 12 May 2006, http://commentisfree.guardian.co.uk/steven_rose/2006/05/why_an_academic_boycott_of_isr.html, downloaded 25 June 2006.

Rosenfeld, Alvin H. (2006) 'Progressive' Jewish Thought and the New Antisemitism,' American Jewish Committee, August 2006, http://www.ajc.org/atf/cf/%7B42D75369-D582-4380-8395-D25925B85EAF%7D/PROGRESSIVE_JEWISH_THOUGHT.PDF, downloaded 25 July 2007.

Roth, Philip (2005) *The plot against America*, London: Vintage.

Saad-Ghorayeb, Amal (2002) *Hizbollah: Politics and Religion*, London: Pluto.

Sacranie, Iqbal (2005) 'Holocaust memorial day is too exclusive', *The Guardian*, 20 September 2005, http://www.guardian.co.uk/comment/story/0,,1573739,00.html, downloaded 17 July 2007.

Said, Edward (1978) *Orientalism*, Harmondsworth: Penguin.

Searle, Chris (2007) 'Interview: Gilad Atzmon', *Morning Star Online*, 12 November 2007, http://www.morningstaronline.co.uk/index2.php/free/culture/music/interview2, downloaded 12 November 2007.

Seymour, David M. (2006) 'On not being criticised', 7 August 2006, http://www.engageonline.org.uk/blog/article.php?id=555, downloaded 24 July 2007.

—— (2007) 'Fantasy and antisemitism', 28 June 2007, http://www.engageonline.org.uk/blog/article.php?id=1190, downloaded 25 July 2007.

Shiblak, Abbas (2005) *Iraqi Jews: a history of mass exodus*, London: Saqi.

Simonon, Alexandra (2006), 'Belgian holocaust memorial deemed inappropriate by Belgian government commission, 22 March 2006, http://www.engageonline.org.uk/blog/article.php?id=317, downloaded 24 July 2007.

Sizer, Stephen, 'Church's share sale is not anti-Semitic', *The Independent*, 20 February 2006, http://comment.independent.co.uk/letters/article346528.ece, downloaded 10 November 2007.

Socialist Worker Online (2006), 'Politics in store at cultures of resistance concert' 2 December 2006, Issue 2029, http://www.socialistworker.co.uk/article.php?article_id=10234, downloaded 28 February 2007.

Soueif, Ahdaf (2006) 'A project of dispossession can never be a noble cause', *The Guardian*, 17 November 2006, http://www.guardian.co.uk/commentisfree/story/0,,1950245,00.html, downloaded 10 December 2006.

Stern, Ken (2006) *A new antisemitism?* New York: American Jewish Committee.

Stoll, Ira (2006), '"Israel Lobby" Caused War in Iraq, September 11 Attacks, Professor Says', *New York Sun*, 29 September 2006, http://www.nysun.com/article/40629, downloaded 29 June 2007.

Strawson, John (2006), 'Zionism and Apartheid: The Analogy in the Politics of International Law', *Engage Journal*, Issue 2, http://www.engageonline.org.uk/journal/index.php?journal_id=10&article_id=34, downloaded 25 July 2007.

Tatchell, Peter (2005) 'Dr Yusuf al-Qaradawi Exposed', *Harry's Place*, http://hurryupharry.bloghouse.net/archives/Qaradawi%20dossier.doc, downloaded 24 February 2007.

WarOnWant.org (2006) 'Roger Waters joins the war on want', http://www.waronwant.org/?lid=8424, downloaded 26 February 2007.

Wheatcroft, Geoffrey (2006) 'After the rhapsody, the bitter legacy of Israel and the left', *The Guardian*, 24 March 2006, http://www.guardian.co.uk/commentisfree/story/0,,1738410,00.html, downloaded 22 February 2007.

Whitaker, Brian (2002) 'Selective Memri', *The Guardian*, 12 August 2002, http://www.guardian.co.uk/elsewhere/journalist/story/0,7792,773258,00.html, downloaded 24 February 2007.

Whitehead, Andrew (2002) '"No common Ground": Joseph Massad and Benny Morris Discuss the Middle East', *History Workshop Journal*, Issue 53.

Woodward, Will (2003) 'Lecturers' union to debate boycott of Israel', *The Guardian*, 5 May 2003, http://education.guardian.co.uk/higher/worldwide/story/0,,949758,00.html, downloaded 14 February 2007.

Yamada, Shirabe (2004) 'Hebrew University to displace Palestinian families', http://electronicintifada.net/cgi-bin/artman/exec/view.cgi/10/3361, downloaded 14 February 2007.

Yeheskeli, Tsadok (2002) 'I made them a stadium in the middle of the camp', *Yediot Aharonot*, 31 May 2002, available at http://gush-shalom.org/archives/kurdi_eng.html, downloaded 8 November 2007.

Yudkin, Michael (2007) 'Is an academic boycott of Israel justified?' *Engage Journal*, Special Issue, April 2007, http://www.engageonline.org.uk/journal/index.php?journal_id=15&article_id=61, downloaded 20 July 2007.

Websites

British Campaign for the Universities of Palestine (BRICUP), http://www.bricup.org.uk
Comment is Free, http://commentisfree.guardian.co.uk/index.html
David Duke's website http://www.davidduke.com
David Irving's website, http://www.fpp.co.uk, Focal Point Publications
Democratiya, http://www.democratiya.com
Dissident Voice, http://www.dissidentvoice.org
Engage, http://www.engageonline.org.uk
Gilad Atzmon's website http://www.gilad.co.uk
Israel Shamir's website http://www.israelshamir.net
Jewish Tribal Review website http://www.jewishtribalreview.org
LabourStart, http://www.labourstart.org
Let's Kick Racism out of Football, http://www.kickitout.org
London Evening Standard, http://www.thisislondon.co.uk
Middle East Online, http://www.middle-east-online.com
Mona Baker's website, http://www.monabaker.com
Palestinian Campaign for the Cultural and Academic Boycott of Israel (PACBI), http://www.pacbi.org
Palestine Solidarity Campaign Gymru-Wales, http://psccymru.org.uk
Palestine Solidarity Campaign, http://www.palestinecampaign.org
Peace Palestine blog, http://www.peacepalestine.blogspot.com
Socialist Worker, http://www.socialistworker.co.uk
Sue Blackwell, http://www.sue.be

Numbered images

Image 1: Blood Orange, 'Boycott Israeli Goods; don't squeeze a Jaffa, crush the occupation', http://www.boycottisrael.co.uk/images/jaffa.jpg, downloaded 23 July 2007.

Image 2: Ariel Sharon eating a baby, Dave Brown, cartoon in *The Independent* newspaper, 27 January 2003, image available at http://www.usefulwork.com/shark/independent_sharon.jpg, downloaded 5 July 2007.

Image 3: Latuff (undated) 'Gaza Strip', http://www.normanfinkelstein.com/img/features/latuff/show.php?nam=39, downloaded 16 February 2007.

Image 4: 'Stars of David and Stripes', *The Independent*, 27 April 2006, http://hurryupharry.bloghouse.net/archives/Independent%20cover.JPG, downloaded 25 July 2007.

Image 5: 'Map of Israeli terror', http://www.respectcoalition.org/?ite=1127, downloaded 5 August 2007.

Reports

Report of the Stephen Lawrence Inquiry, 24 February 1999, http://www.archive.official-documents.co.uk/document/cm42/4262/sli-06.htm, downloaded 26 July 2007.

Association of University Teachers (2005), Recommendations of the Investigative Commission, for recommendation to AUT Council in May 2006, the Investigative Commission's recommendations to Council on international greylisting and boycotts, http://www.aut.org.uk/circulars/html/la7753.html, downloaded 14 February 2007.

Report produced by the Parliamentary All-party Committee against Antisemitism, September 2006, http://thepcaa.org/Report.pdf, downloaded 21 June 2007.

Community Security Trust (2006) *Antisemitic Incidents Reports 2005*, London, http://www.thecst.org.uk/index.cfm?content=7&menu=7, downloaded 21 December 2006.

Community Security Trust (2007) *Antisemitic Incidents Reports 2006*, London, http://www.thecst.org.uk/docs/Incidents%5FReport%5F06.pdf, downloaded 15 February 2007.

ADL report: 'Attitudes towards Jews and the Middle East in Six European Countries', July 2007, First International Resources, http://www.adl.org/anti_semitism/European_Attitudes_Survey_July_2007.pdf, downloaded 27 July 2007.

European Union, *EUMC Working Definition of Antisemitism*, http://fra.europa.eu/fra/material/pub/AS/AS-WorkingDefinition-draft.pdf, downloaded 8 November 2007.

This Green and Pleasant Land: Britain and the Jews

Shalom Lappin[*]

> *I will not cease from mental fight,*
> *Nor shall my sword sleep in my hand,*
> *Till we have built Jerusalem*
> *In England's green and pleasant land.*
>
> from William Blake, *Jerusalem*, 1804

I. INTRODUCTION

In 2006, the United Kingdom celebrated the 350th anniversary of Cromwell's readmission of Jews to England. This concluded a four-hundred-year absence of organized Jewish life in the country following the expulsion in 1290 under Edward I. According to a widely accepted view, held by many British Jews and non-Jews alike, Britain has provided generous sanctuary to waves of Jewish refugees fleeing European antisemitism. It has given them a tolerant, accepting environment in which they have progressed steadily from poverty and exclusion to full integration into British society. Britain is also frequently credited with leading the fight to save European Jews from the onslaught of Nazism and assisting the survivors to rebuild their lives after the Second World War.

Jonathan Sacks, the Chief Rabbi of the United Synagogue of the United Kingdom, expresses this attitude in his reflections on the anniversary of the readmission:

> The Jews who came here loved Britain. They owed it their freedom to live as Jews without fear. In many cases they owed it their lives. Perhaps it takes an outsider fully to appreciate how remarkable Britain is. Jews loved its tolerance, its courtesy, its understated yet resolute commitment to liberty and civility. They loved

---

[*] King's College, London. Earlier versions of this paper were presented in the seminar series of the Yale Initiative for the Interdisciplinary Study of Antisemitism in November 2007 and in the Oxford Hebrew and Jewish Studies Centre Israel Lecture Series in March 2008. I am grateful to the audiences of these forums for thoughtful feedback. I am indebted to Anthony Julius, Rory Miller, and Colin Shindler for invaluable discussion of many of the ideas presented in this paper and for generous assistance with historical research material. I would also like to thank Mitchell Cohen, Lori Coulter, Eve Garrard, Norman Geras, Jonathan Ginzburg, Ariel Hessayon, Edward Kaplan, Yaakov Lappin, Joe Rothstein, Charles Small, Mort Weinfeld, and two anonymous reviewers from the YIISA Working Paper Series for very useful comments on earlier drafts. I bear sole responsibility for the content of the paper and any mistakes that it may contain.

Britain because it was British. It knew who and what it was: the leader of freedom in the modern world, the home of Shakespeare, Newton, the Industrial Revolution and the mother of parliaments. It had confidence in itself, and because it did so, it did not feel threatened by newcomers. Without that confidence, bad things happen.[1]

In fact, there are good grounds for regarding this view of Britain's traditional relations with Jews as largely inaccurate. Recent events have seen the emergence of a distinctly uncomfortable environment for Anglo-Jewry. It might be suggested that this is a relatively new phenomenon conditioned entirely by current demographic and political factors. However, when one consults the historical record it becomes clear that much of what is now taking place bears a clear connection to a well-established pattern of widespread hostility to Jews as members of a cultural and ethnic collectivity that has existed in Britain over many centuries.

The acute hostility to Israel that has become increasingly dominant in large segments of British public discourse is not simply a critical response to Israeli government policy and action, however worthy of criticism these may be. In this paper, I will argue that the current wave of anti-Israel sentiment that is on such prominent display in the press, in academic circles, and among other generators of public opinion must be understood as intimately connected to deeply-rooted social attitudes toward Jews that have been integral to British history. These attitudes have emerged over many centuries, and they have played a major role in conditioning popular social responses to the Jewish community in Britain, as well as to Jews abroad. They have also received direct expression in public policy on Jewish issues throughout Britain's history.

To make the case for this view, I will briefly survey some of the defining events in the history of British Jewry from its origins in the Middle Ages to the postwar years. I sketch this long historical perspective in order to show the depth and consistency of certain clear themes that have characterized Britain's treatment of its Jews. I will also use these events to illustrate the strategies that the leadership of British Jewry have evolved for dealing with the hostility and ambivalence that has frequently greeted their efforts to integrate into the British social fabric. These survival techniques have also made a significant contribution to the situation that British Jewry occupies in its host country, and they continue to characterize the leadership's response to current events.

Before turning to the historical aspect of this discussion, it is necessary to clarify the terms in which much of the contemporary debate on Israel is being conducted in British public discourse.

II. The Current "Debate" on Israel: Lobbies and Boycotts

Since the start of the second Palestinian Intifada in September 2000, the press and public discussion in Britain have been dominated by strident and obsessive attacks on Israel. A part of this comment constitutes legitimate, and in some cases, well-motivated criticism of Israel's policies and conduct toward the Palestinians living

---

[1] Sacks (2006).

under a repressive occupation in the territories beyond its 1967 borders. Vigorous critique is a feature of normal political debate to which any country involved in a bloody and longstanding conflict must expect to be subjected. However, much of this discourse goes well beyond objections to the policies of a government. It paints Israel as a demonic entity whose people are collectively guilty of unprecedented criminality. The country is portrayed as the instrument of an international conspiracy headed by a "Zionist lobby" that dictates American, British, and, in some versions, all of the West's foreign policy.

These claims are no longer the preserve of extremists operating on the fringes of the political spectrum. They have seeped into mainstream discussion, where they are increasingly accepted as unexceptional. Several recent examples give an indication of how far this process has progressed.[2]

Clare Short, Secretary of State for International Development in Tony Blair's government from 1997 until May 2003, posted the following statement on the *Skies are Weeping* website (http://weepingskies.blogspot.com), set up to promote a cantata written in memory of Rachel Corrie, the peace activist killed by an Israeli army bulldozer in Gaza in 2003.

> I am supporting the World Premiere of the Cantata for Rachel Corrie because there has been the usual campaign to silence even a cantata to commemorate a young woman who gave her life in order to stand for justice. I also believe that US backing for Israeli policies of expansion of the Israeli state and oppression of the Palestinian people is the major cause of bitter division and violence in the world. Best wishes, Clare Short MP

In September 2006, the All-Party Parliamentary Inquiry on Antisemitism released its report, in which it pointed to a disturbing increase in antisemitism in Britain in recent years.[3] It identified the frenzied demonization of Israel, to the exclusion of other countries involved in human rights abuses, in the press and on university campuses as a case of a political debate spilling over into group defamation. It also pointed out that this phenomenon was generating alarming levels of hostility to Jews in Britain, some of it realized in increased violence directed at Jewish targets. In fact, the threat of attacks is such that the Jewish community is the only major ethnic or religious group in Britain that is forced to provide a permanent system of guards and surveillance for its schools, religious centers, and communal institutions, which it maintains largely at its own expense.

The report was greeted with widespread indifference. Many on what currently passes for the liberal left in Britain dismissed it as a deliberate attempt to reduce all criticism of Israel to antisemitism. David Clark writing on the report in *The Guardian* said:

> Real anti-semitism is a serious and growing problem, and there is a need for political consensus about how to tackle it. But debate is poisoned and consensus becomes difficult when allegations of anti-semitism are bandied about for reasons that have

---

[2] For additional cases and a detailed discussion of the rise of a demonizing mythology in mainstream British discourse, see Lappin (2003) and (2006).

[3] The report is available from the Committee's website at http://www.thepcaa.org/Report.pdf.

nothing to do with fighting racism. An inquiry that wants to confront anti-semitism should also confront those who cheapen the term through reckless misuse.[4]

This response stands in marked contrast to the near-universal expressions of concern and support for the victims of prejudice that have attended other government inquiries into racism, such as the Macpherson Report, published in February 1999, on the racist murder of teenager Stephen Lawrence in 1993.

Richard Dawkins, who holds the Charles Simyoni Chair for the Public Understanding of Science at Oxford, is well-known for his writings on genetics and evolution. He presents himself as a militant defender of scientific humanism, and he has achieved considerable notoriety for his polemics against religion, which he identifies as the major cause of war and repression.[5] In the course of a recent interview in *The Guardian* on his campaign to promote atheism in America, Dawkins is quoted as saying:

> When you think about how fantastically successful the Jewish lobby has been, though, in fact, they are less numerous I am told—religious Jews anyway—than atheists and [yet they] more or less monopolise American foreign policy as far as many people can see. So if atheists could achieve a small fraction of that influence, the world would be a better place.[6]

Unlike Short, Dawkins has not made the Middle East one of his major public interests. His comment is (if accurately presented in the article) all the more revealing for being an off-handed remark tangential to his primary concerns. Not less significant is the fact that it provoked very little critical reaction. These sorts of remarks carry minimal (if any) cost to the career or public credibility of the people who make them, and they are now generally regarded as unexceptional in public discourse here.

Britain is unique among Western countries in hosting a large, high-profile campaign to boycott Israel. In 2007, four British unions passed boycott motions of one kind or another. These include the National Union of Journalists, UNISON (the public service union), the Transport and General Workers Union (TGWU), and the Universities and Colleges Union (UCU). The latter three are major organizations representing hundreds of thousands of members. The campaign for an academic boycott of Israel within the UCU (and its predecessor unions the AUT and NATFHE) has generated intense controversy both in the United Kingdom and abroad.

Organized labor in the United States and North American academic institutions have, for the most part, strongly rejected the British campaign, particularly the academic boycott.[7] Active hostility to Israel has increased markedly across Western Europe over the past seven years in a manner comparable to the emergence of extreme anti-Israel sentiment in the United Kingdom, and often surpassing it. However, the

---

[4] Clark (2006). The article carries the subtitle text: "Attempts to brand the left as anti-Jewish because of its support of Palestinian rights only make it harder to tackle genuine racism."

[5] Dawkins (2006).

[6] MacAskill (2007).

[7] See the statement of American Labor Unions of July 18 condemning the boycott at http://www.spme.net/cgi-bin/articles.cgi?ID=2647, and Traubmann (2007) on the statement by 300 US university presidents against the boycott.

boycott has gained little if any traction on the Continent. In fact, the Confederation of German Trade Unions has recently spoken out against it.[8]

On September 28, 2007, the UCU announced that it had cancelled its planned year-long debate of the boycott (called for by a resolution passed at its annual conference in May 2007) in light of legal advice stating that the proposed academic boycott of Israel would violate the United Kingdom's anti-discrimination laws.[9] Many boycott supporters greeted this decision with a volley of protest, charging that pressure from external lobby groups had suppressed free speech in the union through legal maneuvers.

Six members of the UCU's Strategy and Finance Committee (the body that took the decision), who are affiliated with the UCU Left group, issued a statement explaining the Committee's reasons for accepting its lawyer's advice. In the course of this clarification they said: "We do not doubt that well-funded groups are ready to engage in legal action against the Union, but even before that stage was reached, the Trustees made it clear that they would feel obliged to fulfill their legal duty to ensure that union funds were only spent on lawful purposes."[10] The hint at the dark workings of an illicit lobby waiting in the wings to bankrupt the union with expensive legal action is unmistakable here.

Interestingly, Anthony Lester, the head of the legal team that advised the UCU to drop the campaign, is a leading human rights lawyer who helped pioneer anti-racism and equal opportunity legislation over the past thirty years. The revelation of this fact seems to have had little impact on those boycott advocates who are describing the union's withdrawal from the motion as another instance of the effectiveness of a powerful international "Zionist" operation to suppress all criticism of Israel.

At its May 2008 conference, the UCU Executive introduced a slightly modified version of the 2007 resolution, and it was passed without opponents of the motion being permitted a significant opportunity to speak against it.[11]

While the influence of the "Israel/Zionist Lobby" is an increasingly prominent theme of public discussion in Britain, other cases of lobbying that affect both British government policy and academic freedom cause little, if any, concern, even when they are widely reported in the press. On December 14, 2006, the Attorney General, Lord Goldsmith, acting on Tony Blair's instructions, cancelled a major criminal investigation by the Serious Fraud Office into allegations that the British arms manufacturer BAE was paying large bribes to Saudi government officials in order to secure military contracts. The inquiry was halted to avoid losing Saudi business and to prevent possible damage to Britain's relations with the Saudi regime. In his statement announcing the decision, Lord Goldsmith said:

---

[8] The Deutsche Gewerkschaftsbund (DGB)'s anti-boycott resolution of September 6, 2007 is reported on the Jewish Labor Committee's website at http://www.jewishlaborcommittee.org/2007/09/german_unions_follow_us_labor.html.

[9] The UCU press release on this decision appears on its website at http://www.ucu.org.uk/index.cfm?articleid=2829.

[10] The full statement is available at http://www.engageonline.org.uk/blog/article.php?id=1456.

[11] See Eve Garrard's account of the process through which this motion was adopted at http://normblog.typepad.com/normblog/2008/05/passing-motion-25-by-eve-garrard.html.

> It has been necessary to balance the need to maintain the rule of law against the wider public interest. No weight has been given to commercial interests or to the national economic interest.
>
> The prime minister and the foreign and defence secretaries have expressed the clear view that continuation of the investigation would cause serious damage to UK/Saudi security, intelligence and diplomatic cooperation, which is likely to have seriously negative consequences for the UK public interest in terms of both national security and our highest priority foreign policy objectives in the Middle East.[12]

The OECD issued a sharp criticism of Britain's action, which, it said, may have violated the country's treaty obligations on the elimination of bribery and corruption in the awarding of international contracts.[13] This affair represents a clear interference in domestic British legal processes by Saudi economic and political interests. It has also damaged Britain's international standing within the OECD. While it was widely covered in the media, it has had little impact on mainstream political debate on the influence of foreign lobbies in British public policy.

In 2006, Cambridge University Press (CUP) published *Alms for Jihad* by J. Millard Burr and Robert O. Collins, both of the University of California at Santa Barbara. The book studies several Islamic charities that, the authors claim, have provided funds to terrorist groups. In the spring of 2007, Sheikh Khalid bin Mahfouz, a Saudi businessman and banker, brought a libel suit in the British courts against CUP over assertions made in the book concerning members of his family. Libel laws in the United Kingdom strongly favor the plaintiff. To avoid a costly court case, CUP withdrew the book from publication, destroyed the remaining unsold copies, and asked libraries to remove it from circulation. It also paid an undisclosed amount in a settlement. Bin Mahfouz has brought previous libel suits in Britain against several other authors and publishers who attempted to link him to financial support for Al Qaeda. All of them were settled without a trial, through the payment of damages. He has not been required to appear in court to provide evidence that the assertions that he has challenged are false.[14]

These suits would seem to constitute an obvious instance of a wealthy businessman using his financial resources and the skewed British libel laws to suppress the publication of material of which he disapproves. They have attracted little, if any, attention in the British media, and no reaction from people who express deep anxiety over the role of pro-Israel pressure groups in Britain and America in restricting discussion on the Middle East.

Given the intensity of this discussion and the deep animosity to Israel on display in much of the British media, the "Lobby" does not appear to be enjoying much success in controlling public debate. Its inability to constrain this debate is further indicated by the best-seller status of Mearsheimer and Walt's *The Israel Lobby and US Foreign Policy* (Farrar, Straus & Giroux, 2007) and the massive publicity generated by their article "The Israel Lobby" in the *London Review of Books* (March 23, 2006). The

---

[12] Leigh and Evans (2007).
[13] Rob Evans (2007).
[14] Donadio (2007).

widespread protests over the putative suppression of criticism at the hands of the "Lobby" are strikingly selective in their concerns and bear little relation to the facts.

Arab and Islamic governments provide substantial funding for Middle East and Islamic studies programs throughout UK and American universities without attracting the stigma of illicit lobbying. Saudi Arabia supports mosques and Islamic religious institutions in Britain and throughout Europe, sometimes with acutely problematic consequences, but this phenomenon does not seem to provoke the same sort of intense anxiety as the "Israel lobby" does among most representatives of what is now packaged as "progressive" opinion in Britain.

The theme of collective Jewish malevolence driving a powerful international conspiracy that subverts the workings of government, the press, the economy, and foreign affairs is a staple of classic anti-Jewish mythology. Its rapid permeation of British public discourse requires explanation. If the popular view of Britain as historically benign in its view of Jews is accurate, then the rise of Jewish conspiracy obsessions in the context of Israel demonology constitutes a new phenomenon in which traditional European attitudes have been imported into a society where they have previously been denied a firm hold. One might seek to explain this event by pointing to the emergence of a multicultural ethic in Britain that, in legitimizing alternative cultural norms, seeks to appease radical Islamist ideas concerning Israel and Jews.

Rabbi Sacks seems to suggest something along these lines when he says:

> The paradox of our time is that multiculturalism, designed to make minorities feel more at home, has had the opposite effect. Britain is a less tolerant society today than it was fifty years ago when I was at school. Never once in those years did I experience anti-Semitism. Many of our children and grandchildren do experience it. Our post-modern culture with its moral relativism and its emphasis on rights rather than responsibilities has, by the law of unintended consequences, made things worse, not better.[15]

In fact, this explanation is not convincing. While the growth of Islamist ideology in Britain has, as in the rest of Europe, played a significant role in promoting anti-Israel and anti-Jewish attitudes, Islamists do not occupy the positions of influence required to account for the current onslaught. The journalists of the British press, the politicians, the academics, and the leaders of the unions who are conducting this campaign and importing it into the political mainstream are, for the most part, neither Islamists nor Muslims. Moreover, "liberal" apologists for radical Islamism do not, in general, embrace its hostility to feminism, gay rights, or Hindus. If they are sympathetic to its deep hatred of Israel and its antisemitism, then it is, apparently, because these resonate with their own beliefs.

The popular notion of Britain as a society tolerant of Jews seriously misrepresents the history of the country's relations with its Jewish population. This history reveals a widespread and deeply-rooted view of Jews as fundamentally alien to British life and illicit as a collectivity. Within the confines of this view, Jews are acceptable to the extent that they can be rendered invisible through Anglicization, and they are problematic in proportion to the explicitness of their Jewish cultural

---

[15] Sacks (2006).

identity. The social entry that Jews have been granted is, in general, conditional upon suppression of one's Jewish associations and cultural properties in the public domain, with those who distance themselves from these associations completely enjoying the highest level of acceptance.

These attitudes have shaped British conduct over many centuries on a wide range of issues, from Jewish immigration to Jewish political rights. That Jews are now fully enfranchised and protected by anti-discrimination laws has not eradicated many of the social views that have stigmatized and excluded them in the past. Moreover, the leadership of the British Jewish community has, over many generations, evolved strategies for surviving in this environment that involve accommodating and cooperating with many of the demands imposed by the non-Jewish framework in which they live.

When considered from this perspective, the current outburst of anti-Israel demonology and Zionist conspiracy-mongering is not an entirely novel phenomenon foreign to traditional British political behavior. Instead it appears as a new version of a longstanding hostility to Jewish collectivity, a hostility to which Israel is the greatest challenge in modern history. The current reaction to Israel, then, mixes legitimate political criticism with deeply held social attitudes toward Jews. It is frequently difficult to disentangle these elements in the debate now occupying such a prominent place in British public discourse. To understand these attitudes more clearly and to trace their sources, it is necessary to recall several important occurrences that have determined the shape of British Jewish history.

III. MEDIEVAL PERSECUTION AND EXPULSION

Organized Jewish life in England began with the Norman invasion in 1066. The Jews came to England in the medieval period largely from France and Germany, and they were concentrated primarily in London.

They were dependent upon money-lending and commerce for their livelihood, due to the restrictions imposed on Jews owning land and their exclusion from craft guilds. They achieved a fair degree of prosperity in their initial century in the country, and they supplied the royal treasury with an important part of its revenue through a special department of the Exchequer (the Jewish Exchequer) devoted specifically to collecting taxes from Jews. Henry III subsequently subjected them to ruinously heavy levies (tallages) to finance his military campaigns and building projects. This resulted in the virtual bankrupting of the community, which greatly undermined the incentive for his successor, Edward I, to continue the royal protection that secured their right of residence in England.[16]

Incitement and violence against the Jews of England began in the twelfth century. The first recorded instance of the blood libel occurred in 1144, when Jews were accused of the ritual murder of William of Norwich during the Passover period.[17]

---

[16] For a detailed and authoritative description of Medieval English Jewry and the expulsion, see Roth (1964, chaps. 1-5).

[17] For a history of the blood libel, see Julius (forthcoming). Julius' book provides a comprehensive social and cultural history of antisemitism in Britain from the Middle Ages until contemporary times.

Further charges of ritual murder were made in, among other places, Gloucester in 1168, Bury St. Edmunds in 1181, and Bristol in 1183, and they were accompanied by escalating attacks against the local Jewish communities. These accusations continued in England throughout the thirteenth century, reaching a climax in 1255, when close to 100 Jews were accused of the alleged ritual murder of a young boy, Hugh of Lincoln. Nineteen were executed, but the remainder were eventually released.

England was the first European country to implement, by royal decree in 1218, a Church directive that Jews wear a badge to distinguish them from Christians. This was part of a series of anti-Jewish measures that the Church authorities mandated at the Fourth Lateran Council in 1215, and England led the rest of Europe in enforcing these measures.

Large-scale violence against the Jews began at the end of the twelfth century, when a Jewish delegation appeared at the gates of Westminster Abbey in an attempt to present gifts to Richard I on the occasion of his coronation on September 3, 1189. They were prevented from entering the cathedral and rioting against Jewish homes throughout London followed, with many killed or injured. The attacks spread to other parts of the country during the next six months, culminating in the bloody assault on the Jews of York during Passover in March 1190, in which over 150 people were killed.

In the next hundred years, numerous attacks occurred in the course of which several small Jewish communities were entirely destroyed. In addition, local exclusions were imposed, banning Jews from many towns and counties. On July 18, 1290, Edward issued an act expelling all Jews from England as of November 1 of that year. This effectively ended the organized Jewish presence in Britain for four hundred years.

Although Jews did not reside openly in England after 1290 until the readmission in 1656, a community of Spanish and Portuguese crypto-Jews (alternatively referred to as "Conversos," "New Christians," and "Marranos"), fleeing the Inquisition in their native countries, established itself in London in the sixteenth century. They lived under cover of their forced conversion to Christianity, and they were in constant fear of being exposed. In 1609, an argument broke out within the Portuguese group, leading one faction to denounce its adversaries as Jews. This resulted in the expulsion of the entire Portuguese Converso community. Interestingly, Shakespeare's *The Merchant of Venice* and Marlowe's *The Jew of Malta* were both written and performed less than twenty years before this event, indicating the persistence of virulently anti-Jewish imagery in the popular imagination of the Elizabethan era.

England's action was the first global deportation of Jews from a country in Europe. It occurred over two hundred years prior to the Spanish expulsion of Jews and Muslims in 1492, and it set a precedent for later events of this kind. The animosity that motivated it was rooted in a toxic combination of religious prejudice and economic resentment that provided the engine for European antisemitism throughout subsequent centuries. While the number of Jews in medieval England was small (Roth (1964) cites an estimate of 16,000 in 1290), the fact that it played a particularly prominent role in the anti-Jewish persecutions of the Middle Ages is significant.[18]

---

[18] See Roth (1964, 91 and 276, note (a)) for a discussion of the size of the Jewish population in England in this period.

This history established a set of cultural attitudes that continued to influence mainstream British perceptions of Jews well beyond the medieval period.

Contemporary popular British approaches to the country's persecution of its Jews in the Middle Ages contrast sharply with the dominant view of the Spanish expulsion. The latter is generally acknowledged as both a Jewish and a European catastrophe. The former does not, in general, figure in the medieval history curriculum for UK schools, and it is rarely mentioned in the many documentaries on medieval English history aired in the British media. It is airbrushed out of most official and unofficial discussions of the monarchs under which the violence and the expulsions took place, and it occupies no real position in the country's understanding of its medieval past, a period that is widely venerated as of formative importance in laying the foundations for British culture and institutions.

IV. CROMWELL AND THE READMISSION

According to a popular account of the readmission, the Puritan revolution produced a more favorable attitude toward Jews, and in 1656 Cromwell extended an invitation to Dutch Jews to settle in England. In fact, no such invitation was issued, and the recognition of the right of Jews to live in the country was not achieved through legislation or executive decree.[19]

In 1655, Rabbi Menashe ben Israel, an influential religious leader of the Amsterdam Jewish community, arrived in London to submit a request to Cromwell for readmission of Jews. He had written a pamphlet describing his proposed conditions for their residence. These included freedom of religious practice, the right to trade and engage in commerce, repeal of the medieval laws enacted against Jews, and communal autonomy for internal issues. The plan also specified the appointment of a special government officer to control the influx of Jewish immigrants, an oath of allegiance to the government, and strict surveillance of the newcomers.

Cromwell was interested in improving Britain's trade and commercial position, and he saw considerable advantage in attracting well-connected Jewish merchants from Amsterdam to relocate their business activities to London. He presented the proposal to the Council of State on November 12, 1655, but the Council was unable to agree on it. It referred the request to an external consultative conference, which met on December 4 and again on December 18 of that year. Various religious figures and business interests in the City of London expressed considerable opposition at these sessions, and noisy popular resentment was also very much in evidence. In the end, the conference did not reach a decision, and Cromwell adjourned it.

At the time of this controversy, a community of Spanish Converso merchants existed in London. England and Spain had been at war since the fall of 1655, and, as a result, this community was in a vulnerable position. Government officials seized the property of a wealthy member of the group, Antonio Rodriguez Robles, when he was denounced as a Spanish national by one of his rivals. He petitioned Cromwell for restoration of his interests on the grounds that he was not Spanish but a Portuguese Jew who had fled the Inquisition. After some delay, the Council of State

---

[19] For descriptions of the readmission and Jewish life in the time of the Restoration see Roth (1964, chaps. 7-8), Katz (1994), and Hessayon (2006).

appears to have approved the petition, and Robles' property was returned to him on May 16, 1656. This action created the informal basis for legalizing the Conversos' status as Jews, and they established a synagogue on Cree Church Lane in London. It was through this individual precedent, then, that the existing Jewish presence in England, previously concealed by forced conversion, was recognized. Immigration of small numbers Jews from the Spanish and Portuguese community in Amsterdam followed.

The precedent on the basis of which the Jewish presence in London was accepted did not provide legal recognition of a Jewish right to live in England. With the restoration of the monarchy under Charles II in 1660 (in fact, immediately after Cromwell's death in 1658), a significant movement of reaction agitated to reverse the readmission policy. Charles had no sympathy for this movement, and he deflected its demands, effectively placing the Jews under royal protection.

In the years following the restoration, the Jewish community in London was able to prosper and slowly expand. They were left largely in peace, and several of its wealthier members achieved a high degree of social acceptance. However, they were subject to numerous economic and political restrictions (thus, for example, they were not permitted to trade in retail as freemen of the City nor could they occupy major political or judicial positions). When attempts were made to rescind the legal constraints imposed on them, widespread popular opposition emerged in which the traditional hostility was on full display.

The Jewish Naturalization Bill (the Jew Bill) of 1753 provides a particularly clear instance of this pattern.[20] Alien residents were subject to a variety of disadvantages, such as prohibitions against owning or inheriting land, owning ships, or trading with overseas plantations. Jews could escape some of these limitations through a costly procedure of partial naturalization known as "endenization," which still did not remove the ban on land inheritance. They were not, however, eligible for full naturalization, as this was open only to Christians. In the spring of 1753, both houses of Parliament passed a bill permitting naturalization of foreign born Jews who had been resident in Britain or Ireland for at least three years, and it became law with royal approval. During the following six months, a massive popular campaign against the law was waged in the press, public meeting places, churches, and the streets. It featured traditional anti-Jewish prejudice and played on the specter of foreign Jews taking control of the country. This campaign was so vociferous that it forced repeal of the law on December 20, 1753.

Pogroms in Poland and the Ukraine in 1768 brought a wave of impoverished Eastern European Jewish immigrants to London, where they were supported by the Jewish community. This influx created social problems and resentments that resulted in the government imposing restrictions on Jewish immigration in 1771 and 1774. The Jewish community itself supported these restrictions because of the negative reaction that the immigrants were attracting and the strain on its charitable resources. The Lord Mayor of London offered free passage to Jewish immigrants willing to return to their countries of origin.[21] Variations on this response to Jewish immigration were to be repeated throughout the first half of the twentieth century.

---

[20] See Roth (1964, 212-23) for the details of the Jew Bill controversy.
[21] See Roth (1964, 235-6).

Popular notions of Cromwell inviting the Jews to return to England and their arriving to a generous welcome have no basis in fact. The opposition that Cromwell encountered in his attempt to secure legislative approval for Rabbi Menashe ben Israel's proposal for readmission led him to abandon it. He succeeded in achieving limited recognition of the legitimacy of an already existing Jewish presence in London through an indirect precedent. This ruling was made in the context of a war with Spain in which Converso Jews fleeing the Inquisition were acknowledged as less problematic than agents of the Spanish monarchy. Once permitted to live openly in the country, the Jews were able to increase their numbers and gradually secure their positions through a series of informal arrangements and incremental improvements. Their willingness to sustain a low public profile was a perennially necessary condition of this process. Their position as a collectivity remained tenuous, and when efforts were made to address this position through progressive legislative changes that would have granted them recognition as a community with guaranteed rights, strong popular opposition and deep prejudice quickly emerged into full view.

V. Political Emancipation

Another popular misconception concerning Anglo-Jewish history is the idea that Jews were granted full political rights by an act of Parliament in 1858. This is by no means the case. Until this date, Jews were excluded from sitting as members of the House of Commons by the requirement that all newly elected MPs take a Christian oath in order to take their seats. Many Jews converted in order to overcome the legal and social obstacles that barred them from a wide variety of professions and many public offices.

Four bills for Jewish emancipation were introduced in Parliament between 1830 and 1836, but none of them passed. The first two were defeated in the House of Commons, while the latter two were overturned in the House of Lords. A Jewish Disabilities Bill was blocked in the House of Lords twice in 1848, and again in 1849, 1851, and each year from 1853 to 1857. Between 1830 and 1858, thirteen bills designed to permit Jewish membership of the House of Commons were rejected because of strong opposition, most of it in the House of Lords.[22]

Between 1847 and 1852, Lionel Rothschild was elected to the Commons three times and, on each occasion, was prevented from taking his seat. In 1858, Disraeli introduced a bill that permitted each chamber to determine its own conditions for membership independently. It encountered significant opposition in the Lords, but it was eventually passed by both Houses. This law resulted in the Commons suspending the required Christian oath for MPs, and Rothschild was finally allowed to enter the House with an alternative pledge, eleven years after first being elected.

Contrary to a widespread impression, no general act of Jewish political emancipation was adopted. Rothschild established an individual precedent that permitted Jews to enter the House of Commons. This precedent applied only to the Parliament in which it was passed, and it would have lapsed with its dissolution. To prevent this from happening, the provisions of the bill modifying the oath for the Commons

---

[22] For an account of the struggle for Jewish political rights in the House of Commons, see Enriques (1968), and Roth (1964, chap. 11 and Epilogue).

were converted to a Standing Order, not bounded in time, in 1860. It was only with the passage of the Parliamentary Oaths Act in 1866 that Jews gained the right to sit in the Lords.

There is a clear analogy between the way in which Jews were readmitted to England in 1656 and the process of their political enfranchisement in the latter half of the nineteenth century. In both cases (as with the Jewish Naturalization Bill of 1753), attempts to extend rights to Jews through legislation failed, due to strong political opposition with a significant popular base. Eventually, an individual precedent was created that was gradually expanded to open the way for incremental Jewish entry into British public life. It might be thought that this pattern is not unique to Jewish issues, but simply constitutes the way in which major social change is achieved in Britain. It is a country without a written constitution or charter of rights, and it has historically relied on case law for its progress to more liberal and democratic institutions. Such a view would miss the sharp contrast that exists between the history of Jewish rights and that of other social causes in this country.

Broadly-based movements for progressive reforms launched large-scale public campaigns from the end of the eighteenth century throughout the nineteenth and twentieth centuries. These were responsible for major changes in British institutions and attitudes. Thus, for example, seven years of protest and agitation throughout Britain by the Catholic Association produced the Catholic Emancipation Act of 1829. A large abolitionist movement with strong support from churches and liberal opinion brought about the Abolition of the Slave Trade Act in 1807 and the Slavery Abolition Act of 1833. A militant, well-organized suffragette campaign achieved the right to vote for women over thirty in 1918, and for women over twenty-one in 1928. Beginning with the Chartists in 1838, the British labor movement waged a continuing struggle for the economic and social rights of workers, which eventually brought about acceptance of collective bargaining, extensive employee protection legislation, and the creation of the welfare state.

It is important to note that there were prominent supporters of Jewish political rights among liberals, dissenting Protestants, and evangelicals.[23] Thomas Babington Macaulay's speech on "Jewish Disabilities," delivered to the House of Commons on April 17, 1833, provides one of the more compelling statements of liberal principle in the nineteenth century. However, no genuine political movement supporting Jewish emancipation of the kind that generated the great reforms of British public life ever emerged in Britain. This matter remained a marginal concern to progressive circles, as well as to other political constituencies in the country.

Moreover, the Jews themselves were deeply ambivalent about the emancipation debate in Parliament, with a significant number not wanting to see it turned into a high-profile public issue for fear of attracting a negative response. Here, as in previous (and subsequent) cases, the Anglo-Jewish leadership preferred to pursue a traditional strategy of protecting Jewish concerns through quiet diplomatic engage-

---

[23] This period also saw the emergence of a small but prominent philo-Semitic element in English literature, as illustrated in some of the work of George Eliot, particularly *Daniel Deronda*, published in 1873. This positive view of Jews co-existed with the persistence of virulently negative images, like Dickens' Fagin in *Oliver Twist* (1838), within English literary culture of the nineteenth century.

ment. They relied on a few prominent members of the community to bring influence to bear on sympathetic figures in the British political elite. This strategy led them to shun public political activism in favor of discreet appeals to authority.

VI. IMMIGRATION AND ANTI-ALIEN RESTRICTIONS

A large wave of Eastern European Jewish immigrants came to Britain in the twenty-five-year period from 1880 until 1905, escaping pogroms in Russia and anti-Jewish government actions in other Eastern European countries. Many of them settled in the East End of London, where they established a major center of Jewish communal life. This influx increased the Jewish population in Britain from 65,000 in 1880 to 300,000 in 1914, with 200,000 concentrated in London.[24]

The arrival of large numbers of generally impoverished Eastern European Jews gave rise to a strong anti-alien response that manifested itself in hostile press comment and popular campaigns demanding that the government restrict immigration. The Conservative government introduced the Aliens Act in April 1905, which was approved by Parliament and passed into law on August 11 of that year. The Act specified a number of criteria by which immigration officials could exclude aliens from entering the country. It was the first of a series of measures adopted in the early years of the twentieth century in order to severely limit the entry of newcomers into the country.

These restrictions were, in large part, motivated by widespread animosity to the presence of Jewish immigrants. Arthur Balfour, the Conservative Prime Minister under whom the Aliens Act was passed (the same Balfour who, as Foreign Secretary, later issued the Balfour Declaration of 1917 for the establishment of a Jewish national home in Palestine), gave clear expression to this current of public opinion in his speech during the debate on the Bill in the House of Commons in July 1905:

> ... it would not be to the advantage of the civilisation of the country that there should be an immense body of persons who, however patriotic, able, and industrious, however much they threw themselves into the national life, still by their own action, remained a people apart and not merely held a religion differing from the vast majority of their fellow country-men, but only inter-married among themselves.[25]

The First World War greatly intensified anti-alien sentiment, with hostility to Jewish immigrants prominent in this movement. There was strong pressure for the mass internment of all people from enemy countries, which would have affected large numbers of German and Austrian Jews. In 1914, the government passed the Aliens Restriction Act, which granted it special emergency powers allowing it to deport aliens and required aliens to register with the police. In 1918, it imposed additional administrative restrictions that included a review of naturalization certificates issued during the war, a ban on civil service positions for people who were neither citizens

---

[24] For a discussion of turn of the century Eastern European Jewish immigration to Britain and the sequence of alien restriction acts that it provoked, see Defries (2002, chaps. 2 and 5) and London (2000, chap. 2).

[25] Quoted in Defries (2002, 28).

of Britain or an Allied country (Russia ceased to be an ally after the Bolshevik revolution of 1917), and the requirement of identity cards for aliens. These restrictions and the conditions of the 1914 Act were extended under the Aliens Restriction Act Amendment of 1919. Additional regulatory procedures were specified in the Aliens Order of 1920. As a result of these bills and administrative provisions, Jewish immigration to Britain was virtually cut off by the end of the First World War.

Agitation against aliens in general, and Jewish immigrants in particular, continued throughout the 1920s. David Cesarani (1989) cites a series of articles published in *The Times* at the end of November 1924 on "Alien London" as expressing the tenor of this campaign. One of the articles contains the following statement:

> They stand aloof—not always without a touch of oriental arrogance—from their fellow citizens. They look upon us with suspicion and a certain contempt. Mixed marriages between orthodox Jews and Gentiles are forbidden. These people remain an alien element in our land.[26]

Throughout this period, William Joynson-Hicks, a leading Conservative politician, promoted anti-Jewish attitudes within the government. In stark contrast to Balfour, he was also a strong opponent of Jewish settlement in Palestine, and he played a leading role in supporting the Palestinian Arab lobby in Britain.[27] He became Foreign Secretary in 1924 in Stanley Baldwin's government. During his tenure (1924-1929), he reinforced the discriminatory practices that the Home Office had been implementing against Eastern European Jewish immigrants prior to assuming his position.

Although the Aliens Act was passed by a Conservative government, it was applied by its Liberal successor. Moreover, significant sections of the labor movement, particularly the Trade Union Congress (TUC), and the left supported the exclusion of Jewish immigrants and participated in the agitation against them that provided public support for anti-alien legislation.[28]

While anti-alien agitators and politicians frequently avoided explicit reference to Jews, they used the rhetoric of xenophobia to press for the curtailment of Jewish immigration and to support the imposition of severe restrictions on Jewish immigrants who had succeeded in entering the country. This form of anti-alien discourse anticipated later campaigns in which antisemitism and other types of racism have been encoded in more indirect and politically palatable terms.

When large numbers of desperate Jewish refugees fleeing the Nazis sought sanctuary in Britain in the 1930s, there was no need for new immigration controls to exclude them. The necessary restrictions had already been installed over the previous two decades to stem the flow from previous anti-Jewish violence in Eastern Europe.

---

[26] *The Times*, November 27, 1924, cited in Cesarani (1989).

[27] See Cesarani (1989) for an account of Joynson-Hicks' activities as an anti-Jewish politician.

[28] See Cohen (1985). Cohen also documents government polices designed to exclude aliens, particularly Jews, from some of the key benefits of the welfare state that emerged in the early years of the last century.

VII. REFUGEES FROM NAZISM AND SURVIVORS OF THE HOLOCAUST

After the Nazis took power in Germany in 1933, Britain, like other Western countries, was besieged by requests from German Jews seeking to escape the escalating violence of the regime. Their numbers were greatly increased in 1938 with Germany's annexation of Austria and the Sudetenland in Czechoslovakia, followed by the *Kristallnacht* pogrom. Austrian, Czech, Slovak, and Polish Jews joined German refugees in their flight from the Nazi onslaught.

Throughout the pre-war period, Britain maintained its system of rigorous controls on immigration, treating Jewish refugees as aliens subject to the existing restrictions.[29] These limited entry to people who were of benefit to the British economy. As the 1930s was a time of economic depression, the prospects for refugees obtaining visas under these conditions were minimal. The German Jewish refugees who did come to Britain were financially supported by the British Jewish community under the terms of a commitment that it made to the government. The community did not extend this commitment to Austrian and Czech refugees after the *Anschluss* of Austria, as it could no longer afford to absorb the expanding numbers of visa applicants.

The labor movement, as represented by the TUC, supported the government's policy of drastically limiting the flow of Jewish refugees. While strongly opposing the Nazi government and its persecution of Jews, it did not feel that it could accommodate an influx of cheap labor at a time of economic hardship.[30]

One area of the economy that did enjoy a robust demand for labor was the market for female servants, and many of the Jewish refugees who came to Britain in the pre-war period gained access under a plan to import foreign domestic workers. As domestics were not heavily unionized and organized labor did not see them as a major area of concern, this was a relatively soft route around immigration restrictions.[31]

There were notable exceptions to the TUC endorsement of government policy. Eleanore Rathbone, a social activist, feminist, and independent MP, campaigned tirelessly throughout the 1930s and the war for government action to save European Jewry. Roy Harrod, an Oxford economist and a member of the Labour Party, argued that immigration promoted growth and urged the labor movement to support a liberalized approach to refugees. However, like other critics, they had little if any impact on either government policy or organized labor's restrictionist position.[32]

Throughout the 1930s and the war years, the British policy on Jewish refugees was driven by the view that only small numbers of individuals who came from cultural and professional backgrounds that facilitated assimilation into British society could be accepted. In general, a program of temporary refuge and resettlement abroad was the strongly preferred option, with most refugees granted only

---

[29] For detailed accounts of Britain's response to Jewish refugees from Nazism, see London (2000), Kushner (1994), and Wasserstein (1979).

[30] For the attitude of the British labor movement to the refugee crisis, see Kushner (1994, chap. 2).

[31] On refugees in domestic service, see Kushner (1994, chap. 3) and London (2000, 75-80).

[32] On Harrod, see Kushner (1994, 74-6). On Rathbone, see Kushner (1994, chap. 6).

transitional status. Government officials argued that if large numbers of the "wrong" kind of refugee were admitted, it would create antisemitism in the country. Hence a "West to East" hierarchy was applied in which Germans were considered more desirable than Austrians, who in turn were ranked above Czechs, followed by Poles and other East Europeans. The Home Secretary Samuel Hoare expressed this attitude in his comments to an Anglo-Jewish delegation on April 1, 1938:

> It would be necessary for the Home Office to discriminate very carefully as to the type of refugee who could be admitted to this country. If a flood of the wrong type of immigrants were allowed in there might be a serious danger of anti-semitic feeling being aroused in this country. The last thing which we wanted here was the creation of a Jewish problem.[33]

Although the Jewish community invested vast efforts and resources in refugee relief, its leadership, for the most part, accepted the government restrictions and the rationale behind them. Otto Schiff, a leading figure in Anglo-Jewish refugee work, responded to Hoare's remark in the following terms:

> It was very difficult to get rid of a refugee ... once he had entered and spent a few months in this country. The imposition of a visa was especially necessary in the case of Austrians who were largely of the shopkeeper and small trader class, and would therefore prove much more difficult to emigrate than the average German who had come to the United Kingdom.[34]

The extent to which the leadership of Anglo-Jewry had internalized the government policy on refugees is indicated by the reservations that a Jewish immigrant liaison officer expressed to the Chief Rabbi, J.H. Hertz, over the hostel for German yeshiva students that the Chief Rabbi was sponsoring:

> How can this loyalty be demanded of any body of young men who are taught nothing about English ways, English history, or the English outlook? If they are not to be trained in this loyalty from the very first week of their arrival, what chance have they of merely comprehending, let alone feeling, that love of England which is the veritable fountainhead of these traditions of Anglo-Jewry of which we English Jews are so proud and which is itself the strongest bulwark against antisemitism in our midst.[35]

This correspondence took place in the context of an effort by the community to resist a government move to intern all refugees from Axis countries after the outbreak of war in 1939.

The *Kindertransports* of 1938 brought approximately 10,000 Jewish children from Germany and Austria to Britain. They are frequently cited as an instance of British generosity toward Jews escaping the Nazis, and indeed they stand as an important act of decency in a dark time. A point that is not generally addressed in discussions of this operation is the fact that the children were forced to come alone because

---

[33] Home Office minutes of the meeting with the Jewish delegation, April 1, 1938, PROHO 213/42. Quoted in London (2000) p. 61.
[34] Ibid.
[35] Rothschild archives, London RAL 000/315C. Quoted in Kushner (1994, 154).

British immigration regulations, rather than German exit controls, prevented their parents from accompanying them. These regulations insured that they became orphans in the course of the war that followed their arrival.

A significant feature of government refugee policy was an insistence on not recognizing Jews as a distinct entity in any official rules or procedures. This was ostensibly motivated by the desire to avoid discrimination among different groups of refugees. In fact, it seriously disadvantaged Jews and created a bizarre paradox. The Jews were a primary target of Nazi racial persecution and genocide, but Britain, as well as other allied countries, refused to acknowledge them as such in their refugee programs. In fact, political refugees, Jewish or non-Jewish, who were pursued for their resistance activities were given strong preference for asylum over economic or "racial" refugees, a class that included most Jewish victims of the Nazis.

During the war, the government continued to enforce its highly restrictive immigration procedures, even for small numbers of Jews who were able to escape Nazi controlled territory to neutral countries like Portugal or Turkey, which accepted them on condition that they be transferred to other venues. At the end of the war, approximately 60,000 Jewish refugees remained in Britain, with another 10,000-20,000 having entered and then re-emigrated or been deported. Therefore, from 1933 to 1945 a total of 70,000-80,000 Jewish refugees received refuge in the United Kingdom.[36] In addition, a net total of 216,000 moved to mandatory Palestine in the 1930s, until the government White Paper of 1939 curtailed Jewish immigration there.

The British response to the refugee crisis before and during the war was not different in kind from that of other Western democracies. The United States also imposed severe limitations on immigration in 1924, which remained in effect throughout the 1930s and the war years. Canada had perhaps the worst record, accepting fewer than 5,000 Jewish refugees between 1933 and 1945.[37]

Britain and the United States co-managed the Evian Conference of July 1938, which was designed to give the appearance of an international effort to assist the refugees while avoiding any substantive measures to accommodate them. Britain was particularly concerned that the conference not create a situation in which Eastern European countries like Poland and Romania could use liberalized immigration policies in the West to unload their large and unwanted Jewish populations. Similarly, the Anglo-American Bermuda Conference in April 1943 was called in response to growing public pressure in both countries to rescue victims of the Nazi genocide, with both governments making certain that it yielded no tangible results.

Significant differences between British and American policy on assistance to victims of the Holocaust began to emerge when President Roosevelt established the War Refugees Board (WRB) in January 1944 at the urging of Henry Morgenthau, the Secretary of the Treasury. The WRB began to pursue a proactive program of aid, primarily in the form of US government currency licenses through which the American Joint Distribution Committee was able to use cash to fund Jewish resistance and escape from concentration camps. The British government opposed these efforts on the grounds that they undermined its economic blockade of Axis territory.[38]

---

[36] London (2000, 11-12).
[37] Abella and Troper (1983).
[38] London (2000, 230-45).

In July 1944, Admiral Horthy, the regent of Hungary, offered to permit large numbers of the remaining Hungarian Jewish population to leave if Allied countries would grant them entry. Both the British and American governments were, in principle, prepared to accept the offer. But while the Americans urged immediate action, the British cabinet delayed a formal commitment over a period of several weeks for fear that it would produce a large flood of refugees. In the end, despite a joint Anglo-American statement in August indicating a willingness to assist Hungarian Jewry, the Germans resumed the deportation of Jews to the death camps.[39]

The shift in the US government attitude that occurred at the beginning of 1944 was, in no small part, due to public pressure exerted by American Jewish groups and their supporters. They held a well-publicized mass rally in Madison Square Gardens in New York on March 1, 1943 to highlight the absence of government support for rescue operations, and they lobbied politicians and government officials. By contrast, the British Jewish community consistently refrained from publicly challenging the British government on its handling of refugees and worked within the restrictions that it imposed. In effect, the British government was able to use the Anglo-Jewish refugee aid committees and their resources as instruments of its policies.

A chasm opened up between British and American responses to Jewish refugees in the post-war period. In the years immediately following the war, the restrictions on Jewish immigration to America remained in place. However, President Truman intervened in 1948 to insure that the Displaced Persons Act of that year was not used to disadvantage Jewish refugees from the DP camps of Europe. As a result, they were permitted to enter the United States in proportion to their numbers in the camps, and over a 100,000 immigrated between 1945 and 1950.

In the period immediately following the war, the British government kept the legal restrictions on the 60,000 Jewish refugees still in the country. This included people who had served in the British army or worked for the war effort in other ways. They remained aliens without full rights to seek employment, and their presence in the United Kingdom was still officially temporary. In fact, there was no solid legal basis for these restrictions after the war, but the refugees were not informed of this fact. They were also frequently not told when some of these constraints were quietly lifted. The government retained hopes of encouraging as many refugees as possible to emigrate. It was not until the end of 1948 that their position in Britain was regularized and they were granted the status of permanent residents.[40]

The post-war Labour government was unwilling to accept survivors in anything but token numbers. The Foreign Secretary Ernest Bevin insisted that Jews were not easily assimilated into British life, and he argued that allowing in a substantial group would intensify the already considerable anti-Jewish sentiment that had arisen as a result of Britain's conflict with the *Yishuv* in mandatory Palestine. As a result, fewer than 5,000 survivors were granted entry from 1945 to 1950, under a family reunification program (the Distressed Relatives scheme). During this period, Britain was

---

[39] Kushner (1994, 194-5).

[40] See London (2000, 260-6) on the post-war status of Jewish refugees in Britain.

experiencing a severe labor shortage and recruited foreign workers. It absorbed approximately 365,000 non-Jewish immigrants, most from Eastern Europe and many from the same DP camps that housed Jewish refugees. The government issued over 600,000 alien work permits. The Eastern European immigrants were not carefully screened, and, as a result, a number of war criminals and Nazi collaborators were permitted entry. It seems that for the British government the non-Jewish foreign workers did not pose the same problems of cultural incompatibility that the Jewish survivors did.[41]

Bevin was committed to repatriating Jewish refugees to the countries from which they had come. Not only was he unwilling to allow them into Palestine, but he also wanted them excluded from Britain. Although post-war pogroms were taking place in Poland in 1946-1947 and most refugees were desperate not to return to hostile environments in Eastern and Central Europe, the Nazi genocide had made little if any impact on Bevin's pre-war hostility to Jewish refugees.[42]

Britain's record on Jewish refugees has been meticulously documented and published in well-known works by mainstream British historians. Oddly, this record remains largely invisible in public discussion of the war. In fact, a self-congratulatory attitude is common in much of this discussion.

The Transport and General Workers Union (TGWU) recently provided a particularly striking example of how this attitude can be recruited into the service of the anti-Israel boycott campaign. When the TGWU passed its resolution calling for the boycott of Israeli products in July 2007, Barry Camfield, the deputy general-secretary of the union, was quoted in *The Jewish Chronicle* as seeking to deflect criticism of the motion by commenting that Britain had stood alone against Hitler and liberated Jewish victims of the Holocaust. "So we will not have the Israeli state telling us that the boycott is antisemitic."[43] Camfield's remarks (if accurately reported) are rich in unintended irony. Bevin was general secretary of the TGWU from 1922 until 1940, and a member of the General Council of the TUC from 1925 to 1940. During this period, he played an important role in shaping organized labor's support for the Conservative government's restrictions on the entry of Jewish refugees. After the war, as Foreign Secretary in the Labour government, he took the lead in excluding survivors from the country. The current leadership of the TGWU, like many other boycott supporters, appear to be either unaware of their historical antecedents or simply indifferent to their significance in the context of the current discussion.

Many of the most vociferous anti-Zionists on the contemporary British "left" insist that a solution to the Jewish refugee problem in the period of the Holocaust should have been found in the Diaspora rather than in Palestine. They remain impressively obtuse to the fact that their own political precursors were instrumental in ruling out such a solution by helping to block Jewish immigration to Britain.

During a debate with the right-wing American commentator Daniel Pipes at the "Clash of Civilizations" conference in London on January 20, 2007 Ken Livingstone, London's former "radical" mayor, claimed that the creation of Israel was a mistake that could have been avoided if the United States and Britain had accepted Jewish

---

[41] Kushner (1994, 229-37).
[42] See Borowicz (1986) on the post-war pogroms in Poland.
[43] Josephs (2007).

refugees from Nazism. In an earlier statement concerning his clash with a reporter from the *Evening Standard*, Livingstone observed that the paper's sister publication, the *Daily Mail*, had campaigned against Jewish immigration in the early part of the twentieth century and expressed sympathies for Nazism in the 1930s.[44] He has carefully avoided acknowledging the part played by the British labor movement and large segments of the British left in keeping Jewish refugees out of the country during this period.

In fact, the successful effort to restrict the entry of Jewish refugees was not the work of a specific political group but a broadly-based enterprise that spanned ideological differences. It was the result of a consensus that ran across the political and social spectrum, from upper class Conservative politicians to working class labor activists and the unions.

VIII. Post-colonialism and Israel

In the past forty years, Britain has developed into a post-colonial society in which it has (in large part) come to recognize the injustices that the British Empire imposed on large portions of the world's population in previous centuries. It has accepted historical responsibility for its role in colonialism and the slave trade, and this process has transformed its understanding of its past. It has also significantly changed the standards of political acceptability determining at least its official relationship to the large post-war immigrant communities from the Indian subcontinent, the Caribbean, Africa, and other parts of its former overseas territories. Mainstream attitudes toward the British colonial presence in Ireland prior to the emergence of the Irish Free State and the establishment of the Irish Republic have been similarly, if less completely, affected by this evolution of historical and social attitudes.

Interestingly, the history of Britain's relationship with its Jewish population has not been subject to a comparable revision. Although the hostility to Jews that figured prominently throughout this history is closely related to the prejudices and the mindset that fuelled colonialism and its attendant racism, it has not been subsumed under the European practices that have formed the main targets of post-colonialist criticism and historiography.

In fact, the Jews have been quickly shuffled away from the status of victims of European racism into the role of the new colonialists. In the 1970s and 1980s, the anti-Zionist left portrayed Israel and its supporters as instruments of Western imperialism in the Middle East. In recent years, they have been promoted to the primary agents of an international imperial project of which the West is increasingly seen as a hapless dupe.

This view was anticipated in the 1960s by Arnold Toynbee, who describes Israel in the following terms:

> Israeli colonialism since the establishment of the state of Israel is one of the two blackest cases in the whole history of colonialism in the modern age; and its blackness is thrown into relief by its date. The East European Zionists have been

---

[44] "Ken Livingstone statement in full," CNN, February 22, 2005, http://edition.cnn.com/2005/WORLD/europe/02/22/livingstone.statement/index.html.

practicing colonialism in Palestine in the extreme form of evicting and robbing the native Arab inhabitants at the very time when the West European peoples have been renouncing their temporary rule over non-European peoples. The other outstanding black case is the eviction of five agricultural Amerindian peoples—the Chickasaw, Choctaw, Creeks, Cherokees, and Seminoles—from their ancestral homes in what are now the states of Georgia, Alabama, Mississippi, and Tennessee to "reservations" in what is now the state of Oklahoma. ... This nineteenth-century American colonialism was a crime; the Israeli colonialism, which was being carried out at the time when I was writing, was a crime that was also a moral anachronism.[45]

It is important to recognize that the basis of Toynbee's objection to Zionism is not, in the end, Israel's behavior toward the Palestinians, but his view of the Jews as an illicit people who have no right to be a nation. Writing of Jewish religious culture he says:

This is a great spiritual treasure which the Jews have to give to all peoples. But one cannot give a treasure and at the same time keep it to oneself. If the giving of this treasure is the Jews' mission, as it surely is, then this mission requires them, now at last, to make that their paramount aim in place of the incompatible aim that they have always put first, so far, ever since their experience of the Babylonish Captivity. They will have to give up the national form of the Jewish community's distinctive identity in order to become, without reservations, the missionaries of a universal church that will be open, on an equal footing, to anyone, Jew or Gentile, who gives his allegiance to Deutro-Isaiah's God and seeks to do His will. In our time the Zionist movement has been travelling in just the opposite direction to this. It has not only clung to, and accentuated, the national form of Jewish communal life. It has also put it back on to a territorial basis.[46]

...

The Jewish religion is meant for all mankind. So far from its being "unthinkable" without the "Chosen People," it cannot fulfil its destiny of becoming a universal religion unless and until the Jews renounce the national form of their distinctive communal identity for the sake of their universal religious mission.[47]

Toynbee is expressing a classic Christian European notion of Jews as a community that ought not to exist as a collectivity. As we have seen, it has been at the core of deeply-rooted mainstream attitudes toward Jews in Britain throughout the centuries. It is also a vintage case of what Edward Said has identified as "Orientalism."[48] Jews are not to be entrusted with the stewardship of their own culture, nor are they entitled to understand themselves in their own terms. The significance of their culture and their place in history is a matter to be determined by those who exercise power over them and have a true understanding of their significance and their needs.

---

[45] Toynbee (1969, 266-7).
[46] Toynbee (1961, 515-6).
[47] Toynbee (1961, 517).
[48] Said (1978).

Most proponents of Said's critique of orientalism (like Said himself) have adopted a variant of Toynbee's view of Jews. Unlike other objects of European (and Middle Eastern) racism, they are not entitled to liberation from external colonial coercion as a national group. They are in no position to decide who they are or where they belong in a properly constituted social order. Political independence and cultural autonomy are inappropriate concessions to a backward-looking particularism for a people that ought not to exist. Instead, they are to achieve "freedom" through dissolution into other peoples' societies, so that their "talents" can be responsibly harnessed. As in the past, their degree of acceptability is to be measured by their willingness to conform to an externally imposed notion of "universalism" that excludes their collective existence in all but the most diffidently unobtrusive and compliant mode.

As in the case of Toynbee, the root objection that contemporary "anti-colonialists," who are now defining mainstream discussion of the Middle East in Britain, bring against Israel is not what it has done (or is doing) but the irredeemable sin of its existence. Australia's ethnic cleansing of its aboriginal population does not undermine its integrity as a country, and America's history of internal colonialism, slavery, and military adventurism abroad has no bearing on the right of its people to constitute a nation. Pakistan's religiously motivated partition of the Indian subcontinent and the associated mass flight of Hindu refugees from its territory is irrelevant to its standing as a state.

By contrast, Jews ought not to have a country, even if it is reformed into a model of secular liberal democracy. To allow them one is to grant legitimacy to a people that has none. The fact that the host societies in Europe, the Middle East, and North Africa through which they were driven for centuries were not able to provide for their basic physical survival is not taken to be a relevant factor in assessing the historical processes that created Israel and populated it with refugees from these societies. Nor is it admitted into consideration when framing the current Israeli-Palestinian conflict in anti-colonialist terms.

Toynbee's approach to Jews was, in turn, anticipated by a small group of militant anti-Zionists within the British Jewish community in the 1940s. The Jewish Fellowship was established in 1942 to combat Zionism and to promote the idea that Jews are a religious group rather than a national community. Their leaders came from the highest economic and social echelons of Anglo-Jewry, and they were heavily influenced by members of the Progressive Movement.[49] The Fellowship compared Zionism to Nazism as early as 1944, just as the nature of the Nazi genocide was becoming fully known in the West. One of the Fellowship's leaders, Colonel Louis Gluckstein, said in testimony to the Anglo-American Committee on Palestine that "to believe this [Jewish suffering] is a justification for Jewish separatism and Jewish nationalism seems to me the adoption of the Hitler doctrine."[50]

The Jewish Fellowship was the antithesis of a radical organization. It represented a largely conservative elite of Jews who were concerned to protect their precarious position as charter, if sponsored, members of the British power structure. They saw in Zionism and the creation of Israel a threat to their own position. They also seem to have been more than a little embarrassed by the Holocaust and its implications for

---

[49] For a detailed and informative history of the Jewish Fellowship, see Miller (2000).
[50] Quoted in Miller (2000, 49).

their idea of a comfortable de-national Jewish life in Europe. In this they followed a long standing pattern in Anglo-Jewry of accommodating themselves to the demand for invisibility as a condition for social acceptance. The idea that failure to conform to this demand will generate antisemitism was shared with British policy makers who invoked it to exclude refugees from the country. The attitudes of the Jewish Fellowship have been echoed by a small but vocal minority of contemporary Jewish anti-Zionists who see Israel as an embarrassment that threatens them with a resurgence of antisemitism.

IX. CONCLUSION

In the second half of the twentieth century, explicit expression of hostility to Jews was rare in Britain. The emerging recognition of the full dimensions of the Holocaust created an environment where even coded anti-Jewish expressions were heavily stigmatized and the traditional imagery of antisemitism was almost entirely banished from public discourse. In recent years, particularly since the end of 2000, increasing animosity toward Israel has been attended with a precipitous decline in the constraints against the language of group defamation, generally formulated in terms of "Zionists" rather than "Jews."

Israel is a country like any other, and, as such, it should be held accountable to the same standards and norms that are applied to other nations. To criticize it on this basis is entirely legitimate, and when the criticisms are accurate, they should be vigorously pursued. But the view of Israel that has emerged recently within the mainstream of British public discourse holds it to be not a normal country at all, but a criminal aberration that is sustained by a malicious conspiratorial lobby of international dimensions. At the foundation of this view is a perception of Jews as an illicit collectivity with no claim to legitimacy or recognition.

This idea is a central element of traditional European (and Middle Eastern) attitudes toward Jews. In this respect, Britain shares its cultural history with the rest of Europe. However, unlike most of continental Europe, Britain continues to promote a largely sanitized and self-laudatory understanding of its past relations with Jews in its own popular imagination, and this has served to misrepresent a history whose details are fully accessible as a matter of public record.

The leadership of the British Jewish community has, for the most part, actively cooperated with this exercise in misrepresentation over the years as part of a strategy for surviving in an environment in which Jews enjoy an acutely conditional acceptance. This strategy is a continuation of the politics of accommodation and low-profile engagement with government power that the community has deployed in pursuit of acceptance and mobility in the face of hostility and social resistance. It contrasts sharply with the self-assertive community activism of American Jews. While the latter have taken their place as one among many ethnic communities that make up the mainstream of an essentially open, immigrant-based society, British Jewry has, in many respects, continued the political and social traditions of pre-war European Jewish communities. Although British Jews enjoy a high level of individual integration within contemporary Britain, Jews as a collective entity remain marginal and subject to cultural stigmas that often find expression in current debates on the Middle East.

While current hostility to Jews in the United Kingdom is frequently packaged as "progressive" political comment, its origins are in traditional social attitudes that have been integral to Britain's history for centuries. The fact that this history has been effectively rendered invisible to the public imagination facilitates the expression of views that might otherwise be identified as prejudicial and ruled out of mainstream discussion. To recognize the origins of these views requires a frank and realistic encounter with an aspect of the country's past that mainstream British opinion has so far managed to avoid.

REFERENCES

Abella, Irving, and Harold Troper. 1983. *None is too Many*, Toronto: Lester and Orpen Dennys.

Borowicz, M. 1986. "Polish-Jewish Relations, 1944-1947." In *The Jews in Poland*, edited by Chimen Abramsky, M. Jachimczyk, and Antonly Polonksy, pp. 190-8. Oxford: Blackwell.

Cesarani, David. 1989. "The Anti-Jewish Career of Sir William Joynson Hicks, Cabinet Minister." *Journal of Contemporary History* 24, pp. 461-82.

Clark, David. 2006. "Accusations of anti-semitic chic are poisonous intellectual thuggery." *The Guardian*, March 6.

Cohen, Steve. 1985. "Anti-Semitism, Immigration Controls, and the Welfare State." *Critical Social Policy*, pp. 73-92.

Dawkins, Richard. 2006. *The God Delusion*. London: Bantam Press.

Defries, Harry. 2002. *Conservative Party Attitudes to the Jews: 1900-1950*. London: Frank Cass.

Donadio, Rachel. 2007. "Libel without Borders." *New York Times*, October 7.

Enriques, H. 1968. "The Jewish Emancipation Controversy in Nineteenth-Century Britain." *Past and Present* 40, pp. 226-46.

Evans, Rob. 2007. "Britain censored over decision to drop BAE Saudi corruption inquiry." *The Guardian*, January 19.

Hessayon, Ariel. 2006. *From Expulsion (1290) to Readmission (1656): Jews and England*. Address to the Jewish Genealogical Society of Great Britain, Goldmith's College, London, December 6, http://www.goldsmiths.ac.uk/history/350th-anniversary.pdf.

Josephs, Brian. 2007. "TGWU joins the campaign." *Jewish Chronicle*, July 5.

Julius, Anthony. forthcoming. *Trials of the Diaspora: A History of Anti-Semitism in England*. Oxford: Oxford University Press.

Katz, David. 1994. *The Jews in the History of England*. Oxford: Oxford University Press.

Kushner, Tony. 1994. The Holocaust and the Liberal Imagination. *Oxford: Blackwell.*

Lappin, Shalom. 2003. "Israel and the New Anti-Semitism," *Dissent* Spring, pp. 96-103.

Lappin, Shalom. 2006. "The Rise of a New Anti-Semitism in the UK." *Engage Journal*, January.

London, Louise. 2000. Whitehall and the Jews, 1933-1948: British Immigration Policy, Jewish Refugees and the Holocaust. *Cambridge: Cambridge University Press.*

Leigh, David, and Rob Evans. 2007. "'National Interest' halts corruption inquiry." *The Guardian*, December 15.

MacAskill, Ewan. 2007. "Atheists arise: Dawkins spreads the A-word among America's unbelievers." *The Guardian*, October 1.

Miller, Rory. 2000. "A Most Uncivil War: The Jewish Fellowship and the Battle over Zionism in Anglo Jewry, 1944-1948." *The Jewish Journal of Sociology* 42, pp. 37-72.

Roth, Cecil. 1964. *A History of the Jews in England*, 3rd ed. Oxford: Clarendon Press.

Sacks, Jonathan. 2006. "Anglo-Jewry at 350." *Jewish Telegraph*, July 7.

Said, Edward. 1978. *Orientalism*. London: Routledge and Kegan Paul.

Toynbee, Arnold. 1961. *The Study of History*, vol. XII, Oxford: Oxford University Press.

Toynbee, Arnold. 1969. *Experiences*. Oxford: Oxford University Press.

Traubmann, Tamara. 2007. "US university heads slam UK boycott of Israeli academe." *Haaretz*, August 8.

Wasserstein, Bernard. 1979. *Britain and the Jews of Europe 1939-1945*. Oxford: Clarendon Press.

Never Again? When Holocaust Memory Becomes Empty Rhetoric, a Diplomatic Tool, and a Weapon against Israel

Walter Reich*

I. Introduction

The Holocaust was the greatest physical outburst of antisemitism the Jews have ever known in a long history of such outbursts—indeed, the Holocaust was the most striking and focused physical outburst of any ethnic hatred the world has ever known. Any aspect of the study of the Holocaust and of the use and abuse of Holocaust memory has a direct bearing on the consideration of antisemitism in general. And it has a direct bearing on the consideration of not only ethnic hatred but also the possibilities and uses of its memorialization.

This paper focuses on the use, often only when it is convenient, of the bold and stirring call of "Never again!" in the realm of international affairs. It will also focus on the ways in which countries use Holocaust symbols to achieve diplomatic ends. Moreover, it will focus on the ways in which Holocaust imagery is hurled at Israel in order to attack it and Jews, as well as the ways in which Holocaust denial, a malady that has afflicted the world for sixty years, has in recent years become wildly popular in the Arab/Muslim world and a key plank of the domestic and foreign policy of one specific country, namely Iran. This phenomenon is well known to much of the world, and was recently highlighted during the visit to the United States of the president of Iran, Mahmoud Ahmadinejad.

II. Rhetoric and Reality: The Place of the Holocaust in Foreign Policy

The main reason that the Holocaust is regularly invoked by leaders in connection with foreign policy matters is probably that it has been designated as a kind of moral touchstone in connection with such matters.

Just about everyone publicly acknowledges, at least in the West, that the international community made a grave moral error in not intervening in the 1930s when

---

* Walter Reich is the Yitzhak Rabin Memorial Professor of International Affairs, Ethics, and Human Behavior, and Professor of Psychiatry and Behavioral Sciences, at George Washington University; a Senior Scholar at the Woodrow Wilson Center; and former Director, United States Holocaust Memorial Museum.

Hitler promised to exterminate the Jews and then spent years squeezing them, hounding them, and finally killing them. During the 1930s, countries could still have intervened to stop that process, but they did not. At the very least, they could have taken in the Jews who, because they were not taken in, were later murdered. As a result, everyone, at least in the West, expresses shame that no such interventions were attempted when they were still possible. So when mass killings are taking place in the world today, the Holocaust is sometimes cited as a justification for intervention.

The problem is that such references to the Holocaust are selective and that they are not necessarily based on any actual similarity between the crisis in question and the Holocaust. For example, to justify the intervention in Kosovo, President Clinton summoned up the Holocaust.[1] But he did not do so in connection with a far more extensive and genuine genocide, one that really did reach proportions that were comparable, in severity and intent if not in numbers and methods, to the Holocaust, namely the genocide in Rwanda. To be sure, President Bush did indeed utter the motto "Never again!" during his visit to the Holocaust Museum in Washington in April 2007, where he devoted most of his talk to the murders in Darfur.[2] It is worth noting that although he did not say that the situation in Darfur was the same as the Holocaust, the setting in which he spoke was designed to add historical gravity to his presentation. Alas, what the United States is actually doing in Darfur has yet to match that gravity, as the killing continues to unfold.

Let me be a little more specific on this matter. Let me focus on Rwanda, and in particular on the phrase "Never again!," which our officials do not hesitate to utter when it costs little or nothing to do so, and on the ways in which they refuse to act on that sentiment when such action is, in fact, seen as inconvenient or costly.

In 2005, the international commemorations of the 60th anniversary of the liberation of Auschwitz were attended by leaders from around the world. The United Nations held one such commemoration; others were held in many other countries. The vow "Never again!" was articulated at nearly all of them.

Unfortunately, this vow, which has been articulated for decades, has not managed in all those decades to mobilize the actions, either national or international, that have been needed when real genocides have occurred.

---

[1] See "Clinton's Remarks in Defense of Military Intervention in Balkans," *New York Times*, May 14, 1999, which cites a reference by President Clinton to the Holocaust in justifying military intervention. Another report on this is by Katharine Q. Seelye, "Clinton Blames Milošević, Not Fate, for Bloodshed," *New York Times*, May 14, 1999. See also Norman Mailer, "Milošević and Clinton," *Washington Post*, May 24, 1999, p. A25, which raises the question whether or not the events in Kosovo constituted a genocide—a question that may also be found in Deb Riechmann, "Some Bristle at Holocaust Parallel," *Associated Press*, May 14, 1999; Lars-Erik Nelson, "Kosovo Is Not the Holocaust," *Daily News* (New York), April 9, 1999; and Elie Wiesel, "The Question of Genocide," *Newsweek*, April 12, 1999, in which Wiesel declines to call what was happening in Kosovo "genocide." See also Steven Erlanger, "Auschwitz Survivor in Belgrade Now Fears NATO," *New York Times*, April 9, 1999, p. A11, which cites a complaint about the use of Holocaust "propaganda" as a justification for policy in the Balkans.

[2] "President Bush Visits the United States Holocaust Memorial Museum," http://www.whitehouse.gov/news/releases/2007/04/print/20070418.html.

The most glaring example involves the response to the 1994 genocide in Rwanda, where some 800,000 human beings, nearly all of them Tutsis, were murdered, mostly by being hacked to death with machetes by Hutu militias.

During the months in which this genocide unfolded, State Department and other Clinton administration officials at the highest levels refused to call it a genocide; they were afraid that doing so would commit the United States to, as an internal memo put it, "actually do something."

In 2000, a member of a panel established by the Organisation of African Unity to study the event and the non-response to it said at a press conference: "The United States ... knew exactly what was going on. ... I don't know how Madeleine Albright lives with it."[3] Albright, who had been America's ambassador to the United Nations during the genocide and later became Secretary of State, responded using an historically resonant and unfortunate phrase, stating that she had merely "followed instructions."[4] Secretary of State Warren Christopher and President Clinton knew exactly what was happening, but it was in fact their unwillingness to act that set the tone for Albright's behavior. In 1998, Clinton apologized in Kigali for his behavior to an audience of genocide survivors.[5]

It is worth recalling, against the background of Clinton's inaction in the case of Rwanda, what he had said just a year before, at the opening of the United States Holocaust Memorial Museum in 1993, when he expressed sorrow that, before World War II had started, the "doors to liberty were shut."[6] It is also worth noting his words at an international Holocaust conference in 2000, where he said: "We must never forget what happened when governments turned a blind eye to grave injustice outside their borders, when they waited too long to act."[7]

For his part, Secretary of State Warren Christopher grudgingly acknowledged that what was happening in Rwanda were "acts of genocide." I recall that two years later, in 1996, at an exhibit mounted by the Holocaust Museum on Capitol Hill about Varian Fry—a brave man who saved about 2,000 human beings from the Holocaust in southern France even as the State Department tried to stop him—Christopher spoke with great feeling. I could sense that feeling because I was standing next to him as the museum's director. "Frankly," Christopher said, "the conduct of our

---

[3] See "West Turned Back on Rwanda Genocide, OAU Report Says," *Washington Post*, July 8, 2000; "Report Says U.S. and Others Allowed Rwanda Genocide, *New York Times*, July 8, 2000."

[4] See "This Week" transcript, July 9, 2000. See also "Albright Disputes Report on Rwanda," *Washington Post*, July 10, 2000.

[5] See "Remarks by the President to Genocide Survivors, Assistance Workers, and U.S. and Rwanda Government Officials," Kigali Airport, March 25, 1998, http://clinton6.nara.gov/1998/03/1998-03-25-remarks-to-survivors-rwanda.html. See also Barbara Crossette, "Report Says U.S. and Others Allowed Rwanda Genocide," *New York Times*, July 8, 2000, p. A4.

[6] See William J. Clinton, "Remarks at the Dedication of the United States Holocaust Memorial Museum," April 22, 1993, The American Presidency Project, http://www.presidency.ucsb.edu/ws/print.php?pid=46468.

[7] "Remarks by the President of the United States for the Stockholm International Forum on the Holocaust," The Stockholm International Forum on the Holocaust, January 26, 2000, http://www.holocaustforum.gov.se/conference/official_documents/messages/clinton.htm.

department was not our finest hour."[8] Indeed, five months earlier, at Yad Vashem, where he had planted a tree in honor of Fry, Christopher had said that we owed Fry "a promise to do whatever is necessary to ensure that such horrors never happen again."[9]

So, if "Never again!" was in their hearts, why did Christopher—or Clinton and Albright—not do what they could to stop the Rwanda genocide when they had the chance? The answer, alas, is that they did not do so because doing so would have come at a cost. No one wanted a repeat of the peacekeeping debacle that had occurred in Somalia six months earlier. Officials assumed that, somehow, things would settle down—and they focused their attention elsewhere.

At the United Nations' commemoration of the 60th anniversary of the liberation of Auschwitz, then Secretary General Kofi Annan acknowledged that "[o]n occasions like this, rhetoric comes easily." He continued, sadly, as follows: "We rightly say, 'Never again.' But action is much harder. Since the Holocaust the world has, to its shame, failed more than once to prevent or halt genocide."[10] Yet Annan himself, who knew all this back in 1994, responded weakly to the Rwanda genocide.[11]

Nor is the disinclination to confront genocide confined to new genocides. It even applies to genocide memory when that memory is politically inconvenient. Take, for example, the first genocide of the twentieth century, the Armenian Genocide during and after World War I. Repeatedly, Armenians have been unable to obtain recognition that that genocide was indeed a genocide—less because of a lack of proof that it happened than because such a recognition would distress modern Turkey. Turkey, of course, has a law that make it a crime to describe the murder of some 1.5 million Armenians a as genocide. Calling it a genocide, or even discussing it in a manner that suggests it was a genocide, even in fiction, can be considered a "crime against Turkishness," a violation of Article 301 of the Turkish penal code. In fact, several Turkish writers have been charged with this crime, including Nobel Laureate Orhan Pamuk. Interestingly, there seems to be an effort within Turkey to this that law, perhaps because it is an international embarrassment. But Turkey's effort to say that the Armenian Genocide never happened has been immensely effective because Turkey has used its political clout to *make* it effective.

In the case of Israel, for example, Turkey has been able to use two political levers to stop the country from recognizing the event. One lever is the fact that it was the first Muslim country to establish full relations with Israel and that it has suggested that recognition of the Armenian Genocide on Israel's part would force it to reconsider those relations. The second lever is Turkey's suggestion that it would not be able to guarantee the safety of Turkey's Jews—a chilling formulation—if Israel should recognize the Armenian Genocide. For Israel, where genocide is of course a

---

[8] Leslie Katz, "Little-known American Rescuer Varian Fry Gets His Due," *Jewish News Weekly of Northern California*, March 6, 1998.

[9] See http://www.almondseed.com/vfry/fryfoun.htm.

[10] Warren Hoge, "UN Listens to Pledges of 'Never Again,'" *International Herald Tribune*, January 26, 2005.

[11] A version of this discussion of the responses by Clinton administration figures to Rwanda, as well as of Warren Christopher's comments about Varian Fry, appeared in Walter Reich, "Useless Commemorations?," *New York Sun*, January 27, 2000.

central concern due to the fact that the country was created soon after—and in part because of—the Holocaust and the fact that a considerable part of its population consists of either Holocaust survivors or the children of Holocaust survivors, this has been an issue of betraying the memory of another genocide's victims in the service of averting the deaths of living Jews. This trade-off has also deterred non-Israeli organizations from recognizing the Armenian Genocide, including, for a long time, the Anti-Defamation League.

In the case of the United States, Turkey has been able to use other political levers to deter American administrations from recognizing the Armenian Genocide. Most recently, on October 5, 2007, Turkish Prime Minister Recep Tayyip Erdogan called President Bush to protest the passage of a Congressional resolution describing the killing of those 1.5 million Armenians as a genocide. Bush told Erdogan that he was against the resolution, saying that its passage would be "harmful" to U.S.-Turkey relations. His spokesman went on to state: "The president has described the events of 1915 as 'one of the greatest tragedies of the 20th century,' but believes that the determination of whether or not the events constitute a genocide should be a matter for historical inquiry, not legislation." Although historical events are indeed properly documented by historical research, not by legislation, it is clear that the president's decision was determined less by the principle that history should be documented by historians than by the fear that, should such legislation pass, Turkey might bar the United States from using its Incirlik airbase in eastern Turkey, which serves as a base for American military efforts in Iraq, and that U.S.-Turkish relations might, in general, suffer.[12] On October 11, after the resolution was passed by the relevant committee of the House of Representatives, Turkey recalled its ambassador to Washington and threatened to stop supporting the Iraq war. "Unfortunately," President Abdullah Gul of Turkey said, "some politicians in the United States have once more dismissed calls for common sense, and made an attempt to sacrifice big issues for minor domestic political games." In response, President Bush's spokesperson said that "we have national security concerns, and many of our troops and supplies go through Turkey. They are a very important ally in the war on terror, and we are going to continue to try to work with them. And we hope that the House does not put forward a full vote." However, Nancy Pelosi, the Speaker of the House, promised to do so.[13] By October 16, though, after a massive lobbying campaign in which Turkey not only threatened to stop allowing the United States to use the airbase to support Iraqi operations but also hinted that it might invade Iraq to go after the Kurdish PKK party, which had carried out terrorist attacks in Turkey, thereby provoking a war between Turkey and Iraq and dragging Iran into the conflict, members of Congress, even those who were cosponsors of the resolution, began to defect. "This happened a long time ago and I don't know whether it was a massacre or a genocide, that is beside the point," said Representative John P. Murtha, a Pennsylvania Democrat

---

[12] Michael Abramowitz, "Turkish Premier Tells Bush Genocide Bill Would Hurt Ties," *Washington Post*, October 6, 2007, p. A11.

[13] Sebnem Arsu, "Turks Angry Over House Armenian Genocide Vote," *New York Times*, October 12, 2007.

who urged the Speaker to keep the resolution from the floor. "The point is, we have to deal with today's world."[14]

Certainly, the act of ignoring the so-called post-Holocaust lesson of "Never again!" is most pernicious when a post-Holocaust genocide unfolds or actually takes place and nothing is done about it because doing something would be politically inconvenient or costly. But as we can see from the case of recognizing the Armenian Genocide, it is also ignored *retroactively*, in terms of its memory, when the act of memorializing a genocide is politically—or militarily—inconvenient or even dangerous.

III. USING THE HOLOCAUST AS A TOOL TO PROMOTE DIPLOMATIC AGENDAS

One of the ways in which the Holocaust figures in the realm of foreign policy is its use to achieve diplomatic ends.

This has already been touched on in connection with President Clinton's use of Holocaust imagery in his effort to justify a military intervention in Kosovo.

But there is also another and very different way of using the Holocaust for diplomatic ends. In this context, the Holocaust is manipulated in order to sway public opinion, especially Jewish opinion, by claiming that someone who is regarded as hostile to Jews and Jewish interests is actually a friend of the Jews who can be trusted because he or she truly feels the pain of the Holocaust. This is held up as proof that the person in question would never harm the Jews.

This is what happened in 1998, when the White House and the State Department tried to manipulate American public opinion, especially American Jewish opinion, about the trustworthiness of Yasser Arafat. They tried to do this by setting up a photo-op of him visiting the United States Holocaust Memorial Museum. The idea was that photos of him mournfully looking at exhibits of dead Jews would make live Jews feel that he understood their pain, as well as the security concerns of the Jewish state, which was created, in part, as a haven for Jews in the wake of the Holocaust. The idea was that seeing Arafat lay a wreath at the museum's eternal flame, which rises above a plinth containing soil from ghettos and death camps, would encourage Jews who were increasingly dismayed by the fatal suicide bombings spreading across Israel and who were ever more convinced that Arafat would do nothing to stop those bombings or even had a hand in them, to reverse their distrust and start believing that he really did care about Jewish suffering and that he could be trusted to make a deal that would ensure a secure Israel.

That invitation to Arafat was a breathtakingly manipulative act. The officials who made it were Jews on the White House's Middle East peace team who were also members of the Holocaust Museum's board of trustees, known as the United States Holocaust Memorial Council. Oddly enough, they had been appointed to the Council by President Clinton as private citizens, even though they were actually government officials. These officials saw the visit as a way to advance their diplomatic agenda, and one of them used his membership to convince the Council's chairman to approve the invitation. And the chairman complied.

---

[14] Carl Hulse, "Support Wanes in House for Genocide Vote," *New York Times*, October 17, 2007.

I was the museum's director at this time. As soon as I learned of the invitation, I objected that it would be an exploitation of the memory of the Holocaust dead to misuse the museum for the purpose of swaying public opinion. The visit, I pointed out, would be a photo-op, with the museum serving as a mere prop. I added that there was no evidence that Arafat wanted to understand the Holocaust. After all, he had been invited to visit Yad Vashem — Israel's memorial to the Holocaust, which is also a museum and every bit as educational as the Holocaust Museum in Washington — but that he had not accepted the invitation, even though he was living a short helicopter-ride away in Gaza. Besides, I said, this was an effort to use the Holocaust Museum as a ritual bath. This week it was Arafat's turn. Would Slobodan Milošević be next in line?

In response to my objections, Arafat was disinvited. Soon enough, pressures for a re-invitation were applied by the Clinton administration. Not only were calls made to the chairman of the museum's board, but Secretary of State Madeleine Albright said on NBC's "Meet the Press" that it was "too bad" that the invitation had been withdrawn and that it would have been appropriate for him to visit the museum as a VIP.[15] Following this and other political pressure, and reportedly fearful that he would lose his job, the chairman then re-invited Arafat, going to the Palestinian leader's hotel room to do so. After he left the hotel, he told reporters that he had invited Arafat "with joy in my heart." As it happens, he failed to tell me that would do so. At a meeting of the Holocaust Council's Executive Committee, one Council member after another asked me to escort Arafat through the museum and even stand there as he laid a wreath before the museum's eternal flame. Each time I refused.

However, on the day that Arafat was supposed to come to the museum, he canceled the visit. The Monica Lewinsky scandal had broken, and Washington's press corps and photographers were at the White House covering it. The opportunity for a photo-op that would sway public opinion was gone. Soon after these events, I resigned as the museum's director, writing to the chairman of the museum's board that I differed with him "on the use of the Museum, and of the memory of the Holocaust, in the context of political or diplomatic circumstances or negotiations."[16]

At the time of the original invitation and re-invitation, there were some — including in the American Jewish community and on the museum's parent body, the United States Holocaust Memorial Council — who desperately wanted to believe that the visit had not been staged as a photo-op, that Arafat really wanted to understand the Holocaust, and that the museum was an educational institution of such great power that Arafat would leave the building a changed man.

But anyone who thinks so now — following Arafat's cancellation of the visit when it became clear that no photographers would be there to cover it, his failure to respond to Yad Vashem's invitations, and his repeated denials in Palestinian Authority

---

[15] See "Transcript: Secretary of State Albright on 'Meet the Press,'" January 20, 1998, http://usembassy-israel.org.il/publish/press/state/archive/1998/january/sd2121.htm.

[16] A short account of this event may also be found in Walter Reich, "No Place for That Photo-Op," *Washington Post*, September 23, 2007, p. B2, as well as in Walter Reich, "A Matter — and a Museum — of Conscience," *Washington Post*, August 28, 1999, p. A18.

publications that the Holocaust ever happened—is simply reinventing history for polemical reasons.

Interestingly, in 2006, the head of the PLO Mission to the United States, Afif Safieh, actually argued, in a letter to the *Washington Post*, that Arafat had had a "strong desire" to visit the museum.[17] Maybe enough time had passed that he thought everyone had forgotten what happened and that he could revise the tawdry history of this episode, manipulating the Holocaust to serve his own needs. Who knows? Maybe he actually believes that this is what happened. Clearly, it is important to remember what really *did* happen—not only to protect the integrity of history but also to recall how even those who are entrusted with the task of preserving Holocaust memory can use that memory to advance political and diplomatic ends.

IV. Promoting Holocaust Memory as a Means to Demonstrate that Anti-Zionism is not Antisemitism

On several occasions, the promotion of Holocaust memory has been used—and in one case continues to be used—to combat the accusation that a certain government or organization is neither against Israel nor antisemitic.

When President Jimmy Carter got into trouble with the American Jewish community in the late 1970s because he sold weapons systems to Saudi Arabia—systems that could be used against the Jewish state—his advisers suggested that he establish a commission to study ways of commemorating the Holocaust. Establishing such a commission would, they felt, mollify the anger toward him among American Jews. That was the origin of the United States Holocaust Memorial Commission, which eventually recommended the creation of a permanent United States Holocaust Memorial Council as well as the United States Holocaust Memorial Museum and the Annual Days of Remembrance Ceremonies. It turns out that Jimmy Carter was not pleased by this outcome. Moreover, how all this happened is a long story that has been documented by others. What is relevant to the theme of this paper, though, is that what some might consider to have been a great act of memory was, one could argue, fundamentally an act of politics. Interestingly, at a White House reception for rabbis called to celebrate the creation of a Holocaust-remembrance body, one of those rabbis, Avi Weiss, when he reached Carter on the receiving line, cut to the political heart of the matter by saying to him: "Mr. President, don't give us the Holocaust at the expense of Israel."

In a current example, the United Nations, which has a poor record anti-Israel activism, has sponsored Holocaust commemorations, including a Holocaust exhibition. Many, including some Holocaust survivors, have been pleased by the United Nations' recognition of Holocaust memory. Others, who are more wary of the organization, suspect that such commemorations and exhibitions, which remain far less prominent than the organization's unrelenting attacks on Israel, are meant to demonstrate that, even if the organization is anti-Zionist, it is not antisemitic. Critics

---

[17] See Afif Safieh, "Arafat and the Holocaust Museum," *Washington Post*, October 19, 2006. See also Walter Reich, "Arafat and the Holocaust Museum (Cont'd)," letter, *Washington Post*, October 30, 2006, p. A16, from which parts of this discussion of the history of Arafat's invitation to visit the Holocaust Museum are drawn.

of the United Nations' behavior toward Israel have noted that it costs little to commemorate dead Jews but that it requires true courage to challenge the demonization, castigation, and excoriation of the Jewish state.

V. USING HOLOCAUST IMAGERY TO ATTACK OPPONENTS, ESPECIALLY ISRAEL

This part of the paper focuses on the use of the Holocaust epithet as a weapon, especially against the country of the victims of the Holocaust, namely Israel.[18]

It is well known that the Holocaust-denial industry has gained a strong foothold in the Arab and Muslim world. After all, Israel is seen as a product of the Holocaust—as having been created on the basis of the justification that, in the wake of the Holocaust, the Jews needed a homeland in which they could defend themselves. What easier way is there to undercut the justification for Israel's existence, especially if you want to end that existence, than by denying that the Holocaust ever happened, instead claiming that it was invented by the Jews in order to steal Muslim and Arab land? Everyone is aware of the claims by Iranian President Mahmoud Ahmadinejad that the Holocaust was a myth. But I could fill page after page citing similar claims by Muslim clerics and leaders saying the same thing.

Ironically, though, even as many Muslim figures insist that the Holocaust never happened, many others, together with their supporters in the West, find it convenient to hurl the epithet "Nazi" at Israel because of the excoriating power of that term. For example, former Israeli Prime Minister Ariel Sharon was regularly called a "Nazi mass murderer" in the Palestinian, Arab, and Muslim media, while a recent Palestinian television program aimed at children showed Israelis "who did the Holocaust" by burning Palestinian children in ovens.

But the epithet "Nazi," and Nazi imagery in general, are also regularly hurled at Israel by European newspapers, editorials, and prominent writers. Many of the examples are well known:

- In May 2001, the Spanish newspaper *El Pais* published a cartoon showing a small figure carrying a rectangular mustache flying toward Sharon's upper lip. The caption: "Clio, the muse of history, puts Hitler's mustache on Ariel Sharon."[19]
- Two days later, another Spanish newspaper, *La Vanguardia*, printed a cartoon showing a building with a sign that read, "Museum of the Jewish Holocaust." Next to that building was another one, still being built, with the sign, "Future Museum of the Palestinian Holocaust."[20]
- In June 2001, three days after a Palestinian suicide bomber killed twenty-one Israelis and wounded 100 others outside a discotheque on the beachfront in Tel Aviv, yet another Spanish daily published a cartoon depicting Ariel Sharon with a hooked nose and sporting a swastika within a star of David, saying, "At least Hitler taught me how to invade a country and destroy every living insect."[21]

---

[18] An earlier version of this discussion, including some of the quotes and observations, may be found in Walter Reich, "Last Word in Anti-Semitism; the Epithet is Hurled at Israel in a Bid to Make Hatred of Jews Respectable," *Los Angeles Times*, May 28, 2004, p. B15.

[19] Cited by Tom Gross, "J'Accuse," *Wall Street Journal Europe*, June 2, 2005.

[20] Ibid.

[21] Ibid.

- In March 2002, the Portuguese Nobel Laureate José Saramago, speaking of Israeli actions in Ramallah, said, "What is happening in Palestine is a crime we can put on the same plane as what happened at Auschwitz...."[22]
- Jewish settlers in the West Bank, the Oxford poet Tom Paulin said a year later, "should be shot dead. I think they are Nazis, racists. I feel nothing but hatred for them."[23]
- That same year, the Irish writer Tom McGurk approved of the comparison between Israel's assault on Jenin with the Nazi destruction of the Warsaw Ghetto. "How extraordinary," he wrote, "that so many in the liberal democratic West should feel so strangely muted, so emotionally strangled in the face of Nazi-style barbarism towards the Palestinians by the State of Israel."[24]
- In a Greek newspaper, a cartoon showed two Israeli soldiers dressed as Nazis stabbing helpless Arabs, with one of the soldiers telling the other, "Do not feel guilty, my brother. We were not in Auschwitz and Dachau to suffer, but to learn."[25]

Alas, the hostility toward Israel in Europe is growing ever stronger, with the Nazi epithet being hurled there with particular venom and frequency during Israel's war with Hezbollah in Lebanon in the summer of 2006.

Why is the Nazi epithet used against Israel? It is used because it is effective. And it is effective with Israel because it instantly and ingeniously turns those who are usually seen as history's victims into history's persecutors, especially if their previous persecution is used to justify the existence of a country that is seen as having caused the victimization of others.

VI. HOLOCAUST DENIAL AS AN IDEOLOGY, A STRATEGY, AND AN INSTRUMENT OF FOREIGN POLICY

It is ironic yet inevitable that, even as the claim is being made that Israel is carrying out a modern-day Holocaust, the claim is also being made, in the same countries, that the Holocaust never happened. It is on this theme that I would like to end this paper.

The most active arena for Holocaust denial is currently Iran. Indeed, the president of Iran, Mahmoud Ahmadinejad, has made questioning the Holocaust a pillar of his presidency—even as a miniseries about an Iranian diplomat who rescued Jews in France during the Holocaust appeared on Iranian television.[26]

---

[22] Quoted in Julian Evans, "The militant magician," *The Guardian*, December 28, 2002, http://books.guardian.co.uk/departments/generalfiction/story/0,,865566,00.html.

[23] Neil Tweedie, "Poet told to apologise for remark on Israelis," *The Telegraph*, April 16, 2002, http://www.telegraph.co.uk/news/uknews/1391035/Poet-told-to-apologise-for-remark-on-Israelis.html.

[24] Tom McGurk, "Israeli Holocaust in Palestine," *Sunday Business Post*, April 14, 2002, http://archives.tcm.ie/businesspost/2002/04/14/story5919628.asp.

[25] See Manfred Gerstenfeld, "An Effective Way to Present Anti-Semitism and Holocaust Inversion," May 28, 2004, http://www.yadvashem.org/yv/en/education/conference/2004/46.pdf.

[26] Nasser Karimi, "Iran Holocaust Show Sympathetic to Jews," *New York Sun*, September 16, 2007.

The claim that the Holocaust never happened has been made throughout the sixty years since the Holocaust ended, both in Europe and in the United States. It is made by antisemites who wanted to accomplish two things.

First, they want to discredit the fact that most discredits antisemitism, namely that it can lead to the mass-murder of Jews. For sixty years, the Holocaust has given antisemitism a bad name. The deniers want to erase this bad name by trying to convince the public that the Holocaust was a big lie. In doing so, they hope to make antisemitism acceptable once again.

In addition, the Holocaust deniers want to discredit the Jews. They argue that the Jews are not only evil people but that they are evil people who have created a myth in order to extort things from the world, including sympathy, money (in the form of Holocaust reparations), and legitimacy for the State of Israel.

Until recent years, Holocaust denial was the province of neo-Nazis and other antisemites, mainly in Europe and North America. Some were kooks. Some were pseudo-scholars. Some, like David Irving, were semi-serious scholars driven by a fanatical antisemitic outlook to try to prove, using what was clearly pseudo-scholarship, that the Holocaust never happened.

All of this was disturbing, but none of it was official on the part of any country, widespread, or, in any immediate way, dangerous. In recent years, however, it has, in one part of the world, become official government policy, very widespread—indeed, endemic—and very dangerous, namely the Arab/Muslim world.

For many years, antisemitic screeds, movies, and cartoons have been a staple in Arab and Iranian media. The forgery claiming a Jewish plot to take over the world, *The Protocols of the Elders of Zion*, and Hitler's *Mein Kampf* are commonly sold in bookstores across the Middle East. Television shows, beamed to millions, show conniving Jews murdering non-Jewish children so that they can use their blood to bake matza. Jews are portrayed as poisoning Arab children, spreading AIDS, and even piloting the airlines that destroyed the World Trade Center. The newspapers and television channels in which much of this antisemitic material appears include those owned by governments, even the government of Egypt, which is at peace—a cold peace, but still a peace—with Israel. Antisemitism has become increasingly virulent. Jews are no longer just being accused of being evil; increasingly, arguments are being made that they should be killed. Antisemitism in the Arab/Muslim world is thus becoming more and more eliminationist.

At the same time, the media in Arab countries and in Iran are focusing ever more on Holocaust denial. Initially, the most common Holocaust-related theme in the Muslim world was the view that the world should be grateful for Hitler's achievement in ridding Europe of its Jews. In the Egyptian government newspaper *Al-Akhbar*, for example, columnist Ahmad Ragab wrote in 2001: "[Give] thanks to Hitler. He took revenge on the Israelis in advance, on behalf of the Palestinians. Our one complaint against him was that his revenge was not complete enough."[27] Increasingly, however, the view has become not that Hitler did not finish the job but

---

[27] Ahmad Ragab, *Al-Akhbar*, April 20, 2001. Cited by the Anti-Defamation League in "Holocaust Denial in the Middle East: The Latest Anti-Israel, Anti-Semitic Propaganda Theme," http://www.adl.org/holocaust/Denial_ME/hdme_genocide_denial.asp#1.

that he never started it. This was heard as far back as the 1970s, but it has become especially common in recent years.

Beginning in the 1990s, Holocaust-denial was expressed very commonly across the Arab/Muslim world. In Syria, it could be found very frequently in the most popular daily, *Teshreen*, which is owned by the Baath Party, the official party of the dictatorship that runs the country. It could also be found in the media of the Palestinian Authority, including its official newspaper and its television station, as well as in the media of Jordan and Egypt.

It is worth citing a few examples of such Holocaust denial from the late 1990s, which have been compiled by the Anti-Defamation League (whose website contains many more examples):[28]

> Israel prospers and exists by right of the Holocaust lie and the Israeli government's policy of intentional exaggeration....[29]

> The entire Jewish State is built on the great Holocaust lie.... What is the proof that Hitler and the Nazis murdered six million Jews in gas chambers? There is no proof at all, except for the conflicting testimonies of a few Jewish "survivors".... At this opportunity mention should be made of the fact that the Jewish state murdered a larger number of Palestinians and Arabs over fifty years. The Holocaust is not what happened to the Jews in Germany, but rather the crime of the establishment of the State of Israel on the ruins of the Palestinian people.[30]

> [The Holocaust is] a tissue of lies, as has been revealed by Western scientists, and it is being used to blackmail the world.[31]

> The Jews invented the myth of mass extermination and the fabrication that 6 million Jews were put to death in Nazi ovens. This was done with the aim of motivating the Jews to emigrate to Israel and to blackmail the Germans for money as well as to achieve world support for the Jews. Similarly, Zionism based itself on this myth to establish the State of Israel.... I continue to believe that the Holocaust is an Israeli myth which was invented to blackmail the world.[32]

The pace of Holocaust denial has, of course, increased markedly across the Arab/Muslim world during the last few years, reaching new heights in the rhetoric of Iran's current president, Mahmoud Ahmadinejad. After the demonstrations in the Muslim world protesting the depictions of the Muslim prophet Muhammad in a

---

[28] These and other examples of Holocaust denial in the Arab/Muslim world are cited on the ADL website at http://www.adl.org/holocaust/denial_ME/default.asp. This website makes several of the observations made here regarding the motivations of those who issue such statements—observations that have been made by many others as well.

[29] Issam Naaman, *Al-Quds Al-Arabi*, April 22, 1998, translated by the Antisemitism Monitoring Forum and cited at http://www.adl.org/holocaust/denial_ME/default.asp.

[30] Mahmoud Al-Khatib, *Al-Arab Al-Yom*, April 27, 1998, translated by the Antisemitism Monitoring Forum and cited at http://www.adl.org/holocaust/denial_ME/default.asp.

[31] Sheikh Mohammad Mehdi Shamseddin in Agence France-Presse, March 22, 1998, cited at http://www.adl.org/holocaust/denial_ME/default.asp.

[32] From "The Holocaust, Netanyahu and Me," *Al-Akhbar*, September 25, 1998, translated by the Antisemitism Monitoring Forum and cited at http://www.adl.org/holocaust/denial_ME/default.asp.

Danish newspaper, including as a terrorist, the Iranian government sponsored a Holocaust cartoon contest that solicited entries that derided the Holocaust. In 2005 and 2006, an Iranian news agency published interviews with Western Holocaust deniers. And on December 11-12, 2006, the Iranian foreign ministry convened a conference of antisemites, anti-Zionists, and Islamic fundamentalists, including David Duke and even the Jewish anti-Zionist group *Neturei Karta*. The conference, like Holocaust denial conferences in the West, was billed as a "scientific" session devoted to the serious and open question of whether or not the Holocaust actually took place. In fact, the speeches emphasized that the Holocaust was a fraud perpetrated by the Jews on the world in the service of forcing the creation of Israel, a country that Ahmadinejad has described as a cancer in the Muslim world that must—and will—be "wiped off the face of the Earth." His statements in the United States during his visit to the United Nations in September 2007 did nothing to mitigate his position.

The story that Ahmadinejad is trying to sell is clear. The Holocaust is a story that was invented by Jews in order to make Westerners, and especially Europeans, feel guilty, so that they would give the Jews both money and a country. The Europeans, who at the time controlled the Middle East, believed the story and, in order to expiate their false guilt, gave them money in the form of reparations and a country in the form of Israel. According to this story, this was a country where the Jews had never lived. Instead, it was stolen from the Palestinians, who as a result experienced a real Holocaust. It is now necessary to show that the Holocaust never happened, as this will justify the elimination of Israel.

Given the mountain of evidence that the Holocaust happened exactly as the world knows that it happened, including the slaughter of six million Jews, Ahmadinejad's beliefs are absurd. But they are also dangerous. This is the same Ahmadinejad whose government is building nuclear installations that are clearly aimed at creating nuclear weapons. This is the same Ahmadinejad who rejects Western pressures to stop building them. And this is the same Ahmadinejad who has assured the true believers not only that will Israel be destroyed, but that the Muslim world will destroy it.

So much for "Never again."

Leo Strauss as a Jewish Thinker

Steven Smith[*]

I

The work of Leo Strauss has never lacked for critics, but until only very recently his work was virtually unknown outside the tight world of academia. But as the great jazz crooner Dinah Washington once observed, what a difference a day makes! In the past couple of years, the work and influence of Strauss has been discussed and debated in every leading newspaper, magazine, and journal. What has made headlines has not been his arcane interpretations of the dialogues of Plato or the intricacies of Maimonides but his alleged influence on the political movement known as neo-conservatism.

Today, Strauss allegedly influences a wide range of Washington policy analysts, journalists, and opinion makers from beyond the grave. Among those most frequently mentioned as disciples of Strauss are former Deputy Defense Secretary Paul Wolfowitz and William Kristol, editor of the neo-conservative *Weekly Standard*. As if this were not enough, his name was mentioned in a recent Broadway play put on by Academy Award-winning actor and anti-war activist Tim Robbins. In this play, entitled *Embedded*, the Iraq war is presented as having been created by a sinister cabal that throughout the play periodically shouts out "hail to Leo Strauss."

However, it is not his contributions—real or apocryphal—to neo-conservatism that I want to talk about today, but Strauss's role as a Jewish thinker, one of the greatest Jewish thinkers of the twentieth century. Strauss's contribution to the world of Jewish thought might at first glance appear relatively uncontroversial. His first book, *Spinoza's Critique of Religion*, was written as a member of the prestigious Berlin Academy for Jewish Research during the 1920s. His second work, *Philosophy and Law*, examined Maimonides and his great Greek and Islamic predecessors. In a large number of essays and lectures, most famously centering on the theme of "Jerusalem and Athens," Strauss explored his lifelong fascination with the differences between biblical thought and Greek philosophy. Finally, in an autobiographical introduction to the English translation of his book on Spinoza, Strauss spoke in no uncertain terms about the various currents of orthodoxy, Zionism, and Jewish liberalism within which he came to maturity.

To describe Strauss as a Jewish thinker obviously means more than that he was simply a thinker of Jewish birth and ancestry. It presupposes that there is something meaningful in the concept of Jewish thought that distinguishes it from other kinds of

---

[*] Alfred Cowles Professor of Political Science, Yale University.

concerns and problems. On the face of it, this something might not be so easy to identify. What, for instance, does the thinking of men such as Rabbi Akiva, Rashi, Judah Halevi, and Maimonides have in common with the thought of such "non-Jewish Jews" as Spinoza, Heine, Marx, and Freud? What can such names possibly do together except appear on a list of Jewish thinkers that is no different from the lists of famous Jewish movie stars or sports figures that regularly appear in books and magazines. It gets us no closer to the thing itself. Before considering this issue, first a little biography.

II

Leo Strauss was born in the Hessian village of Kirchhain in 1899. He was brought up in an observant household where, he remarked later, the Jewish laws "were rather strictly observed." After graduating from a humanistic Gymnasium and a brief service in World War I, Strauss attended university at Marburg, which at that time was the center of the neo-Kantian philosophy inspired by Hermann Cohen. In 1921, Strauss received his doctorate from the University of Hamburg, where he prepared a dissertation under the direction of Ernst Cassirer. A year later, he spent a post-graduate year in Freiburg, where he went to study with Edmund Husserl. It was during this year that Strauss first heard Husserl's student, Martin Heidegger, who left a deep—even lifelong—impression on him.

Strauss worked as a research assistant at the Academy of Jewish Research in Berlin from 1925-1932, where his principle duties were to assist with editing the Academy's jubilee edition of the works of Moses Mendelssohn. During this period, Strauss published some of his earliest writings on Zionism and other Jewish themes in Martin's Buber's journal *Der Jude* and in the *Jüdische Rundschau*. His first book, *Die Religionskritik Spinozas* (Spinoza's Critique of Religion), was dedicated to the memory of Franz Rosenzweig, who had died the year before its publication.

Strauss left Germany in 1932 under the auspices of a Rockefeller Foundation grant and spent a year in Paris before moving to England. Unable to find a permanent position in England, Strauss emigrated to America in 1938. There he joined the faculty of the New School for Social Research, which at this time was a haven for academics in exile from Hitler's Germany. Strauss's New School years were remarkably a productive period in his life where—as we are now beginning to learn fully—his major ideas began to germinate. It was here that Strauss first became a "Straussian."

In 1949, Strauss accepted a position at the University of Chicago, where he spent almost the next twenty years and where his most important books—*Persecution and the Art of Writing* (1952), *Natural Right and History* (1953), *Thoughts on Machiavelli* (1958), and *What is Political Philosophy* (1959)—were written. It was during the Chicago years that Strauss exercised his greatest influence and attracted a remarkable cadre of students. At the invitation of Gershom Scholem, he spent a year at the Hebrew University in Jerusalem, but otherwise devoted himself almost exclusively to teaching and writing. His later works focused increasingly on ancient political philosophy, especially Plato, Xenophon, Aristotle, and Thucydides. Upon his retirement, Strauss spent his last years in Annapolis, Maryland, where he went to join his old friend Jacob Klein on the faculty of St. John's College. Since his death in

1973, several volumes of previously uncollected essays, lectures, and philosophical correspondence have been published. His work, always controversial, has continued to generate debate, arguably more today than during his lifetime. It remains a remarkable monument to twentieth century scholarship and philosophy.

III

The core of Strauss's thought, the theme to which he would return time and again, is what he referred to metaphorically as Jerusalem and Athens. What do these two names signify?

Jerusalem and Athens—the city of faith and the city of philosophy—are the two poles around which Western tradition has evolved. The spirit of Athens has traditionally been understood as the embodiment of rationality, democracy, and science in the broadest sense of the term. The spirit of Jerusalem, on the other hand, represents love, faith, and morality in the broadest sense. For many thinkers—including the great German philosopher Hermann Cohen—modernity itself is predicated upon the synthesis of Jerusalem and Athens, of ethics and science. Modernity and hence progress are only possible with the synthesis of these two great currents of thought. But are they compatible? Is such a synthesis possible? To repeat the question posed by the Church father Tertullian: "What has Athens to do with Jerusalem?"

On the surface it would seem that Jerusalem and Athens represent two fundamentally different, even antagonistic, codes or ways of life. Consider the following. Greek philosophy elevates reason—our own human reason—as the one thing needful for life. Greek philosophy culminates in the person of Socrates, who famously said "the unexamined life is not worth living." Only the life given over to the cultivation of autonomous human understanding is a worthy human life. But the Bible presents itself not as a philosophy or a science, but as a code of law, an unchangeable divine law mandating how we should live. In fact, the first five books of the Bible are known in the Jewish tradition as the Torah, which is perhaps most literally translated as "law."

The attitude taught by the Bible is not one of self-reflection or critical examination but one of obedience, faith, and trust in God. If the paradigmatic Athenian is Socrates, the paradigmatic biblical figure is the Abraham of the *Akedah* (Binding of Isaac), who is prepared to sacrifice his son in response to an unintelligible command.

The difference between Athens and Jerusalem is more than a conflict between the age-old antagonists of faith and reason. These two alternatives express fundamentally different moral and political points of view. Consider once again Greek ethics. The pinnacle of Greek ethical thought is Aristotle's *Nicomachean Ethics*, and the pinnacle of his ethics is the virtue known as *megalopsychia* or greatness of soul. Greatness of soul, as the name implies, is the virtue concerned with honor. The great-souled man is said to claim much because he deserves much. Such a person is concerned above all with how he is seen by others and, of course, how to be worthy of the recognition bestowed on his acts of public service. The great-souled man is haughty in the extreme. But contrast this, if you will, with the typical heroes extolled by the Bible. Such men are typically deeply aware of their own imperfections, their own unworthiness before God, and are haunted by a deep sense of guilt and insufficiency. Recall the following words of Isaiah: "I am a man of unclean lips among a people of unclean lips." Is it even conceivable to think of a Greek philosopher uttering these words? But, more to the point, which of these two is more admirable: Aristotelian man's sense of his own self-worth and pride at his own accomplishments or Biblical man's sense of his unworthiness and dependence on divine love?

These differences go deeper still. The god of the philosophers is Aristotle's famous unmoved mover. The unmoved mover is something like pure thought, which is why both Plato and Aristotle believed that the act of solitary contemplation brought us closest to the divine. *Theoria*—pure contemplation—is the activity the Greeks believed to be most god-like. Needless to say, the Aristotelian unmoved mover, unlike the God of the Bible, is not concerned with man and his fate. The God of Aristotle, whatever else one might say, is not the God of Abraham, Isaac, and Jacob. This God, the God of the Bible, as we will see later, is said to have created us in his image. This means that it is not contemplation or philosophy but repentance and the ruthless demand for purity of heart that is required of us. Repentance— *t'shuva* in Hebrew—means return to an earlier state of purity and simplicity. The omnipotent God of the Bible is not a thinking substance but a being who dwells in the thick darkness and whose ways are not our ways.

The question confronting Strauss was how we can choose between these two alternatives. Each side stakes a claim to our allegiance, but each side also seems to exclude the other. What are we to do? One answer is to say that we are open to both and willing to listen first and then decide. But to suggest that we will make a choice on the basis of our own best judgment already seems to decide the matter in favor of reason over faith. On the other hand, we might say that any answer to the question "who is right—the Greeks or the Jews?" is based on an act of faith. In this case, Jerusalem seems to have triumphed over Athens. A philosophy that is based on faith is no longer a real philosophy.

IV

For Strauss, the abstract problem of Jerusalem and Athens was a very real historical and political problem. The most immediate and urgent manifestation of this problem was expressed as the so-called Jewish Question. The Jewish Question was meant to describe, but was not confined to, the predicament of German Jewry. It was in Germany that the fate of modern Jewry, which Strauss regarded as the major theme of his investigations, was most intensely debated.

Strauss saw the Jewish Question first and foremost as a political question or, to use his own words, a "theologico-political problem." This problem turned on what form or shape Judaism would take in a modern liberal state. German Jewry, perhaps more than the Jews of any other nation, wedded itself to the fate of modern liberalism. The result, as Strauss saw it, was a mixed blessing. The triumph of liberal democracy brought civil equality, toleration, and the end of the worst forms of persecution, if not all forms of private discrimination. At the same time, however, liberalism requires of Judaism—as it does of all faiths—to undergo the privatization of belief, the transformation of Jewish law from a communal authority to the precincts of individual conscience. Arguably, this places harder demands on Judaism than on many other religions. Judaism understands itself, in the first instance, not as a faith or set of beliefs but as a body of laws intended to regulate social and political life.

The liberal principle of the separation of state and society, of public life and private belief, could not but result in the "Protestantization" of Judaism.

The Germany of Strauss's early adulthood was the Weimar Republic. Weimar was a liberal democracy created in the wake of Germany's defeat in World War I. The Weimar Republic was regarded by many intellectuals of Strauss's generation as a foreign import without roots in the German tradition. Furthermore, it was a symbol of Anglo-French domination that could be traced back to the French Revolution. This weakness accounts for the inability of Weimar to protect its most vulnerable minority, namely its Jewish citizens. It was no coincidence that the attack upon Weimar was an attack upon German Jewry. "The Weimar Republic," Strauss later remarked, "was succeeded by the only German regime—the only regime ever anywhere—which had no other clear principle except murderous hatred of the Jews." It was the very weakness and fragility of liberal democracy, its susceptibility to demagoguery, that would become a central problem of Strauss's life's work.

The dilemmas of German Jewry had a long history that Strauss traced back to Spinoza. Spinoza was in effect the godfather of modern Jewry. He made the Jews an offer—actually two offers—that he thought they could not refuse. The first was the promise of emancipation followed by assimilation into a modern democratic society. Liberal democracy, as Spinoza envisaged it, was a society constituted by a universal rational morality. As such, it would be neither Christian nor Jewish. Instead, it would be neutral with respect to the competing denominations. It would be a society where individuals would be encouraged to shed their former religious identities and become citizens of the modern state. This option is explored at length in Mark Lilla's book *The Stillborn God*.

But what if democracy does not solve the Jewish question? Democracies stand or fall on the distinction between the public and private sphere. Democratic governments may be unable to discriminate between individuals on the basis of religion—or along gender or racial lines—but individuals and groups may continue to do so. Rather than solving the problem of persecution, does democracy not simply it move it from the public to the private side of the ledger?

Spinoza thus offered a second option: not emancipation but Zionism. His work holds out the possibility of a re-established Jewish state. To be sure, Spinoza's call for the restitution of Jewish sovereignty is extremely ambiguous. Such a state need not be located in the historical land of Israel but could just as easily be established in Canada or Katmandu. Nor does Spinoza indicate whether such a state would need to be a democracy and, if so, what the status of Judaism would be within it.

Nevertheless, Strauss assigned to Spinoza an honored role among the founders of political Zionism. It was to this creed that he professed allegiance throughout his career. He praised Zionism for its effort to restore a sense of Jewish pride and self-respect in an era of assimilation and loss of traditional values.

He regarded Zionism in some (although not all) respects as a conservative movement seeking to validate Jewish traditions and loyalties. He once compared the Zionist pioneers to the American pilgrim fathers who formed the "natural aristocracy" of the new country.

Strauss's relation to the Zionist movement is a long story that has yet to be fully told. For complicated reasons, however, he came to see the problem of political Zionism as its failure to think through the problems of the modern democratic state.

Early Zionist thinkers like Herzl and Pinsker regarded the solution to the Jewish problem as the creation of a state that would put an end to discrimination and provide full civic equality for the Jews. It would be, in effect, like a European state but created by and for Jews. The Achilles heel of such a solution—so Strauss believed—is that it lacked any intrinsic connection to the moral and spiritual world of Judaism that it was trying to save. A Jewish state without a Jewish culture to support and sustain it would be, in Strauss's words, "an empty shell."

Strauss expressed an appreciation for the cultural Zionists, such as Ahad Ha'am, who argued that a Jewish state would need to be rooted in a vibrant Jewish culture. If political Zionism with its emphasis on states and political institutions was a product of the European Enlightenment, cultural Zionism, with its emphasis on Jewish arts and letters, language, and literature, was a product of European romanticism. The problem with cultural Zionism, however, was revealed in the following anecdote related by Strauss dating from sometime during the 1920s:

> I was myself [he wrote] a political Zionist in my youth and was a member of a Zionist youth organization. In this capacity I occasionally met with [Zev] Jabotinsky, the leader of the Revisionists. He asked me "What are you doing?" I said, "Well, we read the Bible, we study Jewish history, Zionist theory, and of course keep abreast of developments, and so on." He replied, "And rifle practice?" And I had to say, "No."

The point here, beyond the obvious humor, is that a state cannot subsist on culture alone. It requires armies, a police force, young men and women with uniforms and guns.

There is another point at issue. Cultural Zionism conceived of the Jewish tradition not as a divine gift or the product of revelation but as an expression of the Jewish mind possessed of its own unique genius. This was the romantic side of the culturalist movement. But by turning Judaism into just one culture among others, it failed to reflect adequately on the foundations of culture. Had it done so, the cultural Zionists would have realized that the foundation of Jewish culture is in faith, a faith in God's gift of the Torah at Mount Sinai. This faith—not Israeli folk music or dance—is what had sustained the Jews over centuries of dispersion and persecution.

It is only when we consider this foundation in faith—faith in revelation—that cultural Zionism turns into religious Zionism. Strauss was not a religious Zionist and he never for a moment confounded politics with redemption. In an enigmatic passage from his lecture "Why We Remain Jews," he argues that the Jewish people have been chosen to prove the absence of redemption, that redemption is not possible in this world. The creation of the Jewish state may be the most important fact in Jewish history since the completion of the Talmud, but it should not be confused with the coming of the Messianic age and the redemption of all people. So what, then, is the function of the Jewish state? If it is not to be understood as purely secular democratic state, what is its purpose?

In the final analysis, Strauss was grateful for the Jewish state, which he called "a blessing for all Jews everywhere regardless of whether they admit it or not." But not even the Jewish state should be regarded as a solution to the Jewish Question. "The establishment of the state of Israel," he wrote, "is the most profound modification of the *Galut* which has occurred, but it is not the end of the *Galut*; in the religious sense, and perhaps not only in the religious sense, the state of Israel is a part of the *Galut*." What could Strauss have meant by this?

Passages like the above—actually the above is unique in Strauss's writings—call to mind Franz Rosenzweig, "whose name," Strauss would acknowledge, "will always be remembered when informed people speak about existentialism." For Rosenzweig, the Jewish Question was something that ultimately stood outside of politics and history. Judaism is a repository of certain revealed, transhistorical truths that cannot be reduced to politics or culture. Like Cohen, Rosenzweig was a passionate anti-Zionist. The Jewish calling was to remain a people of prayer and study and to resist the entrapments of political power. It is the destiny of the Jewish people both to live in the world but to remain apart from it as part of a unique covenantal community. Strauss's claim to stand apart from both Jerusalem and Athens and to remain an attentive interpreter of each to the other was an echo of Rosenzweig's argument that the modern Jew is torn between two homelands (*Zweistromland*), between faith and reason, law and philosophy, *Deutschtum* and *Judentum*. Rosenzweig's establishment of the *Freies Jüdisches Lehrhaus* (Free Jewish House of Learning) in Frankfurt devoted to the study and translation of traditional Jewish texts could well have served as a model for Strauss's creation of an interpretive community in Chicago many years later.

V

On the basis of his survey of the currents of modern Jewish thought, including Cohenian neo-Kantianism, Zionism, and Rosenzweig's "new thinking," Strauss considered anew the ground of orthodoxy. It was in this context that he put forward what at first appeared to be a fantastic thought-experiment, namely, the return to "medieval rationalism," a term Strauss coined to describe the Maimonidean Enlightenment.

Strauss's discovery of medieval rationalism meant returning to the traditional or at least pre-modern meaning of revelation. Works like Maimonides' *Guide for the Perplexed* were not philosophical books in the manner of Spinoza's *Ethics* or Rosenzweig's *Star of Redemption*. The former were Jewish books insofar far as they accepted the primacy of revelation as their absolute point of departure. The primacy of revelation was connected to the primacy of politics. The prophet, in its original meaning, is a lawgiver, and prophecy is the purest science of the law. The prophet is the creator of the moral and political community within which philosophy is even possible. It follows, then, that revelation belongs to the study of political science.

At least two consequences follow from this discovery. The first is Strauss's assertion regarding the fundamental difference between revelation and philosophy. This put him deeply at odds with those interpreters who stressed the unity—or at least the compatibility—of faith and reason. The belief in the unity of faith and reason is evidence of a "Thomistic" tendency that may hold true for Christian thought but does not hold for the Judeo-Arabic writers. In fact, Strauss's discovery of Avicenna's statement that "the teaching of prophecy and the Divine Law is contained in [Plato's] *Laws*" contains his first and decisive inkling that theology is fundamentally political theology.

The second consequence of Strauss's return to Maimonides and the medieval Enlightenment appears to be merely a literary problem. This concerns the complex and often ambiguous manner of writing in which the ancient and medieval writers chose to reveal—or rather conceal—their deepest and most important teachings from public scrutiny. This doctrine of esotericism or the "double truth" had certainly been noted by Strauss's scholarly predecessors, but none had accorded it the centrality that Strauss attributed to it. Unlike the modern Enlightenment, which set itself the task of removing prejudices and undermining foundations—a kind of race to the abyss—Strauss found in the medieval Enlightenment a different mode of philosophy, one that set out not to destroy society but to maintain religion's political role while obliquely indicating that which favors philosophy.

Strauss's study of the medieval Enlightenment led him to a new understanding of the political. The word "political" as a modifier of philosophy can be understood in two ways. It can designate a distinct branch of philosophy alongside ethics, logic, and metaphysics, or it can designate an attribute of all philosophy. Every philosopher insofar as he desires to communicate to others does so in a way that must take into account the political situation of philosophy, that is to say, what can be said and what needs to be kept under wraps. It is in this sense of the term political that one can speak of the primacy of political philosophy. In the past, such a strategy was undertaken in part out of a need to avoid persecution at the hands of society but more seriously out of the desire to safeguard society from the dangerous, even malignant truths to which philosophy adheres. The medieval Enlighteners took upon themselves the paradoxical task of protecting society from themselves. It was due to their highly elliptical manner of writing that Strauss developed a hermeneutic of his own characterized by "a scrupulous, almost pathological attention to detail" down to the smallest words and articles as containing clues to the deep structure of an author's thought.

Strauss regarded this recovery of the esoteric tradition in Judaism not only as an historical or philological finding but as a key to his own understanding of orthodoxy. By orthodoxy, Strauss did not mean the black hat Haredi community that occupies sections of Crown Heights or Boro Park. Orthodoxy does not refer to the *Neturei Karta* ("Guardians of the City of Jerusalem") or *Agudat Israel* but to a "Maimonidean" strategy that professes outward fidelity to the law and the community of Israel with an inward or private commitment to philosophy and a life of free inquiry. This dual strategy allows one to maintain respect for—even love of—the tradition as a prophylactic to the alternatives of atheism and assimilation. The doctrine of the double truth remains the only way of preserving the viability of Judaism in a post-Nietzschean world that demands intellectual probity at all costs.

It is almost impossible not to read Strauss's understanding of orthodoxy as intended to apply to the situation of contemporary Jewry. To be sure, fundamental differences exist between the theologico-political predicaments of the twelfth century and the twentieth century. To state only the most obvious one, we no longer occupy a world where the primacy of revelation and the immortality of the soul are taken for granted. For this very reason, it has been a source of deep consternation for some readers that Strauss decided to imitate Maimonides by adopting similar modes of expression and practicing the same reticence and deliberate caution in an altogether different world. Why did he do this? What purpose could this serve in the modern "disenchanted world"? Strauss's defense of orthodoxy as little more than a Platonic noble lie—an "heroic delusion," he once called it—violates the one cardinal rule we expect from philosophers: intellectual honesty.

People who live in glass houses should not throw stones. Strauss, who took such evident delight in exposing others, cannot in good conscience complain when the same trick is played on him. Does Strauss's defense of orthodoxy escape the problems that he so ably diagnosed in others? Does his attempt to turn orthodoxy into a legal fiction fulfill the basic requirement of his hermeneutic method: to understand the thought of the past as it understood itself? Or does he import a kind of crypto-Maimonideanism into his understanding of orthodoxy? We can only wish that Leo Strauss were still here to try to answer some of these questions.

The Academic and Public Debate over the Meaning of the "New Antisemitism"

Roni Stauber*

I. INTRODUCTION

From the end of 2000, the number of violent incidents and acts of vandalism against Jews rose quite steadily, reaching a peak in 2006, when about 590 cases of violence and vandalism were registered worldwide. In addition, there was a considerable increase in the number of verbal insults and threats directed against Jews, as well in the publication of antisemitic articles. Thus, between the end of the 1990s and 2006, the number of antisemitic incidents rose by about 300 percent. Moreover, in 2004, Tel Aviv University's Stephen Roth Institute gathered information on more than 500 incidents of violence and vandalism. About 40 percent of these incidents were physical attacks on Jewish individuals, compared to only 20 percent in 1999. This significant shift in the targets of antisemitic attacks is one indicator of the growing involvement of young Muslims in street violence against Jews (see below).[1]

This dramatic escalation has been accompanied by a vigorous discourse regarding the significance of these events to Jews worldwide. Researchers, intellectuals, writers, and public figures have debated several fundamental questions resulting from differing and even contrasting interpretations of the events. The discussion has extended far beyond antisemitism per se to basic questions regarding modern Jewish life in the Diaspora, including the relationship of Jews with various segments of the surrounding society—particularly in Europe, where most of the above-mentioned antisemitic incidents occurred—the relationship and commitment of Jews worldwide to Israel, and the commitment of Israel to the safety and welfare of Jewish communities in the Diaspora. Since the beginning of the debate, dozens of articles as well as several collections of essays and books have been published on these issues.[2] This paper discusses some of the fundamental disagreements revealed during this polemic.

---

* Director and Senior Researcher, Stephen Roth Institute for the Study of Contemporary Antisemitism and Racism, Tel Aviv University. I would like to thank Ms. Sarah Rembiszewski of the Stephen Roth Institute for her most valuable comments.

[1] See http://www.tau.ac.il/Anti-Semitism/statistics/statistics.htm.

[2] See, for example, Ron Rosenbaum, ed., *Those Who Forget the Past* (New York, 2004); Paul Iganski and Barry Kosmin, eds., *A New Antisemitism?* (London, 2003).

II. THE 1990S: THE PREPARATORY YEARS

Antony Lerman, executive director of the Institute of Jewish Policy Research (JPR), is a conspicuous opponent of the view that in recent years Jews have faced a new trend of antisemitism. In his article "Sense on Antisemitism," published in the British magazine *Prospect* in August 2002, he wrote that this argument began with the outbreak of the al-Aqsa intifada in October 2000.[3] This claim is inaccurate. Although the term the "new antisemitism" became common in the public discourse only after the outbreak of the second intifada at the end of 2000, the warnings that Jews worldwide were facing a new form of hate can be traced back to the beginning of the 1990s.

In 1994, Martin Kramer, a prominent Middle East researcher at Tel Aviv University, described in an article entitled "Jihad against the Jews" a dramatic change in the view of many Muslim fundamentalists (hereafter: Islamists) regarding the Jews. He warned of a growing tendency among Islamists toward embracing the concept of a worldwide war, or jihad, against the Jews. "This anti-Semitism seems to me so widespread and potentially violent that it could eclipse all other forms of antisemitism over the next decade," he said.[4]

In the same year, Kramer presented a paper at a conference hosted by JPR (Lerman was one of the main organizers), in which he emphasized that the alleged Jewish worldwide plot to destroy Islam already occupied a central role in the Islamist worldview and that there were clear signs that it was about to become a cornerstone of their teachings. Shortly after the bombing of the AMIA, the Jewish community centre in Buenos Aires, in 1994, Kramer noted that there should no longer be any doubt as to where the most serious threat to Jewish security lay, namely in Islamic fundamentalism: "Hard evidence is rapidly replacing speculation," he warned. "It is evidence we can no longer ignore or deny."[5]

Indeed, at the beginning of the 1990s, there were several indications of the rise of a new type of Islamic antisemitism that perceives Jews as global enemies. In 1993, members of a militant radical Sunni group under the leadership of the Egyptian Sheikh Omar Abdul Rahman carried out the first bombing of the World Trade Center (WTC) in New York. Following their arrest, it was revealed that they had also been planning to attack Jewish targets, among them a Jewish summer camp in the Catskill Mountains.[6] In 1994-1995, the Algerian Groupe Islamique Armé (GIA) attacked a synagogue and a Jewish school in Lyon, France. In pamphlets disseminated in France and Sweden, it called for jihad against the Jews as enemies of Islam.[7] Throughout the 1990s, Islamist leaders in Europe preached and disseminated antisemitic messages, and Osama bin Laden waged his so-called holy war against the Crusaders and the Jews. In addition, antisemitism became a central component in

---

[3] Antony Lerman, "Sense on Antisemitism," in *A New Antisemitism?*, ed. Iganski and Kosmin (London, 2003), http://www.axt.org.Uk/essays/Lerman.htm#About%20the%20.

[4] Martin Kramer, "The Jihad against the Jews," *Commentary*, October 1994, pp. 38-42, http://www.geocities.com/martinkramerorg/JihadAgainstJews.htm.

[5] Martin Kramer, "The Salience of Islamic Antisemitism," *Institute of Jewish Affairs Report*, no. 2, October 1995, http://www.geocities.com/martinkramerorg/Antisemitism.htm.

[6] Ely Karmon, "International Terror and Antisemitism—Two Modern-Day Curses: Is There a Connection?," http://www.tau.ac.il/Anti-Semitism/asw2005/karmon.html.

[7] Database of the Stephen Roth Institute, http://www.tau.ac.il/Anti-Semitism/database.htm.

the ideology of extreme Palestinian and Middle Eastern Muslim groups, both Sunni and Shi'a.[8] There were clear signs, too, of the growing role of young descendants of immigrant families, notably from the Middle East and North Africa, in violent incidents and vandalism against Jewish targets in the early 1990s. Thus, for example, the deportation of Hamas leaders to Lebanon in 1993 and the Baruch Goldstein massacre in Hebron 1994 were followed by a considerable increase in attacks on Jewish individuals and Jewish property in Europe.[9]

However, the emergence of this new type of antisemitism among extreme Muslims and its threat to Jewish communities were not widely discussed in the 1990s. At this time, the spotlight was focused on the formation of new ultra-nationalist and antisemitic groups in the former Soviet bloc, especially in Russia, and the antisemitic incitement of prominent leaders of the Communist party there; the strengthening of nationalist and extreme right-wing parties in Western and Central Europe, particularly the Austrian Freedom Party (FPÖ); the question of Holocaust victims' assets, particularly pre-war deposits in Swiss banks; Holocaust denial; and the growth of hate propaganda of extreme right and neo-Nazi groups on the Internet.

The antisemitism of radical Islam and the threat it posed received only scant attention in the 1990s.[10] Moreover, toward the end of the decade, analyses of antisemitism reported a continuing decline in antisemitic manifestations. Commenting in 1997 on the findings of a joint publication of the JPR and the American Jewish Committee (AJC), the AJC's executive director, David Harris, stated: "We are indeed gratified to see that current trends indicate a decline in antisemitism around the world and that the general population has increasingly little tolerance for this cancerous hatred."[11]

Understanding and defining new historical developments or trends and their potential impact have always been a difficult task for contemporary observers, particularly when longstanding phenomena such as antisemitism lie at the core. The renowned Jewish scholar Jacob Katz called the six years that preceded the eruption of the racial and political antisemitism of 1879 "the preparatory stage" of modern antisemitism.[12] Similarly, the dramatic eruption of antisemitism at the beginning of the new millennium was preceded by ominous manifestations in the last decade of the 20th century. Notwithstanding these signs, the magnitude of the upsurge came as a surprise to almost everyone.

The difficulty of evaluating new political or social developments results from the simple fact that different stages frequently contain previous elements. Ely Karmon,

---

[8] Esther Webman, *Anti-Semitic Motifs in the Ideology of Hizballah and Hamas* (Tel Aviv, 1994).

[9] *Antisemitism Worldwide 1993-1994* (Tel Aviv, 1994).

[10] See, for example, Simon Epstein, "Cyclical Patterns in Antisemitism: The Dynamics of Anti-Jewish Violence in Western Countries since the 1950s," ACTA Occasional Paper, no. 2 (Jerusalem, 1993); *Antisemitism World Report* (London, 1997), http://www.ess.uwe.ac.uk/documents/antsem97.htm; *Antisemitism Worldwide 1999-2000* (Tel Aviv, 2000), http://www.tau.ac.il/Anti-Semitism/asw99-2000/genanalysis.htm.

[11] "Antisemitism World Report 1997 Reveals Declining Levels of Antisemitism Around the World; Increased Use of Internet for Dissemination and Monitoring of Antisemitism," American Jewish Committee, July 1997, http://www.charitywire.com/charity11/00327.html.

[12] Jacob Katz, "The Preparatory Stage of the Modern Antisemitic Movement (1873-1879)," in *Antisemitism Through the Ages*, ed. S. Almog (Oxford, 1988), pp. 279-89.

an expert in international terrorism, pointed out that, from the end of the 1960s, Jewish sites were the target of terror attacks of Palestinian groups, frequently in collaboration with the radical left (German, French, Japanese, and others). Although antisemitism was quite common among members of the French and German extreme left, striking at Jewish targets in Europe was based on the concept that terror against the Jews was part of the war against Israel, conveying the message that the life of Jews would not be safe until the Palestinian problem had been solved. Secular Palestinian terrorist groups targeted some of the same sites later attacked by Islamists. In September 1986, Palestinian terrorists from the Abu Nidal group struck at the Neve Shalom synagogue in Istanbul, killing twenty-two Jews. Seventeen years later, in November 2003, the same synagogue was attacked, this time by Turkish Islamists linked to al-Qaeda. Twenty-three people were killed, among them six Jews, and about 330 were injured.[13]

Nevertheless, even Karmon, who emphasizes the continuum between secular Palestinian terror against Jewish targets and murderous Islamist attacks, accepts Kramer's basic claim regarding the difference between the two group. While Palestinian terror groups perceived their brutal deeds against Jewish targets as part of their war against Israel, Islamist leaders posit the conflict in terms of a struggle between Islam and the Jews—with a new vision of the Jews and Israel as the supreme enemy and an existential threat.[14]

III. Between Demonization of Israel and the War against the Jews

The concept that the Jews were facing a new stage in the history of antisemitism entered the public discourse due mainly to three events:

1. The dramatic increase in numbers of antisemitic incidents, particularly in Western Europe, following the outbreak of the second intifada in October 2000.
2. The 2001 UN World Conference against Racism in Durban, South Africa, where an orchestrated attack of Arab delegations, with the support of numerous NGOs, against the very existence of the State of Israel was accompanied by clear antisemitic motifs. Jewish delegates from various countries were stunned by the level of hatred they witnessed toward Israel and the Jewish people, including cries of "Death to the Jews."[15]
3. The 9/11 attacks by al-Qaeda in New York and Washington, which took place only a short while after Durban.

These events and others that occurred in the following years, including attacks on Jewish targets (see below), demonstrate the global concept of the jihad waged by Islamists. Historians, whose expertise lay in national socialism, the Holocaust, and modern antisemitism rather than oriental studies or Islam, spoke of the genocidal aspect of the antisemitic worldview of Islamists. Yehuda Bauer and Robert Wistrich, for example, emphasized the similarity between the desire for global domination of

---

[13] Karmon, "International Terror and Antisemitism."

[14] Ibid.

[15] Pierre-André Taguieff, *Rising from the Muck* (Chicago, 2004), pp. 70-2; conversation with Dr. Karen Mock who was a member of the Canadian delegation to Durban, February 2006.

radical Islam and the secular totalitarian ideologies national socialism and communism, which caused the deaths of tens of millions.[16] This linkage has been discussed comprehensively by the German researcher Matthias Küntzel and others, who demonstrate how the Nazi war against the Jews was supported during World War II by Palestinian Mufti Muhammad Amin al-Husseini. After the war, the Nazi type of hatred toward the Jews was internalized, particularly in Egypt by the Muslim Brotherhood and by the main teachers of radical Islam Hassan al-Banna and Sayyid Qutb.[17]

Since the end of 2000, there have been several attempted and actual terror attacks against Jewish targets committed by members of Islamist groups, in some cases connected to or inspired by al-Qaeda, such as the strike on the Neve Shalom and Beth Israel synagogues in Istanbul, the attack on the historic synagogue in Djerba, Tunisia, in 2002, and plans to hit Jewish targets in Germany and Norway.[18] However, what characterizes the new wave of the antisemitism is not an increase in the number of terror incidents or large-scale acts of violence organized by groups that sought to hurt as many Jews as possible, but rather assaults on Jewish individuals by persons acting spontaneously even without the use of a weapon and shouting antisemitic slogans in the process.[19] The fact that most incidents were perpetrated randomly is a significant finding that will be discussed in the conclusions.

With the dramatic rise in street violence, an important question has been raised regarding the identification of the perpetrators, an essential element in the effort to explain the upsurge. Although there are few cases in which the police succeeded in establishing the identity of the perpetrators of physical attacks, the involvement of Arabs and Muslims, according to victim testimonies, is significant.[20] Jewish leaders and historians who emphasize the threat posed by radical Islam as a major component of the "new antisemitism" see a clear connection between the street violence perpetrated against Jewish individuals or Jewish property, particularly in Western Europe, and the campaign waged by radical Islam against the Jews. ADL National Director Abe Foxman, for example, states as follows in his book *Never Again?*: "The message of hate preached in the Middle Eastern mosques and broadcasted electronically around the world, is influencing Muslim immigrants in Europe to commit acts of vandalism and violence against Jewish victims." Similarly, in the United Kingdom, Jonathan Sacks, former chief rabbi of the United Hebrew Congregations of the Commonwealth, pointed to "radicalized Islamist youth inflamed by extremist

---

[16] Yehuda Bauer, "From Propagating Myths to Holocaust Research: Preparing for an Education," in *Europe's Crumbling Myths*, ed. Manfred Gerstenfeld (Jerusalem, 2003), pp. 115-7; Yehuda Bauer, "Problems of Contemporary Antisemitism," lecture at UCSC Center for Jewish Studies (2003), http://humanities.ucsc.edu/JewishStudies/docs/YBauerLecture.pdf; Robert Wistrich, *Muslim Anti-Semitism: A Clear and Present Danger* (American Jewish Committee, 2002), pp. 15-22, http://www.ajc.org/atf/cf/%7B42D75369-D582-4380-8395-D25925B85EAF%7D/Wistrich Antisemitism.pdf; Robert Wistrich, "The Old-New Anti-Semitism," *The National Interest* 72 (2003).

[17] Matthias Küntzel, *Jihad and Jew Hatred* (New York, 2007).

[18] Karmon, "International Terror and Antisemitism."

[19] See "Trends in Antisemitic Violence," in *Antisemitism Worldwide 2005*, http://www.tau.ac.il/Anti-Semitism/asw2005/general-analysis.htm.

[20] See "The Perpetrators," in *Antisemitism Worldwide 1994*, http://www.tau.ac.il/Anti-Semitism/asw2004/general-analysis.htm.

rhetoric" as the major perpetrators of violent acts against Jews in Europe in a lecture he gave to the Inter-parliamentary Committee against Antisemitism at the beginning of 2002.[21]

The left, particularly in the United States and Europe, including Jewish intellectuals, has played a significant role in the emergence of the "new antisemitism." Jewish philosophers and researchers such as Peter Pulzer, Alvin Rosenfeld, Pierre-André Taguieff, and Alain Finkielkraut emphasize the impact of the demonization of the State of Israel on the creation of what Pulzer labels an "antisemitic atmosphere."[22] The equation of Israel with Nazi Germany, which in the past was confined to Arab and Soviet propaganda and to the extreme left on the margins of Western society, has infiltrated mainstream newspapers.[23] Thus, for example, in July 2006, Finn Graff, a cartoonist for the popular Norwegian tabloid daily *Dagbladet*, portrayed Israeli Prime Minister Ehud Olmert as a concentration camp commander firing at random at Palestinian inmates. The cartoon was inspired by a scene from Steven Spielberg's movie *Schindler's List*, in which Commandant Amon Goeth of the Plaszow concentration camp fired from his balcony at Jewish prisoners for fun.[24]

Taguieff and others claim that extreme anti-Israel propaganda encourages and even incites violence against Jewish targets.[25] In this respect, the reference made by Lawrence Summer, former president of Harvard University, to "actions that are antisemitic in their effect if not their intent," particularly when accusing Israel of using Nazi methods against the Palestinians, is illuminating.[26] Finkielkraut, Pulzer, and others emphasize the deep identification of intellectuals on the left with both the Palestinian cause and "underprivileged" Muslim youth in Europe—second or third generation immigrants mainly from Africa. In the eyes of these intellectuals, Palestinians and Muslims in Europe have replaced the Jews as the new persecuted minority. They, according to Finkielkraut, are the new "other." Moreover, they have become the new victims of the old ones—the Jews.[27]

As an outcome of this perception, intellectuals on the left tend to tolerate extreme deeds against Israel and the Jews when they are perpetrated by the alleged victims of the Jews and Western civilization. Pulzer writes that, according to the pro-Palestinian

---

[21] Abraham H. Foxman, *Never Again?* (New York, 2003); Jonathan Sacks, "A New Antisemitism?," in *A New Antisemitism?*, ed. Iganski and Kosmin (London, 2003), p. 39-40; see also Bauer, "From Propagating Myths," pp. 116-7; Robert Wistrich "Muslims, Jews and September 11: The British Case," in *A New Antisemitism?*, ed. Iganski and Kosmin (London, 2003), p. 180.

[22] See, for example, Peter Pulzer, "The New Antisemitism, or When Is a Taboo Not a Taboo?," in *A New Antisemitism?*, ed. Iganski and Kosmin (London, 2003), p. 97-112; Taguieff, *Rising from the Muck*; Alain Finkielkraut, "In the Name of the Other: Reflections on the Coming Anti-Semitism," *Azure*, Autumn 5765/2004, No. 18, http://www.azure.org.il/article.php?id=211.

[23] Pulzer, "The New Antisemitism"; Bauer, "Problems of Contemporary Antisemitism"; Roni Stauber, "Anti-Zionism as an Expression of Judeophobia after the War," *Masua* 31 (1993), pp. 37-43 (in Hebrew).

[24] See the 2006 Norwegian report in *Antisemitism Worldwide 2006*, http://www.tau.ac.il/Anti-Semitism/asw2006/norway.htm.

[25] Taguieff, *Rising from the Muck*, pp. 97-100.

[26] Lawrence Summers, "Address at Morning Prayers," in *Those Who Forget the Past*, ed. Ron Rosenbaum (New York, 2004), p. 59.

[27] Finkielkraut, "In the Name of the Other."

left, "[i]f antisemitism is not the fault of the far right, then its perpetrators should be pitied rather than condemned.... They are not the heirs of Vichy."[28]

Based on the arguments supporting the assumption that, particularly since the end of 2001, Jewish communities have faced probably the largest wave of antisemitic manifestations since World War II, the term "new antisemitism" can be defined as a clear conflation of Jewish communities and individuals with Israel, which are perceived as a single evil entity. According to this concept, Israel is at the forefront of Western civilization and world Jewry, which racially oppress underprivileged elements in both Israel-Palestine and Europe. Thus, antisemitism has become interchangeable with anti-Zionism, and the word "Zionist" is identified with Jew. Three groups play a major role in the various manifestations of the "new antisemitism":

1. Islamists, who perceive Israel as the spearhead of Western civilization and world Jewry;
2. young Muslims who are incited by extreme anti-Israel propaganda and the antisemitic messages in the Arab and Muslim media, as well as in the European media, to commit acts of violence and vandalism against Jewish sites and Jewish individuals;
3. left-wing intellectuals and human rights champions who, on the one hand, contribute considerably to the demonization of Israel, occasionally by explicit or implicit use of antisemitic symbols, and, on the other hand, tolerate terror and violent actions against Israel and Jewish targets.

IV. "THE JEWS PAY THE PRICE": ANTI-JEWISH MANIFESTATIONS IN RETALIATION FOR ISRAEL'S DEEDS

The widely-accepted assumption that antisemitism has grown dramatically since the end of 2001 has been rejected by a number of researchers and public figures, prominent among them left-wing Jewish intellectuals who are very disapproving of Israel's policies.[29] They also criticize the Jewish establishment in the Diaspora for what they perceive as its automatic support for Israel and explain the violence against Jews and extreme anti-Israel propaganda in the context of anti-Israel or anti-Zionist activities and not as a new wave in the history of antisemitism.

While Kramer and Karmon point to the Islamist concept of a global war—jihad—against the Jews and Wistrich and others emphasize the impact of this hatred on violence against Jews committed by young descendants of immigrant families, Brian Klug, a senior research fellow in philosophy at St Benet's Hall, Oxford, completely rejects the former claim.[30] Klug is the co-founder of Independent Jewish Voices, a group of British Jewish liberals who seek to create an alternative Jewish voice to the official leadership of the Jewish community in Britain. They accuse the leadership of

---

[28] Pulzer, "The New Antisemitism," pp. 86-7, Finkielkraut, "In the Name of the Other."
[29] Some of these views were expressed in a special collection of articles: A. Cockburn and J. St. Clair, eds., *The Politics of Antisemitism* (Oakland, 2003).
[30] Brian Klug, "The Myth of the New Anti-Semitism," *The Nation*, February 2, 2004, http://www.thenation.com/doc/20040202/klug/5.

Jewish communities and Jewish organizations worldwide, and particularly in the United Kingdom, of abandoning the basic struggle for human rights, "the tradition of Jewish support for universal freedoms, human rights and social justice." Moreover, the Jewish leadership's automatic support for Israel is perceived by them as immoral. According to them, the Jewish leadership "put support for the policies of an occupying power above the human rights of an occupied people."[31]

Klug views the terror attacks against Jewish targets perpetrated by Islamist terror groups, as well as violent attacks by young Muslims, as retaliation against Israel, namely as a continuation of the terror attacks of the 1970s and 1980s, in which the Jews are being forced to pay for Israel's deeds. The war against Israel being waged by Islamic terrorist groups is not, according to Klug, a war against Israel as a Jewish state, but rather as "a European interloper or as an American client or as a non-Arab and non-Muslim entity; moreover, as an oppressive occupying force." According to this view, the Israeli-Palestinian conflict is the only reason for the violent attacks against the Jews of Europe. Similarly, Tony Lerman claims that, in contrast to the antisemitism of the past, "the hostility to Jews is grounded today in a real political grievance; it can increase or decrease according to events."[32]

Michael Neumann, professor of philosophy at Trent University in Ontario, Canada, and author of the book *The Case against Israel,* also explains Arab and Muslim hostility toward the Jews solely as a response to what he calls Israel's racial attitude toward the Palestinians. "The progress of Arab antisemitism fits nicely with the progress of Jewish encroachment and Jewish atrocities. It came to the Middle East with Zionism and it will abate when Zionism ceases to be an expansionist threat."[33] Neumann's article was published in a special collection aimed, according to its editors, at "confront[ing] how the slur of 'antisemite' has been used to intimidate critics of Israel's abuse of Palestinians."[34]

Why did Jews worldwide become a target of Muslim rage? Klug blames Israel. He sees the attacks as an almost reasonable reaction to the basic concept of Israel as the sovereign state of the Jewish people as a whole and to the fact that Jews gather in large numbers in cities of the world to demonstrate their solidarity, as Jews, with Israel.[35]

Tony Judt, professor of European Studies at NYU, expresses this idea more blatantly: "Israel's leaders purport to speak for Jews everywhere. They can hardly be surprised when their own behavior provokes a backlash against Jews." Moreover, according to Judt, violence against Jews in the Diaspora is an outcome with which many Israeli politicians are far from unhappy. They try to delegitimize and silence criticism against Israel by labeling it as antisemitism.[36] Similarly, Neumann blames Israel for "decades-old, systematic and unrelenting efforts to implicate all Jews in its crimes." Furthermore, he not only blames Israel and the Jewish leadership for the

---

[31] "A Time to Speak Out: Independent Jewish Voices," http://jewishvoices.squarespace.com.
[32] Lerman, "Sense on Antisemitism."
[33] Michael Neumann: "What is Antisemitism?," *Counterpunch,* June 4, 2002, http://www.counterpunch.org/neumann0604.html.
[34] Cockburn and St. Clair, eds., *The Politics of Antisemitism.*
[35] Klug, "The Myth of the New Anti-Semitism."
[36] Tony Judt, "Goodbye to All That?," *The Nation,* January 3, 2005, http://www.thenation.com/doc/20050103/judt.

violence committed against Jewish targets but also claims that most Jews living in the Diaspora bear moral responsibility because of their support for Israel. They are being punished for their complicity with Israel's criminal acts. This, according to him, is more serious than German support for the Nazi regime. While many Germans did not know about the crimes committed by their government, Jews worldwide have all the information and still "many, perhaps most adult Jewish individuals, support a state that commits war crimes."[37]

The conceptual linkage between anti-Zionism and antisemitism is one of the most arguable issues between the two camps.[38] Researchers and Jewish leaders who claim that the Jews have suffered a severe wave of antisemitism view anti-Zionism as a major component of this trend. They claim that anti-Zionism, particularly since the establishment of the State of Israel, is identical to antisemitism. Moreover, they associate the current campaign to delegitimize the existence of the State of Israel with the classical antisemitic campaign to deprive the Jewish individual of his civil rights. Wistrich already made this equation in the 1980s, during one of the first serious debates about the conceptual linkage between antisemitism and anti-Zionism, which took place at the residence of the president of Israel.[39] "Anti-Zionism," he said, "seeks to de-emancipate the Jews as an independent nation, much as modern secular European antisemitism insistently sought to de-emancipate the Jews as free and equal individuals"—meaning that they both try to undermine Jewish political achievements.

On the other hand, those on the left who reject the thesis regarding the new threat assert that antisemitism has always been defined as racial or religious hatred against the Jews and Judaism and cannot be confused with political opposition to the Zionist idea and the existence of the State of Israel. Moreover, they claim that, since the establishment of the Zionist movement, anti-Zionism has been part of the internal Jewish debate and has never been labeled as antisemitism. In response to the allegation that anti-Zionism discriminates against the Jews by denying their rights to self-determination as a nation, Klug maintains that the Jewish people do not "constitute a nation in the relevant sense, the sense in which the principle of self-determination applies. Traditionally, the idea of the Jewish people was centered not on a state but on a book, the Torah, and the culture (or cultures) that developed around that book." Thus, denying the right of the Jews to self determination, according to Klug, is a legitimate claim and cannot be defined as an antisemitic manifestation.[40]

V. CONCLUSIONS

The question of continuity and change lies at the core of the debate over the interpretation of violence against Jews, particularly in Europe, as well as of extreme

---

[37] Neumann, "What is Antisemitism?"

[38] On the basic positions in this dispute, see David Hirsh's comprehensive analysis, "Anti-Zionism and Antisemitism: Cosmopolitan Reflections," YIISA Working Paper no. 1 (Yale Initiative for the Interdisciplinary Study of Antisemitism, 2007), which appears in this volume.

[39] Robert Wistrich, *Anti-Zionism as an Expression of Antisemitism in Recent Years* (Jerusalem, 1984).

[40] Klug, "The Myth of the New Anti-Semitism."

anti-Zionist propaganda and demonization of the State of Israel. Left-wing intellectuals reject the assumption that they are antisemitic manifestations, perceiving them as an escalation of the anti-Zionist and anti-Israel campaign from previous decades.

In my opinion, this assertion is a clear misinterpretation of the Islamists' intentions and deeds. It is generally agreed that antisemitism evolved in the Arab and the Muslim world as a consequence of the Arab-Israeli conflict and that some of the main motifs of current antisemitism in the Arab world were absorbed from Europe. Nevertheless, the claim that Islamist terror attacks against Jewish targets are only retaliation for Israel's deeds—"the Jews must pay"—is contradicted by both the statements and deeds of Islamist groups. While secular Palestinian groups, assisted by radical left-wing organizations, were the first to perpetrate terror attacks against Jewish targets at the end of the 1960s, there is a clear distinction between the goals of these attacks, which were part of the struggle against Israel, and the Islamist perception of the Jews and Israel as a single evil entity, a central pillar of corrupt Western civilization. Islamist declarations, anti-Jewish terror, and monstrous plans to strike at Jewish concentrations demonstrate the new genocidal concept. The last words of Daniel Pearl to his Islamist kidnappers in Pakistan, the "confession" "Yes, I am a Jew," is a harrowing expression of the similarity between Nazis and Islamists, with their notion of a global war against the Jews.

The debate over the conceptual linkage of anti-Zionism and antisemitism is not new. The question was discussed widely in the 1980s. The claim that anti-Zionism is a legitimate view, espoused by Jewish leaders and intellectuals since the establishment of the Zionist movement, has always been one of the main arguments of intellectuals on the left, particularly Jews. Moreover, while eminent Jewish figures were the most ardent opponents of Zionism at the end of the 19th century and the first decades of the 20th century, some leading European antisemites supported Zionism as a way to evacuate the Jews from Europe.

Historically, anti-Zionism and antisemitism were indeed antithetical concepts. However, this assertion is irrelevant to the present anti-Zionist campaign and its connections to antisemitism. The aims and motives of current anti-Zionists differ from those of German Jewish liberals at the end of the 19th century, members of the Bund in Eastern Europe, or even Jews in communist parties. German Jewish liberals sought to improve the legal status of the Jews, while members of the Bund and Jewish communists felt that Zionism and Palestine could not be the answer to the miseries of the Jewish masses and only revolution was the cure.

Today, however, in the pluralistic societies of Europe, such confrontations between Zionists and their opponents are irrelevant. The aim of contemporary anti-Zionism is not to improve the Jewish situation but to deprive the Jews of their rights, which at least in principle are given to other nations, whether historical or newly created ones. Today, sixty-one years after the UN resolution to establish an internationally recognized Jewish state, and with most Jews around the world viewing Israel as a Jewish nation, opposition to the right of the Jews to have a state of their own is no longer a theoretical argument but the expression of an actual intention to destroy it. Israel has become the main embodiment, in both Jewish and non-Jewish eyes, of modern Jewish identity. Therefore, delegitimizing Israel is the most effective way of damaging Jewish identity and Jewish political achievements since the Holocaust.

The roots of the equation between Jews and Zionists, and between Judaism and Zionism, can be found in the anti-Zionist propaganda of the Soviet Union as early as the early 1950s, as part of the attack on Jewish nationalism. In 1952-1953, during the so-called Doctors' Plot and Slansky trial in Moscow and Prague, respectively, it became clear that anti-Zionism had provided a new vehicle for the re-emergence of antisemitic attitudes. The accusations of Jewish nationalism and cosmopolitanism were fused by means of an explicitly Zionist conspiracy theory, which linked Israel and Western imperialism. However, while the conflation of Judaism with Zionism in Soviet and Eastern bloc propaganda was part of the struggle against Jewish culture and Jewish nationalism, the Islamist perception has far-reaching and dangerous implications—an all-out war against both Israel and Jews worldwide.

The comparison between Israel and Nazi Germany, which left-wing intellectuals do not define as antisemitic,[41] can also be traced back to the 1950s. Demonization of the Jew and alleged Jewish cruelty, particularly against innocent children, has played a significant role in the history of antisemitism since the early Middle Ages. Again, it was the Soviets who were responsible for the re-emergence of this classic negative Jewish stereotype. The Soviets' attempt to link Nazism and Zionism and to equate Israel with the Third Reich began at the end of the 1950s and early 1960s. Central to their campaign was the allegation that the Zionists collaborated with the Nazis during the war against the interests of their brethren. This attempt to rewrite the history of Jewish suffering during the Holocaust was adopted at the end of the 1960s by the European radical left, who wrote numerous articles about the alleged cooperation between Zionists and Nazis. The Soviet campaign, directed originally against the growing ties between the Federal Republic of Germany and Israel orchestrated by Ben-Gurion and Adenauer, was taken up at the beginning of the 1960s by the Arabs and their delegates to the United Nations, although during the Nazi era and even after the war Arab leaders expressed their admiration for Nazi Germany and some hard-core Nazi war criminals found refuge in Egypt, Syria, and Libya.

The infiltration of anti-Zionist claims, and particularly the equation of Israel with Nazi Germany, into the mainstream discourse in Europe was undoubtedly influenced by the prolonged anti-Zionist campaign of the Soviet Union, the Arab countries, and the radical left in the 1970s and 1980s. In this respect, the Lebanon War should be viewed as a watershed, since it unleashed markedly anti-Jewish reactions in many countries. This process culminated in the last decade with the publication of virulently antisemitic caricatures in mainstream publications. Opinions that had been confined to Arab and Soviet propaganda, as well as to the margins of Western society, had now acquired respectability.

Regarding young Muslims in Europe, as noted, both schools of thought emphasize external factors to explain the violent incidents against Jews in Europe perpetrated in many cases by young people from immigrant backgrounds. Those who support the thesis of the "new antisemitism" view it as part of the campaign waged by radical Islam against the Jewish people and the West in general, stressing the influence of Islamist propaganda. Their opponents, however, claim that it is fury

---

[41] See, for example, Lerman, "Sense on Antisemitism."

against Israel's unjust policies toward the Palestinians that incites young Muslims to commit violence. Thus, according to this assumption, a change in Israeli policy, or a more balanced attitude on the part of European governments to the conflict, could mitigate the violence. Both camps, however, tend to underestimate local socio-economic problems in Europe as a background to acts of violence against Jews, as clearly shown in studies based on findings of the London police and the French interior ministry. These analyses conclude that extreme anti-Israel propaganda is only one cause for the animosity of young immigrants toward Jews. Most of the perpetrators did not belong to an extremist group and carried out their actions spontaneously.[42] These findings lead to a very pessimistic evaluation of the extent to which antisemitic stereotypes are adopted by immigrants and their children in Europe, as demonstrated by the horrendous murder in France of Ilan Halimi in February 2006.

---

[42] P. Ignaski, V. Kielinger, and S. Paterson, eds., *Hate Crimes against London's Jews* (London, 2005); Jean-Christophe Rufin, *Action in the Fight against Antisemitism and Racism* (Paris, 2004); see also Roni Stauber, "Learned Hostility," *Ha'aretz*, July 10, 2005, http://www.haaretz.com/hasen/objects/pages/PrintArticleEn.jhtml?itemNo=632622.

Western Culture, the Holocaust, and the Persistence of Antisemitism

Catherine Chatterley*

INTRODUCTION

In her recent discussion of debt as metaphor, Canadian author and poet Margaret Atwood admits to "assuming that the older a recognizable pattern of behaviour is—the longer its demonstrably been with us—the more integral it must be to our humanness and the more cultural variations on it will be in evidence."[1] This is also my assumption, but in relation to the problem of antisemitism. This essay attempts to begin a conversation about an important subject that is both disheartening and rarely discussed: the persistence of antisemitism in post-Holocaust Western culture.[2] Given the increasing levels of antisemitism throughout the world, one wonders whether Holocaust education, against our very best efforts, and especially those of Holocaust survivors, has failed to educate the public about the specific nature and history of antisemitism. Is it possible that the dominant strategy of Holocaust universalization (a strategy perceived as necessary to make the subject accessible to non-Jews) has worked against the production of an adequate understanding of antisemitism in Western culture, and therefore against the exorcism of antisemitic thinking from Western culture? I would like to suggest that given our current context we begin discussing the following questions: what exactly have we in the West learned from the Holocaust; do these "lessons" have any relationship to the subject of antisemitism; have we perhaps learned the wrong "lessons" when it comes to antisemitism; and, finally, is it possible that this failure to understand the specific nature and history of antisemitism complicates current academic and popular debates about the nature of anti-Zionism and the ongoing significance of antisemitism?

The first section of this essay will discuss a selection of recent cultural observations, which taken together precipitate the questions asked in this paper. The second section diagnoses a paradox in Western culture in which the public appears exhausted by their exposure to the Holocaust but in fact knows very little about the nature and history of antisemitism. In an attempt to explain the reasons for this

---

* Professor, Department of History, University of Winnipeg.
[1] Margaret Atwood, *Payback: Debt and the Shadow Side of Wealth*, 2008 CBC Massey Lectures (Toronto: House of Anansi Press, 2008), p. 11.
[2] I use the phrase Western culture to include the European nations and their national products in the Americas and former British Dominions, which until very recently have defined themselves as sharing a common culture based upon Christianity.

problematic contradiction, the process of Holocaust universalization is scrutinized in a discussion of the two key texts used to educate the public about the Holocaust. This essay is designed to open discussion of these subjects, which require sustained and systematic study.

I. GENERAL CULTURAL OBSERVATIONS

1. Antisemitism: racism against "rich Jews"

As a historian of modern Europe, antisemitism, and the Holocaust, who has taught university courses on these subjects for the last nine years, I must admit that I do not see an adequate understanding of antisemitism, or the Holocaust, for that matter, among the students entering my courses.[3] It is only after taking the course that students begin to understand the unique nature and millennial history of antisemitism, including the Christian European responsibility for its invention and proliferation. A majority of students appear to interpret antisemitism simply as racism against Jews, which they perceive as the product of economic jealousy. In our increasingly secularized Western culture, fewer students seem to have been exposed to the "Christ-killer" accusation that ruled supreme until a generation ago. Instead, today, my students associate "the Jews"[4] with unbridled economic success, and this is how they appear to understand the cultural hostility against Jews. Simply put: people hate Jews because Jews have money. This, unfortunately, is also how they understand the Holocaust: the Germans hated "the Jews" because they had too much money.[5]

Several observations can be made from this dominant student perspective. These students believe that all Jews *are in fact* wealthy and do hold an economic advantage over other groups in society. They assume that this purported Jewish economic reality explains the "racism" that non-Jews direct toward Jews. What appears to be missing from the perspective of my students is a conspiracy theory used to explain this grand level of Jewish wealth, or a revolutionary agenda to redistribute this supposed Jewish wealth. The realities of economic inequality do not appear to trouble the majority of my students, who are as capitalist and materialistic as most North Americans today, but they do see economics as the general source of resent-

---

[3] The University of Winnipeg is a small urban university (9,100 students) catering to undergraduate education in the arts and sciences. The University of Manitoba is a research university with a population of 26,000 students. I have taught courses on the Holocaust and Antisemitism at both campuses. My students tend to share similar characteristics: they are largely non-Jews with a characteristically Canadian multicultural heritage, although many students have German and Slavic backgrounds. Perhaps one third of the population has had an active Christian upbringing, however that number continues to decline. I would estimate the total pool of students informing my discussion to number approximately 2,000.

[4] Placed in quotation marks, this phrase refers specifically to the abstraction created by antisemites, and those who follow unwittingly in their footsteps, which is distinct from Jewish individuals and from the Jewish people in general.

[5] Readers will notice the lack of attention given to Zionism and the State of Israel among these particular students. Generally, there is little anti-Zionist hostility on Canadian campuses in cities with small Arab or Muslim communities, which is the case in Winnipeg. The opposite holds true in cities with larger communities from the Middle East, such as Montreal and Toronto.

ment against Jews in contemporary culture, and one can imagine where their thinking might lead if they felt differently about the nature of society given these problematic assumptions.[6]

In general, I sense in my students both a legitimate curiosity and a near total ignorance about Jews and Judaism, rather than any systematic hostility. Part of this curiosity, however, appears to be connected to a kind of bewilderment at the general hostility directed toward Jews in the world today, especially via the Internet. They wonder why "the Jewish," as many of my students refer to Jews,[7] are hated by so many people in so many different places; why there are so many attacks on Jews and Judaism on the Internet; and why Hitler tried to "wipe them out"? The sense here is that there must be something wrong with the Jews if everyone hates them to such an extent. My sense is that this troubling assumption, *one on which antisemitism feeds*, could be the impetus for their interest in the subject.

Regardless of their level of exposure to Christianity, students begin the course with little awareness of the religious conflict between Judaism and Christianity, or of the discriminatory practices and anti-Jewish legislation resulting from the hateful teachings of Christian theology and its proponents through the ages. And without any knowledge of this religious-historical foundation, students have no understanding of the hostile and exclusionary context that determines the increasing Jewish dependence upon usury and money-occupations in the European Middle Ages. And again, without an understanding of the historical construction of the "rich Jew" mythology in Western history, my students simply continue to accept and reproduce this deeply embedded cultural stereotype, albeit with little apparent personal resentment. If these students have any knowledge of the subject matter, the focus, it seems, is on Nazi racism rather than on European forms of antisemitism. This is confirmed by their astonishment at the fact that everything Hitlerism did to the Jewish people, with the exception of murdering them *en masse* in industrialized killing centers, was already on the books of European Christian history, much of it legislated by Canon Law. Part of the explanation for their familiarity with National Socialism is not simply that it is the result of Holocaust education, but that it is another disturbing example of the undying fascination with Hitler and Nazism,[8] and

---

[6] During this current recession, the Simon Wiesenthal Center wasted no time in taking precautionary measures. See Harold Brackman, *Hatred in Hard Times—And How to Combat It: Lessons from History for the 21st Century* (Los Angeles: Simon Wiesenthal Center, November, 2008). Due to the controlling influence of the Internet on the perceptions of my students, some of them are increasingly sympathetic to contemporary conspiracy theories about 9/11 and the power of global banking elites, as organized through the Bilderberg Group, the Trilateral Commission, and the Council on Foreign Relations.

[7] Students are often uncomfortable using the word Jew in class and in their writing as they believe it to be derogatory; as a result, they go to great grammatical lengths to avoid using this "offensive" term. This, of course, opens up an opportunity for a corrective class discussion, and a lecture on the ubiquity of antisemitism in Western culture, and the effects it continues to have on language.

[8] For example, there is a disturbingly large number of students who design their PowerPoint presentations, regardless of topic, using the Nazi color palette of black, red, and white, as well as those (usually male students) who insist on writing SS in rune font on their final exams. Quite rightly, George Steiner calls this our "corrupting fascination."

thereby may not reflect any real interest in Jews at all or any concern for their fate under antisemitism.

2. *Ideological equality and historical homogeneity*

Another cultural current I have witnessed in class and elsewhere is a tendency for people to freely compare antisemitism to any and all forms of bias or prejudice, and the Holocaust to any and all acts of violence in contemporary culture and human history. In Canada, one of the current problems under discussion is the history of Residential Schools, which were established by the government in the nineteenth century and administered by the Catholic, Anglican, United, and Presbyterian Churches until 1969, when the government again assumed control until 1996, when the last school was closed. These schools, numbering 130 in all, institutionalized 150,000 Aboriginal, Métis, and Inuit children, taking them away from their families and communities, banning their traditions and suppressing their languages, in the effort to "civilize" these children, or more accurately to force their assimilation into Canadian society. Additionally, there was a high degree of physical abuse and sexual molestation experienced by these children at the hands of priests and nuns and this has resulted in an enormous amount of psychological and physiological damage (through alcohol and drug addiction especially) to Aboriginal families and communities. Some now refer to this period of Aboriginal history as "The Canadian Holocaust."[9]

I have observed that those who compare antisemitism, indiscriminately, to other forms of prejudice, and the Holocaust to any violent event in human history, know very little about the events they compare and next to nothing about the specific history and nature of antisemitism or the Holocaust. They *assume* that the similarities between violent disparate historical events far outweigh their differences, largely because human beings are involved and we are now thought to be more alike than different. Very often, these comparisons are reduced to the common theme of human suffering anyway, which few of us want to try to compare. While there are certainly basic similarities in all violence and criminality, I would suggest that the decision to compare Canadian Residential Schools to Auschwitz, as some of my students are now taught to do, has very little to do with the goals of scholarship or any concern for historical accuracy. If accuracy were a priority, then one might engage with the millennial history of Christian European antisemitism (which includes the kidnapping of Jewish children, forced baptism and conversion, compulsory sermons, expulsion, residential segregation, destruction and suppression of religious texts and practices, exclusion from Christian society, mass violence, including rape and murder, and continuous vilification) as the basis for a comparison with the dispossession and destruction of indigenous populations in the Americas. In fact, one can see from this comparison that Jews and Aboriginals have more in common in relation to Christian Europe than many people realize. But this is not the comparison that is made. Few people know or care about the long list of Christian European crimes against the Jewish people and without broad cultural awareness and concern there can be no basis for an effective comparison. This is not the case with the Holocaust. Without knowing much about the actual history of the Shoah, or of the

---

[9] See the following website for an example: http://www.hiddenfromhistory.org.

realities of Auschwitz, people make easy comparisons to both in an attempt to gain sympathetic attention for the suffering of their own people. Many groups assume that their suffering must rival the Holocaust for it to be given respect and consideration in public discourse. Very often, popular comparisons, as opposed to those made by genocide scholars, are not based upon historical understanding or any logical schema, but upon *the content of one's feelings* and the simplistic equation of general human suffering.[10] These easy comparisons, then, reflect both the popular ignorance about the realities of Auschwitz, and our contemporary cultural obsession with equality and inclusion. It is surely one of the ironies of the post-Holocaust period that Holocaust education helped to create our current obsession with racism and its antidote of equality, and it is this same obsession that too often eclipses antisemitism and disfigures the Holocaust.

Comparison, or more accurately equation, allows people to elide difference and to amalgamate all human suffering and therefore build solidarity between people. How can anyone argue with such a humane agenda? Perhaps, historians, obsessed as we are with cultural and temporal specificity, are ill equipped for such an endeavor. However, this impetus for human homogenization appears to be very popular with many people, even some historians. Six years ago, the chair of the history department in which I was teaching told me in no uncertain terms that the Holocaust *should* be taught comparatively. Afterward, I wondered why a Canadian labor historian should have such strong feelings about the nature and contours of my field and why he should feel so empowered to tell me how to teach a course in my specific area of expertise. This experience led me to wonder why it is that after only two decades of existence the academic field of Holocaust Studies is under pressure to abandon its "particularism" and take its rightful place inside Comparative Genocide Studies, especially given the fact that were it not for the Holocaust there would be no legal concept of genocide in the first place.

No doubt, this pressure is the product of a generally humane attempt to represent and unify all the victims of history, but it is also the result of our society's general ignorance about the unique nature of antisemitism and the central role it plays in racism generally and in Nazism in particular. There is also, however, a darker aspect to this problem: the persistence of antisemitic ideas about Jews in Western culture, albeit in forms that are invisible to most people. For many people in post-Holocaust Western culture, Jews continue to be perceived as clannish and selfish, and obsessed with their own suffering. It seems that Holocaust education is increasingly resented as another example of these so-called Jewish tendencies, and this has only exacerbated anti-Jewish attitudes in some quarters. In the world today, Jews are generally not perceived as victims, except perhaps during the Holocaust, but even then they are often casually placed among Hitler's other victims: Roma and

---

[10] See the following examples of comparative scholarship and the central place of the Holocaust within genocide studies: Steven T. Katz, *The Holocaust in Historical Context: The Holocaust and Mass Death before the Modern Age* (Oxford: Oxford University Press, 1994); Frank Chalk and Kurt Jonassohn, *The History and Sociology of Genocide* (New Haven: Yale University Press, 1990); Robert Gellately and Ben Kiernan, eds., *The Specter of Genocide: Mass Murder in Historical Perspective* (New York: Cambridge University Press, 2003); and, Eric D. Weitz, *A Century of Genocide: Utopias of Race and Nation* (Princeton: Princeton University Press, 2003).

Sinti, Slavs, the disabled, gays and lesbians, political and religious dissenters, and anyone else harassed by the regime. Instead, Jews are perceived largely as a people with financial, political ("The Jewish Lobby"), and military power over others who are the actual victims of "Jewish interests." This perception is not new but is a common theme in the history of antisemitism. Regardless of their actual individual circumstances in Western societies, Jews have been perceived collectively as having powerful resources, connections, and an uncanny ability to harm society. Rather than as victims, Jews have been perceived by the West as *victimizers*, beginning with "their murder" of Jesus Christ, which provided the initial template and set this theme into action.

Unfortunately, too many people assume that the Holocaust eliminated antisemitism from our culture root and branch. They also assume that antisemitism is restricted to the Western world, and that what we are witnessing in other regions of the globe is simply anger directed toward Israel for the plight of the Palestinians. For many people today, who know little about the history of antisemitism and its permutations and combinations, the phenomenon is defined strictly in Hitlerian terms, so that unless one is calling for the destruction of the Jewish people one is not really an antisemite. Even calling for the destruction of the Jewish State does not necessarily qualify one as an antisemite today because the call targets Israelis instead of Jews and some see this "emancipatory" call as a legitimate form of progressive politics.

Today, historians talk about taboos against antisemitism thought to have come into existence after World War II. Perhaps it is time for a culturally specific historical analysis of these purported taboos and a proper scholarly evaluation of their cultural significance. Certainly taboos were not produced in Eastern Europe, or in the Middle East, or even in parts of Western and Southern Europe. The taboos of postwar West Germany were official in nature and based upon the self-interested attempt of Germans and their government to re-enter the family of nations after their outrageous assault on humanity. Even the belief that Germans suppressed their memories of Nazism and its antisemitism in the first decades after the war has come under increased scrutiny by historians.[11] In fact, the belief that Jews were *continuing* to harm Germany with their "Holocaust obsession," now funneled through American culture, was common and facilitated the growth of additional forms of German antisemitism. Variations on this same theme existed across postwar Europe, especially in the Soviet republics of Poland and Ukraine. A study of these taboos and their function in postwar societies (primarily as a method of covering up the continued existence of antisemitic attitudes based upon unchanging hostile beliefs about Jews) will call into question the widely held assumption that Auschwitz cured the West of its antisemitism.

3. *Invisible antisemitism*

Is it familiarity or indifference that produces invisibility? In the case of antisemitism it may be both. One of the reasons why people today reject the charge of antisemitism is because, as mentioned, it is largely defined by the Holocaust in the

---

[11] For example, see Alon Confino, *Germany as a Culture of Remembrance: Promises and Limits of Writing History* (Chapel Hill: University of North Carolina Press, 2006).

Western imagination. If one is not prepared to physically attack or attempt to harm Jews one can safely remain aloof to the charge of antisemitism. In Western culture, the beliefs many people still hold about "the Jews" are not seen to be antisemitic (*read* genocidal) but are simply felt to be reflective of everyday reality. In other words, what some of us identify as antisemitic ways of thinking most people see as simply reflective of a reality in which Jews are *in fact* wealthy, *in fact* powerful, *in fact* connected to one another, and *in fact* work together (conspire) to protect their own communal and individual interests, which today include the fate of the State of Israel. Again, this is not new but fully consistent with classic forms of European antisemitism, in which antisemites point to "reality" to illustrate Jewish power, conspiracy, materialism, criminality, or whatever negative association they want to affix to "the Jews." And the "reality" they find then reconfirms their pre-existing antisemitism, as it does today. After almost 2,000 years of indoctrination, which has worked very hard to fix the Western imagination (and the attention of individual Christians) upon this abstract collective called "the Jews," we should not be surprised to discover that Western culture is riddled with antisemitic perceptions and habits of thought about the Jewish people. And this complex invisible reality has not been exorcised by the Holocaust. Negative beliefs and attitudes about Jews are so normal and so ingrained in Western perceptions and attitudes that people (both gentiles and Jews) are simply unable to recognize them for what they are. Like a second skin, *antisemitic thinking has become invisible to most people.*

A striking example of overt antisemitism given wide coverage on American media and yet entirely invisible to the broadcaster, reporter, and the public, was the "Obama Ghost," which aired on American news on October 16, 2008 during the Democratic Primary Campaign.[12] A man named Mike Lunsford from Fairfield City, Ohio, had a Barack Obama ghost hanging from a tree in front of his house. When asked about the ghost, he stated that this was not a political statement; he just did not want an African American president. Obviously, Lunsford was offering the public a symbolic Halloween lynching of Barack Obama. What went entirely unmentioned, however, was the *Magen David* (Star of David) painted on the head of the Obama Ghost, and the SS symbolism (spelled in rune font) used to spell Obama's middle name "Hussain" [*sic*]. No one in the video commented on this; Mike Lunsford was not asked to explain it, nor did the news anchor who introduced the story address the obvious antisemitism involved. It appeared to be completely invisible and obviously irrelevant to one and all. For a culture supposedly inundated with Holocaust education and memorialization, as the United States is often characterized, this lapse of recognition strikes one as rather odd.

With reflection, however, this example is deeply troubling for what it reveals about our contemporary blindness when it comes to antisemitism, and our lack of understanding about the key role it plays in facilitating other forms of racism. This example reveals a cultural fixation on violence against African Americans, which is of course one of the central traumas of American history, but it also reveals a total indifference toward antisemitism. Anyone familiar with the rhetoric of neo-Nazi racism knows that "the Jews" are responsible for orchestrating race mixing and the

---

[12] See the "Obama Ghost" video: http://www.youtube.com/watch?v=MBgR6uO1E_A.

democratic liberation of minorities as part of their conspiracy to weaken white America and bring about its collapse. This is obviously a clear application of Hitlerian thought to the American homeland. All the antisemite has to do to "prove" this conspiracy is to point to David Axelrod as the Jewish mastermind behind the rise of Barack Obama. Lunsford's use of Nazi SS symbolism no doubt reflects his familiarity with contemporary American racist movements, which continue to advocate their Hitlerian mission. It is "the Jew," not African Americans, or any other minority, for that matter, who orchestrates the central threat against the "white race." The world's ethnic and religious minorities, and any emancipatory movement that advances their cause, are the vehicles through which the "Jewish Conspiracy" operates. I would suggest that this example illustrates three cultural tendencies all at once: (1) our general Western fixation on racism, which is a product of the post-Holocaust period; (2) our culturally induced indifference toward antisemitism; and (3) our ignorance of the centrally determinative role played by antisemitism in the racist imagination.

4. Classic and contemporary antisemitism

With our cultural and scholarly focus increasingly fixed upon Islamic antisemitism and the so-called new forms of this hatred, we are ignoring the fact that classic forms of antisemitism continue to persist, and are being reinvigorated by contemporary variations.

On October 12-18, 2008, at Parkway West Middle School in Chesterfield (St. Louis), Missouri, sixth-grade students enjoyed what they called "Spirit Week." This rather benign and inclusive, though obviously Christian-inspired, week began with Hug a Friend Day, moved on to High Five Day, quickly reversed course with Hit a Tall Person Day, and finally devolved into Hit a Jew Day. According to news reports, ten out of thirty-five Jewish students were hit on their backs, and one in the face, during this "Spirit Week" Day. This is obviously a deeply troubling episode in American culture, not least for the children and families targeted by this ritual, which reveals both the ongoing presence of antisemitism and a lack of cultural awareness about the problem. It also may manifest the more familiar antisemitic theme of "the Jew" as an abstraction, as opposed to a real existing human being. However, to properly evaluate this possibility one would have to investigate whether any non-Jewish children were also assaulted. It is telling that there was no Hit a Chinese Day or Hit a Black Day or Hit a Girl Day, although one can imagine that these were in the pipeline had this school ritual continued. The question that we should be asking is why in 2008 in Chesterfield, Missouri (a suburban upper middle class community west of St. Louis) the first ethnic minority group targeted for physical abuse by a group of sixth-graders were Jews. The official response to this eruption of violent antisemitism was not to teach the children, or the larger community that socializes them, about the specific history of antisemitism, but to have the children study the Holocaust later that year. This would allow teachers to convert this experience into "teachable moments" using well-established forms of "anti-bias education" and diversity training.

Last year at the University of North Dakota, aviation student Scott Lebovitz was targeted as a Jew and harassed by fellow students in residence. In addition to swastikas being painted in the dormitory stairwell, Lebovitz was taunted, chased, and threatened with a pellet gun. Finally, "Scott is a Jew" was smeared in ice cream on the elevator door in his dorm. After the staff in residential services refused to register Lebovitz's first complaint, and the university administration ignored the antisemitic nature of his harassment, the Jewish Student's Organization on campus took their case to the media. These students number between 15 and 20 out of a total university population of 13,000 students, the vast majority of whom are Christian and have a European heritage. In addition to its troubled history with the Aboriginal peoples of this region over the ongoing use of the offensive Fighting Sioux mascot, UND is also famous for its acceptance of $100 million dollars in 1990 from casino mogul and alumnus Ralph Engelstad, despite the fact that he had a photograph of Hitler in his office and was known to celebrate the German dictator's birthday. In a 2008 interview with *The Forward*, UND Professor of Philosophy, Jack Weinstein, admitted that he can no longer "in good conscience encourage [Jewish] students to come to UND."[13]

These two examples occurred in American educational environments; precisely the place where many assume antisemitism no longer exists. Is it possible that both Jews and non-Jews, albeit for different reasons, have become immune to specific forms of Western antisemitism? Have we simply accepted certain types of antisemitic attitudes and dynamics as normal in Western culture? Is there so much antisemitism present in the world that our attention and resources have to be directed toward only the most radical forms? One of the problems in the scholarship on antisemitism today is the current conception of antisemitism as old and new. Old antisemitism is precisely the type discussed in this essay, which many assume no longer exists in post-Holocaust Western culture. New antisemitism is believed to be that emanating from the Islamic world (including its European diaspora) and the so-called progressive end of the political spectrum worldwide, despite the fact that both of these forms have well worn histories of their own.[14] This inaccurate conception of old and new antisemitism leads to a minimization, or outright elision, of already existing antisemitism, which never passed away after the Holocaust, and it also blinds us to the connective ties that exist between classic and contemporary forms of antisemitism.

We know that Christian antisemitism was imported into all the regions of the world dominated by European powers beginning in the fifteenth century and continuing for hundreds of years thereafter. Scholars like Matthias Küntzel and Jeffrey Herf are currently investigating the contemporary implications of the very conscious Nazi strategy to export their own version of homicidal antisemitism into the Middle East.[15] The antisemitic fruit of these two European trees planted abroad, Christianity and Nazism, is now being imported back into the West via the Internet. There now appears to be a conscientious strategy on the part of contemporary

---

[13] Anthony Weiss, "Jewish Students Protest Bias in North Dakota," *The Forward*, May 1, 2008, http://www.forward.com/articles/13290, accessed April 19, 2010.

[14] For a brief discussion of these histories, see Jonathan Judaken, "So What's New? Rethinking the 'New Antisemitism' in a Global Age," *Patterns of Prejudice* 42 (2008), pp. 531-560.

[15] See Matthias Küntzel, *Jihad and Jew-Hatred: Islamism, Nazism, and the Roots of 9/11* (New York: Telos Press, 2007). Jeffrey Herf is currently working on a book on Nazi radio broadcasting to the Middle East during World War II.

antisemites in the Islamic world to build an alliance with the West against "the Jews." In fact, the non-Western reading of Western antisemitism (which is obviously millennial and culturally comprehensive in nature) empowers these individuals to use this strategy in their war against Israel. Their strategy is to weaken the relationship between the Western nations and the State of Israel, and between Jews and their non-Jewish neighbors in the West, by reactivating the antisemitic animus in Western culture. Ahmadinejad is the most obvious exemplar of this conscious strategy, and his 2008 address to the UN General Assembly betrays as much:

> The dignity, integrity and rights of the American and European people are being played with by a small but deceitful number of people called Zionists. Although they are a miniscule minority, they have been dominating an important portion of the financial and monetary centers as well as the political decision-making centers of some European countries and the US in a deceitful, complex and furtive manner. It is deeply disastrous to witness that some presidential or premiere nominees in some big countries have to visit these people, take part in their gatherings, swear their allegiance and commitment to their interests in order to attain financial or media support. This means that the *great people of America and various nations of Europe* need to obey the demands and wishes of a small number of acquisitive and invasive people. *These nations are spending their dignity and resources on the crimes and occupations and the threats of the Zionist network against their will* [italics added].[16]

In the Western world, "the Jews" have for millennia been demonized collectively and conceptualized as nihilistic operatives working against the goals of humanity, whether defined as Christian, enlightened, proletarian, or even "Aryan." The Jewish people have been associated in the most concrete and abstract ways with every conceivable form of evil known to Western culture: killing God in the form of Jesus; kidnapping, torturing, and killing children; poisoning, cheating, and conspiring against their neighbors; cannibalism, blood drinking, devil worship, human sacrifice; every form of disloyalty to the state; extortion, blackmail, and all types of financial criminality. This is precisely the context that invented and maintained the lie of the "Worldwide Jewish Conspiracy," which in turn produced the Hitlerian solution, and both have been exported around the world. What is so extremely disturbing about Ahmadinejad's rhetoric, and many others who echo him, is its classic antisemitic depiction of "the Jews," here in the contemporary form of "Zionists," as operating outside the values and interests of common humanity and all that is good. Worse still is the fact that this seems to go unnoticed by the vast majority of people in Western nations, including otherwise progressive academics and members of government. Few seem to notice that the West is being courted by Ahmadinejad to be recruited into his global antisemitic strategy under the banner of humanistic inclusion and spiritual redemption:

> Let us, hand in hand, expand the thought of *resistance against evil and the minority of those who are ill-wishers*. Let's support goodness and the majority of people who are good and the embodiment of absolute good that is the Imam of Time, *The*

---

[16] For the full text of Ahmadinejad's speech to the UN General Assembly on September 23, 2008, see: http://www.un.org/ga/63/generaldebate/pdf/iran_en.pdf.

Promised One who will come accompanied by Jesus Christ, and accordingly design and implement the just and humanistic mechanisms for regulating the constructive relationships between nations and governments. Oh great Almighty, deliver the savior of nations and put an end to the sufferings of mankind and bring forth justice, beauty, and love [italics added].[17]

The leader of Iran is making headway in his strategy. In December 2008, Britain's Channel 4 gave Ahmadinejad the honor of delivering their "alternative Christmas message," stating with characteristic Western democratic aplomb, "we are offering our viewers an insight into an alternative world view."[18] For those of us who study antisemitism, we know that his views are not quite alternative enough but are too common these days. Those familiar with his strategy to unite the Islamic and Christian (or formerly Christian) worlds against "the Jews" see this small Christmas coup as a victory for him and a serious defeat for us. For those who dismiss Christian antisemitism as a thing of the past, two current examples of its continued presence and influence, however muted, should act as a corrective. The first is an unrepentant Bill Moyers, who recently characterized the Israeli assault on Hamas in Gaza as an example of "genetically coded" Jewish violence using the Book of Deuteronomy as his Christian proof text.[19] The second example is the Pope's recent rehabilitation of an antisemitic British bishop who is also a Holocaust denier. Leaving aside the problem that this German Pope was a member of the Hitler Youth, and that this should have disqualified him automatically from becoming "Christ's vicar on earth," the fact that Richard Williamson's antisemitism went unnoticed by the Vatican in their re-assessment of this man's renovation as bishop (the Pope claims not to have known about his views) reveals a disturbing level of antisemitism, or tolerance thereof, in the institution most responsible for it in the first place, as well as an astonishing indifference to the Catholic relationship with the Jewish people.

Given Ahmadinejad's terrible strategy, the lack of Western engagement with the subject of antisemitism, and the resulting ignorance as to its specific nature, history, and ongoing presence in Western culture, is cause for worry and remains a serious problem that requires our scholarly attention.

II. Holocaust Universalization and the Persistence of Antisemitism

Apparently we live in a world that is obsessed with the Holocaust, antisemitism, and Jewish suffering, a world that restricts all negative discussion about Jews and the State of Israel, and censors itself out of fear of being branded antisemitic. The reality, I am afraid, is actually the reverse. We live in a world that knows next to nothing about the detailed planning, purpose, and execution of the Nazi *Final Solution to the*

---

[17] Ibid.

[18] Mark Sweeney, "Iranian President to Deliver Channel 4's Alternative Christmas Message," *The Guardian*, December 24, 2008, http://www.guardian.co.uk/media/2008/dec/24/iranian-president-channel-4-alternative-christmas-message, accessed April 19, 2010. In this address, as well, his obvious aim is to renovate Christian hostility against Jews, albeit in the coded language of contemporary antisemitism.

[19] See the transcript of *Bill Moyer's Journal* broadcast on January 9, 2009, http://www.pbs.org/moyers/journal/01092009/transcript3.html.

Jewish Question, a world that cares little about the problem of antisemitism and the effects of its lies and libels upon Jews and our larger society, because it has not been forced to confront it in any serious and sustained way. With a few exceptions, our world is a world that knows little about the history of Jewish suffering (which has been understood by Christians as a divinely inspired punishment anyway) and cares even less about the suffering of strangers. Far from restricting negative discussion about Jews and Israel, our world is increasingly demonizing and delegitimizing the Jewish State and its people in its attempt to force a solution to the crisis in the Middle East. And instead of self-censoring, people simply now deny and dismiss the label "antisemite" out of hand, thereby erasing the phenomenon as a serious contemporary problem and re-enacting the Western failure to honestly confront and exorcise its own antisemitic demons.

How is all of this possible after decades of exposure to the Holocaust through education in schools and universities, the production of countless Holocaust histories and memoirs, the wide distribution of Holocaust-related films, plays, and television programs, and the construction of Holocaust memorials, including a prominent Federal institution in Washington? How do we explain the apparent paradox of a culture that appears to be suffering from "Holocaust fatigue," so much so that there is growing resentment against the subject and its memorialization, and yet knows very little about the event itself and the pivotal role played by antisemitism in its conception and execution? To answer the question, we must begin to examine the history of Holocaust education and try to assess what exactly people have learned about the Holocaust and antisemitism over the last several decades.

Part of the answer can be found in the material used to teach the subject. The two central texts used by teachers, parents, and professors to educate students about the Holocaust are *The Diary of Anne Frank* and Elie Wiesel's *Night*. Each book records the experience of a child and early adolescent during the years of the Holocaust, one in the occupied Netherlands and the other in Romania (Hungary as of August 1940), and later Auschwitz. Both books have been celebrated for decades[20] but also criticized for their universalization, and not so subtle elision, of the Jewish experience under Nazism. This is especially so in the case of *The Diary of Anne Frank*, first published in Dutch as *Het Achterhuis* [*The House Behind*] in 1947, translated into French and German in 1950, and into English in 1952, with a play staged on Broadway only three years later.[21] Instead of discussing the long and detailed controversies over the book and its theatrical applications,[22] this section will examine several trenchant critiques of the text that deserve our renewed attention. In 1960, Bruno Bettelheim wrote a psychosocial critique of the Broadway play (1955) and Hollywood film (1959) for *Harper's Magazine*, in which he focused his attention not

---

[20] Both books left a deep and bewildering impression upon the author of this essay, who read Anne's diary many times as an adolescent, and was first introduced to *Night* in university.

[21] As of 2001, the book had been translated into fifty-five languages and has sold over twenty million copies.

[22] See Lawrence Graver, *An Obsession with Anne Frank: Meyer Levin and the Diary* (Berkeley: University of California Press, 1995); and Ralph Melnick, *The Stolen Legacy of Anne Frank* (New Haven: Yale University Press, 1997).

so much on Anne's text but upon our use of it and reaction to it. For Bettelheim, the larger culture's "universal and uncritical response" to *The Diary* reflects "our wish to forget the gas chambers," and instead take comfort in the false belief that Jews could retreat "into an extremely private, gentle, sensitive world" despite being surrounded "by a maelstrom apt to engulf one at any moment."[23] Even more offensive is our fetishized treatment of her statement, "In spite of everything, I still believe that people are good at heart," to which the story is often reduced, when in fact Anne had written those optimistic words well before the attic had been sold out by a Dutch informant for about a dollar per person, the inhabitants deported to camps, her mother killed, and she and her sister Margot suffered abject death by typhus in Bergen Belsen in April 1945. This "lesson" about the goodness of people, given the actual history of Anne Frank and her family, is patently false, and Bettelheim believes that it creates an equally false sense of optimism, misleading readers to imagine Anne surviving the war. In fact, recent pedagogical studies of *The Diary* have demonstrated this exact problem. Students have been shown to characterize Anne's diary as more "hopeful than sad," as a story of survival, and even a love story. They appear to manifest a deep-seated resistance to the truth of her death in Bergen Belsen, which was described as "ruining" the story for one student in a classroom study.[24]

Bettelheim also argues that the platitude about human goodness "releases us effectively of the need to cope with the problems Auschwitz presents."[25] Writing in 1960, he does not mention antisemitism specifically, nor does he characterize the specific "problems" Auschwitz presents, but today we know that without antisemitism there would not have been an Auschwitz-Birkenau, and yet *The Diary* allows its readers to disregard this reality entirely. Here, then, is a perfect example of the way students, and the larger culture, are exposed to the Holocaust and yet learn nothing in particular about the problem of antisemitism. Lawrence Langer makes an important observation about the book in this regard. Instead of providing any actual information about the Holocaust or antisemitism, Langer argues, *The Diary* "enacts in its very text a designed avoidance of the very experience it is reputed to grant us some exposure to." And, "[t]hus her work helps us to transcend what we have not yet encountered, nonetheless leaving behind a film of conviction that we have."[26] And it is this false conviction that both impedes an honest cultural engagement with antisemitism, and, as we shall see, actually reproduces antisemitism in relation to Israel.

In a devastating critique by Cynthia Ozick, *The Diary* is described as "bowdlerized, distorted, transmuted, traduced, reduced ... infantilized, Americanized, homogenized, sentimentalized, falsified, kitschified, and, in fact, blatantly and arrogantly

---

[23] Bruno Bettelheim, "The Ignored Lesson of Anne Frank," *Harper's Magazine* (November 1960), pp. 45-50 at p. 45.
[24] See Karen Spector and Stephanie Jones, "Constructing Anne Frank: Critical Literacy and the Holocaust in Eighth-Grade English," *Journal of Adolescent & Adult Literacy* 51:1 (September 2007), pp. 36-48.
[25] Bettelheim, "The Ignored Lesson," p. 47.
[26] Lawrence Langer, "Anne Frank Revisited," in *Using and Abusing the Holocaust* (Bloomington: Indiana University Press, 2006), pp. 16-29 at pp. 20-21.

denied."[27] Like Bettelheim and Langer, Ozick denies the value of this text as a Holocaust document. To make her point, she proceeds to reconstruct the actual fate of the Frank girls, based upon the testimony of Belsen survivors, including Anne's schoolmate Hannah Goslar: "[Margot] fell dead to the ground from the wooden slab on which she lay, eaten by lice, and Anne, heartbroken and skeletal, naked under a bit of rag, died a day or two later."[28]

Equally important to Ozick's graphic truth-telling is her revelation of the very real dejudaization of the book, revealed by the publication in 1995 of additional diary material removed by Anne Frank's father Otto, subsequent publishers, and translators.[29] Comparing editions now reveals that Otto Frank removed Anne's numerous references to Judaism, including those describing Yom Kippur. Additionally, the Zionism of Anne's sister Margot as well as the Hebrew the family sung at Hanukkah were deleted from the Hackett Broadway script approved by Frank. Additions that distort Anne's story were invented by producer Lillian Hellman, who inserted lines like "we're not the only people that've had to suffer ... There've always been people that've had to ... sometimes one race ... sometimes another."[30] Even worse, Otto Frank allowed the translator of the German edition, Anneliese Schütz, to either remove or revise Anne's passages about Germans. For example, in her list of house rules, Anne writes, "*Use of Language*: It is necessary to speak softly at all times. Only the language of civilized people may be spoken, thus no German." The German translation reads: "Alle Kultursprachen ... aber leise!" — "All civilized languages ... but softly!"[31] Schütz justified her methods of distortion and exculpation as necessary because a book "for sale in Germany ... cannot abuse the Germans."[32] Ozick tells us that a German drama critic admitted that the theatrical version of *The Diary* allowed Germans to see "our own fate—the tragedy of human existence per se."[33] And so, as Alvin Rosenfeld observed, "Anne Frank has become a ready-to-hand formula for easy forgiveness,"[34] and of all things, Ozick argues, a "vehicle of German communal identification."[35] One is reminded of Theodor Adorno's discussion of a German woman who left the play in 1959 saying, "Yes, but really, at least *that* girl ought to have been allowed to live."[36] The fact that Adorno

---

[27] Cynthia Ozick, "Who Owns Anne Frank," in *Quarrel & Quandary* (New York: Vintage, 2000), pp. 74-102 at p. 77.

[28] Ibid., p. 79.

[29] This is in addition to Otto Frank's removal of material that embarrassed the family, including Anne's discussion of the Frank marriage, and material that would have been outside the bounds of decency in the 1950s, such as her discussion of contraceptives, female genitalia, and lesbianism.

[30] Ozick, "Who Owns Anne Frank," p. 95.

[31] Ibid., p. 90.

[32] Ibid.

[33] Ibid., p. 98.

[34] Alvin Rosenfeld, "Popularization and Memory: The Case of Anne Frank," in *Lessons and Legacies: The Meaning of the Holocaust in a Changing World*, edited by Peter Hayes (Evanston: Northwestern University Press, 1996), pp. 243-278 at p. 271.

[35] Ozick, "Who Owns Anne Frank," pp. 98-99.

[36] Theodor Adorno, "What Does Coming to Terms with the Past Mean?" in *Bitburg in Moral and Political Perspective*, edited by Geoffrey Hartman (Bloomington: Indiana University Press, 1986), pp. 114-129 at p. 127.

characterizes this remark as a "first step toward insight," for which he appears to be grateful, illustrates the pervasive antisemitism in postwar German society and the ongoing complicity of Germans in these crimes as late as fourteen years after the war. It would not be until 1991 that Germans would have the opportunity to discover the original content of Anne's diary.

Cynthia Ozick describes Otto Frank in what are thought to be typically German Jewish terms: secular, assimilated, and bourgeois, but also accommodating, even deferential in relation to non-Jews and especially toward Germans. She interprets his primary role in distorting *The Diary of Anne Frank* as the result of his "social need to please his environment and not to offend it."[37] It has always been, and remains today, safer for Jews to avoid confronting gentiles about their antisemitism, and this reality, Ozick argues, is what led him to "speak of goodness rather than destruction," and to allow *The Diary* to be "accommodated to expressions like 'man's inhumanity to man,' diluting and befogging specific historical events and their motives."[38] Furthermore, the memorial he chose to honor his daughter was the Anne Frank Foundation[39] and International Youth Center, both located in Anne Frank House in Amsterdam. Ozick argues that this memorial, dedicated to the humanistic goal of bringing young people across the globe into contact with one another, "nevertheless washed away into do-gooder abstraction the explicit urge to rage that had devoured his daughter."[40] Here, she is referring to Anne's diary entry from May 3, 1944: "There's a destructive urge in people, the urge to rage, murder, and kill."[41] Obviously, our choice to ignore these words and fetishize their very opposite, and then to present our choice as the epitome of Anne Frank and her experience, says more about the problematic needs of post-Holocaust Western culture than anything else. One can see how truly deceitful this cultural fetish is when the lines immediately following Anne's comments about human goodness read: "I simply can't build up my hopes on a foundation consisting of confusion, misery, and death. I see the world gradually being turned into a wilderness, I hear the ever approaching thunder, which will destroy us too, I can feel the sufferings of millions."[42] Our misuse of her words is actually perverse, as suggested by Griselda Pollock, in that we make the victim herself provide bystanders (and even perpetrators) "with comfort in our distress at encountering her suffering."[43]

The second Holocaust text used in the classroom is *Night*, Elie Wiesel's memoir of his experience as a young Hasidic boy in Sighet, Romania, the destruction of his family and community, his struggle to survive in Auschwitz, and the liberation of Buchenwald. The book was first published in French in 1958, with the help of French Catholic writer François Mauriac, and translated into English two years later. Despite

---

[37] Ozick, "Who Owns Anne Frank," p. 85.

[38] Ibid., p. 86.

[39] Today the Anne Frank Foundation fights discrimination against minorities in Europe, with a specific focus on protecting the rights of Turks and immigrants.

[40] Ozick, "Who Owns Anne Frank," p. 86.

[41] Ibid., p. 85.

[42] Martha Ravits, "To Work in the World: Anne Frank and American Literary History," *Women's Studies* (1997), pp. 1-30 at p. 16.

[43] Griselda Pollock, "Stilled Life: Traumatic Knowing, Political Violence, and the Dying of Anne Frank," *Mortality* 12 (May 2007), pp. 124-141 at p. 139.

the fact that the Jewish child in this text is Hasidic, and therefore less familiar to readers than the more assimilated Anne of *The Diary*, the major trope of *Night* is nevertheless universal: the collapse of faith in a God who can no longer possibly exist after Auschwitz. Moreover, the book is Christological in places, such as the image of the hanging (crucified) Jewish boy in Auschwitz, which serves to make the text accessible and meaningful to a Christian audience. Mark Anderson interprets this Christology as a conscious strategy with problematic implications: "Evoking Christ's crucifixion even as it denies the existence of God, Wiesel's account of Auschwitz turns it into a religious drama accessible to all readers, Jews and Christians. It becomes a moral tale about the sanctity of 'angelic' children rather than a historical meditation on Nazi crimes and gentile complicity."[44]

Like *The Diary of Anne Frank*, we now know that there is an earlier version of this text, which is not dominated by universal themes but articulates a Jewish point of view that is justifiably furious at the non-Jewish world. Elie Wiesel wrote an 800-page manuscript in Yiddish immediately after the war, and 250 pages of it were published under the title *Un di velt hot geshvign* [*And the World Kept Silent*] in 1956 in Buenos Aires. In this earlier text Wiesel describes the Jewish context of his childhood in elaborate detail, which reflects the Jewish process of memorialization and the early documentation of destruction,[45] but he also conveys the realities of Jewish rage and the desire for revenge. In her study of the two Wiesel texts, Naomi Seidman explains that instead of the lack of vengeful thoughts found in *Night*, the Yiddish version states that newly liberated "Jewish boys ran off to Weimar to steal clothing and potatoes. And to rape German girls."[46] There is also additional material at the end of the text, nonexistent in *Night*, which conveys Wiesel's anger and frustration at the antisemitic continuity of postwar Europe:

> Now ten years after Buchenwald, I see that the world is forgetting. Germany is a sovereign state, the German army has been reborn. The bestial sadist of Buchenwald, Ilsa Koch, is happily raising her children. War criminals stroll the streets of Hamburg and Munich. The past has been erased. Forgotten. Germans and anti-Semites persuade the world that the story of the six million Jewish martyrs is a fantasy, and the naive world will probably believe them, if not today, then tomorrow or the next day. So I thought it would be a good idea to publish a book based on the notes I wrote in Buchenwald. I am not so naive to believe that this book will change history or shake people's beliefs. Books no longer have the power they once had. Those who were silent yesterday will also be silent tomorrow.[47]

This, unfortunately, is not the Elie Wiesel the world has come to know. This Jewish survivor who accuses Europe of complicity and condemns a silent world, Seidman argues, was "supplanted by the [French Catholic] survivor haunted by metaphysics

---

[44] Mark M. Anderson, "The Child Victim of the Holocaust: An American Story," *Jewish Social Studies* 14 (Fall 2007), pp. 1-22 at p. 6.

[45] For a discussion of this subject, see Laura Jockusch, "*Khurbn Forshung*: Jewish Historical Commissions in Europe, 1943-1949," *Simon Dubnow Institute Yearbook* (2007).

[46] Naomi Seidman, "Elie Wiesel and the Scandal of Jewish Rage," *Jewish Social Studies* 3 (Fall 1996), pp. 1-19 at p. 6.

[47] Ibid., p. 7.

and silence." And so, as with Anne Frank's diary, the specificity of Jewish experience, which is determined by antisemitism, is sacrificed to the wants and needs of the dominant gentile world. What is worse, the Jewish survivor is then co-opted by his surrounding Christian culture as a "potent emblem of martyrdom ... of suffering silence,"[48] thereby enacting and reinforcing a tradition responsible for antisemitism in the first place.[49]

CONCLUSION

This essay has tried to suggest that the primary Holocaust texts used to teach the subject both universalize and Christianize the experience of Jewish suffering in an attempt to make the subject matter accessible and meaningful to non-Jews. This was perceived as necessary after the war due to the antisemitic nature of postwar Western culture. There was a general hope that non-Jews would somehow imbibe that antisemitism was wrong from reading these stories and eventually from a curriculum that focused on the general evils of discrimination and racism and promoted a doctrine of universal human rights. Today, Holocaust education forms the basis for a new type of civic education. Instead of learning about the nation, our provinces or states, or even one's city, young people learn about war and genocide, increasingly in a comparative framework, and the new civic values of peaceful reconciliation and human rights. In countries like Canada and the United States this also presents an opportunity to celebrate ourselves in the form of the *American Constitution*, the *Canadian Charter of Rights and Freedoms*, and our Allied role in liberating Europe from Hitler. This is precisely the conclusion presented in the permanent exhibit of the *United States Holocaust Memorial Museum*, and it is the basis for the conception of the new *Canadian Museum for Human Rights*,[50] scheduled to open in Winnipeg in 2012.

There is no doubt that Holocaust education has had a positive influence on Western society. It has helped to create our contemporary concern with fighting racism and promoting human rights and has generated our current interest in the historical and contemporary problems of genocide and war crimes. The problem, however, is that *it has not produced a corresponding concern about antisemitism*, and this has created serious problems for the State of Israel and for Jews worldwide. What we have produced in contemporary Western culture is a general conviction, to use Langer's term, that we have learned the "lessons" of the Holocaust when in fact few people outside the academic field know anything in particular about the Nazi *Final Solution*, its systematic destruction of Jewish Europe, and the nature and history of the antisemitism responsible for this catastrophe, which continues to exist in our

---

[48] Ibid., p. 16.

[49] For a discussion of the Christian influence on Holocaust memory in Western culture, see Tom Lawson, "Shaping the Holocaust: The Influence of Christian Discourse on Perceptions of the European Jewish Tragedy," *Holocaust and Genocide Studies* 21 (Winter 2007), pp. 404-420.

[50] It should be noted that Israel Asper, the original creator of the Museum, initially proposed a Holocaust Museum, but due to protests coming from Aboriginal and Ukrainian organizations, the Museum was reconceptualized as a human rights museum. How the conflict in the Middle East will be represented by this museum is no doubt one of its future controversies.

culture.[51] This paradoxical reality has a detrimental effect on Western culture and on the role Western nations play in contemporary politics. Academic and popular discussions of the ongoing war in the Middle East are increasingly dominated by a human rights ideology, which is understood to rest upon the universal historical "lessons" of the Holocaust. This same ideology lacks an equal interest in the problem of antisemitism, which is the key factor animating the ideological war against Israel and provoking the often aggressive (defensive) Israeli response to violence and provocation, which cycles over and over again in this conflict. The widespread willful denial of the fundamental role played by antisemitism in this conflict guarantees that the cycle of killing will continue. By erasing antisemitism from the equation of the Middle East and refusing to understand and accept the effects of the Shoah on the people of Israel, and Jews in general, both the Western and Islamic worlds will continue to mischaracterize Israel as irrational, violent, and inhumanly cruel. They will also be responsible for helping to fuel, and therefore prolong, this terrible conflict.

Moreover, the human rights under discussion in this conflict are increasingly identified as Palestinian instead of *civilian*, which again manifests the antisemitic impulse of excluding Jews from common humanity. Lacking an adequate knowledge about the nature and history of antisemitism, and of the Nazi *Final Solution to the Jewish Question*, people make and accept false and deeply offensive equations between Israel and Nazi Germany and dismiss the ferocious antisemitism of the Arab and Muslim worlds as merely righteous anger at the Israeli violation of their human rights. And so, in what can only be characterized as a tragically ironic development, contemporary hostility against Israel is further legitimized by a growing perception that Jews (of all people) have failed to learn the universal "lessons" of their own Holocaust.[52] And for this, Jews are once again guilty (collectively) for advancing their own particularism in violation of the new universal religion of humanity.[53]

Given this current scenario, one wonders if Holocaust survivors and the others involved in creating public Holocaust education would agree with Cynthia Ozick, who suggested at the end of her critique of *The Diary of Anne Frank* that it may have been better for Anne's diary to have been lost, and thereby "saved from a world that made of it all things, some of them true, while floating lightly over the heavier truth of named and inhabited evil."[54]

---

[51] One reason for the problematic chasm in knowledge and perception between the public and Holocaust scholarship is the exclusive focus on the Jewish victims in public Holocaust education, especially Anne Frank and Elie Wiesel, whose experience has been universalized, Christianized, and Americanized. This kind of universalization would be impossible if one's focus was also on the perpetrators, whose entire ideology and program specifically targeted the Jewish people for destruction.

[52] For an examination of contemporary Israeli attitudes toward the Holocaust, see Dalia Ofer, "The Past That Does Not Pass: Israelis and Holocaust Memory," *Israel Studies* 14 (Spring 2009), pp. 1-35.

[53] For an explanation of the rage against Israel we are now witnessing in some progressive circles, see Bernard Harrison, *The Resurgence of Anti-Semitism: Jews, Israel, and Liberal Opinion* (London: Rowman & Littlefield, 2006). For an interpretation of European attitudes on this so-called Jewish betrayal of humanity, see Alain Finkielkraut, "The Religion of Humanity and the Sin of the Jews," *Azure* (Summer 5765/2005), pp. 23-32; and, "In the Name of the Other: Reflections on the Coming Anti-Semitism," *Azure* (Autumn 5765/2004), pp. 21-33.

[54] Ozick, "Who Owns Anne Frank," p. 102.

Demonizing Israel:
Political and Religious
Consequences among Israelis

Yossi Klein Halevi*

I. INTRODUCTION

Like the people it vilifies, antisemitism is astonishingly adaptable. The growing international movement to demonize Israel and even equate it with Nazi Germany accomplishes the seemingly impossible: mobilizing the Holocaust, the final barrier against relegitimizing antisemitism, to empower its latest permutation.

The antisemitism of mere prejudice is unremarkable, tending to resemble the dislike of any "other." But there is another—unique and potentially lethal—form of antisemitism, which transforms the Jew into the embodiment of whatever a given society defines as its worst quality or sin and the enemy of its highest good. This is the antisemitism of symbols: Christ-killer under Christianity, murderer of prophets under Islam, capitalist under Communism, and race polluter under Nazism.

The Holocaust prompted widespread revulsion, at least in the West, toward the antisemitism of symbols. The most far-reaching result of that revulsion was the Vatican's *Nostra Aetate*, absolving the Jews of deicide. But the antisemitism of symbols has been revived by anti-Zionism, which turns the Jewish state into a symbol of colonialism, oppression, and militarism—a violator of contemporary society's most lofty norms. There is an acute irony in the growing popularity of anti-Zionism. The founders of political Zionism envisioned a Jewish state as the solution to lethal antisemitism. The irony is not merely the inability of the Jewish state to achieve that goal; it is that the Jewish state has become the pretext and the target for the re-empowerment of lethal antisemitism.

The return of the antisemitism of symbols, with its focus on the Jewish national rebirth, has profound political and religious repercussions within Israeli society. The more demonized the Jewish state, the more Israelis tend to withdraw into old patterns of Jewish isolationist thinking, developed under conditions of exile and ghettoization. The result is a weakening of the secular Zionist ethos that founded Israel with the promise of "normalizing" the Jews by transforming them into a nation among nations.

---

* Senior fellow at the Adelson Institute for Strategic Studies of the Shalem Center in Jerusalem; contributing editor of *The New Republic*.

II. Political Consequences of Demonization

The first wave of demonization of Israel on an international scale—beyond the Arab world and the Soviet bloc—occurred after the 1973 Yom Kippur War and the Arab oil boycott. Many Third World countries severed diplomatic relations with the Jewish state. By the end of the war, more nations were maintaining diplomatic relations with the PLO, which was frankly committed to destroying Israel, than with the Jewish state. When Yasser Arafat received a standing ovation in the UN General Assembly, Israelis sensed that the right of the Jews to statehood was being symbolically revoked.

Despite the atmosphere of religious and nationalist euphoria generated among Israelis by the Six Day War, the *Gush Emunim* settlement movement did not arise until the bitter aftermath of the Yom Kippur War, in a near-apocalyptic atmosphere of fear for the future of Israel. Part of that fear—and rage—centered on the growing isolation of Israel.

Gush Emunim's greatest triumph coincided with the precise moment when most Israelis felt that the world had once again become a hostile place. On November 10, 1975, the UN General Assembly voted to declare Zionism a form of racism. In his address to the General Assembly, Israel's UN ambassador, Chaim Herzog, spoke for most Israelis when he compared the Zionism-Racism resolution to the Nazi assault on the Jewish right to exist. "It is symbolic," he began, "that this debate ... should take place on November 10. Tonight, thirty-seven years ago, has gone down in history as Kristallnacht, the Night of the Broken Crystals." The UN, he continued, was "on its way to becoming the world center of antisemitism. Hitler would have felt at home on a number of occasions during the past year, listening to the proceedings in this forum."

Less than three weeks later, on November 30, *Gush Emunim* mobilized thousands of supporters to march on Sebastia, the ancient Israelite capital of Samaria, in an attempt to force the Labor government of Yitzhak Rabin to permit Jewish settlement in the northern West Bank. This was *Gush Emunim*'s eighth such attempt to settle in Samaria, but by far the most ambitious. Though the demonstration, which coincided with Hanukkah, had been planned before the Zionism-Racism resolution passed at the UN, the passion roused by the resolution won *Gush Emunim* unprecedented public support. Participants in the march included iconic figures long identified with Labor Israel—like Naomi Shemer, composer of Israel's most popular songs, including the Six Day War anthem, Jerusalem of Gold, and Meir Har-Zion, the Israeli army's most famous commando. Ehud Olmert, then a young Likud member of the Knesset who also joined in the march, told a reporter that the demonstration was the Zionist response to the UN.

Unlike previous occasions, this time the government did not order the army to evacuate the squatters. The reason provided by Rabin was that a solidarity conference of world Jewish leaders protesting the UN resolution was convening that same week in Jerusalem. How would it appear, after all, for Israeli soldiers to be fighting Israeli civilians when the Jewish people was uniting in response to the UN? The hard-line backlash within the Israeli public may well have contributed to the government's hesitation. Even after the solidarity conference ended, Rabin hesitated to evict the squatters. Finally, the government found a face-saving formula that was in effect a capitulation to *Gush Emunim*, and Samaria was opened for Jewish settlement.

The rise of the Likud to power two years later insured the success of the settlement movement. But *Gush Emunim* was psychologically empowered by its breakthrough at Sebastia, which settlers rightly regard as the turning point for their movement.

International hostility toward Israel over the years has deepened the siege mentality among Israelis and heightened public support for the right. When Israelis sense unjustified hostility from the international community, their wariness toward the peace process increases. Conversely, when Israelis sense a measure of acceptance toward the Jewish state, their willingness to compromise and take risks for peace grows.

The beginning of the Oslo process in 1993 was preceded by several crucial events that led to an easing of the siege against Israel. First was the collapse of the Soviet Union, which had been the major center, outside of the Arab world, for disseminating anti-Zionism. (Indeed, the equation of Zionism with racism and of Israelis with Nazis were constant themes of the Soviet media.) The liberation of Eastern Europe led to the renewal of diplomatic relations between former Soviet bloc countries and Israel. China and India initiated ties. African countries that had severed relations with Israel following Arab oil pressure following the 1973 war now renewed them. The Vatican's recognition of Israel ended lingering Jewish fears that the Church still opposed Jewish statehood based on the pre-Vatican II theological concept of the "wandering Jew." Finally, when the UN General Assembly rescinded the Zionism-Racism resolution on December 16, 1991, Israelis felt that the nightmare of re-ghettoization that had begun in 1973 was ending.

"No longer is it true that the whole world is against us," Yitzhak Rabin declared to the Knesset in the inaugural speech of his second term as prime minister on July 13, 1992. "We must overcome the sense of isolation that has held us in its thrall for almost a half a century. We must join in the international movement for peace, reconciliation and cooperation that is spreading over the entire globe these days—lest we be the last to remain, all alone in the station."

Israelis reciprocated the overtures of the international community by tempering their defiant independence with a sense of global interdependence. With far greater enthusiasm than in the past, they joined international relief efforts, raising funds for Somali famine victims and Turkish earthquake survivors. The Israeli press even debated whether the Israeli army should participate in international peacekeeping missions. A new prosperity allowed Israelis to become passionate travelers. Tens of thousands of young Israelis participated in the post-army ritual of backpacking in India and South America. In their new identification with far-off places, Israelis displayed a new embrace of the world. Younger Israelis stopped using the derogatory Yiddish word "goy" to describe gentiles and stopped referring to the nations outside Israel as "the world," as if Jews inhabited a separate planet. The Holocaust began to fade from mainstream political discourse, confined to the rhetoric of the hard right.

This new, expansive atmosphere helped create the psychological conditions that emboldened Israel to initiate contacts with the PLO. Despite profound misgivings about Yasser Arafat's intentions, a majority of Israelis initially supported the Oslo process. The optimism among Israelis ended in September 2000, with the collapse of the Oslo process and the renewal of Palestinian terrorism. Israelis have since experienced two forms of siege: jihadist-inspired terrorism accompanied by an intellectual assault around the world on Israel's right to exist. The Israeli media keenly follows attacks on Israel's legitimacy, like attempts in England to boycott Israeli academics and cartoons in European newspapers comparing Israelis to Nazis. On April 3, 2002, when the Israeli army laid siege to terrorists barricaded inside Bethlehem's Church of the Nativity, the Italian newspaper *La Stampa* published a cartoon on its front page showing an Israeli tank moving toward the Baby Jesus, who exclaims: "Surely they don't want to kill me again?" For Israelis, that cartoon symbolized the true motives of Israel's critics—and served as a reminder of the need for Israel to be strong in a hostile world.

While the renewed strength of the Israeli right is mostly a reaction against Arab terrorism, the anti-Israel campaign abroad, especially in Europe, has also contributed to a hardening of Israeli attitudes. During the Israeli election campaign of 2009, I interviewed supporters of the anti-Arab party, *Yisrael Beiteinu* (Israel Our Home), headed by Avigdor Lieberman. When I noted that strengthening Lieberman would weaken Israel's standing in the international community, one supporter responded vehemently: "They'll hate us no matter what we do." Variations of that comment are typical among right-wing voters.

The outrage and despair are not confined to the right. Amos Oz, novelist and peace activist, notes that graffiti in pre-Holocaust Europe demanded: "Jews to Palestine!" while the graffiti now demands "Jews out of Palestine!" The message to Jews, concludes Oz, is: "Don't be here and don't be there. That is, don't be."

III. Religious Implications of Demonization

Arguably no ideology from within the Jewish mainstream ever managed to so successfully challenge the traditional notion of Jewish chosenness as did secular Zionism. Like the elders of Israel who demanded of Samuel the Prophet to anoint a king over Israel so that it could become a nation like all nations, secular Zionists set out to free the Jews from the cycle of divine chosenness and human ostracism—what could be called the "Joseph Syndrome" after the biblical Joseph, beloved by his father but despised by his brothers. After the Holocaust, that excess of "chosenness," most Jews embraced Zionist normalization as the means of healing the Jewish people. Zionism became the final, desperate strategy of the Jews for ending their radical alienation from the nations.

Zionism in effect aimed at two forms of "return": the return of the Jews to the land of Israel, along with their return to the international community. Addressing the UN General Assembly on May 11, 1949, Israeli Foreign Minister Moshe Sharett declared that Israel's admission into the world body was "the consummation of a people's transition ... from exclusion to membership in the family of nations."

Dr. Leon Pinsker, a 19th century forerunner of political Zionism, offered perhaps the most compelling Zionist critique of antisemitism and of how a return to the land of Israel would cure it. The Jews, he wrote, were a disembodied nation haunting humanity, whose fear of ghosts results in antisemitism. Only by restoring their collective physical existence would humanity stop imposing its dark fantasies on the Jews. "The ghostlike apparition of a living corpse," wrote Pinsker, of a people without unity or organization, without land or other bonds of unity, no longer alive, and yet walking among the living—this spectral form without precedence in history, unlike anything that preceded or followed it, could but strangely affect the imagination of the nations. And if the fear of ghosts is something inborn, and has a certain justification in the psychic life of mankind, why be surprised at the effect produced by this dead but still living nation.[1]

Now, though, it is the re-embodied Jew who haunts humanity. Israel is the only country that has no permanent home in any regional grouping in the United Nations, in effect a wanderer among the nations. And like Pinsker's Diaspora ghost, the Jewish state attracts fear and rage: Israel is the target of more UN denunciations than any other nation, indeed of all other nations combined.

Pinsker would no doubt be confounded by one more twist in the Jewish story: anti-Zionists now celebrate the pre-state Jewish "ghost" as the upholder of ethical values that have been betrayed by Zionism. Just as the Church denounced the post-biblical Jews for betraying their spiritual calling as a people entrusted with redemption, so do anti-Zionists denounce the post-Holocaust Jews for betraying their spiritual calling to serve as a victim people upholding human rights, in effect carriers of the mission of secular redemption. Jews have gone in a single generation from being despised as cowards and race-polluters to being despised as aggressors and racists—precisely because they now behave as any "normal" people would in their place, defending themselves against threat. Israel's offense is in adopting the norms of the nations, its insistence on the right to normalization.

Demonizing Zionism, the ideology of normalization, not only reinforces the political right but also those religious forces advocating a return to ghetto Judaism. Indeed, the theological implications of the imposition on the Jewish state of an enforced "chosenness" have not been lost on the Haredim, or ultra-Orthodox Jews, Zionism's traditional opponents. Several prominent Haredi spokesmen, especially those who spread the faith among secular Israelis, invoke the hatred directed against Israel as proof that secular Zionism's goal of normalization is a failure, and that the only alternative for Israeli Jews is to voluntarily embrace the ghetto. For popular "outreach" rabbis like Amnon Yitzhak and Uri Zohar, the anti-Israel assault reinforces an historic opportunity to reverse the victory of secular Zionism over Orthodox Judaism. In trying to transform the Jews into a nation among nations, they insist, secular Zionism was nothing more than an assimilationist movement cleverly masked as a movement of Jewish affirmation. Herzl, notes Zohar in a video aimed at secular Israelis, initially hoped to end antisemitism by leading the Jews to the steps of St. Peter's, where they would convert en masse to Christianity. But all assimilationist movements are destined to fail. If Israel now finds itself cast in the role of the Jew of the nations, it is because the Jews are inherently different.

In the ongoing culture war between Haredi isolationists and Israelis open to the world, the burden of proof has shifted to the normalizers. Jonathan Rosenblum, a Haredi writer and columnist, cogently summed up how the assault against Israel confirms Jewish chosenness. "It is time to embrace our abnormal existence," he wrote.

---

[1] Arthur Herzberg, ed., *The Zionist Idea* (Meridian Books, 1964), p. 184.

> The enduring, irrational, and protean nature of the hatred directed at us in all generations and all places is the greatest proof of that we have been singled out for a unique mission. ... Rather than depressing us, we should view the rapid metamorphosis of anti-Zionism into the same old Jew-hatred as one of the clearest proofs of our chosenness, and, incidentally, of the world's unconscious recognition of that fact. Not by accident does the UN Human Rights Commission occupy itself with no subject other than Israel, or every European paper seemingly devote two or three articles to Israel every day.[2]

That argument resonates far beyond the Haredi community. Writing during the wave of suicide bombings that followed the collapse of the Oslo process, Peggy Cedor, a former left-wing activist, considered the unthinkable:

> The suspicion slips into the heart that maybe the Haredim were right when they warned that a sovereign state for Jews would annoy the nations and bring annihilation on the remnant of the Jewish people. ... The State of Israel, which was intended to give the Jews an entry ticket into the family of nations, didn't deliver the goods: We're still being judged by separate standards; there is still no proportion between our actions (in themselves severe) and the responses around the world. ... It was nice to feel like everyone else for a while, but that seems to be over.[3]

The most extreme example of the impact of the demonization of Zionism on Jewish religious sensibilities is the theology known as Kahanism, named for the late Rabbi Meir Kahane. The radical, Brooklyn-born rabbi, who emigrated to Israel in 1971, clarified his theology of rage and despair in the immediate aftermath of the Yom Kippur War, and in response to the post-Yom Kippur assault on Israel's legitimacy.

The purpose of Jewish existence, wrote Kahane, was to bring the messiah, but that mission could be fulfilled only when the Jews cut themselves off from pretend-allies among the gentiles and relied only on the protection of Heaven. The Jews and the rest of humanity were meant to be in a state of perpetual war, just as the rabbinic phrase insisted: "Esau hates Jacob"—that is, Esau the gentile hates Jacob the Jew. Kahane advocated provocative acts like expelling the Arabs residents of Israel and blowing up the Dome of the Rock on the Temple Mount—acts that would leave Israel in splendid isolation and that would sanctify God's name by showing fearlessness and contempt for the world's judgment. Rather than endure constant denunciations in the UN, Israel should quit the world body. Finally, Kahane saw the arrival of the messiah as ushering in not an era of brotherly love but of vengeance against the nations that humiliated the Jews, God's people, and thereby desecrated God's name.[4]

While Kahanism has attracted few followers, Kahane's ideas—both political and theological—resonate far beyond his limited circle. Graffiti throughout the country proclaims: "Kahane was right." And within some religious Zionist circles, Kahanism is no longer taboo. In Israel's most recent elections, a Kahanist was elected to the Knesset through the National Union—the first time a political party (aside from the banned Kahanist party, "Kach") legitimized Kahanism.

---

[2] "Embrace the Abnormal," *Jerusalem Post*, March 22, 2007.

[3] Peggy Cedor, "Time to Shut the Business," *Kol Hazman*, October 22, 2002.

[4] See, for example, Meir Kahane, *Forty Years* (Institute of the Jewish Idea, 1983); and Meir Kahane, *The Jewish Idea* (Institute for Publication of the Writings of Rabbi Meir Kahane, 1998).

IV. Conclusion

The growing pessimism among Israelis about their country's place in the community of nations threatens Zionism's great psychological achievement: protecting the Jews from a fatal, post-Holocaust bitterness. Israel's founding pre-empted a massive Jewish rejection of the non-Jewish world, allowing survivors to turn rage into reconstruction. Israel even forced the Jews to make their peace with Europe. When David Ben-Gurion negotiated the German reparations agreement in the early 1950s, resisting the violent opposition led by Menachem Begin, he compelled Israelis to choose pragmatism over history. But that choice should not be taken for granted. Perhaps the Holocaust's deepest long-term wound on the Jewish psyche is the sense that "the world" did not care whether the Jews lived or died. Jews must continually resist the suspicion that even the enlightened world cares little for their survival. The consequences—political and theological—of feeding that suspicion could be shattering.

Israel's psychological struggle is between the optimism of the 1990s and the despair of the 1970s. One popular Israeli bumper sticker sums up the current mood: "There is no one on whom to rely, except on our Father in Heaven"—an all encompassing cry of despair directed at institutions ranging from the Knesset to the UN.

To be sure, Palestinian terror attacks and Arab enmity generally have a greater impact on the rightward shift of the Israeli public than even the harshest criticism from nations outside the Middle East. Still, the impact of the renewed and intensified demonization of Israel should not be underestimated. International detractors who turn every Israeli act of war into a war crime and subject the Jewish state to a level of moral judgment not applied to any other nation are inciting the very hard-line forces they deplore. And as the results of the most recent Israeli elections prove, those forces are growing.

Uncivil Society: Ideology, the Durban Strategy, and Antisemitism

Gerald M. Steinberg*

I. INTRODUCTION

Civil society organizations are widely seen as important actors in policy making, both within countries and in the wider framework of international relations. These non-governmental organizations (NGOs)—which are also known as third-sector organizations, non-profits, and charities—are viewed as independent of government and political considerations, and not subject to the selfish interests of the marketplace and business sector.[1] In international issues, this NGO network is particularly influential in the areas of human rights, humanitarian aid, and related issues.[2] NGO reports, press releases, and political lobbying campaigns constitute a powerful source of "soft power," and they have a significant influence in the United Nations, the media, and academia.[3]

Much of this influence stems from the image of NGOs as altruistic organizations, promoting the common good.[4] In this spirit, the causes they espouse cover a wide spectrum, including environmental objectives, disarmament, gender equality, human rights, and the elimination of poverty. Among the most powerful groups, Amnesty International was awarded a Nobel Peace prize, adding to its prestige and influence. Amnesty's mission statement explicitly claims that this NGO "does not support or oppose any government or political system.... It is concerned solely with

---

* President of NGO Monitor and Professor of Political Studies at Bar Ilan University.

[1] See Mary Kaldor, "A Decade of Humanitarian Intervention: The Role of Global Civil Society," in *Global Civil Society 2001*, ed. H. Anheier, M. Glasius and M. Kaldor (Oxford: Oxford University Press, 2001); Mary Kaldor, *Global Civil Society: An Answer to War* (Cambridge: Polity, 2003).

[2] Anne Florini, "Transnational Civil Society," in *Global Citizen Acton*, ed. M. Edwards and J. Gaventa (London: Earthscan, 2001); Jessica Mathews, "Power Shift," *Foreign Affairs* 76, no. 1 (1997), pp. 50-66.

[3] Joseph S. Nye, Jr., *Soft Power: The Means to Success in World Politics* (New York: Public Affairs, 2004); see also Joseph S. Nye, Jr., "The Decline of America's Soft Power," *Foreign Affairs* 83, no. 3 (2004).

[4] Robert Putnam, *Making Democracy Work: Civic Traditions in Modern Italy* (Princeton: Princeton University Press, 1993); J. Cohen and A. Arato, *Civil Society and Political Theory* (Cambridge, MA: MIT Press, 1992).

the impartial protection of human rights."[5] Similarly, Human Rights Watch (HRW) pledges to uphold objectivity and condemn human rights abuses on all sides.

However, as some independent analysts have shown, many of these organizations and the officials that control their resources "are hardly neutral on issues of policy formation."[6] Powerful NGOs claiming to promote human rights and humanitarian aid contribute significantly to the campaigns to label and isolate Israel as a pariah, "racist," and "apartheid" state. This NGO agenda is closely related to the agenda of the UN Human Rights Council (UNHRC) and to the 2001 UN Conference against Racism, held in Durban. NGOs have helped to promote the allegation (increasingly questioned as the evidence is belatedly examined[7]) that the IDF was responsible for the death of Mohammed Al-Dura, the false charges of "massacre" and "war crimes" during the Israeli military's anti-terror operation in Jenin (Defensive Shield) in April 2002, the portrayal of Israel's separation barrier as "the apartheid wall," the academic boycott efforts of the UK's Association of University Teachers (AUT) and others, the divestment campaign of a number of Protestant church groups, and the "collective punishment" allegations related to events in Gaza.

Appropriating the rhetoric of universal human rights and humanitarian aid to pursue narrow political and ideological goals, many publications, statements, and campaigns run by political NGOs have been shown to be false or based on evidence that is not credible. "The problem is that this information can be unsystematic, unreliable, and/or tainted by the interests of those who are disseminating it."[8]

In parallel, NGO critics, such as James McGann and Mary Johnstone, warn of a "crisis of transparency and accountability, an issue that looms on the horizon for the entire NGO sector. ... NGOs as an international community lack the transparency and accountability in terms of finances, agenda, and governance necessary to effectively perform their crucial role in democratic civil society."[9] Other analysts have identified the "democracy deficit" in NGOs, reflecting the fact that officials of these powerful organizations, many of which have budgets of tens, and in some cases, hundreds of millions of dollars, are either self-perpetuating or selected by a small and closed elite, and not subject to any forms of checks and balances.[10]

The problem is exacerbated by the fact that many donors "do not probe deeply into what exactly is being done with grant funds.... Grant makers ... often do not

---

[5] "Editorial Guidelines," Amnesty International, accessed February 10, 2009, http://www.amnesty.org/en/editorial-guidelines.

[6] James McGann and Mary Johnstone, "The Power Shift and the NGO Credibility Crisis," *The International Journal of Not-for-Profit Law* 8, no. 2 (2005), accessed March 22, 2009, http://www.icnl.org/research/journal/vol8iss2/art_4.htm.

[7] Philippe Karsenty, "We Need to Expose the Muhammad al-Dura Hoax," *Middle East Quarterly*, Fall 2008, pp. 57-65, http://www.meforum.org/article/1998; Nidra Poller, "A Hoax?," *Wall Street Journal*, Europe edition, May 27, 2008; "Al-Durra Case Revisited," *Wall Street Journal*, Europe edition, May 27, 2008.

[8] McGann and Johnstone, "The Power Shift."

[9] Ibid.

[10] Gary Johns, "The NGO Challenge: Whose Democracy Is It Anyway?" (Melbourne: Institute for Public Affairs, 2003), available at http://www.aei.org/files/2003/06/11/20040402_20030611_johns.pdf; P. Niggli and A. Rothenbuhler, "Do the NGOs Have a Problem of Legitimacy?," December 2003, http://www.globalpolicy.org/ngos/credib/2003/1203problem.htm.

even read grant proposals, and program officers are often 'too busy' with grant applications to read reports on projects' impact. Thus, while funders are in a prime position to demand accountability from NGOs, this opportunity is often lost."[11]

However, these problems are largely hidden, and as a result of the "halo effect" the NGO community has largely avoided critical analysis, despite the power that it wields.[12] The "halo effect" is the term used to refer to the degree to which reports and statements made by prominent NGOs are routinely accepted at face value by donors and foundation officials, as well as journalists, diplomats, academics, and others, who act as force multipliers for the NGOs' agendas.[13]

This immunity can be traced to the belief in the veracity of human rights norms, including post-Holocaust conventions and treaties such as the Convention on the Prevention and Punishment of the Crime of Genocide and the Universal Declaration of Human Rights, both of which were adopted in 1948.[14] The emphasis on these norms has grown continuously, and, as Irwin Cotler has noted, human rights have become the global secular religion.[15] As a result, the institutional responsibility for implementing human rights norms has been expanded from the United Nations and individual governments to include and, in many cases, be led by the NGO network.

II. THE EXPANSION OF NGOS' IMPACT ON THE HUMAN RIGHTS DISCOURSE

The most powerful NGOs—including Amnesty International, HRW, the International Commission of Jurists (ICJ), Christian Aid (UK), and the International Federation for Human Rights (FIDH) (France)—exert immense influence in the UN, the EU, and Western capitals. In 1948, sixty-nine NGOs had consultative status at the UN; by 2000, the number was over 2,000, with many claiming to promote "universal human rights" in their mission statements.[16] (By the end of 2008, this number had grown to 4,000.)

Much of this growth in numbers and influence took place in the context of the Cold War, particularly during the 1970s. Groups such as Amnesty International and what was to become HRW were instrumental in the Helsinki process and the Conference on Security and Cooperation in Europe (CSCE). They protested on issues such as the situation of political prisoners and the denial of human rights to Jews in the Soviet Union and the Communist countries of Eastern Europe, including the denial of the right to emigrate.

---

[11] McGann and Johnstone, "The Power Shift."

[12] Hugo Slim, "By What Authority? The Legitimacy and Accountability of Non-Governmental Organisations" (paper presented at the International Meeting on Global Trends and Human Rights—Before and After September 11, International Council on Human Rights Policy, Geneva, January 10-12, 2002).

[13] Robert Charles Blitt, "Who Will Watch the Watchdogs? Human Rights Non-Governmental Organizations and the Case for Regulation," *Buffalo Human Rights Law Review* 10 (2004).

[14] Available at http://www.un.org/Overview/rights.html.

[15] Irwin Cotler, "Beyond Durban," *Global Jewish Agenda*, June 17, 2003, http://www.jafi.org.il/agenda/2001/english/wk3-22/6.asp.

[16] "The Growth in the Number of NGOs in Consultative Status with the Economic and Social Council of the United Nations," accessed March 1, 2009, http://www.staff.city.ac.uk/p.willetts/NGOS/NGO-GRPH.HTM#graph,2002, originally published in P. Willetts, ed., *"The Conscience of the World": The Influence of Non-Governmental Organisations in the UN System* (London: Hurst, 1996), p. 38.

By the mid-1980s, these organizations were very powerful international actors and, like other actors, continuously sought to maintain or increase their influence and resources. When the Cold War ended, their agendas necessarily shifted and expanded.[17] Due to its high media visibility, the Middle East, and the Israeli-Arab conflict in particular, proved to be a good venue for maintaining and even increasing their influence, as well as their funding and, thus, their power. A study by the United States Institute of Peace (USIP) examines 160 international NGOs (INGOs) with a combined annual revenue of $2.3 billion, "almost all of which comes from private donors."[18]

III. Post-colonial Ideology and Antisemitism

In parallel to its expanding influence, the ideology of post-colonialism has become increasingly dominant in the NGO community, in concert with much of the media, academia, and diplomatic networks. This ideology, articulated by Noam Chomsky, Edward Said, Joseph Massad, and many others, assigns virtue to chosen "victims" and condemns others, including the United States and Israel, as neocolonialist aggressors and "hegemons."[19] In contrast to liberalism and the marketplace of competing ideas, post-colonial adherents eschew examination of evidence, variables, and different theories used to explain complex political processes. Instead of focusing on behavior, they promote a form of "essentialism," based on *a priori* judgment regarding the inherent nature and characteristics of the political actors. Similarly, in this ideological framework, liberal democracy is not considered a virtue but rather a means of manipulation and "marginalization."[20]

In this framework, the West in general, and the United States and Israel in particular are defined by nature as evil manipulators responsible for the world's problems. Hirsch observes that "the United States and Israel occupy subject positions in the ideology that go far beyond their actual empirical roles."[21] And as Donna Robinson Divine has observed, "postcolonialism typically uncovers traces of Western power lurking in the world's economy, its politics, and its so-called Western defined culture; and ... projects the national heirs of former colonies as innocents and still powerless."[22] Power and the use of military force (including for self-defense against terror) are confused with immorality, while the image of weakness (a central

---

[17] On the transformation of missions and survival of organizations, see David L. Sills, "Voluntary Associations: Sociological Aspects," in *International Encyclopedia of the Social Sciences* (New York: Macmillan and Free Press, 1968); and Peter M. Blau and W. Richard Scott, *Formal Organizations: A Comparative Approach* (San Francisco, CA: Chandler, 1962).

[18] Pamela R. Aall, *NGOs and Conflict Management* (Washington, D.C.: United States Institute of Peace, 2000), cited in McGann and Johnstone, "The Power Shift."

[19] See, for example, Josef Joffe, "The Demons of Europe," *Commentary* 117, no. 1 (January 2004), pp. 29-34.

[20] Noam Chomsky, "The Disconnect in US Democracy," *Khaleej Times*, October 29, 2004.

[21] Cited in David Hirsh, "Anti-Zionism and Antisemitism: Cosmopolitan Reflections" (YIISA Working Paper Series, no. 1, Yale Initiative for the Interdisciplinary Study of Antisemitism, New Haven, 2007), p. 7.

[22] Donna Robinson Divine, "Introduction," in *Postcolonial Theory and the Arab-Israel Conflict*, ed. Philip Carl Salzman and Donna Robinson Divine (Oxford: Routledge, 2008), p. 5.

element of pro-Palestinian imagery, erasing the prevalence of terror) is seen as a virtue.

Antipathy to Zionism is further heightened by the ideological opposition to nation states resulting from Western Europe's history of aggressive nationalism (adopted by academics in North America, despite a very different historical basis). Western nationalist movements are perceived through this Euro-centric filter as "backward" and regressive, in contrast to the supposedly "enlightened" post-nationalism of post-Holocaust Europe.

Beyond the distortions resulting from this ideological framing, Divine also notes the degree to which post-colonialism's limited "analytical rigor is particularly compromised by its advocacy function" in the attacks on Zionism.[23] Similarly, Karsh traces the impact of this narrative in erasing the history of Islamic imperialism, which is inconsistent with post-colonialism,[24] and Steinberg examines the ideological influence on the sub-field of peace studies.[25]

The post-colonial ideological frame also explains the embrace of Yasser Arafat and the PLO, who were seen as the leaders of the Palestinian struggle against Israel, Later, as Arafat's influence waned and Hamas became more powerful, the allegiance of academics, political leaders (particularly among the European Left), and NGO officials changed. By 2008, during its confrontation with Israel, the post-colonial leadership had switched its support (ranging from tacit to active) to Hamas, while continuing to condemn Israel with allegations of "racism." In contrast, there is no criticism of the Hamas charter, which includes statements such as: "The Islamic Resistance Movement aspires to implement Allah's promise: 'The Day of Judgment will not come about until ... the Jews hide behind rocks and trees, which will cry: Oh Muslim! Oh Abdullah! There is a Jew behind me, come on and kill him.' [Article 7] ... There is no solution for the Palestinian question except through jihad. All initiatives, proposals, and international conferences are a waste of time and vain endeavors." [Article 13][26]

The intensive use of demonizing terms such as "apartheid" and "racism" with reference to Israel is a central expression of post-colonial "essentialism" and expresses the goal of reversing the establishment of Israel as a sovereign state. Hirsh's examination of the sources of modern anti-Zionism shows that this rhetoric is "part of a movement" that encompasses different and often conflicting discourses, including "'anti-imperialism' and post-colonial theory," as well as "the nationalist discourses of Arab and Palestinian anti-colonialism, the Christian and Muslim religious discourses of antisemitism...." In the intensity of the debates and political campaigning, "[c]oncepts and commonsense notions developed within one kind of

---

[23] Divine, "Introduction," pp. 4-5.

[24] Efraim Karsh, "The Missing Piece: Islamic Imperialism," in *Postcolonial Theory and the Arab-Israel Conflict*, ed. Philip Carl Salzman and Donna Robinson Divine (Oxford: Routledge, 2008).

[25] Gerald M. Steinberg, "Postcolonial Theory and the Ideology of Peace Studies," in *Postcolonial Theory and the Arab-Israel Conflict*, ed. Philip Carl Salzman and Donna Robinson Divine (Oxford: Routledge, 2008).

[26] See http://middleeast.about.com/od/palestinepalestinians/a/me080106b.htm; see also David G. Littman, "The Genocidal Hamas Charter," *National Review Online*, September 26, 2002, http://www.nationalreview.com/comment/comment-littman092602.asp.

discourse tend to slip and slide, and metamorphose, into those of the other terrains."[27]

The metamorphosis of post-colonial ideology into anti-Zionism and antisemitism is expressed in denying the Jewish people the right of sovereign equality among the nations. As Cotler has stated, "the call for the dismantling of Israel as an apartheid state ... is not limited to talk about divestment—it is about the actual dismantling of Israel based upon the notion of apartheid as a crime against humanity." Cotler adds that this

> ideological antisemitism involves the characterization of Israel not only as an apartheid state—and one that must be dismantled as part of the struggle against racism—but as a Nazi one. And so it is then that Israel is delegitimized—if not demonized—by the ascription to it of the two most scurrilous indictments of twentieth-century racism—Nazism and apartheid—the embodiment of all evil.[28]

IV. NGOS AND ANTI-ISRAEL IDEOLOGY

The influence, logical fallacies, and political biases of post-colonial ideology are magnified in the resource-rich and unaccountable realm of civil society and NGOs. Indeed, the power of NGOs and their ability to determine agendas and government policies is a reflection of the core doctrines and beliefs of post-colonialism, such as opposition to state power and "hegemonism."

In their activities, many NGOs that claim human rights or humanitarian missions reflect the post-colonial ideology and rhetoric, particularly in their campaigns and publications related to Israel. For example, a group of radical Israeli and Palestinian NGOs (many funded by the European Commission under the façade of the Partnership for Peace program—see discussion below) submitted a statement to the United Nations in 2008 using such rhetoric. The statement began with normative terms, in which the NGOs claimed to be "civil society movements and organizations who share a deep commitment to freedom, justice and equality and the combat of racism, racial discrimination, xenophobia and related intolerance worldwide." Reflecting the democracy deficit, these "civil society movements" made no attempt to demonstrate legitimacy, which is assumed to be automatic.

Using this foundation to claim legitimacy, the signatories launched their attack against Israel using the language of post-colonialism, merged with antisemitism, as defined by Cotler, in the UK Parliamentary Study on Antisemitism,[29] Hirsh,[30] and others. "We also share practical experience derived from our struggles for ending foreign domination, colonialism, apartheid, slavery and their legacies and current

---

[27] Hirsh, "Anti-Zionism and Antisemitism."

[28] Irwin Cotler, "Global Antisemitism: Assault on Human Rights" (YIISA Working Paper Series, no. 3, Yale Initiative for the Interdisciplinary Study of Antisemitism, New Haven, 2009).

[29] All-Parliamentary Group Against Antisemitism, "Report of the All-Party Parliamentary Inquiry into Antisemitism," September 2006, available at http://www.antisemitism.org.uk/wp-content/uploads/All-Party-Parliamentary-Inquiry-into-Antisemitism-REPORT.pdf.

[30] "If some people are treating Israel as though it were demonic, if they are singling out the Jewish state for unique hostility and if they are denouncing 'Zionists' as Nazis or racists or identifying them with apartheid, then in doing so, they may be playing with the fire of antisemitism." Hirsh, "Antisemitism and Anti-Zionism," p. 6.

manifestations in numerous regions of the world, with and alongside the United Nations."[31] Other sections referred to "Jewish colonization" and policies "to change the demographic composition of the country for the exclusive benefit of its Jewish population through policies and practices which are in blatant violation of international law and public law norms...."[32]

Similarly, the Applied Research Institute Jerusalem (ARIJ)—a major Palestinian NGO—publishes reports and submits statements to the United Nations with the same emphasis. One of ARIJ's main projects is "Monitoring Israel's Colonizing Activities," which

> aims at disseminating information on Israeli *colonization* by monitoring Israeli *colonization* activities through the collection of primary and secondary data and the analysis of *colony's* land use changes. Additionally, the project will study the political and socio-environmental consequences of the establishment of Israeli *colonies* on surrounding Palestinian communities. This project is continuing to serve as a platform for reliable data on Israeli *colonization* needed in the course of negotiations. [emphasis added]

In this brief paragraph, the word "colony" and variations thereof are used five times, highlighting the ideological message in this group's activities, while the history of the conflict and the context of war and terror directed at Israel is completely erased.[33] (This "anti-colonial" project is funded by the European Commission under its Partnership for Peace program, the Swiss Agency for Development and Cooperation, and other European governments. ARIJ's publications also refer to the "apartheid wall" and describe terrorists and suicide bombers as "martyrs,"[34] while accusing Israel of "war crimes," "massacres," and "ethnic cleansing."[35])

ARIJ's publications also systematically erase context and history: the background to the 1967 war and the war itself are completely ignored, leaving the post-war occupation as an example of pure "colonization." Similarly, this post-ideological distortion of history also excises the many cases in which Palestinian leaders refused to negotiate a compromise agreement that would have ended the "occupation," including the failed Oslo process and the July 2000 Camp David summit, as well as the discussions that followed.[36] This invented history allows ideological NGOs such

---

[31] Palestinian Boycott, Divestment and Sanctions National Committee (BNC), "United Against Apartheid, Colonialism and Occupation: Dignity & Justice for the Palestinian People," final draft, October 2008 (Palestinian Civil Society's Strategic Position Paper for the Durban Review Conference, Geneva, April 20-24, 2009), p. 3, http://bdsmovement.net/files/English-BNC_Position_Paper-Durban_Review.pdf.

[32] Ibid, p. 7, para. 11.

[33] ARIJ website, http://www.arij.org/index.php?option=com_content&task=view&id=322&Itemid=30&lang=en.

[34] ARIJ, *Report on the Israeli Colonization Activities in the West Bank & the Gaza Strip* 53 (December 2002), accessed March 1, 2009, http://www.arij.org/index.php?option=com_content&task=view&id=227&Itemid=35&lang=en.

[35] POICA, "Ethnic Cleansing in Jenin Camp," August 15, 2002, http://www.poica.org/editor/case_studies/view.php?recordID=233; ARIJ, "Report: The Apartheid Wall Campaign," http://www.arij.org/pub/Separation%20wall%20Campaign/Separation%20wall.pdf.

[36] See Dennis Ross, *The Missing Peace: The Inside Story of the Fight for Middle East Peace* (New York: Farrar, Straus and Giroux, 2004).

as ARIJ and many others to preserve and reinforce the essentialist image of Palestinians as victims and Israelis as aggressors.

This post-colonial and anti-imperialist or anti-hegemonic ideological rhetoric is prominent among many NGOs that claim to advance humanitarian objectives. For example, War on Want, Christian Aid, and Oxfam—which are all based in Britain—lead political campaigns under banners such as opposition to the "root causes of global poverty, inequality and injustice."[37] The perceived "root causes" are cast as resulting from Western democracy, the nation state, and capitalism. Similarly, an official from the powerful FIDH organization, which is funded by the French government, referred to international justice as "white justice, a justice that serves only to reproduce neo-colonial patterns. What's worse, those fighting nationally or internationally for the recognition of victims' rights to justice are stigmatized and accused of playing into the hands of northern countries."[38]

Many of the NGO that reflect this ideological agenda also take leading roles in anti-Zionist campaigns that systematically single out Israel for condemnation, as noted by Hirsch and others. This conflation "is the reason why a century ago August Bebel, the German Social Democratic leader, characterized [antisemitism] as the socialism of fools. Given its subsequent development, it could also have been called the anti-imperialism of fools."[39]

Another example is provided by the activities Pierre Galand, a socialist senator in Belgium and a leading member of the NGO network that advocates a radical ideological agenda in Europe and the UN. Galand gained public visibility as head of Oxfam Belgium for three decades.[40] Oxfam is a powerful NGO confederation providing humanitarian aid while often espousing a distinct political agenda and ideology. In 2003, Oxfam Belgium produced an anti-Israel poster based on the theme of the blood libel, which, following intense criticism, was later withdrawn (see discussion of NGO antisemitism below).[41] Galand continues to be involved in many different political NGOs and is the European chairman of the Coordinating Committee for NGOs on the Question of Palestine (ECCP), a Brussels-based association of NGOs cooperating with the UN Committee on the Inalienable Rights of the Palestinian People. He is also president of the Forum des Peuples (People's Forum NGO) and the Belgo-Palestinian Association. All of these so called "civil society" organizations are active in virulent anti-Israel activities.

In the United States, New York-based Human Rights Watch (HRW) is headed by Kenneth Roth, a former prosecutor whose rhetoric often reflects post-nationalist and

---

[37] War on Want, accessed January 18, 2009, http://www.waronwant.org. In April 2009, War on Want was an active sponsor of the demonstrations against the meeting of the G20 in London. "War on Want in G20 City Protest," press release, March 31, 2009, http://www.waronwant.org/news/press-releases/16508-war-on-want-in-g20-city-protest.

[38] Sidiki Kaba, "White Justice?," accessed March 27, 2009, http://blog.gardonslesyeuxouverts.org/post/2009/02/04/White-Justice.

[39] Cited in Hirsh, "Anti-Zionism and Antisemitism," p. 7.

[40] NGO Monitor, "Pierre Galand (Belgium): Using Political NGOs to Promote Demonization and Anti-Semitism in the UN & EU," July 28, 2004, http://www.ngo-monitor.org/editions/v2n11/v2n11-5.htm.

[41] NGO Monitor, "Oxfam Belgium Produces Political Poster," June 24, 2003, http://www.ngo-monitor.org/editions/v1n09/v1n09-3.htm.

post-colonialist ideology. Under Roth's leadership, HRW has devoted a highly disproportionate percentage of its resources to condemnations of Israel, reflected in numerous statements and activities in which the context of terrorism is all but erased.[42]

This disproportionate focus on Israel also reflects the ideologies of Roth's inner circle at HRW, which includes a number of individuals with radical political backgrounds such as Sarah Whitson; Joe Stork and Darryl Li, both of whom were affiliated with the strongly anti-Israel Middle East Report (MERIP); and Reed Brody, who led the HRW delegation at the Durban conference and was active in promoting the attempt to bring Prime Minister Sharon to trial in Belgium. In addition, Lucy Meir, hired in 2005 as a researcher for Israel and the West Bank, had previously been affiliated with the radical Electronic Intifada website.[43] In 2008, HRW added Nadia Barhoum, a Palestinian campus activist, to its staff.[44] For this group of people and many others, NGOs that claim to promote human rights and international law are an effective vehicle for gaining influence and promoting their radical political objectives, without the restraints of democratic processes and accountability.

Many NGO activities reflect the post-colonial conflation of Israel and the United States. An October 2008 statement submitted to a UN committee, headlined "United Against Apartheid, Colonialism and Occupation: Dignity & Justice for the Palestinian People" and signed by a number of anti-Israel NGOs such as Ittijah, the Anti-Apartheid Wall Campaign, the Alternative Information Center, and ICAHD, stated that by "[s]haring the racist agenda of justifying foreign domination through the propagation of Islamophobia, the United States and its allies have supported Israel's policy of aggression."[45]

The post-colonial agenda is also prominent among much of the humanitarian aid community, including many NGOs active in the Israeli-Palestinian conflict zone. Many of these organizations are also linked to churches, and, in some prominent cases, their post-colonial rhetoric and pro-Palestinian bias include elements of theological antisemitism, as shown in many of the examples below.

The UK-based charity Christian Aid is one of Europe's most powerful charities. The significant funding it receives from the UK government[46] and the widespread support it enjoys from a wide range of major UK churches, including the Church of England, Baptist and Lutheran churches, provides it with considerable influence. Christian Aid has been centrally involved in numerous anti-Israel efforts, some of

---

[42] NGO Monitor, "Report On Human Rights Watch: A Comparative Analysis of Activities in the Middle East 2002-2004," revised: June 30, 2005 and appendix (documentation), http://www.ngo-monitor.org/archives/news/HRWReportDocumentation.pdf.

[43] Official biographies of some of the HRW officials can be found at http://www.hrw.org/about/info/staff.html. Additional information is available at http://www.ngo-monitor.org/archives/infofile.htm#hrw.

[44] NGO Monitor, "HRW Hires Another Pro-Palestinian Activist," October 29, 2008, http://www.ngo-monitor.org/article/hrw_hires_another_pro_palestinian_activist.

[45] BNC, "United Against Apartheid," p. 10, para. 21.

[46] NGO Monitor, "Analysis of NGO Funding: UK Department For International Development (DFID)," November 3, 2005, http://www.ngo-monitor.org/editions/v4n03/DFID.htm.

which reflect theological antisemitic themes.[47] As Kaplan and Small show, there is a close correlation between anti-Israel ideology and classical European antisemitism, and the theological Christian references trigger these manifestations. In the context of Christian Aid's anti-Israel campaigning, examples include the Christmas 2003 film ("Peace Under Siege") and a poster campaign around the theme of the IDF operation in Jenin in 2002,[48] as well as the Christmas 2004 campaign based on the headline of "Bethlehem's Child." This campaign purported to tell the story of a Palestinian girl who had lost her vision in one eye after allegedly being struck by a bullet fired by an Israeli soldier and being unable to reach a hospital due to Israeli checkpoints. In this and other depictions, Israeli/Jewish violence is portrayed as gratuitous—once again, the numerous terror attacks from the Bethlehem area have been cleansed from the historical record.[49] Other church-based humanitarian NGOs involved in anti-Israel divestment that use this artificial ideological framing include Trócaire[50] (Ireland) and Caritas.[51]

Antisemitic theological themes that promote anti-Israel agendas are also highlighted in the activities of another UK-based charity, War on Want. This organization has also combined references to Bethlehem with depictions of Palestinians (in the form of the central figures from the Nativity) and Israelis as carrying out entirely unjustified acts of violence.[52] And, as noted above, an Oxfam poster (2003) supporting a boycott of Israeli products, reads: "Israeli fruits have a bitter taste … reject the occupation of Palestine, don't buy Israeli fruits and vegetables." Well-known Israeli brands and logos are pictured as unfit for consumption, including a large orange dripping blood and invoking the theme of the blood libel.[53]

The rhetoric of the "Protocols of the Elders of Zion" and other Jewish conspiracies is also prevalent in some NGO activities. ADRID, which is part of the Ittijah NGO network, issued a "manifesto" in 1999 that referred to "Zionist conspiracies" and claimed that the establishment of Israel was "gained with the support of international Zionist and imperialist forces." Similarly, the head of the Palestine

---

[47] Edward H. Kaplan and Charles A. Small, "Anti-Israel Sentiment Predicts Anti-Semitism in Europe: A Statistical Study," *Journal of Conflict Resolution* 50, no. 4 (2006).

[48] NGO Monitor, "Christian Aid: 'Child of Bethlehem' Exploits Christmas to Promote Anti-Israel Campaign; 'Pressureworks' Pulls Teens into Radicalism," *NGO Monitor Digest* 3, no. 4, December 15, 2004, http://www.ngo-monitor.org/article.php?id=743.

[49] "Senior terrorists hiding in a psychiatric hospital arrested in Bethlehem," Israel Ministry of Foreign Affairs, April 1, 2004, http://www.mfa.gov.il/MFA/Terrorism-+Obstacle+to+Peace/Terrorism+and+Islamic+Fundamentalism-/Arrest+Tanzim+terrorists+in+Bethlehem+1-Apr-2004.htm; Ali Waked, "Report: IDF kills mastermind of Jerusalem Terror Attack," *Ynet News*, March 12, 2008, http://www.ynetnews.com/articles/0,7340,L-3518374,00.html.

[50] NGO Monitor, "Trócaire: Misdirected Catholic Aid from Ireland Fuels Conflict," March 18, 2009, http://www.ngo-monitor.org/article/tr_caire_misdirected_catholic_aid_from_ireland_fuels_conflict_.

[51] NGO Monitor, "Caritas Representative to Head UN NGO Conference," March 15, 2005, http://www.ngo-monitor.org/article.php?id=774.

[52] NGO Monitor, "'Hijacked by Hatred': British NGOs Use Christmas for anti-Israel Attacks," December 23, 2008, http://www.ngo-monitor.org/article/_hijacked_by_hatred_british_ngos_use_christmas_for_anti_israel_attacks.

[53] NGO Monitor, "Oxfam Belgium produces political poster."

Children's Relief Fund (PCRF) speaks of the "Zionist lobby and Zionist influence" that manipulates the US government, its citizens, and its media.[54]

NGO use of theological themes of antisemitism in the context of anti-Israel campaigns are central to the activities of the Palestinian-based Sabeel Ecumenical Liberation Theology Center, which is closely linked to Christian Aid in the United Kingdom and to the church-based divestment movement under the Durban strategy. (Christian Aid helps to promote and amplify Sabeel's activities, and a number of Christian Aid officials were also involved in the UK Friends of Sabeel.) Sabeel's leader, Naim Ateek, routinely uses antisemitic imagery to condemn Israel. "[I]t seems to many of us that Jesus is on the cross again with thousands of crucified Palestinians around him," Ateek said in Sabeel's Easter message. "The Israeli government crucifixion system is operating daily."[55]

As this record shows, far from promoting universal moral objectives, such as peace, human rights, and the elimination of poverty, the actions of the post-colonial NGO network are counterproductive to the advancement of these goals. In this inverted racism, legitimate criticism of Israel has been overwhelmed and buried by the essentialist form of racism of post-colonial ideology, which has morphed into a virulent form of antisemitism.

V. Antisemitism at the NGO Forum of the 2001 Durban Conference

The NGO Forum of the 2001 Durban World Conference on Racism provided the central venue for exercising NGO power and promoting its dominant post-colonial ideological and political objectives. Responding to an invitation issued by the UNHRC,[56] it is estimated that as many as 7,000 delegates from 1,500 NGOs participated in this event, funded by the Ford Foundation, European governments, Canada, and other sources.[57]

The main result of the Durban NGO Forum was the relaunching of the "Zionism is racism" campaign of the 1970s. Journalists reported that, "[a]n Amnesty press release handed out during the NGO conference cited several examples of racism and human rights abuses around the world, but mentioned only Israel by name."[58] In a

---

[54] NGO Monitor, "Politics or Altruism: An Analysis of Palestinian Children's NGO's," January 15, 2004, http://www.ngo-monitor.org/editions/v2n05/v2n05-2.htm.

[55] NGO Monitor, "Sabeel's Ecumenical Façade," January 10, 2005, http://www.ngo-monitor.org/editions/v3n11/SabeelsEcumenicalFacade.htm.

[56] See http://www.unhchr.ch/html/racism/05-ngolist.html; Jeffrey Andrew Hartwick, "Non-Governmental Organizations at UN-Sponsored World Conferences: A Framework for Participation Reform," *Loyola of Los Angeles International & Comparative Law Review* 26, no. 2 (2003), pp. 217-280.

[57] Office of the United Nations High Commissioner for Human Rights, Statement by Mary Robinson, High Commissioner for Human Rights and Secretary-General of the World Conference Against Racism, Racial Discrimination, Xenophobia, and Related Intolerance, September 4, 2002, http://www.unhchr.ch/huricane/huricane.nsf/0/81BEC2394E67B11141256 ABD004D9648?opendocument; Gerald M. Steinberg, "Soft Powers Play Hardball: NGOs Wage War against Israel," *Israel Affairs* 12, no. 4 (October 2006), pp. 748-768.

[58] Michael J. Jordan, "Jewish Activists Stunned by Hostility, Anti-Semitism at Durban Conference," *Jewish Telegraphic Agency News*, September 5, 2001, http://www.ujc.org/content_display.html?ArticleID=15621.

preparatory conference, HRW representatives defended "calls for violence," claiming this clause was "justified if against apartheid or on behalf of the Intifada."[59] In a radio interview, HRW head Kenneth Roth rejected criticism, declaring: "Clearly Israeli racist practices are an appropriate topic."[60]

The conference took place against the backdrop of intense violence that escalated into major Palestinian mass terror attacks against Israeli civilians, injuring and killing thousands, including hundreds of women and children. But, following the post-colonial formula, in the spirit of Chomsky and Said, the NGOs systematically portrayed the Palestinians sympathetically as victims and Israelis as powerful aggressors and occupiers. Israeli victims of terrorism were largely invisible, while the image of Mohammed al-Dura, the Palestinian child filmed with his father attempting to avoid what was portrayed as Israeli gunfire, became a central symbol—including at the NGO Forum.[61]

Hanan Ashrawi, a prominent Palestinian official who also heads Miftah (a prominent NGO recipient of EU funding), and a main speaker at the NGO Forum, reinforced these images: "The Palestinians today continue to be subject to multiple forms and expressions of racism, exclusion, oppression, colonialism, apartheid, and national denial."[62] Marchers through the conference area chanted "What we have done to apartheid in South Africa, must be done to Zionism in Palestine."[63]

The NGO Forum's declaration predictably took the form of an indictment, using the binary post-colonial rhetoric to condemn Israel. This document asserted that the "targeted victims of Israel's brand of apartheid and ethnic cleansing methods have been in particular children, women, and refugees" and called for "a policy of complete and total isolation of Israel as an apartheid state … the imposition of mandatory and comprehensive sanctions and embargoes, the full cessation of all links (diplomatic, economic, social, aid, military cooperation, and training) between all states and Israel."[64] A small group of NGOs, particularly from Eastern and Central European post-communist countries, attempted to dissent, rejecting the chapter "Palestinians and Palestine" as well as the deliberate distortions made to the chapter "Anti-Semitism," which, they declared "is extremely intolerant, disrespect-

---

[59] Reported by Dr. Shimon Samuels, Director for International Liaison of the Simon Wiesenthal Centre and Chair of the Jewish Caucus at the World Conference Against Racism, "Antisemitism in the Anti-racist Movement: The Road to Durban," Simon Wiesenthal Center, August 15, 2001, http://www.wiesenthal.com/site/apps/nl/content2.asp?c=bhKRI6PDInE&b=296323&ct=350160.

[60] Anne Bayefsky, "Human Rights Watch Coverup," *Jerusalem Post*, April 13, 2004

[61] Later analysis indicated that the shots could not have been fired by Israeli troops, that the entire episode had been staged, and that the child may not even have been killed. See Nidra Poller, "Myth, Fact, and the al-Dura Affair," *Commentary* 120, no. 2 (September 2005).

[62] Hanan Ashrawi, address to World Conference Against Racism World Conference Against Racial Discrimination, Xenophobia, and Related Intolerances—NGO Forum, Durban, August 28, 2001, available at http://i-p-o.org/palestine-ashrawi.htm.

[63] Anti-Defamation League, "Dateline Durban: Anti-Semitic Materials/Slogans Proliferate on Opening Day of UN Conference," August 31, 2001, http://www.adl.org/durban/durban_083101.asp.

[64] "WCAR NGO Forum Declaration," September 3, 2001, available at http://www.unwatch.org/atf/cf/%7B6DEB65DA-BE5B-4CAE-8056-8BF0BEDF4D17%7D/durban_ngo_declaration_2001.pdf.

ful and contrary to the very spirit of the World Conference Against Racism, Racial Discrimination, Xenophobia and Related Intolerance."[65] But this effort had little impact.

The NGO declaration also condemned Israel's "perpetration of racist crimes against humanity including ethnic cleansing, acts of genocide." It redefined antisemitism to include "anti-Arab racism." Noticeably absent from the declaration was any reference to Palestinian incitement to genocide and terror, or to the Palestinian policy of deliberately endangering civilians through the use of populated Palestinian areas as launch pads for attacks on Israel. In full compliance with post-ideological essentialism, Palestinian violations of human rights norms were ignored by most NGOs.

Many participants and observers have described this event as characterized by vitriolic antisemitism.[66] According to Cotler, Durban

> became the "tipping point" for the emergence of a new anti-Jewishness. Those of us who witnessed the "Durban Speak" festival of hate in its declarations, incantations, pamphlets, and marches—seeing antisemitism marching under the cover of human rights—have forever been transformed by this experience. "Durban" is now part of our everyday lexicon as a metaphor for racism and antisemitism. ... A World Conference Against Racism turned into a conference of racism against Israel and the Jewish people. ... Never have I witnessed the kind of virulence and intensity of anti-Jewishness—mockingly marching under the banner of human rights—as I found in the festival of hate at Durban.[67]

Some of the antisemitism was directed at representatives of Jewish NGOs at Durban. When the representatives of groups such as the International Association of Jewish Lawyers and Jurists (IAJLJ) sought to participate in the discussions of the caucus of international human rights NGOs, HRW's advocacy director Reed Brody joined the move to expel them. According to Prof. Anne Bayefsky, an IAJLJ delegate, Brody declared that representatives of Jewish groups were unwelcome.[68] Similarly, Congressman Lantos, a member of the US delegation to the intergovernmental forum, declared: "What is perhaps most disturbing about the NGO community's actions is that many of America's top human rights leaders—[including] Reed Brody of Human Rights Watch ... participated. Although most of them denounced the NGO document that was adopted, it was surprising how reluctant they were to attack the anti-Semitic atmosphere...."[69]

Physical violence against Jewish delegates was also documented by some of the participants:

---

[65] "Joint Statement by Eastern and Central Europe NGO Caucus and other NGOs at the NGO Forum of the World Conference Against Racism," September 2, 2001, http://www.icare.to/wcar/statement111.html.

[66] Tom Lantos, "The Durban Debacle: An Insider's View of the World Racism Conference at Durban," *The Fletcher Forum of World Affairs* 26, no. 1 (Winter/Spring 2002).

[67] Irwin Cotler, "Global Antisemitism: Assault on Human Rights."

[68] Ibid.

[69] Tom Lantos, "The Durban Debacle"; Canadian Jewish Congress, "WCAR Canadian Jewish Congress Final Report" (unpublished, 2001), p. 1-6.

In response to the hostility, which resulted in many of the Jewish delegates hiding their name tags and even to some of the kippa-wearing male delegates wearing caps out of fear, the Jewish caucus convened a media conference, inside the media tent, as this was regarded as the least likely place in which Jewish delegates would be physically attacked. However, before the opening statements could be completed, a group of shouting, jeering, fist-waving, shoving demonstrators, including a number wearing media badges, forced the abandonment of what had been hoped would be a rare opportunity for Jewish voices to be heard.[70]

The virulence of the attacks on Israel led UN High Commissioner for Human Rights, Mary Robinson, who was responsible for the entire framework, to reject the "hateful, even racist" antisemitic atmosphere of the NGO Forum. And in contrast to standard practice, she decided against commending the final declaration to governments.

However, this response came far too late, and the Durban strategy was launched. The themes have been highlighted in numerous examples, including promoting the false claim of the Jenin "massacre" (2002); campaigns against Israel's West Bank security barrier (2004); the attempt to impose an academic boycott on Israel (2005); the church-based anti-Israel divestment campaigns (2006); and spreading disinformation about the Israel-Hezbollah war (2006) and Israel's military response to rocket fire from Gaza (2007-2009).[71] Additionally, the "lawfare" strategy used by NGOs to harass Israeli officials with civil lawsuits and criminal proceedings is part of the Durban strategy. These cases are designed to amplify the negative image of Israel, advance boycotts, and promote delegitimization.[72]

From late 2007 to March 2009 (the completion date of this paper), the focus of the Durban strategy was on condemning Israeli responses to attacks from Gaza, which is controlled by Hamas. Over fifty NGOs active in the Arab-Israeli conflict issued reports, press releases, and "urgent calls" in condemnation of Israel (300 statements in 2008, and another 500 during the three-week war that began on December 28). Many falsely invoked international humanitarian law by labeling the policy as "collective punishment" and repeated a PLO "legal opinion" claiming that Gaza remained "occupied."[73] Under the façade of morality and universality, they exploited international legal terminology and erased Hamas' genocidal objectives and its many violations of international humanitarian law, such as the extensive use of human shields.

---

[70] Jeremy Jones, "Durban Daze—When antisemitism becomes 'anti-racism.'" *The Review*, October 2001, http://www.durbanreview.org/Durban_2001_NGO_forum/durban_daze.shtml; Herb Keinon, "'Zionism is racism'—a Dead Issue," *Jerusalem Post*, September 2, 2001, available at http://www.ngo-monitor.org/article.php?id=1027.

[71] Gerald M. Steinberg, ed., "The NGO Front in the Gaza War: The Durban Strategy Continues," NGO Monitor Monograph Series, February 2009, http://www.ngo-monitor.org/article/the_ngo_front_in_the_gaza_war.

[72] Anne Herzberg, "NGO 'Lawfare report': Exploitation of Courts in the Arab-Israeli Conflict," NGO Monitor Monograph Series, September 2008, http://www.ngo-monitor.org/article/ngo_lawfare_exploitation_of_courts_in_the_israeli_arab_conflict.

[73] Abraham Bell, "Is Israel Bound by International Law to Supply Utilities, Goods, and Services to Gaza?," Jerusalem Center for Public Affairs, February 2008, http://www.jcpa.org/JCPA/Templates/ShowPage.asp?DBID=1&TMID=111&LNGID=1&FID=378&PID=0&IID=2037.

In the short Gaza war at the end of 2008, which followed the resumption of Hamas' rocket bombardment of Israel, NGOs organized anti-Israel demonstrations in many European cities. European newspapers published articles and editorial cartoons attacking Israel and reprinted NGO condemnations. Allegations included "collective punishment," "indiscriminate attacks," "disproportionate force," "violations of international law," "war crimes," etc.[74] Following the NGO lead, European diplomats made similar statements, and academics renewed campaigns calling for a boycott of Israeli universities.

These NGO statements largely erased Hamas's aggression and war crimes, including thousands of cross-border rocket attacks designed explicitly to strike civilians, exploitation of human shields, and mass suicide bombings in which hundreds of Israelis were killed. In parallel, little mention was made of Hamas' declared genocidal objectives, as stipulated in the movement's charter.[75]

This intense "soft war" directed against Israel followed the pattern set during earlier confrontations, including the 2006 conflict initiated by Hezbollah, Israeli defensive actions against the suicide bombing campaign from 2001 to 2005, the Mohammed Dura affair, and elsewhere. In these and numerous other examples, the Palestinian narrative and version of history is dominant, following the framework of post-colonial ideology, which defines Palestinians as victims, irrespective of their behavior, and singles out Israel, *a priori*, as the aggressor. The timing of this NGO campaign coincided with the preparations of the Durban Review Conference, held in Geneva in April 2009. This provided an opportunity to repeat the rhetoric of the 2001 conference.

VI. NGOs AND THE JENIN "MASSACRE" MYTH

The implementation of the NGO Durban strategy can be seen in the responses to the IDF's "Defensive Shield" operation, which took place in March 2002, following several Palestinian terror attacks, including the Park Hotel bombing on Passover, which killed thirty Israelis and injured 160. The IDF's goal was to disrupt and destroy the bases of the terror network located in densely populated urban areas, such as the Jenin refugee camp. During the Jenin operation, Palestinian spokesmen such as Saeb Erekat accused Israel of a "massacre." Much of the media immediately repeated the claim,[76] demonstrating the power of the Durban strategy of demonization and the singling-out of Israel.

The NGO community played a major role in promoting false reports of a massacre. Immediately after Erekat's statements were broadcast, officials from Amnesty International and the UN gave credence to the myths, as shown in Martin Himel's documentary "Jenin: Massacring Truth." Professor Derrick Pounder of Amnesty International was quoted by the BBC as saying that the signs point to a massacre.[77]

---

[74] Steinberg, "The NGO Front."
[75] See http://middleeast.about.com/od/palestinepalestinians/a/me080106b.htm; see also Littman, "Genocidal Hamas Charter."
[76] See "Jenin Camp 'Horrific Beyond Belief,'" *BBC News*, April 18, 2002, http://news.bbc.co.uk/2/hi/middle_east/1937387.stm; "UN says no massacre in Jenin," *BBC News*, August 1, 2002, http://news.bbc.co.uk/2/hi/middle_east/2165272.stm.
[77] "Jenin 'massacre evidence growing,'" *BBC News*, April 18, 2002, http://news.bbc.co.uk/1/hi/world/middle_east/1937048.stm.

Irene Khan (also from Amnesty International) and Kenneth Roth (HRW) were more careful, but their public comments, as well as press releases and detailed reports, included numerous ideologically-based allegations of Israeli "war crimes" and violations of international law.[78] In addition to demonstrating the degree to which the language of international law is used subjectively and inconsistently to promote narrow agendas, these examples highlight the prominent role played by officials of such political NGOs.[79]

Months later, these NGOs published lengthy reports with similar claims, resulting in another round of headlines alleging Israeli violations of human rights.[80] In June 2002, Adalah, an NGO based in Israel and funded by the Ford Foundation, the European Commission, and the New Israel Fund, issued a report entitled "Israeli Military Attacks on the Occupied Palestinian Territories," which repeated much of the ideological and post-colonial rhetoric, including war crimes allegations.[81] Similar terms were used when Amnesty International and HRW published high profile reports.[82] While acknowledging that the massacre claims had been fabricated, these reports followed the Durban strategy, erasing the context of the terror that justified Israeli actions and using the rhetoric of international law selectively.[83]

The NGO network has continued to use the false allegations regarding Jenin to advance the Durban strategy of demonization. In HRW's 2004 "World Report" (published in 2005, three years after Jenin), Kenneth Roth repeated claims of "indiscriminate" attacks that "cause disproportionate harm to civilians."[84] Similarly, NGOs claiming to provide humanitarian aid also promoted this image. Christian Aid produced a film on Defensive Shield ("Peace under Siege") as part of its Christmas campaign in 2003. Scenes of Palestinian suffering as a result of "Israeli

---

[78] HRW's numerous reports on Jenin include: "Jenin: IDF Military Operations," report, May 2002; "Israel/Occupied Territories: Jenin War Crimes Investigation Needed," press release, May 3, 2002; "Israel: Don't Coerce Civilians to Do Army's Work," joint statement given in Jerusalem with Amnesty International and the International Commission of Jurists, April 7, 2002; "Live from Jenin Online Chat in *Washington Post* with Peter Bouckaert," press release, April 18, 2002.

[79] Gerald M. Steinberg, "The UN, the ICJ and the Separation Barrier: War by Other Means," *Israel Law Review* 38, nos. 1-2 (2005), pp. 331-347.

[80] HRW, "Israel: West Bank Barrier Endangers Basic Rights: U.S. Should Deduct Costs from Loan Guarantees," October 1, 2003, http://www.hrw.org/press/2003/10/israel100103.htm.

[81] Adalah, "Israeli Military Attacks on the Occupied Territories," http://www.adalah.org/eng/optagenda.php; NGO Monitor, "Adalah and the Impact of Legal-Based NGOs in the Arab-Israeli Conflict," October 23, 2003, http://ngo-monitor.org/editions/v2n03/v2n03-1.htm.

[82] Amnesty International, "Israel/Occupied Territories: Wanton destruction constitutes a war crime," press release, October 13, 2003, http://web.amnesty.org/library/Index/ENGMDE 150912003?open&of=ENG-ISR; HRW, "Israel, the Occupied West Bank and Gaza Strip, and the Palestinian Authority Territories: Jenin: IDF Military Operations," May 2002, http://www.hrw.org/reports/2002/israel3/israel0502.pdf; Amnesty International, "Israel and the Occupied Territories: Shielded from Scrutiny: IDF Violations in Jenin and Nablus," November 2002, http://www.amnesty.org/en/library/info/MDE15/143/2002.

[83] Yagil Henkin, "Urban Warfare and the Lessons of Jenin," *Azure* 15 (Summer 5763/2003).

[84] Kenneth Roth, "Drawing the Line: War Rules and Law Enforcement Rules in the Fight against Terrorism," *Human Rights Watch World Report 2004: Human Rights and Armed Conflict* (January 2004), p. 177, http://www.hrw.org/legacy/wr2k4/download/wr2k4.pdf.

aggression" were given prominence, including images of tanks pushing ambulances. Images of Israeli victims were practically non-existent—these would have been incompatible with the post-ideological definitions of Palestinians as victims and Israelis as aggressors.[85]

Furthermore, the timing of this campaign—during the Christmas season—as well as other aspects of Christian Aid's anti-Israel campaigning, suggested the influence of classical theological antisemitism, as discussed above.

VII. NGO LEADERSHIP IN THE "APARTHEID WALL" CAMPAIGN

The 2004 NGO campaigns condemning the separation barrier again portrayed Israel as an all-powerful aggressor and Palestinians as powerless victims. Like the Defensive Shield operation, this barrier was erected in the wake of and in order to prevent mass terror attacks. An intensive media campaign led by prominent NGOs, in cooperation with the Palestinians and Arab governments, promoted a UN General Assembly resolution couched in these essentialist terms. This resolution referred the issue to the International Court of Justice for an "advisory opinion," providing a façade of international legitimacy for imposing "a policy of complete and total isolation of Israel as an apartheid state ... [and] the imposition of mandatory and comprehensive sanctions and embargoes," as adopted by the NGO Forum at Durban.[86]

This campaign again reflected the transformation of the universal principles of human rights and international law into particular criteria used to condemn and marginalize Israel. Many of the governments that submitted briefs to the ICJ condemning Israel's policy have erected their own barriers with similar impacts on the local population, yet the NGOs that issued the reports condemning Israel on this issue did not mention these numerous other examples.[87] This is another example of the singling-out of Israel and double standards, consistent with the dominant ideological framework.

The ICJ, a political body with a judicial façade,[88] issued its advisory opinion in July 2004. As expected, the majority claimed that the Israeli policy was a violation of international law—while Judge Buergenthal issued a strong dissent.[89] In September 2005, the Israeli High Court of Justice ruled that the ICJ's advisory opinion was biased and lacked validity as a basis for policy making.[90]

---

[85] NGO Monitor, "Christian Aid's Political Campaign Continues: 'Peace Under Siege,'" October 23, 2003, http://www.ngo-monitor.org/editions/v2n03/v2n03-2.htm.

[86] "Declaration and Programme of Action," NGO Forum, World Conference Against Racism, Racial Discrimination, Xenophobia and Related Intolerance, Durban, South Africa, August 27-September 1, 2001, available at http://academic.udayton.edu/race/06hrights/WCAR 2001/NGOFORUM/.

[87] For detailed analyses of the different aspects of the ICJ process on this issue, see articles published in the special issue of the Israel Law Review: "Domestic and International Judicial Review of the Construction of the Separation Barrier," *Israel Law Review* 38, nos. 1-2 (2005).

[88] Steinberg, "The UN, the ICJ and the Separation Barrier."

[89] *Legal Consequences of the Construction of a Wall in the Occupied Palestinian Territory*, Advisory Opinion, Declaration of Judge Buergenthal, *ICJ Reports* (2004), p. 240, http://www.icj-cij. org/icjwww/docket/files/131/1687.pdf.

[90] *The Judgment on the Fence Surrounding Alfei Menashe*, HCJ 7957/04, Israel Government Press Office, September 15, 2005.

Once again, HRW was among the most active international NGOs in this campaign, distributing press releases and mass emails as well as issuing calls to the US government and the EU to penalize Israel for building this barrier.[91] HRW's statements repeated Palestinian claims that the barrier impedes "freedom of movement," endangers "access to food, water, education, and medical services," and appropriates land, without even engaging with the Israeli rationale.[92] The evidence in this, as in most other HRW reports and publications regarding Israel, was provided by Palestinian "eyewitnesses," carefully selected journalists, and other sources whose credibility could not be verified.[93]

As in other cases, the NGO reports on the separation barrier provided little or no analysis of the Israeli security environment or the role of the Palestinian officials in promoting terror; HRW's single major report on terror absolved Arafat of responsibility.[94] This framework, as well as the rhetoric and repetition of Palestinian claims, couched in the language and claims of human rights, was adopted and reinforced by the UN General Assembly resolutions and the ICJ's majority opinion.[95]

Other major NGOs were also very active in this phase, including: Christian Aid, Amnesty International, World Vision,[96] the Palestinian NGOs assembled under the Palestinian Environmental NGO Network (PENGON), the Palestinian Grassroots Anti-Apartheid Wall Campaign (www.stopthewall.org), Palestinian affiliates of the International Commission of Jurists,[97] the UK-based War on Want,[98] the Mennonite Central Committee,[99] and Médecins du Monde (based in France).[100]

The language and terms of reference that they used were very similar to those used by HRW and were also consistent with post-colonial ideology. Christian Aid launched a campaign opposing the British government's position, which viewed the ICJ as an inappropriate forum for consideration of the barrier. In a press release entitled "Why the Israeli 'Barrier' Is Wrong," this NGO belittled "Israel's legitimate fears about terrorism," in two sentences, while twenty-one paragraphs described Palestinian hardships resulting from Israel's "land grab."[101] Similarly, Amnesty

---

[91] HRW, "Israel: West Bank Barrier Endangers Basic Rights."

[92] Ibid. See also NGO Monitor, "HRW's Political Condemnation of Israel's Separation Barrier," October 4, 2003, http://www.ngo-monitor.org/editions/v2n02/v2n02-3.htm.

[93] NGO Monitor, "HRW's Political Condemnation."

[94] HRW, "Erased in a Moment, Suicide Bombing Attacks Against Israeli Civilians," October 2002, http://www.hrw.org/reports/2002/isrl-pa/.

[95] See, for example, the critique by Michla Pomerance, "Jurisdiction and Justiciability," *Israel Law Review* 38, nos. 1-2 (2005), p. 134-164.

[96] Tim Costello, "For the Children's Sake, Tear Down This Wall!," *The Age* (Melbourne), July 14, 2004.

[97] NGO Monitor, "Palestinian Affiliates of the International Commission of Jurists (ICJ)," March 31, 2003, http://www.ngo-monitor.org/editions/v1n06/v1n06-1.htm.

[98] NGO Monitor, "War on Want's War Against Israel," August 5, 2004, http://www.ngo-monitor.org/editions/v2n11/v2n11-6.htm.

[99] NGO Monitor, "Mennonite Central Committee Campaign & Newsletter Promotes Anti-Israel Propaganda," October 15, 2004, http://www.ngo-monitor.org/editions/v3n02/v3n02-1.htm.

[100] Simon J. Plosker, "Médecins du Monde Report Lacking in Credibility," *NGO Monitor*, March 7, 2005, http://www.ngo-monitor.org/article/_medecins_du_monde_report_lacking_in_credibility_.

[101] Christian Aid, "Why the Israeli 'Barrier' is Wrong," February 24, 2004, http://www.christian-aid.org.uk/news/features/0402barrier.htm.

International published a detailed report accusing Israel of "violat[ing] international law and ... contributing to grave human rights violations."[102]

These activities demonstrated that for these NGOs the details that led to the construction of the barrier, the discussion in the UN, and the ICJ advisory opinion were of little importance. The objective was to use these activities to single out Israel, condemn its actions, and promote sanctions, consistent with the Durban strategy.

Concurrent with the publicity given to the ICJ's "advisory opinion" in the second half of 2004, preparations began in Britain to promote an academic boycott via the major faculty unions. In addition, a campaign was launched to pressure selected commercial firms, such as the Caterpillar Corporation, to stop doing business with Israel. This boycott effort was accompanied by a great deal of publicity, including press conferences and rallies in which NGO officials took an active role. Similarly, the drive calling for divestment from Israel began in a number of churches in the United Kingdom, the United States, and Canada.

The momentum based on the NGO-led campaign against the "Apartheid Wall" faltered, despite the degree to which the International Court of Justice followed the script, when some governments that had supported the initial UN General Assembly resolution, including the EU and Canada, lost enthusiasm. As a result, the next phase, in which the General Assembly was expected to adopt the advisory opinion as the basis for considering sanctions, was delayed and watered down. However, the NGO network quickly found other ways to promote boycotts and sanctions.

VIII. BOYCOTT CAMPAIGNS IN THE DURBAN STRATEGY

In October 2004, following the model of the Jenin and "Apartheid Wall" campaigns, HRW released a 135-page glossy publication entitled "Razing Rafah," which condemned Israeli policy along the Egyptian border with Gaza.[103] This report focused primarily on allegations that Israeli responses to the smuggling of weapons and explosives in this area led to the unjustified demolition of Palestinian houses. HRW head Kenneth Roth came to Jerusalem's American Colony Hotel for a press conference and other media events to gain the widest possible coverage.[104] The largely unverified allegations in this report, based on Palestinian eyewitness accounts, provided the basis for the next stage, in which HRW promoted the effort to force Caterpillar to end its sales to Israel. HRW's activities also included mass emails and public letters, as well as participation in rallies outside a meeting of Caterpillar shareholders in Chicago.[105]

---

[102] Amnesty International, "Israel and the Occupied Territories: The Place of the Fence/Wall in International Law," February 19, 2004, http://web.amnesty.org/library/index/engmde 150162004.

[103] HRW, "Razing Rafah: Mass Home Demolitions in the Gaza Strip," October 2004, http://www.hrw.org/reports/2004/rafah1004/.

[104] NGO Monitor, "HRW's Report on Gaza: Lacking Credibility and Reflecting a Political Agenda," NGO Monitor Special Edition, October 18, 2004, http://www.ngo-monitor.org/editions/v3n02/ResponsetoHRWPressRelease.htm.

[105] "Speakers for Press Conference in Chicago, Biographies and Contact Information," no date, http://www.catdestroyshomes.org/article.php?id=298; HRW, "Israel: Caterpillar Should Suspend Bulldozer Sales," November 21, 2004, http://www.hrw.org/en/news/2004/11/21/israel-caterpillar-should-suspend-bulldozer-sales.

HRW was joined by many other NGOs in these activities, including Amnesty International, the Israeli Committee Against Housing Demolitions (ICAHD), Sabeel Ecumenical Liberation Theology Center, and War on Want, which enlisted entertainment celebrities in its high-profile campaign against the "wall" and in favor of divestment.[106] Caterpillar was the public relations focus of the effort to impose economic sanctions and boycotts on Israel.

In parallel, other NGOs supported a group of anti-Israel extremists in the United Kingdom, including Sue Blackwell and Hillary Rose, seeking to gain approval from the Association of University Teachers (AUT) for a boycott of Israeli universities.[107] The AUT boycott effort was initiated in 2002 as part of the Jenin "massacre" campaign and was revived in the context of the separation barrier campaign and the ICJ decision. The language of the boycott resolution was written and publicized by the Palestinian NGO network (PNGO).[108] Many members of PNGO were active in Durban, and PNGO co-sponsored a conference held in London during December 2004 that relaunched the boycott movement. Although initially successful, this effort also faltered when AUT delegates voted to rescind earlier decisions.[109] In terms of public relations and propaganda, however, the momentum behind the demonization process was maintained.

In the wake of the boycott campaigns, another front was opened based on a series of anti-Israel divestment resolutions and debates adopted and publicized by Lutheran, Anglican, and other politicized Protestant church groups. The church-based divestment campaign was promoted by many of the active Palestinian NGOs, such as MIFTAH, BADIL (a radical group that promotes refugee claims), Al-Mezan (based in Gaza); ADRID; Ittijah (an Israeli-Arab NGO), the Applied Research Institute Jerusalem (ARIJ), and others.

The divestment campaign also gained visibility through the activities of Christian-based NGOs, such as the Mennonite Central Committee, which is based in North America and receives significant Canadian government funding, Sabeel, and groups such as Christian Peacemaker Teams (CPT)[110] and the Ecumenical Accompaniment Programme in Palestine and Israel (EAPPI).[111] The church-based divestment campaign illustrates the "soft power" influence of NGOs over institutional actors.

---

[106] NGO Monitor, "HRW and Amnesty Promote Caterpillar Boycott," April 13, 2005, http://www.ngo-monitor.org/editions/v3n08/HRWAndAmnestyPromoteCaterpillarBoycott.htm; NGO Monitor, "War on Want's War against Israel."

[107] For a detailed study of the forces that contributed to the academic boycott movement, see Manfred Gerstenfeld, ed., *Academics against Israel and the Jews* (Jerusalem: Jerusalem Center for Public Affairs, 2007). More specifically on the UK, see the essays by Fraser and Gerstenfeld in the same book.

[108] NGO Monitor entry on PNGO, http://www.ngo-monitor.org/archives/infofile.htm#pngo.

[109] Ronnie Fraser, "The Academic Boycott of Israel: Why Britain?" (Papers in Post-Holocaust and Anti-Semitism 36, no. 1, Jerusalem Center for Public Affairs, September 2005), http://www.jcpa.org/phas/phas-36.htm.

[110] NGO Monitor, "Christian Peacemaker Teams (CPT)," no date, http://www.ngo-monitor.org/article/christian_peacemaker_teams_cpt_.

[111] NGO Monitor, "Ecumenical Accompaniment Programme in Palestine and Israel (EAPPI)," no date, http://www.ngo-monitor.org/article/ecumenical_accompaniment_programme_in_palestine_and_israel_eappi_.

For example, War on Want,[112] Christian Aid, and Sabeel were instrumental in the Church of England's initial vote for "morally responsible investment" (essentially divestment) in relation to Caterpillar. Christian Aid's films and Christmas campaigns, such as "Peace Under Siege" and "Child of Bethlehem," and War on Want's "alternative" report on Caterpillar influenced the Church debate in 2005 and laid the foundations that Sabeel exploited the following year. In January 2006, Rev. Stephen Sizer, vice-chair of Friends of Sabeel UK and a proponent of "replacement theology," introduced a resolution on divestment at the meeting of the Synod. The participants—including the head of the Church, the Archbishop of Canterbury, who also sits in the House of Lords—approved this move.[113]

Thus, NGO influence on the Synod's motion on divestment was tangible: the vocabulary of "morally responsible investment" was coined by Sabeel, and the text called for members to visit "recent house demolitions."[114] Sabeel was joined by the small EU-funded NGO ICAHD, which provides a platform for Jeff Halper, an Israeli who regularly appears alongside Ateek. As a Jew and an Israeli, Halper's appearances are seen as providing "legitimacy" for Sabeel's extremist agenda, in the form of a counter to allegations of antisemitic motivations.

As in the case of the AUT academic boycott, the furor following the adoption of this resolution led to a declaration by the Church's decision-making body stating that it would not implement the motion. But the threat, as well as the promotion of this form of anti-Israeli boycott activity in the overall Durban strategy, gained additional attention.

IX. Responding to NGO Post-Colonialism and Antisemitism

The activities of politicized NGOs active in the Israeli-Palestinian conflict reflect the post-ideological essentialism in which Palestinians are automatically identified as victims and Israel is always the aggressor. The campaigns that promote this ideology exploit the rhetoric of human rights, humanitarian assistance, and international law in an effort to delegitimize Israel through the apartheid label. Protected by the "halo effect" and the absence of accountability, the NGO network has provided a foundation for campaigns designed to promote international condemnation of Israel, followed by embargoes, boycotts, and, eventually, dismemberment. By using unique criteria to judge and condemn and erasing the context of terrorism and legitimate self-defense, the process of singling out Israel and promoting antisemitism is extended.

As the evidence presented in this study shows, the central role of NGOs that claim to promote human rights and humanitarian aid in the demonization of Israel can be explained, to a significant degree, by the combination of two ideological

---

[112] Bernard Josephs, "War on Want Urges Sanctions Against Israel," *Jewish Chronicle*, May 18, 2005, available at http://www.ngo-monitor.org/archives/news/WaronWantUrgesSanctions AgainstIsrael.htm.

[113] Ruth Gledhill, "Synod in Disinvestment Snub to Israel," *The Times* (UK), February 7, 2006, http://www.timesonline.co.uk/tol/news/uk/article728027.ece. For details on the roles of Sabeel and Sizer, see entry and references at NGO Monitor, "Sabeel Ecumenical Liberation Theology Center," http://www.ngo-monitor.org/article/sabeel_ecumenical_liberation_theology_center.

[114] Sabeel, "A Call for Morally Responsible Investment: A Nonviolent Response to the Occupation," May 2005, http://www.sabeel.org/pdfs/A%20nonviolence%20sabeel%20website.pdf.

dimensions that are often found in this community: the ideology of civil society and the ideology of post-colonialism. This combination, along with the huge resources available to the political NGO network, allows these organizations to promote campaigns of one-sided condemnation and singling-out of Israel using the rhetoric of human rights, global morality, and international law.

However, this ideological combination is increasingly inconsistent with the observable empirical evidence, and NGOs need to go to greater and greater lengths to argue convincingly that Israel is purely an aggressor and that Palestinian groups like Hamas, Islamic Jihad, or the Fatah-based Al Aqsa Martyrs' Brigades, are powerless victims. (The same is true with respect to Hezbollah and the 2006 Lebanon War.) The cognitive dissonance necessary to sustain these images is growing and will eventually become unsustainable.

Furthermore, many of the ideological elements in this framework are internally contradictory. As these contradictions gain greater exposure, the NGOs that promote this process will be forced to use resources to defend their records. In particular, the allocation of *a priori* labels to the Palestinians ("victims") and Israel ("aggressor"), regardless of actual behavior, is antithetical to the universal norms of human rights and international law. Similarly, the context of Palestinian and Arab violence that is systematically erased in these accounts must be restored.

As a result of the growing debate on this missing context, the blatant ideological bias in NGO reports has begun to attract critical attention. While the decision-making process regarding the allocation of resources to NGOs remains very secretive—yet another example of the lack of transparency among NGOs—there have been some important changes. For example, HRW's reconstituted Middle East Advisory Board instituted significant changes to offset the extreme imbalance in this NGO's focus on condemnations of Israel between 2000 and 2004. In 2005, HRW's reports on the Middle East were more evenly distributed, including analyses of human rights abuses in Libya, Saudi Arabia, Iran, and elsewhere. In 2006, however, the Lebanon War initiated by Hezbollah provided HRW with an opportunity to return to its former pattern,[115] as did the Gaza war in late 2008.

To continue this process of exposure, it will be necessary to remove the "halo effect" that has protected the ideological biases of NGO officials from scrutiny. Powerful individuals, such as Kenneth Roth of HRW and Irene Kahn of Amnesty International, are frequent commentators on radio and television, and their analyses appear in the pages of major newspapers. These analyses and claims regarding allegations of human rights abuses are repeated in the media, where they are presented as unbiased, objective, and credible.[116]

In December 2005, based on NGO Monitor reports, growing criticism of Christian Aid's biases was voiced in the *Jewish Chronicle* (London) and echoed by prominent Jewish figures, prompting the heads of this powerful NGO to request a meeting with the Chief Rabbi of the United Kingdom, Jonathan Sachs. As a result of

---

[115] NGO Monitor, "Report on HRW's Activities in 2006: Political Bias Undermines Human Rights," June 26, 2007, http://www.ngo-monitor.org/article/report_on_hrw_s_activities_in_political_bias_undermines_human_rights.

[116] Fiamma Nirenstein, "The Journalists and the Palestinians," *Commentary* 111, no. 1 (January 2001).

this meeting and a desire to demonstrate that Christian Aid's leaders were not antisemitic and anti-Israel, a consultation agreement was reached on future Christian Aid reports and activities related to Israel.

Indeed, NGO Monitor has observed a decrease in Christian Aid's use of theological themes and a limited decline in direct anti-Israel activity, although its cooperation with groups like Sabeel and the Alternative Information Center continues.[117] Nevertheless, to a limited degree, the consultation agreement and the meeting itself reflect a weakening of the "halo effect."

Detailed NGO Monitor reports and analyses on the role of government funding of radical anti-Israel NGOs in Canada and Europe have also begun to have an impact. Beginning in January 2006, the EU pledged to implement transparency in providing information on the funding of Israeli NGOs, including political groups such as the Arab Association for Human Rights, PHR-I, and Machsom Watch. In Canada, members of the opposition Conservative Party raised the issue of funding for politicized NGOs by the government funding agency, known as CIDA [now DFATD—Ed.], which has provided funding for BADIL and the pro-Palestinian Mennonite Central Committee, which, in turn, supports other NGOs.[118] The Conservative Party's victory in the January 2006 elections led to some changes in this area, and CIDA has ended funding for BADIL and some other NGOs.

Perhaps most importantly, during the preparations for the 2009 Durban Review Conference (DRC), UN officials and representatives of several governments took measures to prevent a repetition of the ideological attacks that took place in 2001. Most importantly, no NGO Forum was authorized for 2009, and many funders limited support for NGO participation in the side events and the government forum. The Ford Foundation, which had been the main source of resources for the most radical NGOs at Durban, prevented the use of its funding for participation in the DRC. The government of Canada adopted similar restrictions.

Beyond the NGO dimension, a number of governments announced that they would not send official delegations to an antisemitic conference based on the Durban model. Canada was the first to adopt this position, and the government was backed by the two main opposition parties, demonstrating that this was not a partisan political decision. Later, as the draft declaration under negotiation was filled with language that reflected the 2001 NGO Forum, again singling out Israel for condemnation, the Israeli government announced its withdrawal. In the United States, the newly elected Obama administration attempted to apply its policy of engagement to the DRC, but when this failed to alter the text of the draft declaration, it also withdrew, followed by Italy, while other European governments threatened to withdraw.

The combined impact of these policies will take some time to become apparent, but this opposition to a repetition of the 2001 Durban experience and the rejection of a draft text singling out Israel may signal the weakening of the dominant ideological

---

[117] NGO Monitor, "Christian Aid 2008 Update: Promoting Conflict," November 25, 2008, http://www.ngo-monitor.org/article/christian_aid_update_promoting_conflict.

[118] NGO Monitor, "Assessing Canadian International Development Agency (CIDA) Funding for Political NGOs," September 22, 2005, http://www.ngo-monitor.org/editions/v4n02/CIDA.htm.

framework. This strategy must be sustained over many years and be able to mobilize significant resources in order to successfully restore the universality of human rights norms, in opposition to the dominant post-colonial ideologies that merge into anti-semitism.

Victims of Success:
How Envious Antisemitism Foments Genocidal Intent and Undermines Moral Outrage

Peter Glick*

I. INTRODUCTION

Why, still, the Jews? How can we understand not only more than two thousand years of antisemitic hostility, but the persistent belief in a diabolical Jewish conspiracy that controls world events? Antisemitism makes strange bedfellows; besides belief in Jewish conspiracy, is there any other ideological point of agreement between the likes of Martin Luther and Mahmoud Ahmadinejad, Henrich Himmler and Gore Vidal, or Richard Nixon and London's left-wing former mayor Ken Livingstone? What other conviction threads through the historical heart of Christianity, Nazi fascism, and Muslim extremism; or connects the traditional reactionary Right with the contemporary radical Left?

This essay explores the social psychological roots of anti-Jewish sentiment, arguing that the Jews are, in many ways, *victims of their own success*. As a result of their unique position in world history, the Jews have repeatedly been targets of envy, resulting in an especially virulent, volatile, and often violent form of prejudice toward a group perceived as a powerful, manipulative competitor. Conceptualizing antisemitism as an envious prejudice helps to explain: (a) its propensity to turn genocidal; (b) its tenacious persistence across millennia; (c) its focus on conspiracy theories; (d) its contemporary spread across the globe as well as both ends of the political spectrum; and (e) its failure to provoke the same moral outrage reserved for other forms of injustice.

One might presume that a high-achieving minority group would elicit universal admiration. In one sense, this is true: socio-economically successful minorities are viewed as extremely competent (see Fiske, Cuddy and Glick 2007). For example, consider the question "Who most fervently believes that the Jews are extremely clever?" The answer: Jews and antisemites. For Jews, ingroup competence is a point of pride—group esteem is enhanced by celebrating Jewish successes. Antisemites, however, interpret Jewish competence as menacing. Their suspicion of Jews' intentions makes Jewish competence a grave, even existential threat because it feeds into Jews' alleged abilities to control world events.

---

* Professor of Psychology, Lawrence University.

Why, then, do antisemites exaggerate Jewish competence and power? The Freudian view suggests that antisemites project their own repressed desires onto the Jews, who serve as a projective screen. Thus, "I want to control the world and indulge my animal urges" becomes "The Jews want to control the world and indulge their animal urges." This essay offers an alternative view, that stereotyping and attributional processes produce antisemites' exaggerated views of Jewish competence and malign intent. These stereotypes begin with a kernel of truth, namely observations of Jewish success which, in turn, lead to attributed competence. Stereotypes of Jewish competence remain relatively benign until combined with suspicions about Jews' motives. These suspicions foster antisemitic conspiracy theories ranging from exaggerated views of the Jews' role in a realistic conflict (e.g., the Israeli-Palestinian conflict) to demonstrably false fabrications (e.g., the *Protocols of the Elders of Zion*).

II. Envious Prejudice

Understanding "Why the Jews?" requires understanding that all prejudices are not alike. My colleagues Susan Fiske, Amy Cuddy, and I (Cuddy, Fiske, and Glick 2008; Fiske, Cuddy, and Glick 2007) have challenged the long-standing social psychological view of prejudice as a univalent antipathy toward outgroups (Allport 1954). Instead, we have shown that many prejudices are inherently ambivalent across two fundamental dimensions of stereotype content: *competence* and *warmth*. Some groups are stereotyped positively on one dimension but negatively on the other. Competence and warmth represent fundamental dimensions because they address two crucial questions about others: What are they capable of? Are they friends or foes?

Specifically, our Stereotype Content Model proposes that groups' social and economic status drives inferences about competence: People assume that successful or powerful groups *must* be highly competent (i.e., ambitious, intelligent, and skillful) and disadvantaged groups incompetent. However, perceived structural relations between groups determine warmth stereotypes. Minorities viewed as cooperative with (or, at least, not threatening to) mainstream society are stereotyped as *warm* (i.e., good-natured, well-intentioned, sincere) and groups viewed as having competing interests as cold, their motives toward others distrusted.

This approach yields a 2 x 2 classification scheme that encompasses but also expands on older views of prejudice. Prior conceptions of prejudice assumed that people have wholly positive stereotypes of dominant ingroups, viewing them as competent and warm, resulting in *admiration*. By contrast, outgroups were assumed to elicit completely negative stereotypes as incompetent and cold, resulting in *contempt*. The Stereotype Content Model additionally proposes two types of ambivalent prejudice. In the first, low status groups that are perceived as cooperative or non-threatening (e.g., traditional women, the elderly, and the disabled) are stereotyped as incompetent, but also as warm, eliciting *paternalistic prejudice*. Paternalism combines affection with patronizing behavior, such as "the soft bigotry of low expectations."

The second type of ambivalence occurs toward minorities viewed as both successful and competitors, such as Jews. Their socio-economic success fosters stereotypes of competence. But whether competence is admired or elicits hostility depends on whether it is paired with perceived warmth or coldness; competence represents a favorable trait in an ally, but a threatening trait in an enemy. The successful but competitive combination yields a competent but cold stereotype, resulting in *envious prejudice*. Kierkegaard defined envy as an "unhappy admiration," noting that it motivates attempts to cut the other down to size.

III. Envious Prejudice, Scapegoating, and Genocide

Even if envied, successful minorities may be tolerated for their perceived skills when times are good. But such minorities are especially likely to be suspected of maliciousness when times are bad, eliciting scapegoating or blame for having caused societal misfortunes (Glick 2002). This contention differs sharply from past scapegoating theory. Classic scapegoating theory (see Allport 1954) suggests that frustrations, whether individualized or shared (e.g., an economic crisis) create an irrational, frustration-induced aggression "vented" onto innocent, weak, and vulnerable outgroups, just as a child might attack a helpless family pet rather than the powerful parent who induced frustration by punishing her. In this view, conspiracy theories represent *post hoc* rationalizations of an automatic and infantile aggressive response to frustration.

The frustration-aggression theory of scapegoating misses some crucial points. My ideological model of scapegoating (Glick 2002, 2005, 2008) expands on the Stereotype Content Model to explain not only why scapegoating occurs but which types of groups face particular risk of becoming targets of scapegoating and genocide. Ervin Staub (1989, 2008) has persuasively shown that collective frustrations precede genocides. Such frustrations elicit a propensity to blame someone or some group, but not just anyone or any group will do. Scapegoating represents a *collective attribution process* initiated by shared or society-wide frustrations rather than isolated individual problems. When shared crises occur, rather than blindly lashing out, people collectively search for *culturally plausible* narratives about why circumstances have deteriorated. This desire to know who or what caused shared problems represents a generally adaptive process. Only by diagnosing the source of problems can people work toward effective solutions. Widespread social problems, however, tend to have complex, diffuse, impersonal causes. Therefore, the rational motive to explain these problems can be overwhelmed by the difficulty of finding an answer.

Scapegoating, then, can be viewed as a form of social attribution. Heider (1958) noted that when making attributions about who might have caused an outcome, perceivers consider both capability and intent: who has the ability to cause the effect and might also want to bring it about? To deliberately engineer widespread, complex social misfortunes (e.g., an economic crisis) requires both a high degree of competence and the cold intent to cause widespread harm. Stereotypes, unfortunately, may provide culturally plausible, even if completely wrong-headed answers. Groups that are widely perceived as competent but cold fit the attributional logic of blame, predisposing them to be chosen as scapegoats.

Other factors also weigh in. A history (even if ancient) of conflict or continuing conflict increases the likelihood of scapegoating. Realistic conflict—for territory or other resources—or past exploitation by a minority elite reinforces suspicions about another group's intentions. Additionally, there are many psychological reasons why people find scapegoat ideologies attractive. For example, it is much more appealing to blame an outgroup than one's own group as the source of societal misfortunes.

To be effective at explaining a crisis, scapegoat ideologies must necessarily exaggerate the perceived competence of the scapegoated group. At the same time, they propose how the enemy, once unmasked, can be overcome. Thus scapegoating ideologies not only fuel resentment but motivate and organize mass violence. When shared misfortunes are viewed as the result of intentional maliciousness by a powerful minority, eliminating this group becomes the "logical" solution. A competent and powerful "enemy" cannot be controlled but must be destroyed, psychologically justifying genocidal attacks as "self-defense" against an implacable foe.

Genocides do not spontaneously erupt as people vent frustrations. The bureaucratic and systematized killing in the Holocaust most vividly illustrates this fact. Although the Rwandan genocide, with its low-tech use of mobs with machetes, may seem like a counter-example, the killings were highly coordinated, directed by the government through radio broadcasts (Gourevitch 1998). Genocidal movements undoubtedly both permit and spawn individual's voluntary acts of sadism as people incorporate themselves into a brutal system, but the bulk of the violence is top-down and highly organized.

In the view offered here, scapegoating represents a mix of relatively "rational" and "irrational" processes. On the one hand, it is adaptive and rational to try to diagnose the causes of a persistent social crisis and, if there is a history of realistic conflict between groups, suspecting an established foe makes sense. On the other hand, cultural biases in the form of exaggerated stereotypes, along with heightened psychological needs—for certainty, for self and group esteem—can lead people to scapegoat an innocent group.

IV. VICTIMS OF SUCCESS

The ideological model of scapegoating specifies why some groups, like the Jews, face greater risk of blame for social misfortunes. In general, successful minorities—so-called "model minorities," middle-man minorities, or what Chua (2003) refers to as market-dominant minorities—are most at risk for scapegoating. The irony is that the more successful such groups are, the more at risk they become when a crisis occurs. For example, it has long been noted that prior to the Nazi regime, Jews had greater success in Germany than most other European nations. The Nazis used the Jews' relative prominence as "evidence" of their alleged perfidy, that they had "infiltrated" and "corrupted" German society.

A number of historical examples of genocides and mass killings provide support for this model, with victims ranging from Armenians in Turkey, Jews in Germany, intellectuals and professionals in Cambodia, and the Tutsi in Rwanda (see Glick 2008). Comparing the Holocaust and Rwanda is especially instructive, because the propaganda toward the targets of these genocides is so well documented. Both the Nazis and Hutu *genocidaires* characterized their victims as powerful manipulators who had "stabbed us in the back." The imagery and written propaganda in these two cases is eerily, but not coincidentally similar. For example, the "Tutsi Ten Commandments" published in the newspaper *Kagura* in the 1990s (Mamdani 2001) was virtually identical to Nazi (and prior European antisemitic) characterizations of the Jews. The Tutsi were labeled as "blood and power thirsty," wanting to "impose their hegemony on the Rwandan people," and "dishonest in business."

V. But why always the Jews? An interdisciplinary approach

But how does this model account for the persistent targeting of Jews across millennia and its spread to new parts of the globe? By focusing on the consequences of a minority group's *structural position* in society, the Stereotype Content Model and the Ideological Model of Scapegoating provide frameworks for an interdisciplinary approach to this question. Looking through the social psychological lens these models provide reveals how, despite changes in historical particularities, the position of the Jews has consistently been in the "successful competitor" quadrant that reinforces competent but cold stereotypes and envious prejudice.

The saying that "the more things change, the more they remain the same" applies all too well to stereotypes about Jews. This is not because cultural stereotypes, once created, never change, but because the Jews have repeatedly occupied social positions that evoke and reinforce envious prejudice. Consider the origins of Christian antisemitism, which began when Christianity was a small break-away sect from Judaism; in other words, a time when Judaism had relatively greater status and power (Sandmel 1976). From an early Christian perspective, most Jews' rejection of Jesus' divinity represented a potentially fatal threat to their religious view. If Jesus was the Messiah, how could his own community, God's Chosen People, reject him? The psychological solution was to view the Jews as "children of the devil" who engineered Christ's death, manipulating the Roman authorities, creating a template for the many Jewish conspiracy theories that followed (Rubenstein 1966). What could represent a more powerful or evil conspiracy than killing the very Son of God?

From a structural stereotyping perspective, the later economic role of Jews in Europe as middle-men merchants and especially as money-lenders once again cast them in the stereotypically competent but cold role. Money-lenders are readily resented as profiting from others' misery. While this economic niche originated in prohibitions against Christians engaging in usury, it became an independent, secular complement to religiously-based antisemitism (Rubenstein 1966). From a social structural standpoint, the general effect was the same as religiously motivated anti-Judaism: Jews were seen as powerful, conspiratorial, self-interested competitors.

Money-lending, of course, later developed into banking, and the great wealth amassed by a few, such as the Rothschilds, has long fostered financial conspiracy theories about the Jews. The Nazi's later antisemitism featured continued resentment of the Jews' economic role, combined with a backlash against perceptions of their growing cultural influence in Germany. In the propaganda film *The Eternal Jew*, the Nazis bitterly complained about Jews' prominence in German industry, high status professions, the media, art, and culture. While perceived as ultimately inferior to Aryans, Nazis viewed the Jews as diabolically clever and fervently believed in an "international Jewish conspiracy." In the 1930s, initial actions against the Jews were only gradually ratcheted up as the Nazis attempted to feel out not only how fellow Aryans would react but also how the rest of the world, believed to be manipulated by powerful Jews, would respond.

In the past sixty years, obviously, the establishment of the modern Israeli state through colonial partition has inflamed and continues to exacerbate antisemitism. Israel's military and economic success provides support for stereotypes of Jews as hyper-competent and powerful. Realistic conflict with Palestinians and Arab nations hardens characterizations of Jews as cold and malevolent. To say that Israel's close relationship with the United States does not help the situation is a gross understatement. Whether Israel is viewed as the hand-maiden or the tail that wags the dog (Mearsheimer and Walt 2007), its special relationship with the world's hyperpower—itself not universally viewed as benevolent or warm—buttresses antisemitism in large swaths of the globe. Finally, as a group, the Jews have overcome displacement and oppression to attain economic success in the United States as well. The relative success of Jews in finance, the media, government, and academia means that, as a minority group, contemporary American Jews remain positioned in ways that reinforce envious stereotyping.

Thus, it is no surprise that the economic crisis that emerged in 2008 amplified antisemitism. An internet conspiracy theory not only blamed Jewish bankers but linked them with Israel, claiming that Lehman Brothers sent four hundred billion dollars to Israel just prior to the firm's collapse (a May 2009 Google search for Israel + Lehman + conspiracy yielded 148,000 hits). Indeed, reactions to the current economic crisis nicely illustrate the shortcomings of older scapegoating theory. A *Wall Street Journal* article (Stoll 2009) cited former Secretary of Labor Robert Reich's worry that the economic crisis would spawn populist rage against various minorities: Jews, homosexuals, and Blacks. Should homosexuals or Blacks be particularly worried about receiving the blame for an economic recession? While social stressors may increase all forms of prejudice, Blacks and homosexuals are not stereotyped as competent but cold conspirators or viewed as uniquely well-positioned to have deliberately caused economic havoc.

By contrast, the Jews, even without the infamous shyster Bernie Madoff as a poster-boy, remain likely targets. A May 2009 Google search for "Jewish bankers" + "conspiracy" yielded about 13,800 hits. Invoking the major ethnicity of U.S. bankers by searching for "White bankers" + "conspiracy" yielded considerably fewer hits at 2,940. "White male bankers" + "conspiracy" turned up only 74 hits. What about the other minorities Robert Reich frets about? "Black bankers" + "conspiracy" yielded 129 hits, and "homosexual bankers" + "conspiracy" just 3. Interestingly, *restricting* the last two searches by adding "Jewish" revealed almost the same number of hits; 120/129 hits for "Black bankers" and 2/3 of hits for "homosexual bankers." A closer look showed that Black bankers were typically viewed as puppets or tools in an explicitly Jewish conspiracy to sell mortgages in poor neighborhoods. And the isolated "homosexual bankers" conspiracy typically referred to *Jewish* homosexual bankers. The Jews remain the scapegoat of choice not because they are general targets of prejudice but because they are targets of envious prejudice, stereotyped as both capable and willing to have caused (and profited by) an economic meltdown.

VI. Conspiracy Theories: Biased, But Not Exactly "Crazy"

The unfortunate fact is that because scapegoating is partly rooted in kernels of truth combined with deeply entrenched suspicions, it can be extraordinarily difficult to draw a sharp dividing line between rational mistrust and antisemitic rant or between realistic conflict and misplaced hostility. At what point on a continuum between the observation that "There are a number of Jews prominent in investment banking and the government" and the claim that "The Jews control Wall Street and the U.S. government" has the antisemitic line been crossed?

This is not merely a rhetorical question, but a difficult and vexing debate. Consider the controversy over a 2006 Harvard working paper and later 2007 book, *The Israel Lobby and U.S. Foreign Policy* by John Mearsheimer and Stephen Walt, policy experts from the University of Chicago and Harvard. Some commentators viewed Mearsheimer and Walt's thesis about how the Israeli lobby has hijacked U.S. policy to have crossed the line into antisemitic conspiracy mongering. The *Washington Post* trotted out dueling *Cohanim*, with one Op-Ed piece by Eliot Cohen claiming "Yes, it's antisemitic" (E. Cohen, 2006) followed by another in which Richard Cohen (R. Cohen, 2006) came to precisely the opposite conclusion.

Whether or not one believes that this particular analysis of the pro-Israel lobby was fair scholarship or infected with antisemitism, it is unhelpful to simply dismiss anti-Jewish conspiracy theorists as psychotically "out of touch with reality." Rather, conspiracy theories rest on a few facts—the reality of Jewish success—combined with largely untestable suspicions about Jews' intentions. Factually, Jews *have* achieved prominent roles out of proportion to their numbers. If they were clannish, coldly self-interested, and conspiratorial surely they would be clever enough to deny and hide it. How can such suspicions possibly be disproved? Conspirators can be expected to mask their intentions, presenting a smiling face to those they want to manipulate. In short, a few facts combined with entrenched suspicions lend conspiracy theories an undeniable logic among believers.

Further, there is a basic asymmetry between how easy it is to establish warmth (or perceived good intent) versus coldness (or bad intent). People generally hide immoral behavior, so when it emerges, perceivers pay attention (Hamilton and Gifford 1976). Further, perceivers realize that it is more costly to trust an unscrupulous person than to be wary of someone who turns out to have good intent. As a result, negative behavior more strongly influences perceivers' attitudes than positive behavior. Nicole Tausch and her colleagues (Tausch, Kenworthy, and Hewstone 2007) have recently shown that people demand many "nice" behaviors to confirm the impression that someone is warm. By contrast, it takes relatively few anti-social behaviors to decide that someone is cold.

The opposite is also true—it is extremely difficult to combat established impressions of cold intent. If one suspects that another person has manipulative intent, it makes sense to look at apparent demonstrations of good will (e.g., a telemarketer's apparent friendliness or "free offer") with a jaundiced eye. Apparent good will could represent a clever attempt to get close enough for a stab in the back. Even repeated demonstrations of good behavior are easily undermined by one or two salient negative instances. Being caught committing fraud one time, for example, outweighs many instances of honest dealing. For a group historically stereotyped as cold manipulators, the salient bad behavior of one member, such as Bernie Madoff, does tremendous damage. As a result, combating stereotypes of coldness and related suspicions about intent is like trying to crawl out of quicksand. The difficulty of disconfirming suspicions through positive acts and the ease with which isolated negative instances can reactivate old suspicions partially explains the stubborn persistence of conspiracy theories about Jews.

VII. Globalization and the Spread of Antisemitism from West to East, Right to Left

Once established, conspiracy theories can easily spread, especially in a world that is now connected through instantaneous and cheap communication. But the fact that people *can* spread these ideas does not explain which ideas will be ignored or embraced, which internet conspiracy theory will languish or "go viral." The Stereotype Content Model stresses the importance of interdependence, whether cooperative or competitive in motivating people to attend to others. Perceivers can afford to ignore groups whose actions have no implications for their own outcomes, but experience strong motivation to "figure out" and characterize groups or nations whose actions have personal consequences. Thus, conspiracy theories about Jews have found buyers in new markets (e.g., in the Far East, see Huang 2008) not just because the world is increasingly interconnected but because the world is increasingly *interdependent*.

As current events amply illustrate, what happens on Wall Street, in Washington D.C., and in the Middle East can quickly produce huge effects across the globe. In the past, the average Chinese person may not have cared much about figuring out Wall Street. But after experiencing a drop in standard of living due to a global economic crisis that originated from Wall Street speculation, suddenly understanding Wall Street matters. From this perspective, it is not surprising that a book peddling a conspiracy theory about how Jews on Wall Street control international finance has become a best-seller in China (Huang 2008). The book, *Currency Wars*, has not only sparked general interest in China, but gained particular popularity among government officials. That the author Song Hongbing has defended himself against claims of antisemitism by noting that, like most Chinese, *even he* thinks the Jews are "really smart, maybe the smartest people on earth" is hardly reassuring, As noted above, belief in the Jews' (diabolical) cleverness merely reinforces, rather than dispels, the charge.

The contemporary position of Jews also explains why antisemitism has spread not just geographically, but warps the political landscape so that the two ends of the spectrum meet. Israel's conflict with the Palestinians and the Israeli-U.S. alliance represent a double strike against the Jews for many on the Left. As a result, antisemitism has spread from its traditional (and continuing) home among the authoritarian Right to those in the contemporary political Left who associate Israel, and therefore Jews, with oppression and U.S. hegemony (e.g., see M. Cohen 2007). For example, a 2004 article in *Adbusters* (a leftist magazine) claims that of the "50 most influential neocons in the US ... half of them are Jewish." Its title asks "*Why won't anyone say they are Jewish?*" Antisemitism of the Left partially explains how the United Nations' 2009 anti-racism conference could begin with an opening-day address by Mahmoud Ahmadinejad, a Holocaust denier who has said that Israel should be "wiped off the map." Antisemitism in the demagogic guise of concern about the Jews' alleged racism hogged center stage while other problems, such as genocide in Darfur, took a back seat.

In short, Jews' social position puts them at risk of attack from both sides of the political spectrum. Both Left and Right-wing antisemites see the Jews as having infiltrated, even taken over, the traditional power structure. Antisemites of the Right resent Jews as a perceived threat to traditional White, European, Christian dominance. Antisemites of the Left, who want to topple the traditional power hierarchy, see the Jews as traitors to the cause, transforming from oppressed victims of the Holocaust to today's oppressors in Gaza and the West Bank and in the halls of power in the United States.

VIII. Lack of Moral Outrage

Finally, Jews' position as a powerful minority suggests why antisemitism may elicit less moral outrage than other prejudices. It is much more socially acceptable to express hostility toward a successful or powerful group than toward a clearly disadvantaged minority. Power elicits envy rather than sympathy. Hostile comments or jokes about dominant groups, such as white men, tend not to elicit charges of racism, except among the likes of Rush Limbaugh. Similarly, because they do not seem to be oppressed, successful minorities, such as Jews, may not receive the same protections accorded to disadvantaged groups. It makes sense to exclude successful minorities from social policies, such as affirmative action, that are designed to address socioeconomic disadvantage. But successful minorities may also be psychologically excluded from sympathy, concern, and outrage over verbal attacks, even though they face an insidiously dangerous kind of prejudice that, history tells us, can rapidly turn genocidal.

IX. Conclusions

Unfortunately, the approach outlined here does a better job of diagnosing the problem than suggesting solutions. And the diagnosis seems rather grim. The good news? Elements of the radical Right and Left, Islamic and Christian fundamentalists, and conspiracy theorists all over the world all agree on something. The bad news? That "something" is that the Jews are probably up to no good. This is not to say that antisemitism is universally shared. Even though Jews may face increased danger from individual hate crimes during crises, such as the current economic meltdown, it seems extremely unlikely that Jews will experience another attempt at genocide in a contemporary Western democracy.

But antisemitic conspiracy theories pose a clear and present threat—not just to the Jews, but the world as a whole—because they harden the Middle Eastern conflict, with suspicion constantly undermining negotiated solutions. The persistence of Jewish conspiracy theories clearly does not help the chances that Western governments will muster the political will to pressure both sides to accept a resolution. In the end, as the Holocaust recedes further and further into history, the general perception of Jews and Israel as successful and powerful may undermine any sense of urgency to address worldwide antisemitism even as this same belief in Jewish success sews the seeds for future scapegoating.

REFERENCES

Adanir, F. 2001. "Armenian deportations and massacres in 1915." In *Ethnopolitical warfare: Causes, consequences, and possible solutions*, edited by E. Chirot and M.E.P. Seligman, 71-81. Washington, DC: American Psychological Association.
Allport, G.W. 1954. *The nature of prejudice*. Reading, MA: Addison-Wesley.
Chua, A. 2003. *World on fire: How exporting free market democracy breeds ethnic hatred and global instability*. New York: Doubleday.
Cohen, E.A. 2006. "Yes, it's antisemitic." *The Washington Post*, April 5, A23.
Cohen, M. 2007. "Antisemitism and the Left that doesn't learn." *Dissent* (Fall). http://www.dissentmagazine.org/article/?article=972.
Cohen, R. 2006. "No, it's not antisemitic." *The Washington Post*, April 25, A23.
Cuddy, A.J.C., S.T. Fiske, and P. Glick. 2008. "Warmth and competence as universal dimensions of social perception: The Stereotype Content Model and the BIAS Map." In *Advances in Experimental Social Psychology* vol. 40, edited by M.P. Zanna, 61-150. Thousand Oaks, CA: Academic Press.
Fiske, S.T., A.J.C. Cuddy, and P. Glick. 2007. "Universal dimensions of social cognition: Warmth and competence." *Trends in Cognitive Science* 11: 77-83.
Glick, P. 2002. "Sacrificial lambs dressed in wolves' clothing: Envious prejudice, ideology, and the scapegoating of Jews." In *Understanding genocide: The social psychology of the Holocaust*, edited by L.S. Newman and R. Erber, 113-142. New York: Oxford University Press.
Glick, P. 2005. "Choice of scapegoats." In *On the nature of prejudice: 50 years after Allport*, edited by J.F. Dovidio, P. Glick and L.A. Rudman 244-261. Malden, MA: Blackwell Publishing.
Glick, P. 2008. "When neighbors blame neighbors: Scapegoating and the breakdown of ethnic relations." In *Explaining the breakdown of ethnic relations: Why neighbors kill*, edited by V.M. Esses and R.A. Vernon, 123-146. Malden, MA: Blackwell.
Gourevitch, P. 1998. *We wish to inform you that tomorrow we will be killed with our families: Stories from Rwanda*. New York: Farrar, Strauss and Giroux.
Hamilton, D.L., and R.K. Gifford. 1976. "Illusory correlation in interpersonal perception: A cognitive basis of stereotypic judgment." *Journal of Experimental Social Psychology* 12: 392-407.
Heider, F. 1958. *The psychology of interpersonal relations*. New York: John Wiley & Sons.
Huang, H. 2008. "China, antisemitic conspiracy theories and Wall Street." *New York Times*, October 2. http://economix.blogs.nytimes.com/author/hung-huang.
Mamdani, M. 2001. *When victims become killers: Colonialism, nativism, and the genocide in Rwanda*. Princeton, NJ: Princeton University Press.
Mearsheimer, J.J., and S.M. Walt. 2007. *The Israel Lobby and U.S. Foreign Policy*. New York: Farrar, Strauss, and Giroux.
Rubenstein, R.L. 1966. *After Auschwitz: Radical theology and contemporary Judaism*. Indianapolis, IN: Bobbs-Merrill Educational Publishing.
Sandmel, S. 1978. *Antisemitism in the New Testament*. Philadelphia: Fortress Press.
Staub, E. 1989. *The roots of evil: The psychological and cultural origins of genocide*. Cambridge: Cambridge University Press.

Staub, E. 2008. "The origins of genocide and mass killing: Prevention, reconciliation, and their application to Rwanda." In *Explaining the breakdown of ethnic relations: Why neighbors kill*, edited by V.M. Esses and R.A. Vernon, 245-268. Malden, MA: Blackwell.

Stoll, I. 2009. "Antisemitism and the economic crisis." *Wall Street Journal*, April 6. http://online.wsj.com/article/SB123906114937094859.html.

Tausch, N., J. Kenworthy, and M. Hewstone. 2007. "The confirmability and disconfirmability of trait concepts revisited: Does content matter?" *Journal of Personality and Social Psychology* 92: 542-556.

"Why won't anyone say they are Jewish?" 2004. *Adbusters Magazine* (March/April). http://canadiancoalition.com/adbusters01.

Why Well-Intentioned Westerners Fail to Grasp the Dangers Associated with Islamic Antisemitism: Some Arguments Considered

Neil J. Kressel*

I. INTRODUCTION

Many observers of the Middle East and world affairs—some of whom are Jewish themselves—have dismissed warnings about the rise of a dangerous new antisemitism in the Middle East as unjustified, overblown, or otherwise unworthy of significant attention. Although some in this group of skeptics, are unconcerned because—despite their political interests—they remain uninformed about what is really going with regard to the Jews, others view warnings from mainstream Jewish organizations as the by-product of an overly sensitive Jewish psychology or, worse, as a nefarious political move designed to divert the gaze of honorable people from Israel's own human rights abuses. Even among those who agree that a virulent form of Jew-hatred has, indeed, taken hold in the Middle East, some maintain that, for a variety of reasons, this bigotry should not become a focal point of world attention.

All in all, human rights activists, progressive academics, social scientists, left-leaning political leaders, and others whom one might expect to stand stalwartly opposed to overt and extreme bigotry have been largely silent. Surprising to some, former President Bush (2003)—hardly a darling of progressive forces—did take some steps to focus world attention on Jew-hatred back in November 2003 when he called on world leaders to "... strongly oppose antisemitism, which poisons public debates over the future of the Middle East." But, on the whole, right-leaning American politicians have not been notably more concerned about antisemitism than those on the left. There has been no alarm, almost no research, and precious little concern from outside the Jewish community and allied organizations. My own field of social psychology, once a leader in the battle against segregation and anti-black racism in the United States, has failed even to begin to address problems associated with Muslim and Arab antisemitism (Kressel 2004).

My purpose here is to begin to answer the question why this is the case. Holocaust movies command huge audiences, and books and educational programs documenting the Nazi assault on European Jewry are still a growth industry. Social

---

* Visiting Associate Professor, Yale Initiative for the Interdisciplinary Study of Antisemitism (YIISA); Professor, Department of Psychology, William Paterson University.

scientific studies in the United States show fairly low levels of antisemitism when judged by historical standards (ADL 2002).[1] Students in many schools are taught the fundamentals of "racism and sexism," even before they are taught the fundamentals of reading and writing. Both major political parties in the United States claim an unshakeable commitment to the state of Israel. Why then, under such circumstances, have so few observers from outside the Jewish community been able or willing to grasp the dangerous nature of revitalized antisemitism in the Middle East?

An answer to this question requires: (1) documentation that dangerous Muslim antisemitism exists; (2) documentation that the world has not been devoting sufficient attention to this problem; (3) examination of the arguments offered by those who do not deem Muslim antisemitism a matter of major concern; (4) refutation of these arguments; and (5) exploration of the underlying ideological, psychological, social, and political sources of the failure to confront Muslim antisemitism. All of these issues are addressed to some degree in this paper, but the main focus is on the examination and refutation of arguments offered by those who think that the world need not focus on Muslim antisemitism.

II. DANGEROUS ANTISEMITISM REALLY EXISTS

It is not my goal here to make a systematic, airtight case that a dangerous and potentially genocidal hatred of the Jews has captured large segments of the Muslim and Arab world. For evidence supporting this position, which I believe is correct, one might examine works by Yossef Bodansky (1999), Robert Wistrich (2002), Marvin Perry and Frederick Schweitzer (2002), Phyllis Chesler (2003), Abraham Foxman (2003), Kenneth Timmerman (2003), Gabriel Schoenfeld (2004), Denis MacShane (2008), and Bernard Henri-Levi (2008), as well as various reports produced under the auspices of the Middle East Media Research Institute (MEMRI) (MEMRI 2002a; 2002b; 2002c; 2004a; 2004b; Solnick 2002; Milson 2004). One might also review the carefully documented study issued by the Israel-based Intelligence and Terrorism Information Center (ITIC) in 2008, which concludes, according to center director Reuven Erlich (quoted in Gur 2008), that: "This [Arab-Muslim antisemitism] isn't ordinary prejudice. This prejudice is evil because it isn't theoretical. It is ideological incitement by states and organizations with the practical means of translating it into action." It is also not the goal of this paper to present a full-blown explanatory theory of the origins of Muslim and Arab antisemitism. Still, some summary evidence concerning the depth, scope, and potential destructiveness of Muslim Jew-hatred in necessary in order to show just what it is that I am contending many observers in the West have failed to observe. Moreover, it is necessary to offer the rough frame of an explanatory framework, precisely because, as we shall see, several grounds for downplaying Middle Eastern Jew-hatred rest on disagreements over its origins rather than arguments about the existence of the phenomenon.

---

[1] There probably has been some increase in antisemitic beliefs in the United States in recent years, accounted for mainly by higher levels of prejudiced thinking about Jews among Blacks and Hispanics. Even so, the overall level of antisemitic beliefs remains substantially lower than it was in the first half of the twentieth century.

To the extent that few Westerners are fluent in Middle Eastern languages and many Middle Eastern antisemites speak differently to different audiences, it is perhaps best to start with evidence of Jew-hatred coming from translations of Middle Eastern media that were originally intended for Middle Eastern audiences, rather than with statements made directly for Western consumption. Such evidence is easy to find.

For example, a 2009 Hamas Friday sermon that was broadcast on al-Aqsa TV cited as an authoritative source the classic antisemitic *Protocols of the Elders of Zion*, a notorious forgery by the Czarist secret police in which "the Jews" plot to take over the world. According to the April 3 sermon (MEMRI 2009):

> ... [The Jews'] famous book, the existence of which is denied by the reasonable people among them, the so-called *Protocols of the Elders of Zion*—but we call it the Protocols of the Idiots of Zion.... In this book, the Jews included their plan to besiege the whole world by land, by air, by sea, by ideology, by economy, and by the media, as is happening today, my brothers in the nation of the Prophet Muhammad. The Jews today are weaving their spider webs in order to encircle our nation like a bracelet encircles the wrist, and in order to spread corruption throughout the world.

But the *Protocols* were not the only source that was cited as a basis for anti-Jewish sentiment. One might expect anger, whether justified or not, to stem from the winter 2008/2009 Israeli military action in Gaza, but the sermon cites a more distant and eternal source of fury: "We Muslims know best the nature of the Jews, because the Qur'an has informed us about this, and because the pure Sunna of the Prophet Muhammad has devoted much space to informing the Muslims of the truth about the Jews and their hostility to Islam and its Prophet." Of course, the Hamas sermon is hardly the final authority on what the Qur'an really says. But the sermon's policy recommendation was clear: "Allah willing, the moment will come when their property will be destroyed and their sons annihilated, until not a single Jew or Zionist is left on the face of the Earth."

Similar dehumanizing and genocidal sentiments can also be found in a poem published by the Saudi poet S'ad Al-Bawardi (quoted in Chernitsky and Glass 2009) in the Saudi daily newspaper, *Al-Jazirah*:

> You were merciful, oh Hitler.
> [That is my conclusion] when I see around me
> The cruel acts
> Of the descendants of apes.
> You were wise, oh Hitler
> To rid the world
> Of some of these wild pigs.
> [But] they have spawned a gang
> [Whose heart] is filled with blind hatred...
> Oh Hitler,
> The descendents of apes—
> None are more cruel and horrifying than they are....

Now, of course, poets are given some license to express their views, and this poem was written in early 2009 in the midst of the Gaza war—which opened the gates to new levels of bigotry. But the sentiments in the poem date back to well before that war. Indeed, back in 1999, Israel had for several years been deeply involved in pursuing a peace process that would culminate the following year in Ehud Barak's offer to establish a two-state solution on terms generally judged favorable to the Palestinians. At that very time, *Mein Kampf* became a best-seller in the Palestinian territories, presumably not because of an upsurge in local interest in European history. Even in liberal Turkey, in 2005, *Mein Kampf* made it on to bestseller lists. And the *Protocols of the Elders of Zion* are frequently referenced in many Arab and Muslim countries, having been the subject of a 41-part TV series in 2002 in Egypt and, more recently, another one in Iran (MEMRI 2002c; ITIC 2009b). More and more often, the *Protocols* are cited as an unchallenged, respected historical source in Arab print and broadcast media.

Also, consider the importance of some of the religious and political leaders publicizing antisemitic ideas:

- In 2002, Sheikh Abdur-Rahman al-Sudais, an imam of the most important mosque in Mecca and a man described by the BBC as a moderate, sermonized that Jews are "... killers of prophets and the scum of the earth" (Kressel 2007b). The sheikh had explained that, "Allah had hurled his curses and indignation on them and made them monkeys and pigs and worshipers of tyrants." In this sermon, Al-Sudais described Jews as: "... a continuous lineage of meanness, cunning, obstinacy, tyranny, evil, and corruption...." It was not a new theme for the imam, who in November 2002 had called upon Allah to annihilate the Jews. He further advised Arabs to abandon all peace initiatives with the Jews.
- A Syrian Defense Minister, Mustafa Tlass, published a book, *The Matza of Zion*, attempting to revive medieval blood libel charges against the Jews. According to Tlass, "With the publication of this book, I intended to illuminate some of the secrets of the Jewish religion by [describing] the actions of the Jews, their blind and repugnant fanaticism regarding their belief, and the implementation of the Talmudic precepts compiled in the Diaspora by their rabbis who distorted the principles of the Jewish belief (the religious law of the Prophet Moses), as it is said in the Koran [2:79]..." (MEMRI 2002d).
- In 2003, just prior to his retirement, Mahathir Mohammed (2003), Malaysia's longest serving prime minister told a sympathetic assembly of Muslim leaders from across the globe that: "We [Muslims] are actually very strong, 1.3 billion people cannot be simply wiped out. The Nazis killed 6 million Jews out of 12 million [during the Holocaust]. But today the Jews rule the world by proxy. They get others to fight and die for them. They invented socialism, communism, human rights and democracy so that persecuting them would appear to be wrong so they may enjoy equal rights with others. With these they have now gained control of the most powerful countries" (ADL 2003).
- Speaking before the United Nations in September 2008, Iranian President Ahmadinejad declared: "The dignity, integrity and rights of the European and American people are being played with by a small but deceitful number of people called Zionists. Although they are miniscule minority, they have been dominating an important portion of the financial and monetary centers as well as the political decision-making centers of some European countries and the U.S. in a

deceitful, complex and furtive manner.... This means that the great people of America and various nations of Europe need to obey the demands and wishes of a small number of acquisitive and invasive people."
- In March 2009, on the al-Jazeera network, Sheikh Dr. Muhammad Yussuf al-Qardawi (quoted in ITIC 2009a), an influential Sunni religious authority, offered his own interpretation of a controversial *hadith* (i.e., a saying attributed to Muhammad.) Responding to a question about the role of the righteous in liberating the holy places of Islam, al-Qardawi said (according to a paraphrase by Memri.org) that the Prophet Muhammad said: "You will therefore continue to fight the Jews, and they will fight you until they are killed by the Muslims. The Jew is hiding behind the rock and the tree. The rock and the tree say, 'Oh, slave of Allah, oh, Muslim, here is the Jew behind me, come and kill him.'" Al-Qardawi interprets this *hadith* by saying that everything standing next to those who fight the Jews and liberate the lands, even the rock and the tree, will point out (the hiding places of) the Jews.

On any given day, one can find new instances of dehumanizing bigotry coming from high and diverse places. Prominent political and religious leaders have taken the lead. They popularize conceptions of Jews as "pigs and apes," a notion derived from an arguably misunderstood passage in the Qur'an (Solnick 2002). They portray Jews as immorality incarnate.

The conspiratorial component of recent antisemitic ideology deserves special attention, for it has received sanction from high places in the Arab world and reveals much about the anti-Jewish mindset (Kressel 2003). Conspiracy theories are needed to reconcile the claims of the hate ideology with the facts about Jews and Israel as they are generally presented in responsible Western circles. The basic idea is that the Jews are bent on taking over and ruling the world, though sometimes—to avoid the charge of antisemitism—the word "Zionist" is substituted for "Jew." Facts and historical occurrences are manufactured to buttress claims of conspiracy. Thus, to support the theory that Jews perpetrated the 9/11 attacks, elements in the mainstream Arab media reported nonexistent events including: arrests in America of Jews rejoicing in the streets, American media confirmation that 4,000 Jews had not shown up for work at the World Trade Center, and arrests of Israelis in Florida with large quantities of anthrax.

Another important point is that Middle Eastern antisemitic conspiracy theorists count as Jews many people who do not classify themselves as such; they typically publish lists of "Jews" occupying positions of influence in the American government, determining religious affiliation apparently on the basis of surnames. See, for example, postings on the Radio Islam web site such as one that first ran in January 1998 under the headline: "USA's Rulers—They are all Jews! Clinton's list." A key debate that surfaces periodically among the theorists concerns whether the Jews are king and America is pawn, or vice versa.

Increasingly, the point is to show the Jews as eternal and dangerous enemies of Muslims, making use of controversial passages in the Qur'an that appear to offer religious sanction for genocidal hatred of the Jews (Kressel 2007b, 139-198). The most virulent antisemites, such as Ahmadinejad, are often controversial figures who sometimes face strong domestic opposition, but this opposition very rarely focuses on their positions regarding the Jews. While intense hatred of the Jews is not consensual, few leaders see much point in mounting a defense that is bound to be unpopular. Indeed, the lack of locally-based, loud, prominent voices denouncing Muslim and Arab Jew-hatred is even more ominous than the presence of the voices of hate themselves. In July 2009, it was headline news when King Mohammed VI of Morocco declared the Holocaust one of the most tragic chapters of modern history; throughout much of the Muslim world the Nazi assault on European Jewry is unknown, disbelieved, diminished, or viewed as yet another crime in which the Zionists participated. So it took considerable bravery for a king simply to declare what every high school student in the West accepts as a basic truth. The king was only able to do so because he essentially criticized European Jew-haters of the past and stopped short of addressing the consequences on contemporary antisemitism in the Islamic world (Montesquiou 2009).

Quantitative data on Muslim antisemitism is hard to find. Elsewhere, I have offered some thoughts on why very little such data is available and why social scientists, for the most part, have neglected the study of one of the most severe and potentially dangerous forms of hatred in the contemporary world (Kressel 2004). Still, some fairly clear data do support the contention that some level of antisemitic sentiment is now very widely held by the populations of some Muslim-majority countries. For example, a report by The Pew Global Attitudes Project (2005), a group with no readily apparent agenda with regard to the topic, found 77% of Americans holding *favorable* views of Jews and only 7% holding unfavorable ones. The percentage of Germans holding favorable views of Jews was 67%. Similarly, Spaniards (58%), Frenchmen (82%), and Russians (63%) held favorable views of Jews. The percentage of Jordanians and Lebanese holding favorable views drops to zero, with 99-100% holding *unfavorable* views. In Morocco, a moderate, pro-Western Arab country, 88% of people hold negative views of Jews. In Pakistan, 74% are negatively inclined and in Indonesia, 76%. Even in Turkey, a potential member of the European Union, 60% hold negative views of Jews.

Muslim antisemitism is clearly global in scope, but just how dangerous is it? As I have written elsewhere:

> Some of the raw materials of mass hate can be found in almost every society on earth, often in plentiful supply. People everywhere tend to think in terms of 'us' and 'them,' and to prefer their own group. Across the globe, even the most tolerant people sometimes rely on simplistic stereotypes. No society has yet been able to free itself of sociopaths, extreme bigots, and aggressive personalities. And frustrating life conditions of one sort or another exist in every nation. [Moreover,] [f]anatics always seem to be sprouting evil schemes (Kressel 2002, 213).

Still, bigotry reaches murderous proportions in only a relatively small number of societies. To assess the danger of Muslim and Arab antisemitism, we must address how raw materials of mass hatred can combine in an explosive mixture. No simple formula can account for the many routes by which societies grow destructive. Each travels down its own idiosyncratic path colored by history, politics, culture, tradition, and leadership. Yet there are certain societal characteristics that distinguish relatively normal (though, of course, undesirable) animosities from those likely to erupt into murderous hatred. Some characteristics of potentially genocidal societies include: (1) widespread and intense public anger directed against a scapegoat; (2) dissemination by leaders of dehumanizing rhetoric; (3) cultural norms and values that tolerate or encourage violence against outgroups; (4) the existence of special cadres prepared to carry out violent acts; and (5) the lack of a strong constitutionally-based tradition of tolerance and checks and balances. Perhaps most important, there is great danger when ideologies of hatred capture large numbers of supporters, convincing them that the hated group is the source of their problems and that elimination of that group is the solution. There is even greater danger when such ideologies lack vocal domestic opponents (Kressel 2003).

No conclusive data can determine the extent to which the Muslim and Arab world exhibits these dangerous predisposing societal conditions. Yet few fair analysts who attend to media reports from the Middle East would argue against the proposition that there is widespread and intense public anger, dehumanizing rhetoric directed against the Jews, and a lack of a constitutionally-based tradition of checks and balances.

There are many grounds for pessimism. Few are more serious than the presence of Jew-hatred and the religious and educational socialization practices that prevail in some Muslim-majority countries (American Jewish Committee 2003; B'nai B'rith Foundation, n.d.; Harris 2003; Stalinsky 2003).

And then there are demagogues like Ahmadinejad and those in the Iranian leadership who will continue to promote his agenda even after he leaves the scene. Ahmadinejad has made no secret of his hatred for Jews or his desire to destroy Israel, possibly using the nuclear weapons that he or his associates seem destined to control in the near future. Opposition to Israel is not inherently antisemitic, but—as former Israeli ambassador to the United Nations Dore Gold (quoted in Mosgovaya 2008) notes—"[Ahmadinejad's] talk amounts to a violation of the genocide convention."

Putting all this together, it seems hard to deny that a more-than-garden-variety antisemitism prevails in many parts of the Muslim and Arab world—and that it has been spreading rapidly to the Muslim and Arab communities in Europe. The only reasonable matters for debate are: (1) whether this bigotry is merely serious, or whether it has become—or may soon become—murderous in intensity; and (2) whether countervailing forces, including (but not limited to) Israeli military power, Western liberal sentiments, the implicit threat of reprisals, religious and political restraints inside the Muslim world, the intrusion of other, more reality-based concerns of Muslims and Arabs, and lack of easy access to large numbers of Jews will serve to limit the damage caused by the widespread antisemitic ideology.

III. LISTENING TO THOSE WHO DENY THE SIGNIFICANCE OF MUSLIM AND ARAB ANTISEMITISM

During the past few years, I wrote several articles focusing on antisemitism in the Muslim and Arab world, and a book that touched on the topic as part of a broader study of the nature and origins of religious extremism. Although each work had its own objective, all sought to raise consciousness in the academic community about the dangers of the new antisemitism. In one piece (2004), I sought to explain the paucity of social scientific research on the topic. In another (2003), I explored the dangers associated with Muslim antisemitism and tried to identify the factors that were keeping it from becoming genocidal. The third piece (2007) aimed to elucidate the roots of Muslim and Arab antisemitism in four sources: (a) reactions to the Arab-Israeli conflict; (b) the legacy of Islamic history and theology; (c) the effects of frustration, anger, and scapegoating in an ailing culture; and (d) the results of widespread socialization of hatred. Though I am not a psychoanalyst, this last piece was published as the lead article in a special issue of the *International Journal of Applied Psychoanalytic Studies*, and others were asked to write responses to it. Ira Brenner (2007), a co-editor of the issue, wrote in his introduction that the paper:

> ... [threw] down the gauntlet and [offered] ... a documented view of the institutional initiative to promulgate hatred of Jews.... From the indoctrination of young children in schools and hate-mongering sermons from fiery clergymen to exploitation of the media through music, videos, TV shows and films, Dr. Kressel provides a very disturbing picture of a systematic poisoning of minds in Islamic regions today throughout the Middle East and beyond.

However, Nadia Ramzy (2007), the other co-editor, and several other respondents to my other writings on Muslim antisemitism were far less sympathetic.

It is useful to start with a few examples of how Muslim antisemitism and the dangers associated with it can be minimized. Writing in the *Chronicle of Higher Education*, Shabana Mir (2004)—a graduate student in educational policy—avers that:

> Neil Kressel worries that Islamic antisemitism is falling under the radar of social scientists. Perhaps in addition to studying antisemitism, they could study the efforts of numerous Muslims to combat antisemitism, sexism, homophobia, classism, exploitation, and neocolonialism. ... Some of the Muslim women I spoke to during my dissertation research would like to bring to your attention the anti-Muslim biases of Israeli and Jewish professors of political science and Middle Eastern studies at elite universities. These women feel that Islamophobia is still one of the most politically correct forms of hatred in academe today. Let's study hatred—but all forms of it, instead of just kicking the underdog when he's down.

Stanley Morse (2004), a professor of psychology and sociology at the Kuwait campus of the University of Maryland, writes—also in the *Chronicle of Higher Education*—that:

> Neil Kressel says we need to study Middle Eastern antisemitism, which he describes as a "dangerous form of contemporary bigotry." He couches his argument in seemingly reasonable terms. It is difficult to disagree without being labeled anti-intellectual, if not antisemitic.... [But] [a]ntisemitism in the Middle East is the result of Zionist activities that culminated in the establishment of Israel. It has nothing to do with primordial, group-based hatred. ... Kressel's essay thus can be seen only as an example of historical and cultural ignorance, if not also Jewish paranoia. It is a not-so-subtle attempt to dismiss—by pathologizing them—the entirely rational concerns of the vast majority of people in the Middle East. That better educated people may show more rather than less antisemitism, as Kressel suggests, may merely reflect their presumably better knowledge and understanding of existing realities.

Gregory Starrett (2004), a University of North Carolina anthropologist and Islam expert who has presented his research to audiences at the U.S. Department of State, the Library of Congress, and major universities across the country, agrees that antisemitism is "... an unalloyed evil" and that I am right that studies of European historical antisemitism will not tell us much about antisemitism in the Middle East. Moreover, he concedes that there are no moral excuses for hating Jews. But Starrett suggests that we need not look to social psychology for an explanation when "... residents of the region can see on television Palestinian children shot, their houses bulldozed, their institutions destroyed, and their fields uprooted, seized, or blocked off by representatives of the Israeli state." Moreover, he objects to my coining the label "Daniel Pearl effect"—for the consequences of the fear that saying the wrong things or asking the wrong questions in the Middle East, especially for Jews, can lead to real danger. I used this notion to explain in part why some journalists and scholars working in the Middle East might be reluctant to openly study Jew-hatred. Starrett says:

> As for 'the Daniel Pearl effect,' Kressel might want to talk to some of the thousands of scholars, journalists, development workers, and other foreigners, Jewish and non-Jewish alike, who live in the Middle East, dining with, working among, and asking 'probing questions' of both the right and the wrong people, without being slaughtered for their efforts....

Antisemitism is surely evil, but so is the broad characterization of Arabs and Muslims as barbarians who would just as soon slit your throat as talk to you.

Nadia Ramzy (2007), a self-described Egyptian-Coptic-American psychoanalyst and co-editor of the special issue on antisemitism agreed that: "... the hatred and bigotry that Kressel describes as currently extant is Arab and Muslim cultures toward the Jewish people is both horrifying and deeply disturbing...." However, she suggests that Muslim and Arab "... prejudice is a political one—it is the prejudice that people feel toward their enemies in war—not a prejudice embedded in a racist ideology directed toward an entire ethnic group...." She expresses some discomfort with the term antisemitism since "... the vast majority of Arabs eschew the term 'antisemitism' as applied to them as being nonsensical because to suggest that the Arabs are antisemitic is to suggest that they are, as a cultural grouping, anti-themselves." More substantially, she objects that I "... ignore both the social-psychological impact of occupation and the long established tradition of tolerance in Islamic culture, which is tragically neglected in Western social science in general." She then suggests that Maimonides fled from "Christian intolerance in Inquisition riddled Spain" to a safe haven in northwest Africa. (Maimonides, in reality, fled from the Muslim Almohades from Africa who conquered Córdoba in 1148, and threatened the Jewish community. This Inquisition was several centuries in the future.)

Ramzy then argues that "[t]o claim that 'the roots of contemporary Jew-hatred are deep and, as in the case of Christian antisemitism, part of the blame belongs to the religious tradition' is simply not correct when applied to Islamic culture." She concludes by quoting Uri Avneri who wrote in 2006 that: "Every honest Jew who knows the history of his people cannot but feel a deep sense of gratitude to Islam, which has protected the Jews for fifty generations, while the Christian world persecuted the Jews and tried many times 'by the sword' to get them to abandon their faith."

Finally, consider the commentary on my paper offered by Joseph Montville (2007), a former diplomat—well-respected in some circles for advocacy of Track II, non-official diplomacy—and also a director of the Center for the Study of Islam and Democracy. Montville begins his critique:

> Well yes, antisemitism in the Muslim world is worthy of study. But Neil Kressel is not the person to take the lead. I have read the paper four times in the months I have had it, always ending with a very negative reaction. In struggling to find one word to describe the paper, I have decided on an unspectacular but, for me, generally telling adjective. It is disrespectful.

Montville then proceeds to develop his argument. First:

> Muslim-Jewish antagonism in its political form is nuclear armed.... To understand the genesis and underlying dynamics of Arab and Muslim expressed public hatred of Israel in particular and by extension Jews in general requires the most profound—and respectful—scholarship so that the enormity of the nuclear threat and ways to transform it can be discovered.

Next, he explains:

> Any identity group that has been beaten militarily and politically and has suffered traumatic loss of life and homes and the existential faith in the idea of justice is enraged. They have suffered unbearable blows to their sense of collective self-worth. And this sense of narcissistic wounding and justice denied becomes a key component of the group identity that is passed.... Understanding narcissistic rage and the violence it often generates is not rocket science—and should not be for a professor of psychology.

Third, Montville considers my paper "... stunning in the way it shortchanges readers" on the positive aspects of life under Islam for the Jews, and denigrates my reliance on Princeton University professor emeritus Bernard Lewis (1987; 2002; 2003), Yossef Bodansky (1999), and Bat Yeor (2002) as sources. Finally, he concludes with a seemingly unrelated devotional passage that all God's children deserve mercy and compassion.

While some of these responses focus on the particulars on my approach, similar criticism will be directed against anyone who attempts to classify antisemitism in the Middle East as a virulent, widespread, and dangerous form of bigotry. The arguments voiced in these letters and elsewhere can be divided into fairly distinct categories, though many writers offer a mix of objections. Ten useful categories include:

- Definitional arguments (What we say is antisemitism is not really antisemitism.)
- Civility arguments (Nice people don't look for trouble by focusing on the negative.)
- Islamophobia arguments (Criticizing Muslims and Arabs who hate Jews is a form of bigotry against Arabs and Muslims.)
- Political spillover arguments (Antisemitism is merely an expected spillover from the Arab-Israeli conflict.)

- Bad history arguments (Claiming that antisemitism has roots in the history and theology of Islam is just bad scholarship.)
- Bad motives and *ad hominem* arguments (Those who raise charges of Muslim antisemitism are really operating out of inappropriate and unstated motivation.)
- Benign neglect theories (Yes, there's plenty of antisemitism but it's better not to focus on it.)
- Intensity disagreements (There is some antisemitism but not a dangerous amount.)
- Antisemitic arguments (The Jews are the problem — not antisemitism.)
- Distractions (What we really should be talking about is something else.)

Of course, several of these categories have associated sub-arguments and variants. In the next section, we consider the validity of the arguments and offer some counter-arguments.

IV. Answering Those Who Deny the Significance of Muslim and Arab Antisemitism

1. Definitional matters

These are attempts to end the discussion of Islamic and Arab antisemitism before it starts.

Muslims can't be antisemites.

It is surprising how many supposedly serious scholars deem this essentially ridiculous point worthy of consideration. Back in 1987, Bernard Lewis offered a response that should have put the matter to rest:

> [T]he term 'Semite' has no meaning as applied to groups as heterogeneous as the Arabs or the Jews, and indeed it could be argued that the use of such terms is in itself a sign of racism and certainly of either ignorance or bad faith.... [Moreover,] antisemitism has never anywhere been concerned with anyone but Jews, and is therefore available to Arabs as to other people as an option should they choose it.

Historian Robert Wistrich (2002) pointed out that the membership of Palestinian Arab leader Haj Amin al-Husseini in "... the Arabic-speaking branch of the 'Semitic' linguistic family did not deter Heinrich Himmler, the ruthless head of the SS, from wishing ... [him] every success in his fight 'against the foreign Jew.'" The only thing gained from applying the antisemitism label to anti-Arab and anti-Islamic discrimination, abhorrent in their own right, is to confuse matters and take attention away from Jew-hatred. This happened in 2001 at the first United Nations World Conference Against Racism in Durban, South Africa, when non-governmental organizations (NGOs) declared Zionism to be a form of racism and anti-Arab racism to be another form of antisemitism.

All criticism of Israel is not antisemitic.

Here, the best answer comes from British scholar David Hirsh who says: "No, of course not, but who says that it is? There are very few Jewish communal spokespeople or Israeli politicians who are prepared to make such an evidently false claim.

The contention that criticism of Israel is necessarily antisemitic nearly always functions as a straw-man argument." Moreover, antisemitism in the contemporary Middle East and in Muslim and Arab communities in Europe sounds more like classic, old-fashioned bigotry than politically-based criticism of Israel.

Moreover, there are times when criticism of Israel crosses the line into antisemitism. Numerous writers have attempted to develop workable criteria for distinguishing between legitimate (though, still, possibly incorrect) criticism of Israel and antisemitism. One of the best-known and most reasonable of these comes from Natan Sharansky (2005), who lists the 3-Ds of the new antisemitism: demonization, double standards and delegitimization. Demonization presents Israel as the embodiment of evil, often describing the Jewish state as Nazi in nature. The test for double standards is to see whether Israel is being judged by different criteria than other states under similar circumstances. Another manifestation of double standards is the devotion of more attention to Israeli transgressions than to similar ones by other states in similar circumstances. Finally, attempts to deny Israel the right to exist and to turn it into a pariah state are also antisemitic, according to Sharansky. It is no simple matter to distinguish reliably between reasonable criticism of Israel (which may be valid or invalid) and antisemitism, but it is important to make the effort rather than to advance all-or-none judgments.

No one hates the Jews; they only hate the Zionists.

As a matter of empirical fact, this distinction often means very little to many Muslims and Arabs with strong opinions on either Jews or Zionists. Rarely is the distinction articulated at all, except occasionally in response to questions from Western journalists. Thus, one finds in the Middle Eastern media many instances of "Zionists" doing things well before the start of the Zionist movement. And Zionists are frequently seen by Arab critics to act from motivation that is clearly Jewish rather than political. For example, in a recent article in the Saudi daily *Al-Watan*, journalist Ashraf Al-Faqi (quoted in Chernitsky and Glass 2009) claims that the current Israeli policies are based on "the Jewish interpretation of the Torah." And writing in the Saudi edition of the daily *Al-Hayat*, Islamic researcher 'Abd Al-Rahman Al-Khatib (quoted in Chernitsky and Glass 2009) describes the Jews as religious fanatics, and claims that their ideology—which is reflected in *The Protocols of the Elders of Zion*—stems from the Torah and the Talmud, and is currently being implemented in Gaza. He further explains that "Jewish ideology has only two sources: the Torah and the Talmud. This ideology has spawned many secondary texts, including *The Protocols of the Elders of Zion* by Matvei Golovinski, *The Jewish State* by [Theodor] Herzl and [oddly] *The Prince* by [Niccolo] Machiavelli...."

British antisemitism scholar David Hirsh (2007) suggests yet another narrowing of the gap between leftist anti-Zionism and antisemitism—this time emanating from the political left. He writes that:

> ... if an anti-Zionist worldview becomes widespread, then one likely outcome is the emergence of openly antisemitic movements. The proposition is not that anti-Zionism is motivated by antisemitism; rather that anti-Zionism, which does not start as antisemitism, normalizes hostility to Israel and then to Jews. It is this hostility to Israel and then to Jews, a hostility which gains some of its strength

from justified anger with Israeli human rights abuses, that is on the verge of becoming something which many people now find understandable, even respectable. It is moving into the mainstream.

2. Civility

It's more constructive to focus on the positive.

Sumbul Ali-Karamali (2008a) recently wrote a book, *The Muslim Next Door*, that sought to correct misimpressions about Islam. Khaled Abou El Fadl, a brave and responsible Muslim writer who knows much about Islamic extremism, praised her book highly, saying "I wish I could send ... [it] not just to every Muslim extremist, including Bin Laden and his likes, but also to the President of the United States and his staff, to all policy makers, and also to every single Islamophobe or self-hating Muslim in the world." Yet Ali-Karamali (2008b), who asserts that she is not antisemitic and has many Jewish friends, is deeply disturbed that people identify significant antisemitism in the Muslim world. She cites a wide variety of Islamic rules and traditions that she perceives as sympathetic to the Jews, noting—for example—that, "... in the seventh century, Muhammad urged his followers to fast on Yom Kippur, in solidarity with the Jews. The Qur'an states that fasting is prescribed for Muslims, just as it was prescribed for those (the Jews) before them...." She explains that:

> Antisemitism has no place in Islam, just as Islamophobia has no place in Judaism. For their time, these two religions sought to decrease violence and bigotry in the world. The weight of history, if we can but remember it, is on the side of pluralism. Islam accepts Judaism, as well as Christianity, as part of the Islamic tradition.

Moreover, she argues that "Because Islam is part of the Judeo-Christian tradition, the Qur'an grants Jews and Christians an exalted status." After all this, she concludes:

> I'm not saying that any of our histories are perfect. My local bookstore prominently featured a book on how some Muslim preacher allied himself with the Nazis to spread antisemitism. Well, I find that disgusting. But where's the balance? Why focus on this guy and not on the Muslim king of Morocco, who refused to give up his Jewish population to the Nazis? Why not focus on the Albanians, a country of seventy percent Muslims, who hid their Jewish neighbors from the Nazis so that—remarkably—all but five Albanian Jews survived the Nazi occupation of Albania? Why not remember that fifty thousand Spanish Jews fled the Inquisition to settle in the Muslim Ottoman Empire, where most stayed for another four centuries? We can either focus on the conflicts in history, proving only that human beings are imperfect; or, we can focus on the countless cooperative, cross-religious acts of generosity instead, using those to drive forward our vision of the future. It's up to us.

Ali-Karamali's essay highlights several of the barriers a people face if they seek to explain the nature of contemporary Islamic antisemitism to well-intentioned liberals and Islamic moderates. The first is that those seeking constructive encounters between human beings often prefer not to focus on conflict, especially when such conflict has its roots in religion or tribal identity. There is a strong tendency to assume benign relations even when none exist. Second, Karamali invokes a rosy image of the past that, quite simply, is not borne out by the facts. Third, Karamali tells a very one-sided story about the treatment of Jews in Islamic sacred writings, yet to correct this misimpression requires one to venture into dangerous waters. Fourth, Karamali speaks about "a preacher" who sided with the Nazis; most probably, she is referring to the Mufti of Jerusalem, the official head of Palestinian Muslims at the time and a very prominent leader in the Arab Islamic world of his day. Fifth, she misleadingly implies that Islamophobia is just as prevalent in contemporary Judaism as antisemitism is in contemporary Islam. All of Ali-Karamali's misconceptions can be corrected, but—in a world where so many Muslims hate Jews passionately—what is the point of engaging in this unpleasant discussion with someone whose heart seems to be in the right place? The problem is that although Ali-Karamali is trying to bring about the right kind of world, she can't get very far by simply assuming it is already here. Nor will focusing on the positives do much to eliminate the negatives in the world. Recognizing a problem is the first step to solving it.

Nice people don't criticize other people's religious beliefs.

This is a variant of the above argument. The problem is that terrible things have been done throughout history under the banner of religion. To maintain that criticism of religion is out of bounds is to offer a screen behind which evil-doers may operate with impunity (see Dacey 2008; Hamilton 2005).

3. *Islamophobia*

Criticizing Muslims or Islam is Islamophobia.

Islamophobia is the real problem.

The answer here is that hostility toward Muslims *is* sometimes a big problem, not least to those of us who believe—as I do—that part of the battle against religious extremist violence depends on convincing large numbers of Muslim believers that the West can offer them a hospitable home. As to which is worse, antisemitism or anti-Muslim feeling, Jewish historian Deborah Lipstadt (quoted in Durbach 2008) offers the not unreasonable opinion that:

> This is too broad a question to answer easily. It depends where—what country—and what situation. I think there is more overt anti-Muslim feeling in the U.S. today and a far greater fear of Muslims than Jews. I think the situation in France or the United Kingdom is quite different.

On the other hand, the sort of widespread, venomous hatred—sanctioned by high-level political and religious leaders—that has been directed against Jews is nowhere evident against Muslims at present. In any case, as a tiny group, Jews are—despite antisemitic fantasies—far less able to defend their interests than the hundred-times-larger Muslim and Arab communities.

More important, religion and ethnicity do not confer a protective shield behind which one may engage in inappropriate and destructive behavior. If a large segment of a group is antisemitic, saying so does not make one a bigot. If religious leaders preach hatred, saying so does not make one a hater.

Aren't Jews anti-Muslim?

Of course some are. Some evidence may exist showing that Jews are more anti-Muslim than other Westerners, but I have not seen any. It may also be possible that Jews—with their prevailing liberal political sympathies—are less Islamophobic than Western populations as a whole. In either case, it is incumbent upon Jewish leaders to continue to fight anti-Muslim bigotry in their group, just as it is incumbent upon non-Jewish leaders to do the same. But opposing bigotry against Muslims does not require closing one's eyes to Jew-hatred that is being perpetrated by many Muslim religious leaders and large portions of their flocks in the name of the faith.

Those who call attention to Islamic and Arab antisemitism are painting with too broad a brush.

There is a danger that charges of antisemitism might be interpreted to imply that all Muslims are antisemitic or that Muslims are necessarily antisemitic. Such inferences, obviously, would be unjust, incorrect, and insulting to millions of Muslims who do not harbor such hatred. They would also reflect ignorance insofar as some Muslim theologians have found in Muhammad's message the basis for positive relations with Jews and some Muslim leaders at some points in history have been relatively tolerant toward Jews in their midst.

It is logically, morally, and strategically important to establish in some detail the topography of antisemitism in the Muslim world (Thienhaus 2004). Where is antisemitism more prevalent and why? Where has it not taken hold? Those who object to a description of the Islamic world as monolithic are certainly right. Hostility toward Jews is very strong in some Islamic countries and among some Islamic populations, for example, in Egypt, Syria, Iran, and Saudi Arabia. It is very likely far weaker and less central to the mindset of many Muslims living, for example, in Southeast Asia or, say, in the United States. Still, serious instances of virulent Jew-hatred can be observed in parts of the Muslim world far removed from the center of the Arab-Israeli conflict. Moreover, we do not have the luxury—especially for such a tremendously under-researched topic—to await well developed, systematic, and comprehensive studies before speaking out.

Finally, there are those who suggest that antisemitism is only endorsed by a tiny handful of Muslims. Though we do not have conclusive data on the extent of diffusion of antisemitic hatred into the population of Muslims, we have enough evidence already to say that these "handful" theorists are wrong. Moreover, if the "handful" quantification applies to any subgroup of the Muslim population, it applies to those who speak out loudly and clearly in denunciation of antisemitism. Indeed, with regard to the state of Israel, the Arab or Muslim leader who stands up in some Muslim nations and says "I think there is some justice in Israel's claim" will almost certainly be committing political suicide and may, in fact, be putting his or her life in danger. Once again, recognizing reality does not make one anti-Muslim. It might make one Islamophobic, if it that term implies fear. But fear of venomous hatred is not a form of bigotry.

4. Political spillover

The real issue is not hostility toward Jews, but sometimes there's a little understandable spillover from the Arab-Israeli conflict.

This argument comes in many forms, all of which attribute the rise in Muslim antisemitism to some aspect of the Arab-Israeli conflict. When such arguments deny altogether the existence of the seeds of anti-Jewish sentiment in the pre-Zionist period, they misread the history and theology of Islam. However, it is difficult to deny the role of Zionism and the rise of Israel in changing fundamentally the way Muslims think about Jews. It is a complicated matter to specify precisely the causal relationship between the rise of Muslim antisemitism and the progression of the Arab-Israeli conflict. It is equally difficult to speculate about how Muslim-Jewish relations might have progressed had there never been a state of Israel. But, in sum, Israel's existence and the Arab-Israeli conflict have surely contributed importantly to the rise in Muslim antisemitism.

Still, a problem arises when political scientists, psychologists, and others use this relationship as an excuse. Consider Joseph Montville's (2007) point:

> Any identity group that has been beaten militarily and politically and has suffered traumatic loss of life and homes and the existential faith in the idea of justice is enraged. They have suffered unbearable blows to their sense of collective self-worth. And this sense of narcissistic wounding and justice denied becomes a key component of the group identity that is passed on from generation to generation.

There is some merit in this explanation. (I make a similar point about damaged self-worth, group identity, and extremism in my own work (Kressel 2007b, 216-31)). But what Montville suggests doesn't always happen. Jews don't hate Germans, today. Nelson Mandela made peace with whites in South Africa. Montville thinks the idea of scapegoating is not important in understanding the Arab/Muslim psychology with regard to the Jews. I disagree. As I have written elsewhere:

> For many, Israel has become a central element in a collective obsessional delusion. With no shortage of injustices close to home in countries such as Pakistan, Indonesia, Sudan, Libya, Saudi Arabia, and elsewhere, one wonders how so many people find so much energy to devote to a conflict so far away. Even if Israel were conducting itself as unjustly as its detractors maintain, it remains to be explained why its particular infractions should loom so large in Muslim and Arab public consciousness.

Part of the reason is that hostility toward the Jewish state is what Bernard Lewis calls a licensed grievance: "... the only one that can be freely and safely expressed in those Muslim countries where the media are either wholly owned or strictly overseen by the government. Indeed, Israel serves as a useful stand-in for complaints about the economic privation and political repression under which most Muslim peoples live, and as a way of deflecting the resulting anger." This license sometimes extends to "the Jews" as such, but sometimes stops short, at least officially, with Israel. Anti-American hostility can play a similar, safety-valve role, though—sometimes— governments view antagonizing the United States as a costlier approach.

Anger is not necessarily directed at true sources of a problem. The many misfortunes, injustices, and "narcissistic wounds" experienced by large numbers of people in the many parts of the Arab world have a plethora of sources. Most (but not all) of the time, blaming Israel has been little more than a form of irrational scapegoating rather than an accurate direction of anger toward the source of the troubles.

How else would we expect people to react to all those Israeli transgressions?

Israeli journalist Yossi Klein Halevi has expressed his vigorous opposition to claims, frequently made by Israel's supporters, that the Israeli army is "the most moral in the world." In questions following a paper he delivered at Yale University, Halevi (2009) asserted that the Israeli army was a good one but that "an army is an army" and isn't perfect. He argued that Israel need not be the best in order to free it from the attacks of those who see it as the worst. His point is important. Moreover, most nations in the world do not appear to be judged at all in international forums. But, to the extent that a nation is judged, it should be judged by the totality of its record. It would be hard to argue, I think, that Israel's record is *worse* on just about any human rights dimension than the nations with whom it has been struggling—and a reasonable case could be made that its record is far better (Dershowitz 2004). Yet, for much of the human rights community, the issue of Israeli human rights abuses against Palestinians has loomed much larger on the agenda than even Palestinian human rights abuses against Palestinians, let alone that of Jewish or Israeli rights—and hence there has been a disproportionate focus on Israeli "transgressions" (Pollak 2009). The structure of the international community (with many Arab states and one Jewish one), of human rights organizations (with a preference for losers over winners and a dislike of the use of military power), and world media (again reflecting population imbalances—among other things) has created a situation where the focus on Israeli transgressions has been way out of proportion to the dimensions of these transgressions. There is also the matter of the media seeking "man-bites-dog" stories; examples of once-victimized Jews being abusive seem to fit the bill.

In Lebanon, Gaza, and elsewhere, Israeli actions have resulted in a substantial number of civilian deaths. But in an Arab world where Israel and Jews are demonized, we would hardly expect to find a population likely to consider the role of its own leadership in creating the circumstances under which these deaths occurred. Moreover, in some areas, pointing out the culpability of local leaders can be a dangerous undertaking.

The Left's propensity for opposing Zionism has consequences that have been spelled out clearly (in terminology addressed to leftist academics) by David Hirsh (2007), who writes that one real danger

> ... is that antiracist anti-Zionism is creating commonsense discourses which construct antisemitism as thinkable and possible. There are some people who are prepared to experiment openly with antisemitic ways of expressing themselves and are nonetheless accepted as legitimate by some antiracist organizations and individuals.... It is a serious mistake to view this surge of antisemitism only as a response to the United States and Israel. This empiricist reduction would be akin to explaining Nazi antisemitism simply as a reaction to the Treaty of Versailles. While American and Israeli policies have doubtlessly contributed to the rise of

this new wave of antisemitism, the United States and Israel occupy subject positions in the ideology that go far beyond their actual empirical roles.

5. Bad history

Muslims have always treated the Jews well, so how can we say that what we are witnessing now is a serious instance of dangerous bigotry?

The first answer to this argument is that even if the roots of antisemitism were all relatively recent, it would not negate the importance of the current manifestation of hatred. A second, more important, answer is that Islam's record of tolerance has been greatly overstated by many sources. At best, Islam's historical treatment of the Jews has been a very mixed bag. Bernard Lewis, who has authored many volumes on Islamic history, several of which specifically revisit the question of Muslim-Jewish relations, explains that: "It was not until comparatively modern times that the idea was imported from Europe that the Jews are a separate race, with evil and enduring racial characteristics" (Lewis 1987, 132) and that "[w]ith rare exceptions, where hostile stereotypes of the Jew existed in the Islamic tradition, they tended to be contemptuous and dismissive, rather than suspicious and obsessive" (Lewis 2002, 154). The situation of the Jews "… was never as bad as in Christendom at its worst, nor as good as in Christendom at its best" (Lewis 1987, 121). In recent years, however, several volumes have appeared that have maintained that there were many more instances of hostility to Jews in some eras of Muslim history than historians, in the past, have noted (see Bostom 2007; Bat Yeor 2002; Ibn Warraq 2007). In truth, the argument concerning the extent and depth on anti-Jewish treatment under Islam is partly an argument over which sources to trust but mainly a glass half-full or half-empty problem. Being on average considerably better for the Jews than the Christian world may not be saying all that much. There appears to be a "will to believe" in many contemporary retellings of tales of Muslim kindness to the Jews, witness the frequent error about Maimonides fleeing from the Christian Inquisition. But there is also a kernel of truth behind such tales, and there were times when Jews under Islam fared reasonably well.

Recent works have also documented the prevalence of antisemitism in the twentieth century in some parts of the Muslim world. For example, Dalin and Rothman (2007) have recently recounted the tale of Hitler's relationship with the very influential and popular Mufti during World War II. Clearly, the two men had a similar mindset with regard to the Jews, as Hitler recognized when he honored the Mufti by making him one of the first non-Germans to learn of the Final Solution. The relationship did not cost the Mufti (who might well have been tried as a war criminal) any points with his constituency and may have helped him reassert his authority in the postwar period. Moreover, the Mufti had no trouble assembling the Hanzar division to fight on behalf of National Socialism. As Leon Cohen (2008) writes in his review of several new books on the history of Muslim-Jewish relations: "The state of Israel exists every bit as much in response to Muslim civilization's prejudices and crimes against the Jewish people and Judaism as because of anything that happened in Christian Europe." This judgment is overstated and incorrect to the extent that historically it was Jews fleeing from Europe who felt the urgency to launch the state. However, an honest review of Muslim history shows a long tradition of discrimination that should establish some degree of moral responsibility.

A particularly insightful explanation of the role of Islamic history and theology in contributing to modern-day antisemitism comes from Mortimer Ostow (2007; see, also, Ostow 1996):

> The obvious source of current Arab and Muslim resentment against the Jews derives from the establishment of the State of Israel in 1948 on land claimed by the Muslim Arabs.... But the Jews also represented a mythic enemy, a principle of cosmic evil. It was only because of that satanic power, the Arabs argued, that they were able to defeat the Arab armies which had come to wipe them out in recent years. Throughout the history of Jewish-Muslim coexistence in Muslim countries, both Jews and Christians were tolerated only as long as they acknowledged the subservient status to which they were assigned, and which they accepted. That the Jew, who, in Muslim eyes, was seen as weak, cowardly and ineffectual, could impose such a quick and definitive military defeat upon the Arab enemy could not be explained except by the theory that the Jews embodied a principle of cosmic evil, a satanic element, whose worldwide conspiracies would some day be disclosed and defeated.

It is historically inaccurate to say Islam contains the seeds of antisemitic belief.

Identifying scriptural sanctions for hatred and unethical behavior is always a delicate matter, especially regarding religions that see their scriptures as inerrant guides. Judaism, Christianity, and Islam all have such so-called "difficult passages." The existence of these passages does not, *ipso facto*, make believers evil. Adherents of all religions have used "interpretation" and various other methods to render their "difficult verses" harmless (Kressel 2007b).

We of course know very little from objective sources about what transpired in Arabia in the seventh century. But we do know that contemporary Muslim antisemites have found several passages in the sacred works that they need not twist very much to support antisemitic visions. Muhammad's wars against Jewish tribes in Arabia provide much precedent. One hadith, for example, has Muhammad ordering (or endorsing) the decapitation of hundreds of Jewish non-combatants (from the Banu Qurayza) following an unconditional surrender. Afterward, Muhammad took a wife from among the widows of the slaughtered Jews.

The Qur'an itself picks up and develops one theme from Christian antisemitism, namely that of the Jews as the killer of Jesus. Addressing the Jews, the sacred book states:

> We gave Jesus the son of Mary veritable signs and strengthened him with the Holy Spirit. Will you then scorn each apostle whose message does not suit your fancies, charging some with imposture and slaying others? They say: "Our hearts are sealed." But Allah has cursed them for their unbelief. They have but little faith. And now that a Book confirming their own has come to them from Allah, they deny it, although they know it to be the truth.... Evil is that for which they have bartered away their souls. [2:87-89]

This passage proceeds to challenge the Jews: "Why did you kill the prophets of Allah, if you are true believers?" [2:91] The text further offers "proof" that the Jews know they are wrong, suggesting that, if they were true believers, they would long for death and the rewards it brings. Yet the Jews, readers are told, "... will never long for death, because of what they did; for Allah knows the evil-doers. Indeed, you will find that they love this life more than other men; more than the pagans do. Each of them would willingly live a thousand years." [2:94-96] To modern ears in the West, this is an odd insult. Yet, it was comprehensible and meaningful to early believers. No doubt, the words continue to resonate in the thoughts and feelings of many Muslims who provide a more current rationale for their animosity toward Jews and Israel (Kressel 2007b, 185).

Perhaps little is gained by pulling such passages outside of their historical context. Though the Qur'an and hadiths include numerous statements that might be interpreted as anti-Jewish, the passages cited above (and others like them) did not lead to fierce antisemitic behavior in many parts of the Islamic world for much of Islamic history. Importantly, there are also numerous positive counterweights regarding the Jews in Islamic sacred writings. According to Reuven Firestone (2007) — an observant Jew who has spent a sabbatical year with his family in Egypt —

> The question that remains, therefore, is what activates the latency of scriptural antisemitism into an operational state? This is an important question because the vital core scriptural authority of the New Testament and Qur'an that can and has been invoked to authorize and justify violence against Jews can never be eliminated from the consciousness of those that accept the divine origin of these scriptures. One can always point to certain scriptural texts that justify antisemitism. Antisemitism, therefore, will always remain potential. What makes it actual?

Firestone's question is an important one, worthy of far more attention than it has received to date.

The extremist Christians are the deeper enemies of the Jews.

A related objection is that we — Jews, Christians, and Muslims — should get together and fight the right-wingers and neo-Nazis who are the real enemies of both the Jews and the Muslims.

True, no one knows where the next wave of antisemitism might originate. And there has long been a disturbing amount of hatred coming from the extreme right and neo-Nazis. However, Islamic Jew-hatred is currently the more pressing concern. Moreover, Christianity has taken many constructive steps during the past half century to limit and control its antisemitic potential. As Christopher Hitchens (2008) recently noted in reference to the Muslim nations of the Middle East: "In point of fact, there is only one area of the world where pure, old-fashioned undiluted Jew-hatred is preached from the pulpit, broadcast on the official airwaves, given high-level state sanction and taught in the schools."

6. Bad motives and ad hominem *arguments*

Those who charge Muslims with antisemitism are really seeking to score points for Israel and to distract observers from its abysmal human rights record.

This or that person or group is disqualified to speak on the matter of antisemitism because of his — or its — background, biases, character flaws, etc.

As a consequence of their unfortunate history, traumatized Jews are always finding antisemites everywhere and always worrying about another Holocaust.

David Hirsh (2007) calls the first argument the "Livingstone Formulation" "... after Ken Livingstone, the [former] Mayor of London. He said: 'for far too long the accusation of antisemitism has been used against anyone who is critical of the policies of the Israeli government....'" Such arguments about motivation are secondary and do not dispense with the need to address charges of antisemitism on their merits. Worry about antisemitism and another Holocaust may be part of the psychology of many Jews, but that, too, hardly constitutes a refutation of manifest evidence that such antisemitism exists.

7. Benign neglect

These theories generally start by acknowledging the existence of at least some antisemitism in the Muslim world and then proceed to explain why we should deliberately ignore it for one reason or another.

Focusing on antisemitism is not in the interest of the Arab-Israeli peace process; pursuing that process ardently is the best way to reduce Arab and Muslim antisemitism.

The basic argument here is that if only we could solve the Arab-Israeli conflict, Arab antisemitism would begin to dissipate and antisemitism in the non-Arab Muslim world would rapidly disappear. First of all, this approach underestimates the future impact of massive antisemitic socialization that has already occurred in many parts of the Middle East and also in some other parts of the Muslim world. More important, the argument bears resemblance to the old story about a person landing on a desert island with only an economist for companionship and several crates of canned food for sustenance. How, you ask the economist, can we open the cans? He replies: "First, assume a can-opener." How can the Arab-Israeli conflict be resolved when an irrational hostility to Jews possessing power and partial control over Jewish destiny forms a key barrier to the resolution of that conflict? Shall we first *assume* a solution to the Arab-Israeli conflict? Absent anti-Jewish irrationality and bigotry, the conflict would have ended with the Israeli offer for a two-state solution in 2000, or indeed much earlier.

Focusing on antisemitism is not a good idea if we hope to encourage Muslim moderates; it does not advance President Obama's new plan to reach out to the Muslim world.

Focusing on antisemitism is not in the interests of America's war on terrorism.

The core idea in both of these positions is that, in the strategic pursuit of America's goals, the less said about the Jews and antisemitism, the better. Wisdom, after all, dictates that America has varying interests throughout the vast and diverse Muslim world and that these interests may not be advanced by putting Israel and the Jews at the top of the agenda. Especially given the prevalent state of delusional thinking about the Jews, some argue that it would be best to make progress on other issues first. Then, there would be a cooperative foundation on which the matter of antisemitism might be addressed. If, for example, Obama can make progress with the Iranians, then America will have more influence to discourage Iranian Jew-hatred. Similarly, if Europe can arrive at understandings with ever-so-slightly antisemitic—

but otherwise moderate—Muslims at home and abroad, then such Muslims will be more willing and able to abandon their antisemitic ways.

In principle, such approaches seem pragmatic. But there remains the possibility that delusional thinking also exists in the West. Putting aside the oxymoronic aspects of the "antisemitic moderate," there is a chance that Europe and America may be misleading themselves about the extent to which such individuals wish to deal. The proposed benign neglect may also be less benign than theorists imagine. As Robert Wistrich (n.d.) has written:

> The annihilation of Israel is the precursor to a successful Jihad, as was Hitler's war against the Jews, which is also viewed as the opening salvo in gaining world domination. The Nazis, like Stalin in the final years of his rule, accused World Jewry of having the same ambitions they themselves fostered. They are reminiscent of the Nazis because of their hatred of liberalism, of freedom of thought, of non-conformism, of women's liberation, and other decadent expressions of modernism and civilization.... Arab and Muslim antisemitism is the Trojan Horse designed to undermine the West's belief in its own values. Islam is at present winning this war because Europe is cooperating—because of its lust for oil, because of electoral considerations with the increased Muslim populations in their countries, because of past colonialist sins, and because of the naive belief that the weak is always right. But the West must not sacrifice Israel on any altar of appeasement.... Europe is liable to find itself once more entrapped in a complex of partners in destructive crime, and Israel has not yet begun to relate to this serious problem through a coherent strategic policy, frequently playing into the enemy's hands. Both of them—Europe and Israel—must change their ways.

8. *Intensity disagreements*

There is some antisemitism but not a dangerous amount.

This is a legitimate area for debate. However, it must rely far more heavily on data emanating from the Middle East and an analysis of vulnerabilities and protective factors. Wishful thinking and ideology should recede to the background.

9. *Antisemitism*

The charges about the Jews are largely true, and it is only political correctness that prevents others from saying so.

Such arguments appear more often than one might suspect in Muslim media. Needless to say, there is no point arguing with an antisemite.

10. *Distraction*

We should really be talking about global poverty or just about anything else.

This is a debating tactic, not an argument, and it should be recognized as such.

V. Conclusion

The main goal of this paper has been to offer responses to those who claim that Muslim and Arab antisemitism is not real or important, thereby taking a step toward overcoming conceptual impediments to understanding and confronting the bigotry. The expressed reasons for holding a position do not necessarily constitute the real reasons. Even so, one must start by answering critics rather than by explaining them away. Only then is it justifiable to move to the next level of explanation.

One might offer all manner of speculation about the underlying reasons why observers often refuse to acknowledge the extent and danger of Muslim antisemitism. Many—including Jews—I suspect, simply have not seen enough of the evidence and, instead, extrapolate from their assessments of the extent of antisemitism in the West. Others are influenced by what they perceive to be an overly defensive Jewish psychology. To some extent, these sorts of judgments reflect a failure of the mainstream mass media to assign adequate prominence to empirical evidence of Muslim antisemitism.

Of course, other observers—who knows how many?—may themselves dislike Jews, though they feel bound by the rules of social behavior that prevail in the West to keep such biases out of public discourse. Still others are influenced mainly by their sympathies and loyalties to Arab, Palestinian, and Muslim causes, which they feel may be tarnished by the charge of antisemitism. No doubt many who empathize with the Palestinians may also dislike the antisemitism that has become associated with various Arab causes and hope that it will disappear when their objectives are realized. For these people, it is simply a matter of priorities.

The recognition of Muslim and Arab antisemitism poses certain intellectual inconveniences for parts of the intellectual left, though the situation varies greatly depending on the particularities of allegiances and orientations (Siegel 2004). As political scientist Andrei Markovits (quoted in Gerstenfeld 2004) has noted: "Anti-Americanism and antisemitism relate to each other and empirically are almost always in close proximity, even if not totally identical. The overlap between them has become more pronounced since the end of World War II." (at p. 2) Anti-Israel sentiments also correlate with antisemitism. Thus, to oppose antisemitism puts one in bed to some extent with the Americans and the Israelis, and this—for some on the far left—is not a comfortable place to be. Markovits further explains that:

> In Western Europe as well as the United States, left-wing intellectuals began to perceive Israel as America's pit bull after the Six-Day War. Israel became America's tool in the latter's imperialist designs on the Middle East and beyond.... [More recently,] [t]he European and American Left—as well as the right—have come to view the current war against Iraq as a thinly disguised American proxy for Israel's purposes. ... European antisemitism has changed in the sense that it is illegitimate to express hatred for powerless Jews, i.e., Jews living in Europe. The resentment is now reserved almost exclusively for Israel—of late—Jews in America, the much-maligned "East Coast."

As a result, Markovits contends, "... the threshold of shame about antisemitism has been lowered significantly over the past decade" (see also Markovits 2007).

Many on the left prefer underdogs and see their role as helping those who have not achieved political, economic, and military success. There is a strong desire to help the failed Arab and Muslim states and societies, and it does not seem to some that a wholesale assault on the culture's rampant antisemitism would be consistent with that agenda. Israel and the Jews lost sympathy when they stopped being victims.

Concern for Palestinian rights and opposition to Israel can even override many other traditional leftist considerations. As British writer Nick Cohen (2009) puts it: "When brave feminists, gays, democrats and liberals in the Muslim world and in Britain's Muslim communities make a stand [against Muslim intolerance toward them], they too are accused of being tools of the Zionists." And in some circles of the anti-racist left, nobody speaks out in their support.

Some others on the left (e.g., Deutsch 2001) and elsewhere on the political spectrum understandably hope to achieve a "just, peaceful, humane, and sustainable world" by encouraging leading Islamic religious figures to broadcast statements of moderation. Their objective, above all, is to keep the West from ending up in a conflict with Islam or Muslims. Unfortunately, gaining the cooperation of many Muslim religious leaders has proved far more difficult than expected, and hostility toward the United States appears more broad-based than initially believed in the days following 9/11. In this context, to focus attention on widespread bigotry emanating from large segments of the Muslim and Arab world is seen by some as fanning the flames of conflict by identifying negative characteristics of the community with which we seek to get along. There is a strong impulse to leave just this one stone unturned in the battle against bigotry. Even when antisemitism is unearthed, some—especially in Europe—try very hard to deflect blame from the Muslim community, though this may mean assigning it where it does not belong (Morris 2004).

Another problem is that, if we face up to the existence of venomous Jew-hatred in Iran, then we also need to face up to what will happen when this bigotry becomes nuclear armed. The prospect is frightening, not only because such a weapon might well be used on Israel. The presence of such extreme hatred in such high places leads us to doubt the mental stability of the leaders who would control such weapons and to suspect that they might use newly acquired power to foment all sorts of trouble in the region. That such fear might beget denial of the threat, as some psychoanalysts might predict, is a possibility. In any case, many on the left regard the use of military force by Israel in conjunction with Western powers as anathema, no matter what the reason—and they are afraid of where thinking about an almost-nuclear-armed, genocidal antisemitic power might lead.

There is a very clear answer about what must not be done about antisemitism in the Muslim and Arab world. It must not be given a pass. World leaders must assert core principles, even when they relate to Jews and even when they may prove costly. If the notion of international community means anything at all, it means that Israel must be treated like other countries—and principled nations must realize that more than the fate of the Jews hangs on whether this happens. As many have said, antisemitism is the canary in the coal mine, and what starts with the Jews rarely ends with the Jews. For specifics on how to proceed, the declaration of the London Conference on Combating Antisemitism (2009) provides a very good beginning. And keeping nuclear weapons away from nations that espouse genocidal ideologies is certainly the next step.

REFERENCES

ADL. 2002. *Anti-Semitism in America 2002*. Retrieved April 2, 2009. http://www.adl.org/anti_semitism/2002/as_survey.pdf.

———. 2003. *Fallout from Mahathir: Muslim and Arab reaction*. Retrieved June 29, 2004. http://www.adl.org/anti_semitism/malaysian_fallout_1.asp.

———. 2008. *Reaction to the financial crisis in the Arab world*. Retrieved April 13, 2009. http://www.adl.org/main_Arab_World/Financial_Crisis.htm.

Ahmadinejad, M. 2008. Excerpts from speech at the United Nations General Assembly. Retrieved April 26, 2009. http://www.haaretz.com/hasen/spages/1024097.html.

Ali-Karamali, S. 2008a. *The Muslim next door: The Qur'an, the media, and that veil thing*. Ashland, OR: White Cloud Press.

Ali-Karamali, S. 2008b. *Antisemitism through the lens of Islamophobia*. Retrieved April 13, 2009. http://www.muslimnextdoor.com/writings/anti_semitism.html.

American Jewish Committee. 2003. *The West, Christians and Jews in Saudi Arabian schoolbooks*. New York: American Jewish Committee. Retrieved August 5, 2003. http://www.ajc.org/InTheMedia/Publications.asp?did=750.

B'nai B'rith Foundation. n.d. *The portrayal of Israel and Jews in school textbooks of the Palestinian Authority*. Brochure. Washington, D.C.: B'nai B'rith Foundation.

Bodansky, Y. 1999. *Islamic antisemitism as a political instrument*. Houston, TX: Freeman Center for Strategic Studies.

Bostom, A.G. 2007. *The Legacy of Islamic antisemitism: From sacred texts to solemn history*. Amherst, NY: Prometheus.

Brenner, I. 2007. "Guest editorial." *International Journal of Applied Psychoanalytic Studies* 4(3), pp. 187-90.

Bush, G.W. 2003. Text of Bush speech of November 19. Retrieved April 27, 2009. Lexis-Nexis Academic Database.

Chernitsky, B., and E. Glass. 2009. *Antisemitic statements and cartoons in the wake of the Gaza war*. MEMRI Inquiry and Analysis #507. Washington, D.C.: MEMRI. Retrieved March 30, 2009. http://www.memri.org/bin/articles.cgi?Page=archives&Area=ia&ID=IA50709.

Chesler, P. 2003. *The new antisemitism: the current crisis and what we must do about it*. San Francisco: Jossey-Bass.

Cohen, L. 2008. "New books probe reality of Muslim antisemitism." *The Wisconsin Jewish Chronicle*, July 17. Retrieved April 13, 2009. http://www.jewishchronicle.org/article.php?article_id=10346.

Cohen, N. 2009. "Hatred is turning me into a Jew." *The JC.com*, February 12. Retrieved March 2, 2009. http://www.thejc.com/print/11905.

Dacey, A. 2008. *The Secular conscience*. Amherst, NY: Prometheus.

Dalin, D.G., and J.F. Rothman. 2008. *Icon of evil: Hitler's Mufti and the rise of radical Islam*. New York: Random House.

Dershowitz, A. 2004. *The Case for Israel*. NY: Wiley.

Deutsch, M. 2001. "Response to the terrorist actions: The Best long-term strategy for a just, peaceful, humane, and sustainable world." A Letter from Morton Deutsch, Ph.D., September 20. Retrieved July 10, 2003. http://cpa.ca/epw/epw/Deutsch.html.

Durbach, E. 2008. "Prof sees mixed picture on hatred, Shoa denial." *New Jersey Jewish News*, September 28. Retrieved March 24, 2009. http://www.njjewishnews.com/njjn.com/092508/cjProfSees Mixed.html.

Firestone, R. 2007. "Contextualizing antisemitism in Islam: Chosenness, choosing, and the emergence of new religion." *International Journal of Applied Psychoanalytic Studies* 4(3), pp. 235-54.

Foxman, A.H. 2003. *Never again? The threat of the new antisemitism*. New York: HarperCollins.

Gerstenfeld, M. 2004. "European anti-Americanism and antisemitism: similarities and differences—An interview with Andrei S. Markovits." *Post-Holocaust and Antisemitism* 16. Retrieved March 27, 2009. http://www.jcpa.org/phas/phas-16.htm.

Gur, H.R. 2008. "Report: Muslim antisemitism 'strategic threat.'" *Jerusalem Post Online Edition*, April 22. Retrieved April 13, 2009. http://www.jpost.com/servlet/Satellite?cid=1208422652742&pagename=JPost%2FJPArticle%2FPrinter.

Halevi, Y.K. 2009. "Demonizing Israel: Political and religious consequences among Israelis." Paper presented at YIISA, Yale University, New Haven, CT, April 2, 2009. Retrieved April 26, 2009. http://www.yale.edu/yiisa/yossikleinhalevipaper 4209.pdf.

Hamilton, M.A. 2005. *God versus the gavel*. New York: Cambridge.

Harris, D. 2003. "Palestinian education." Testimony of David Harris in hearing before the Subcommittee on Labor, Health and Human Services, and Education of the Appropriations Committee, Senate. 108th Cong., 1st Sess. (2003), October 30.

Hirsh, D. 2007. "Anti-Zionism and antisemitism: Cosmopolitan reflections." YIISA Working Paper No. 1, Yale University. Retrieved April 1, 2009. http://www.yale.edu/yiisa/workingpaper/hirsh/David%20Hirsh%20YIISA%20Working%20Paper 1.pdf.

Hitchens, C. 2008. "The New antisemitism?" *Times Literary Supplement*, November 19. Retrieved March 24, 2009. http://entertainment.timesonline.co.uk/tol/arts_and_entertainment/the_tls/article5186954.ece.

Ibn Warraq. 2007. "Islamic antisemitism." *New English Review*. Retrieved October 1, 2008. http://www.newenglishreview.org/custpage.cfm?frm=6628&sec_id=6628.

Intelligence and Terrorism Information Center (ITIC). 2008. *Contemporary Arab-Muslim antisemitism, its significance and implications (updated to March 2008)*. Israel Intelligence and Heritage Commemoration Center. Retrieved April 20, 2009. http://www.terrorism-info.org.il/malam_multimedia/English/eng_n/html/a_s_170408e.htm.

———. 2009a. *Antisemitism on Arab media*. Israel Intelligence and Heritage Commemoration Center. Retrieved April 20, 2009. http://www.terrorism-info.org.il/malam_multimedia/English/eng_n/html/as_e002.htm.

———. 2009b. *The Hate industry*. Israel Intelligence and Heritage Commemoration Center. Retrieved April 20, 2009. http://www.terrorism-info.org.il/malam_multi media/English/eng_n/html/hamas_e069.htm.

Kressel, N.J. 2002. *Mass hate: the global rise of genocide and terror*, rev. ed. Boulder, CO: Westview. Originally published in 1996.

———. 2003. "Antisemitism, social science, and the Muslim and Arab world." *Judaism* 52(3-4), pp. 225-45.

———. 2004. "The urgent need to study Islamic antisemitism." *The Chronicle of Higher Education*, March 12, pp. B14-B15.

———. 2007a. "Mass Hatred in the Muslim and Arab World: The Neglected Problem of Antisemitism." *International Journal of Applied Psychoanalytic Studies* 4(3), pp. 197-215.

———. 2007b. *Bad Faith: The Danger of Religious Extremism*. Amherst, NY: Prometheus Books.

Levy, B. 2008. *Left in dark times*. Translated by B. Moser. New York: Random House.

Lewis, B. 1987. *Semites and anti-Semites*, paperback ed. New York: Norton.

———. 2002. *What went wrong?* New York: Oxford University Press.

———. 2003. *The Crisis of Islam*. New York: Modern Library.

London Conference on Combating Anti-Semitism. 2009. "The London Declaration on Combating Anti-Semitism." Retrieved April 26, 2009. http://antisem.org/downloads/The-London-Declaration-on-Combating-Antisemitism.pdf.

MacShane, D. 2008. *Globalising hatred: The new antisemitism*. London: Orion.

Mahathir, M. 2003. Speech by Prime Minister Mahathir Mohamad of Malaysia to the Tenth Islamic Summit Conference, Putrajaya, Malaysia, October 16. Retrieved April 26, 2009. http://www.adl.org/Anti_semitism/malaysian.asp.

Markovits, A.S. 2007. *Uncouth nation: Why Europe dislikes America*. Princeton, NJ: Princeton.

MEMRI. 2002a. *A new antisemitic myth in the Middle East media*. Special Report No. 8. Washington, D.C.: MEMRI. Retrieved July 3, 2003. http://www.memri.org/bin/articles.cgi?Page=subjects&Area=antisemitism&ID=SR00802.

———. 2002b. *The events of September 11 and the Arab media*. Special Report No. 9. Washington, D.C.: MEMRI. Retrieved July 3, 2003. http://www.memri.org/bin/articles.cgi?Page=subjects&Area=antisemitism&ID=SR00902.

———. 2002c. *Arab press debates antisemitic Egyptian series: "A Knight without a Horse"—Part II*. MEMRI Inquiry and Analysis No. 113. Washington, D.C.: MEMRI. Retrieved August 4, 2003. http://www.memri.org/bin/articles.cgi?Page=subjects&Area=antisemitism&ID=IA11302.

———. 2002d. *The Damascus Blood Libel (1840) as Told by Syria's Minister of Defense, Mustafa Tlass*. MEMRI Inquiry and Analysis No. 99. Retrieved April 26, 2009. http://memri.org/bin/articles.cgi?Page=archives&Area=ia&ID=IA9902.

———. 2004a. *Former al-Azhar Fatwa Committee head sets out the Jews' 20 bad traits as described in the Qur'an*. Special Dispatch No. 691. Washington, D.C.: MEMRI. Retrieved June 24, 2004. http://www.memri.org/bin/articles.cgi?Page=archives&Area=sd&ID=SP69104.

———. 2004b. *Leading Egyptian journalist: the Jews are behind every disaster or terrorist act*. Special Dispatch No. 700. Washington, D.C.: MEMRI. Retrieved June 24, 2004. http://www.memri.org/bin/articles.cgi?Page=archives&Area=sd&ID=SP70004.

———. 2009. *On Hamas TV*. Special Dispatch No. 2318. Washington, D.C.: MEMRI. Retrieved April 20, 2009. http://www.memri.org/bin/latestnews.cgi?ID=SD231809.

Milson, M. 2004. *What is Arab antisemitism?* MEMRI Special Report No. 26. Washington, D.C.: MEMRI. Retrieved June 11, 2004. http://www.memri.org/bin/articles.cgi?Page=archives&Area=sr&ID=SR2604.

Mir, S. 2004. "Letters to the editor: looking beyond stereotypes of Jews and Muslims in the Middle East." *The Chronicle of Higher Education*, April 23, p. B4.

Montesquiou, A. de. 2009. "Morocco challenges Mideast Holocaust mindset." *Associated Press Online*, July 26. Retrieved July 31, 2009. http://news.yahoo.com/s/ap/20090725/ap_on_re_mi_ea/af_mideast_muslims_holocaust.

Montville, J.V. 2007. "Commentary of 'Mass hatred in the Muslim and Arab world: The Neglected problem of antisemitism." *International Journal of Applied Psychoanalytic Studies* 4(3), pp. 216-20.

Morris, M. 2004. "EU whitewashes Muslim antisemitism." *American Thinker*. Retrieved April 13, 2009. http://www.americanthinker.com/2004/04/eu_white washes_muslim_antisemi.html.

Morse, S.J. 2004. "Letters to the editor: looking beyond stereotypes of Jews and Muslims in the Middle East." *The Chronicle of Higher Education*, April 23, p. B4.

Mozgovaya, N. 2008. "Charge Ahmadinejad with incitement to genocide, say former U.S., Israeli envoys to UN." *Ha'aretz*, September 23. Retrieved April 26, 2009. http://www.haaretz.com/hasen/spages/1023773.html.

Ostow, M. 1996. *Myth and madness*. New Brunswick, NJ: Transaction.

———. 2007. "Commentary of 'Mass hatred in the Muslim and Arab world: The Neglected problem of antisemitism.'" *International Journal of Applied Psychoanalytic Studies* 4(3), pp. 221-34.

Perry, M., and F.M. Schweitzer. 2002. *Antisemitism*. New York: Palgrave Macmillan.

Pew Global Attitudes Project. 2005. *Islamic extremism: Common concern for Muslim and Western publics*. Retrieved April 21, 2009. http://pewglobal.org/reports/display.php?ReportID=248.

Pollak, N. 2009. "Double standards and Human Rights Watch." *The Wall Street Journal*, July 30. Retrieved July 31, 2009. http://online.wsj.com/article/SB10001424052970204619004574318344040299638.html.

Radio Islam. n.d. "USA's Rulers—They're All Jews! Clinton's List." Retrieved on August 4, 2003. http://www.abbc2.com/islam/english/toread/collect.htm.

Ramzy, N. 2007. "Editor's Response to Kressel." *International Journal of Applied Psychoanalytic Studies* 4(3), pp. 191-6.

Schoenfeld, G. 2004. *The return of antisemitism*. San Francisco: Encounter.

Sharansky, N. 2005. "3-D test of Antisemitism." *Jewish Political Studies Review* 17(1-2). Retrieved on April 27, 2009. http://www.jcpa.org/phas/phas-sharansky-s05.htm.

Siegel, R. 2004. "Anti-Zionism is Anti-Semitism: A Response to Judith Butler." *Bad Subjects* 70, October. Retrieved on April 20, 2009. http://bad.eserver.org/issues/2004/70/siegel.html.

Solnick, A. 2002. "Based on Koranic verses, interpretations and traditions, Muslim clerics state: the Jews are descendants of apes, pigs, and other animals." MEMRI Special Report No. 11. Washington, D.C.: MEMRI. Retrieved July 3, 2003. http://memri.org/bin/articles.cgi?Page=subjects&Area=antisemitism&ID=SR01102.

Stalinsky, S. 2003. "Inside the Saudi classroom." *National Review Online*, February 7. Retrieved June 24, 2004. Lexis-Nexis Academic Database.

Starrett, G. 2004. "Letters to the editor: looking beyond stereotypes of Jews and Muslims in the Middle East." *The Chronicle of Higher Education*, April 23, p. B4.

Thienhaus, O.J. 2004. "Communications." *Judaism* 53(1-2), p. 159.

Timmerman, K.R. 2003. *Preachers of hate*. New York: Crown Forum.

Wistrich, R.S. 2002. *Muslim antisemitism*. New York: American Jewish Committee. Retrieved August 5, 2003. http://www.ajc.org/InTheMedia/PublicationsPrint.asp?did=503.

Wistrich, R. n.d. *Muslim antisemitism*. The Coordination Forum for Countering Antisemitism. Retrieved April 27, 2009. http://www.antisemitism.org.il/eng/articles/7932/Muslim_Antisemitism_-By_Robert_Wistrich.

Yeor, B. 2002. *Islam and dhimmitude*. Cranbury, NJ: Fairleigh Dickinson University Press/Associated University Presses.

Trauma in Disguise:
The Effects of Antisemitism

Hadar Lubin*

I. INTRODUCTION

The persistence of antisemitism in its overt and covert forms continues to challenge those who seek a coherent model of prejudice and bigotry. This paper will utilize the trauma construct to elucidate the responses, dynamics, and consequences of antisemitism. Addressing these challenges from a trauma perspective may offer a helpful model that describes the experience of the victim, the dynamics between the victim and the perpetrator, and the role that society plays in sustaining and perpetuating prejudice.

Antisemitism can be defined as the hatred of Jews because they are Jews. Although presumably antisemitism arose from or involved a conflict over religious beliefs, over the years it seems to have evolved into a deep fear and hatred of the Jews *as a people*, and has become a systematic attack on political and social levels reinforced by policies of isolation and exclusion (Chanes 1995). Acts may range from violent attacks on individuals, Jewish institutions, or, of course, all Jews (as in the Holocaust), to *microaggressive* incidents within supposedly tolerant societies, such as language idioms and jokes. Contemporary antisemitism in the West may appear in anti-Zionist references on internet sites and blogs or couched in political opinions about the Middle East conflict (Chanes 2000).

In the field of trauma, debate continues regarding the range of events from obviously life-threatening experiences to less obvious incidents of neglect, subtle bullying or teasing, and social isolation. More and more clinicians and researchers are discovering that even apparently minor incidents, especially if occurring frequently, over long periods of time, or from multiple sources, may have as devastating an impact on the thoughts, behaviors, and self-perceptions of the victim (Herman 1992; Van der Kolk 1987). In a similar way, the effects of antisemitic acts may range from transient distress to the development of psychopathology, depending on the severity, persistence, and nature of the antisemitic event.

II. THE TRAUMA PERSPECTIVE

Trauma overwhelms the person's capacity to respond to the event. Often the individual freezes and is unable to respond or the individual remains in a state of

---

* Assistant Clinical Professor, Department of Psychiatry, Yale University School of Medicine; Director of the Post Traumatic Street Center, LLC in New Haven, Connecticut.

shock and disbelief that the event actually occurred. Trauma evokes a profound sense of helplessness and fear. It can cause physical, psychological, and emotional harm. Given the power differential between the perpetrator and the victim, the experience may lead to a sense of defeat and lack of control. The effects of the trauma reverberate throughout the person's life (Lubin and Johnson 2007). Likewise, the experience of antisemitism can evoke a sense of helplessness, fear, lack of control, or shock, resulting in emotional harm. Individuals who have been targeted by antisemitism testify to the longevity of the effect and its potency years later. These reactions are common and characteristic of the experience of trauma. Understanding these dynamics can shift the blame and the sense of failure from the victim to the perpetrator.

III. Responses to the Spectrum of Traumatic Events

There are predictable and universal responses to trauma, which, if understood, can be expected when antisemitism is directed at the individual. These responses may develop into a constellation of symptoms recognizable as a disorder, such as post-traumatic stress disorder, depression, or an anxiety disorder. However, especially in response to the more covert forms of antisemitism, individuals may also use a variety of strategies that tend to minimize, deny, or internalize the stress that is created.

Avoidance is commonly employed to ward off the effects of the experience. Often avoidance includes withdrawal from activities and places that are associated with the antisemitic event, which may include attending Jewish religious services, celebrating Jewish holidays, or participating in activities in which one's Jewish identity may be revealed. These avoidant efforts are often justified for other reasons unrelated to fears of antisemitism. Isolation from supportive communities may be one result (Peterson, Prout, and Schwarz 1991).

The experience of antisemitism often evokes high *anxiety* that tends to reappear when avoidance fails (McCann and Pearlman 1990; Everly and Lating 1995). It is not surprising that an unprovoked and unjustified attack will produce heightened anxiety. Often individuals will deny or minimize the effects of the antisemitic experience in order to lower the anxiety associated with its recollection. As we learned from the work with trauma, the person's anxiety is fueled by fear, avoidance, lack of control, and the anticipation of a repeated experience. Those same mechanisms are responsible for sustaining the anxiety that the antisemitic experience may reoccur and in turn enhances the avoidance of the original experience. The result is often a commitment to silence, including a failure to report the incident to authority, a failure to communicate the event to family and friends, a tendency to minimize the negative effects of the experience, and a desire to hide one's Jewish identity.

In addition to avoidance and anxiety, the targeted individuals report a sense of *shame and humiliation*, and the associated feelings of inadequacy, self-blame, and guilt (McCann and Pearlman 1990; Everly and Lating 1995). There are several factors that lead to the experience of shame and humiliation. Being singled out and put down lead to a sense of shame. Since the initial response to the event is of shock and disbelief, often the targeted individuals feel that they failed to respond appropriately and therefore attribute the experience to themselves. The experience of helplessness during the antisemitic experience may evoke distorted beliefs such as "I am weak." Seeing or hearing Jews portrayed in negative and demeaning ways often leads to displacing the bad feelings associated with the antisemitic experience to the feeling of being a Jew. This is particularly common among children who are the targets of antisemitism at school or other social and public settings.

Antisemitic jargon and stereotypes are dehumanizing, objectifying and demonizing, which may become internalized as a *sense of inadequacy*. During the encounter with antisemitism, the sense of pride in oneself is overshadowed by hateful words and negative characterizations. The failure to preserve that sense of self during the encounter leads to a sense of inadequacy. As a result, victims become critical of how they handled the event, and may conclude that somehow they are to blame for it. The blame is shifted from the perpetrator to the victim. The larger society may collude with this shift. When members of society collude with silencing the wrong, with blaming the victim, and with explaining away the acts of the perpetrator, then collectively society become a collaborator to prejudice.

The most extreme, though not uncommon response among victims of antisemitism may be actually identifying with the perpetrator and developing secretly-held collusive beliefs that Jews are responsible for some of the reactions to them. Victims may distance themselves from Jewish culture or traditions, they may become overly critical of Israel, and they may not identify themselves as Jews in public settings or with new acquaintances. Among Jews outside of Israel, this identification with the perpetrator may take the form of splitting allegiances: maintaining one's support for Jews while demonstrating objectivity by condemning the State of Israel. This stance, of course, is also taken by certain antisemitic groups.

IV. Modes of Antisemitic Acts

There are different ways to target an individual by antisemitism: in private or public contexts, emotionally or physically, and overtly or covertly. The following are examples of the different ways antisemitism is transmitted:

1. Private or public context

An unwitnessed encounter with antisemitism is likely to evoke the individual's helplessness and isolation. The victim must make a judgment whether to reveal the event or not, and considerations of one's own credibility, in relation to the power position of the perpetrator, come to the fore. However, when the attack occurs in public, the potential failure of witnesses to stand by the victim adds substantial risk to the victim's experience of isolation. Often the failure of the bystander to support the victim is as painful and damaging as (or sometimes even more than) the actual antisemitic attack. It communicates to the individual that there is an unstated, collusive agreement with the perpetrator's actions or words. The isolation and alienation therefore deepens.

2. Emotional vs. physical

Humiliating or demeaning remarks about Jews (emotional abuse) have significantly different effects than harm to self or properties (physical abuse). Portraying Jews in demeaning and negative ways creates tension between the individual's sense of pride about their Jewish identity and the views of the perpetrator. For example, if you feel proud about your mitzvah contributions, the portrayal of Jews as being obsessed with money or cheap is incongruent with the sense of pride and therefore creates an internal psychic tension. It can eat at you from the inside. In contrast, a physical attack or act of vandalism is intrusive, visible, and violent. The perpetrator succeeds at scarring, branding, or altering the victim and their body: the violent act rests on the skin or the possessions of the victim. Feelings of being soiled, ruined, marked, or targeted are likely to arise.

3. Overtly vs. covertly

An explicit antisemitic remark such as "you are a dirty Jew" is quite different from being indirectly excluded from activities or groups because of the Jewish faith, for example, when an activity at school is scheduled on a Jewish holiday. On the one hand, the overt attack seems worse. But because it is explicit, it is often easier to address it or counter it with legal action. The covert act, though apparently less violent, is much more difficult to address, as the perpetrator will deny intention and in fact counter with claims that the victim is being "too sensitive." The victim is left injured and embarrassed.

V. METHODS OF ADDRESSING ANTISEMITISM FROM A TRAUMA PERSPECTIVE

Similar to the work with trauma victims, the healing process for victims of antisemitism involves direct empowerment (Herman 1992). Trauma does strip the individual from power; thus the antidote to trauma is a restoration of power in the targeted individual. The path to empowerment comprises of multiple avenues such as reporting, education, advocacy, and support.

1. Reporting

The goal of the perpetrator is to isolate the victim and to keep him/her silent. The more isolated and silent the victim, the more powerful the perpetrator becomes. Breaking the silence by reporting, telling, and talking about the event weakens the position and the power of the perpetrator. Alerting the system and the relevant authorities neutralizes both the power of the perpetrator and the effect of the perpetration. The more the victim talks about the event with friends and family, the more support is available to buffer the toxic effects of antisemitism. Victims of antisemitism are advised to counter and resist the avoidance that fuels the negative consequences of the event. Confronting the perpetrator's actions, directly if safe or indirectly through reporting, restores the sense of control within the victim and shifts the control away from the perpetrator. The witnesses to the antisemitic event also have the obligation to report the event. By doing so, they take an active role in combating it, shifting their position from bystanders to allies.

2. Education

Knowledge is a powerful tool not only against ignorance but also in locating the fault in the perpetrator. Holding the perpetrator accountable for his/her actions is the first step toward reparation, the first step toward countering the devastating effects of injustice. Learning about the effects of antisemitism and the common responses to it helps people understand its universality. Addressing the negative consequences of antisemitism in the context of the human condition normalizes the responses to it and therefore facilitates the recovery from such a painful experience. Efforts to educate the perpetrator are of prime importance because some antisemitic actions are the result of ignorance and misinformation. Both the perpetrator and the targeted individual benefit from the power of increased knowledge. Understanding through education is the cornerstone of healing society from prejudice.

3. Advocacy

During the antisemitic event, the power differential is strong and decisive: the perpetrator holds the power and the victim is powerless. This power differential shifts as the victim takes on the position of an advocate. Helping others understand the experience of being a target of antisemitism empowers the victim and puts him/her in the position of an educator. Helping others deal with the consequences of antisemitism through advocacy actively counters the corrosive effects of hatred and bigotry. Giving testimonies about the experiences of antisemitism is a powerful antidote for the senseless act of antisemitism and improves the societal milieu for all people. By supporting efforts of advocacy and by listening to the testimonies of antisemitism, members of society can be actively involved in combating prejudice.

4. Support

Though the act of perpetration can occur in isolation or in public, the act of healing must occur in a social context. We all suffer when antisemitism targets a member of society. We are all responsible for countering its effects (Lubin and Johnson 2007; Figley 1986). Providing support to the victim at the time of the event by being an ally rather than a bystander is an act of defiance against prejudice. Providing support to the victim after the event helps validate the suffering associated with the antisemitic experience and shares the burden of the event. It is important that the victim allows an ally to provide the necessary support. By doing so both benefit: the victim by alleviating the pain of the perpetration and the ally by having an opportunity to do the right thing. If educating the perpetrator fails, distancing oneself from him/her preserves one's safety. Support is also available through the Anti-Defamation League, which provides access to resources, guidance, and educational programs (Anti-Defamation League 2008). Only through a collective effort can society succeed in ameliorating the devastating consequences of hatred and prejudice.

VI. Special Challenges

Now that antisemitism and its consequences are better understood through the construct of trauma, it is prudent to review a few specific challenges. Understanding what we are up against helps us to respond effectively to acts of discrimination and bigotry.

1. Fear of retribution

As mentioned earlier, the perpetrator is in the position of power. Fearing the perpetrator is a natural human response, and it is common to fear retribution. Any action or inaction has its consequences. Fear of retribution often leads to and fuels the avoidance that results from the antisemitic event. The avoidance not only isolates the victim but reinforces the perpetrator. What protects the victim is the acknowledgement of the event. The more the authority is involved and the more the victim is supported, the less likely the retribution becomes. The fear of retribution also strengthens the perpetrator. Preparing for the retribution with the help of the authority and with the support of the community actually weakens the perpetrator. That is not to say that caution should not be exercised; recognizing the difference between the two enhances everyone's safety.

2. Lack of support

Unfortunately, support is not always readily available. However, its absence can be minimized through education and understanding. During the antisemitic event, the presence of bystanders is common. Many times witnesses of the antisemitic event also fear the perpetrator and are unable to respond in an effective way or fail to recognize that what they have witnessed is indeed antisemitism. Educating people about the nature of the experience affords them more options to respond in a timely fashion and in an effective manner. Addressing the importance of being an ally either during the antisemitic event or afterwards reinforces the support that is available. Bystanders need to understand that their passivity of action and their muted response support the perpetrator and antisemitism. That is also true when institutions, like schools, fail to react appropriately and decisively when antisemitism takes place on their premises. The institution itself becomes a proxy for the perpetrator.

3. Sub-threshold events

When the antisemitic event is extreme, the reaction to it is more likely to be uniformly decisive. The harm is more out in the open. However, more often the experience of antisemitism is cumulative and insidious, consisting of small moments of innuendo, nonverbal gestures, and supposed humor. The effect of these microaggressive events tends to build up over time and may reach a threshold, the victim bursting out in an emotional reaction. At that point, the targeted individual may be viewed as being "overly sensitive." Often, the victim himself/herself also judges their response as an over-reaction. It is a perfect situation for condoning the antisemitic behavior and for over-looking the effects on the victim. With this arrangement, both the victim and society are colluding with inaction. The inaction then fuels further action by the perpetrator or other perpetrators.

Sub-threshold events are also excused or redirected by other strategies, supported by either the victim or society or both. They may be excused by the *cycle of violence argument*. Here, the perpetrator's actions may be excused by the recognition that the perpetrator was a victim in the past. It is true that a significant number of perpetrators were victimized at one point in their lives. This information is particularly important in the context of educating perpetrators and in the effort to rehabilitate them. However the perpetrator must be held accountable for the actions if any reparation or healing is to take place. No chance for recovery exists if society condones this perpetrator's action because of someone else's perpetration. By doing so, we fail twice. By doing so we fuel this vicious cycle. The cycle of violence has to break in order to change the course of prejudice. That can only be done by holding the perpetrators responsible for their actions and by providing the necessary support to the perpetrator-as-victim. The message is also intended for the victims, who should be discouraged from perpetuating the violence by becoming perpetrators themselves.

The second strategy redirects the sub-threshold event onto the political arena, transforming an act of prejudice into a "political opinion." Here, the phenomenon of the identification with the aggressor can be best used to understand the anti-Israeli sentiment when it is a form of antisemitism. Clearly, criticism of Israeli policy is appropriate within a civil dialogue about the Middle East. However, when it is cloaked as criticism but in fact is a form of antisemitism or anti-Zionism, it is useful to understand the dynamic of identification with the aggressor. Israel is often viewed as the aggressor even when it responds to persistent violence against its citizens. This distortion is based on the historical knowledge that the Jews were victims and are now taking the position of the perpetrator. Israel, as the more powerful force in comparison with the Palestinians, now takes on the role of the perpetrator. Defensive responses by Israel after suicide or missile attacks are characterized as "over-reactions." Victim and perpetrator roles become reversed and confused, to the delight of the antisemitic person. Untangling this merging of political debate and ethnic hatred is nearly impossible, leaving this strategy an unfortunately effective one.

VII. Summary

In summary, utilizing a trauma perspective to understand the effects of antisemitism and other forms of prejudice sheds light onto some of the common reactions to bigotry, helps to understand the dynamics among the perpetrator, victim, bystander, and ally, and provides guidance to effective ways of responding to hatred. Trauma can be viewed as a cancer of the psyche: it is aggressive, invasive, and sometimes fatal. Prejudice, such as antisemitism, is the cancer of society. It violently invades the healthy matrix of society, it destroys its vitality, and it needs to be countered by decisive measures.

References

Anti-Defamation League. 2008. *Confronting Anti-Semitism.* Washington, DC: Anti-Defamation League.

Chanes, J. 2000. *A dark side of history: Antisemitism through the ages.* New York: Anti-Defamation League.

Chanes, J. 1995. *Antisemitism in America today: Outspoken experts explode the myths, Part 1.* New York: Birch Lane Press.

Everly, G., and J. Lating, eds. 1995. *Psychotraumatology. Key papers and core concepts in post-traumatic stress.* New York: Plenum Press.

Figley, C., ed. 1986. *Trauma and its wake. Volume II: Traumatic stress: Theory, research, and intervention.* New York: Brunner/Mazel, Publishers.

Herman, J. 1992. *Trauma and recovery.* New York: Basic Books.

Lubin, H., and D. Johnson. 2007. *Trauma-centered group psychotherapy for women. A clinician's manual.* Binghamton, NY: Haworth Press.

McCann, L., and L. Pearlman. 1990. *Psychological trauma and the adult survivor: Theory, therapy, and transformation.* New York: Brunner/Mazel, Publishers.

Peterson, K., M. Prout, and R. Schwarz. 1991. *Post-traumatic stress disorder. A clinician's guide.* New York: Plenum Press.

Van der Kolk, B. 1987. *Psychological trauma.* Washington, DC: American Psychiatric Press.

Mixed Emotional Needs of Israeli-Jews as a Potential Source of Ambivalence in Their Response to the Iranian Challenge

Nurit Shnabel* and John F. Dovidio**

I. INTRODUCTION

One of the famous quotes of David Ben-Gurion, the first prime minister of Israel, is that "the fate of Israel depends on its strength and on its justice." This quote may still be relevant today, in which Israel's future may depend, on the one hand, on its military power to defend itself from organizations such as the Hezbollah and, on the other hand, on acting in a just and moral way to avoid both its isolation from the international community and its internal divide due to Israelis' loss of faith in their country's righteousness. Furthermore, from a social psychological perspective, we believe Ben-Gurion's quote to perceptively capture two fundamental dimensions of groups' identities: power and morality. In the present paper, we will use our perspective as social-psychologists to analyze the experience of threat to these dimensions of identity among Israeli-Jews, and we consider the particular historical and psychological influences that produce a duality of emotional needs for Israeli-Jews and its implications for their response to existential threats, including the current Iranian challenge. After putting forward our general theoretical perspective, we present the Needs-Based Model, a socio-psychological model that explains how threats posed to certain identity dimensions (i.e., power and morality) bring about specific emotional needs for empowerment and social acceptance. We then present empirical data showing that Israeli-Jews experience an enhanced need for either empowerment or acceptance in different intergroup contexts, suggest that this dual psychological experience may lead to an ambivalent response of Israeli-Jews to existential threats, and discuss the implications of this ambivalence.

We begin by elucidating what "a social-psychological perspective" means. Since its emergence as an independent scientific discipline, social psychology as a field has devoted considerable attention to understanding the processes involved in intergroup conflict and has accumulated valuable insights and knowledge on this subject, particularly in recent decades (Jones 1998). The theoretical and empirical research in social psychology focuses on *formulating general principles* that operate in conflicts rather than on analyzing the particular characteristics of specific conflicts. For example,

---

* Post-Doctoral Fellow in Social Psychology, Yale University.
** Professor of Psychology, Yale University.

social psychologists may point to the general tendency of adversaries to devaluate offers made by the other party compared to the ones made by one's own party (Ross 1995) rather than analyzing the particular responses to a specific offer (e.g., the Israeli response to the Saudi peace initiative).

In their analysis of conflicts, including their causes and resolution, social psychologists have generally used two theoretical perspectives. The Realist approach to conflict (see Scheff 1994) suggests that conflicts originate from groups' competition over scarce tangible resources, such as land or money. This approach is often contrasted with that of Psychological Needs approach (Burton 1969), which emphasizes that during conflict parties inflict humiliation and pain on each other that produce threats to basic psychological needs such as the need for positive esteem, worthy identity, autonomy, security, and justice. These threats bring about emotions and motivations (e.g., the motivation of revenge, Frijda 1994) that contribute to the maintenance of conflicts. Rather that representing competing positions, the theoretical perspectives of the Realist and the Psychological Needs approaches may be viewed as complementary, illuminating the different aspects and processes that operate in conflicts.

The Needs-Based Model (Nadler and Shnabel 2008; Shnabel and Nadler 2008; Shnabel et al. 2008; Shnabel et al. 2009), which is presented and applied in this paper to analyze the emotional mechanisms that influence the Israeli-Jewish response to Iran, is theoretically anchored in the Psychological Needs perspective on conflict. Thus, even though we acknowledge that instrumental factors and considerations influence the Israeli-Jewish response to Iran, our analysis exclusively focuses on psychological aspects and processes that affect this response. We believe that the theoretical perspective suggested by the Needs-Based Model, as well as the empirical data collected within its framework, can provide valuable insights for understanding the psychological mechanism underlying the reaction of Israeli-Jews to situations of intergroup conflict in general and to the one with Iran in particular.

II. THE NEEDS-BASED MODEL AND ITS APPLICATION TO THE JEWISH-ISRAELI CASE

The Needs-Based Model is a theoretical model that seeks to explain why certain social roles are more strongly associated with an enhanced need for acceptance, whereas other social roles are associated with an enhanced need for empowerment, and to illuminate how the satisfaction of these needs can improve intergroup relations. One key foundational element of the model is the tenet that, following an episode in which one side has victimized another, both the victims (i.e., group members[1] who perceive their group as having been victimized by the outgroup) and the perpetrators (i.e., group members who perceive their group as having perpetrated harm and suffering on others) experience a threat over certain unique psychological dimensions of their identities. This threat is posed at the group level, and therefore it may be experienced by group members regardless of whether or not they were personally involved in the victimization episode. For example, historical events

---

[1] The Needs-Based Model also relates to the context of interpersonal transgressions, but this is beyond the scope of the present paper.

may arouse collective-based feelings of guilt or victimization among group members due to their identification with their ingroup (e.g., Wohl, Branscombe, and Klar 2006).

The Needs-Based Model further suggests that the psychological threat posed to the identities of victims and perpetrators is asymmetrical. Specifically, victims suffer a basic psychological threat to their identity as *powerful social actors*: they feel inferior with respect to their level of power (Foster and Rusbult 1999), honor (Scheff 1994), self-esteem (Scobie and Scobie 1998), and perceived control (Baumeister, Stillwell, and Heatherton 1994), and therefore they typically experience feelings of anger (McCullough et al. 1998). In contrast, perpetrators experience a threat to their identity as *moral social actors*: they suffer from a sense of moral inferiority (Exline and Baumeister 2000; Zechmeister and Romero 2002) and generally, although not always, feel guilt (Baumeister et al. 1994), shame (Exline and Baumeister 2000), or remorse (North 1998). This array of emotional states has been said to reflect perpetrators' "anxiety over social exclusion" (Baumeister et al. 1994, 246), because, if perpetrators are viewed as guilty by others, they face the threat of being rejected from the moral community to which they belong (Tavuchis 1991).[2]

The idea that power and morality are fundamental dimensions of groups' identity is reflected in the Stereotype Content Model (Fiske et al. 2002), which demonstrates that most group stereotypes are captured by two dimensions: competence and warmth. Perceptions of competence are related to respect towards other groups; perceptions of warmth are associated with liking them. These dimensions are often negatively related (Judd et al. 2005). For example, groups that elicit "envious stereotypes," such as Jews and Germans (Phalet and Poppe 1997), are depicted as high in competence but low in warmth (e.g., they are perceived as relatively immoral and unsocial). A similar notion is reflected in Loughnan and Haslam's (2007) proposition that outgroup members may be likened to animals (i.e., high in warmth and low in competence) or automata (i.e., high in competence and low in warmth). Although the Stereotype Content Model relates to stereotypes in general rather than to the specific social roles of victims and perpetrators, its perspective and evidence are highly relevant to that of the Needs-Based Model, because the dimensions of competence and warmth in the first correspond to those of power and morality (respectively) in the latter.

The differential threat to victims' and perpetrators' dimensions of identities arouses corresponding motivations. Victims are motivated to restore their sense of power. A unilateral way to achieve this goal would be to take revenge on their perpetrators (Nadler and Shnabel 2008). A bilateral way would be to pursue the perpetrators' acknowledgement of their responsibility for causing the injustice, which returns

---

[2] The concept of "moral community" consists of psychologically relevant others who make up one's significant social relationship and who share with one a specific set of norms and values. Membership in this "moral community" is "predicated upon our knowledge, acceptance and conformity to specific and general norms" (Tavuchis 1991, 8). Most "moral communities" hold that we should not harm another person or group of people unjustifiably or disproportionately. Consequently, the perception that perpetrators had inflicted such harm may threaten the validity of their membership in the relevant "moral community" and arouse fears of being excluded from it.

control to victims who may determine whether to cancel the moral "debt" (Minow 1998). Palestinian and Jewish terror attacks against each other illustrate a unilateral attempt of restoring power, whereas raising demands for recognition (by Israelis) in Palestinians' right of return or acknowledgment (by Palestinians) in Israel's right to exist reflect bilateral attempts to restore power.

Perpetrators, in contrast, are motivated to remove the threat to their moral image. A unilateral way to reduce this threat would be to deny the painful consequences of their actions and/or their responsibility for having caused them (Schönbach 1990). A bilateral way would be to seek forgiveness, empathy for their emotional distress, and understanding of the circumstances that compelled them to act in a socially unacceptable way (Nadler and Liviatan 2006), or social connections with the victim (e.g., forming friendships). Such responses restore perpetrators' moral image, help them feel "rehumanized" (Staub et al. 2005, 328), and make them feel as acceptable social actors despite their transgressions. Dehumanization of the outgroup (e.g., of Palestinians by Jews and of Jews by Palestinians, Bar-Tal 2007) illustrates a unilateral attempt to reduce the threat to the ingroup's moral image, whereas public apologies (e.g., Pope John Paul II's apology to the Jews for two millennia of persecution by the Catholic Church) exemplify a bilateral attempt to remove such a threat.

From a broader theoretical perspective, the psychological motivations of victims and perpetrators may be subsumed under the basic human needs for *status*, that is, the need for relative power, control, autonomy, sense of competence, influence, and respect, on the one hand, and *relatedness*, that is, the need for social acceptance and belongingness, on the other (Bennis and Shepard 1956; Foa and Foa 1980). In the following sections, we use the terms *acceptance* and *empowerment* to relate to these respective needs and present empirical data from two experiments that examined the experience of these needs by Israeli-Jews. These experiments (Shnabel et al., 2009) used two contexts of intergroup relations—those between Jews and Germans and between Israeli-Jews and Arabs—to examine the threats posed to the dimensions of power and morality in the collective identity of Israeli-Jews and the emotional needs experienced by them as a result.

The first experiment focused on relations between Germans and Jews (Shnabel et al., 2009). In line with the Needs-Based Model, we hypothesized that reminding college-age Israeli-Jewish participants of the Holocaust would arouse feelings of a threat to their group's sense of power and therefore create an enhanced need for empowerment. Accordingly, these Israeli-Jewish participants would respond more positively to an empowering compared to an accepting message from a German representative. The opposite pattern was predicted for German participants reminded of the Holocaust, who were hypothesized to experience a threat to their group's moral image and therefore feel an enhanced need for acceptance. Consequently, German participants were expected to respond more positively to an accepting compared to an empowering message from a Jewish representative.

To test these hypotheses we measured Israeli-Jewish and German participants' collective sense of power and moral image after reminding them of events associated with the Holocaust. We then exposed them to two speeches, allegedly made by their outgroup's representatives. The central message conveyed in each speech was either the empowerment or the acceptance of the participants' ingroup. The messages used were identically phrased for Jewish and German participants and each participant was exposed to both kinds of messages. The Empowerment message conveyed the idea that "Nowadays, it is the [Germans'/Jews'] right to be strong and proud of their country and to have the power to determine their own fate," whereas the Acceptance message conveyed the idea that "We, the [Germans/Jews], should accept the [Jews/Germans] and remember that we are all human beings." We then measured participants' responses to each message (e.g., its effects on their support for reconciliation with the other group). As expected, Israeli-Jewish participants had a lower sense of power and responded more positively to a message of empowerment that satisfied their psychological need for empowerment, while German participants had a lower moral image and responded more positively to a message of acceptance that satisfied their psychological need for social acceptance.

The second experiment that investigated the emotional needs of members of different groups focused on the context of the relations between Israeli-Jews and Israeli-Arabs. The relations between Jews and Arabs are characterized by "competitive victimhood" (Noor, Brown, and Prentice 2008), that is, both Jews and Arabs often claim that they are the "real" victims of the Jewish-Arab conflict (Nadler 2002) and that they have suffered *more* than the outgroup. To complement the previous experiment, though, we focused on an historical event for which there is a consensus among Jewish and Arab Israelis as to the victimization of Arabs by the Jewish side: the Kafar Kassem massacre. In this event, which took place in October 1956, 43 unarmed Arab civilians were killed by the Israeli border patrol for violating a curfew that had recently been imposed. Thus, whereas the previous study emphasized the role of Jews as victims, this experiment focused on their role, in this instance, as perpetrators.

Using the same experimental design as the one used in the German-Jewish study, we measured Israeli Arabs and Jews sense of power and moral image and then exposed them to speeches conveying messages of empowerment or acceptance ostensibly made by representatives of their outgroup on the 50th anniversary of the massacre. In contrast with the first experiment, in this context Israeli-Jews had a lower moral image and responded more positively to a message of acceptance, while Israeli-Arabs had a lower sense of power and responded more positively to a message of empowerment.

Taken together, these findings suggest that in different contexts Israeli-Jews experience threats over differential dimensions of their identities and consequently experience fundamentally divergent emotional needs. In the context of Holocaust, in which Jews identify with the social role of the victim, the threat is over their sense of power resulting in an enhanced need for *empowerment*, whereas in the context of the Kafar Kassem massacre, in which Jews identify with the social role of the perpetrator, the threat is over their moral image resulting in an enhanced need for *acceptance*. Furthermore, as mentioned above, while the context of the Kafar Kassem massacre is clear cut in terms of the identity of victims and perpetrators, the general context of Jewish-Arab relations is not (see Nadler 2002). Consequently, Israeli-Jews are likely to experience differential emotional needs in different situations within this context; for example, terror attacks vs. counter-attacks are likely to enhance their need for empowerment vs. acceptance, respectively. In conclusion, *the Israeli-Jewish identity is characterized by the psychological experience of duality, in terms of social roles (i.e., victims and perpetrators), experienced threats, and emotional needs.*

Admittedly, it is possible that members of many groups—other than Israeli-Jews—also experience one type of threats and emotional needs in some contexts and another type of threats and emotional needs in other contexts. For example, members of some European countries may experience a threat over their group's moral image when discussing the period of colonialism, and a threat over their group's sense of power when discussing the Second World War. Yet, it is important to note that both contexts used in our experiments involve *existential conflicts* that play a central role in shaping the Israeli-Jewish identity and are reflected in language, images, myths, and collective memory: the Holocaust, which threatened the right and ability of Jews to exist, is considered a major group trauma (e.g., Maoz and Bar-On 2002), and the Israeli-Arab conflict, as an intractable conflict, is violent, prolonged, and affects many aspects in the lives of the involved parties (Bar-Tal 1998). Thus, the experience of dual, opposing social roles and consequent threats and needs is likely to be particularly pronounced among Israeli-Jews compared to members of other groups.

Further contributing to the experience of this duality is the particularly charged response of other (i.e., non-Jewish) groups (e.g., Europeans) towards Jews and Israelis when placed in one of these two social roles (victims or perpetrators). For example, following the Second World War, the allies pressured the Germans to aid the Jewish people, but seemed less concerned about other groups, such as homosexuals or Romany people (Gypsies) who were also targeted by the Nazis for elimination (Brooks 1999). Then again, violations of human rights by Israel seem to receive more attention and criticism from the international community compared to parallel violations conducted by other groups. For example, Turkish Prime Minister Recep Tayyip Erdogan condemned Israel's actions during Operation Cast Lead as a crime against humanity but did not make similar accusations towards the Vice President of Sudan, Ali Osman Mohammed Taha, who was hosted by Turkey at about the same time, despite his role in the Darfur genocide. The intense emotional response of other groups towards victimized or perpetrating Jews and Israelis is likely to further intensify their experience of threats to the different dimensions of the Jewish and Israeli identity as well as the resultant psychological needs and duality.

The experience of such a dual, ambivalent identity is likely to affect the reaction of Israeli-Jews to various intergroup situations, including the present conflict with Iran. First, it raises the political dilemma of which type of threat is more crucial and requires a more pressing response. For example, the statement of Mahmoud Ahmadinejad, the president of the Islamic Republic of Iran, that the Israeli regime is a "disgraceful stain on the Islamic world" that should be "wiped from the pages of history,"[3] is likely to threaten Israeli-Jews' sense of autonomy and enhance their need for empowerment. At the same time, the repeated use of equalization between the Star of David, the symbol of the Israeli-Jews, and the swastika, the symbol of the Nazi regime, in different international contexts (e.g., in anti-Israeli demonstrations or graffiti) is likely to threaten Israeli-Jews' moral image and enhance their concern of

---

[3] There is a controversy over the exact translation of Ahmadinejad's speech, but in any case, because the alternatives are equivalent in terms of the type of threat they pose to the *power dimension* of the Israeli identity, we will refrain from addressing this issue in the present chapter.

social rejection (e.g., fear of boycott or embargo, like the one imposed on South Africa) and consequent need for acceptance. Different group members (e.g., holders of left-wing vs. right-wing ideologies) may have different estimations of the gravity of each threat, leading to a difficulty in finding and making a clear, cohesive group voice regarding these issues.

Second, each type of response—aggressive versus restrained—is likely to satisfy one need at the expense of the other. The emotional responses to Operation Cast Lead may illustrate this "damned if you do, dammed if you don't" trap regarding Israel's foreign policies. Prior to the operation, when cities and villages in south Israel were bombed, Israeli-Jews experienced a threat to their sense of control and autonomy, leading an enhanced need for power and an embracing support of a military operation. Yet, following the operation, and in light of the worldwide criticism of it as violating Palestinians' human rights (which even led, among other consequences, to the severance of diplomatic relations with several countries), it is likely that the threat over moral image and resultant enhanced need for acceptance were more heavily weighted and experienced by Israeli-Jews.

Finally, the Theory of Ambivalence-Amplification (Katz 1981) suggests that inconsistent and opposing cognitive or emotional elements (e.g., a mixture of sympathy and aversion felt towards members of a stigmatized group) create psychological tension that can be resolved, in the terms of Freudian psychodynamic theory, by a "reactive displacement of cathexis." Specifically, the responses in a situation in which conflicting needs are experienced would tend to be amplified as the "energy" drawn from one need would be added to the other. Applying this theory to the case of Israeli-Jews, we would expect a phase of vacillation in response to a threat to their autonomy, sense of control, or right to exist (such as the one posed by Iran) followed by an amplified forceful response. The fact that much of the criticism (e.g., by Israeli human rights organizations) of Israel's actions during both the Second Lebanon War and Operation Cast Lead did not concern its right to react to the attacks initiated by Hezbollah and Hamas, but rather the *magnitude and forcefulness* of these reactions, may imply that a psychological mechanism similar to the one suggested above was operating in these cases as well.

III. Summary

We opened this paper by presenting the theoretical perspective of the Needs-Based Model, which suggests that empowerment and acceptance are two fundamental human needs that are enhanced among victims and perpetrators (respectively). We then provided empirical data suggesting that Israeli-Jews, who continually face threats to both their collective sense of power and their moral image, experience enhanced needs for empowerment and acceptance in different contexts of intergroup relations that are central to their collective identity. We suggested that the consequences of this psychological duality (i.e., the experience of inconsistent and opposing emotional needs) are Israeli-Jews' difficulty in finding and expressing a clear voice regarding the Israeli-Iranian conflict due to the augmented political dilemma regarding the relative weight that should be given to each type of threat; a "trap" in which the satisfaction of one need leads to the dissatisfaction of the second, opposing need; and a pattern of response that involves a phase of vacillation followed by an amplified powerful response.

In conclusion, group identities are shaped by general social-psychological processes, such as group members' motivation to maintain positive ingroup identity (Tajfel and Turner 1979), as well as by groups' unique historical and geopolitical conditions. Integrating the two, as done in the present paper, can thus add an important aspect to the analysis of groups' identities and consequent emotions and behavior, by illuminating their psychological dynamic. We hope that the present paper has contributed to the understanding of the unique psychological dynamic of Jewish Israeli identity, how it is affected by the social roles that Jews filled through history or are filling today, and in what way it influences their response to current existential challenges.

REFERENCES

Bar-Tal, D. 1998. "Societal beliefs in times of intractable conflict: The Israeli case." *International Journal of Conflict Management* 9: 22-50.

Bar-Tal, D. 2007. "Sociopsychological foundations of intractable conflicts." *American Behavioral Scientist* 50: 1430-1453.

Baumeister, R.F., A.M. Stillwell, T.F. and Heatherton. 1994. "Guilt: An interpersonal approach." *Psychological Bulletin* 115: 243-267.

Bennis, W.G., and H.A. Shepard. 1956. "A theory of group development." *Human Relations* 9: 415-437.

Brooks, R.L., ed. 1999. *When sorry isn't enough: The controversy over apologies and reparations for human injustice.* New York: New York University Press.

Burton, J.W. 1969. *Conflict and communication: The use of controlled communication in international relations.* New York: Free Press.

Exline, J.J., and R.F. Baumeister. 2000. "Expressing forgiveness and repentance: Benefits and barriers." In *Forgiveness: Theory, research and practice,* edited by M.E. McCullough, K.I. Pargament, and C.E. Thoresen, 133-155. New York: Guilford Press.

Fiske, S.T., A.J.C. Cuddy, P. Glick, and J. Xu. 2002. "A model of often mixed stereotype content: Competence and warmth respectively follow from perceived status and competition." *Journal of Personality and Social Psychology* 82: 878-902.

Foa, E.B., and U.G. Foa. 1980. "Resource theory: Interpersonal behavior as exchange." In *Social exchange: Advances in theory and research,* edited by M.E. McCullough, K.I. Pargament, and C.E. Thoresen, 77-94. New York: Plenum Press.

Foster, C.A., and C.E. Rusbult. 1999. "Injustice and powerseeking." *Personality and Social Psychology Bulletin* 25: 834-849.

Frijda, N.H. 1994. "The lex talionis: On vengeance." In *Emotions: Essays on emotion theory,* edited by S.H.M. Van Goozen, N.E. Van de Poll, and J.A. Sergeant, 263-289. Hillsdale, NJ: Lawrence Erlbaum.

Jones, E. 1998. "Major developments in five decades of social psychology." In *The handbook of social psychology* vol. 1, 4th ed., edited by D.T. Gilbert, S.T. Fiske, and G. Lindzey, 3-57. New York: McGraw-Hill.

Judd, C.M., L. James-Hawkins, V. Yzerbyt, and Y. Kashima. 2005. "Fundamental dimensions of social judgment: Understanding the relations between judgments of competence and warmth." *Journal of Personality and Social Psychology* 89: 899-913.

Katz, I. 1981. *Stigma: A social psychological analysis.* Hillsdale, NJ: Lawrence Erlbaum.

Loughnan, S., and N. Haslam. 2007. "Animals and androids: Implicit associations between social categories and nonhumans." *Psychological Science* 18: 116-121.

Maoz, I., and D. Bar-On. 2002. "From working through the Holocaust to current ethnic conflicts: Evaluating the TRT group workshop in Hamburg." *Group* 26: 29-48.

McCullough, M.E., K.C. Rachal, S.J. Sandage, E.L Worthington, S.W. Brown, and T.L. Hight. 1998. "Interpersonal forgiving in close relationships: II. Theoretical elaboration and measurement." *Journal of Personality and Social Psychology* 75: 1586-1603.

Minow, M. 1998. *Between vengeance and forgiveness: Facing history after genocide and mass violence.* Boston: Beacon Press.

Nadler, A. 2002. "Post resolution processes: Instrumental and socio-emotional routes to reconciliation." In *Peace education: The concept, principles, and practices around the world*, edited by G. Salomon and B. Nevo. Mahwah, NJ: Lawrence Erlbaum.

Nadler, A., and I. Liviatan. 2006. "Intergroup reconciliation: Effects of adversary's expressions of empathy, responsibility, and recipients' trust." *Personality and Social Psychology Bulletin* 32: 459-470.

Nadler, A., and N. Shnabel. 2008. "Intergroup reconciliation: The instrumental and socio-emotional paths and the need based model of socio-emotional reconciliation." In *Social Psychology of Intergroup Reconciliation*, edited by A. Nadler, T. Malloy, and J.D. Fisher, 37-56. New York: Oxford University Press.

Noor, M., J.R. Brown, and G. Prentice. 2008. "Precursors and mediators of intergroup reconciliation in Northern Ireland: a new model." *Journal of British Social Psychology* 47: 481-495.

North, J. 1998. "The 'ideal' of forgiveness: A philosopher's exploration." In *Exploring forgiveness*, edited by R.D. Enright and J. North, 15-34. Madison, WI: University of Wisconsin Press.

Phalet, K., and E. Poppe. 1997. "Competence and morality dimensions of national and ethnic stereotypes: A study in six eastern-European countries." *European Journal of Social Psychology* 27: 703-723.

Ross, L. 1995. "Reactive devaluation in negotiation and conflict resolution." In *Barriers to Conflict Resolution*, edited by K. Arrow, R.H. Mnookin, L. Ross, A. Tversky, and R. Wilson, 26-43. New York: W.W. Norton Company.

Scheff, T.J. 1994. *Bloody revenge: Emotions, nationalism and war.* Boulder, CO: Westview Press.

Schönbach, P. 1990. *Account episodes: The Management or escalation of conflict.* New York: Cambridge University Press.

Scobie, E.D., and G.E.W. Scobie. 1998. "Damaging events: The perceived need for forgiveness." *Journal for the Theory of Social Behaviour* 28: 373-401.

Shnabel, N., and A. Nadler. 2008. "A needs-based model of reconciliation: Satisfying the differential emotional needs of victim and perpetrator as a key to promoting reconciliation." *Journal of Personality and Social Psychology* 94: 116-132.

Shnabel, N., A. Nadler, J. Ullrich, J.F. Dovidio, and D. Carmi. 2009. "Promoting reconciliation through the satisfaction of the emotional needs of victimized and perpetrating group members: The Needs-Based Model of Reconciliation." *Personality and Social Psychology Bulletin* 8: 1021-1030.

Staub, E., L.A. Pearlman, A. Gubin, and A. Hagengimana. 2005. "Healing, reconciliation, forgiving and the prevention of violence after genocide or mass killing: An intervention and its experimental evaluation in Rwanda." *Journal of Social and Clinical Psychology* 24: 297-334.

Tajfel, H., and J.C. Turner. 1979. "An integrative theory of intergroup conflict." In *The social psychology of intergroup relations*, edited by W.G. Austin and S. Worchel, 33-48. Monterey, CA: Brooks/Cole.

Tavuchis, N. 1991. *Mea culpa: A sociology of apology and reconciliation*. Stanford, CA: Stanford University Press.

Wohl, M.J.A., N.R. Branscombe, and Y. Klar. 2006. "Collective guilt: Emotional reactions when one's group has done wrong or been wronged." *European Review of Social Psychology* 17: 1-37.

Zechmeister, J.S., and Romero, C. 2002. Victim and offender accounts of interpersonal conflict: Autobiographical narratives of forgiveness and unforgiveness. *Journal of Personality and Social Psychology* 82: 675-686.

Global Antisemitism: Assault on Human Rights

Irwin Cotler*

[May I] share with you the feeling of urgency, if not, emergency, that we believe antisemitism represents and calls for. I must confess to you, I have not felt the way I feel now since 1945. I feel there are reasons for us to be concerned, even afraid ... now is the time to mobilize the efforts of all of humanity.

Elie Wiesel[1]

The rise of antisemitism anywhere is a threat to people everywhere. Thus, in fighting antisemitism, we fight for the future of all humanity.

Kofi Annan[2]

It is this recent intensification and escalation of antisemitism that underpins and necessitates this International Parliamentary Coalition to confront and combat this oldest and most enduring of hatreds. Silence is not an option. The time has come not only to sound the alarm, but to act. For as history has taught us only too well, while it may begin with Jews, it does not end with Jews.

Irwin Cotler

We're meeting because antisemitism is on the rise. There must be a fight-back and we parliamentarians are willing to lead from the front. Jewish communities across the world should know that they are not alone ... We are proud to be joined by national leaders across the political spectrum, who stand united and ready to confront this oldest hatred in the newest of settings.

John Mann, MP[3]

---

* Irwin Cotler is a Canadian MP and former Minister of Justice and Attorney-General of Canada. He is Professor of Law (on leave) from McGill University who has written extensively on matters of hate, racism, and human rights. He is a co-founder of the International Parliamentary Coalition to Combat Antisemitism with UK MP John Mann.

[1] Elie Wiesel, Remarks to *the International Commission for Combating Anti-Semitism* (ICCA), May 2002, http://www.mfa.gov.il/MFA/AntiSemitism+and+the+Holocaust/Documents+and+communiques/The+International+Commission+for+Combatting+Anti-S.htm?DisplayMode=print.

[2] Former UN Secretary-General Kofi Annan, "Throughout History Anti-Semitism Unique Manifestation of Hatred, Intolerance, Persecution Says Secretary-General in Remarks to Headquarters Seminar," Press Release, Opening Remarks at the Department of Public Information (DPI) Seminar on Anti-Semitism, New York, June 21, 2004, http://www.un.org/News/Press/docs/2004/sgsm9375.doc.htm.

[3] John Mann, MP, "Britain—UK Pledges to Combat antisemitism," *The Coordination Forum for Combating Antisemitism* (CFCA), February 17, 2009, http://www.antisemitism.org.il/eng/struggle/38660/Britain-UKpledgestocombatantisemitism.

I. Introduction: Antisemitism Old and New—Definition and Distinction

What we are witnessing today—and what has been developing incrementally, sometimes imperceptibly, and even indulgently for some thirty-five years now—is a new, sophisticated, globalizing, virulent, and even lethal antisemitism, reminiscent of the atmospherics of the 1930s and without parallel or precedent since the end of the Second World War.

The new anti Jewishness overlaps with classical antisemitism but is distinguishable from it. It found early juridical, and even institutional, expression in the UN's "Zionism is Racism" resolution but has gone dramatically beyond it. This new antisemitism almost needs a new vocabulary to define it; however, it can best be identified using a rights-based juridical perspective.

In a word, classical or traditional antisemitism is the discrimination against, denial of, or assault upon the rights of Jews to live as equal members of whatever host society they inhabit. The new antisemitism involves discrimination against the right of the Jewish people to live as an equal member of the family of nations—the denial of, and assault upon, the Jewish people's right even to live—with Israel as the "collective Jew among the nations."

Observing the complex intersections between the old and the new antisemitism and the impact of the new on the old, Per Ahlmark, former leader of the Swedish Liberal Party and Deputy Prime Minister of Sweden, pithily concluded:

> Compared to most previous anti-Jewish outbreaks, this [new antisemitism] is often less directed against individual Jews. It attacks primarily the collective Jews, the State of Israel. And then such attacks start a chain reaction of assaults on individual Jews and Jewish institutions.... In the past, the most dangerous antisemites were those who wanted to make the world Judenrein, "free of Jews." Today, the most dangerous antisemites might be those who want to make the world Judenstaatrein, "free of a Jewish state."[4]

Regrettably, indices of measurement for the new antisemitism have yet to be developed. Indeed, this may account for the disparity between the visceral feelings of Jews and the reports of social scientists still following the old antisemitism paradigm. According to the traditional indicators—such as discrimination against Jews in housing, education, or employment, or access for Jews to major positions in the political, economic, scientific, and academic arenas—it would appear, falsely, that antisemitism is in decline.

What follows is the missing conceptual and analytical framework—a set of eight indicators—to identify, pour content into, monitor, unmask, and combat this global threat whereby the new antisemitism builds upon—and incites to—traditional hatred. We need this paradigm shift in our thinking.

Two important caveats underpin this analysis. First, none of the indicators are intended to suggest that Israel is somehow above the law or that it is not to be held

---

[4] Per Ahlmark, "Combating Old-New Antisemitism," speech at *International Conference on the "Legacy of Holocaust Survivors,"* Yad Vashem, April 11, 2002, http://www1.yadvashem.org/about_yad/what_new/data_whats_new/whats_new_international_conference_ahlmark.html.

accountable for any violations of law. On the contrary, Israel, like any other state, is accountable for any violations of international law or human rights. The Jewish people are not entitled to any privileged protection or preference because of the particularity of Jewish suffering.

Second, I am not referring to critiques—even serious critiques—of Israeli policy or Zionist ideology, however distasteful or offensive some of these critiques might sometimes be. But the converse is also true: antisemitic critiques cannot mask themselves under the exculpatory disclaimer that "if I criticize Israel, they will say I am antisemitic." In the words of *New York Times* commentator Thomas Friedman: "Criticizing Israel is not anti-Semitic, and saying so is vile. But singling out Israel for opprobrium and international sanctions—out of all proportion to any other party in the Middle East—is anti-Semitic, and not saying so is dishonest."[5]

II. INDICATORS OF THE STATE OF GLOBAL ANTISEMITISM TODAY

1. State-sanctioned genocidal antisemitism

The first indicator—and the most lethal type of anti-Jewishness—is what I would call genocidal antisemitism. This is not a term that I use lightly or easily; rather, I am using it in its juridical sense as set forth in the Convention on the Prevention and Punishment of the Crime of Genocide. In particular, I am referring to the Convention's prohibition against the "direct and public incitement to genocide."[6] If antisemitism is the most enduring of hatreds and genocide is the most horrific of crimes, then the convergence of this genocidal intent embedded in antisemitic ideology is the most toxic of combinations.

There are three manifestations of this genocidal antisemitism. The first is the state-sanctioned—indeed, state-orchestrated—genocidal antisemitism of Ahmadinejad's Iran. This intent is further dramatized by the parading in the streets of Teheran of a Shihab-3 missile draped in the emblem "Wipe Israel off the Map," while demonizing both the State of Israel as a "cancerous tumor to be excised" and the Jewish people as "evil incarnate."

A second manifestation of this genocidal antisemitism is in the covenants and charters, platforms, and policies of such terrorist movements and militias as Hamas, Islamic Jihad, Hezbollah and al-Qaeda, which call not only for the destruction of Israel and the killing of Jews wherever they may be but also for the perpetration of acts of terror in furtherance of that objective. For instance, Hamas leader Mahmoud al-Zahar proclaims that "before Israel dies, it must he humiliated and degraded," while Hezbollah leader Hassan Nasrallah has said that "if all the Jews were gathered in Israel it would be easier to kill them all at the same time."[7]

In a lesser-known, but no less defamatory and incendiary expression, Nasrallah has said that "if we searched the entire world for a person more cowardly, despicable,

---

[5] Thomas L. Friedman, "Campus Hypocrisy," *The New York Times*, October 16, 2002, http://www.nytimes.com/2002/10/16/opinion/16FRIE.html.

[6] Article 3 of the Genocide Convention expressly prohibits "direct and public incitement to genocide."

[7] Quoted in Amal Saad-Ghorayeb, *Hezbollah: Politics and Religion* (Pluto Press, 2001).

weak, and feeble in psyche, mind, ideology, and religion, we would not find anyone like the Jew. Notice, I do not say the Israeli." Shi'ite scholar Amal Saad-Ghorayeb, author of the book *Hezbollah: Politics and Religion*, argues that such statements "provide moral and ideological justification for dehumanizing the Jews." In this view, she adds, "the Israeli Jew becomes a legitimate target for extermination and it also legitimizes attacks on non-Israeli Jews."[8]

The third manifestation of this genocidal antisemitism takes the form of the religious *fatwas* or execution writs in which these genocidal calls in mosques and the media are held out as religious obligations and Jews and Judaism are characterized as the perfidious enemy of Islam. Israel emerges here not only as the collective Jew among the nations but as the Salman Rushdie among the nations.

In a word, Israel is the only state in the world today—and the Jews the only people in the world today—that are the object of a standing set of threats by governmental, religious, and terrorist bodies seeking their destruction. And what is most disturbing is the seeming indifference—even the sometimes indulgence—in the face of such genocidal antisemitism.

2. Political antisemitism: Denial of fundamental rights

If genocidal antisemitism is a public call for—or incitement to—the destruction of Israel, political antisemitism is the denial of Israel's right to exist to begin with or the denial of the Jewish people's right to self-determination, if not their very denial as a people. There are four manifestations of this phenomenon.

The first is the denial of the Jewish people's right to self-determination—the only right consecrated in both the International Covenant on Civil and Political Rights and the International Covenant on Economic, Social and Cultural Rights. Jews are being singled out and discriminated against when they alone are denied this right. As Martin Luther King, Jr. put it: "this is the denial to the Jews of the same right, the right to self-determination, that we accord to African nations and all other peoples of the globe. In short, it is anti-Semitism."[9]

The second feature of political antisemitism involves denying the legitimacy, if not the existence, of the State of Israel itself. Just as classical antisemitism was anchored in the denial of the very legitimacy of the Jewish religion, the new anti-Jewishness is anchored in the denial of the very legitimacy of the Jews as a people, as embodied by the Jewish state, Israel. In each instance, then, the essence of anti-semitism is the same—an assault upon whatever is the core of Jewish self-definition at any given moment in time—be it the Jewish religion or Israel as the "civil religion" or juridical expression of the Jewish people.

A third manifestation of political antisemitism is the denial of any historical connection between the Jewish people and the State of Israel, a form of Middle East

---

[8] Jeffrey Goldberg, "In the Party of God: Are Terrorists in Lebanon Preparing for a Larger War?," *The New Yorker*, October 14 and 21, 2002.

[9] Martin Luther King, Jr., quoted in Seymour Martin Lipset, "The Socialism of Fools: The Left, the Jews and Israel," *Encounter*, December 1969, p. 24. See also John Lewis, "I Have a Dream for Peace in the Middle East: Martin Luther King, Jr.'s Special Bond with Israel," *San Francisco Chronicle*, January 21, 2002, http://www.upjf.org/detail.do?noArticle=1796&noCat=127&id_key=127.

revisionism or "memory cleansing" that seeks to extinguish or erase the Jewish people's relationship to Israel, while "Palestinizing or Islamicizing" the Arab and Muslim exclusivist claim. If Holocaust revisionism is an assault on Jewish memory and historical experience, "Middle East revisionism" constitutes no less of an assault on Jewish memory and historical experience. It cynically serves to invert the historical narrative so that Israel is seen as an "alien" and "colonial implant" in the region that "usurped" the Palestinian homeland—leading to the conclusion that its people are a "criminal" group of nomadic Jews whose very presence "defiles" Islam and must be expurgated.

It is not surprising that this revisionist Middle East narrative should lead to the final variant of political antisemitism: the "demonizing" of Israel or the attribution to Israel of all the evils of the world. This is the contemporary analogue to the medieval indictment of the Jew as the "poisoner of the wells," as Israel—portrayed as *the* metaphor for a human rights violator—is indicted as the "poisoner of the international wells" with no right to exist.

Distinguished British jurist Anthony Julius, often understated in his characterization and critique of antisemitism, sums it up as follows:

> To maintain that the very existence of Israel is without legitimacy, and to contemplate with equanimity the certain catastrophe of its dismantling ... is to embrace—however unintentionally, and notwithstanding all protestations to the contrary—a kind of antisemitism indistinguishable in its compass and its consequences from practically any that has yet been inflicted on Jews.[10]

3. Ideological antisemitism: Antisemitism under the cover of anti-racism

While the first two indicators are overt, public, and clearly demonstrable, ideological antisemitism is much more sophisticated and arguably a more pernicious expression of the new antisemitism. Indeed, it may even serve as an "ideological" support system for the first two indicators, though these are prejudicial and pernicious enough indicators in their own right.

Here, ideological antisemitism finds expression not in any genocidal incitement against Jews and Israel or an overt racist denial of the Jewish people and Israel's right to be; rather, ideological antisemitism disguises itself as part of the struggle *against* racism. Indeed, it marches under the protective cover of the UN and the international struggle against racism.

The first manifestation of this ideological antisemitism was its institutional and juridical anchorage in the "Zionism is Racism" resolution at the UN, a resolution that, as the late US Senator Daniel Moynihan said, "gave the abomination of antisemitism the appearance of international legal sanction." Notwithstanding the fact that the resolution has been formally repealed, "Zionism is Racism" remains alive and well in the global arena, particularly in the campus cultures of North America and Europe, as confirmed by the recent British All-Party Parliamentary Inquiry into Antisemitism.

---

[10] Anthony Julius, "Don't Panic," *The Guardian*, February 1, 2002, http://www.guardian.co.uk/uk/2002/feb/01/britishidentity.features11.

The second manifestation is the indictment of Israel as an apartheid state. This involves more than the simple indictment of Israel as an apartheid state. It also involves the call for the *dismantling* of Israel as an apartheid state as evidenced by the events at the 2001 UN World Conference against Racism in Durban. This indictment is not limited to talk about divestment—it is about the actual dismantling of Israel based upon the notion of apartheid as a crime against humanity.

The third manifestation of ideological antisemitism involves the characterization of Israel not only as an apartheid state—and one that must be dismantled as part of the struggle against racism—but as a Nazi one.

And so it is that Israel is delegitimized—if not demonized—by the ascription to it of the two most scurrilous indictments of twentieth-century racism—Nazism and apartheid—which serve to portray it as the embodiment of all evil.

The labeling of Zionism and Israel as "racist, apartheid, and Nazi" supplies the criminal indictment. No further debate is required. The conviction that this "triple racism" warrants the dismantling of Israel as a moral obligation has been secured. For who would deny that a "racist, apartheid, Nazi" state should not have any right to exist today? What is more, this characterization allows terrorist "resistance" to be deemed justifiable—after all, such a situation is portrayed as nothing other than *occupation et resistance*, where "resistance" against a racist, apartheid, Nazi occupying state is legitimate, if not mandatory.

There is no more dramatic example of the danger of the "Nazification" of Israel and the inflammatory inversion of the Holocaust than the dual demonizing indictments arising from the recent Israel-Hamas conflict. On the one hand, Jews are blamed for perpetrating a Holocaust on the Palestinians, as in the appalling statement of Norwegian diplomat Trine Lilleng that "the grandchildren of Holocaust survivors are doing to the Palestinians exactly what was done to them by Nazi Germany."[11] On the other hand, crowds are incited to another Holocaust against the Jews, as in the chants of protesters who scream "Hamas! Hamas! Jews to the gas!"

What is so disturbing about this ideological antisemitism is not simply the use of these defamatory and delegitimating indictments to call for the dismantling of die Jewish state itself but in particular the masking of this ideological antisemitism as if it were part of the struggle against racism, apartheid, and Nazism, thereby transforming an antisemitic indictment into a moral imperative with the imprimatur of international law.

4. *"Legalized antisemitism": Discriminatory treatment in the international arena*

If ideological antisemitism seeks to mask itself under the banner of anti-racism, this fourth indicator of the new anti-Jewishness—legalized antisemitism—is even more sophisticated and insidious. Here, antisemitism simultaneously seeks to mask itself under the banner of human rights, to invoke the authority of international law, and to operate under the protective cover of the UN. In a word—and in an inversion of

---

[11] Etgar Lefkovitz, "Norwegian envoy equates Israel with Nazis," *Jerusalem Post*, January 21, 2009.

human rights, language, and law—the singling-out of Israel and the Jewish people for differential and discriminatory treatment in the international arena is "legalized."

The first case study is the 2001 UN World Conference against Racism in Durban, which became the "tipping point" for the emergence of a new anti-Jewishness. Those of us who witnessed the "Durban Speak" festival of hate in its declarations, incantations, pamphlets, and marches—seeing antisemitism marching under the cover of human rights—have forever been transformed by this experience. "Durban" is now part of our everyday lexicon as a metaphor for racism and antisemitism.

It should have been otherwise. Indeed, when Durban was first proposed some ten years ago, I was among those who greeted it with anticipation, if not excitement. And yet what happened at Durban was truly Orwellian.[12] A World Conference Against Racism turned into a conference of racism against Israel and the Jewish people. A conference intended to commemorate the dismantling of South Africa as an apartheid state resonated with the call for the dismantling of Israel as an apartheid state. A conference dedicated to the promotion of human rights as the new secular religion of our time singled out Israel as the meta-human rights violator of our day—indeed—as the new anti-Christ of our time. A conference that was to speak in the name of humanity ended up as a metaphor for hate and inhumanity. Never have I witnessed the kind of virulence and intensity of anti-Jewishness—mockingly marching under the banner of human rights—as I found in the festival of hate at Durban.

Another example of legalized antisemitism occurred annually for over thirty-five years at the UN Commission on Human Rights. The importance of the Commission's work derived from the fact that the UN exerts enormous influence around the world.

Yet, this influential body consistently began its annual sessions with Israel being the only country singled out for country-specific indictment—even before the deliberations started—in breach of the UN's own procedures and principles.[13] In this "Alice in Wonderland" situation, the conviction and sentence were pronounced even before the hearings commenced. Some 30 percent of all the resolutions passed at the Commission were indictments of Israel.

It was a hopeful sign when a reform panel of eminent persons appointed by UN Secretary General Kofi Annan referred to the Commission's "eroding credibility and professionalism" and "legitimacy deficit that casts doubts on the overall reputation of the United Nations."[14] But after the Commission was replaced in June 2006 by the UN Human Rights Council, the new body proceeded to condemn one member state—Israel—in 80 percent of its twenty-five country-specific resolutions, while the major human rights violators of our time enjoyed exculpatory immunity. Indeed,

---

[12] I have documented this elsewhere in my writings.

[13] See Gregg J. Rickman, "Contemporary Global Antisemitism: A Report Provided to the United States Congress," US Department of State, pp. 50-1: "Resolutions with Negative Country-Specific References (2001-2007)" and "Resolutions Criticizing Countries' Human Rights Records (2001-2007)," (March 2008), http://www.state.gov/documents/organization/102301.pdf.

[14] "A more secure world: Our shared responsibility," report of the High-Level Panel on Threats, Challenges and Change (United Nations, 2004), http://www.un.org/secureworld.

five special sessions, two fact-finding missions, and a high level commission of inquiry have been devoted to a single purpose: the singling-out of Israel.[15]

These case studies are not the only examples of the international "legal" character of the new antisemitism. Indeed, an entire paper—if not book—can be devoted to the systematic, if not systemic, denial to Israel and the Jewish people of equality before the law and international due process in the international arena. The tragedy is that all this is taking place under the protective cover of the UN, thereby undermining international law and human rights. The fact is that there have been more resolutions adopted, committees formed, deliberations held, speeches made, and resources expended in the condemnation of Israel than on any other state or combination of states.

5. European antisemitism on the rise—including the far right

In speaking of European antisemitism, I do not wish to suggest that Europe—or any of its countries—is antisemitic. On the contrary, Europe as a whole is committed to the promotion and protection of democracy, human rights, and the rule of law. But the documentary record in Europe since the dawn of the new millennium suggests that we are witnessing a serious rise of antisemitism in Europe almost without parallel or precedent since the Second World War.

Over much of the past decade, governments, international institutions, and NGOs have noted an increase in antisemitic incidents, including attacks on Jewish people, property, community institutions, and religious facilities. For example, Resolution 1563 of the Parliamentary Assembly of the Council of Europe noted that "far from having been eliminated, antisemitism is today on the rise in Europe. It appears in a variety of forms and is becoming relatively commonplace."[16]

During my visits to European capitals these past eight years I can personally attest to some of the following events that occurred, all of which were reported upon in the media during these visits:

- Physical assaults upon and desecration of synagogues, cemeteries, and Jewish institutions.
- Desecration of Holocaust memorials, as in Slovakia, where Jewish memorials were desecrated in what an official described as "the biggest attack on the Jewish community since the Holocaust."
- Attacks upon identifiable Jews, be they orthodox Jews or Jews wearing a skullcap, a Star of David, or other visible Jewish symbols.
- Convergence of the extreme left and the extreme right in public demonstrations calling for "death to the Jews."
- Atrocity propaganda against Israel and Jews, for example, the accusation that Israel has injected Palestinians with the AIDS virus, as well as the demonizing Nazi and Holocaust metaphors.

---

[15] See also Hillel C. Neuer, "Statement at a Hearing before the Subcommittee on Africa, Global Human Rights, and International Operations of the Committee on International Relations—House of Representatives," Serial No. 109-221, September 6, 2006.

[16] "Resolution 1563: Combating Antisemitism in Europe," *Parliamentary Assembly of the Council of Europe* (2007), http://assembly.coe.int/Mainf.asp?link=/Documents/AdoptedText/ta 07/ERES1563.htm.

- The ugly canard of double loyalty, described as follows by Professor Joel Kotek of the University of Brussels: "One's position on the Arab-Israeli conflict has become a test of loyalty. Should he express solidarity with Israel he becomes a supporter of a Nazi state."[17]
- The belief—held by close to 50 percent of Europeans—that Jews are more loyal to Israel than to their own country and the belief—held by more than one-third—that Jews have "too much power" in business and finance.[18]

As discussed throughout this paper, there has been an emergence of a new global and virulent antisemitism. It is also important to make note of the strong resurgence of extreme right-wing groups, particularly throughout Europe. Extreme nationalist parties in some European countries—successfully—started to use antisemitic slogans and ideas that were previously deemed unacceptable. This antisemitism has even become a central campaign platform by combining anti-Jewish epithets with a broader message of hatred and exclusion, which has resulted in violent and hateful anti-Jewish and anti-immigrant public demonstrations.

The overt and conscious antisemitism of the old Neo-Nazi groups is easily identified, and yet it still exists—and thrives—in contemporary society. In the Netherlands, the *Racism and Extremism Monitor* observed that the contribution of extreme right-wing participants to racial violence as a whole—particularly incidents of antisemitism—had risen sharply from 38 incidents in 2005 to 67 in 2006 and was continuing to increase at an exponential rate. "Loosely organized extreme right-wing groups," including informal movements of right-wing young people (often termed "Lonsdale youth" or skinheads) and neo-Nazi groups are reportedly gaining ground and influence.[19]

In its November 2007 report, the Dutch monitoring organization Centre Documentation and Information on Israel expressed concerns about the numerous incidents reported on the anniversary of the German surrender in 1945—observed on May 4 and 5—during which Holocaust monuments were defaced or destroyed. These actions were seen to be directly related to the rise of the extreme right, with memorials covered with hate symbols such as swastikas and neo-Nazi slogans. In another example, on December 8, 2007, supporters of the Freedom Party and the Patriots of Ukraine organization took part in a torch-lit march through Kiev, chanting antisemitic, anti-immigrant, and pro-white power slogans, including "one race, one nation, one motherland,"[20] which were frighteningly reminiscent of the hateful slogans of Nazi Germany.

In response to changing circumstances and challenges, many right-wing groups have transformed their approach by incorporating the old, traditional form of antisemitism into the new, more tolerable antisemitism. Antisemitic adherents of the far right seek to portray their views as anti-Zionist or anti-Israel, on the grounds that this is more politically acceptable than open advocacy of Nazi positions. For

---

[17] Daniel Ben Simon, "Haunted by ill winds of the past," *Ha'aretz*, January 2, 2002.

[18] Anti-Defamation League, "ADL Survey in Seven European Countries Finds Anti-Semitic Attitudes Steady; 31 Percent Blame Jews for Financial Crisis," New York, February 10, 2009.

[19] Human Rights First, "2008 Hate Crime Survey: Antisemitism," http://www.humanrights first.org/discrimination/pages.aspx?id=157.

[20] Ibid.

instance, in its 2007 annual report on antisemitism, the League for Human Rights of B'nai Brith Canada cites a bulletin of the neo-Nazi website *Stormfront*, imploring followers to "remember to say 'Zionists' or 'Israeli Firsters' instead of 'Jews' when making public speeches or writing articles." In this way, the radical right makes explicit the convergence of the old/new antisemitism that remains unspoken in other contexts.

6. Cultural antisemitism

Cultural antisemitism refers to the *mélange* of attitudes, sentiments, innuendo, and the like in academia, in parliaments, among the literati, public intellectuals, and the human rights movement—in a word, *la trahison des clercs*. As UK MP Denis MacShane has noted: "The most worrying discovery is that anti-Jewish sentiment is entering the mainstream, appearing in everyday conversations of people who consider themselves neither racist nor prejudiced."[21]

Such antisemitic attitudes include: the remarks of the French Ambassador to the United Kingdom questioning why the world should risk another world war because of "that shitty little country Israel,"[22] the observation of Petronella Wyatt that "antisemitism is respectable once more, not just in Germany or Catholic-central Europe, but at London dinner tables,"[23] the distinguished British novelist A.N. Wilson dredging up another ugly canard in accusing the Israeli army of "the poisoning of water supplies,"[24] Tom Paulin, Oxford Professor and poet, writing of a Palestinian boy "gunned down by the Zionist SS,"[25] or Peter Hain, a former Minister in the British Foreign Office, stating that the present Zionist state is by definition racist and will have to be dismantled.

Indeed, according to the US State Department Report on Contemporary Antisemitism, drawing comparisons between contemporary Israeli policy and that of the Nazis is increasingly commonplace in intellectual circles, as illustrated by the frequent media images of Israel as a "Nazi-state" during the July 2006 war with Hezbollah,[26] as well as during the more recent war in Gaza, wherein repeated reference was made at the UN Human Rights Council to the "Holocaust perpetrated by the Israelis." ADL head Abraham Foxman stated that "this is the worst, the most intense, the most global that it's been in most of our memories," citing "an epidemic, a pandemic of anti-Semitism."[27]

---

[21] UK Labour MP Denis MacShane, Chair of the 2006 UK *All-Party Parliamentary Inquiry Into Antisemitism*, as quoted in *The Guardian* on September 7, 2006.

[22] "'Anti-Semitic' French envoy under fire," BBC Online, December 20, 2001, http://news.bbc.co.UK/2/hi/europe/1721172.stm.

[23] Petronella Wyatt, "Poisonous Prejudice," *Spectator*, December 8, 2001, http://www.spectator.co.uk/the-magazine/cartoons/9580/poisonous-prejudice.thtml.

[24] A.N. Wilson, "A demo we can't afford to ignore," *Evening Standard*, April 15, 2002.

[25] Tom Paulin, "Killed in Crossfire," *The Observer*, February 18, 2001.

[26] This upsurge was documented in the US Department of State's *2006 Country Reports on Human Rights Practices*, http://www.state.gov/g/drl/rls/hrrpt/2006/index.htm, as well as its *2006 Report on International Religious Freedom*, http://www.state.gov/g/drl/rls/irf/2006/index.htm.

[27] Rabbi Levi Brackman and Rivkah Lubitch, "ADL sees 'pandemic of anti-Semitism,'" *Y-net News*, February 7, 2009, http://www.ynetnews.com/articles/0,7340,L-3667928,00.html.

In summary, antisemitism appears to be "the right and only word," in the words of Gabriel Schoenfeld, for a cultural antisemitism "so one-sided, so eager to indict Israel while exculpating Israel's adversaries, so shamefully adroit in the use of moral double standards, so quick to issue false and baseless accusations and so disposed to invert the language of the Holocaust and to paint Israelis and Jews as evil incarnate."[28] That was six years ago, even before the present pandemic.

7. Discrimination and exclusion: globalizing the boycott

There is a growing incidence of academic, university, trade union, and related boycotts and divestments—whose effect in practice if not in intent—is the singling-out of Israel, Israeli Jews, and supporters of Israel for selective opprobrium and exclusion. Indeed, what began as a British phenomenon has now become a global one, with universities, organizations, and unions from South Africa to Canada, Norway to the United States, and Turkey to Italy moving from the boycott of Israeli goods and services to restrictions and bans on Israeli academics. As the UK All-Parliamentary Inquiry into antisemitism reported: "The singling-out of Israel is of concern. Boycotts have not been suggested against other countries.... The discourse around the boycott debate is also cause for concern, as it moved beyond reasonable criticism into anti-Semitic demonization of Israel."[29]

Labour MP John Mann, chair of the All-Party Parliamentary Group against Antisemitism, stressed the motion's discriminatory character against British Jews: "boycotts do nothing to bring about peace and reconciliation in the Middle East but leave Jewish students, academics, and their associates isolated and victimized on university campuses."[30]

8. The old/new Protocols of the Elders of Zion

For over a hundred years, the world has been suffused with the most pervasive, persistent, and pernicious group libel in history, the *Protocols of the Elders of Zion*—the tsarist forgery proclaiming an "international Jewish conspiracy" bent on "world domination." Today, the "lie that wouldn't die"[31] underpins the most outrageous of international conspiracy thinking and incitement targeting first the Jews and then the "international Zionist conspiracy."

The following examples represent just a small sample of such thinking: the Jews were behind the 9/11 attacks and had forewarning, Jewish doctors are responsible for infecting Palestinians with the AIDS virus, Jewish scientists are responsible for

---

[28] Gabriel Schoenfeld, "Israel and the Anti-Semites," *Commentary Magazine*, June 2002, http://www.commentarymagazine.com/viewarticle.cfm/israel-and-the-anti-semites-9468?search=1.

[29] "Report of the All-Party Parliamentary Inquiry into Antisemitism," *All-Party Parliamentary Group Against Antisemitism*, September 2006, p. 41, pts. 210-211, available at: http://www.thepcaa.org/report.html.

[30] Jonny Paul, "Ex-EU Official Condemns UK Academic Boycott Call," *Jerusalem Post*, June 1, 2008, http://www.jpost.com/servlet/Satellite?pagename=JPost%2FJPArticle%2FShowFull&cid=1212041440272.

[31] Hadassah Ben-Itto, *The Lie that Wouldn't Die—A Hundred Years of the Protocols of the Elders of Zion* (Tel Aviv: Dvir Publishing, 1998), pp. 338-9.

the propagation of the Avian flu, a Jewish astronaut was responsible for the explosion of the Columbia space shuttle, the Jews were behind the publication of the Danish cartoons and the Pope's defilement of Islam, the Jews are responsible for the war in Iraq, "genocides" such as the one in Darfur are orchestrated by the Jews, and so on.

It was not long before the same libelous inheritance of the Jews was transferred to the Jews of Israel—to the international Zionist conspiracy—bringing together the old and new protocols in a conceptual and linguistic symmetry that blamed Israel and Zionists for all the above things that were once blamed on the Jews.

But it is in the Arab and Muslim world that the Protocols have taken hold, not unlike the incitement accompanying the anti-Jewish pogroms in tsarist Russia and the murders of the Third Reich. The Protocols are propagated in mosques, taught in schools, published by states, sold in bookstores, and, most compellingly, have secured a captive audience in the daily broadcast media.

9. The resurgence of global antisemitism: Evidentiary data

The data unsurprisingly confirm that antisemitic incidents are very much on the rise. Still, the available figures only show half the picture—they demonstrate an increase in this old/new antisemitism by concentrating on the traditional antisemitic paradigm targeting individual Jews and Jewish institutions, while failing to consider the new antisemitic paradigm targeting Israel as the Jew among nations and the resulting fall-out for traditional antisemitism. This caveat is important—for the rise in traditional antisemitism cannot be viewed solely in the context of the traditional paradigm. Rather, the rise in traditional antisemitism should be seen as a complement to—and consequence of—the rise in the new antisemitism, insidiously buoyed by a climate receptive to attacks on Jews because of the attacks on the Jewish state.

– For instance, a trend can be noted in the statistical data of a rise in antisemitic incidents correlating with the situation in the Middle East, particularly with respect to the Arab-Israeli conflict. Data from the 2007 Report of Tel Aviv University's Stephen Roth Institute for the Study of Contemporary Antisemitism and Racism illustrate an upsurge in violence and related antisemitic crimes in the years 2000 and 2006, which correspond to the beginning of the Second Intifada and the Israel-Hezbollah war.[32] More recent reports, such as from the ADL, have shown a major increase in anti-Jewish and anti-Israel attacks and demonstrations since the recent 2009 Israel-Hamas war, which have even been characterized as a "pandemic."[33]
– The 2006 Pew Global Attitudes Project Poll noted that the percent of people polled with an unfavorable view of Jews in various Muslim countries was exceptionally high. In Egypt, it was as high as 97 percent and in Jordan 98 percent.[34]

---

[32] Dina Porat and Esther Webman, eds., "Antisemitism Worldwide 2007: General Analysis," Tel Aviv University, Stephen Roth Institute for the Study of Contemporary Antisemitism and Racism (in cooperation with the World Jewish Congress), http://www.tau.ac.il/antisemitism.

[33] Ibid., p. 33.

[34] Pew Global Attitudes Project, Poll on Anti-Semitic Attitudes in Selected Muslim Countries, 2005 to 2006, http://pewresearch.org.

- In 2007, overall levels of violent antisemitic attacks against persons increased in Canada, Germany, Russia, Ukraine, and the United Kingdom, according to official statistics and reports of nongovernmental monitors. Indeed, there is a trend that antisemitic incidents increasingly take the form of physical attacks on individuals. A "constant pressure to conceal one's [Jewish] identity" has been noted, while Jewish leaders have been singled out for violence.[35]
- A disturbing number of victims of antisemitic attack are school students. Children and young people have been assaulted and threatened in the streets, on public transport, and even in and around their schools. Physical assaults have taken place in France, Germany, Russia, the United Kingdom, and the United States. Children in playgrounds have been pelted with stones. With respect to universities, Jewish students and student centers, dormitories, and Jewish clubs have been assaulted.[36] For example, in February 2009, a hundred anti-Israel activists descended upon the York University Hillel student club shouting slogans such as "Zionism is racism," threatening and intimidating Jewish students.[37]
- Jewish institutions have been particularly susceptible to attacks as "centers of Jewish life became the main targets for those seeking to express their hatred and strike a symbolic blow against Jews as a people."[38] Synagogues, cemeteries, and Holocaust memorials have been reported vandalized and desecrated in no less than twenty-six different countries.[39]
- A report from Human Rights First notes that "in some countries, the frequency and severity of attacks on Jewish places of worship, community centers, schools, and other institutions resulted in a need for security measures by representatives of both the Jewish community and local or national government." The human rights NGO credited such "enhanced security"—and not a decrease in antisemitic sentiment—with a reduction in serious attacks, commenting that "the reality in which such protection is required on an everyday basis is, however, perhaps the truest indicator of just how far the revival of antisemitism has progressed since 2000."[40]
- In 2007, 1,042 antisemitic incidents were reported to the League for Human Rights of B'nai Brith Canada, constituting an overall increase of 11.4% from the previous year. A five-year view shows that the number of incidents has almost doubled since 584 incidents were reported in 2003, while a ten-year view shows a dramatic upward trend with incidents multiplying more than four-fold since 1998, when there were 240 reported cases.[41]

---

[35] Human Rights First, "2008 Hate Crime Survey: I. Antisemitism," http://www.humanrightsfirst.org/discrimination/reports.aspx?s=antisemitism&p=index.

[36] Porat *and* Webman, "Antisemitism Worldwide 2007," p. 25.

[37] Jonathan Blake Karoly, "An eyewitness account of this week's aggressive intimidation of Jewish students at York University," posted by Jonathan Kay, *The National Post*, February 12, 2009, http://network.nationalpostxom/np/blogs/fullcomment/archive/2009/02/12/an-eyewitness-account-of-this-week-s-aggressive-intimidation-of-jewish-students-at-york-university.aspx.

[38] Porat and Webman, "Antisemitism Worldwide 2007," p. 33.

[39] Ibid.

[40] Ibid.

[41] Anita Bromberg and Ruth Klein, "2007 Audit of Antisemitic Incidents: Patterns of Prejudice in Canada," *League for Human Rights of B'nai Brith Canada*, p. 2, http://www.bnaibrith.ca/publications/audit2007/audit2007.pdf.

III. Conclusion

The thesis of this paper, global antisemitism as an assault on human rights, is that we are witnessing today an old/new, escalating, sophisticated, global, virulent, and even lethal antisemitism. In its benign (if it can be called benign) form, the old/new antisemitism refers to increased hostility toward and attacks on Jewish people and property and Jewish communal, educational, and religious institutions; "the mendacious, dehumanizing, or stereotypical allegations about Jews or the powers of Jews as a collective";[42] Holocaust denial and inversion; conspiracy theories where Jews and Israel are blamed as "poisoners of the wells"; boycotts of Jews and Israeli nationals; accusations of dual loyalty; and the singling-out of Israel and the Jewish people for differential and discriminatory treatment in the international arena and denial of fundamental rights.

In its more virulent and lethal form, it refers to the delegitimization and demonization of the Jewish people—of the emergence of Israel as the collective Jews among the nations—and to state-sanctioned genocidal antisemitism that constitutes a contemporary warrant for genocide.

It is this escalation and intensification of antisemitism that underpins—indeed necessitates—the need to understand, confront, and combat this oldest and most enduring of hatreds. Silence is not an option. The time has come not only to sound the alarm—but to act. For, as history has taught us only too well, while it may begin with the Jews, it does not end with the Jews. Antisemitism is the canary in the mineshaft of evil, and it threatens us all.

---

[42] As stated by the European Monitoring Center for Racism and Xenophobia (EUMC), in Gregg J. Rickman, "Contemporary Global Antisemitism: A Report Provided to the United States Congress," US Department of State, March 2008, p. 19.

BIBLIOGRAPHY

Ahlmark, Per. "Combating Old-New Antisemitism." Speech at International Conference on the "Legacy of Holocaust Survivors," Yad Vashem, April 11, 2002. http://www1.yadvashem.org/about_yad/what_new/data_whats_new/whats_new_international_conference_ahlmark.html.

Annan, Kofi. "Throughout History Anti-Semitism Unique Manifestation of Hatred, Intolerance, Persecution Says Secretary-General in Remarks to Headquarters Seminar." Press Release, Opening Remarks at the Department of Public Information (DPI) Seminar on Antisemitism, New York, June 21, 2004. http://www.un.org/News/Press/docs/2004/sgsm9375.doc.htm.

Anti-Defamation League. "ADL Survey in Seven European Countries Finds Anti-Semitic Attitudes Steady; 31 Percent Blame Jews for Financial Crisis." February 10, 2009. http://www.adl.org/PresRele/ASInt_13/5465_13.htm.

BBC Online. "'Anti-Semitic' French envoy under fire." December 20, 2001, http://news.bbc.co.uk/2/hi/europe/1721172.stm.

Ben-Itto, Hadassah. *The Lie That Wouldn't Die—A Hundred Years of the Protocols of the Elders of Zion*. Tel Aviv: Dvir Publishing, 1998.

Ben Simon, Daniel, "Haunted by ill winds of the past," *Ha'aretz*, January 2, 2002.

Bromberg, Anita, and Klein, Ruth. "2007 Audit of Antisemitic Incidents: Patterns of Prejudice in Canada." *League for Human Rights of B'nai Brith Canada*. http://www.bnaibrith.ca/publications/audit2007/audit2007.pdf.

Convention on the Prevention and Punishment of the Crime of Genocide. UN General Assembly resolution 260 A (III), December 9, 1948. Office of the High Commissioner for Human Rights. http://www.unhchr.ch/html/menu3/b/p_genoci.htm.

Friedman, Thomas L. "Campus Hypocrisy." *New York Times*, October 16, 2002. http://www.nytimes.com/2002/10/16/opinion/16FRIE.html.

Goldberg, Jeffrey. "In the Party of God: Are Terrorists in Lebanon Preparing for a Larger War?" *The New Yorker*, October 14 and 21, 2002.

Human Rights First. "2008 Hate Crime Survey." http://www.humanrightsfirst.org/discrimination/reports.aspx?s=antisemitism&p=index.

Julius, Anthony. "Don't Panic." *The Guardian*, February 1, 2002. http://www.guardian.co.uk/uk/2002/feb/01/britishidentity.features11.

Kay, Jonathan. "An eyewitness account of this week's aggressive intimidation of Jewish students at York University." *The National Post*, February 12, 2009.

Lefkovitz, Etgar. "Norwegian envoy equates Israel with Nazis." *The Jerusalem Post*, January 21, 2009.

Lewis, John. "I Have a Dream for Peace in the Middle East: Martin Luther King, Jr.'s Special Bond with Israel." *San Francisco Chronicle*, January 21, 2002. http://www.upjf.org/detail.do?noArticle=1796&noCat= 127&id_key=127.

Lipset, Seymour Martin. "The Socialism of Fools: The Left, the Jews and Israel." *Encounter*, December, 1969.

Mann, John, MP. "Britain—UK Pledges to Combat antisemitism." The Coordination Forum for Combating Antisemitism (*CFCA*), *February 17*, 2009. http://www.antisemitism.org.il/eng/struggle/38660/Britain-UKpledgestocombatantisemitism.

Neuer, Hillel C. "Statement at a Hearing before the Subcommittee on Africa, Global Human Rights, and International Operations of the Committee on International Relations—House of Representatives." Serial No. 109-221, September 6, 2006.

Paul, Jonny. "Ex-EU Official Condemns UK Academic Boycott Call." *Jerusalem Post*, June 1, 2008.

Paulin, Tom. "Killed in Crossfire." *The Observer*, February 18, 2001.

Pew Global Attitudes Project, Poll on Anti-Semitic Attitudes in Selected Muslim Countries, 2005 to 2006, http://pewresearch.org.

Porat, Dina and Webman, Esther, eds. "Antisemitism Worldwide 2007: General Analysis." Tel Aviv University: Stephen Roth Institute for the Study of Contemporary Antisemitism and Racism (in cooperation with the World Jewish Congress). http://www.tau.ac.il/antisemitism.

"Report of the All-Party Parliamentary Inquiry into Antisemitism," All-Party Parliamentary Group Against Antisemitism, September 2006. http://www.thepcaa.org/report.html.

"Resolution 1563: Combating Antisemitism in Europe," Parliamentary Assembly of the Council of Europe, 2007. http://assembly.coe.int/Mainf.asp?link=/Documents/AdoptedText/ta07/ERES1563.htm.

Rickman, Gregg J. "Contemporary Global Antisemitism: A Report Provided to the United States Congress." US Department of State, March 2008. http://www.state.gov/documents/organization/102301.pdf.

Saad-Ghorayeb, Amal. *Hezbollah: Politics and Religion*. Pluto Press, 2001.

Schoenfeld, Gabriel. "Israel and the Anti-Semites." *Commentary*, June 2002.

United Nations. *A more secure world: Our shared responsibility*. Report of the High-Level Panel on Threats, Challenges and Change. 2004. http://www.un.org/secureworld.

US Department of State. *2006 Country Reports on Human Rights Practices*.

Wiesel, Elie. Remarks to the International Commission for Combating Anti-Semitism (ICCA), May 2002. http://www.mfa.gov.il/MFA/AntiSemitism+and+the+Holocaust/Documents+and+communiques/The+International+Commission+for+Combatting+Anti-S.htm?DisplayMode=print.

Wilson, A.N., "A demo we can't afford to ignore." *Evening Standard*, April 15, 2002.

Wyatt, Petronella. "Poisonous Prejudice." *Spectator*, December 8, 2001.

Y-net News, February 7, 2009.

The Principles and Practice of Iran's Post-Revolutionary Foreign Policy

Brandon Friedman*

I. INTRODUCTION

Western scholars and statesmen working on issues related to Iran's post-revolutionary foreign policy continuously address the question of whether Iran acts pragmatically or ideologically. The question is often expressed or phrased in several variations: Does Iran act based on its interests or religious dogma? Is Iran pragmatic or fanatical? Does the regime make its decisions based on a cost-benefit analysis? Does the Iranian regime recognize the imperatives of *realpolitik* or is it an ideological regime? This paper will modestly challenge the utility of this simple either/or proposition, and instead argue that the regime's foreign policy has been and continues to be both pragmatic and revolutionary. Further, Iran's 1979 revolution has not ended,[1] and over the past thirty years Iran's foreign policy has been a primary battleground for the ruling elites of Iran to assert their vision of the state's revolutionary identity.[2] This, in part, explains the more provocative approach of current President Ahmadinejad, in contrast to his predecessors 'Ali Akbar Rafsanjani (1989-1997) and Mohammad Khatami (1997-2005).

R.K. Ramazani, a leading scholar of Iranian foreign policy, has written that the "balance of ideology and pragmatism in the making of Iranian foreign policy decisions has been one of the most persistent, intricate, and difficult issues in all Iranian history...."[3] So what, exactly, do scholars mean when they begin talking about Iran's pragmatism? Is everyone talking about the same thing? According to the Western liberal canon of political philosophy, John Stuart Mill has described the flexibility behind the pragmatist's view of action: "It can be experimental because it trusts the grand direction of the underlying pattern of change."[4] In contrast to Western liberal thought, an Iranian scholar has characterized the "Islamic Shi'ite pragmatism" of Iran as capable of being "experimental because it teleologically

---

* Research Fellow, Center for Iranian Studies, Tel Aviv University.

[1] Said Arjomand, "Has Iran's Islamic Revolution Ended?," *Radical History Review*, no. 105 (Fall 2009), pp. 132-8.

[2] Arshin Adib-Moghaddam, "Islamic Utopian Romanticism and the Foreign Policy Culture of Iran," *Critique: Critical Middle Eastern Studies* 14, no. 3 (Fall 2005), pp. 265-92.

[3] R.K. Ramazani, "Ideology and Pragmatism in Iran's Foreign Policy," *Middle East Journal* 58, no. 4 (Autumn 2004), p. 549.

[4] K.L. Afrasiabi, *After Khomeini: New Directions in Iran's Foreign Policy* (Boulder, San Francisco and Oxford: Westview Press, 1994), p. 11.

trusts the grand direction of the underlying pattern of values."[5] This suggests that the post-Khomeini leadership in Iran has derived its pragmatism from what it perceives as a dynamic ideology. And this definition of pragmatism is conceptually different from the Western definition of pragmatism. In other words, Western scholars and statesmen and Iranian diplomats and elected officials may be using the same terms but referring to different concepts.

A leading scholar based in the Islamic Republic, Kaveh Afrasiabi, argues that the conventional Western assumption of a "pragmatic/fundamentalist" dichotomy fails to account for the pragmatic qualities and ethos of Islamic fundamentalism, and that what is considered pragmatic action occurs on the basis of submerged values.[6] That is to say, for Iran, pragmatic behavior can also be value-driven or ideological behavior. For Iranian officials, pragmatism and ideology are not mutually exclusive. Ideological goals and material and strategic interests can be pursued in parallel, where one is mutually reinforcing the other, and it is not an either/or, zero-sum proposition as Ramazani and others suggest.

This clarification of concepts is important because, when Western statesmen and scholars perceive Iran's behavior as pragmatic,[7] there may be a temptation to conclude that Iran's regime has reoriented itself and is no longer strictly adhering to its revolutionary identity or ideological principles. This conclusion is problematic because it presupposes a previous phase of behavior that was not pragmatic and based entirely on ideological reasoning and does not differentiate between changes in means and changes in ends.[8]

As a result of this misconception, there is a tendency to mistake Iran's tactical concessions for regime reorientation[9] and therefore to conclude that the regime is moderating its objectives rather than applying different tactical maneuvers, or means, to achieve the same revolutionary goals. The shift from using subversive military plots in the 1980s to advancing instruments of soft power—financial, religio-political and cultural influences—in the late 1990s and first decade of the twenty-first century to spread its revolutionary ideals exemplify Iran's change in tactical means rather than ends.

The danger of confusing a change in means for a change in ends also has the potential to lead to confusion regarding how the Islamic Republic of Iran perceives its interests. There may be some in the West who assume there is an inverse relationship between national interests and revolutionary Islamic values. In contrast, post-revolutionary Iran conceives religio-cultural norms and values as a constitutive component of national interests and not independent of them.[10]

---

[5] Afrasiabi, *After Khomeini*, p. 11.

[6] Ibid.

[7] Anoushiravan Ehteshami, "The Foreign Policy of Iran," in *The Foreign Policies of Middle Eastern States*, ed. Raymond Hinnebusch and Anoushiravan Ehteshami (Boulder, Colorado: Lynne Rienner Publishers, Inc., 2002), pp. 283-309.

[8] Afrasiabi, *After Khomeini*, p. 12.

[9] For example, see Anoushiravan Ehteshami, *After Khomeini: The Iranian Second Republic* (London and New York: Routledge, 1995), pp. 143-5. Ehteshami hedges his analysis with a broad disclaimer on p. 142.

[10] Afrasiabi, *After Khomeini*, p. 12.

Most Western observers of Iran tend to conceive of rationality (often used euphemistically with pragmatism in the West) as behavior based on national interests defined in terms of military, territorial, geographic, demographic, and economic strength. Or, in other words, interests are defined in material terms and viewed as distinct and super-ordinate to ideology. In light of this conception of interests, Western observers conventionally conceive of Iran's ideological behavior as either irrational or cynically instrumental and serving the ends of material interests.

Meanwhile, in contrast to the way some Westerners perceive Iran's interests, some scholars and statesmen in the Islamic Republic argue that there is a "religio-cultural" dimension to national interests, as well as "politico-religious" and "communicative" interests that focus on cultural authenticity and national pride.[11]

In other words, strategic interests in the Islamic Republic of Iran are framed in terms of both the Imam Khomeini's revolutionary objectives and material interests. In short, Iran's post-revolutionary foreign policy has maintained a consistent revolutionary identity since 1979, with changing means, which has both served and defined its strategic goals since 1979. These goals, derived from Khomeini's ideology and the 1979 Constitution, have four central components: first, social justice in tandem with economic growth and development (material interests often described in terms of the revolutionary objective of social justice); second, preserving national sovereignty and territorial integrity (strategic material interest); third, defending the rights of Muslims and supporting liberation movements (oppressed peoples) and confrontation with Israel and the U.S. (revolutionary objective); and, fourth, the establishment of an Islamic polity based on Shi'i principles (revolutionary objective).[12] There is a coexistence and reinforcement between revolutionary and material interests in the Islamic Republic of Iran's foreign policy; they are not mutually exclusive of one another, where one can be set at odds against the other.

In order to better understand the context for Iran's foreign policy under President Ahmadinejad, particularly his antagonistic and provocative statements toward Israel and about the Holocaust, it is important to understand the overarching themes in Iran's revolutionary discourse and its influence on how the current Iranian regime perceives and expresses its interests.

II. Themes in Iran's Revolutionary Discourse

Iran's foreign policy discourse and behavior was aggressive and revolutionary during the first decade after the Islamic Revolution, a period during which Iran was fighting a long and bloody war with Iraq and struggling to consolidate control over state institutions. In the late 1980s, following the death of Imam Khomeini and the end of the Iran-Iraq War, the executive branch of the Iranian government was strengthened by constitutional reforms.

The new President, Ali Akbar Hashemi Rafsanjani (1989-1997), inherited an economic crisis and attempted to soften Iran's image in the international community in order to rebuild the state's decimated economic and military capabilities.

---

[11] Ibid.
[12] Ibid.

This effort reached its peak in the late 1990s under former President Khatami (1997-2005). Both Rafsanjani and Khatami focused much of their efforts on a diplomatic offensive that attempted to improve Iran's relations with the community of states through confidence-building statements, strengthen relationships with international organizations, such as the IMF and World Bank, and present the Islamic Republic of Iran as a rule-abiding actor in the international system.[13]

These efforts were offset by Iran's steadfast opposition to any progress in the Palestinian-Israeli peace process beginning in October 1991. Iran actively offered financial and logistical support for militant activity carried out by Hezbollah, Hamas, Palestinian Islamic Jihad, and other groups throughout the 1990s, and began to develop its undeclared nuclear program during the period of Rafsanjani's and Khatami's presidencies. In the 1990s, it was the tension between Iran's relatively moderate presidential statements and subversive military and financial support for militant non-state actors beyond its borders that made analyzing Iran's foreign policy a challenge.[14]

In contrast to the 1990s, one of the central themes of Iran's third revolution, as the Ahmadinejad period (2005- present) has come to be known, has been its relentless public attacks on the international system. Henry Kissinger, in his book *A World Restored* (1964), observed that, "whenever there exists a power which considers the international order or the manner of legitimizing it oppressive, relations between it and other powers will be revolutionary." In these cases, Kissinger noted, "it is not the adjustment of differences within a given system which will be at issue, but the system itself."[15] Iran's current foreign minister, Manouchehr Mottaki, authored an article in the spring of 2007, entitled "What is a Just Global Order," in which he stated that "the order in the context of [the] international system is a discriminative and, hence not functional any more." Mottaki also argued that "the order in the international society is a combination of imposed concepts which defines structure of the same international system based on power without principle and justice."[16] Later, in the same article, Mottaki claims that: "A multicultural global order controlled by one pole, in which the relation between this pole and the world remains to be ethnocentric, is not acceptable."[17] Mottaki, who may be said to represent the president as one part of a complex decision-making consensus in Iranian foreign policy, is clearly attacking the system itself and not the differences within the system.

Ahmadinejad's opposition to the current international system is rooted in Iran's revolutionary discourse, which has three main elements: resistance, justice, and independence.[18] Despite the Imam Khomeini's historical denunciation of the Western

---

[13] Homeira Moshirzadeh, "Discursive Foundations of Iran's Nuclear Policy," *Security Dialogue* 38, no. 4 (December 2007), p. 527.

[14] Joseph Kostiner, *Conflict and Cooperation in the Gulf Region* (Wiesbaden, Germany: VS Verlag für Sozialwissenschaften, 2009), p. 173.

[15] *Henry Kissinger*, A World Restored: Europe after Napoleon: The Politics of Conservatism in a Revolutionary Age (1964), pp. 1-3.

[16] Manuchechr Mottaki, "What is a Just Global Order," *Iranian Journal of International Affairs* 19, no. 2 (Spring 2007), pp. 1-7.

[17] Ibid.

[18] Moshirzadeh, "Discursive Foundations"; Adib-Moghaddam, "Islamic Utopian Romanticism."

notion of nationalism,[19] Iran's emphasis on independence is often interpreted in the West as "Iranian nationalism,"[20] because Iran's emphasis on independence has been a consistent element of Iran's political discourse throughout the twentieth century, from Reza Shah Pahlavi to Imam Khomeini and his followers. Iran's emphasis on independence stems from: (1) its proud historical legacy as a Safavid-Shi'i power (16th to 18th centuries); (2) its pre-modern defeats at the hands of foreign invaders (Greeks, Turks, and Mongols); and (3) its encounters with imperial powers (Russia, Britain, and the U.S.), which Iran holds responsible for its dependence and underdevelopment.[21] In particular, Iran's collective memory of nineteenth century defeats at the hands of foreign powers is still a very powerful discursive theme that had an important impact on the course of development in nineteenth and twentieth century Iran.

Iran's emphasis on independence is different from the Western understanding of nationalism in international politics[22] and has led scholars to classify it as a "maximalist" independence or "hyper-independence" or "true independence."[23] One creative characterization of this phenomenon is "the arrogance of non-submission."[24] This emphasis on hyper-independence manifests itself in two principal ways: first, it causes Iran to resist what it perceives as foreign dominance in the international system; and, second, it causes Iran to place an unusual emphasis on self-reliance in the security realm.[25] Moreover, these are principles enshrined in Articles 2, 3, and 153 of Iran's 1979 Constitution, which explicitly reject any form of dependence or submission to foreign states. For example, during President Ahmadinejad's speech to the U.N. General Assembly in New York in 2005, he attacked "[t]hose hegemonic powers, who consider the scientific and technological progress of independent and free nations as a challenge to their monopoly on these instruments of power and who do not want to see such achievements in other countries…."[26] Ahmadinejad perceives himself as defending Iranian independence from foreign domination.

The second principal element of Iran's revolutionary discourse is the demand for justice (*'adl*). In Shi'i Islam, justice is considered "of overwhelming importance" and is demanded from Muslims in their day-to-day life.[27] One of the central themes of Ayatollah Khomeini's revolutionary ideology was the triumph of the oppressed in the face of injustice. This populist sentiment called for supporting the powerless, disadvantaged masses of people (*mostaz'afin*) in their struggle to escape oppression from the world's oppressive superpowers (*mostakhbarin*). Khomeini included the

---

[19] Farhang Rajaee, *Islamic Values and World View: Khomeyni on Man the State and International Politics*, vol. 7 (Lanham, New York, London: University Press of America, Inc., 1983), pp. 71-2.

[20] Ehteshami, "Foreign Policy of Iran," p. 284.

[21] Ibid., p. 285; Moshirzadeh, "Discursive Foundations," p. 529.

[22] Afrasiabi, *After Khomeini*, pp. 16-18.

[23] Moshirzadeh, "Discursive Foundations," p. 530; R.K. Ramazani, *Revolutionary Iran: Challenge and Response in the Middle East* (Johns Hopkins University Press, 1988), p. 28.

[24] Ehteshami, "Foreign Policy of Iran," p. 285.

[25] Moshirzadeh, "Discursive Foundations," p. 530.

[26] Kasra Naji, *Ahmadinejad: The Secret History of Iran's Radical Leader* (London: I.B. Tauris, 2008), p. 126.

[27] Nikkie Keddie, *Modern Iran: Roots and Results of Revolution* (New Haven and London: Yale University Press, 2003), p. 18.

capitalists, socialists, Phalangists, Zionists, fascists, and communists into the group of oppressors. Khomeini insisted that "[t]he dispossessed must triumph over the dominant elements."[28]

Justice is viewed as a universal value and obligation, and this principle is articulated in Article 154 of the Islamic Republic's Constitution, which states that the Islamic Republic of Iran considers the rule of justice to be the right of all the people of the world.[29]

It is through the prism of their principle of justice that Ahmadinejad and his supporters relentlessly attack the Holocaust, attempt to delegitimize Israel, support the Palestinians and other "liberation" movements, and criticize the U.S.-led international system for mobilizing support on behalf of Israel.[30] On December 9, 2005, in Mecca, Saudi Arabia, the seat and symbol of Islam, Ahmadinejad said: "Some European countries insist on saying that, during World War II, Hitler burned millions of Jews. And they insist so strongly on this issue that anyone who denies it is condemned and sent to prison." He continued: *"Although we don't believe this claim,* let's suppose what the Europeans say is true ... let's give some land to the Zionists in Europe or in Germany or Austria. We will also support it. They faced injustice in Europe, so why do the Palestinians have to pay the consequences."[31] The clause, "Although we don't believe this claim," is Holocaust denial.

It is argued that Ahmadinejad uses his foreign policy bombast to: (1) generate domestic political support from hard-line religious figures; (2) signal to domestic political opponents the tone and direction of Iran's foreign policy; (3) create a leadership role for Iran in the Palestinian-Israeli conflict, which provides Iran with regional prestige and geopolitical leverage vis-à-vis the West; and (4) generate popularity for the Islamic Republic among the populations of the Arab states whose leaders are supported by the West, therefore creating domestic pressure on Arab leaders to act more aggressively on the Palestinian-Israeli issue and delegitimizing their regimes. However, despite these arguments, to claim that Ahmadinejad's Holocaust denial is strictly instrumental is nothing more than sophisticated and apologetic acceptance of Ahmadinejad's self-serving misunderstanding of history.

Ahmadinejad's attacks on the Holocaust are part of the erroneous perception that the Holocaust led directly to the establishment of the State of Israel. He asserts that there is a causal link between the Holocaust and the creation of Israel. However, this account is a misreading of history. The Zionist enterprise began long before the Holocaust. For example, the 1917 Balfour Declaration recognized the Zionist efforts to establish a Jewish homeland in Palestine more than fifteen years before the Holocaust.

Ahmadinejad was not the first Iranian high official engage in Holocaust denial. The Supreme Leader (*rahbar*) of the Islamic Republic, Ayatollah 'Ali Khamene'i, also attacked Israel by attempting to cast doubt on the atrocities of the Holocaust. In April 2001, he said: "There is proof that the Zionists had close relations with German Nazis. The presentation of astronomical figures on the massacre of the Jews was, in

---

[28] Ramazani, *Revolutionary Iran*, pp. 23-4.
[29] Moshirzadeh, "Discursive Foundations," p. 533.
[30] Ibid.
[31] Naji, *Ahmadinejad*, pp. 154-156.

itself, a means of making the people express sympathy with them and prepare the ground for occupying Palestine and justifying the Zionists' crimes."[32]

The political leaders in Iran have used Holocaust denial as one element of broader "vehement anti-Zionist position" that reflects "traditional anti-Jewish themes in Iran's national and religious culture."[33] Meir Litvak has astutely noted that, as opposed to the modern scholarly literature on nationalism, Jews are not viewed as a nation but rather as a scattered religious community that rejected the message of the Prophet Muhammad.[34] These themes are an important part of the teachings of Ayatollah Ruhollah Khomeini, the ideological founder and leader of the Islamic Republic of Iran and "have guided the Iranian government ever since the 1979 Revolution."[35]

Ayatollah Khomeini, the leader of the 1979 revolution, wrote with a distinct anti-Jewish theme, which combined Shi'i ideology with elements of European anti-semitism. In the opening paragraphs of his book *Islamic Governance* (*Al-Hukumah al-Islamiyyah*), Khomeini claimed that "[f]rom the very beginning, the historical movement of Islam has had to contend with the Jews," who "first established anti-Islamic propaganda and engaged in various stratagems, and as you can see, this activity continues down to the present."[36] In Khomeini's earlier book, *Clarification of the Questions* (*Touzih al-Masa 'el*), he emphasized the Shi'i doctrine of the ritual impurity of unbelievers (*nejasat*), whom he considered contaminated. He directed his followers not to purchase products that could not be purified (such as food) from unbelieving infidels.[37]

It would seem that President Ahmadinejad and the Supreme Leader, in the spirit of Imam Khomeini's ideology, believe that a just solution for the Palestinians is the elimination of the Jewish State of Israel. This is the view of many officials in the Islamic Republic, who believe that Zionism is part of Western imperialist designs against Islam[38] and that these designs are supported by an unjust international system.[39]

On October 26, 2005, in Tehran, Ahmadinejad gave a speech at a student conference, and for the first time he called for the elimination of Israel (literally: "this Jerusalem occupying regime must vanish from the pages of time.") This language was not new in the history of the Islamic Republic of Iran. Indeed, Hossein Shariatmadari, the editor of the Iranian daily newspaper *Kayhan* and advisor to the Supreme Leader, stated: "The honorable President has said nothing new about Israel that would justify all this political commotion. ... We declare explicitly that we will

---

[32] "Iran: Khamene'i says Zionism exaggerated Holocaust," Vision of the Islamic Republic of Iran Network 1, *BBC Worldwide Monitoring*, April 24, 2001.

[33] Meir Litvak, "What is Behind Iran's Advocacy of Holocaust Denial?," *Iran Pulse*, no. 3 (Tel Aviv University: Center for Iranian Studies, 2006).

[34] Ibid.

[35] Ibid.

[36] Imam Khomeini, *Islam and Revolution*, translated and annotated by Hamid Algar (Berkeley, California: Mizan Press, 1981), p. 27.

[37] David Menashri, "Iran, the Jews, and the Holocaust," in *Annual Country Report* (Stephen F. Roth Institute for the Contemporary Study of Antisemitism and Racism, 2005).

[38] Litvak, "Iran's Advocacy of Holocaust Denial."

[39] Rajaee, *Islamic Values*, p. 87.

not be satisfied with anything less than the complete obliteration of the Zionist regime from the political map of the world."[40]

In January 2001, the Supreme Leader, Ayatollah Khamene'i, said that Israel was a cancerous tumor that needed to be removed from the region. In December 2001, former President Rafsanjani, while leading a Friday prayer service in Tehran, threatened Israel with nuclear destruction and said "if one day, the Islamic world is also equipped with weapons like those that Israel possesses now, then the imperialists' strategy will reach a standstill because the use of even one nuclear bomb inside Israel will destroy everything. However, it will only harm the Islamic world. It is not irrational to contemplate such an eventuality."[41] It is through the revolutionary principle of justice viewed through the prism of Imam Khomeini's ideology that Iran relentlessly attempts to delegitimize and threaten Israel.[42]

Iranian officials also employ the principles of justice and equality to attack the hierarchy of powers in the international system. For example, in September 2005, when Ahmadinejad referred to the attempt of Western nuclear powers to prevent Iran from enriching uranium as "nuclear apartheid," and said to the Turkish Prime Minister "[w]ith respect to the needs of Islamic countries, we are ready to transfer nuclear know-how to these countries," he was attacking what he perceives as the injustice and inequality in the double-standards of the international system. Iranian officials argue against the injustice and double-standard of the U.S. posture toward the nuclear program of Iran, on one hand, and that of India, Israel, and Pakistan, on the other. These arguments are also part of the ideology of Imam Khomeini, who argued that it is only the logic of the oppressors that rules over the relations between nations.[43] According to this ideology, Iran was part of the oppressed nations and the U.S. was the oppressor.

Resistance is the third element or theme of the Islamic Republic's revolutionary ideology. The idea of resistance is and has been a powerful theme in the discourse of many of the Islamic Republic's institutions, such as the Revolutionary Guards (*Sepah-e Pasdaran*), the hard-line media, the Guardian Council, the *Basij*, and the Islamic associations.[44] The Islamic Republic's rejection of the Western-dominated international order is deeply rooted in its discourse of resistance. Israel, which the Islamic Republic views as a colonial tool of the West artificially implanted into the heart of the Muslim territory, is a core focus in its discourse of resistance. The Islamic Republic's foreign policy has actively cultivated relations with Islamic resistance movements throughout the Middle East. These movements have drawn inspiration from the Iranian revolution in 1978 and 1979, and in turn the Islamic Republic has provided support to these movements. Hizbullah in Lebanon has embraced Khomeini's ideology and has maintained a close relationship and identification with the Islamic Republic. Furthermore, Hizbullah and to a lesser degree Islamic Jihad

---

[40] *Kayhan*, October 30, 2005, as quoted in Naji, *Ahmadinejad*, p. 149.

[41] Agence France-Presse, December 14, 2001; "Iran: Rafsanjani warns of high cost of US support for Israel," *BBC Worldwide Monitoring*, December 15, 2001.

[42] David Menashri, *Post-Revolutionary Politics in Iran: Religion, Society and Power* (London and Portland, Oregon: Frank Cass, Ltd., 2001), pp. 262-263.

[43] Rajaee, p. 80.

[44] Moshirzadeh, "Discursive Foundations."

and Hamas have provided the Islamic Republic with a means to project the Islamic revolution beyond its immediate borders. The Islamic Republic's ability to influence events in the Palestinian-Israeli arena provides it with an important lever to manipulate public opinion in the conservative Arab states. Therefore, pursuing its revolutionary agenda concerning Israel has provided the Islamic Republic with concomitant instrumental points of leverage to use in its relations with its Arab neighbors. In other words, by pursuing its ideological agenda vis-à-vis resistance to Israel, Iran is both reinforcing its revolutionary commitment to resistance and concurrently developing instruments of regional influence that provide it with diplomatic leverage. Resistance is a theme that goes hand in hand with the idea of independence, which was discussed earlier.

Iran's troubled history of experience with Western powers reinforces the idea that Iran must resist foreign powers that threaten its sovereignty or independence.[45] Iran lionizes its historical episodes that focus on political resistance in order to preserve its independence, such as the tobacco protests (1891-1892), the constitutional revolution (1905-1911), the oil nationalization movement, and the Islamic resistance to American capitulations in 1963, which are episodes explicitly referred to in the preamble of the 1979 Constitution. On the other hand, compromising on Iran's independence in any form or in exchange for any reward has often resulted in vilification in Iran's domestic political arena.[46] For example, President Ahmadinejad's supporters vilified the previous administration's decision to suspend nuclear uranium enrichment (November 15, 2004) as an embarrassing surrender comparable to the treaty signed with Russia at Turkmenchai in 1828. This treaty forced the ruling Qajar dynasty to cede huge portions of Iranian territory to Russia. This territory was never regained and today forms part of present-day Armenia, Azerbaijan, and Georgia.[47]

III. THE ISLAMIC REPUBLIC'S REVOLUTIONARY PRAGMATISM

To return to the initial point of reference for this essay, rather than asking if the Islamic Republic is a pragmatic or revolutionary actor in an either/or, zero-sum proposition, the question one should ask is how, and in what context, has the Islamic Republic's pragmatism historically manifested itself in its foreign policy? Or, in other words, how has it adjusted its means to meet its revolutionary goals?

The historical record has demonstrated that Iran's leadership has followed the Imam Khomeini's dictate: "The preservation of the Islamic Republic is a divine duty which is above all other duties."[48] What did Khomeini mean? He was alluding to those situations where the Islamic Republic's leadership believes the survival of the regime is at stake, in which case the Islamic Republic may compromise on its ideological principles to protect the Islamic state.[49]

In the early days of the Islamic Republic, the Imam Khomeini's rhetoric regarding exporting the Iranian revolution threatened Iran's Gulf neighbors. In addition to

---

[45] Ibid., p. 536.
[46] Ibid.
[47] Naji, pp. 123-124.
[48] Afrasiabi, p. 17.
[49] Menashri, *Post-Revolutionary Politics*, p. 14.

broadcasting regional radio messages in Arabic that attacked neighboring regimes that Khomeini believed to be corrupt or pawns of U.S. imperialism, the Islamic Republic was suspected of training and arming a group of Shi'ites who plotted to overthrow the ruler of Bahrain in 1981. The Islamic Republic was also suspected of complicity in the multiple bombings carried out by Shi'ites in Kuwait in December 1983 and the hijacking of a Kuwaiti airliner flying from Dubai to Karachi in 1984. The Islamic Republic also used its delegation to the *hajj* in Mecca to politicize the event and to incite believers against the Saudi regime. In 1987, Rafsanjani inveighed against the Saudi regime, claiming that Iran should "uproot the Saudi rulers in the region and divest the control of the holy shrines from the contaminated existence of the Wahhabis, those hooligans."[50] Furthermore, the Islamic Republic used ideology to mobilize its young teenagers during the war against Iraq. Young Iranian men and boys were sent to the front in the war against Iraq, where they were employed as human waves to cross minefields and serve as human detonators in advance of Iranian troops carrying out military offensives. During the first ten years of the Islamic Republic, Iran's foreign policy was perceived by the West as being revolutionary and ideological.[51] Iran's foreign policy posture was also influenced by its relative isolation during its decade-long war against Saddam Hussein's Iraq beginning in 1980.[52]

In July 1982, Iran, which had succeeded in driving Iraqi forces from Iranian territory in 1981, went on the offensive, taking the war into Iraq. Iraq, facing increasing losses, attempted to internationalize the war by attacking Iran's shipping and oil tanker traffic in the Gulf. Since Iraq was not shipping oil through the Gulf, Iran responded by attacking the shipping and oil traffic of the Arab Gulf states. This initiated the "Tanker War" phase of the conflict, which ultimately resulted in the U.S. Navy entering the Gulf to protect tanker traffic to and from Kuwait. With the support of many of the Gulf rulers, as well as the West, the war began to turn in Iraq's favor in the mid-1980s, and Iran became increasingly isolated, lacking adequate supplies of advanced weapons. It was in the context of facing the possibility of losing a long, bloody war against Iraq, and perhaps even the end of the regime, that elements within Iran entered into an agreement with the U.S. and Israel to exchange kidnapped American hostages in Lebanon for Israeli and American arms and equipment. Iran depended on oil revenues to finance its war effort. In 1986, the market for oil declined sharply, seriously damaging Iran's capability to sustain the war against Iraq. Furthermore, Iraqi attacks on Iran's oil-producing infrastructure exacerbated fluctuating market conditions. Iran's wartime economy had already been stretched thin; it relied on subsidies, rationing, and price controls to manage rapidly declining resources. By 1988, the war was absorbing nearly half of all state revenue, leaving little money for anything else. It was the politics of preserving the Islamic regime that forced Khomeini to give up "war until victory" and drink the "poisoned chalice," accepting, with great reluctance, U.N. Resolution 598, which ended the Iran-Iraq war on August 20, 1988. As one analyst noted, Iran's "acceptance of the United Nations Security Council Resolution 598 calling for ceasefire with Iraq

---

[50] David Menashri, "Iran," in *Middle East Contemporary Survey*, ed. Itamar Rabinovich and Haim Shaked, vol. 11 (Boulder, San Francisco and London: Westview Press, 1987), p. 417.

[51] Ramazani, *Revolutionary Iran*.

[52] Ehteshami, *After Khomeini*.

was the revolutionary leader's [Khomeini's] single greatest submission to the logic of realpolitik."[53] In other words, with the existence of the regime at stake, the Imam Khomeini reversed himself to preserve the Islamic Republic.

Six months after Khomeini ended the war with Iraq, and three days after the tenth anniversary of the 1979 revolution, on February 14, 1989, Khomeini announced that it was the duty of Muslims everywhere to kill author Salman Rushdie for his book *The Satanic Verses*, which was published in the summer of 1988. In May 1989, Rafsanjani was encouraging Palestinians to retaliate against Israel by attacking Westerners. He said: "If, in retaliation for every Palestinian martyred in Palestine they kill ... five American or Britons or Frenchmen," then the Israelis "would not continue their wrongs."[54] Khomeini's decree and Rafsanjani's statement may be interpreted as the regime's reassertion of its revolutionary identity following the compromises required to end the Iran-Iraq war and begin reconstructing the nation.

1989 was an important year for the Islamic Republic of Iran. In June 1989, the Imam Khomeini died and Sayyid Ali Khamene'i somewhat controversially succeeded Khomeini as the new *rahbar* of the Islamic Republic. The government also amended its constitution in 1989, eliminating the position of prime minister and vesting the office of the president with much stronger executive powers. Rafsanjani was elected president and faced the steep challenge of reconstructing Iran's depleted, war-torn resources.

A critical component of Rafsanjani's plan to rehabilitate Iran's economy, which was on the brink of disaster following a decade of war, was improving relations with the West so that the Islamic Republic would be eligible to receive loans from the World Bank and IMF. Rafsanjani understood that reconstructing Iran's economy required achieving three primary goals: (1) developing "normal" diplomatic relations with the outside world; (2) improving Iran's access to Western technology, particularly in the area of oil infrastructure; and (3) integration of Iran into the world economy to increase Iran's socio-economic development.[55] These pragmatic tactics were necessitated by Iran's economic crisis. These goals entailed changing the image that Iran presented to the world rather than changing the revolutionary identity of the regime.[56] Rafsanjani implemented a tactical shift in order to soften the revolutionary image of the regime—which in the words of one scholar based in the Islamic Republic was a form of dissimulation or *taqiyya*[57]—rather than a fundamental reorientation of the regime's revolutionary identity. In a December 1991 Friday sermon, President Rafsanjani called for a prudent policy (*tadbir*) in domestic and foreign affairs, "so that we can help people without being accused of engaging in terrorism, without anyone being able to call us fanatics."[58] David Menashri noted

---

[53] Ahmed Hashim, *The Crisis of the Iranian State* (Oxford: Oxford University Press, 1995), p. 30.

[54] Quoted from David Menashri, *Post-Revolutionary Politics*, p. 197.

[55] Hashim, *Crisis of the Iranian State*, p. 30.

[56] For a serious theoretical treatment on how states manipulate their images for their desired ends in international relations, see Robert Jervis, *The Logic of Images in International Relations* (Princeton: Princeton University Press, 1970).

[57] Afrasiabi, *After Khomeini*, p. 11.

[58] Radio Tehran, December 20, 1991—Daily Report, December 23, 1991, as quoted in David Menashri, "Iran," in *Middle East Contemporary Survey*, ed. Ami Ayalon, vol. 15 (Boulder, San Francisco and Oxford: Westview Press, 1993), p. 385.

that Rafsanjani was not rejecting terror, he "only wished that his country would not be identified with such actions and not be viewed as fanatic. This was the nature of his 'pragmatism' if this was the correct word for such an approach."[59]

The regime adopted a two-track foreign policy during the 1990s. On the one hand, it pursued the aforementioned goals of softening its image in the West to expedite desperately needed socio-economic development and global market integration; on the other hand, it supported the Islamist regime in Sudan and Hizbullah in Lebanon, rejected the Israeli-Palestinian peace accords, supported militant Islamic organizations in the Palestinian territories, conducted assassinations of prominent opponents of the regime throughout the world, and developed a secret nuclear energy program.[60]

Iran's foreign policy posture during the 1990s was shaped, in large measure, by the security arrangements that emerged in the Persian Gulf region following Operation Desert Storm, the U.S.-led international war to undo Iraq's invasion of Kuwait in 1990-1991. The Islamic Republic maneuvered through the Kuwait crisis as a neutral party seeking to take advantage of the war between its two major enemies, Iraq and the U.S. It condemned Iraq's invasion of Kuwait and opposed U.S. military build-up in the region.

Iran also benefited from Iraq's vulnerability in the period following Saddam's invasion of Kuwait and prior to Operation Desert Storm. In mid-August 1990, Saddam, eager to insure that Iran would remain on the sidelines, made several immediate and important concessions to the Islamic Republic to settle unresolved issues related to the Iran-Iraq war. Saddam agreed that: (1) territorial rights to the Shatt al-Arab waterway would be governed by the 1975 Algiers Accord; (2) Security Council Resolution 598 would be accepted; and (3) Iraq and Iran would carry out an exchange of prisoners of war, of which there were nearly three times as many Iranian ones. As a gesture of goodwill, Saddam also agreed to withdraw from 26,000 square miles of occupied Iranian territory. These were significant concessions from Iraq, and ultimately presented Iran with the victor's spoils from its long war with Iraq.

Following the war, Iran was eager to play an important role in the post-war regional security of the Gulf. The Islamic Republic believed that the Gulf's coastal states should be responsible for Gulf security, and the region should be free from foreign interference.[61] It advocated a regional system of collective security (*amniyat-e dast-e jam 'ii*).[62] Furthermore, the leaders of the Islamic Republic believed that any regional security system that excluded Iran was illegitimate. However, Iran's prudent neutrality during the Kuwait crisis was a product of its post Iran-Iraq war weakness. By remaining on the sidelines during a critical security episode for the region, the Islamic Republic marginalized its own position in any future regional security cooperation.

---

[59] Menashri, "Iran" (1993), p. 385.
[60] Ali Banuazizi, "Iran's Revolutionary Impasse: Political Factionalism and Societal Resistance," *Middle East Report (MERIP)*, no. 191 (November-December 1994), p. 4.
[61] Menashri, "Iran" (1993), p. 403.
[62] Afrasiabi, *After Khomeini*, p. 101.

Following Saddam's defeat in 1991, the Gulf Cooperation Council (GCC) states[63] announced a preliminary security plan for the Gulf, the Damascus Declaration, which included the six GCC states plus Egypt and Syria. Iran was excluded from this new security arrangement. However, when the Damascus Declaration fell apart in the spring of 1991, each one of the GCC states made separate bilateral security deals with U.S. to guarantee their security, which not only excluded Iran from any role in regional security but also entrenched the Great Satan's military forces in its backyard. It is hard to overstate the effect of these developments. Iran's national identity is deeply tied to its historical self-perception as the dominant regional power in the Gulf. The build-up and long-term presence of U.S. forces in the Gulf and the Arab Gulf states' preference for U.S. security rather than a regional arrangement antagonized the Islamic Republic, which felt it was being slighted.

For Iran, this issue was not simply a matter of its self-image or regional policy regarding its Arab Gulf neighbors; the sustained post-war U.S. military presence in the region put its historical oppressor in its backyard and presented a direct challenge to the Islamic Republic's revolutionary principle of resistance to an increasingly U.S.-dominated regional and world security order. The Islamic Republic's first opportunity to demonstrate its symbolic resistance to the U.S. regional agenda came in October 1991, when it organized and sponsored an Islamist conference in Tehran (October 19-22) to oppose the U.S. organized Arab-Israeli peace conference in Madrid, to be held later that same month. Apart from the Islamist government of Sudan, the parties that attended the conference in Tehran consisted primarily of militant Islamist organizations from the Middle East and Africa that rejected peace with Israel.

It is important to bear in mind that the Islamic Republic was still extremely vulnerable in 1991, just two years after the end of the Iran-Iraq war. Moreover, before the Kuwait crisis, Iran and Iraq were still negotiating over the terms of their post-war agreement. And while Iran's cash reserves had received a boost from the rise in oil prices during the war against Saddam, the Iranian economy was still vulnerable and its military was weak and poorly armed. President Rafsanjani was desperately fighting political battles at home to advance his economic reforms and integrate Iran into the global marketplace. The October 1991 anti-peace conference in Tehran provided the Islamic Republic with a pragmatic, low-risk opportunity to reassert its revolutionary identity of resistance to the U.S. order and Israel's legitimacy. Rather than direct military confrontation however, which was Iran's approach during the 1980s, it adapted new tactics in the 1990s, choosing to express its resistance through diplomatic initiatives, while at the same time providing covert financing, logistics, weapons, and training to proxy Islamist groups that were ready to confront American and Israeli interests asymmetrically. This tactical shift allowed the Islamic Republic to pursue a revolutionary foreign policy that was less likely to jeopardize the Islamic regime's survival. Combining savvy public diplomacy with covert and deniable militancy, Iran was able to pursue a foreign policy that was *both* pragmatic and revolutionary during the 1990s.

---

[63] The six GCC states include Bahrain, Kuwait, Oman, Qatar, Saudi Arabia, and the UAE.

IV. Conclusion

Henry Kissinger noted that the motivation of the revolutionary power may well be defensive, and Iran may well be sincere and justified in its claims of feeling threatened by the West. However, the key distinguishing feature of a revolutionary power, as Kissinger pointed out, "is not that it feels threatened—such feeling is inherent in the nature of international relations based on sovereign states—*but that nothing can reassure it*. Only absolute security—the neutralization of the opponent—is considered a sufficient guarantee, and thus the desire of one power for absolute security means absolute insecurity for all the others."[64] R.K. Ramazani, a leading scholar of Iranian foreign policy, observed that Iranian leaders, during the first decade of the Islamic Republic, almost never used the word security by itself—it was always preceded by "such adjectives as real, true, and genuine."[65]

Indeed, it is the Islamic Republic's quest for regime security that has historically come into conflict with its revolutionary principle of independence. A prominent scholar in the Islamic Republic of Iran, noting the rigid criteria that "true independence" demanded, argued that "a balance needs to be struck between preserving political sovereignty (and not independence) and stable and permanent cooperation with the West." This scholar also argued that "[t]here is no such concept as political independence," and urged the Iranian elites "to move from the anti-colonial tendencies of the 1950s to the realities of statecraft of the 21st century."[66] Iran, which is still in the throes of its revolutionary development,[67] does not appear to have completed this transition.

---

[64] Kissinger, *A World Restored*, pp. 1-3.
[65] Ramazani, *Revolutionary Iran*, p. 27.
[66] Mahmood Sariolghalam, "Theoretical Renewal in Iranian Foreign Policy (Part I)," *Discourse: An Iranian Quarterly* 3, no. 3 (Winter 2002), p. 75.
[67] Arjomand, "Has Iran's Islamic Revolution Ended?"

BIBLIOGRAPHY

Adib-Moghaddam, Arshin. "Islamic Utopian Romanticism and the Foreign Policy Culture of Iran." *Critique: Critical Middle Eastern Studies* 14, no. 3 (Fall 2005), pp. 265-92.

Afrasiabi, Kaveh L. *After Khomeini: New Directions in Iran's Foreign Policy*. Boulder, San Francisco, and Oxford: Westview Press, 1994.

Arjomand, Said. "Has Iran's Islamic Revolution Ended?" *Radical History Review*, no. 105 (Fall 2009), pp. 132-8.

Banuazizi, Ali. "Iran's Revolutionary Impasse: Political Factionalism and Societal Resistance." *Middle East Report (MERIP)*, no. 191 (November-December 1994).

Ehteshami, Anoushiravan. "The Foreign Policy of Iran." In *The Foreign Policies of Middle Eastern States, edited by* Raymond Hinnebusch and Anoushiravan Ehteshami, pp. 283-309. Boulder, Colorado: Lynne Rienner Publishers, Inc., 2002.

———. *After Khomeini: The Iranian Second Republic*. London and New York: Routledge, 1995.

Hashim, Ahmed. *The Crisis of the Iranian State*. Oxford: Oxford University Press, 1995.

Khomeini, Ruhoullah. *Islam and Revolution*. Translated and Annotated by Hamid Algar. Berkeley, California: Mizan Press, 1981.

Kissinger, Henry. A World Restored: Europe after Napoleon: The Politics of Conservatism in a Revolutionary Age. 1964.

Kostiner, Joseph. *Conflict and Cooperation in the Gulf Region*. Wiesbaden, Germany: VS Verlag Fur Sozialwissenschaften, 2009.

Litvak, Meir. "What is Behind Iran's Advocacy of Holocaust Denial?" *Iran Pulse*, no. 3. Tel Aviv University: Center for Iranian Studies, 2006.

Menashri, David. "Iran, the Jews, and the Holocaust." In *Annual Country Report*. Stephen F. Roth Institute for the Contemporary Study of Antisemitism and Racism, 2005.

———. Post-Revolutionary Politics in Iran: Religion, Society and Power. *London and Portland, Oregon: Frank Cass, Ltd., 2001.*

———. "Iran." *In Middle East Contemporary Survey*, edited by Itamar Rabinovich and Haim Shaked, vol. 11. Boulder, San Francisco and London: Westview Press, 1987.

Moshirzadeh, Homeira. "Discursive Foundations of Iran's Nuclear Policy." *Security Dialogue* 38, no. 4 (December 2007).

Mottaki, Manuchechr. "What is a Just Global Order." *Iranian Journal of International Affairs* 19, no. 2 (Spring 2007), pp. 1-7.

Naji, Kasra. *Ahmadinejad: The Secret History of Iran's Radical Leader*. London: I.B. Tauris, 2008.

Rajaee, Farhang. *Islamic Values and World View: Khomeyni on Man the State and International Politics*, vol. 12. Lanham, New York, London: University Press of America, Inc., 1983.

Ramazani, R.K. "Ideology and Pragmatism in Iran's Foreign Policy." *Middle East Journal* 58, no. 4 (Autumn 2004), pp. 549-59.

———. Revolutionary Iran: Challenge and Response in the Middle East. *Johns Hopkins University Press, 1988.*

Sariolghalam, Mahmood. "Theoretical Renewal in Iranian Foreign Policy (Part I)." *Discourse: An Iranian Quarterly* 3, no. 3 (Winter 2002).

Missing from the Map: Feminist Theory and the Omission of Jewish Women

Jennifer Roskies[*]

I. Introduction

This paper examines a topic at the beginning stages of its investigation. It attempts to shed light on an apparent omission within feminist theory in the United States and discusses its implications for contemporary feminism—as well as for feminists who are American Jewish women.

As described below, feminists of diverse racial and ethnic backgrounds have developed theoretical models that articulate their uniquely situated standpoints in relation to the sexism of their respective racial/ethnic groups, on the one hand, and what has been termed "mainstream" or "white" feminism, on the other. This is not so when it comes to Jewish women, notwithstanding the involvement of many Jewish women in the women's movement, including as leading theorists, leaving a gap in both feminist and multicultural theory, as well as in identity studies. This paper presents a comparison of existing theoretical approaches and demonstrates the absence of a comparable depiction of Jewish women as case studies within multicultural feminism. It poses the following query:

If one were to try to develop a theoretical model of multicultural Jewish feminist identity where there now is none, how would one do so? How might such a theory explain the following questions:

(a) If Jewish women are missing from the map of feminist theory—both as subjects and as authors—why might this be, and where do they place *themselves* when it comes to their Jewish and feminist identities?
(b) Is one possible explanation of this absence from the map that Jewish women locate themselves within so-called mainstream feminism, that is, as white, and unencumbered by an extraneous identity of any consequence?
(c) If so, how do Jewish feminists view expressions within the women's movement that pertain to Jewish issues or Israel, including expressions that appear to be antisemitic? How do their identities as mainstream members of this movement coexist with their identities as members of the Jewish people?

This paper draws upon Black feminist theory as a point of contrast with current scholarship related to feminism and American Jewish women. With that contrast in

---

[*] Researcher, YIISA and Bar-Ilan University. I wish to acknowledge Dina Feldman, David Chinitz, and Arlene R. Chinitz for their valuable comments.

mind, the paper puts forth the thesis that, while there may be an overall identification among Jewish women with the feminist mainstream, their position in the women's movement may nevertheless reflect the eternal puzzle of Jews viewed as "Other"—as a race, as a religion, as both, as neither, as a composite projection of the host population's fantasies. This absence of a theoretical model reflects the absence of a secure standing within the movement as an ideological home. While this specific paper will not grapple with the issue of "Jew as Other" in this age of multiculturalism, it will conclude with the sketching of a road map for exploration, which, however preliminary, can act as a starting point for additional research in the future.

II. Background

My journey into the world of Gender Studies originated with the wish to understand a certain trait among numerous contemporaries and friends—women, some of whom live in Israel like me, some of whom do not. I noticed an inconsistency between a strong conviction on behalf of women's issues, on the one hand, and a conviction regarding the defense of the legitimacy of the State of Israel, on the other. My own deep conviction held that the two issues—both based on the principles of equal opportunity and self-determination, and both facing the threat of Islamist fundamentalism—go hand in hand. Yet often, these friends did not seem to recognize threats facing Israel as being on par with problems facing women, or they felt that concern for Israel was parochial compared to the more universal condition of gender issues, and therefore ranked as a less immediate priority. I wondered why this might be.

My studies of feminist theory, enlightening on many levels, brought a particular revelation in my encounter with Black feminist and multicultural feminist thought. Black feminist and multicultural theorists initiated an abrupt departure from leading feminist theorists of the 1980s, who had defined the challenges to all women in uniform terms, stemming from their own perspectives as white middle-class women. Black feminist thinkers asserted that the experience of being female—however universal it is in many respects—differs significantly depending upon one's racial, ethnic, cultural, and socio-economic background. Thinkers such as bell hooks [sic],[1] Patricia Hill Collins, Audre Lorde, Barbara Christian, and others pointed to the history and experience of African-American women, which resulted in a distinct social condition with an equally distinct set of needs. In recognizing that these differences had been overlooked and discounted by feminists who had claimed the experience of middle-class white women as the norm and as the mainstream and in articulating a theoretical model—an "Afrocentric feminist standpoint"[2]—Black feminists' landmark contribution enriched feminist theory as a whole. Their writings spoke to the enduring nature of the ties that bind many people to their own ethnic,

---

[1] bell hooks, *Feminist Theory: From Margin to Center* (Boston: South End Press, 1984); Patricia Hill Collins, *Black Feminist Thought: Knowledge, Consciousness and the Politics of Empowerment* (New York: Routledge, Chapman and Hall, Inc., 1991); Audre Lorde, *Sister Outsider: Essays and Speeches* (Berkeley: Crossing Press, 1984); Barbara Christian, "The Race for Theory" (1987), in *New Black Feminist Criticism 1985-2000*, by Barbara Christian, ed. Gloria Bowles, M. Giulia Fabi and Arlene R. Keizer (Urbana and Chicago: University of Illinois Press, 2007).

[2] Collins, *Black Feminist Thought*, pp. 115-117.

racial, or national groups and demonstrated that these ties often claim an allegiance over political or ideological affiliations—and that this may be seen as both natural and legitimate. Their message was one of validation, the validity of staking ground for one's own group, bringing benefit to that group but to others as well in the process. In the words of writer Sonia Sanchez: "I've always known that if you write from a Black experience, you're writing from a universal experience as well ... I know you don't have to whitewash yourself to be universal."[3]

With these ideas in mind, I set out in search of the equivalent academic literature regarding Jewish women's experience of their connections to their Jewishness and their feminism, looking for ways to apply the theoretical model I would find to the situation of my friends and myself. This, I ventured, would bring theoretical underpinning to a project that seemed to require justification, namely, seeing the fight for the legitimation of Jewish self-determination and women's self-determination as linked.

To my great surprise and puzzlement, however, the comparable body of literature was not to be found. Despite existing research on the subjects of feminist identity and multicultural feminist studies, few studies look at Jewish women as case studies in this context.[4] Put differently, the experience of Jewish women, whose role in the women's movement has been highly visible and active, is not reflected in scholarship of multicultural feminist theory. Jewish women are missing from the map.

This paper explores why this may be so.

III. "Jewish Feminism"

Saying that Jewish women are missing from the map of multicultural feminist theory does not mean to say that a search combining the words "Jewish" and "feminism" will yield nothing. On the contrary, within popular literature, one may find personal accounts describing examples of Jewish women's activism in the battle for women's rights and in the feminist movement.[5] Furthermore, when it comes to academic scholarship, searches linking the words "Jewish" and "feminism," do yield studies—pertaining primarily, though, to the theme of women within the Jewish world: women and Jewish religious law, ritual, and communal life. The term "Jewish feminism" itself describes attempts by Jewish women to find a place within or alongside normative Jewish tradition. Scholars such as Rachel Adler,[6] Judith Plaskow,

---

[3] Claudia Tate, ed., *Black Writers at Work* (New York: Continuum Publishing, 1983), p. 142.

[4] Michelle Friedman, "Toward an understanding of Jewish identity: An ethnographic study" (Ph.D. diss., State University of New York, 2002).

[5] See, for example, Judith Plaskow and Donna Berman, eds., *The Coming of Lilith: Essays on Feminism, Judaism and Sexual Ethics, 1972-2003* (Boston: Beacon Press, 2005); Susan Weidman Schneider, *Jewish and Female: Choices and Changes in Our Lives Today* (New York: Simon and Schuster, 1985); Letty Cottin Pogrebin, *Deborah, Golda and Me: Being Female and Jewish in America* (New York: Crown Publishers, 1991); Laura Levitt, *Jews and Feminism: The Ambivalent Search for Home* (New York: Routledge, 1997).

[6] Rachel Adler, *Engendering Judaism: An Inclusive Theology and Ethics* (Boston: Beacon Press, 1999); Judith Plaskow, *Standing Again at Sinai: Judaism from a Feminist Perspective* (New York: Harper One, 1991); Plaskow and Berman, *The Coming of Lilith*; Susannah Heschel, ed., *On Being*

Susanna Heschel, Elyse Goldstein, Tova Hartman, Blu Greenberg, Rivka Haut, Tamara Cohn Eskenazi and Andrea Weiss, Tamar Ross, Danya Rutenberg, and others have contributed toward attempts to realize and define a Jewish religiosity, spiritual fulfillment, dignity, and inclusion for Jewish women in the contemporary Jewish world.

Jewish feminism in the above context has its parallel in works by feminists of other faiths—Christian, Moslem, Hindu—who struggle with similar issues of women's participation, ordination, or changes in theologies and liturgy that range from standard androcentric to outright misogynist. Within Jewish feminism, thinkers and theorists have inspired notable changes in religious and communal life, prompting Sylvia Barack Fishman to remark that these "profound transformations have already become so mainstream as to appear unremarkable."[7] Indeed, these changes are apparent in areas such as synagogue worship, with egalitarianism common practice in the vast majority of American congregations (the vast majority of which are Reform and Conservative), and the integration of female-centered rituals into Jewish life, as well as within the organized Jewish community.[8]

IV. BLACK FEMINIST THOUGHT—DUAL PERSPECTIVES

If existing Jewish feminist scholarship emphasizes issues of women within the Jewish world, Black feminist theory—despite the substantial difference in experiences between the two groups—provides a relevant point of contrast. For the latter, the feminist struggle takes place within African-American society while extending well beyond the "home" community to American society as a whole. Black feminist theorists have explored and reflected African-American women's perceptions of their unique position at a nexus of discrimination on the basis of race, gender, and class. In coining the term "matrix of domination," Patricia Hill Collins spoke of

---

a Jewish Feminist: A Reader (New York: Schocken Books, 1983, 1995); Elyse Goldstein, ed., *The Women's Haftarah Commentary: New Insights from Women Rabbis on the 54 Weekly Haftarah Portions, the 5 Megillot and Special Shabbatot* (New York: Jewish Lights Publishing, 2008); Tova Hartman, *Appropriately Subversive: Modern Mothers in Traditional Religions* (Cambridge: Harvard University Press, 2003); Tova Hartman, *Feminism Encounters Traditional Judaism: Resistance and Accommodation*, HBI Series on Jewish Women (Waltham, MA: Brandeis University Press, 2008); Blu Greenberg, *On Women and Judaism* (New York: Jewish Publication Society of America, 1991); Rivka Haut and Susan Grossman, eds., *Daughters of the King: Women and the Synagogue* (Philadelphia: Jewish Publications Society, 1992); Tamara Cohn Eskenazi and Rabbi Andrea Weiss, eds., *The Torah: A Women's Commentary* (Philadelphia: Union for Reconstructionist Judaism Press, 2007); Tamar Ross, *Expanding the Palace of Torah: Orthodoxy and Feminism*, Brandeis Series on Jewish Women (Waltham, MA: Brandeis University Press, 2004); Danya Rutenberg, ed., *Yentl's Revenge: The Next Wave of Jewish Feminism* (Boston: Seal Press, 2001).

[7] Sylvia Barack Fishman, "Women's Transformations of Public Judaism: Religiosity, Egalitarianism and the Symbolic Power of Changing Gender Roles," in *Studies in Contemporary Jewry Vol. XVII: Who Owns Judaism? Public Religion and Private Faith in America and Israel*, ed. Peter Medding (New York: Oxford University Press, 2001).

[8] Sylvia Barack Fishman, *A Breath of Life: Feminism in the American Jewish Community* (Waltham, MA: Brandeis University Press, 1995); Sylvia Barack Fishman, *Matriarchal Ascent/Patriarchal Descent: The Gender Imbalance in American Jewish Life* (Waltham, MA: Brandeis University Press, 2008); Sylvia Barack Fishman, "The Impact of Feminism on American Jewish Life," in *American Jewish Year Book* (1989).

creating a new paradigm. "The significance of seeing race, class and gender as interlocking systems of oppression is that such an approach fosters a paradigmatic shift of thinking inclusively about other oppressions ... and the economic, political and ideological conditions that support them."[9]

Black feminist theory also emerges from a recognition that the condition of Black women is distinct from that of African Americans as a group as well as from women as a group; therefore, their solutions emanate neither from Afrocentric theory nor from feminist theory but from a uniquely Afrocentric feminist position. Ultimately, the goal of Black feminist theory is to articulate Black women's standpoint, making full use of "access to both the Afrocentric and the feminist standpoints ... [expecting that it] should reflect elements of both traditions, but be distinct—a search for the distinguishing features of an alternative epistemology."[10]

If one were to attempt to depict this objective of Black feminist theory as a diagram, it would look like this:

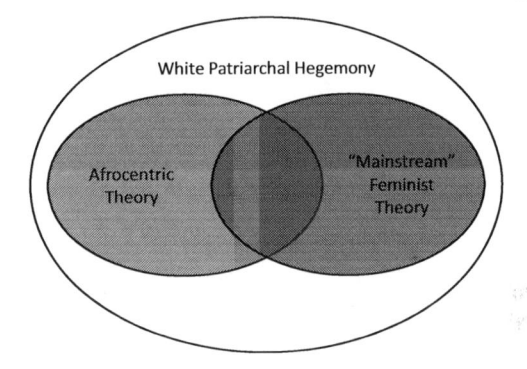

Figure 1: Intersection: the Afrocentric feminist standpoint

and its caption might quote bell hooks's observation:

> White women and black men have it both ways. They can act as oppressor or be oppressed. Black men may be victimized by racism, but sexism allows them to act as exploiters and oppressors of women. White women may be victimized by sexism, but racism enables them to act as exploiters and oppressors of black people. Both groups have led liberation movements that favor their interests and support the continued oppression of other groups.[11]

The intersection of the two inner-circles above depicts what Collins termed "accessing both the Afrocentric and the feminist standpoint while maintaining distinctiveness"—all three sections operating within the general context of the system's white patriarchal hegemony. Feminist theorists of other racial and ethnic backgrounds have reached similar conclusions and prescribe a theoretical model that combines a similar dual focus—on sexism within their respective racial/ethnic group as well as

---

[9] Collins, *Black Feminist Thought*, p. 232.
[10] Ibid., p. 206.
[11] hooks, *Feminist Theory*, p. 15.

on the racism that flows from mainstream white feminism.[12] A schematic representation of Jewish feminism, in contrast, might look more like this:

Figure 2: Jewish feminism

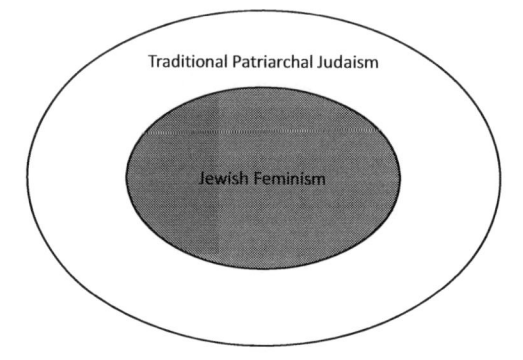

reflecting its focus as rooted within the Jewish world. Missing is the comparable "oval," the attempt at self-definition vis-à-vis traditional androcentric Judaism *and* vis-à-vis non-Jewish feminism, with the attempt to identify a standpoint unique to Jewish women. Such a model would be represented as follows:

Figure 3: Intersection: feminist Jewish women's standpoint

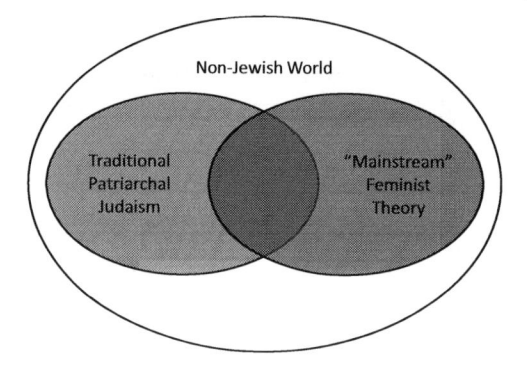

---

[12] See, for example, Shirley Geok-lin Lim, "Feminist and Ethnic Theories in Asian American Literature" (1993), in *Feminisms: An Anthology of Literary Theory and Criticism*, ed. Robyn D. Warhol and Diana Price Hernd (New Brunswick, NJ: Rutgers University Press, 1997), pp. 807-826; Amy Ling, "I'm Here: An Asian American Woman's Response" (1987), in *Feminisms: An Anthology of Literary Theory and Criticism*, ed. Robyn D. Warhol and Diana Price Hernd (New Brunswick, NJ: Rutgers University Press, 1997), pp. 776-783; Gloria Anzaldua, "La conciencia de la mestiza: Towards a New Consciousness" (1986), in *Feminisms: An Anthology of Literary Theory and Criticism*, ed. Robyn D. Warhol and Diana Price Hernd (New Brunswick, NJ: Rutgers University Press, 1997), pp. 765-775; Biddy Martin and Chandra Talpade Mohanty, "What's Home Got to Do with It?" (1986), in *Feminisms: An Anthology of Literary Theory and Criticism*, ed. Robyn D. Warhol and Diana Price Hernd (New Brunswick, NJ: Rutgers University Press, 1997), pp. 293-310; Rosaura Sanchez, "Discourses and Gender: Ethnicity and Class in Chicano Literature" (1992), in *Feminisms: An Anthology of Literary Theory and Criticism*, ed. Robyn D. Warhol and Diana Price Hernd (New Brunswick, NJ: Rutgers University Press, 1997), pp. 1009-1028.

V. Where do Jewish Women—Jewish Feminists—Locate Themselves?

This contrast in orientations is all the more intriguing when one considers the active role that Jewish women have played in the women's movement, including thinkers and writers whose works hold a central place in the canon of feminist and gender theory. A selected list includes Betty Friedan, Adrienne Rich, Susan Moller Okin, Andrea Dworkin,[13] as well as ground-breaking feminist thinkers and writers in the disciplines of history (Gerda Lerner, Natalie Zemon Davis, Joan Wallach Scott),[14] literary criticism (Sandra Gilbert and Susan Gubar, Elaine Showalter),[15] psychology (Nancy Chodorow, Phyllis Chesler, Carol Gilligan),[16] feminist research methodology (Shula Reinharz),[17] and queer theory (Judith Butler, Eve Kosofsky Sedgwick).[18] Yet, we do not see a body of scholarship comparable to that of Black feminists describing the encounter between Jewish women and feminism, echoing observations regarding the "conspicuous absence of theory and research [related] to the Jewish people within the general literature on multiculturalism."[19]

How might this situation have come to be? One explanation may be that this search for a "Jewish women's feminist standpoint" simply was not necessary. At first glance, this point may seem so obvious as to be barely noteworthy. In as race-conscious a society as the United States, a Black woman—or man—will face a greater level of discrimination than someone white. If Jewish women's feminism has not evolved the same kind of differentiation and self-definition as Black women's, this may well reflect the lack of a sense of urgency to do so: an absence of that same experience of discrimination and, just as surely, a sense of identification with the American white majority. The fact that works of the Jewish theorists cited above were incorporated into the core feminist oeuvre provides further evidence of their identification and sense of belonging within the feminist white mainstream.

---

[13] Betty Friedan, *The Feminine Mystique* (New York: Dell Mass Market Paperback, 1964); Adrienne Rich, "Disloyal to Civilization: Feminism, Racism, Gynophobia," *On Lies, Secrets and Silence: Selected Prose 1966-1978* (New York: W.W. Norton, 1991), pp. 275-310; Susan Moller Okin, *Justice, Gender and the Family* (New York: Basic Books, 1989); Andrea Dworkin, *Pornography: Men Possessing Women* (New York: Plume Books, 1991).

[14] Gerda Lerner, *The Creation of Patriarchy* (New York: Oxford University Press, 1986); Natalie Zemon Davis, *Women on the Margins: Three Seventeenth-Century Lives* (Cambridge: Belknap Press of Harvard University Press, 1997).

[15] Sandra Gilbert and Susan Gubar, *The Madwoman in the Attic* (New Haven: Yale University Press, 1979); Elaine Showalter, *New Feminist Criticism: Women, Literature and Theory* (New York: Pantheon, 1985).

[16] Nancy Chodorow, *The Reproduction of Mothering* (Berkeley: The Regents University of California Press, 1978); Nancy Chodorow, *Feminism and Psychoanalytic Theory* (New Haven: Yale University Press, 1991); Phyllis Chesler, *Women and Madness* (New York: Doubleday and Co., 1972); Carol Gilligan, *In a Different Voice: Psychological Theory and Women's Development* (Cambridge: Harvard University Press, 1982).

[17] Shulamit Reinharz, *Feminist Methods in Social Research* (New York: Oxford University Press, 1992).

[18] Judith Butler, *Undoing Gender* (New York: Routledge Press, 2004); Judith Butler, *Gender Trouble: Feminism and the Subversion of Identity* (New York: Routledge, 2006); Eve Kosofsky Sedgwick, *The Epistemology of the Closet* (Berkeley: The Regents of University of California Press, 1990).

[19] Friedman, "Toward an understanding of Jewish identity."

Likewise, the feminist Jewish women's viewpoint is virtually indistinguishable from the mainstream in the context of multicultural feminist theory. Much of multicultural feminist theory relates to the negotiation of women's standing alongside a multitude of cultural contexts. It upholds the avoidance, as in Black Feminist theory, of "white solipsism,"[20] that is, the implicit tendency to take the white perspective as universal. It focuses, rather, on the issue of women's rights in societies and cultures around the world in their respective contexts. Accordingly, one finds calls for greater awareness of the diversity among American Jewish women, with appeals for greater sensitivity and inclusion of Jewish women of color, for example, or of Sephardic women, in keeping with a spirit of multiculturalism.[21]

VI. WHITENESS: THE FLUIDITY OF RACIAL CATEGORIZATION

It bears recalling, therefore, that Jews as a group have only recently come to be considered white. As demonstrated by Jacobson, Gilman, J. Boyarin, Brodkin, and Cheyette,[22] race is a "social construct" and has been a remarkably fluid form of categorization over the past centuries. Gilman notes that

> for the eighteenth and nineteenth-century scientist, the "blackness" of the Jew was taken as fact and as mark of racial inferiority [in addition to] ... an indicator of [his] diseased nature.... By the midcentury, being black, being Jewish, being diseased and being "ugly" came to be inexorably linked ... one bore the signs of one's diseased status on one's anatomy, and by extension, in one's psyche.[23]

Gilman underlines that "the boundaries of race were one of the most powerful social and political divisions evolved in the science of the period." Ironically, Jewish in-marrying, rather than marking Jews a pure race, marked them as impure and

---

[20] Rich, "Disloyal to Civilization"; Linda Martin Alcoff, *Race, Gender and the Self* (New York: Oxford University Press, 2005).

[21] Marla Brettschneider and Dawn Robinson Rose, "Engaging Jewish Feminist Diversity Issues," *Nashim: A Journal of Jewish Women's Studies and Gender Issues*, no. 8 (Fall 5765/2004), pp. 180-188; Yolanda Shoshana, "Am I My Sister's Keeper?," *Nashim: A Journal of Jewish Women's Studies and Gender Issues*, no. 8 (Fall 5765/2004), pp. 154-164; Rosa Maria Pegueros, "Radical Feminism—No Jews Need Apply," *Nashim: A Journal of Jewish Women's Studies and Gender Issues*, no. 8 (Fall 5765/2004), pp. 174-180.

[22] Matthew Frye Jacobson, *Whiteness of a Different Color: European Immigrants and the Alchemy of Race* (Cambridge: Harvard University Press, 1998, 2002); Sander L. Gilman, "Are Jews Multicultural Enough?," *Multiculturalism and the Jews* (New York: Routledge, 2006); Sander L. Gilman, "The Jewish Nose: Are Jews White? Or, the History of the Nose Job," in *The Other in Jewish Thought and History: Constructions of Jewish Culture and Identity*, ed. Laurence J. Silberstein and Robert L. Cohn (New York: New York University Press, 1994); Jonathan Boyarin, "The Other Within and the Other Without," in *The Other in Jewish Thought and History: Constructions of Jewish Culture and Identity*, ed. Laurence J. Silberstein and Robert L. Cohn (New York: New York University Press, 1994); Karen Brodkin, *How the Jews Became White Folks: And What That Says about Race in America* (New Brunswick, NJ: Rutgers University Press, 1999); Bryan Cheyette, "Neither Black Nor White: The Figure of 'the Jew' in Imperial British Literature," in *The Jew in the Text*, ed. Linda Nochlin and Tamar Garb (London: Thames and Hudson, 1995), pp. 31-42.

[23] *Gilman, "Are Jews Multicultural Enough?," p. 370.* Note: Blackness of skin was thought to be a result of congenital syphilis—JR.

"mongrel," due to interbreeding with Africans during the period of the "Alexandrian exile."[24]

Literature documenting race in America dates the designation of Jews as white as recently as the 1920s—recalling the contrast Al Jolson drew of himself between blackface entertainer as opposed to white cantor's son in "The Jazz Singer" (see below)

Image 1: Al Jolson in "The Jazz Singer"

—or the period following World War II. With the awareness and horror of Nazi Germany's racial policies, "the 1940s produced a profound revision in the taxonomy of the world's races."[25] This is reflected in examples such as Arthur Miller's 1945 novel *Focus* or Laura Z. Hobson's 1947 *Gentleman's Agreement*, later adapted into a film starring Gregory Peck (see below), whose message was not just that Jews are difficult to tell apart from non-Jews but also that their similarity to "real" Americans reflects their essential worthiness of racial equality as well.

Image 2: Gregory Peck in "Gentleman's Agreement"

Expanding the definition of "whiteness" brought obvious benefits in terms of relative power within American society. The perceived differentiation from other racial groups coupled with the identification with mainstream white America positioned Jews to attain greater financial security and power during the second half of the 20th century.

---

[24] Gilman, "The Jewish Nose," pp. 369-370.
[25] Jacobson, *Whiteness of a Different Color*, p. 188.

Yet in sources even more recent, Jews are described as "not quite white" or as "a different shade of white," in other words, not quite blending in. A telling study involving white American women on the subject of their white identities[26] notes statements by Jewish participants indicating that

> several points must be made about the intersection of Jewishness and whiteness... Ashkenazi Jews for much of this century in the US and Europe have been placed at the borders of whiteness, at times viewed as cultural outsiders, at times as racial outsiders, but in any case never as constitutive of the cultural norm.[27]

This study, by Ruth Frankenberg, is revealing in other ways as well. In the relatively short section she devotes to the Jewish aspect of those women among her participants who were Jews (numbering 11 out of 30), the theme of experiencing antisemitism arises among every single one of them. Frankenberg picks up on statements by the Jewish women in her interviews that describe their sense of identity as Jews over different stages in their lives.

This study is significant in that it is among the only ones I have been able to locate that explores women's identities together with their Jewish identities not on the subject of their religiosity or spirituality but in the context of the wider world. Another equally informative study, by Debra Kaufman,[28] indicates how much one can glean when one asks questions that pertain directly to the missing parts of the Venn diagram in Figure 3, in that she alludes to exactly this intersection of identities. When Kaufman's subjects express that their identity as Jewish women "is grounded in their experience as 'the Other' within Judaism," for example, it speaks directly to and in concert with the experience of being a Jewish woman vis-à-vis Jewish men, as well as vis-à-vis their experience of the greater world's perception of the Jew as Other.

VII. An Uncertain Sisterhood—The Women's Movement and Antisemitism

A brief examination will reveal that the experience of feeling like a "cultural outsider" (Frankenberg) and "Other" (Kaufman) is far from uncommon within the women's movement itself, leaving one to wonder what tenuousness may accompany Jewish feminist women's identification and sense of belonging within the mainstream of the movement.

One such strand is evident within Christian feminism.[29] Judith Plaskow critiques the myth that accuses the Jews of inventing and inflicting patriarchal religion on the

---

[26] Ruth Frankenberg, *White Women, Race Matters: The Social Construction of Whiteness* (Minneapolis: University of Minnesota Press, 1993).

[27] Ibid., pp. 216, 224.

[28] Debra Kaufman, "Measuring Jewishness in America: Some Feminist Concerns," *Nashim: A Journal of Jewish Women's Studies and Gender Issues*, no. 10 (Fall 5766/2005).

[29] Annette Daum, "Blaming the Jews for the Death of the Goddess," in *Nice Jewish Girls: A Lesbian Anthology*, ed. Evelyn Torton Beck (Boston: Beacon Press, 1982, 1989), pp. 298-302; Heschel, *On Being a Jewish Feminist*, p. xix; Judith Plaskow, "Blaming the Jews for the Birth of Patriarchy," in *Nice Jewish Girls: A Lesbian Anthology*, ed. Evelyn Torton Beck (Boston: Beacon Press, 1982, 1989) pp. 303-309.

world, banishing the Goddess who had "reigned in matriarchal glory." The myth continues, she states, claiming that when Jesus then tried to "restore egalitarianism, [he] was foiled by the persistence of Jewish attitudes within Christian tradition."[30] This portrayal of "the Hebrews as ruthlessly supplanting Goddess worship with the monotheistic male Hebrew deity" acts as a feminist incarnation of the old charge of deicide.[31] "Christian feminism gives a new slant to the old theme of Christian superiority ... deeply rooted in Christian theology," according to Plaskow, while, Daum adds, "singl[ing] out [Jews] ... as the source of society's sexism."

Within feminist activism, Jewish-targeted enmity commonly takes the form of anti-Zionism and vituperative hostility toward Israel The interconnected nature of these two bigotries has been demonstrated by Kaplan and Small.[32] Examples include the exclusion or expulsion of Israelis and Jews from participation in women's conferences or organizations,[33] the exclusion of material that depicts Israel in a favorable light from feminist publications,[34] the adoption of anti-Israel and anti-Zionist resolutions in conferences convened to discuss women's issues,[35] the formation of women's organizations whose central purpose is the defamation of Israel, which is invoked as an actual expression of feminism.[36]

The message, implicit and explicit, is that vilification of Zionism is integral to feminist ideology, to the point that the two goals are deemed indistinguishable. The option of being a feminist and a supporter of Israel is rendered mutually incompatible, a contradiction in terms.

Painting Jews as responsible for egregious forms of racism (adding responsibility for the slave trade to the indictment to boot[37]) would be almost comical were it not so stinging. Scholars of American Jewry relate the overwhelming degree to which American Jews identify with left-wing and liberal ideologies,[38] the Jewish communal

---

[30] Plaskow, "Blaming the Jews," p. 298.

[31] Daum, "Blaming the Jews," pp. 304-305; Heschel, *On Being a Jewish Feminist*, p. xix.

[32] Edward Kaplan and Charles A. Small, "Anti-Israel Sentiment Predicts Anti-Semitism in Europe," *Journal of Conflict Resolution* 50 (2006), pp. 548-561.

[33] Phyllis Chesler, *The New Anti-Semitism: The Current Crisis and What We Must Do About It* (San Francisco: Jossey-Bass, 2003) pp. 67, 70; Pegueros, "Radical Feminism."

[34] Stewart Ain, "Feminist Moment of Truth," The Jewish Week, January 16, 2008, http://www.thejewishweek.com/ features/'feminist_moment_truth'. "Ms. Magazine Blocks Ad on Israeli Women," American Jewish Congress, January 10, 2008, http://www.ajcongress.org/site/News2?page=NewsArticle&id=6709. Links were active at time of this publication.

[35] Chesler, *The New Anti-Semitism*, p. 53; Letty Cotton Pogrebin, "Attention Must Be Paid: How a Jewish Feminist Fought Against Anti-Semitism in the Women's Movement," *Journey*, Spring 2003, pp. 15-19; Pogrebin, *Deborah, Golda and Me*; Letty Cottin Pogrebin, *Ms. Magazine* (1982).

[36] Coalition of Women for Peace: http://coalitionofwomen.org/?lang=en; Women in Black: http://www.womeninblack.org/en/vigil; Code Pink: http://codepinkalert.org. Links were active at time of this publication.

[37] Chesler, *The New Anti-Semitism*, p. 57.

[38] Steven M. Cohen and Leonard J. Fein, *Annals of the American Academy of Political and Social Science*, vol. 480, Religion in America Today (July 1985), pp. 75-88; Steven M. Cohen and Charles S. Liebman, "American Jewish Liberalism: Unraveling the Strands," *The Public Opinion Quarterly* 61, no. 3 (Autumn 1997), pp. 405-430; John Podhoretz, ed., "Why Are Jews Liberals? A Symposium," *Commentary Magazine*, September 2009; Norman Podhoretz, *Why Are Jews Liberals?* (New York: Doubleday, 2009).

establishment in the 1960s going so far as to maintain that a Jew's position on the issue of civil rights formed a primary measure of his very Jewish identity.[39] That being a member of the Jewish community could mark one as suspect of racism recalls the condition termed by Steven M. Cohen as "the unbearable whiteness of being Jewish."[40] Or, as Gilman noted in observing this irony, "multicultural discourse has marginalized Jews while using Jewish experience as one of the models for the multicultural."[41]

VIII. SUPPLEMENTING THE GAP IN THEORY — AND SUBSTANCE

How, then, do Jewish women deal with this situation? On a more fundamental level, if Jewish women experience animosity, how do they describe its impact, a rejection by sisters within the sisterhood?

Chandra Talpade Mohanty, a postcolonial feminist theorist, observes a frequent conflict between feminism and the "home" community, criticizing allegiance to the home community as "revisionism [that] severely limit[s] ... feminist inquiry and struggle." She describes

> the risk of rejection by one's own kind, by one's family, when one exceeds the limits.... *The fear of rejection by one's own kind refers not only to the family of origin, but also to the potential loss of a second family; the women's community*, with its implied and often unconscious replication of the conditions of home.[42]

Personal reflections of Jewish women regarding this conflict between their Jewish and feminist ties provide telling and poignant expressions of this very sense of loss of their "second family [in] the women's community." Letty Cottin Pogrebin, referring to the anti-Israel and antisemitic diatribes at the 1980 United Nations Women's Conference in Copenhagen, states: "Jewish women have two battles to fight: against sexism and against anti-Jewish beliefs ... identifying as Jews within the feminist movement with as much zeal as we identify as feminists in Judaism."[43]

Others, like Phyllis Chesler, decry the demonization of Israel and of Jewish self-determination as an abandonment of the feminist struggle itself, sacrificing the well-being of Islamic women — and of all women — in the face of encroaching Islamist fundamentalism on Western shores in a rush of appeasement that stands to imperil all.[44]

Testimonials of this kind cast light on this under-studied area in scholarship. A more complete "feminist Jewish standpoint" in the model of Black feminist thought would serve to illuminate the anatomy of antisemitism in the women's movement and its effect on Jewish women. We lack more studies such as Debra Kaufman's and

---

[39] Steven M. Cohen, "The Unbearable Whiteness of Being Jewish: Desegregation in the South and the Crisis of Jewish Liberalism," *Journal of American Jewish History*, June 1997.

[40] Ibid.

[41] Gilman, "Are Jews Multicultural Enough?," p. 179.

[42] Chandra Talpade Mohanty, *Feminism Without Borders: Decolonizing Theory, Practicing Solidarity* (Durham: Duke University Press, 2003), pp. 103-104 (emphasis added).

[43] Letty Cottin Pogrebin, *Ms. Magazine* (1982).

[44] Chesler, *The New Anti-Semitism*, p. 12; see also Gloria Greenfield, "Statement," Jewish Women's Archive, 2008, http://jwa.org/feminism/html/JWA101.htm. Link was active at time of this publication.

Ruth Frankenberg's to augment the data on how Jewish women experience these meeting points in their own words.

To go back to the original question regarding the missing theoretical model describing Jewish women's multicultural feminist identity, a more comprehensive understanding of the points of encounter between Jewish women and the non-Jewish world would complement the existing works related to women within the Jewish world. The present situation, Jewish women's absence from feminist theoretical models, underscores an element of "homelessness." To borrow Elaine Showalter's image in her essay, "Feminist Criticism in the Wilderness," without a theoretical basis, Jewish women risk remaining "an empirical orphan in the theoretical storm."[45] Bereft of theoretical belonging or anchor, not even the most loyal, committed or radical feminists are exempt from bias, slurs, and innuendo. An increased analysis could serve to right this imbalance. Such findings might increase awareness and understanding of current trends regarding the impact of feminist ideology as it relates to the connection between feminism—a movement conceived in order to fight bias—and the age-old bias of antisemitism.

IX. Conclusion

The above documentation illustrates the lack of correspondence between the basic focus of "Jewish feminism" within the Jewish world and between Black feminist thought and that of other racial and ethnic groups, oriented both within their respective ethnic groups and beyond their groups to deal with "mainstream" feminism. Jewish women as a whole may have felt no need for such a dual orientation, evidenced by a sense of belonging and identification within mainstream feminism. Yet one need not scratch very deeply beneath the surface to behold an undercurrent that can prove unsettling to Jewish women. Expressions of anti-Zionism and of outright antisemitism raise the question of how Jewish women experience an apparent attack that calls their feminist allegiance into question. New research, with the aim of recording and analyzing Jewish women's perceptions in their own words, stands to add a new dimension to what we currently know about Jewish women's experience and identities.

In 1984, bell hooks wrote incisively of mainstream feminism at that time, saying: "Feminism has its party line and women who feel a need for a different strategy, a different foundation, often find themselves ostracized or silenced."[46]

Could an equivalent body of scholarship by feminist Jewish women create a space for a distinct standpoint that addresses the concerns of women within the Jewish world as well as within the world of mainstream feminism? The answer to this question is complicated, given that it is linked to persistent efforts through the centuries to see the Jew as Other in every conceivable context. The anatomy of antisemitism in the women's movement lies within feminist theory itself. A new theoretical model to supplement what is currently missing may act as a starting point for additional exploration in the future and as a source of change in rhetoric as well as in practice.

---

[45] Elaine Showalter, "Feminist Criticism in the Wilderness," *Critical Inquiry* 8, no. 2: Writing and Sexual Difference (Winter 1981), pp. 179-205 at p. 180.

[46] hooks, *Feminist Theory*, p. 9.

Bibliography

Adler, Rachel. *Engendering Judaism: An Inclusive Theology and Ethics*. Boston: Beacon Press, 1999.

Ain, Stewart. "Feminist Moment of Truth." *The Jewish Week*, January 16, 2008. http://www.thejewishweek.com/features/'feminist_moment_truth'.

Alcoff, Linda Martin. *Race, Gender and the Self*. New York: Oxford University Press, 2005.

Anzaldua, Gloria. "La conciencia de la mestiza: Towards a New Consciousness." 1986. In *Feminisms: An Anthology of Literary Theory and Criticism*, edited by Robyn D. Warhol and Diana Price Hernd, pp. 765-775. New Brunswick, NJ: Rutgers University Press, 1997.

Boyarin, Jonathan. "The Other Within and the Other Without." In *The Other in Jewish Thought and History: Constructions of Jewish Culture and Identity*, edited by Laurence J. Silberstein and Robert L. Cohn. New York: New York University Press, 1994.

Brettschneider, Marla and Dawn Robinson Rose. "Engaging Jewish Feminist Diversity Issues." *Nashim: A Journal of Jewish Women's Studies and Gender Issues*, no. 8 (Fall 5765/2004), pp. 180-188.

Brodkin, Karen. *How the Jews Became White Folks: And What That Says about Race in America*. New Brunswick, NJ: Rutgers University Press, 1999.

Butler, Judith. *Undoing Gender*. New York: Routledge Press, 2004.

Butler, Judith. *Gender Trouble: Feminism and the Subversion of Identity*. New York: Routledge, 2006.

Chesler, Phyllis. *Women and Madness*. New York: Doubleday and Co., 1972.

Chesler, Phyllis. *The New Anti-Semitism: The Current Crisis and What We Must Do About It*. San Francisco: Jossey-Bass, 2003.

Cheyette, Bryan. "Neither Black Nor White: The Figure of 'the Jew' in Imperial British Literature." In *The Jew in the Text*, edited by Linda Nochlin and Tamar Garb, pp. 31-42. London: Thames and Hudson, 1995.

Chodorow, Nancy. *The Reproduction of Mothering*. Berkeley: The Regents University of California Press, 1978.

Chodorow, Nancy. *Feminism and Psychoanalytic Theory*. New Haven: Yale University Press, 1991.

Christian, Barbara. "The Race for Theory." 1987. In *New Black Feminist Criticism 1985-2000*, by Barbara Christian, edited by Gloria Bowles, M. Giulia Fabi, and Arlene R. Keizer. Urbana and Chicago: University of Illinois Press, 2007.

Cohen, Steven M. and Charles S. Liebman. "American Jewish Liberalism: Unraveling the Strands." *The Public Opinion Quarterly* 61, no. 3 (Autumn 1997), pp. 405-430.

Cohen, Steven M. and Fein, Leonard J. *Annals of the American Academy of Political and Social Science*, vol. 480, Religion in America Today (July 1985), pp. 75-88.

Cohen, Steven M. "The Unbearable Whiteness of Being Jewish: Desegregation in the South and the Crisis of Jewish Liberalism." *Journal of American Jewish History*, June 1997.

Cohn Eskenazi, Tamara and Rabbi Andrea Weiss, eds. *The Torah: A Women's Commentary*. Philadelphia: Union for Reconstructionist Judaism Press, 2007.

Collins, Patricia Hill. *Black Feminist Thought: Knowledge, Consciousness and the Politics of Empowerment*. New York: Routledge, Chapman and Hall, Inc., 1991.

Daum, Annette. "Blaming the Jews for the Death of the Goddess." In *Nice Jewish Girls: A Lesbian Anthology*, edited by Evelyn Torton Beck, pp. 298-302. Boston: Beacon Press, 1982, 1989.

Dufour, Lynn Resnick. "Sifting Through Tradition: The Creation of Jewish Feminist Identities." *Journal for the Scientific Study of Religion* (2002), pp. 98-103.

Dworkin, Andrea. *Pornography: Men Possessing Women*. New York: Plume Books, 1991.

Fishman, Sylvia Barack. "Women's Transformations of Public Judaism: Religiosity, Egalitarianism and the Symbolic Power of Changing Gender Roles." In *Studies in Contemporary Jewry, Vol. XVII: Who Owns Judaism? Public Religion and Private Faith in America and Israel*, edited by Peter Medding. New York: Oxford University Press, 2001.

Fishman, Sylvia Barack. *A Breath of Life: Feminism in the American Jewish Community*. Waltham, MA: Brandeis University Press, 1995.

Fishman, Sylvia Barack. *Matriarchal Ascent/Patriarchal Descent: The Gender Imbalance in American Jewish Life*. Waltham, MA: Brandeis University Press, 2008.

Fishman, Sylvia Barack. "The Impact of Feminism on American Jewish Life." In *American Jewish Year Book* (1989).

Frankenberg, Ruth. *White Women, Race Matters: The Social Construction of Whiteness*. Minneapolis: University of Minnesota Press, 1993.

Friedan, Betty. *The Feminine Mystique*. New York: Dell Mass Market Paperback, 1964.

Friedman, Michelle. "Toward an understanding of Jewish identity: An ethnographic study." Ph.D. diss., State University of New York, 2002.

Geok-lin Lim, Shirley. "Feminist and Ethnic Theories in Asian American Literature." 1993. *Feminisms: An Anthology of Literary Theory and Criticism*, edited by Robyn D. Warhol and Diana Price Hernd, pp. 807-826. New Brunswick, NJ: Rutgers University Press, 1997.

Gilbert, Sandra and Susan Gubar. *The Madwoman in the Attic*. New Haven: Yale University Press, 1979.

Gilman, Sander L. "Are Jews Multicultural Enough?" In *Multiculturalism and the Jews*. New York: Routledge, 2006.

Gilman, Sander L. "The Jewish Nose: Are Jews White? Or, the History of the Nose Job." In *The Other in Jewish Thought and History: Constructions of Jewish Culture and Identity*, edited by Laurence J. Silberstein and Robert L. Cohn. New York: New York University Press, 1994.

Gilligan, Carol. *In a Different Voice: Psychological Theory and Women's Development*. Cambridge: Harvard University Press, 1982.

Goldstein, Elyse. *New Jewish Feminism: Probing the Past, Forging the Future*. New York: Jewish Lights Publishing, 2008.

Goldstein, Elyse, ed. *The Women's Haftarah Commentary: New Insights from Women Rabbis on the 54 Weekly Haftarah Portions, the 5 Megillot and Special Shabbatot*. New York: Jewish Lights Publishing, 2008.

Greenberg, Blu. *On Women and Judaism*. New York: Jewish Publication Society of America, 1991.

Greenfield, Gloria. "Statement." Jewish Women's Archive, 2008. http://jwa.org/feminism/_html/JWA101.htm.

Hartman, Tova. *Feminism Encounters Traditional Judaism: Resistance and Accommodation*, HBI Series on Jewish Women. Waltham, MA: Brandeis University Press, 2008.

Hartman, Tova. *Appropriately Subversive: Modern Mothers in Traditional Religions*. Cambridge: Harvard University Press, 2003.

Haut, Rivka and Susan Grossman, eds. *Daughters of the King: Women and the Synagogue*. Philadelphia, Jewish Publications Society, 1992.

Heschel, Susannah, ed. *On Being a Jewish Feminist: A Reader*. New York: Schocken Books, 1983, 1995.

hooks, bell. *Feminist Theory: From Margin to Center*. Boston: South End Press, 1984.

Jacobson, Matthew Frye. *Whiteness of a Different Color: European Immigrants and the Alchemy of Race*. Cambridge: Harvard University Press, 1998, 2002.

Kaplan, Edward and Charles A. Small. "Anti-Israel Sentiment Predicts Anti-Semitism in Europe." *Journal of Conflict Resolution* 50 (2006), pp. 548-561.

Kaufman, Debra. "Measuring Jewishness in America: Some Feminist Concerns." *Nashim: A Journal of Jewish Women's Studies and Gender Issues*, no. 10 (Fall 5766/2005).

Lavie, Aliza, ed. *A Jewish Woman's Prayer Book*. New York: Spiegel and Grau, 2008.

Lerner, Gerda. *The Creation of Patriarchy*. New York: Oxford University Press, 1986.

Levitt, Laura. *Jews and Feminism: The Ambivalent Search for Home*. New York: Routledge, 1997.

Ling, Amy. "I'm Here: An Asian American Woman's Response." 1987. In *Feminisms: An Anthology of Literary Theory and Criticism*, edited by Robyn D. Warhol and Diana Price Hernd, pp. 776-783. New Brunswick, NJ: Rutgers University Press, 1997.

Lorde, Audre. *Sister Outsider: Essays and Speeches*, Berkeley: Crossing Press, 1984.

Martin, Biddy and Chandra Talpade Mohanty. "What's Home Got to Do with It?" 1986. In *Feminisms: An Anthology of Literary Theory and Criticism*, Robyn D. Warhol and Diana Price Hernd, pp. 293-310. New Brunswick, NJ: Rutgers University Press, 1997.

Mohanty, Chandra Talpade. *Feminism Without Borders: Decolonizing Theory; Practicing Solidarity*. Durham: Duke University Press, 2003.

"Ms. Magazine Blocks Ad on Israeli Women." American Jewish Congress, January 10, 2008. http://www.ajcongress.org/siteNews2?page=NewsArticle&id=6709.

Okin, Susan Moller. *Justice, Gender and the Family*. New York: Basic Books, 1989.

Pegueros, Rosa Maria. "Radical Feminism—No Jews Need Apply." *Nashim: A Journal of Jewish Women's Studies and Gender Issues*, no. 8 (Fall 5765/2004), pp. 174-180.

Plaskow, Judith. *Standing Again at Sinai: Judaism from a Feminist Perspective*. New York: Harper One, 1991.

Plaskow, Judith and Donna Berman, eds. *The Coming of Lilith: Essays on Feminism, Judaism and Sexual Ethics, 1972-2003*. Boston: Beacon Press, 2005.

Plaskow, Judith. "Blaming the Jews for the Birth of Patriarchy." In *Nice Jewish Girls: A Lesbian Anthology*, edited by Evelyn Torton Beck, pp. 303-309. Boston: Beacon Press, 1982, 1989.

Pogrebin, Letty Cotton. "Attention Must Be Paid: How a Jewish Feminist Fought Against Anti-Semitism in the Women's Movement." *Journey*, Spring 2003, pp. 15-19.

Pogrebin, Letty Cottin. *Deborah, Golda and Me: Being Female and Jewish in America*. New York: Crown Publishers, 1991.

Pogrebin, Letty Cottin. *Ms. Magazine.* 1982.
Podhoretz, John, ed. "Why Are Jews Liberals? A Symposium." *Commentary Magazine*, September 2009.
Podhoretz, Norman. *Why Are Jews Liberals?* New York: Doubleday, 2009.
Reinharz, Shulamit. *Feminist Methods in Social Research.* New York: Oxford University Press, 1992.
Rich, Adrienne. *Of Woman Born: Motherhood as Institution and Experience.* New York: W.W. Norton and Co., 1976.
Rich, Adrienne. "Disloyal to Civilization: Feminism, Racism, Gynophobia." *On Lies, Secrets and Silence: Selected Prose 1966-1978*, pp. 275-310. New York: W.W. Norton, 1979.
Ross, Tamar. *Expanding the Palace of Torah: Orthodoxy and Feminism*, Brandeis Series on Jewish Women. Waltham, MA: Brandeis University Press, 2004.
Rutenberg, Danya, ed. *Yentl's Revenge: The Next Wave of Jewish Feminism.* Boston: Seal Press, 2001.
Rutenberg, Danya. *Surprised by God: How I Learned to Stop Worrying and Love Religion.* Boston: Beacon Press, 2009.
Sanchez, Rosaura. "Discourses and Gender: Ethnicity and Class in Chicano Literature." 1992. In *Feminisms: An Anthology of Literary Theory and Criticism*, edited by Robyn D. Warhol and Diana Price Hernd, pp. 1009-1028. New Brunswick, NJ: Rutgers University Press, 1997.
Schneider, Susan Weidman. *Jewish and Female: Choices and Changes in Our Lives Today.* New York: Simon and Schuster, 1985.
Scott, Joan Wallach. *Gender and the Politics of History.* New York: Columbia University Press, 1999.
Sedgwick, Eve Kosofsky. *The Epistemology of the Closet.* Berkeley: The Regents of University of California Press, 1990.
Shoshana, Yolanda. "Am I My Sister's Keeper?" *Nashim: A Journal of Jewish Women's Studies and Gender Issues*, no. 8 (Fall 5765/2004), pp. 154-164.
Showalter, Elaine. "Feminist Criticism in the Wilderness." *Critical Inquiry* 8, no. 2: *Writing and Sexual Difference* (Winter 1981), pp. 179-205.
Showalter, Elaine. *New Feminist Criticism: Women, Literature and Theory.* New York: Pantheon, 1985.
Tate, Claudia, ed. *Black Writers at Work.* New York: Continuum Publishing, 1983.
Zemon Davis, Natalie. *Women on the Margins: Three Seventeenth-Century Lives.* Cambridge: Belknap Press of Harvard University Press, 1997.

1948 as Jihad

Benny Morris*

Midway through the first Israeli-Arab war, in August 1948, Emil Ghoury, a member of the Arab Higher Committee, the "Cabinet" of the Palestinian Arab national movement, blamed the Arab states for creating the Palestinian refugee problem. He argued that the Arab states had pushed and cajoled the Arabs of Palestine into launching hostilities against the Jewish community in Palestine, then known as the *Yishuv*, in defiance of the United Nations partition resolution, while the Palestinians were disorganized and unprepared for war, and that they themselves launched their invasion of Israel, in May 1948, while disunited and insufficiently prepared. The war had resulted in the creation of the refugee problem. Ghoury rejected a solution of the problem by way of repatriation, arguing that the Jews "would [then] hold them hostage and torture them severely." He assumed that a refugee return would be achieved through negotiations with Israel and that an agreement so achieved would mark the beginning of Arab acquiescence in Israel's existence. "We must inculcate in the heart of every Arab," he said, "hatred for the Jews" and we must the renew "the jihad against Israel." The refugees, he concluded, would return to their places only after Palestine was reconquered.[1]

Months earlier, in January 1948, just after the start of hostilities, Matiel Mughannam, head of the Arab Women's Organization, a female affiliate of the Arab Higher Committee, told an interviewer: "The UN [partition] decision [of 29 November 1947] has united all Arabs, as they have never been united before, not even against the Crusaders. ... [A Jewish state] has no chance to survive now that the 'holy war' has been declared. All the Jews will eventually be massacred."[2] Ms. Mughannam, it should be noted, was a Lebanese Christian who had moved to Jerusalem in the 1930s after marrying a Palestinian.

Following the pan-Arab invasion of Palestine in May 1948, the Saudi regime organized jihadi festivals around the kingdom, in the towns and oases, to mobilize volunteers for the war in Palestine. According to Madawi Al-Rasheed, an expert on Saudi Arabia and 1948, 2,000 men were registered within two days, and it was said that 200,000 were "ready to perform jihad and sacrifice their lives." As it turned out, only several hundred reached Palestine. The Saudi religious authorities, the *ulama*,

---

* Professor of History, Department of Middle East Studies, Ben-Gurion University.

[1] "Emil Ghoury's Response to the Telegraph on the Matter of the Refugees," August 1948, Haganah Archive (HA) (Tel Aviv) 105/102.

[2] Nadia Lourie, "Interview with Mrs. Mogannam [Mughannam]," January 10, 1948, Central Zionist Archive (CZA) (Jerusalem) S25-9005.

played a major part in the mobilization for jihad.[3] The call for jihad also vibrated around the Maghreb, and in the spring and summer of 1948 thousands of Moroccan, Algerian, and Tunisian Muslims set off to fight in the hills of Palestine (though only hundreds actually reached the battlefields due to French, British, and Egyptian interdiction along the way).

Historians of 1948 have tended to view the first Arab-Israeli war as a milestone and a turning point in a national struggle between two peoples or ethnic groups, the Jewish-Zionist and Palestinian-Arab collectives, over a piece of territory called the Land of Israel or Palestine. A cull through the available documentation, essentially through Israeli and Western records, points to an additional and perhaps important—and for some of the Arab participants in that war dominant—perspective, namely the religious face of that war.

In light of the available records, it would appear that many of the Arab participants in the 1948 war saw that onslaught against the *Yishuv*/Israel as a holy war, a jihad, against a foreign and infidel invader. It is possible that the opening of Arab state archives and a thorough trawl through the press of the region stretching from Yemen to Iraq to Rabat will only reinforce the impression that the political and military leaders of the Arab states, the "street" in Cairo, Baghdad, Sana, and Marrakesh, and the soldiers who actually fought in the war saw it as a holy war and not only, or perhaps even not mainly, as a war between two national movements or peoples.

Several methodological problems arise here. The first and most obvious is that the archives of the Arab states, of the main Arab political parties, royal courts, and armies, are all closed—all the Arab states are dictatorships of one sort or another, and dictatorships, as is well known, do not open archives. This means that anyone interested in understanding the Arab side in the 1948 war is forced, in the main, to view it through the eyes and documentation of Western and Israeli diplomats, analysts, and intelligence officers.

The second problem is in defining what constitutes a jihad. Is a war a jihad when the religious authorities in a given state or society define it as such? Or when their leaders, or some of their leaders—and in the case of the pan-Arab invasion of Palestine on May 15, 1948 we are dealing with dozens of political and military leaders hailing from different states—deem it so? Or is it necessary for the bulk of the population of a state or states or societies to give voice to this characterization to make it so?

When it comes to the Arab masses—civilians and soldiers—in 1947-1948, it is near impossible to make out what they thought or felt. There were few if any opinion polls, and, again, we are talking about authoritarian states, not democracies, in which the vast majority of the population was illiterate. For all intents and purposes, these masses were silent (and, historiographically speaking, remain silent). Occasionally, a newspaper or leader at the time would refer to what the "street" thought or to a slogan brandished in a street demonstration. But that is all. We have no records, or almost no records, about what peasants, the urban poor, and soldiery thought or felt, certainly not from their own pens or mouths. The problem of lack of

---

[3] Madawi Al-Rasheed, "Saudi Arabia and the 1948 Palestine War: Beyond Official History," in *The War for Palestine*, 2nd ed., ed. Eugene Rogan and Avi Shlaim (Cambridge: Cambridge University Press, 2007), p. 240.

free expression also pertains to the more literate, numerically small middle and upper classes—we do not really know what they thought or felt.

And a problem of definition also relates to the leaders. When this or that Arab leader described the ongoing war in 1948 as a jihad, does that "prove" that we are dealing with a jihad or even a jihadi mindset? Did King Farouk of Egypt, in sending his army across Sinai to attack Israel, believe in May 1948 that he was carrying out Allah's will and command and that he was engaged in a holy war? Or did he use the characterization because he understood that this would get his countrymen's attention and ignite their warlike passions—whereas talk of abstract (Western) concepts such as nationalism and sovereignty would have had little purchase with the Cairo "street" or among the Nile Delta's *fellaheen*? Perhaps he used the term to appease his opponents among the Muslim Brotherhood or other political radicals. We do not have the internal memoranda or protocols of Arab court or cabinet discussions, diaries of government ministers and kings, or the internal correspondence of the leaders to tell us what was really in their minds.

A third problem arises from the political culture or the culture of discourse that characterized—and in some ways still characterizes—Arab governments and countries, where there was and is no real separation between church and state. Often, the rhetoric of politicians—the description or explanation of this or that policy or practice—will be couched in religious, Islamic terminology. Does this necessarily signify real religious motive or zeal, or is it just a superficial patina born of tradition and discursive culture, as when President Anwar Sadat of Egypt, appearing before the Knesset in Jerusalem in November 1977, opened his historic speech with the phrase *bismillah* (in the name of God)?

There is no simple answer to these questions and the historiographic problems they pose. What we can say for now is that the historian must recognize that all his conclusions in this sphere must remain tentative. Perhaps the opening of Arab archives, if this ever occurs and if these archives prove chockfull of the type of documentation we find in the archives of Western democracies, will help to resolve these questions. And perhaps, given that the basic question—what makes a war a jihad—is problematic, a question of mindset and psyche of millions of people rather than a question of "fact," we may still remain largely in the dark or at least in territory where there are no certain signposts and milestones.

For the present, all that one can safely say is that historians and students of the Arab world in 1948 should treat seriously what the available records are telling us about what certain people in that world, including some of its leading politicians, said and not abruptly dismiss their jihadi utterances as so much hot air just because they do not match the contemporary historian's or student's historical and political views, preferences, or prejudices. When Arab leaders in 1948—religious, military, and political—tell us something, we should pay attention. Perhaps they are giving voice to a major truth or reality.

The history of the Islamic world is replete with holy wars against infidel peoples and polities. The rise of Islam, in the seventh and eighth centuries, was characterized by an enormous, aggressive jihadi surge that saw the Arab conquerors sweep over the Middle East and North Africa, as far as Spain and southern France. A second eruption of jihad, defensive in nature, occurred in the Middle Ages, when Muslim warriors contained and then drove back the Crusaders and destroyed their kingdoms in the Levant. A third, aggressive wave of jihad occurred in the Early Modern period, when Turkic armies, from the middle of the 15th century until the end of the 17th century, assaulted the Balkans and central Europe, reaching the gates of Budapest and Vienna. Today, we are in the throes of the fourth wave of jihad—and there is a dispute in the West about whether to attribute it to Islam as a whole or just to radical Islam and Islamists—a wave directed against the West and its promontories around the world, stretching from the Philippines and Mumbai through East and West Africa and Darfur to London and Madrid and the Twin Towers in New York. At the center of this wave are the wars against infidels (and their local helpers) in Afghanistan/Pakistan, Iraq, and Palestine. One can view the current jihadi wave as aggressive or defensive—there are strong arguments for both positions. Be that as it may, it is possible that, in several hundred years' time, the war between the Arabs and the Jews over Palestine in 1948 will be seen as the beginning of, or at least as a major milestone in, this wave that confronts the West in our time.

The Arabic word jihad means to "make an effort" and, in its religious connotation, has been defined as "a bloodless striving in missionary zeal for the spread of Islam." Meaning, if you like, an effort at religious persuasion. There are analysts who focus on this meaning of the word jihad and denude it of all political and military meaning.

And there are commentators who argue that the Islamic doctrine of jihad is essentially a defensive doctrine: the believers embark on jihad only when first assailed by infidels.

But a more honest and discerning look at the deeds of Mohammed and his successors and at the mainstream exegeses of Islamic scholars during the following centuries leaves little room for doubt or evasion about the meaning of the word jihad (to most Muslims and non-Muslims) and the doctrine of jihad.

In the Koran, the believers are enjoined to wage holy war against the infidel: "Fight those who do not believe in Allah or in Judgment day ... and who do not accept the true religion even if they be the Peoples of the Book, until they pay the *jizya* [poll tax] in submission, and feel themselves submissive" (Koran 29:9).

In most of the exegetic texts, there is an obligation, before doing battle, to call on the infidels to convert to Islam or at least to submit to Muslim rule. And only if the infidels reject this call are the believers obliged to open hostilities. But be this as it may, Allah commands all Muslims, individually and as a collective, to wage jihad against the infidel. As it says in the Koran: "Battle is your duty, even if you do not like it" (Koran 216:2).

Now it is true that the Koran is often vague and obscure and that one can find in it sentences pointing the reader and believer in varying directions. But among the major Muslim theologians in the millennium following Mohammed's death a more or less consensual mainstream emerged about the main pillars of the religion. This also holds true for the doctrine of jihad. Ibn Khaldum, the great Sunni philosopher and historian of the 14th century, put it this way:

> In the Muslim community, jihad is a religious obligation, because of the universality of the [Muslim] mission and [the duty] to Islamize all [mankind] or through persuasion or through force. ... Other religious groups did not have a universal mission, and holy war was not a religious duty for them, save in self-defense. ... [But] Islam, [on the contrary] is bound to rule over other peoples.

In Shia Islam, jihad is seen in the same way: "Islamic jihad against the believers in other religions, for example the Jews, is an obligation, save if they convert to Islam or pay the *jizya*," as Al-Amili, a prominent Persian theologian of the 16th and 17th centuries, put it.

The belief that jihad, in order to forcibly convert or at least vanquish the rest of humanity, is obligatory for the believers is based on the sentence: "We have sent you out to all mankind" (Koran 28:34). And definitive world peace is only attainable if the whole world accepts or bows to Islam. In the course of the struggle, truces, even long-term ceasefires (*hudnas*), are possible, but the fight against the infidels must be maintained until they are defeated.

In Western eyes, this posture is seen as aggressive or unjust. But in the eyes of classical Islam, it appears self-evident and just—as the truth is found only in Islam and the award of the truth to others, also by way of the sword, is sensible and just.

It is possible that Muhammad's wars against the Jewish and pagan tribes in Hijaz at the dawn of Islam are interpretable as defensive. It is quite likely that, in the 620s and 630s, Muhammad and his followers believed that, without victory, Islam would be vanquished and they themselves would end up being put to the sword. But Muhammad's successors, from the caliphs onwards, initiated wars of expansion and conquest against the Christian world with the aim of converting the whole of humanity to Islam.

And this holds true for Christians and Jews as well as pagans. According to all Koranic texts, the aim of jihad against the Peoples of the Book is to convert them to Islam or obtain their submission to Islam. And participation in jihad is the duty of all adult Muslim males unencumbered by physical or mental handicap—though the believers were ordered not to kill "children, madmen, women, priests, impotent old men, the sick, the blind, [and] the mentally infirm, so long as they do not take part in the battle," as one 13th century exegesist, Ibn Qudama, put it.

According to Ibn Taimiya, a major 13th and 14th century theologian, "the obligation to participate in jihad appears innumerable times in the Koran and the Sunna. Therefore, that is the most important willed [religious] activity a man can undertake. All the sages agree that it is more important than the haj. ... The prophet said 'the supreme issue is Islam ... and its peak is the jihad' ... jihad is obligatory both if we began it and if undertaken in defense." Indeed, one major 12th century exegesist, Al-Ghazali, wrote that "one should undertake jihad at least once a year" (which sounds a bit tiring, but that is what he wrote).

In the days after the UN General Assembly passed the partition resolution (No. 181) on November 29, 1947, providing for the establishment of Jewish and Arab states in Palestine, waves of rioters hit the streets of the large towns in the Arab world and attacked Jews and Europeans and their property. Some of the rioting may have been spontaneous, while some of it may have been organized by governments or political parties. At the beginning of December 1947, there were pogroms in Aden, Bahrain, and Aleppo and a variety of assaults on Jews in Cairo and Damascus. The rioters commonly shouted *idbah al-yahud* (kill the Jews) and, in most cases, the authorities failed to rein them in, certainly not expeditiously. Dozens of Jews were murdered, some were raped, and hundreds of houses were torched.

On December 2, 1947, three days after the UN vote, the *ulama*—the leading scholars of theology—of the University of Al-Azhar in Cairo, perhaps the most important arbiters and authorities in the Sunni Muslim world, declared a "worldwide jihad in defense of Arab Palestine."[4] In the course of the war, the *ulama* of Al-Azhar periodically renewed their fatwa and call to jihad. "The liberation of Palestine [is] a religious duty for all Muslims without exception, great and small. The Islamic and Arab governments should without delay take effective and radical measures, military or otherwise," pronounced the *ulama* at the end of April 1948.[5] On the day of the Egyptian Army's invasion of Palestine on May 15, Muhammed Mamun Shinawi, the rector of Al-Azhar, declared: "The hour of jihad has struck. ... A hundred of you will defeat a thousand of the infidels. ... This is the hour in which ... Allah promised paradise...."[6]

And, in December 1948, on the eve of the final bout of hostilities between the Israel Defense Forces and the Egyptians in the Negev and Sinai, the *ulama* of Al-Azhar renewed their call for jihad and cautioned the Arab kings—this was directed primarily at Abdullah, the king of Jordan, who was suspected of colluding with the Jews—against deviating from "the way of the believers." Otherwise, they faced "damnation."[7]

The jihadism of 1948 was accompanied by a strong dose of antisemitism. In 1947, well before the outbreak of the war, the *ulama* of Al-Azhar issued a fatwa prohibiting all commercial contact with "the Jews," and defined anyone doing so as "a sinner and criminal ... who will be regarded as an apostate to Islam."

Samir Rifa'u, the prime minister of Jordan, told visitors in Amman that year that "the Jews are a people to be feared ... Give them another 25 years and they will be all over the Middle East, in our country and Syria and Lebanon, in Iraq and Egypt. ... They were responsible for starting the two world wars. ... Yes, I have read and studied, and I know they were behind Hitler at the beginning of his movement."[8]

Rifa'i's observations reflected beliefs that spread through the Middle East at the end of the 19th century and the early 20th century, beliefs that added a "modern" layer to the classic antisemitic utterances embedded in the Koran (where the Jews are designated, inter alia, as "a base people" and "murderers of the prophets"[9]). There is "religious hostility ... between the Moslems and the Jews from the beginning of Islam ... which arose from the treacherous conduct of the Jews towards Islam and Moslems and their prophet," King Ibn Saud of Saudi Arabia explained to President Roosevelt in 1943.[10] The Muslim Brotherhood defined it thus: "Jews are the historic enemies of Muslims and carry the greatest hatred for the nation of Muhammad."[11]

---

[4] "Partition of Palestine and Declaration of Jihad," undated, British National Archive, Public Record Office (PRO), FO 371-61583.

[5] Campbell to FO, May 1, 1948 (no. 536), PRO FO 371-68371.

[6] Shai, "Report of Monitoring Arab Radio Stations for 15.5.1948," HA 105/90.

[7] Campbell to FO, December 13, 1948, PRO FO 371-68644.

[8] "Off-the-Record Talks in Transjordan of Two British Correspondents," unsigned, Amman, October 21, 1947, CZA S25-9038. Incidentally, the charge that the Jews were responsible for starting the two world wars remains a staple in the Arab world (for example, it is repeated explicitly in the Hamas Charter of August 1988).

[9] Benny Morris, *Righteous Victims: A History of the Zionist Arab Conflict, 1881-2001* (New York: Vintage Books, 2001), pp. 8-13.

[10] Ibn Saud to Roosevelt, April 30, 1943, PRO CO 733/443/18.

[11] Abd Al-Fattah Muhammad El-Awaisi, *The Muslim Brothers and the Palestine Question 1928-1947* (London/New York: Tauris Academic Studies, 1998), p. 8.

In April 1948, Sheikh Muhammad Mahawif, the mufti of Egypt, issued a fatwa calling on all Muslims to participate in the jihad in Palestine. He maintained that the Jews intended "to take over ... all the lands of Islam."[12]

It is no wonder, then, that during the 1930s and 1940s different variants of the following *hadith* were quoted in Islamic tracts: "The day of resurrection does not come until Muslims fight against Jews, until the Jews hide behind trees and stones and until the trees and stones shout out: 'O Muslim, there is a Jew behind me, come and kill him.'"[13]

Alongside its traditional antisemitic basis, the 1948 call to jihad had another historical pedigree. Before and during 1948, the Zionists were often compared by Arab spokesmen to the Crusaders—and almost always it was said that their end would be similar. As the secretary general of the Arab League, Abdul Rahman Azzam Pasha, put it in 1947, "you [the Jews] are a temporary phenomenon. Centuries ago, the crusaders established themselves in our midst against our will, and in 200 years we ejected them."[14]

Shukri al-Quwatli, the president of Syria, said similar things the following year, on the eve of the pan-Arab invasion: "Overcoming the Crusaders took a long time, but the result was victory. There is no doubt that history is repeating itself."[15] Riad al-Sulh, the prime minister of Lebanon, told a British diplomat in the course of the war that "it had taken the Arabs over a century to expel the Crusader[s] but they had succeeded in the end."[16] The Palestinian Zaafer Dajani, the head of the Jaffa Chamber of Commerce, said similar things to a Jewish interlocutor in 1947.[17] The Egyptian Muslim Brotherhood announced that the death of martyrs in Palestine conjured up "the memories of the Battle of Badr ... as well as the early Islamic jihad for spreading Islam and Salah al-Din's [Saladin's] liberation of Palestine" from the Crusaders.[18]

Perhaps it is worth noting that the first Arab to publicly make the comparison was Shukri al Asali, the Ottoman governor of Nazareth, during the 1910-1911 struggle over the lands of Fula, an Arab village in the Jezreel Valley built around the ruins of a Crusader castle. The land had been bought by Zionist institutions and, shortly afterward, Kibbutz Merhavia was established on the site. Since then, Arab spokesmen have often referred to the Zionists as "the new Crusaders." In 1945, Azzam Pasha argued that the clash between the Arabs and Zionism might trigger a new war between the Christian and Muslim worlds, as did the Crusades.[19]

The banner of jihad was raised aloft, or the notion was at least mentioned, with regard to the *Yishuv*, in the decades before 1948. In March 1936, the speaker of the

---

[12] *Al-Difa'a*, April 8, 1948, p. 2.

[13] El-Awaisi, *Muslim Brothers*, p. 15.

[14] "Meeting: A. Eban and D. Horowitz—Abdul Rahman Azzam Pasha (London, 15 September 1947)," London, September 19, 1947, *Political Documents of the Jewish Agency*, vol. 2, January-November 1947, ed. Nana Sagi, pp. 669-672.

[15] Shai, "In the Arab Public," May 5, 1948, Israel Defense Forces Archive (IDFA) 1196/52//1.

[16] Trefor Evans to FO, 21 September 1948, PRO FO 371-68376.

[17] E.L., "Talk with Zaafar Dajani, Chairman of the Jaffa Chamber of Commerce," 26 November 1947, CZA S25-3300.

[18] El-Awaisi, *Muslim Brothers*, 15.

[19] J.C. Hurewitz, *The Struggle for Palestine* (New York: Schocken Books, 1976), p. 229.

Iraqi parliament, Said al-Haj Tabith, while on a visit to Palestine, called for jihad against the Zionists.[20] A decade earlier, Haj Muhammad Said al-Husseini, the mufti of Gaza, issued a fatwa against land sales to Jews, arguing that, as a result of Zionism, the Jews had lost their status as *dhimi* or wards of Islam and any Muslim or Christian who helped them would be regarded as an apostate or infidel. In 1935, the first *ulama* or gathering of Muslim religious scholars issued a similar fatwa.[21]

During the Palestine Arab Revolt of 1936-1939, the discourse among the rebels, to judge by their publications, was often religious (as well as political-nationalist), and the struggle was seen at least in part as religious. Indeed, the 1936 announcement of the establishment of the Arab Higher Committee—the leadership body of the national movement that in effect orchestrated the revolt—included the following typical sentence: "Because of the general feeling of danger that envelops this noble nation, there is a need for solidarity and unity and a focus on strengthening the holy national jihad movement."[22] Preachers in the Nablus area were prominent among those mobilizing the population for combat.

It was no surprise, then, that when the Arab states launched their assault on the *Yishuv* in 1948, the campaign was regarded by many as a jihad and was reinforced with fatwas by the religious leadership that embraced holy war. And it was only to be expected that the Arab leaders would fall into step. Both King Farouk of Egypt and his foreign minister, Ahmed Muhammad Khashaba, said during the summer of 1948 that for "the whole Arab world," the struggle was a matter of religion—"it was for them a matter of Jewish religion against their own religion." According to Farouk, the Arab masses were gripped by "widespread religious fervor ... and men ... were keen to enter the fray—as the shortest road to heaven."[23] Even Abdullah King of Jordan, the most clear-headed and pragmatic of the Arab leaders, adopted the language of holy war when, on May 14, he addressed his troops about to cross the Jordan into Palestine: "He who will be killed will be a martyr; he who lives will be glad of fighting for Palestine ... I remind you of the jihad and of the martyrdom of your great-grandfathers."[24]

The defeat of the Arab armies failed to reduce the fervor of their spiritual guides. In December 1948, the *ulama* of Al-Azhar renewed their call for jihad. They reiterated the need to free Palestine from the Jewish gangs, proclaiming that the Arab armies "had fought victoriously" in "the conviction that they were fulfilling a sacred religious duty." And those who failed to undertake jihad would be "damned."[25]

Let me conclude by saying that the foregoing is in the nature of suggesting a lead; it is not the result of wide-ranging, lengthy, systematic research. I have not thoroughly and fully studied and searched the available records in terms of "1948 as

---

[20] Michael Eppel, *The Palestine Conflict in the History of Modern Iraq: The Dynamics of Involvement, 1928-1948* (London: Frank Cass, 1994), p. 31.

[21] Hillel Cohen, *Army of Shadows: Palestinian Collaboration with Zionism, 1917-1948* (Berkeley: University of California Press, 2008), pp. 46-49.

[22] Ibid., p. 97.

[23] Campbell to Bevin, April 17, 1948, PRO FO 371-68370, and Campbell to FO, May 19, 1948, PRO FO 371-68506.

[24] Benny Morris, *1948: A History of the First Arab-Israeli War* (New Haven: Yale University Press, 2008), p. 209.

[25] Campbell to FO, December 13, 1948, PRO FO 371-68644.

jihad." Scholars and students still need to look long and hard at Western and Israeli archives to plumb the jihadi aspect of 1948. For example, I have a feeling that British Foreign Office files from the 1930s and 1940s relating to Saudi Arabia, Egypt, Iraq, and Syria (all deposited with the Public Record Office) may well prove enlightening. The opening of the Arab states' archives, needless to say, would greatly facilitate research in this area. But even if this unlikely event does not come to pass, researchers might usefully begin to trawl through the Arab press, from Morocco to Iraq and Yemen, as well as through published memoirs. My feeling, based on the material I discovered without looking for it and quite by chance, is that great reinforcement will be afforded for the thesis that 1948, in the eyes of many in the Middle East, was a jihad as well as being a politically motivated war.

Jews in China: Legends, History, and New Perspectives*

Pan Guang**

I. Jews in Ancient China: The Case of Kaifeng

It was during the Tang dynasty (around the 7th-8th century) that the earliest groups of Jews came to China via the overland Silk Road. Others may have subsequently come by sea to the coastal areas before moving inland. A few scholars believe that Jews came to China as early as the Han dynasty (206 B.C.-220 A.D.)—some even go so far as to place their arrival earlier, during the Zhou dynasty (around the 6th century B.C.)—though there have been no archaeological discoveries that prove such claims. After entering China, Jews lived in many cities and areas, but it was not until the Song dynasty (960-1279) that the Kaifeng Jewish community was formed.

During the Northern Song dynasty, a group of Jews came to the then capital Dongjing (now Kaifeng, as it will be referred to below). They were warmly received by the authorities and allowed to live in Kaifeng as Chinese while keeping their own traditions and religious faith. Thereafter, they enjoyed, without prejudice, the same rights and treatment as the Han peoples in matters of residence, mobility, employment, education, land transactions, religious beliefs, and marriage. In such a safe, stable, and comfortable environment, Jews soon demonstrated their talents in business and finance, achieving successes in commerce and trade and becoming a rich group in Kaifeng. At the same time, their religious activities increased. In 1163, the Jews in Kaifeng built a synagogue right in the heart of the city. After more than 100 years, with the support of the government of the Yuan dynasty (1279-1368), the synagogue was renovated. During the Ming dynasty (1368-1644), the Jewish community in Kaifeng reached its most prosperous period. It included more then 500 families, with a total population of about 4,000-5,000. The Jews' social status also continued to rise. At that time, some of them had become government officials after passing imperial examinations, some had grown extraordinarily wealthy through business, some had become skilled craftsmen or hard-working, prosperous farmers, and still others had become doctors or clergymen. At the same time, the Jews were

---

* Previously published in Peter Kupfer, ed., *Youtai—Presence and Perception of Jews and Judaism in China*, Publikationen des Fachbereichs Translations-, Sprach- und Kulturwissenschaft der Johannes Gutenberg-Universität Mainz in Germersheim, vol. 47 (Frankfurt am Main: Peter Lang, 2008).

** Director and Professor of the Shanghai Center for International Studies; Dean of the Center of Jewish Studies Shanghai (CJSS); Walter and Seena Fair Professor of Jewish Studies.

407

almost unconsciously becoming assimilated into the mainstream of Chinese Confucian culture. They took part in the imperial examinations, changed their Hebrew names to Chinese ones, used Chinese for speech and study, started to intermarry with other nationalities, dressed like Chinese, and absorbed Chinese habits and traditions while their own gradually faded away. In 1642, Kaifeng Synagogue was destroyed and many religious scriptures lost in a major flood of the Yellow River. The Jews in Kaifeng rebuilt their synagogue in 1663 and recovered some of the scriptures, but the number of the Jewish community had decreased to less then 2,000.

By the late 17th century, the Jewish community had essentially lost contact with the Jewish world outside. By the mid-19th century, the Kaifeng Synagogue lay in ruins, and the Jews in Kaifeng had lived without a rabbi for many years. They could not read Hebrew and had ceased performing religious rituals. Just around that time, Western missionaries "discovered" the descendants of Jews in Kaifeng, provoking a frenzy of research by Europeans and Americans into the Kaifeng Jews. Later, the Jews in Shanghai also tried in vain to help the descendants of Jews in Kaifeng to restore Jewish traditions. In the end, the Jewish community in Kaifeng was integrated into Chinese culture.

II. From Baghdad to Hong Kong and Shanghai: the Sephardi experience in China

Sephardi Jews arrived in China as a result of the Opium War and the subsequent upsurge of trade with Britain. Coming to China from British-controlled places such as Baghdad, Bombay, and Singapore, most of them were merchants and businessmen with British citizenship. Originally from Baghdad, the Sassoon family first shifted their operations eastward to India and then went on to become the first Jews to establish firms and engage in business in Hong Kong and Shanghai. In the wake of the Sassoons, other Sephardi merchants originally from Baghdad, such as the Hardoons and the Kadoories, came to China to seek their fortunes. As external trade centers open to foreign countries, Hong Kong and Shanghai became their leading bases for business. They soon revealed their commercial talents, taking advantage of their traditional contacts with various British dependencies as well as the favorable geographic location of Shanghai and Hong Kong to develop a thriving import-export trade from which they quickly amassed a great amount of wealth. They then turned around and invested this wealth in real estate, finance, public works, and manufacturing, gradually becoming the most active foreign consortium in Shanghai and Hong Kong, whose influence spread throughout China and the entire Far East.

They were also engaged in public welfare and charity work within the community, building synagogues, establishing schools, and providing aid to Russian Jewish immigrants and European Jewish refugees. They supported the Zionist movement and, in order to safeguard their own interests, occasionally became involved in Chinese politics. Some of them, like Mr. Silas Aaron Hardoon, also patronized Chinese arts and culture. Basically, they maintained friendly relations with the social and political groups in China.

But the Sephardi merchants' interests in China sustained great losses following the Japanese invasion of China in 1937. When Japan occupied Shanghai and Hong Kong after the Pearl Harbor incident in December of 1941, the Sephardi merchants lost all their property in those territories. After the war, with the resumption of the Chinese Civil War and the founding of the People's Republic of China, the Sephardi merchants gradually transferred their property to Hong Kong and abroad. After 1949, they continued to forge ahead, taking advantage of Hong Kong's position as the main trading channel between China and the West. Since the implementation of reform policies and the "opening" of China to foreign businesses after the "Cultural Revolution," many Sephardi merchants have once again begun to make investments on the Chinese mainland, promising that their relations with China will continue to further strengthen and expand.

III. THE SECOND HOMELAND: RUSSIAN (ASHKENAZI) JEWS IN CHINA

Unlike the Sephardic Jews, Russian (Ashkenazi) Jews came to China not mainly for trade, but rather because of rising antisemitism in Russia and Eastern Europe from the 1880s onward. This wave led to the migration of millions of Russian Jews to North America, and tens of thousands also crossed Siberia, reaching northeast China, Inner Mongolia, and further to southern parts of China. During this period, the construction of the China Eastern Railway, the expansion of Russian power in China, the Russo-Japanese War, and the two Russian revolutions of 1905 and 1917 all propelled the migration of Russian Jews to China. In the beginning, they lived mainly in Harbin and neighboring areas, where they formed the largest Jewish community in the Far East. After Japan's invasion of northeast China, they moved southward and settled in communities in cities such as Shanghai, Tianjin, and Qingdao.

Most of these Russian Jews initially lived in poverty, able only to eke out a meager living by running small businesses. Later they rose to the middle class through their own efforts. Because they greatly outnumbered the Sephardic Jews, they became an active force in community activities and the Zionist movement. Some of them were technicians and intellectuals and contributed to China's economic and cultural development by working in enterprises and organizations set up by Chinese, Russians, Sephardic Jews, and other foreigners.

Long-resident Russian Jews looked upon China as their second motherland. Some studied hard and were integrated into Chinese culture, playing a positive role in promoting Chinese-Jewish and Chinese-Russian cultural exchanges. After the founding of the People's Republic of China in 1949, a number of Russians Jews stayed on, and some of them obtained USSR passports. The last group of Russian Jews did not leave until the beginning of the Cultural Revolution.

IV. HAVEN FOR HOLOCAUST VICTIMS FROM NAZI EUROPE

While the Nazis were conducting their furious persecution and slaughter of European Jews seventy years ago, many individuals upheld justice and boldly rescued the Jewish victims of the Nazi terror. At the same time, however, the governments of many nations imposed strict restrictions on the immigration of Jewish refugees. Especially after 1938, almost all countries closed their doors to the desperate Jews. Looking back at what was done to the Jews by the "civilized world," the people of China can be proud of the fact that, when Jewish people were on the verge of death and struggling for survival, the Chinese city of Shanghai provided them with a vital haven and all possible forms of relief. From 1933 to 1941, Shanghai accepted over 30,000 European Jewish refugees. Excluding those who went on from Shanghai to other countries, by the time of the Japanese attack on Pearl Harbor in December 1941 the city was sheltering 20,000-25,000 Jewish refugees. According to the Simon Wiesenthal Center, Shanghai took in more Jewish refugees than Canada, Australia, New Zealand, South Africa, and India combined. Before Pearl Harbor, Sephardic Jews, Russian Jews, and Jewish refugees from Nazi Europe in Shanghai amounted to over 30,000, forming the largest Jewish community in the Far East. The prosperous community had its own communal association, synagogues, schools, hospitals, clubs, cemeteries, chamber of commerce, more than fifty publications, active political groups (from Utopian socialism to revisionist Zionism), and a small fighting unit, the Jewish Company of Shanghai Volunteer Corps, which was at the time the world's sole legal Jewish regular army.

The Nazis and their accomplices not only killed six million Jews in Europe but also seriously menaced Jewish communities outside Europe, including the Jewish communities in China and especially in Shanghai. In July 1942, eight months after the outbreak of the Pacific War, Colonel Josef Meisinger, chief representative of the Gestapo in Japan, arrived in Shanghai and proposed a "Final Solution in Shanghai" to the Japanese occupation authorities. Although the "Meisinger Plan" was not put into effect due to differences between the Japanese and German governments' attitudes toward Jews, the Japanese authorities proclaimed a "Designated Area for Stateless Refugees," ordering refugees who had arrived in Shanghai from Europe after 1937 to move into the area within a month. The pressure of Nazi Germany and the vagaries of Japanese policy toward the Jews kept Shanghai's Jews in difficult, unpredictable, and sometimes dangerous straits for nearly four years. But, in the end, almost all Shanghai's Jews, not only Central European Jewish refugees but also the Sephardic congregation and Russian Jews, survived the Holocaust and the war, mainly depending upon their own mutual aid as well as the great support of American Jews and Chinese people.

Like "Schindler," "Wallenberg," and "Sugihara," the name "Shanghai" has now become synonymous with "rescue" and "haven" in the annals of the Holocaust.

V. THE HISTORICAL PAGES OF TRADITIONAL FRIENDSHIP BETWEEN THE CHINESE AND JEWISH PEOPLE

The Jews who came to China were nurtured in some cases by the breadth and profundity of Chinese culture; likewise, their own cultural traditions had an influence on Chinese society. The important point is that although many Jews inhabited China from ancient to modern times, no indigenous antisemitic activity has ever taken place on Chinese soil. Why has China never witnessed any spontaneous and native antisemitic activity? I think the main reasons are as follows:

1. Antisemitism originated from deep-rooted religious prejudice, which is more conspicuous in Christian Europe. However, as a whole, the Chinese are influenced by Confucianism, Buddhism, and Taoism, and this kind of strong antisemitic fanaticism with deep religious bias therefore does not exist in China, and never has.

2. From a cultural point of view, the Chinese and Jewish cultures have a lot in common. For example, both heavily emphasize the role of family ties and the value of education, and although both have absorbed various exotic cultures their central core has never changed since birth. On a stone monument erected in 1489, the Kaifeng Jews wrote: "Our religion and Confucianism differ only in minor details. In mind and deed both respect Heaven's Way, venerate ancestors, are loyal to sovereigns and ministers, and filial to parents. Both call for harmony with wives and children, respect for rank, and for making friends." All these contributed to the prevention of the impact of antisemitism on Chinese people.
3. Since the middle of last century, the Chinese people have suffered as much devastation as the Jews did. Nearly 35 million Chinese were killed and wounded by Japanese fascists during the war. In addition, anti-Chinese atrocities that have occurred in various parts of the world in the past several centuries—and even in Indonesia in 1998—remind us of similar anti-Jewish outrages that occurred in Europe in previous centuries, especially between 1933 and 1945. This shared experience engendered in the Chinese people a deep sympathy for Jewish people and made them oppose firmly any kind of antisemitism.

What is especially worth mentioning is mutual respect, sympathy, and support between Jews and Chinese people. As early as December 14, 1918, in a letter to Mr. E.S. Kadoorie, Mr. Chen Lu, Vice-Minister of Foreign Affairs of the Chinese government, stated that China endorsed the establishment of a Jewish national home in Palestine. On April 24, 1920, Mr. N.E.B. Ezra, another leader of Shanghai Jewish community, received a letter from Dr. Sun Yat-sen, founder of the Republic of China. In this letter, Dr. Sun wrote: "All lovers of democracy cannot help but support the movement to restore your wonderful and historic nation, which has contributed so much to the civilization of the world and which rightfully deserves an honorable place in the family of nations."

Soon after Hitler's anti-Semitic campaign started, Madame Sun Yat-sen (Song Qingling) headed a delegation to meet with the German Consul in Shanghai and lodged a strong protest against Nazi atrocities. Her delegation included all the important leaders of the China League for Civil Rights. As recently discovered materials indicate, Dr. Feng Shan Ho, Chinese Consul General in Vienna, Austria, from 1938 to 1940, was one of the first diplomats to save Jews by issuing them visas that enabled them to escape the Holocaust. Also, documents have been found indicating that in 1939 the Chinese government planned to set aside territory in Yunnan for the resettlement of Jewish refugees from Europe. For various reasons, the plan was never carried out.

While thousands of Jewish refugees arrived in Shanghai between 1937 and 1941, millions of Shanghai residents themselves became refugees following the Japanese occupation of Shanghai. However, in spite of this, the natives of Shanghai tried their best to help Jewish refugees in various ways. In the hardest days in Hongkew, from 1943 to 1945, Jewish refugees and their Chinese neighbors enjoyed mutual help and shared weal and woe. Though largely separated by linguistic and cultural barriers, they found themselves bound together by mutual suffering.

It is important to emphasize here that the Jews in China also did their best to support the Chinese national-democratic movement and resistance against Japanese aggression. Some Jewish individuals joined the anti-Japanese war or cooperated with the Chinese underground, and even gave their lives for the cause of the liberation of the Chinese people. There are many examples that our worthy of deep respect. The well-known Morris "Two-Gun" Cohen was aide-de-camp to Dr. Sun Yat-sen in 1922-1925. Following Sun's death, he worked for a series of Chinese leaders and rose to the rank of general in the Chinese army. Mr. Hans Shippe, a writer and reporter from Germany, was the first Jewish volunteer to fall in battle on China's soil during its war against Japanese aggression. He left Shanghai and joined the Chinese army in 1939. On November 30, 1941, several days before Pearl Harbor, he died with a gun in his hand in an engagement with Japanese troops in Shandong province. Chinese people erected a monument for him near the battlefield. Another such individual was Dr. Jacob Rosenfeld, who came to Shanghai from Austria as a Jewish refugee in 1939 and left Shanghai to join the anti-Japanese war in 1941. He served in the ranks of the Chinese army for ten years, obtaining the rank of Commander of the Medical Corps as a foreigner. Had he not died abruptly of a heart attack in Tel Aviv in 1952, it is speculated that he would have been appointed as a high-level officer in the Ministry of Health of the PRC.

VI. "JEWS FROM CHINA" AND JEWS IN TODAY'S CHINA

After the Second World War, China descended into civil war, and a number of Jews left China for a variety of reasons. Following the establishment of the People's Republic of China, many Jews continued to live and work in peace on Chinese soil, and it was not until the outbreak of the "Cultural Revolution" that they were forced to leave. Jewish communities have continuously thrived in Hong Kong and Taiwan as part of China. Today, "Chinese Jews" live throughout the world. While their natures, pursuits, and occupations differ, they nevertheless have a common bond, recalling China as their "home" and considering themselves "old China hands." In order not to forget the memorable years they spent in China, they have established associations that frequently hold events and issue various publications.

Since the introduction of China's policies of reform and openness, they have returned with their children to their "home city" in order to seek their roots, visit old friends, and travel. Some have come to China to invest and do business, participating in their former home's new upsurge of development. After revisiting China in 1978 after an absence of thirty years, Lord Lawrence Kadoorie wrote: "We are grateful to the country where we grew up." He met Mr. Deng Xiaoping during his visit to Beijing in 1985. When Michael Blumenthal, U.S. Secretary of the Treasury, returned to Shanghai in 1979, he showed off his old Shanghai haunts in Hongkou to the press. One change he noted after arriving in Shanghai from Germany in 1939: "There are now no people dying in the street." Ambassador Yosef Tekoah (Tukachinsky) said at a banquet when he revisited China in 1989: "The most wonderful time of the life is youth. I spent the time in China. Now I am back with the purpose of looking for something that is the best." The late Shaul Eisenberg came to China as a refugee during the Second World War and later went on to become a noted businessman. He actively invested in Shanghai enterprises, establishing, for example, the Y.P. Glass Factory. During his life, he energetically supported the project to establish the Pudong Diamond Exchange Center in Shanghai, which is now coming true.

In 1992, China and Israel established diplomatic relations, further encouraging the return flow of Jews to China. At present, Beijing and Shanghai have begun to see the emergence of new Jewish communities made up of business people, technical experts, diplomats, and foreign students. Since Hong Kong's return to China, the Jewish community there has once more come to life.

VII. Jews in China: A Hot Topic of Academic Research and Public Interest

Since the mid-20th century, there has been a steady increase in books on Jews in China, and during the 1980s and 1990s this subject became a "hot topic" at international level. Particularly since the establishment of Sino-Israeli diplomatic relations in 1992, academic conferences have regularly been devoted to the subject, and a large number of books on the topic have appeared. This enthusiasm for the subject is not limited to academic circles but extends to the mass media, television, and movies. To a certain degree, interest in the subject carries social and political connotations. First, this "Oriental" page in the history of the Jewish people has academic value in the fields of Jewish studies, sinology, history, religious studies, ethnic studies, cultural anthropology, and philosophy. Moreover, this topic has important practical significance in opposing racism and fascism, furthering friendly relations and cultural harmony between all peoples, and preserving peace in the world. Since the subtext of this topic is the special friendship between the Chinese and the Jews, it also plays a unique role in furthering the continued opening-up of China and developing relations between China and nations like Israel and the United States.

On behalf of the Israeli people, the late Yitzhak Rabin, when he visited Shanghai in 1993, expressed his heartfelt thanks to Shanghai for providing a haven for Jewish refugees from Nazi Europe. During his visit to Shanghai in 1995, Austrian President Thomas Klestil paid a special visit to Hongkew (today's Hongkou) to lay a wreath in memory of the Holocaust victims from Austria. In 1998, U.S. First Lady Hillary Clinton and U.S. Secretary of State Madeleine Albright visited Shanghai's Ohel Rachel Synagogue. In 1999, Israeli President Ezer Weizmann paid a visit to a photo exhibit at Shanghai's Ohel Rachel Synagogue, where he once again thanked the Chinese people for rescuing Jewish refugees. Also in 1999, German Chancellor Gerhard Schroder visited Shanghai's Ohel Rachel Synagogue. His visit is especially significant, because the majority of Shanghai's Jewish wartime refugees came from the Nazi Germany and its occupied territories. When his short visit came to an end, Mr. Schroder wrote in the distinguished visitors' book: "A poet once wrote 'death is an envoy coming from Germany'. We know that many victims of persecution found a haven in Shanghai. We never forget this history. Today, we are here to show our appreciation and praise to those who provided every possible relief for the victims of persecution."

These pages of history, composed on Chinese soil by many ordinary Chinese and Jews and cataloging the traditions of Sino-Jewish friendship, form a chapter in the history of human progress that will forever shine.

Our World of Contradictions: Antisemitism, Anti-Tutsi-ism, and Never Again

Berthe Kayitesi*

It happened, therefore it can happen again: this is the core of what we have to say. It can happen, and it can happen everywhere.

Primo Levi[1]

I. ANTIRACISM OR ANTISEMITISM?

From April 20 to April 24, 2009, a conference which had the goal of combating racism, was held at the United Nations in Geneva. However, the racism that was expressed from the first day, and which had a more important impact than the rest of the conference, necessitates a questioning of anti-racism. This conference confirmed, more than ever, that anti-racism is not necessarily opposed to racism, but that it can also be another form of it (Taguieff 1988). Through the comments of the Iranian president, Mahmoud Ahmadinejad, the conference confirmed that Godin (2008) was right when he said that "today, anti-racism may be the principle vector of antisemitism" (p. 142). This factor should not delegitimize the whole anti-racist movement, but the notion of anti-racism must nevertheless be considered carefully.

In his speech at the United Nations on April 20, 2009, the Iranian president directed inflammatory words at those who were in the room and especially at Israel and the West. The accusations against the State of Israel contained a form of antisemitism that is unique in many ways. It is a state-owned antisemitism, in which one state accuses another state of having a genocidal character, when in fact this characteristic is more true of the accusing state. Thus, Ahmadinejad, who had also mentioned his intention of wiping Israel off the world map, declared that "it is all the more regrettable that a number of Western governments and the United States have committed themselves to defend those racist perpetrators of genocide...." This particularity is in line with the genocidal logic that, in order to justify extermination, one attributes criminality and hate to those one wants to eliminate (Ternon 2001; Sémelin 2005). The genocidal antisemitism that the Iranian president and radical Muslims adhere to perpetuates the classic antisemitism that involves discrimination

---

* PhD Candidate, University of Ottawa. With gratitude to Professor Charles A. Small, Jeanine Munyeshuli Barbé, Taylor Krauss, Noam Schimmel, Rosine Urujeni, Aisha Rahamatali, Cynthia Kamikazi, and Esther Mujawayo. Many thanks to Megan Russell for the translation into English.

[1] Levi (1989, p. 196).

and hostility against Jews (Godin 2008; Cotler 2009; Wieviorka 2008; Bauman 2002). The comments of the Iranian president extend and go beyond classic antisemitism because of the added state-owned characteristic. Classic forms of antisemitism can be counted in millenia, as Bauman (2002) points out:

> Among all the other cases of hostility directed towards a collectivity, antisemitism occupies a separate place because of its unprecedented systemization, its ideological intensity, its supranational and supra-territorial scale, and its unique mix of sources and local and ecumenical ramifications. (p. 21)

This consistency over time leads Godin (2008) to describe antisemitism as "total racism" (p. 75). However, the displacements and the forms that run through antisemitism do not change the root of the problem, which is that of hostility toward Jews. This population, which was racialized in the past, is now being accused of racism, or even of Nazism, and a form of apartheid that they themselves had denounced (Taguieff 1986). Relating the situation to France, Wieviorka (2008) attests that when

> Jews are hated and denounced, it is no longer as a race, but more because of their connection to the State of Israel, for their place in society, or even because they would manipulate to their advantage, the historical tragedy in which they were victims to Nazism. (pp. 16-17)

These explanations go hand-in-hand with the Iranian president's speech at the Durban Review Conference, in which he said: "after the second World War, they resorted to military aggression in order to make an entire nation homeless, on the pretext of Jewish sufferings and the ambiguous and dubious question of the Holocaust." This speech brings to mind the response of a French politician, Jean-Marie Le Pen, who answered the question, "what do you think of Faurisson's and Roques' arguments" [two notorious French Holocaust negationists] by saying:

> I am terribly interested in the history of World War II. I have asked myself a certain number of questions about it. I do not say that the gas chambers did not exist. I myself was not able to see them. I have not made a special study of the matter. But I believe they are a footnote in the history of World War II. (Herszkowicz 2003, p. 190; Frossard 1987, p. 44)

To say that the gas chambers are a footnote in the history of World War II is not simply grotesque and inadmissible. Above all, it gives the green light to perpetrators of genocide, who, in most cases, hide under the banner of war in order to complete their extermination projects. It is also to voluntarily ignore what differentiates war from genocide. This is why it is necessary to clarify the distinction between the two. Ternon (2007) differentiates genocide from war in the following terms:

> In a genocide, the annihilation is one-way. Of course, war can lead to the annihilation of the adversary, but the difference is that losses are considerable on both sides. War is plural, genocide singular: it is neither classic nor limited, but an absolute, extreme point.... (p. 22)

One deduces from these comments that the particularity of genocide lies in the absence of an adversary. On the one hand, this absence results from the total innocence of the victims. On the other hand, it results from the total non-consideration of the victims, robbed of everything that makes them members of the human race, even their names. Primo Levi (1987), a survivor of and witness to the Nazi barbarity, completes this distinction by insisting upon the pointlessness of genocidal violence in following terms:

> Wars are loathsome, they are the worst method of resolving controversy between nations and factions, but one cannot define them as pointless: they have a goal, inequitable or destructive, they are not gratuitous, they do not set out to inflect suffering; suffering is there—collective, agonizing, unfair, but it is a by-product, one of many. And yet, I believe that the Hitler years have shared their violence with many other historical spaces and times, but that they are characterized by a wide-spread pointless violence, which became a means to an end with the sole purpose of inducing pain. (pp. 104-105)

The antisemitism of the Iranian president and his acolytes prefers to ignore this distinction in order to strike where it hurts the most. Even more serious is the Iranian president's strategy to imprison the memory of the Holocaust and fuse it to the establishment of the State of Israel. If it is undeniable that the Holocaust is part of the history of Israel, it is not healthy to freeze and maintain an entire state in the horrific experience of the Jews of Europe. Since Israel is a sovereign state among nations, any criticism directed toward it must take its sovereignty into consideration. Like other states, if it is engaged in a war, and one wants to advocate for a cease-fire, it is inappropriate to attribute guilt to Israel by accusing it of genocide and questioning the Holocaust. Denial of the evidence of the Holocaust refutes the accusations brought against Israel. Because, by following this false route of denial, the Iranian president clouds the issue and affirms his antisemitism more than he pleads for the Palestinian cause. The cause that he claims to defend serves as an alibi. His denial of the Holocaust is a new call to murder. As Godin states, "if Muslim antisemites fanatically deny the historical reality of the Shoah, it is obviously because they would like to re-edit it." (p. 106)

Let us also note the contradiction that is implicit in not recognizing an event while at the same time keeping a word that originates from it in one's lexicon. Indeed, Ahmadinejad cannot evoke the word genocide in his discourse without recognizing the Shoah, which situates it historically. The Armenian genocide that preceded it only received, a "biased acknowledgement ... as a 'crime against humanity' in 1919" (Kalisky 2004). The term genocide goes back to the work of Lemkin (1944), who created and defined it, following the extermination of the Jews by the Nazis, all the while including other crimes that were in accordance with his definition. Lemkin upholds the reference to Nazi crimes in these terms:

> It is clear that the German experience is the most manifest, the most deliberate, and that it was pushed the farthest; however, history provides us with other examples of destruction of national, ethnic, and religious groups.[2]

In view of the Nazi horror, Lemkin reported that one was confronted with an exceptional crime that merited an exceptional designation. Thanks to his efforts, the United Nations recognized the term genocide on December 9, 1948, as

---

[2] See http://www.preventgenocide.org/fr/lemkin/legenocide1946.htm.

any of a number of the following acts committed with the intent to destroy, in whole or in part, a national, ethnic, racial, or religious group, as such:

(a) Killing members of the group;
(b) Causing serious bodily or mental harm to members of the group;
(c) Deliberately inflicting on the group conditions of life calculated to bring about its physical destruction in whole or in part;
(d) Imposing measures intended to prevent births within the group;
(e) Forcibly transferring children of the group to another group.[3]

This preliminary work, along with that of others who followed in the same direction, created a foundation for later genocide studies. Waintrater (2003) affirms the inevitability of this definition in the following terms:

> The start of the twentieth century was marked by the Armenian genocide, in 1915, immediately followed by World War I, then by the Shoah, and, more recently, by the long line of Cambodian, Rwandan, and Yugoslavian genocides, to name a few. However, the Shoah remains in this century the paradigm of social and psychological catastrophe. The experience acquired through the testimonies of the survivors of the Shoah allows us to understand other extreme experiences, whether they be posterior or anterior; the scale of the catastrophe, and the scale of the studies dedicated to it and which continue to grow, make up a fundamental corpus for the understanding of the genocidal phenomenon, which, for that matter, annoy some, who, periodically, attempt to "sit on" the destruction of the Jews of Europe by the Nazis. (p. 10)

Taking into account the conditions surrounding the creation of the word genocide, it would be unacceptable to use it while denying the context that created it. In short, Ahmadinejad contradicts himself. When he mentions the word genocide, he admits evidence of the Holocaust in spite of himself and his duplicity. One cannot deny what has been.

Furthermore, one cannot deny the Holocaust without calling other genocides—which are defined in relation to the Holocaust—into question and, especially, without creating an opportunity for future genocides. This denial should worry us all.

II. Colonial antisemitism and anti-Tutsi ideology

As Cotler (2009) clearly reminds us, "while it may begin with Jews, it does not end with Jews" (p. 15). This phrase invites us to return to the past in order to try to identify how antisemitism is an evil that affects us all. Reading it reminded me of the time between April and July 1994, when, over the course of three months, innocent blood was shed over the beautiful hills of Rwanda, and, fifty years after the Shoah, a genocide was committed openly while the entire world watched. Everyone admits that it was a genocide that could have been prevented, a genocide that shows that we have learned nothing in spite of the abundance of research on other genocides, a genocide that leads us to question the concept of "Never Again," and a genocide that has a particular connection to the Shoah and, therefore, to antisemitism (Kalisky

---

[3] Convention on the Prevention and Punishment of the Crime of Genocide, article 2.

2004). In a study entitled "From One Genocide to Another: References to the Shoah in Scientific Approaches to the Genocide of the Tutsis," Aurelia Kalisky underlines the importance of a comparative approach between the two genocides by referring to evidence of crimes that have a genocidal nature, on the one hand, and taking into account the specific and internal elements of these two tragedies, on the other. In relation to this evidence, she notes that:

> For the first time since 1945, a crime with an obvious genocidal nature was committed in such a "consensual" way.... This "evidence" is what brings together the genocide of the Jews and that of the Tutsis in a number of analyses and what designates the common usage of the Shoah as a reference when it is a question of the genocide in Rwanda. (p. 412)

This evidence was ignored when the genocide began to take place because of the different roles that certain Western leaders played in it. Among these leaders was the then president of France, François Mitterrand. In this connection, Mugiraneza brings up the discourse of Mitterrand, who declared: "What do you want to change if the Hutus and the Tutsis decided to fix their problems by wielding machetes?" Similarly, Charles Pasqua, then minister of the interior, refused to talk about these "tribal brouhahas" when questioned by a journalist during the genocide (Mugiraneza 2007, p. 95). This duplicity and lack of tact in relation to breaking up a genocide in the war between African tribes attests to an ever-present racism in regard to the African continent. It is a racism that tries to cover up responsibility for the colonialism that planted the roots for what was to become the last genocide of the twentieth century. Fortunately, when one person denies, another confirms. Of those who acknowledge these facts, French philosopher Bernard Henri Lévy, in his book *La pureté dangeureuse*, states:

> What was true of Auschwitz is true, mutatis mutandis, of Rwanda. One cannot acknowledge the use of Zyklon B, or maintain that the gas chambers existed (it goes without saying), or (more difficultly) that this existence was constitutive of the novelty, of the horror of the Hitlerian project, without admitting that the rule follows equally for Kigali, and that the choice of one procedure rather than another, the self-managing and "popular" quality of the carnage, the crushing of faces by voices, the absence of a visible figure of it own to incarnate the disaster, had a decisive impact and importance here too. (Lévy 1994, p. 60)

Those who denied and continue to deny have opened the doors to a negationism that is displayed under the banner of double genocide. This system of misinformation slows down the process of justice, builds impunity, and protects those involved in the genocide and their accomplices. Ternon (2003) explains this state of affairs in the following way:

> The UN's refusal to intervene in January 1994 to disarm soldiers and militia who declared their volition to kill the Tutsis, the withdrawal of UNAMIR troops in April 1994, the UN's refusal to order a vast peace-keeping operation in April and May, the refusals of the Security Council to identify the massacres as genocide, the declarations of heads of state and high-ranking Western officials speaking about the genocide that had just taken place in terms of "double genocide," comparing the exile of the Hutus ordered by the Hutu Power and the humanitarian

disaster that it engendered to another genocide, these evasions, these cover-ups, these lies, were only the facets of the same phenomenon of negationism, of international amnesia according to political interests. (p. 216)

Much like Ternon and Lévy, those who acknowledged proof of the genocide of 1994 went further in their analyses of the process that made it possible. In this connection, Rutayisire asserts that "anti-Tutsi racism is recent, it is fueled by colonial racism" (p. 63). At the beginning, there were explorers, settlers, and Catholic missionaries. Later on, before 1994, the Rwandan government had its own ideology and militia. The Europeans arrived in Rwanda at a time when, back home, racial theories prevailed. They carried out their colonial project with this racist outlook. In the case of Rwanda, they did it by means of violence, which resulted in the deposing of King Musinga, who refused to be baptized and to adhere to what was being imposed on him by the settlers. Kayishema describes this fierce determination to uproot all Rwandan culture in order to replace it with that of the settlers and the missionaries as cultural genocide:

> The genocide of Rwanda in 1994 was made possible by a cultural genocide. Everything starts with the arrival of colonialism and of missionaries and white priests who imported racial delirium from the West into this small country in Africa. The Rwandan elite ended up re-appropriating this fateful ideology and broke national solidarities conserved in their culture: myths, rituals, beliefs, taboos, etc. Since then, nothing could ever stand in the way of the crime of crimes. (Kayishema 2009, p. 9)

It is in through the racial frenzy of settlers and missionaries that antisemitism and anti-Tutsi-ism met for the first time and, later, that this anti-Tutsi-ism would lead to a "final solution" in Rwanda. In the beginning, it was a symbolic expulsion of the Tutsis from their own land by settlers and missionaries through a poisoned chalice. This false gift was to make the Tutsis believe that they were superior and more intellectually suited to govern than their congeners and that, for this reason, they were not totally black but of some other origin. They therefore excluded them from Rwanda without necessarily anticipating the long-term consequences. In order to get what they wanted, the settlers and the missionaries described the Tutsis of Africa as being of Hamitic descent. In this connection, Coquio states:

> In the twentieth century, Tutsis coming from the Great Lakes region were likened to Egyptians or to Ethiopians with their fiery faces, but also as related to Jews. The Abyssinian Houmas, according to Speke, were of Semitic descent on the paternal side, and of Hamitic descent on the maternal side. The "Hamite" people were called the Jews of Africa for a long time. (Coquio 2004, p. 45)

Elsewhere, one can read that for "John Hanning Speke, their ancestors were the Galla from southern Ethiopia; for Father Pagès, Tutsis came from ancient Egypt, while De Lacger situated the origin of the Tutsis in Melanesia or in Asia Minor" (Prunier 1999, pp. 16-17). Prunier also cites the views of a missionary, in which the reference to antisemitism is obvious:

> The Bahima (a Tutsi clan) differ completely, by the beauty of their traits and their light-colored skin; Bantou farmers are an inferior variety. Tall and well proportioned, they have long, thin noses, large foreheads, and fine lips. They say that

they come from the North. Their intelligent and delicate appearance, their love of money, and their ability to adapt to any situation seem to indicate a Semitic origin. (Prunier 1999, p. 17)

Prunier, after finding that settlers, explorers, and missionaries had assigned different origins to the Tutsis in various writings from colonial Rwanda, falls into the same trap when he attests:

Yes, our feeling is that the Tutsis are not natives of the Great Lakes region, and it is even possible that they come from a distinct racial lineage. ... Their physical particularities most likely point to a Cushitic origin, that is to say, somewhere in the Horn of Africa, possibly in southern Ethiopia, where the Oromo have proven for a long time that they are both nomadic and adventurous. (Ibid., p. 27)

This insistence upon the Jewish origins of Tutsis goes back to a hidden antisemitism that colonizers, missionaries, and explorers of Rwanda brought with them. It is necessary, however, to note that this validating form of antisemitism came with a certain ambiguity, since it referred to the superiority of the Tutsis. It is equally important to be careful to limit it to the context of colonialism, while noting the consequences that it had during the 1994 genocide. In this context, Léon Mugesera's speech always comes to mind. This man, who was recognized by the Canadian government for being guilty of inciting hate, murder, and genocide in Kabaya in 1992, once declared: "It is time to chop off the heads of Tutsis and throw them into the Nyabarongo river in order to send them back to their native land, Abyssinia (Ethiopia)."

Taking into account the absence of sufficient documentation before the colonization of Rwanda, it is difficult to take sides. However, the confusion about Tutsi origins leads us to support Rutayisire (2009), who states that "Rwandan Tutsis did not come from the outside, they became Tutsis in the heart of Rwanda. So did the Hutus." (p. 62)

Another important fact that shows that antisemitism fueled certain aspects of anti-Tutsi-ism is the "Colonization Plan of Kivu," allegedly discovered in 1962 and published in 1981, which is the Tutsi equivalent of "The Protocols of the Elders of Zion." (Kalisky 2004). Kalisky points out several contradictions in this infamous document, which identifies Tutsis and Jews as the chosen people, but also compares Tutsis to the Nazis, who saw themselves as a master race destined to dominate the world. Kalisky explains that this comparison to Nazis refers to the inversion of the victim/torturer status that began with the exclusion and discrimination of the Tutsis from 1950.

A combination of modern antisemitism, anti-Hamitic ideology, and a denial of the genocide committed against the Tutsis appears in an article by Roland Hureaux, entitled "Obama: A White Man Disguised as a Black Man."[4] In this article, this French politician and essayist goes back to colonial thinking, more specifically the belief in Nilo-Hamitic domination. From this starting point, he tries to explain Obama's ascendancy to the American presidency. According to him, the forty-forth president of the United States came to power because of his father's Nilo-Hamitic origins.

---

[4] See http://www.marianne.net/Obama-un-blanc-deguise-en-noir_a83684.html.

In this argument, references to Jews are at the forefront. Hureaux notes as follows:

> The Luos belong to this great family of shepherd people of Eastern Africa called "Nilo-Hamites." If the expression that de Gaulle once applied to Jews as 'self-confident and dominating', makes sense—it is certainly this way in this part of the world.

Part of the article is dedicated to the denial of the genocide against the Tutsi, in which Hureaux justifies the role of the perpetrators of the genocide:

> Indeed, by linking themselves to the Nilo-Hamitic people, the Tutsis of Rwanda and Burundi—a "noble" minority making up between 5 and 10 percent of the population, ruled the Hutu (or Bantu) majority in these two kingdoms for a long time. The Tutsi minority, overthrown in Rwanda in 1960, was helped by the Ugandan President Museveni, and came back to power under the aegis of Paul Kagame in 1994. The army of the "old regime," exiled for over thirty years, returned to the country massacring left, right, and center. The ruling Hutu majority panicked, and so they began to massacre all the Tutsis on the inside, and their real or supposed friends—that was the genocide of 1994.

III. THE NEGATION OF THE GENOCIDE COMMITTED AGAINST THE TUTSIS AT DURBAN REVIEW CONFERENCE

From April to July 1994, a genocide was committed against the Tutsis of Rwanda under the eyes of the international community. This genocide should have been prevented, or at least limited in its magnitude. In the space of a hundred days, a million people of every age and every level of society were killed. However, like other genocides that preceded it, this genocide has not escaped revisionist views of history. The inversion of the victim/perpetrator status is one of many forms of negationism. This form of denial found support at the United Nations during the Durban Review Conference.

A presentation of the testimony of a survivor of the genocide committed against the Tutsis of Rwanda was planned as one of the side events of the conference. In reality, however, the woman in question was not a survivor. She was the daughter of a former minister of the Habyarimana regime who had planned and executed the genocide. The active role that her father, Aloys Nsekalije, had played in the discrimination and the exclusion of the Tutsis was such that he could not be counted as one of the moderate Hutus who were opposed to the genocide. Nsekalije, a former minister of education, played a key role in the exclusion of Tutsi children from the educational system in Rwanda before 1994. Here is a quote from 1986 in which he defends this discrimination under the guise of so-called "ethnic equilibrium":

> I am going to tell you the truth, because all Rwandans are intelligent. Telling lies is not good. If, for example, on the one hand, a commune like Kigoma had 30 intelligent Batwa students who all passed, the Minister of Education posts that list at the Commune. On the other hand, let's say that in the Nyamabuye, there is only a list of Tutsis who passed posted at the Commune. Elsewhere only Hutu students pass their exams. Can that list of Tutsis stay there? Let us tell the truth. That list will be burned, and the schools where they will study will be burned. It is for this reason that there has to be "equilibrium," or a quota system.

Other than the discrimination against Tutsi students, Nsekalije played a key role in the massacre of Tutsis in Cyangugu in 1963 (Mugesera 2004). Accused of genocide, he was cleared in the Gacaca court, part of the community justice system. Certain witnesses said that he even rescued Tutsis in 1994. To bring up Nsekalije's role in the events that plunged Rwanda into mourning goes to show that his daughter cannot claim to be a genocide survivor. However, that does not mean that one can make the child carry the responsibilities of the father. On this point, I am of the same opinion as Wiesel, who maintains, at the time of his conversation with Semprun, that "only the guilty are guilty, the children of the guilty are children. Guilt is limited or limitless, for those in that category, for those who participated in this crime" (Semprun and Wiesel 1995, p. 32). One therefore cannot reproach Nsekalije's daughter for his acts. Nor can one prevent another person from talking about genocide: no one has the right to monopolize this conversation. However, it is necessary to be vigilant about how and under what guise these conversations are held. A person cannot speak as a genocide survivor unless he or she is a survivor, whether directly or indirectly. That is why the survivors and the friends of the survivors of the genocide committed against the Tutsis of Rwanda were opposed to Milly Nsekalije's testimony at the United Nations. As soon as she heard of this opposition, she withdrew. By not presenting herself as a survivor, she still has the right to talk about the genocide, which she witnessed like every other person who was in Rwanda at the time of the genocide.

The appropriation of the status of genocide survivors by their persecutors and those associated with them is part of the process of negationism (Ternon 2001). Having been dehumanized before and having escaped—often through sheer luck—during the genocide, the survivors, when deprived of their unique victim status, are once again excluded in the aftermath. This attempt to occupy their place erases them all over again. As Waintrater (2003) points out, however, survivor testimony is a way to reintegrate victims into the human community, after their membership was cut off during the persecution. The responsibility to make sure that survivors are able to return to life with as few obstacles and as little suffering as possible falls to those who are interested in safeguarding their future. This is because the appropriation of the status of the survivor, just like all other forms of negationism, imprisons the latter in his status as a victim. In trying to prove that this status really belongs to him, the survivor is forced to go back to the period of persecution, to go over it again, and to describe the images. By forcing him into a position of perpetual complaint, the process of healing is compromised. As Lecomte (2004) notes, recognition of wrongdoings facilitates the healing process, while the opposite impedes it.

In order to overcome this problem, it has proven necessary to understand the causes that drive some people to present themselves as victims of genocide when they are not. This has occurred frequently in the case of the genocide committed against the Tutsis of Rwanda. In this case, there are several causes to explore. For example, there is the cultural proximity that unites the victims with their persecutors as well as the way events unfolded after 1994. In addition, the loss of the war and the end of their political monopoly shattered the lives of the Hutus who, while slaughtering the Tutsis, believed that everything would belong to them, so much so that they would sing *Iyi si n'ibiyirimo byose n'ibyabahutu* (This world and all that it holds belongs to the Hutus). In more exceptional cases, the children of the perpetrators live in shame because of their parents' actions, at least those who face up to reality. This leads some of them to take refuge in the identity of the victim. They do not deny the reality of what happened, but they maintain that they did not take part in these crimes or distort reality in order to live with it. On the basis of Milly Nsekalije's testimony,[5] one can place her in this category. When one has read and heard testimonies of survivors, it is obvious that her testimony does not reflect the experience of a true genocide survivor. It is about her fear of war and gunshots, but not about discrimination, exclusion, the fear of machetes, the loss of family members, separation, Interahamwe militia attacks, hiding, hunger, and thirst. The superficiality of this testimony not only attests to the identity of the speaker but, more seriously, dilutes the size and scale of the genocide.

The desire to belong to the community of victims may come from the status of victimhood, which, in the modern world, can have certain advantages (Chaumont 1997; Ternon 2001). However, these advantages and alleged glory are debatable. For those who have seen and lived through genocide, it is difficult to attach great importance to what victim status has to offer, because even positive events bring back the horror. This is where the relativism of many survivors comes from. There is nothing to be gained from living through a genocide, other than a loss of confidence in humanity. This confidence is gradually restored to survivors each time they make a friend. However, those who appropriate the status of genocide survivors can make the most of this status with ease, because they are not brought back to the period of persecution and pain that goes along with it.

IV. "Never Again"

It is hard not to be pessimistic when you are from Rwanda and have lived through the "Again" fifty years after the introduction of the word "genocide" in the lexicon of the international community. It is difficult not be pessimistic when the United Nations, which should support the application of "Never Again," welcomes and gives the floor to those who call for repetition and deny past genocides. This points to a major contradiction within this institution, which is intended to protect us. Denial paves the way for repetition. And what we forget is that it can happen to anyone, and for this reason we are all affected by the "Never Again" project as well as the collection of ideologies that dehumanize and animalize the "Other."

Beyond pessimism, it is impossible not to ask why the "Again" is coming back and what to do about it. The Senegalese writer Boubacar Boris Diop suggests an answer about not recognizing a genocide:

> We only perceive what our mind was made to conceive. If a death, a thousand deaths are, alas, able to be imagined because we are accustomed to it as part of our historical memory, the damage to the principle of humanity that the idea of genocide encompasses is strictly not representable. The refusal to accept it leads to the refusal of recognizing it. (Diop 2009, p. 189)

To this fine analysis, I will add that the "Again" comes back because people still believe that genocide is unthinkable, even when it is depicted before their eyes.

---

[5] See http://www.iheu.org/racism----road-genocide.

However, if one can admit that genocide is in fact imaginable and that, if it was imagined yesterday by certain people, it can be imagined today or tomorrow by someone else, then we may be able to protect future generations.

Why? Because we forget the simple fact that none of the past victims chose to be born Armenian, Jewish, Gypsy, Cambodian, or Tutsi.

Why? Because political and economic interests take precedence over everything, whether there was a genocide or not. And in thinking thus, we forget that each life of a child killed, just for being born, cannot be assessed in terms of such interests but that it surpasses them all. And we refuse to admit that this child could have been our own. And, especially, that this child was and remains innocent in the absolute sense of the word. That it is only by trying to shorten the psychological distance between people that we can accomplish the "Never Again."

Why? Because we forget that the best way to grieve for the dead and to seek justice for their suffering is to give rise to acts of redemption for other people.

V. Conclusion

In this paper, I felt it was necessary to return to the context that opened the door for me to the study of antisemitism. In this regard, Ahmadinejad's speech at the Durban Review Conference serves as the common thread. The relationship between antisemitism and anti-Tutsi-ism is reflected in this noteworthy quote from Irwin Cotler: "While it may begin with the Jews, it does not end with Jews." Such comparisons must be performed with extreme lucidity in order not to confuse the elements of one genocide or one ideology with the other. Therefore, it would be inappropriate to look for all the elements of antisemitism in anti-Tutsi-ism. One speaks of antisemitism in terms of centuries, while for anti-Tutsi-ism the timeframe is measured in decades. Since the two contexts differ, certain factors are not necessarily transposable, and they should be treated as unique to each case. Nevertheless, a detailed examination of the different aspects and facets of antisemitism is valuable for those who are interested in anti-Tutsi-ism and anti-Hamite-ism in terms of lessons to be learned about limiting their magnitude, since these ideologies did not disappear when the genocide ended.

The denial of the genocide committed against the Tutsis of Rwanda has shown us another side of negationism, namely appropriation of victim status. The "Never Again" project is constituted from personal reflections. The contradictions that I refer to in this paper essentially come from the United Nations, which continues to provide a platform for negationism.

References

Bauman, Z. 2002. *Modernité et Holocauste*. Paris: La Fabrique.
Chaumont, J.-M. 1997. *La concurrence des victimes: génocide, identité et reconnaissance*. Paris: La Découverte & Syros.
Coquio, C. 2004. *Rwanda: Le réel et le récit*. Paris: Belin.
Cotler, I. 2009. "Global Antisemitism: Assault on Human Rights." YIISA Working Paper no. 3, Yale Institute for the Interdisciplinary Study of Antisemitism, Yale University, New Haven.

Diop, B.B. 2009. "Génocide et devoir d'imaginaire." In "Rwanda. Quinze ans après. Penser et écrire l'histoire du génocide des Tutsi." Special issue, *Revue d'Histoire de la Shoah* 190, pp. 365-395. Paris: Mémorial de la Shoah.
Frossard, A. 1987. *Le crime contre l'humanité*. Paris: Robert Laffont.
Godin, C. 2008. *Le racisme*. Nantes: Éditions du Temps.
Herszkowicz, A. 2003. "L'antisémitisme aujourd'hui. Au-delà de la négation." In *L'histoire trouée. Négation et témoignage*, edited by C. Coquio, pp. 189-205. Nantes: Librairie d'Atlante.
Kalisky, A. 2004. "D'un génocide à l'autre: référence à la Shoah dans les approches scientifiques du génocide des Tutsi." In "Génocides, lieux (et non-lieux) de mémoire." Special issue, *Revue d'Histoire de la Shoah* 181, pp. 411-438. Paris: Mémorial de la Shoah.
Kayishema, J.-M. 2009. "Aux origines du génocide des Tutsi du Rwanda: l'ethnocide culturel." In *Le génocide des Tutsi. Rwanda, 1994: Lectures et écriture*, edited by C. Sagarra, pp. 9-32. Québec: Les Presses de l'Université Laval.
Lecomte, J. 2004. *Guérir de son enfance*. Paris: Odile Jacob.
Lemkin, R. 1944. *Axis Rule in Occupied Europe*. New York: Howard Fertig.
Levi, P. 1989. *Les naufragés et les rescapés. Quarante ans après Auschwitz*. Translated from Italian by André Maugé. Paris: Gallimard.
Levy, B.H. 1994. *La pureté dangereuse*. Éd. Grasset & Fasquelle.
Mugesera, A. 2004. *Imibereho y'abatutsi kuri Repubulika ya mbere n'iya kabiri 1959-1990*. Kigali: Les Éditions Rwandaises.
Mugiraneza, A. 2007. "Le négationnisme: un piège pour le citoyen, un défi pour l'intellectuel." *La nuit Rwandaise* 1, pp. 91-100. Paris: L'Esprit frappeur & Izuba.
———. 2009. "Négationisme au Rwanda post-génocide." In "Rwanda. Quinze ans après. Penser et écrire l'histoire du génocide des Tutsi." Special issue, *Revue d'histoire de la Shoah* 190, pp. 285-298. Paris: Mémorial de la Shoah.
Prunier, G. 1999. *Rwanda: le génocide*. Paris: Dagorno.
Rutayisire, P. 2009. "Le remodelage de l'espace culturel rwandais par l'Église et la colonisation." In "Rwanda. Quinze ans après. Penser et écrire l'histoire du génocide des Tutsi." Special issue, *Revue d'histoire de la Shoah* 190, pp. 83-103. Paris: Mémorial de la Shoah.
Sémelin, J. 2005. *Purifier et détruire: usages politiques des massacres et de génocides*. Paris: Seuil.
Semprun, G. and E. Wiesel. 1995. *Se taire est impossible*. Paris: Éditions mille et une nuits & Arte Éditions.
Taguieff, P.-A. 1986. "Racisme et anti-racisme: modèles et paradoxes." In *Racismes, Antiracismes*, edited by A. Béjin et J. Freund, pp. 253-302. Paris: Librairie des méridiens.
Ternon, Y. 2001. *L'innocence des victimes au siècle des génocides*. Paris: Desclée de Brouwer.
———. 2003. "Le spectre du négationnisme: analyse du processus de négation des génocides du XX siècle." In *L'histoire trouée. Négation et témoignage*, edited by C. Coquio, pp. 207-221. Nantes: Librairie d'Atlante.
———. 2007. *Guerre et génocides au XX siècle*. Paris: Odile Jacob.
Waintrater, R. 2003. *Sortir du génocide: témoigner pour réapprendre à vivre*. Paris: Payot.
Wieviorka, M. 2008. *L'antisémitisme est-il de retour?* Paris: Larousse.

Two Steps Forward, One Step Back: Diplomatic Progress in Combating Antisemitism

Michael Whine*

I. INTRODUCTION

During the late 1990s—forty years after the end of World War II—international organizations became aware of the recrudescence of antisemitism on a major scale. This was combined with the growing awareness that it was now coming from new and different directions, although the traditional sources had not gone away.[1]

For Jewish organizations, this was vividly highlighted by the events at the UN World Conference Against Racism at Durban in 2000, where a noxious combination of states, mostly Middle Eastern and led by Iran, and many so-called human rights organizations conspired to demonize Israel and Zionism and to intimidate Jewish and Israeli delegates.[2]

Whether this is "new" antisemitism or whether it is just the old anti-Jewish myths and tropes dressed up in a new disguise is immaterial. Their increasing acceptance by new audiences who have no memory of the Holocaust or the events that led to the creation of the State of Israel, as well as an increasing opposition to the United Stats and to globalization, pose significant dangers to Jews.

Against this background, governments themselves, spurred by some Jewish organizations, came to realize that there was a need for action at the international level. Their interest was quickened in the aftermath of the Intifada and Al Qaeda's attacks on the United States, when antisemitic incidents around the world rose alarmingly.

These developments led certain Jewish organizations to seek redress at the international level, and the resultant diplomatic offensive against antisemitism has therefore been carried on through the medium of various intergovernmental organizations. Some organizations have played a greater and more effective role than others, but most initiatives have been more than declaratory. They involve

---

* Director of Government and International Affairs, Community Security Trust; Consultant, European Jewish Congress.

[1] See the *Antisemitism Worldwide* annual reports published by the Stephen Roth Institute for the Study of Contemporary Antisemitism and Racism, http://humanities.tau.ac.il/roth/2012-09-10-07-07-36/antisemitism.

[2] For the best account, see Joelle Fiss, *The Durban Diaries* (American Jewish Committee, 2005), also available at http://www.eujs.org/news/article/25.

programs at ground level and within territories that have historically provided fertile ground for antisemitism.

II. ORGANIZATION FOR SECURITY AND CO-OPERATION IN EUROPE (OSCE)

Among international organizations, the first to recognize and react to the changing circumstances was the OSCE, which at its December 2002 Foreign Ministerial Conference in Porto noted concern over the "manifestation of aggressive nationalism, racism, chauvinism, xenophobia, anti-Semitism and violent extremism, wherever they may occur."[3]

The statement did more than express concern, however. It went on to authorize the OSCE to take action and to ensure effective follow-up via the annual Human Dimension meetings and seminars organized by the agency's human rights affiliate, the Office for Democratic Institutions and Human Rights (ODIHR).

One consequence of this was the 2003 Vienna meeting on antisemitism, the first high-level conference devoted specifically to antisemitism.

More than 400 participants from governments and NGOs considered means to prevent antisemitism, such as raising awareness, education, anti-discrimination legislation, and legal and law enforcement initiatives. The meeting was preceded by a two-day seminar on human rights and antisemitism organized by the Jacob Blaustein Institute, at which Jewish representatives sought to engage with and enlist the support of some of the major international human rights groups, including Human Rights Watch and Amnesty International. That meeting was less than successful, and in the end the Jewish groups were unable to enlist any real support from the international human rights groups, a situation that still prevails.[4]

The Vienna meeting needed a proper follow-up: an event that would engage governments at the highest level and ensure continuing support for programs. This led to the Berlin Conference of 2004. Initially, there was resistance to such a meeting at the highest levels, but US diplomatic pressure, a change in the attitude of the French government, which had begun to react to the rise in anti-Jewish violence, and a resolution adopted by the OSCE Parliamentary Assembly (a parallel body of parliamentarians elected by member states) in July 2004 overcame the opposition of other states.[5]

A "quid pro quo" had been demanded for holding the antisemitism meeting in Vienna, and this took the form of a separate meeting on racism, Islamophobia, and other forms of intolerance. While some disappointment was expressed at the time, it is now deemed to strengthen Jewish activists' arguments to be able to point to the

---

[3] Tolerance and Non-Discrimination, Decision No. 6, OSCE Ministerial Council, December 7, 2002, Porto.

[4] "OSCE Participating States Ready and Willing to 'Take Up the Gauntlet' and Fight Anti-Semitism," Press release, Chairman-in-Office, Vienna, June 19, 2003; Recommendations of the Seminar on Human Rights and Anti-Semitism, Convened by the Jacob Blaustein Institute for the Advancement of Human Rights, Vienna, June 19-20, 2003.

[5] Michael Whine, "Progress in the Struggle Against Anti-Semitism in Europe: The Berlin Declaration and the European Union Monitoring Centre on Racism and Xenophobia's Working Definition of Anti-Semitism," *Post-Holocaust and Anti-Semitism*, no. 41, Jerusalem Center for Public Affairs, February 1, 2006.

singularity of antisemitism while at the same time rooting it within the general arena of racism.

The Declaration of the Berlin Conference, which noted "unambiguously that international developments or political issues, including those in Israel or elsewhere in the Middle East, never justify anti-Semitism," broke a logjam in pointing to the source of much "new" antisemitism. The Declaration also committed OSCE participating states to collect and maintain reliable information and statistics on antisemitic and other hate crimes and to work with the Parliamentary Assembly to determine appropriate periodic reviews of antisemitism. It tasked ODIHR to work systematically on collecting and disseminating information, identifying best practices for preventing and responding to antisemitism, and if requested, offering advice to participating states.[6]

The first step in pursuing these aims was the Paris Meeting on cyberhate two months later, which examined the increasing use of the internet to promote antisemitism and other forms of hatred.[7] On this occasion, the OSCE failed to follow up the recommendations, and it took until March 2010 for the organization to hold its second expert meeting on the same subject. Here some delegates noted that no progress had been made in the intervening six years and that the issues had become more complicated with the development of social networking sites.[8]

The Berlin conference was followed by two more high-level conferences, in Cordoba and Bucharest, and a third is planned for Astana in 2010. The purpose is to provide a high-level forum for states' representatives to demonstrate governments' progress in combating antisemitism and equally to press recalcitrant states to increase their efforts. Intermittent experts' meetings are also held to draw attention to emerging concerns and to assist the Personal Representative on Antisemitism to the OSCE Chairman-in-Office.[9]

The concept of the Personal Representative follows the practice of intergovernmental agencies to appoint high-level experts tasked with approaching governments in a more discrete and effective manner than may be possible via conferences, where time and space may be at a premium. In this regard, the two Personal Representatives appointed so far, Professor Gert Weisskirchen and Rabbi Andrew Baker, have sought to help some member states to recognize and counter antisemitism within their borders.[10]

---

[6] Berlin Declaration, Second OSCE Conference on Anti-Semitism, Berlin, April 28-29, 2004, http://www.osce.org/cio/31432?download=true.

[7] OSCE Meeting on the Relationship between Racist, Xenophobic and Anti-Semitic Propaganda on the Internet and Hate Crimes, OSCE, Paris, June 2004, http://www.osce.org/documents/cio/2004/09/3642end.pdf; Conclusions by the Chair of the OSCE Meeting on the Relationship between Racist, Xenophobic and Anti-Semitic Propaganda on the Internet and Hate Crimes (PC.DEL/514/04), OSCE, Paris, June 16-17, 2004.

[8] Expert meeting "Incitement to hatred vs. freedom of expression: Challenges of combating hate crimes motivated by hate on the Internet," ODIHR, Warsaw, March 22, 2010. The meeting report had not been published at the time of writing, but modalities and so forth are available at http://tandis.odihr.pl?p=qu-ev,events,1003expcyb&id=0.

[9] Cordoba Declaration, OSCE Conference on Anti-Semitism and on Other Forms of Intolerance, Cordoba, June 9, 2005, http://www.osce.org/cio/15548?download=true.

[10] Recent reports by Rabbi A. Baker are available at http://tandis.odihr.pl/?p=qu-pr. Other reports are available on the TANDIS website at http://tandis.odihr.pl.

ODIHR now publishes a series of important reports, including the annual *Hate Crimes in the OSCE Region* report, which collects and analyses data from member states and NGOs and includes a substantial section on antisemitism. The report also measures progress against agreed targets, such as adherence to national and international instruments.[11] In addition, ODIHR publishes other reports, including *Education on the Holocaust and Antisemitism, Hate Crime Laws—A Practical Guide*, and a series of school books for high school students in various OSCE languages.[12] The ODIHR Tolerance and Non-Discrimination Information System (TANDIS) database contains national legislation against hate crimes, model legislation for states that have yet to draft such legislation, and over two million other pieces of relevant information for governments to use.[13]

III. EUROPEAN UNION

Parallel initiatives by the EU and its associated bodies were fraught with problems in the early stages, but real efforts have since been made to redress the balance.

A report on antisemitism, *Manifestations of Antisemitism in the European Union 2002-2003*, published by the European Monitoring Centre on Racism and Xenophobia (EUMC)—renamed the European Union Fundamental Rights Agency (FRA) in 2007—was in fact two reports: a country analysis prepared by the Berlin University Centre for Research on Antisemitism (ZfA) and a report on *Perceptions of Antisemitism in the European Union*.[14] These reports were reasonable given the short time allowed for their preparation, but controversy erupted when the EUMC sought to bury the first report, delay publication of the second, and then publish both with a press release at variance with the assessments made by the reports' authors.[15] The EUMC had failed to understand that antisemitism is now frequently a consequence of the overspill of Middle East tension and is increasingly promoted by Islamists. Muslim communities also suffer from prejudice, and the EUMC, a body established to monitor this phenomenon, found difficulty in reconciling the fact that victims of one sort of prejudice could be responsible for promoting another form of prejudice.

Since 2004, the FRA has published an annual review of antisemitism within the EU based on reports submitted by its RAXEN network of national focal points. But, as with the annual OSCE report, it fails to provide a complete picture as too many

---

[11] *Hate Crimes in the OSCE Region—Incidents and Responses*, http://www.osce.org/odihr/item11_41314.html.

[12] *Education on the Holocaust and on Anti-Semitism in the OSCE Region—An Overview and Analysis of Educational Approaches* (Warsaw: OSCE-ODIHR, 2005); *Hate Crime Laws—A Practical Guide* (Warsaw: OSCE-ODIHR, 2009); *International Action Against Racism, Xenophobia, Antisemitism and Intolerance in the OSCE Region—A Comparative Study* (Warsaw: OSCE-ODIHR, 2004). ODIHR also publishes books for high school students on antisemitism, the Holocaust, and Jewish history, in conjunction with the Anne Frank House, Amsterdam, and Yad Vashem, Jerusalem, in an increasing number of OSCE languages.

[13] Tolerance and Non-Discrimination Information System, http://tandis.odihr.pl.

[14] *Manifestations of Antisemitism in the EU 2002-2003* (Vienna: European Monitoring Centre on Racism and Xenophobia, 2004).

[15] See Michael Whine, "International Organizations: Combating Anti-Semitism in Europe," *Jewish Political Studies Review* 16, nos. 3-4 (Jerusalem Center for Public Affairs, Fall 2004).

states are still unable or unwilling to submit data. Nevertheless, the annual *Summary Overview of Antisemitism in the European Union* is a useful guide.[16]

A second initiative, undertaken by the European Jewish Congress and the Council of European Rabbis, involved a series of meetings with elected European Commission leaders. These meetings were designed to demonstrate that the direction from which antisemitism was coming was changing and that anti-Jewish violence rose when tension in the Middle East increased.[17] These meetings continue intermittently. The most recent, held at the Commission in Brussels in 2009, featured speakers from FRA, Jewish communities, and a British Muslim leader whose working focus is on Muslim antisemitism.[18]

However, what has been of real lasting benefit is the EUMC Working Definition of Antisemitism. When the EUMC considered its first report in 2003, it found that many respondents could not define antisemitism in today's political climate. It also lamented the fact that no two experts could define antisemitism in the same way.[19] It therefore asked a selection of Jewish NGOs and academics to provide a simple working definition that would encompass antisemitic demonization of Israel and could also be used by its own RAXEN network of national focal points and by law enforcement agencies. The international consultation involved many of the major Jewish agencies and prominent Jewish and non-Jewish academics. The result led to final draft negotiations between representatives of the American Jewish Committee and European Jewish Congress, the EUMC director and head of research, and the ODIHR Tolerance and Non-Discrimination program director and antisemitism expert.[20]

Following acceptance by the EUMC, the definition was circulated to interested parties with the expectation that it would assist their work. Although it was never intended that it be legislated, it has nevertheless been adopted by the OSCE and by the US State Department as a working guide.[21]

Another major step forward within the EU is expected when the Common Framework Decision on Combating Racism and Xenophobia comes into effect in November 2010. Although much watered down from the original stronger draft, it nevertheless places on all EU member states a requirement to legislate against the promotion of hatred (including antisemitism), holocaust denial, and denial of genocide.[22]

---

[16] *Antisemitism—Summary overview of the situation in the European Union* (Vienna: FRA, 2009), http://fra.europe.eu/fraWebsite/attachments/antisemitism_Update_2009.pdf.

[17] "Europe against Anti-Semitism for a Union of Diversity," joint seminar of the EJC, European Commission, Conference of European Rabbis, Brussels, February 19, 2004.

[18] "MEPs to EJC Symposium: We Have to Combat All Forms of Anti-Semitism, Even from the EU Parliament itself," European Jewish Congress, March 31, 2009, http://www.eurojew cong.org/ejc/print.php?id article=3828.

[19] Ibid.; *Manifestations of Antisemitism in the EU*, pp. 320-322.

[20] Working Definition of Antisemitism, EUMC, Vienna, http://fra.europa.eu/fraWebsite/material/pub/AS/AS-WorkingDefinition-draft.pdf.

[21] *Hate Crimes in the OSCE Region: Incidents and Responses*, OSCE-ODIHR, http://www.osce.org/odihr.

[22] Council Framework Decision on Combating Racism and Xenophobia, 8180/2/07REV 2DROIPEN2a, Justice and Home Affairs Council of the European Union, Strasbourg, April 17, 2007.

IV. COUNCIL OF EUROPE

The Council of Europe, with a larger membership than the EU, has also acted by passing policy resolutions condemning antisemitism.[23] Its racism monitoring body, the European Commission against Racism and Intolerance (ECRI), has taken on the issue in an effective and business-like manner. The ECRI mission is to monitor member states' adherence to European legislation and the European Convention on Human Rights, in particular. It does so by means of four-yearly reviews of states' compliance with European and their own national legal instruments, as well as occasional thematic recommendations. Member states are expected to act on ECRI recommendations, and the current third cycle of country reports is paying particular attention to the improvements made by members over the entire twelve-year cycle. In 2004, ECRI also published a *General Policy Recommendation on Combating Antisemitism*, which gave advice to member states on legislation and the action required by national criminal justice agencies.[24]

ECRI's 2010 review of progress notes that its three-pronged program of activities (country reports, thematic reports, and engagement with civil society) has allowed it to promote real legislative progress, effective use of legislation, and the spread of best practices between member states.[25]

V. UNITED NATIONS

Despite the well-founded belief that the United Nations has latterly been ineffective in defending human rights, it has nevertheless made a contribution to combating antisemitism. Several denunciations of antisemitism, within the context of denouncing racism, in 2002 and 2005, were followed by the more practical decision to establish the International Day of Commemoration for Holocaust victims on January 27 and an unequivocal condemnation of Holocaust denial, signed by all member states except Iran, in 2005.[26]

Even the ridiculous 2009 Durban Follow-Up Conference in Geneva attempted to move on from the ill-fated 2001 United Nations World Conference against Racism, Racial Discrimination, Xenophobia and Related Intolerance by calling on member states to counter antisemitism (and anti-Arabism and Islamophobia), to take measures to prevent the emergence of movements promoting hatred, and to

---

[23] Combating Anti-Semitism in Europe, Parliamentary Assembly, Council of Europe, Strasbourg, 2007, http://assembly.coe.int/Documents/WorkingDocs/Doc07/EDOC11292.htm; see also ECRI Declaration on the Use of Racist, Anti-Semitic and Xenophobic Elements in Political Discourse, March 17, 2005, http://www.coe.int/t/E/human_rights/ecri/1-ECRI/4-Relations_with_civi_society/1-Programme_of_act.

[24] General Policy Recommendation No. 9 on the Fight against Anti-Semitism, European Commission against Racism and Intolerance, Strasbourg, 2004.

[25] Lanna Hollo, *The European Commission against Racism and Intolerance (ECRI) — Its first 15 years* (Strasbourg: Council of Europe Publishing, 2009).

[26] Resolution adopted by the General Assembly on Holocaust remembrance, A/RES/60/7, New York, November 1, 2005, http://www.un.org/holocaustremembrance/docs/res607.shtml; Resolution adopted by the General Assembly on Holocaust denial, A/RES/61/255, January 26, 2007, http://www.un.org/en/holocaustremembrance/docs/res61.shtml.

implement General Assembly resolutions on Holocaust commemoration and Holocaust denial.[27]

VI. Stockholm Declaration

Among the most practical and long-lasting outcomes of international diplomacy, which stemmed not from Jewish urging but the concerns of statesmen, was the declaration adopted by the Stockholm International Forum on the Holocaust in 2000.[28]

Initiated by the then Swedish Prime Minister, the conference agreed to establish an international taskforce to ensure that states recognize the magnitude of the Holocaust and its lasting scarring effect on the Jews and humanity as a whole. So far, twenty-seven states have signed the Stockholm Declaration and put in place annual Holocaust commemorations and educational programs.

To ensure enlargement and consistency, a permanent office was established in Berlin, funded by the German government, and a revolving chairmanship shared by signatory states was established.[29]

VII. Assessment

It might be argued that ten years' diplomatic effort to counter antisemitism has been of little avail given the dramatic increase in incidents and deterioration in discourse following the 2009 Operation Cast Lead.

This would, however, miss the point. At the turn of the millennium, governments were reluctant to even recognize that antisemitism was once again growing. Since then, states have recognized the dangers to society's health by not combating the phenomenon, have agreed a common yardstick by which antisemitism can be defined and measured, and have recognized that it now also comes from new and different directions. Many have also legislated against incitement of antisemitism in its various forms, including Holocaust denial. Those that have not yet done so, in Europe at least, will have to do so by the end of 2010.[30]

If there have been setbacks, it is because some states are still unable to measure antisemitism for various reasons, despite having agreed to do so The picture is therefore lacking in total clarity, although the broad outlines are apparent. However, the monitoring role is increasingly filled by NGOs, and the EU, the Council of Europe and the OSCE recognize this and rely on their vital work in this regard. Also, a certain fatigue is apparent, and the progress made has not always been continuous or consistent. But without the determination of a handful of individuals and their governments, the progress made thus far would not have been possible.

---

[27] See Michael Whine, "Durban 11: Rescuing Human Rights from the United Nations," *The Israel Journal of Foreign Affairs* 3, no. 2 (2009).

[28] Declaration of the Stockholm International Forum on the Holocaust, Stockholm, January 26-28, 2000, http://www.holocaustforum.gov.se/conference/official_documents/declaration.

[29] Task Force for International Cooperation on Holocaust Education, Remembrance and Research, http://www.holocausttaskforce.org.

[30] For the list of states criminalizing Holocaust denial and recent criminal cases, see Michael Whine, "Expanding Holocaust Denial and Legislation Against It," *Jewish Political Studies Review* 20, nos. 1-2 (Jerusalem Center for Public Affairs, May 2008).

Memetics and the Viral Spread of Antisemitism through "Coded Images" in Political Cartoons

Yaakov Kirschen*

PREFACE

For more than forty years, I have been putting ideas into people's heads. It is what I do. I am a political cartoonist. Some of my cartoonist colleagues define the purpose of our work as showing the "truth," others as "expressing our opinion," but the fact is that what we do is to attempt to put our own ideas into other people's heads ... and we use cartoons to do it.

When a portion of the cartoonist's readership cries foul about a cartoon, he defends his work as being a valid political statement. But effective cartoons can go far beyond being "just" political statements. A cartoon can use the power of graphic signals, which are embedded with subliminal messages, to transmit deeper, more visceral meanings than any verbal description of the cartoon might imply.

The intense political focus on Israel and the frustrating search for peace in the Middle East have become favorite topics for editorial cartoonists. Inevitably, when a portion of the cartoonist's readership cries "antisemitism," the cartoonist attacks his critics as "right-wing defenders of Israel" ... and defends his work as a valid political statement.

The rich and extensive use of antisemitic cartoons by the National Socialist Party as part of their strategies in the prelude to the Holocaust gives today's debate an added importance and, perhaps, urgency. It is in light of the extensive use of antisemitic cartoons by the Nazis that I undertook, both as a fellow of the Yale Initiative for the Interdisciplinary Study of Antisemitism and as a political cartoonist dedicated to freedom of expression, to address the contemporary controversy and to examine the question of how to distinguish between valid political commentary and antisemitism in contemporary political cartoons.

At the beginning of the study, it became apparent that the cartoons that are the most undeniably antisemitic can be recognized even if they are in a language that the observer cannot read. The graphic images themselves speak clearly without the words of the cartoon, as many of the same powerfully communicative images appear over and over again in the work of different cartoonists. They are like a familiar cast of characters. It is the intent of this paper to explain what the examination of this set of antisemitic graphic images has revealed.

---

* Political cartoonist and YIISA Artist in Residence. With thanks to Rachel DeFilipp for assistance in the cartoon research and preparation of this paper.

I. Introduction

Antisemitic propaganda is a valuable tool for aspiring mass movements and totalitarian regimes. By portraying Jews as a powerful, secretive, demonic threat, such movements employ a common enemy as a unifying force for the recruitment of new members. Totalitarian governments, including those of Nazi Germany, Stalinist Russia, and Revolutionary Iran, and radical organizations such as Hamas, the PLO, Hezbollah, White Supremacists, and Black Muslims have all defined Jews as a threat which only they themselves can confront.

In the twentieth and twenty-first centuries, antisemitic political cartoons have used an identical set of graphic images to portray an assortment of viral beliefs. In the digital age, antisemitic cartoons have been particularly pervasive in a growingly "post-literate" society.

These image-codes can be divided into three distinct families. The first two families were codified in the twentieth century and are taken from ancient and medieval libels along with newly developed twentieth century codes. The *dehumanization* codes work in such a way as to portray Jews as undeserving of the empathy that humans naturally feel for one another. These codes spread the belief that Jews are vermin, blood drinkers, or demons in league with evil forces. The *stereotyping* codes describe Jews as rich, ugly, money-grubbing, powerful, and secretly controlling the banks, the media, and the world. Combined, the two families of codes instruct that Jews are rich, ugly, demonic, powerful, and enemies of the social order.

The Holocaust proved Jews to be victims and powerless. The environment in much of the West then became hostile to open antisemitism. From a memetic point of view, antisemitism can be seen as a virus, which in order to survive developed a Holocaust-resistant strain. The *moral inversion* codes simply repackage the horror by inverting it: Jews are portrayed as the perpetrators rather than the victims. In this case, Jews are essentially depicted as Nazis. This new and virulent strain is now infecting cartoonists and their cartoons in pandemic proportions.

This paper describes the identification and examination of antisemitic image-codes embedded in contemporary political cartoons.

II. The Function of Antisemitic Propaganda

During the twentieth century, two major European anti-democratic mass movements employed antisemitic propaganda in political cartoons. On the extreme left, the Stalinist Soviet state and, on the extreme right, Hitler's Nazi movement both used antisemitic messages to attempt to advance their own agendas. This brings to the forefront their shared motivation for promoting antisemitism. In order to gain acceptance and purpose within a population, all mass movements must find a function and role to play. As Erich Hoffer observed:

> The technique of a mass movement aims to infect people with a malady and then offer the movement as a cure ... mass movements can rise and spread without belief in a God, but never without belief in a devil.[1]

---

[1] Erich Hoffer, *The True Believer: Thoughts on the Nature of Mass Movements* (New York: Perennial Classics, 2002). First published in 1951.

Both Stalin's Communist party and Hitler's Nazi movement demonized the Jewish people. The goal of the propaganda distributed was to build a unifying, shared hatred in the public's mind. This shared hatred and obsession with eradicating the "devil" gave purpose to the Nazi and Communist parties. These mass movements created the "Jewish problem," a problem that only the regime could solve.

> Jews are a valuable hostage given to me by the democracies. Antisemitic propaganda in all countries is an almost indispensable medium for the extension of our political campaign. You will see how little time we will need in order to upset the ideas and the criteria of the whole world, simply and purely by attacking Judaism.[2]

III. IMAGE-CODES AND POLITICAL CARTOONS

In the twentieth century, graphic images were widely used to efficiently and effectively infect the masses with a viral hatred of Jews. In the pre-Holocaust pages of Nazi newspapers and in post-World War II pages of Soviet humor magazines, cartoons were used to focus the attention of readers on the common enemy of the Jews. These cartoons spoke through a specific set of graphic codes rich in anti-Jewish meaning. However, the fall of Stalinism and Nazism did not spell the end of these powerful graphic codes. They continued to live, embedded in cartoons spread by groups such as the Ku Klux Klan, Russian Fascists, Neo-Nazis, and White Supremacists. These aspiring mass movements, eager to attract followers, utilized the spread of antisemitic beliefs through graphic images to further their grasp on the public.

Even today, cartoons from openly antisemitic regimes such as Iran and Syria regularly make use of a specific set of antisemitic image-codes. The purpose of the codes is to define Jews, Judaism, and the Jewish people as a powerful force corrupting and secretly controlling human society. This in turn, creates the imaginary threat, real to the population, that only the "movement" can defeat.

The widespread dissemination of these codes has now virally entered the consciousness of political cartoonists in democratic societies throughout the world, and the antisemitic codes embedded in their cartoons are presented as valid political comments. These meme-carrying images are a graphic vocabulary of the same anti-Jewish libels that were originally codified and mass distributed by Hitler's Nazi movement and later employed by Stalinist communism.

As evident from cartoons around the globe, the use of these image-codes in the metaphors of political cartoons has expanded beyond the groups traditionally identified with transmitting antisemitic images. The principal of memetics explains the vast and far-reaching presence of these image-codes today.

IV. MEMETICS

A computer virus is a software program. The word "virus" is derived from "viral" because of a virus's shared characteristic with all other viral entities—the ability to replicate or reproduce itself. "Computer viruses" spread copies of themselves from one computer to millions of other computers. Just as viruses spread, beliefs, ideas,

---

[2] Hermann Rauschning, *The Voice of Destruction: Conversations with Hitler* (New York: G.P. Putnam's Sons, 1940) p. 236.

and notions can also spread, moving from one person to many others. A successful self-replicating entity, whether a life form, a computer virus, or a viral belief, is one which succeeds in reproducing and avoids extinction. Successful viral beliefs are replicated as they proliferate through a population, in effect spreading copies of themselves from one brain to millions of other brains. Replicating beliefs that spread throughout a human population have been called "brain viruses" or "memes." The word "meme" is derived from Greek, meaning "to imitate or mime."

> Memetics provides new insight into the way our minds, societies, and cultures work. Rather than look at the development of culture as a sequence of ideas and discoveries that build upon one another, what would it be like to look at culture as a meme pool, where the ideas in our heads are shaped and transported by various forces including mind viruses? Are they helping or harming us? Can we control them? Can our enemies create new ones and infect us with them?[3]

Memes spread through a population like a biological virus: sweeping cultural changes and new belief systems can be understood if they are examined as epidemics.

> Returning to the abstract model of epidemia, it becomes evident that this model can be applied to phenomena that have nothing to do with disease: the circulation of objects, money, customs, or the propagation of affects and information. Fashion, the circulation of violence and even rumors, those contagions passing from mouth to ear, are all epidemics.[4]

Although memes are frequently transmitted by "word of mouth," they can be dispersed through other mediums as well. There are two general types of memophores (i.e. conveyors of memes): auditory and image-based. Auditory memophores includes jingles, sayings, and nicknames, whereas image-based examples include idols, icons, paintings, and cartoons.

V. MEMETICS AND ANTISEMITISM

As a viral belief system, antisemitism has historically used image-based memophores to spread its constituent memes. In the past, these memophores appeared in woodcuts, etchings, paintings, murals, and stained glass windows. Twentieth century mass movements used image-codes taken from these medieval works alongside newly created image-codes in cartoons, which were mass produced in newspapers and magazines and presented as valid political commentary.

What was considered mass production in the age of twentieth century mass movements is dwarfed by the potential "viral" distribution afforded by our twenty first century digital reality. The most successful distribution systems of information at present are computer viruses and spam email. Second to those is the forwarding of content by users to a list of their friends and contacts, which is commercially exploited as "viral marketing."

---

[3] Richard Brodie, *Virus of the Mind: The New Science of the Meme* (Seattle, WA: Integral Press, 1996), p. 64.

[4] M. Guillaume, "The metamorphoses of epidemia," in *Zone 1-2: The Contemporary City*, ed. M. Feher and S. Kwinter (Cambridge, MA: The MIT Press, 1987), p. 60.

Viral marketing describes any strategy that encourages individuals to pass on a marketing message to others, creating the potential for exponential growth in the message's exposure and influence. Like viruses, such strategies take advantage of rapid multiplication to explode the message to thousands, to millions.[5]

When a professional newspaper or magazine cartoonist draws a cartoon, it will be replicated on the pages of that newspaper or magazine. It will be seen by readers of that publication. However, once on the Internet, the cartoon can be distributed virally, without cost or limit, to millions of viewers. Like a chain letter, an emailed page of jokes, a YouTube video, or a computer virus, it is replicated by being forwarded and re-forwarded over and over again. Each replicated copy carries the same impact and message of the original. Viral distribution has revolutionized the way information and memes move throughout the world. What once might have only circulated around a small city, state, or even country can now freely cross international boundaries and leap across continents.

Image-based memophores are more important than ever. We used to speak of literacy and illiteracy, but digital society seems to be post-literate. People can read, but reading has become a chore. Increasingly, virally forwarded content consist mainly of photographs, videos, and cartoons.

[Communication] is moving toward a mixed model of written/audio and visual communication that focuses, where possible, on visual communication more than on written text or audio. Users prefer to watch more than to read.[6]

Visual content is the new medium of choice. Keeping up with modern preferences, vehicles carrying antisemitic memes are not longer transmitted by woodcuts and paintings but instead by cartoons, perfectly repackaged for viral distribution.

VI. Contemporary Cartoons and Infected Cartoonists

Most cartoons communicate in metaphors. The immense power of the metaphor is its ability to set the terms and backdrop of the discussion. The graphic codes of incitement created by twentieth century mass movements, which have their roots in medieval art, can increasingly be found in contemporary twenty-first century editorial cartoons. They are not hidden but are displayed in plain view, posing as original metaphors and defended as valid political comments. The image-codes, which are primarily metaphors, are used in political cartoons, which are also largely metaphorical. Their power to virally transmit is enhanced by use of the metaphor form. A response to an allegation presented as a metaphor, such as a political cartoon, is framed in terms of the acceptance or rejection of the metaphorical premise. The viewer is restricted to the framing of the metaphor regardless of its irrelevance to a proper or wider discussion of the topic.

---

[5] R.F. Wilson, "The six simple principles of viral marketing," *Web Marketing Today* (2000/2005), http://www.wilsonweb.com/wmt5/viral-principles.htm.

[6] Alfredo M. Ronchi, *eCulture: Cultural Content in the Digital Age* (Heidelberg: Springer, 2009), p. 42.

> Metaphors produce ideological effects because they are selective accounts of experience. Understanding X in terms of Y emphasizes only some features and discounts others. It organizes our imagination about X in one way rather than another. We model X according to the features and relationships between elements found in Y, although we might have modeled it on a completely different set of elements and relations.[7]

Viewed memetically, these image-codes transmit antisemitic memes to the viewer. These memes attempt to replicate in the brains of viewers, just as a software virus attempts to replicate in the memory of each new computer it comes into contact with. In the digital world, people forwarding "infected" cartoons to others can be understood as people being used as hosts by the meme-bearing codes to spread their message.

> Memes "use" people for the purpose of their own propagation. We should not understand such anthropomorphic language literally: memes no more than genes have wants, desires, purposes, or interests. Rather, this is merely a shorthand way of describing how natural selection works on units of cultural transmission.[8]

In contemporary use, antisemitic memophore image-codes are incorporated into cartoons both with and without willful intent to "infect" the viewer. Users with intent include contemporary anti-democratic movements such as the Islamic Republic of Iran, Hamas, Al Qaeda, Hezbollah, and Arab dictatorships, whereas contemporary cartoonists from countries such as the United States or Australia unwittingly produce cartoons containing image-codes that transmit hidden antisemitic memes.

A cartoonist infected with these viral meme codes of antisemitism will use these memophores in his cartoons (such as the "devourer of children," "blood-drinking," or "money-hungry" memophore). A twenty-first century cartoonist who is infected may have no more control over his compulsion to insert infectious antisemitic image-codes in his or her drawings than a person with a cold can control his sneezing out of germs potentially infecting other human hosts. Such cartoonists may become serial creators of antisemitic cartoons while sincerely believing that they are creating fair and honest work.

> Memes are like symbionts that alter the behavior of their hosts, much as the rabies virus alters the behavior of a dog by making it more aggressive, increasing its salivation, and preventing it from swallowing. Just as the genes in the rabies virus make use of the host to spread their genetic information, memes use their hosts to spread their own memetic information.[9]

Any critical study of antisemitism in contemporary art must include the examination and identification of the specific memophoric image-codes used and the meme/beliefs they transmit.

---

[7] J.N. Balkin, *Cultural Software: A Theory of Ideology* (New Haven: Yale University Press, 1998), p. 245.

[8] Ibid., p 61.

[9] Ibid., p 62.

VII. CODE ORIGINS AND CODIFICATION

Medieval antisemitism was a belief system that incorporated the beliefs that Jews had sexual contact with pigs, drank the blood of abducted Christian children, were in league with the devil, and had horns. Artists of the time used their artwork to depict hate-provoking, blood curdling images of such scenes. Twentieth century totalitarian states and mass movements adapted and organized these inflammatory depictions into a collection of codes and used them in political cartoons. These image-codes, and the varieties and variations that they have spawned, can now be found, disguised as metaphors, in current political cartoons. Each code carries a specific antisemitic libel.

The original image-codes, as codified by the Nazi movement, can be organized into two broad families based on the nature of the memes they transmit.

One family, *dehumanization*, houses the codes that spread the dehumanizing memes. For example, the belief that Jews are vermin, blood drinkers, or demons in league with demonic forces. The second family, *stereotyping*, portrays Jews as rich, ugly, money-grubbing, powerful, and secretly controlling the banks, the media, and the world. These memes resonate with existing antisemitism in the minds of potential host populations. Combined, the two families teach that Jews are rich, demonic, powerful, and enemies of the social order.

The Holocaust forced the codes to evolve. Images of the extermination of European Jewry, the horrendous piles of skeleton-thin bodies, photographs of men and women standing in line, stripped naked, waiting to be shot and thrown into an open pit, circulated around the world. The Jews were undeniably targeted and powerless victims of the Nazi Holocaust. As a result, antisemitism was deemed unacceptable throughout the West. In response, like any successful viral entity, the virus of antisemitism adapted to the new conditions and evolved a new "Holocaust-resistant" strain. This new strain is now infecting cartoonists and their cartoons in pandemic proportions.

The Holocaust-resistant codes do not deny the existence of the Nazi death camps or the Holocaust. Instead, they simply repackage the horror by "inverting" it. Jews are presented as the perpetrators rather than the victims. The new codes carry memes including: "the Jews are acting like Nazis," "the Jews perpetrated a Holocaust," "the Jews operate an Auschwitz-type death camp," "the piles of skeletal victims are not Jewish but rather the victims of Jews," and "the Jews are Nazis." These new and infectious Holocaust-resistant codes are hereafter collectively referred to as the *moral inversion* codes.

The moral inversion codes are new, fresh, and rapidly spreading their memes. Moral inversion has taken its place alongside the two earlier pre-Holocaust families of codes. While the pre-Holocaust codes have become dated and to a certain extent politically incorrect, the moral inversion codes are easily swallowed, readily believed, and increasingly part of an accepted vocabulary.

The Arab destruction of ancient Jewish holy sites has given birth to a new strain of moral inversion codes. Parallel to the Holocaust-resistant moral inversion codes, these new memophores carry the inverted belief that it is the Jewish state that is destroying holy Islamic sites. In this scenario, Muslims are perceived as the victims.

Diagram 1

The Three Families of Antisemitic Image Codes Found in Contemporary Political Cartoons

- Dehumanizing
- Moral Inversion
- Stereotyping
- Post-Holocaust
- Holocaust
- 20th century Pre-Holocaust
- Paintings
- Medieval Roots
- Deicide
- Blood Libels
- Superstitions

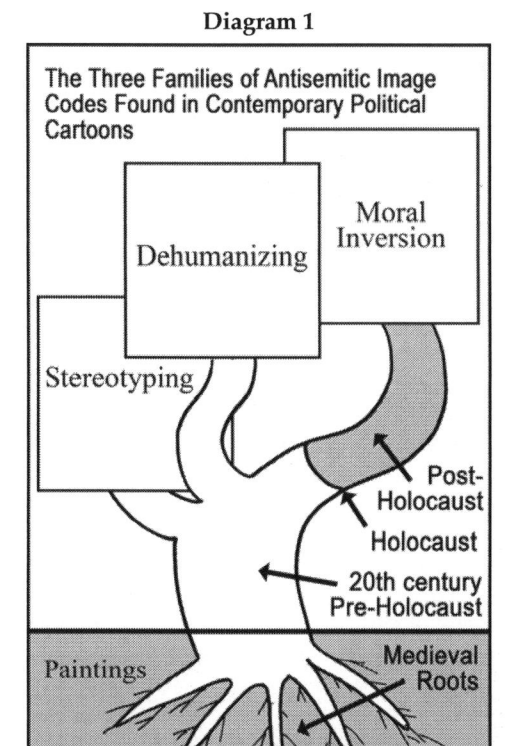

VIII. CODES FROM GENERATION TO GENERATION

The following three figures illustrate the ability of image-codes to survive and remain potent over time, even through radical changes in society. Each of the following figures is a sample of a single antisemitic image-code that has remained active, continuing to replicate and infect from the moment of its appearance in:

1. pre-Holocaust Nazi cartoons
2. post-Holocaust Soviet cartoons
3. contemporary work.

The first two examples contain zoomorphic image-codes. The first is the "Jew as a vulture" code and the second the "Jew as a spider" code. The third example shows instances of the pairing of the "money-hungry Jew" and "hook-nosed Jew" codes as they move from the pre-Holocaust Nazi period to the post-war Soviet era and finally to contemporary work.

MEMETICS AND THE VIRAL SPREAD OF ANTISEMITISM 443

Figure 1: The "Jew as a Vulture" code

1. In a Nazi cartoon

"The Vulture" (from *Der Stürmer*)

2. In a Soviet cartoon

"The Vulture" (from *Zarya Vostoka*, 1980)

3. In a contemporary cartoon

February 26, 2007 (Jordan)

Figure 2: The "Jew as a spider" code

1. In a Nazi cartoon

Der Stürmer (Nazi Germany), February 1930

2. In a Soviet cartoon

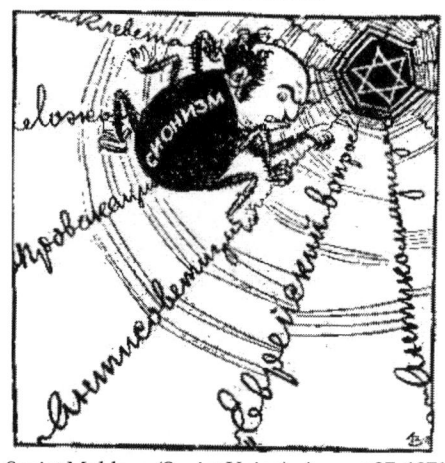

Soviet Moldova (Soviet Union), August 27, 1971

3. In a contemporary cartoon

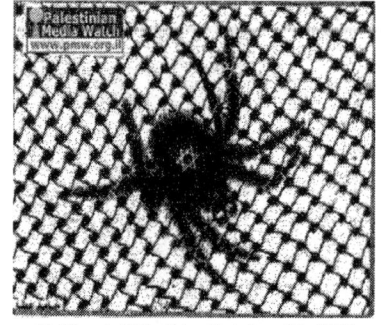

Al-Hayat Al-Jadida, October 21, 2001

Figure 3: The "Money-Hungry Jew" and "Hook-Nosed Jew" codes

1. In a Nazi cartoon

"Roosevelt against High Finance,"
Der Stürmer, 1938, Vol. 4

2. In a Soviet cartoon

"The Modern Prayer Coat,"
Vechernyaya Moskva, 1973

3. In a contemporary cartoon

Chicago Tribune, May 30, 2003

IX. CODE FAMILIES

There are three broad families of codes:
1. the dehumanizing family
2. the stereotyping family
3. the moral inversion family.

See Figure 4.

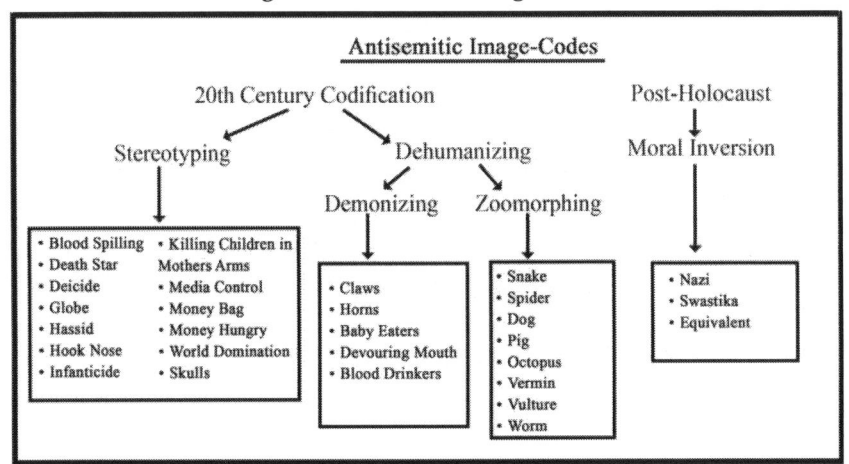

Figure 4: Antisemitic Image Codes

```
                        Antisemitic Image-Codes
                    ╱              ╲
        20th Century Codification        Post-Holocaust
            ╱         ╲                      ↓
    Stereotyping    Dehumanizing         Moral Inversion
         ↓           ╱      ╲                 ↓
                Demonizing  Zoomorphing
                    ↓           ↓
┌──────────────┬──────────────┐ ┌──────────────┐ ┌──────────────┐ ┌──────────────┐
│• Blood Spilling│• Killing Children in│ │• Claws        │ │• Snake       │ │• Nazi        │
│• Death Star  │  Mothers Arms │ │• Horns        │ │• Spider      │ │• Swastika    │
│• Deicide     │• Media Control│ │• Baby Eaters  │ │• Dog         │ │• Equivalent  │
│• Globe       │• Money Bag    │ │• Devouring Mouth│ │• Pig         │ └──────────────┘
│• Hassid      │• Money Hungry │ │• Blood Drinkers│ │• Octopus     │
│• Hook Nose   │• World Domination│ └──────────────┘ │• Vermin      │
│• Infanticide │• Skulls       │                   │• Vulture     │
└──────────────┴──────────────┘                   │• Worm        │
                                                  └──────────────┘
```

1. The dehumanizing family of codes

Dehumanizing codes answer the question "who are the Jews?" in such a way as to prevent others from feeling empathy toward them. There are two sub-families within the dehumanizing family of codes: zoomorphic codes and demonization codes. The zoomorphic codes are metaphorical. They transmit the belief that Jews are like spiders, snakes, rats, vultures, and other animals that are generally perceived negatively. The demonization codes portray Jews as clawed demons, horned devils, cannibals, baby eaters, devouring mouths, blood drinkers and blood-sucking vampires.

The images in Figures 5 and 6 transmit the ancient "blood libel" message that Jews are vampire-like drinkers of blood. The first (Figure 5) is a photograph of a Polish wood panel carving from about 1900. It depicts a group of Jews sucking the blood (through straws) from a child victim. The blood-sucking image code is used again in a contemporary cartoon more than a century later by an Indian artist (Figure 6).

Figure 5

Figure 6

2. *The stereotyping family of codes*

Stereotyping codes address the question "what are Jews like?" These codes transmit the belief that there is a set of traits and characteristics that is common to all Jews. They then define those "Jewish" characteristics and present them graphically. Stereotyping codes depict Jews as controlling the world and the media and as being money-hungry, brutal, blood-spilling murderers of everyone from Jesus to Palestinian babies in Gaza.

One of these image codes, the "hook-nosed Jew" code, carries the meme that Jews can be identified by their uniquely big noses. Another, the "money-hungry Jew" code carries the belief that Jews are motivated by their avarice, greed, and love of money. In Figure 7, a 2003 cartoon published in *The Chicago Tribune* drawn by Dick Locher, a Pulitzer Prize-winning artist, addresses the question of how to bridge the gulf in Middle East negotiations. The cartoon features a Jew with a huge beak-like nose being tempted to follow a trail of dollar bills.

Figure 7

3. The moral inversion family of codes

The Holocaust and the contemporary targeting of Jews and Jewish institutions by terrorist organizations are an impediment to the portrayal of the Jew as the powerful "devil," referred to earlier as the unifying force needed by mass movements in their quest for power. Memetically, antisemitism and the antisemitic image-codes needed to evolve into a form that denied Jewish victimhood. Moral inversion codes depict the victims as the perpetrators. Thus, the Jew becomes the Nazi or the terrorist suicide bomber, rather than the target or victim!

In Figure 8, a cartoon from Brazil depicts Arabs and a Muslim mosque inside of a "Jewish Prison Camp" with the Israeli guards dressed as Nazis and German writing on the gate.

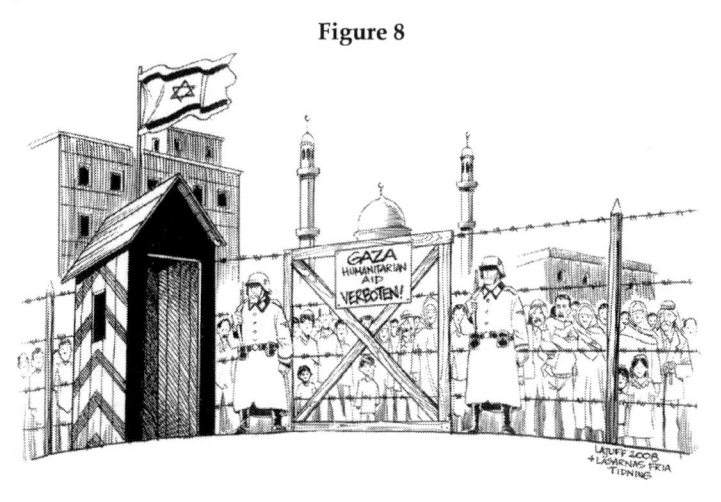

Figure 8

Figure 9

Figure 9 shows the Nazi code in a cartoon from Lebanon.

X. The Star and the Codes

The six-pointed star has been a Middle Eastern, occult, and kabbalistic symbol for centuries, but the use of the six-pointed star to represent Jews and Judaism is a relatively new phenomenon. It was only in the late eighteenth century that the "Star of David" was first used as a Jewish symbol. Today, the Jewish star carries a much broader meaning than the simple identification of a religion or church—it represents Jews, the Jewish people, and Judaism. This is mainly due to the pervasive use of the graphic symbol by the Nazis.

> The most prominent symbol of Judaism throughout the Early Middle Ages was the Torah Shrine. While the Menorah often appeared together with it, the Ten Commandments on tablets, the hands of the Kohanim giving the priestly blessing and even the Temple were more significant than the Star of David and the Menorah. But clearly at the end of the 19th century with the birth of a new more secular definition of Judaism, and as a Jewish nation emerged, symbols were sought which would be easily identifiable, did not have excessive religious connotations (although some was necessary) and which could hearken back to political/national settings without a religious emphasis. The Menorah, which had been a symbol of the Maccabean revolt (the Maccabees were a favorite of the early Zionists and nationalists although the symbol was clearly associated with the Temple), was chosen, and the rather abstract and ignoble "Star of David" whose checkered past was known to only a few scholars, but whose international and universal themes had already emerged as significant among late 19th and early 20th century thinkers.[10]

As a symbol, the "Jewish star" is agglutinative. In other words, when "glued on to" other symbols, it forms a derivative or compound symbol to expresses a single definite meaning. For example, a Jewish star on a spider or an octopus forms a compound code that transmits the dehumanizing zoomorphic message that the Jewish people, the Jewish state, Judaism, and, by extension, the Jewish shopkeeper down the block, for example, are spider-like or octopus-like. See Figures 10 and 11 below.

Figure 10

Die Ausgesaugten

---

[10] Michael Berkowitz, *Nationalism, Zionism and Ethnic Mobilization of the Jews in 1900 and Beyond* (Leiden: Brill, 2004), p. 286.

Figure 11

"Death star" code: In addition to its use in conjunction with other symbols, the "Jewish star" appears independently as a specific code. The "death star" code portrays the star (and hence the Jews, the Jewish state, the Jewish people, and Judaism) as murderous, imprisoning, agents of death, strangling, back-stabbing, and so forth. See Figure 12 from 1930s Nazi propaganda and Figure 13 from *The Seattle Times* in 2003.

Figure 12

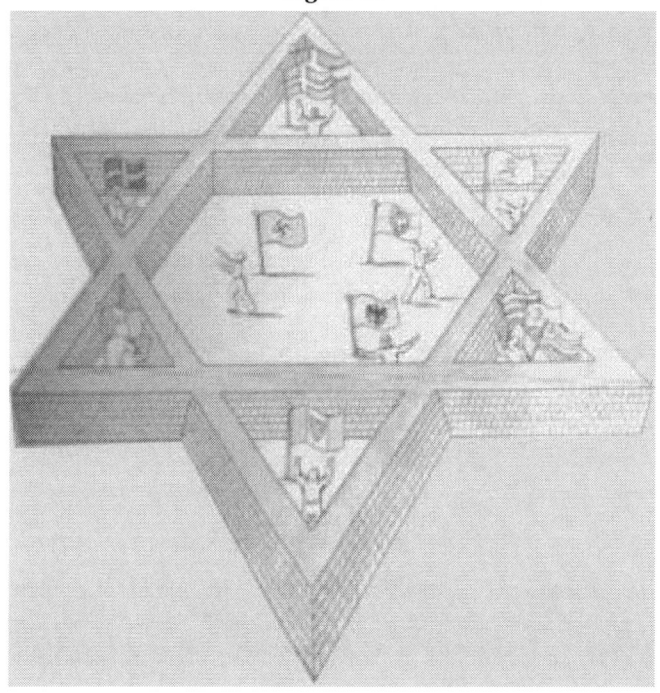

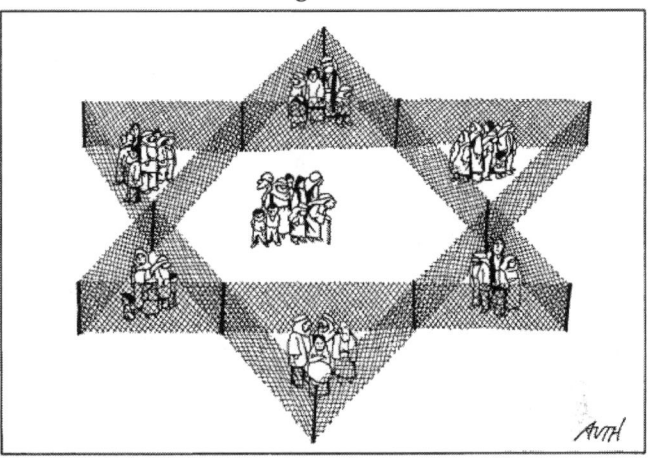

MEMETICS AND THE VIRAL SPREAD OF ANTISEMITISM 451

Figure 13

Clusters: In contemporary political cartoons, the codes often appear in clusters, delivering a set of visual messages. See, for example, the cartoon distributed by the Arab media in Figure 14 below (with an explanation of the individual codes clustered within).

Figure 14

a. The star is a visual tag to indicate that the eater is "the Jews" (or the Jewish state, the Jewish people, or Judaism).
b. The glass of blood is the "blood drinkers" libel code.
c. The dead baby on the plate is the "infanticide" code.
d. The child about to be eaten is the "baby eaters" code.
e. The American flag fork in the hand of "the Jew" communicates the Jewish "world domination" code.

XI. A REPRESENTATIVE SAMPLE

The meme-carrying antisemitic image-codes have survived and replicated themselves in cartoons for more than eighty years, through major social changes. It is equally important to note their viral spread to varied artists of our digital age. Below (Figure 15) is a representative sample of contemporary instances of the "devouring mouth" image-code, which carries the message that Jews devour everything in their path. The "devouring mouth" image relays a basic childhood image of a cannibalistic fiend.

Figure 15

2008 (Syria)

2008 (Jordan)

2007 (Jordan)

MEMETICS AND THE VIRAL SPREAD OF ANTISEMITISM 453

2009 (Jordan)

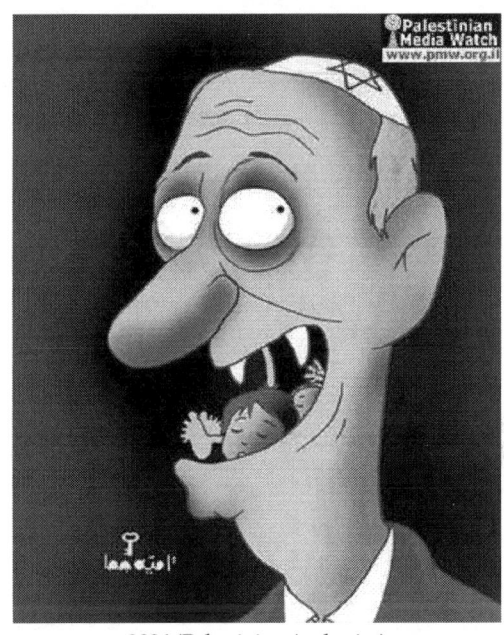

2006 (Palestinian Authority)

2007 (Palestinian Authority)

2007 (Palestinian Authority)

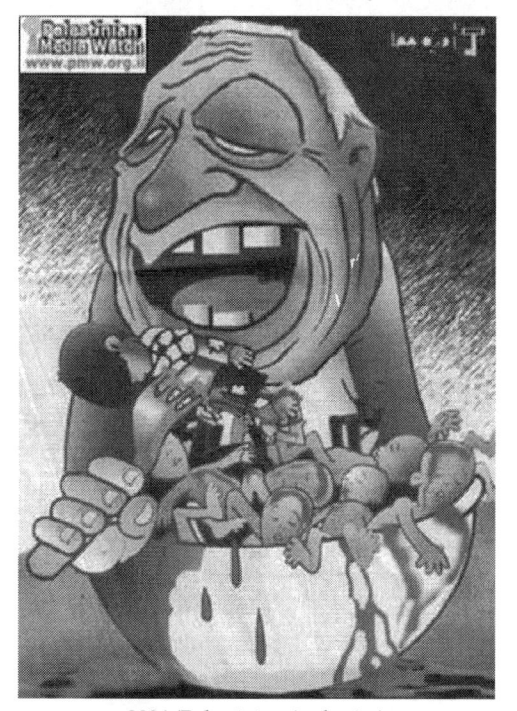

2004 (Palestinian Authority)

2004 (Palestinian Authority)

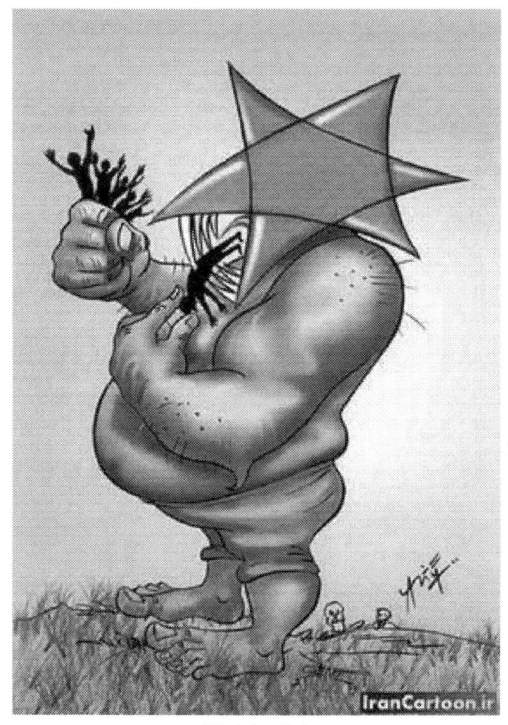

MEMETICS AND THE VIRAL SPREAD OF ANTISEMITISM 455

2006 (India)

2009 (US): A sophisticated cartoon by Pat Oliphant, the most widely syndicated political cartoonist in the world. Note the use of the "devouring mouth" code inside the "death star" code with the moral inversion "Jew as Nazi" code coupled with the "killing children in their mothers' arms" code. The entire cluster of codes can be absorbed subliminally as an image of the flag of Israel, with the two horizontal bars and the star between them. The wheel at the bottom of the star tricks the eye into not seeing the flag.

XII. Conclusions

This paper has demonstrated that there are simple, direct, and fair criteria for diagnosing the presence of antisemitism in political cartoons. Given the fact that the Internet is a natural environment for viral communication and the fact of a post-literate public, we can expect a radical explosion of viral antisemitism fueled by cartoons. The contamination of professional cartoonists in Western countries by the image-codes, and their resultant replication of the codes in their own work, can and should be approached as society approaches any communicable disease. A fundamental element of the defense against contamination is the identification of the viral strains and the conditions and factors involved in the spread of the disease. This paper can serve as the beginning of such a defense.

From Sayyid Qutb to Hamas: The Middle East Conflict and the Islamization of Antisemitism*

Bassam Tibi**

I. INTRODUCTION

The distinguished Princeton historian Bernard Lewis is a leading authority on antisemitism. Earlier in his career, he was honored as the "Dean of Islamic Studies," but this title was abandoned when the field was overtaken by the followers of Edward Said. In both capacities, Lewis has stated in his work that—despite existing tensions—antisemitism is alien to Islam, but that it has been successfully transplanted from Europe to the world of Islam.[1] In my research, I identify this process as the Islamization of European antisemitism. The carrier of this process has traditionally been Sunni Islamism, embodied in the Movement of the Muslim Brothers.[2] An offspring of this movement is Hamas, which has ruled Gaza since 2006. In addition, there is also the Shi'i variety of Islamist antisemitism. While I acknowledge for two reasons that the latter is becoming more dangerous, the present study focuses mainly on the origin of Islamist antisemitism, namely Sunni-Islamist antisemitism, and on the Middle East conflict. The two reasons are that Shi'i Islamists are already in control of Iran and that this state is becoming a nuclear power that targets the Jewish State of Israel.[3] This threat represents an imagined genocidal nuclear antisemitism. However, I will leave this issue aside in order to focus on the above-mentioned problem, which will be dealt with in three steps: (1) identifying the Islamization of antisemitism; (2) introducing the *rector spiritus* of this genocidal ideology; and finally (3) an analysis of the Hamas Charter—the antisemitic agenda of an organization falsely presented as a movement of liberation.

The contemporary Islamization of European antisemitism places additional obstacles in the way of a solution to the conflict in the Middle East. Islamist anti-

---

* Previously published in Charles A. Small, ed., *Global Antisemitism: A Crisis of Modernity* (New York: ISGAP, 2013).
** Professor Emeritus of International Relations, University of Goettingen, Germany; A.D. White Professor-at-Large, Cornell University; Senior Research Fellow, YIISA.

[1] Bernard Lewis, *The Jews of Islam* (Princeton, NJ: Princeton University Press, 1984).
[2] The standard work on this movement is Richard Mitchell, *The Muslim Brothers* (London: Oxford University Press, 1969).
[3] See Shahram Chubin, *Iran's Nuclear Ambitions* (Washington, DC: Carnegie Endowment for International Peace, 2006) and the more recent study by Alireza Jafarzadeh, *The Iran Threat: President Ahmadinejad and the Coming Nuclear Crisis* (New York: Palgrave, 2008).

semitism complicates the search for peace. Based on this assumption, I establish a link between the two elements indicated in the title of this study. First of all, on the grounds of the evidence presented, this study claims to see in this process a direct line from Sayyid Qutb, the intellectual father of Islamism, to Hamas. Second, the tradition and practice of Islamist antisemitism has had—and continues to have—a significant impact on the Middle East conflict.

II. THE CONTEXT

Islamism forms a challenge to the United States.[4] The Bush administration failed to deal with it properly. The inauguration of President Barack Obama was accompanied by the promise of a sea change in U.S. politics. President Obama's first address to the Muslim world in Ankara on April 6, 2009 was lauded by the *New York Times* as a transition from a presidency of the "clash of civilizations" to one of dialogue, combined with the promise of "an active effort to resolve the Israeli-Palestinian conflict."[5] This conflict is examined extensively in the present study.[6] In his second address to the Islamic world in Cairo on June, 4 2009, President Obama listed seven sources of tension, including the Middle East conflict. The president did not shy away from mentioning the Holocaust and antisemitism in this context. However, he did not mention Islamism, despite the need to recognize the fact that this movement and its ideology only deepen the conflict. In the name of peace, Hamas' politics of "resistance" engage in the Islamization of antisemitism. Nevertheless, President Obama's two visits to the Islamic world reflect a serious change in Washington. On the positive side, Turkey is one of the few Islamic states that recognize Israel, and this recognition is bolstered by various security agreements, while Egypt signed a peace treaty with Israel in 1979. On the other hand, Turkey is changing under the Islamist rule of the AKP (see *infra* note 29), and the Muslim Brotherhood has gained control in Egypt since the fall of Mubarak.

It is understandable that President Obama restricted the first step in his attempt to reach out to the Islamic world to underlining what he described as "mutual interest and mutual respect," but in his speech in Ankara he shied away from referring to any conflictual issues, including the Middle East conflict. The above-mentioned article predicted a second step in which the president was expected to acknowledge "not just common ground, but important differences ... including the issues of women's right and freedom of religion" (see *supra* note 5). This second step duly took place in Cairo on June 4, 2009. However, neither President Obama nor the

---

[4] This is the title of and the main idea behind my YIISA lecture delivered at Yale University on April 1, 2009, which is incorporated in the present study. On this Islamist challenge, see Bassam Tibi, *Political Islam, World Politics and Europe: Democratic Peace and Euro-Islam versus Global Jihad* (New York: Routledge, 2008).

[5] See the report "America Seeks Bonds to Islam, Obama Insists," in *The New York Times*, April 7, 2009, p. A1.

[6] On this conflict, see Deborah J. Gerner, *One Land, Two Peoples: The Conflict over Palestine* (Boulder, CO: Westview, 1991). Gerner already states what the conflict is about in the title of her book, which is still valid today. The land has to be shared, but the Islamists reject this vision. For an overview, see Ian Brickerton and Carla Klausner, *Concise History of the Arab-Israeli Conflict* (Upper Saddle River, NJ: Prentice Hall, 1995).

article took account of the pivotal issue of the "Islamization of antisemitism." In the context of the Middle East conflict, this process involves a combination of antisemitism and anti-Americanism. The *New York Times* article is evasive, but the present study is not. It argues that no solution to the Israeli-Palestinian conflict can ever be successful if Islamist antisemitism is not addressed and dealt with candidly. The present study goes beyond these evasions and argues that the religionization of the conflict is rendering it intractable. Conflict resolution requires negotiation, but religious beliefs are non-negotiable. When politics is religionized, the end result is a form of neo-absolutism that dismisses dialogue and compromise.

Hamas' behavior in the Israeli-Palestinian conflict is a case in point. As stated, Hamas is an offspring of the first Islamist-fundamentalist movement in Islam, namely the Movement of the Muslim Brotherhood. This origin is acknowledged in all of Hamas' pronouncements and documents.[7] Hamas has not only religionized the conflict but has also Islamized antisemitism, thus closing the door to a peace based on mutual recognition. The political and secular representative movement of the Palestinians, the Palestine Liberation Organization (PLO), did not have great difficulty in recognizing the State of Israel at the outset of the Oslo Peace Process in 1993. Today, Hamas rejects the recognition of Israel in its Charter and rebuffs all negotiation over Palestine, which is viewed as *waqf* (religious property). From Hamas' perspective it would be a betrayal of Islam to negotiate over sharing the holy land. In short, there is no place for the Jews and their state. The present study examines this polarizing mindset, which results from the Islamization of Palestinian politics and undermines all prospects of Islamic-Jewish reconciliation and peace.[8]

Although it focuses on the Islamization of antisemitism and its effects on the Israeli-Palestinian conflict, the present study does not aim to analyze day-to-day issues. Nevertheless, it is important to touch, in passing, on the post-Gaza war developments, which give rise to misgivings concerning the potential for an appeasement of Hamas. In the West, and particularly in Europe, there is a belief in "the changing face of Hamas." This belief is echoed in the title of an article by Paul McGaugh in the *International Herald Tribune*. In this article, McGaugh quotes from an interview with Hamas leader Khalid Mishal, in which the latter advances the notion that "Hamas has already changed." Nonetheless, Mishal stubbornly responds to questions about "rewriting the Hamas Charter" with the following clear response: "not a chance."[9] It is through this Charter that the Islamization of antisemitism, as initiated by the *rector spiritus* of Islamism, Sayyid Qutb, is continued and politically established. As will be demonstrated in the present study, antisemitism is inherent to a form of Islamist ideology of which the Hamas Charter is not only an expression but also a powerful source.

---

[7] See the excellent study by Matthew Levitt, *Hamas, Politics, Charity and Terrorism in the Service of Jihad* (New Haven, CT: Yale University Press, 2006). Some biased scholars in the U.S. Middle East studies community complained when Yale University Press published this well-researched and revealing study and unjustly accused it of being "anti-Arab."

[8] Beverly Milton-Edwards, *Islamic Politics in Palestine* (London: Tauris, 1996).

[9] Paul McGaugh, "The Changing Face of Hamas," *International Herald Tribune*, April 13, 2009, p. 13.

The idea of a shift from the bullet to the ballot box as applied to Hamas has repeatedly been contradicted by the movement's own actions. In practice, it has not abandoned terrorism and has maintained its commitment to the bullet. After a landslide electoral victory in 2006, Hamas used the military force of its militias to remove all opposition and jail 450 PLO members in 2007.[10] Is this representative of the shift of Islamism to democracy? Unfortunately, there are many precedents for arguing that Islamists cannot be democratic (e.g. Hezbollah in Lebanon and Islamist Shi'i parties in Iraq).[11]

It is unfortunate that the Israeli government did not learn much from the IDF's unsuccessful dealings with Hezbollah in the irregular warfare that characterized the Second Lebanon War of 2006.[12] The same mistakes were repeated in the Gaza War of 2007-2008 with Hamas. In both cases, the outcome was similar. Despite their military losses, both Islamist-Jihadist movements were politically victorious and boasted of their success in the aftermath of the war.[13] As in the case of Hezbollah, the call not to legitimate and strengthen Hamas went unheeded.[14]

The newly envisioned U.S. approach to the Middle East and the Islamic world of the Obama administration must take account of the reality of the combination of anti-Americanism and antisemitism in contemporary Islamist ideology. If it does not, any new policies adopted under this approach will simply represent wishful thinking. One cannot reduce existing anti-Americanism without addressing the antisemitism that underlies it.[15]

To illustrate the point, I refer to a report concerning the Gaza War that appeared a few months after the fighting had ended. In March 2009, *The New York Times* reported that in January 2009, during the Gaza War, Israeli warplanes had bombed a convoy of trucks in Sudan. The convoy was carrying Iranian arms bound for Gaza. Understandably, the Sudanese government kept silent about the incident simply for the sake of convenience. When the arms shipment and the related air strike were disclosed, a Sudanese government spokesman condemned the bombing during a press conference. The attack was described as a "genocide committed by U.S. forces."[16] In this context, one is reminded of the real genocide committed by the Islamist government of Sudan against its own non-Muslim population in Darfur.[17] The Sudanese president, Omar Al-Bashir, is the first sitting president in history to be issued with an arrest warrant by an international court on charges of genocide. The bombing of the Iranian convoy that was smuggling arms to Gaza was a military

---

[10] On the PLO, see Helena Cabban, *The Palestinian Liberation Organization: People, Power, Politics* (New York: Cambridge University Press, 1987).

[11] This argument is elaborated upon by Bassam Tibi, "Islamic Parties: Why Can't They Be Democratic?" in *Journal of Democracy* 91(3) (2008) pp. 43-48.

[12] On the 2006 Lebanon War, see Arnas Harel and Avi Issacharoff, *34 Days: Israel, Hezbollah and the War in Lebanon* (New York: Palgrave, 2008).

[13] See the cover story of *The Economist* of August 19-25, 2006: "Nasrallah Wins the War".

[14] Mark Heller, "Don't Strengthen Hamas," *International Herald Tribune*, January 30, 2009, p. 9.

[15] Bassam Tibi, "Public Policy and the Combination of Anti-Americanism and Antisemitism in Contemporary Islamist Ideology," *The Current* 12(1) (Fall 2008) pp. 123-146.

[16] See "U.S. Officials Say Israel Struck in the Sudan," *New York Times*, March 27, 2009, p. A7.

[17] On political Islam in Sudan, see Dan Patterson, *Inside Sudan: Political Islam, Conflict and Catastrophe* (Boulder, CO: Westview, revised edition, 2003).

action, not genocide. In contrast, the killing in Darfur supported and facilitated by the Sudanese government was an act of genocide. At the aforementioned press conference, various journalists confronted the Sudanese government spokesman with the fact that the bombing was undertaken by Israeli rather than U.S. warplanes. He responded by saying: "We don't differentiate between the U.S. and Israel. They are all one."

It is hard to think of stronger evidence for the combination of anti-Americanism and antisemitism. As will be demonstrated in more detail below, Islamists from Sayyid Qutb to Hamas believe that "the Jews rule America." Today, these Islamists are able to cite a study completed by two U.S. professors alleging that the Israel lobby in Washington designs U.S. foreign policy.[18] This study represented a huge boost for Islamist propaganda. The two professors may not have anything in common with Hamas, but the fact that they are being cited by those who believe in the alleged conspiracy that the Jews rule America demonstrates where this kind of work can lead.[19]

III. WHAT IS THE ISLAMIZATION OF ANTISEMITISM?

The subject of this study is the Islamization of antisemitism and its place in the Middle East conflict. As stated in the introduction, the Islamization of antisemitism was initially a Sunni phenomenon. Several decades later, Ayatollah Khomeini combined enmity toward the United States with Jew-hatred. In doing so, he established a Khomeinist Shi'i variety of antisemitism. This strain of antisemitism, which is incorporated into anti-Americanism, is based on a belief in an alleged Israeli conspiracy to destroy Islam. *The Protocols of the Elders of Zion* are cited as evidence in this context.[20] However, in the Shi'i variety of Islamist antisemitism, "the Jews" do not act for themselves but as a proxy for the United States. Under this approach, the Jewish State of Israel is "identified as an alien essentially Western colonial element in the region and a policeman."[21] This policeman acts in to advance American interests, and for this reason Israel and the Jews are viewed by Iran as a proxy. In spite of this, Iranian President Mahmoud Ahmadinejad has publicly contemplated the extermination of Israel but not of the United States! This suggests that antisemitism is stronger than anti-Americanism.

Even though the present study does not deal directly with Shi'i and Iranian antisemitism, but rather with the Sunni phenomenon, it does not overlook the links that exist between the two. Among these is the fact that Hamas is also supported by Iran.[22] Experts on Iran acknowledge the "latent antisemitism ... that the Islamic

---

[18] The book by John Mearshheimer and Stephen Walt, *The Israel Lobby and U.S. Foreign Policy* (New York: Farrer and Strauss, 2008) is highly contentious. Its impact is also potentially dangerous in terms of its support for Islamist contentions.

[19] On antisemitic conspiracy-driven thinking, see Jeffrey Bale, "Political Paranoia vs. Political Realism: On Distinguishing Between Bogus Conspiracy Theories and Genuine Conspiratorial Politics," *Patterns of Prejudice* 41(1) (2007) pp. 45-60.

[20] Ervand Abrahamian, *Khomeinism* (Berkeley: University of California Press, 1993) pp. 124-125.

[21] Graham Fuller, *The Center of the Universe: The Geopolitics of Iran* (Boulder, CO: Westview, 1991) p. 123.

[22] See Levitt, *supra* note 7, at pp. 172-178.

Republic [of Iran] brought out."[23] In contemporary Sunni Islamism, the anti-Jewish sentiments are different in that they regard the Jewish State of Israel as the "Big Satan," rather than the "Little Satan" acting on behalf of the United States. In contemporary Sunni Islamism, the Islamization of European antisemitism takes a different form. Unlike earlier secular ideologies in the Middle East,[24] Islamism is anti-secular and bases its claims of authenticity on this fact.[25] Islamists have placed a program of purification that targets the Jews on their agenda. In Islamist ideology, the Jews are viewed as those who manipulate others—including the United States—as part of a conspiracy to rule the world.[26] According to this Islamist argument, the Jews are "evil" and contaminate the world to the extent that they deserve to be annihilated. It is important to note that the distinction between Islamism and Islam is essential to this study and guides its argumentation.[27] The very notion of "Islamization" suggests that contemporary antisemitism in the Islamic world rests on an import from Europe. The Islamists equate what has been Islamized with what is authentic, but Islamized antisemitism is not authentic to Islam. Rather, antisemitism is alien to Islam. This statement is supported by Bernard Lewis (see *supra* Introduction). Of course, I do not deny the existence of Judeophobia in traditional Islam, but this is a racist prejudice. Antisemitism is different in view of its genocidal nature. The argument that the Jews are "evil" leads genocidal antisemitism. This ideology was imported from Europe and has been indigenized in process of Islamization. These historical facts contradict Andrew Bostom's contention that "Islamic antisemitism is as old as Islam."[28] This incorrect view of the history has significant consequences because it closes the door to better Jewish-Islamic understanding combined with mutual recognition.

The Obama administration must take account of the existing connection between antisemitism and anti-Americanism in its dealings with Islamism. In Cairo, President Obama unequivocally condemned antisemitism, but in Ankara he ignored the fact that the so-called moderate Turkish AKP supports Hamas and that it is actually an Islamist party.[29] Any dialogue with representatives of the Islamic world must acknowledge this connection as a political reality. This study aims to address the fact

---

[23] Fuller, *supra* note 21, at p. 123.

[24] See Bassam Tibi, "Islam and Modern European Ideologies," in Shahram Akbarzadeh, ed., *Islam and Globalization: Critical Concepts in Islamic Studies*, Vol. 1 (New York: Routledge, 2009) pp. 206-222.

[25] See the chapter on authenticity—a notion often put at the service of Islamist antisemitism in its purification agenda—in Bassam Tibi, *Islam's Predicament with Modernity* (New York: Routledge, 2006) pp. 237-264.

[26] The interesting book by Emmanuel Sivan, *Radical Islam: Medieval Theology and Modern Politics* (New Haven, CT: Yale University Press, 1985) fails to address these issues in Islamism, which Sivan perceives as "radical Islam."

[27] On the distinction between Islam and Islamism, see *Islamism and Islam: A Study of a Significant Distinction* (New Haven, CT: Yale University Press, 2010), which I completed during my time as a Senior Research Fellow at YIISA.

[28] Andrew Bostom, ed., *The Legacy of Islamic Antisemitism* (Amherst, NY: Prometheus, 2008).

[29] On Turkey's AKP Islamists, see Bassam Tibi, "Turkey's Islamist Danger: Islamists Approach Europe," *Middle East Quarterly* 16(1) (Winter 2009) pp. 47-54; see also Zeyno Baran, "The Muslim Brotherhood's U.S. Network," *Current Trends in Islamist Ideology*, Vol. 6 (Washington, DC: The Hudson Institute, 2008) pp. 95-122.

that there is little understanding of the importance of this distinction in the United States. In a Cornell/Princeton study on anti-Americanism in world politics, Katzenstein and Keohone acknowledge that "antisemitism and anti-Americanism often blend seamlessly into one another."[30] This point having been clearly established, the focus of this study now returns to the phenomenon of antisemitism in the Sunni part of the Islamic world.

The aforementioned distinction between Islamist ideology and Islam must be made sharply and strictly not only for academic reasons but also for the sake of pursuing proper policies. Islam and Islamism are not to be confused. The outcome of such confusion would be highly detrimental to the prospects of peace between Islam and Judaism. As already noted, Islamism religionizes politics in the world of Islam, exacerbates conflicts, and places obstacles in the way of their solution. The Islamist obsession with an alliance between the West and Israel, perceived in terms of "crusaderism" (the West) and world Jewry,[31] is even supported in certain U.S. academic works. As already discussed, one work on the Israel lobby supports the Islamist narrative that the Jews rule the United States. The Islamists have gratefully incorporated this contention in their own antisemitism narrative. A similarly useful work on the United States and the West, published by a prominent Ivy League press, is entitled *The New Crusaders*.[32]

In three decades of studying Islamism, I have made an effort to conceptualize my findings with the help of Hannah Arendt's major work, *The Origins of Totalitarianism*.

Arendt argues that antisemitism is an essential element of any totalitarian ideology.[33] In this light, I view Sunni Islamism as the most recent variety of totalitarianism.[34] At this point, I wish to present the hypothesis that Islamism is not only a right-wing ideology in which an Islamization of antisemitism has taken place but also an ideology of polarization that makes conflicts intractable. The new totalitarian ideology of Islamism is based on the politicization of Islam, not traditional Islam. Unlike Christianity,[35] in which European antisemitic ideology is rooted, Islam has no such tradition. Nevertheless, the ideology of Sunni-Islamic fundamentalism has introduced this antisemitism into Islam, and it has been able to take root. The corner-

---

[30] Peter Katzenstein and Robert Keohane, eds., *Anti-Americanisms in World Politics* (Ithaca, NY: Cornell University Press, 2007) p. 22. The volume includes a chapter by Marc Lynch on "Anti-Americanisms in the Arab World" that does not reach the standard of the rest of the volume: it ignores the connection between antisemitism and anti-Americanism, which—as noted—is acknowledged by the editors.

[31] See, for example, the views of Saudi professors Mohammed Jarisha and Yusuf al-Zaibaq, *Asalib al-Ghazu al-fikri lil-alam al-Islami* [Methods of the Intellectual Invasion of the World of Islam] (Cairo: Dar al-I'tisam, second printing, 1978).

[32] Emran Queshi and Michael Sells, eds., *The New Crusaders* (New York: Columbia University Press, 2003) use a slogan employed from the Islamist war of ideas as the title of their book.

[33] The book by Hannah Arendt, *The Origins of Totalitarianism* (New York: Harcourt Inc., 1951, reprinted 1976) served as an inspiration for the present study on the political nature of Islamism. For an earlier example of its impact on my work, see Bassam Tibi, *Der neue Totalitarismus* (Darmstadt: Primus, 2004).

[34] See Tibi, *supra* note 33, as well as Bassam Tibi, "The Totalitarianism of Jihadist Islamism," *Totalitarian Movements and Political Religions* 8(1) (2007) pp. 35-54.

[35] On the medieval Christian roots of antisemitism, see Walter Laqueur, *The Changing Face of Antisemitism* (New York: Oxford University Press, 2006) ch. 3.

stone was laid by Sayyid Qutb, and the effort is continued today by Hamas. Both combine their Jew-hatred with anti-Americanism and believe that the Jews rule the United States through the Israel lobby, which is in control of U.S. foreign policy.

Not only in my capacity as a scholar, but also as a practitioner, who along with the late Rabbi Albert Friedlander established the Jewish-Islamic dialogue,[36] I believe it is essential to keep a community of 1.6 billion Muslim believers free from Islamist antisemitism. In order to do so, it is important to protect Muslims from a susceptibility to this mindset. In this context, I draw attention to the disillusion of moderate Islamism that has developed into a transnational movement in Sunni-Islamism known as "The Moderate Muslim Brotherhood."[37] This movement has been a key source of Islamized antisemitism. The Muslim Brothers have gained a toehold in the United States,[38] and their movement cannot be mollified—as some U.S. academics in the field of Islamic studies who are apologetic to Islamism like to believe.

Having argued that Islamism is the political force that Islamizes antisemitism, I am aware that I am running against the mainstream. In various books and articles published in the West, one encounters many errors and distortions made by scholars who present a false image of Islamism. In a reader on "liberal Islam," for example, one finds the distortion that the Egyptian Muslim Brother Yussaf al-Qaradawi is liberal,[39] whereas al-Qaradawi is in fact the heir of Sayyid Qutb. The following statement of Islamized antisemitism was made by al-Qaradawi in his weekly al-Jazeera TV broadcast: "There is not dialogue between us and the Jews except by the sword and the rifle."[40] Is this the "liberal Islam" that some U.S. pundits present to Western readers? Al-Qaradawi's mentor is Sayyid Qutb. The latter laid the foundations for Islamist antisemitism in combination with anti-Americanism. The narrative of a crusader conspiracy instigated by "the Jews" to destroy Islam is rooted in Qutb's work.[41]

Before introducing Qutb, I wish to touch on the dismissal of antisemitism by the European liberal left, which argues that there is no antisemitism at work, but rather

---

[36] On the Jewish-Islamic dialogue, see Bassam Tibi, *Krieg der Zivilisationen* (Hamburg: Hoffman und Campe, 1995) ch. 6. This dialogue runs counter to the sentiment that Islam is under siege. See Graham Fuller, *A Sense of Siege: The Geopolitics of Islam and the West* (Boulder, CO: Westview, 1995).

[37] See the outrageous allegations made in Robert Leikin and Steven Brooke, "The Moderate Muslim Brotherhood," *Foreign Affairs* (April 2007) 107-121. The allegations are on all counts and by all criteria wrong. Empirically they lack any evidence.

[38] On the Muslim Brothers, see *supra* note 2; on their links in the United States, see Baran, *supra* note 29.

[39] It is astonishing to see the heir of Sayyid Qutb, Yusuf al-Qaradawi, being upgraded to the rank of a "Muslim liberal" through his inclusion in Charles Kurzman, ed., *Liberal Islam: A Sourcebook* (New York: Oxford University Press, 1998) pp. 196-204. Qaradawi's major work, a trilogy entitled *al-Hall al-Islami* (The Islamic Solution) was published in Cairo and Beirut and enjoys frequent reprints. It has been widely disseminated in the Islamic world and is one of the main sources of contemporary totalitarian Islamism.

[40] Qaradawi, quoted in Laqueur, *supra* note 35, at p. 199.

[41] On conspiracy-driven thought, see note 19. On the Arab variety, see Bassam Tibi, *Die Verschwörung. Das Trauma arabischer Politik* (Hamburg: Hoffman & Campe, 1993, expanded second edition 1994). Similar observations are found in Daniel Pipes, *The Hidden Hand, Middle East Fears of Conspiracy* (New York: St. Martin's Press, 1996).

outrage about injustice or opposition to Zionism. Historian Jeffrey Herf edited an excellent volume that came to the conclusion that a new variety of antisemitism is at work.[42] Neither Qutb nor Hamas distinguish between Judaism and Zionism: to them they both mean the same.

The antisemitism of the Islamic Diaspora in Europe is also dismissed as a protest against Israeli policies in the context of the Middle East conflict. In France, antisemitism is rampant in the Islamic Diaspora to the extent that it poses a real security threat to French Jews. U.S. pundit Jonathan Laurence asks whether there is such a thing as specific Muslim antisemitism and answers his own question by stating that, "in the overwhelming majority of cases, antisemitic acts were not elaborate affairs."[43] Together with his co-author, he contends that such acts are based on "anti-Israel" sentiments and a sense of "solidarity with oppressed Palestinians," combined with "feelings of injustice and resentment."[44] In other words, this is not even real antisemitism!

IV. SAYYID QUTB'S NARRATIVE OF ISLAMIST ANTISEMITISM IN *OUR BATTLE AGAINST THE JEWS*

Now that the overall context for the inquiry into the Islamization of antisemitism has been established, it is time to explain why Qutb receives so much attention in the present study? Is he the authoritative source on Islamism and the Islamization of antisemitism? In view of this question, it is important to present some evidence of Qutb's impact. Roxanne Euben, a scholar of Islam, rightly states that

> Qutb's prominence seems an accepted fact....
>
> Qutb's influence is undisputed....
>
> He has altered the very terms of Islamic political debates....[45]

Another scholar of Islam, David Cook, maintains that

> Qutb ... has founded the actual movement...
>
> [He] was the very center of the Arab Muslim political, intellectual and religious debate...
>
> His works have been cited by radical Muslims from the 1960s until the present and his influence upon the movement is significant.[46]

To be sure, Qutb was no lone wolf, and the Movement of the Muslim Brothers committed to his thought is not a band of radical Muslims operating on the fringes of

---

[42] Jeffrey Herf, ed., *Antisemitism and Anti-Zionism in Historical Perspective* (New York: Routledge, 2007) in particular the Introduction by Herf (pp. x-xix) and the chapter by Markovits (pp. 71-91).

[43] Jonathan Laurence and Justin Vaisse, *Integrating Islam* (Washington, DC: Brookings Institution, 2006) p. 233.

[44] Id., at p. 237.

[45] Roxanne Euben, *The Enemy in the Mirror: Islamic Fundamentalism and the Limits of Modern Rationalism* (Princeton, NJ: Princeton University Press, 1999) ch. 3, p. 55.

[46] David Cook, *Understanding Jihad* (Berkeley: University of California Press, 2004) pp. 102-103.

Islam. In fact, there is a powerful mass movement inspired by Qutb's views on the Jews and the United States. Anti-Jewish resentments, identified here as Judeophobia, have existed throughout history. Unlike this traditional anti-Jewish bias, however, the basic feature of Islamist antisemitism is the implicit desire to annihilate the Jews, who are characterized as "evil." I therefore distinguish between antisemitism as a murderous ideology and the racist prejudices of Jew-hatred known as Judeophobia. Antisemitism is associated with a call for genocide. Nothing like contemporary Islamist antisemitism ever existed in classic Islamic history or thought.

The story of antisemitism, in the modern understanding of the term, did not start with Islamism in the Middle East, the core of the Islamic world, but rather with the secular pan-Arab nationalist ideologies. The antisemitism of the pan-Arab nationalists has been converted through the prism of Islamism into an Islamist form of antisemitism.[47] As a result of its Islamization, this ideology can no longer be regarded as a foreign import, although its roots are still in European antisemitism. The carrier of this trend is political Islam, which is also known as Islamism or Islamic fundamentalism. The main ideological source of political Islam is the work of Sayyid Qutb. Qutb spent two years in the United States (1948-1950) and became a major Islamist figure after joining the Muslim Brotherhood upon his return to Egypt. Based on his sojourn in the United States, Qutb developed a hatred of the West. He also claimed to know America from the inside, concluding that the Jews rule the United States. Qutb is thus one of the main propagators of this image of the role of the Jews in the United States.

The ideas of Sayyid Qutb have placed an authoritative stamp on Islamism. All the basic features of Islamism emanate from Qutb's work, including his Jew-hatred. In contrast to the secular pan-Arab nationalists, Qutb did not confine his efforts to "translating" European antisemitism into a local form of antisemitism. He wanted more: the Islamization of antisemitism was meant to imbue it with authenticity. Qutb was executed by the Egyptian authorities in 1966, a year before the country's devastating military defeat in the 1967 Six-Day War. This defeat contributed to the end of pan-Arab nationalism and the spread of Islamist ideas across the Middle East at the expense of the region's defeated secular regimes. These authoritarian regimes, which had been legitimized by secular pan-Arabism, lost their legitimacy in the post-1967 developments.[48] In this environment, the Islamist antisemitism became increasingly powerful. This summary does not deliberately ignore the fact that Islamism has existed since 1928, prior to the emergence of the current Israeli-Palestinian conflict. At that time, however, Islamism was not yet as mainstream as it is today. Islamism did not become visible or appealing until the 1967 defeat. Both

---

[47] For more details, see Matthias Küntzel, *Jihad and Jew-Hatred: Islamism, Nazism and the Roots of 9/11* (New York: Telos Press, 2007) pt. 2.

[48] The best study of these developments is Fouad Ajami, *The Arab Predicament* (New York: Cambridge University Press, 1981). For more details on the history of Arab nationalism, see Bassam Tibi, *Arab Nationalism: Between Islam and the Nation-State* (New York: Macmillan, 3rd edition, 1997). On the political thought of Husri, see parts III and IV of the same book. On the 1967 Six-Day War and its repercussions (e.g. delegitimization), see Bassam Tibi, *Conflict and War in the Middle East: From Inter-State War to New Security* (New York: St. Martin's Press, 2nd edition, 1998) ch. 3 and 4.

Islamism and Islamist antisemitism are based on the legacy of Sayyid Qutb, although he never witnessed this success. In a 65-page pamphlet, Qutb laid down the aforementioned foundations for the Islamization of antisemitism. It is worth noting that his execution in Cairo in 1966 was ordered by the most popular pan-Arabist hero of the day, Gamal Abdel Nasser. A year after Qutb's death, his ideas moved from the fringe to become a mobilizing ideology not only in the Middle East but also throughout the Islamic world.[49]

In his antisemitic pamphlet *Our Battle Against the Jews*, Qutb pays tribute to the young people that joined forces with his movement "not for the sake of any material benefits, but simply to die and sacrifice one's own life."[50] This glorification of death, earlier emphasized by the founder of the Muslim Brothers, Hasan al-Banna, in his *Essay on Jihad*,[51] is alien to the ethics of life in Islam. In fact, it more closely reflects Sorel's fascist *Réflections sur la violence* (1908). This Islamist glorification of death is also what justifies suicide terrorism.

According to the Islamist ideology of al-Banna and Qutb, Muslims are supposed to die in a "cosmic" war against the Jews. According to Qutb, Muslims have no choice in this regard because the Jews themselves launched this war after the birth of Islam in Medina in 622. Qutb refrains from referring to the year 610 as the real beginning of Islam with Mohammed's revelation. There are two reasons for this. First, between 610 and 622, the Prophet was positive about the Jews. He viewed them as allies and prayed in the direction of Jerusalem, not Mecca. That changed in 622. The second reason is that Meccan Islam (610-622) was purely spiritual, whereas Medina Islam from 622 onward also incorporated politics.

Qutb regarded the Jews as "evil" and viewed them as the main enemy of Islam since the beginning of its history. Qutb accused the Jews of using their *la'ama* or wickedness to destroy Islam. Qutb claimed that

> this is an enduring war that will never end, because the Jews want no more no less than to exterminate the religion of Islam.... Since Islam subdued them [in Medina] they are unforgiving and fight furiously through conspiracies, intrigues and also through proxies who act in the darkness against all what Islam incorporates.[52]

The Islamists believe that they must fight back in the so-called "cosmic" war allegedly launched by the Jews. This war, as the work of Sayyid Qutb suggests, targets not only the Jews but also "America."[53]

---

[49] Carrie Rosefsky Wickham, *Mobilizing Islam: Religion, Activism and Political Change in Egypt* (New York: Columbia University Press, 2002).

[50] Sayyid Qutb, *Ma'rakatuna ma'a al-Yahud* [Our Battle with the Jews] (Cairo: Dar al-Shuruq, 10th legal edition, 1989) p. 15.

[51] Hasan al-Banna's *Risalat al-Jihad* [Essay on Jihad] is the cornerstone of the development from classical Jihad to Jihadism. The essay is included in al-Banna's collection of essays: Hasan al-Banna, *Majmu'at Rasail al-Imam al-Shahid* [Collected Writings of the Martyr Imam] (Cairo: Dar al Da'wa, legal edition, 1990), pp. 271-291.

[52] Qutb, *supra* note 50, at p. 33.

[53] For more details on this issue, see Salah A. al-Khalidi, *Amerika min al-dakhil bi minzar Sayyid Qutb* [America Viewed from the Inside Through the Lenses of Sayyid Qutb] (al-Mansura (Egypt) and Jedda (Saudi Arabia): Dar al-Manara, 3rd edition, 1987).

The "cosmic" war is also a "war of ideas." This notion has become popular in the West since 9/11.[54] However, this idea is Islamist in origin rather than being a Western creation. In support of this contention, it is possible to quote Qutb, who argues: "The Jews do not fight in the battlefield with weapons ... they fight in a war of ideas through intrigues, suspicions, defamations and maneuvering," thus demonstrating their "wickedness and cunning." This 0quote reveals that Qutb was also an early proponent of the concept of the "war of ideas," which is also a war of propaganda.[55]

Despite Qutb's attempt to portray Islamist antisemitism as an authentic ideology, he does not refrain from explicitly drawing on one infamous European source, namely the fraudulent *Protocols of the Elders of Zion*. Qutb quotes this "source" repeatedly in support of his allegations. The Protocols are quoted throughout Islamist writing. However, Qutb incorporates European antisemitism into Islamic history to imbue it, through selective religious arguments, with an authentic Islamic shape. This fabricated authenticity is reflected in the narrative that appears in Qutb's *Ma'arakatuna ma'a al-Yahud* (Our Battle Against the Jews). As already mentioned, Islamic-Jewish enmity, as described by Qutb, begins in 622 with the establishment of the Islamic polity of Medina. There is no talk about Palestine. According to Qutb, this enmity prevails throughout Islamic history, stretching all the way to the present. These facts undermine the claim that the conflict over Palestine is the source of wider conflict, which is allegedly *not* antisemitic.

The first Arab antisemites were Christians, followed by Muslim secular pan-Arabists who had studied in Europe. Their antisemitism was simply a reproduction of the imported European view. The Islamization of this murderous ideology, which gives antisemitism an authentic Islamic shape, is the work of Qutb. In this way, it becomes a public choice in Islamist ideology. Antisemitism is no longer restricted to secular Westernized elites.

Qutb was a well-educated Muslim who knew the Qur'anic distinction between *ahl-al-kitab* or "people of the book" (namely Jews and Christians)—who are acknowledged as believers—and the *kuffar* or "unbeliever." However, he spoke of *al-kaffar al-Yahud* or the "Jewish unbeliever," which in Qur'anic terms is a contradiction. Qutb legitimated this deviation from the religious doctrine by alleging that they "who were originally in fact included in *ahl-al-kitab* community diverted, however, from the very beginning.... They committed *shruk* or unbelief and became the worst enemies of believers."[56] Based on this interpretation, Qutb used religious terms to paint a picture of enmity between Islam and the Jews in order to justify a cosmic war against the Jews. This enmity allegedly commenced: "From the very first moment, when an Islamic state was established in Medina, as it was opposed by the Jews, who acted against Muslims on the first day when those united themselves in one *umma*."[57] Qutb continued this propaganda on two levels. The first was his invented

---

[54] Walid Phares, *The War of Ideas: Jihadism against Democracy* (New York: Palgrave, 2007); Zeyno Baran, "Fighting the War of Ideas," *Foreign Affairs* (November/December 2005) pp. 68-78. See also Eric Patterson, ed., *The War of Ideas* (New York: Palgrave, 2010).

[55] Qutb, *supra* note 50.

[56] Id., at p. 31.

[57] Id., at p. 31.

history of the interaction of Jews with Islam. The second level of Qutb's antisemitism involved psychological and anthropological aspects, such as the description of *simat al-Yahud* or the basic traits of the Jews. In his unequivocally antisemitic language, expressed through an invented "history" and "anthropology" of the Jews, Qutb laid the foundations for an Islamized antisemitism. According to this ideology, the Jews are the source of all evil. The clear implication is that the annihilation of the Jews is a requirement for ending the aforementioned "cosmic war". This is what Qutb regards as an "Islamic peace."[58]

It is important to recall that Qutb began his narrative with the foundation of the polity of Medina in 622, which he wrongly labeled as *dawla* or "state." It is an historical and philological fact that the term "state" was not used in those times, nor does it appear in the vocabulary of the Qur'an or the *hadith* (the authoritative canonical records of the prophet). The war with the Jews must be continued throughout Islamic history. Qutb summed up the reasons for the war in a passage that deserves to be quoted at length. The text begins with a question concerning the source of "evil" and answers this question with one word: *Yahudi* or a "Jew." The following quote seems to implicitly legitimate a purification—a kind of a new Holocaust. However, this is an imaginary Holocaust, because Islamists still lack the power and resources to implement their Islamist ideology. Qutb asks:

> Who tried to undermine the nascent Islamic state in Medina and who incited Quraish in Mecca, as well as other tribes against the foundation of this state? It was a Jew! Who stood behind the *fitna*-war and the slaying of the third caliph Osman and all the tragedies that followed hereafter? It was a Jew! And who inflamed national divides against the last caliph and who stood behind the turmoil that ended the Islamic order with the abolition shari'a? It was Ataturk, a Jew! The Jews always stood and continue to stand behind the war waged against Islam. Today, this war persists in the Islamic revival in all places on earth.[59]

In the next section, there is a similar quote from the Hamas Charter, which closely follows the style and substance of this text by Qutb. The Hamas Charter also supports the annihilation of Jews in order to erase the main "source of evil" in the world. Historically speaking, the aforementioned antisemitic beliefs, which are couched in religious terms, are wrong in that they run counter to all historical records and facts. These beliefs serve to underpin the view that there can never be a settlement, reconciliation, or compromise with the Jews. Qutb believed that the Jews "use all weapons and instruments employed in their genius of Jewish cunning."[60] He adds to this *amaqariyyat al-makr* or "genious of cunning" the pursuit of their "malicious conspiracy." According to this mindset, it is the Jews, not the Muslims, who are committed to waging this never-ending cosmic war. Jihad is merely a defensive measure. The aggressors are the Jews. In response to the question why the Jews would want to carry out all of these "assaults" against Islam Qutb's answer is the "Jewish character."

---

[58] Sayyid Qutb, *al-Salam al-alami wa al-Islam* [World Peace and Islam] (Cairo: Dar al-Shuruq, 10th legal edition, 1992).

[59] Qutb, *supra* note 50, at p. 33.

[60] Id., at p. 32.

The nature of this "Jewish character" can de deduced from Qutb's depiction of "the Jews," in which attributes such as "evil" and "wickedness" prevail. The logical conclusion is that the solution to the problem lies in the annihilation of the Jews. The Islamic world's approval of what happened in Europe between 1933 and 1945 has clear implications. Qutb repeats the accusation that "they [the Jews] killed and massacred and even dismembered the bodies of a number of their own prophets.... So what do you expect from people who do this to their prophets other than to be blood-letting and to target all of humanity!"[61] This accusation amounts to a sanction to "liberate humanity" from this "evil." This genocidal antisemitism was alien to classical Islam and cannot be compared with pre-existing Islamic Judeophobia. The notion of an "Islamic legacy of antisemitism" is therefore fundamentally wrong.

In short, the "Islamization" of this European ideology refers to an undertaking more dangerous than any of its secular precedents because the action in question has turned an alien ideology into a supposedly authentic Islamist ideology. In its local version, antisemitism is no longer an import from Europe and is therefore more appealing. This explains why the Islamized ideology has been able to take root and gain strength from the popular sentiment of anti-Americanism. Thus combined, the ideology today prevails throughout the Islamic world. Islamists believe that the alliance between the United States and Israel has given rise to a "crusader-Zionist" *harban salibiyya-sahyuniyya* or "war against every root of the religion of Islam."[62] This perception is also at the root of the concept of "Islam under siege." Islamists following Qutb believe in a "conspiracy" against Islam hatched by "world Jewry" and "world Zionism," in alliance with the United States. This belief conflates the "Zionists" and "the Jews" to describe the same people. In Islamist writing, these terms are used interchangeably, while Americans are described as the "new crusaders." Qutb is firmly convinced that "the Jews were the instigators from the outset. The crusaders only followed later."[63] Thus the *salibiyyun* are downgraded to "executioners of the Jews."

The main source of Islamist antisemitism in the Islamic world is Qutb's writing. The findings in this section contradict the allegation that the Bush administration's flawed Middle East policy and Israeli injustices against the Palestinians in the occupied territories explain Jew-hatred. The truth is that the conflation of "world Jewry" and "world Zionism," which are viewed as the instigators of the U.S.-led war against Islam, predates President Bush. In short, the real issue is the "Islamization of antisemitism" as carried out by Qutb.

In terms of policy, the issue can be articulated in the following manner. Islamized antisemitism was introduced by the political thought of Sayyid Qutb. In order to counter it, it is necessary to engage in a Jewish-Christian-Muslim trialogue. This is more promising than the failed policy of an indiscriminate "war on terror," as unsuccessfully pursued by the Bush administration and ended by President Obama. Even though the U.S. Holocaust museum is a federal agency, it acts independently and has supported the efforts of John Roth and Leonard Grob to establish a tria-

---

[61] Id., at p. 27.
[62] Id., at p. 33.
[63] Id., at p. 23.

logue.[64] In such a trialogue, one cannot be silent about political Islam being the source of the racist "new antisemitism" nor about the inappropriate policies pursued by the United States in order to deal with it.

The Islamist notion of "Islam under siege,"[65] fighting a Jihad against a Jewish-American conspiracy, finds its origins in the work of Qutb. Those who belittle the impact of Qutb overlook his powerful characterization of "the Jews" as "evil" and the implication of an imagined Holocaust as a solution. Qutb's antisemitism is not a minority view. Qutbism has become the cornerstone of the political and religious thought of most contemporary Islamist movements. One can safely state that Qutb's ideas have become the main source for the Islamist worldview that serves as a basis for Islamized antisemitism and anti-Americanism.

Once again, it is important to recall the distinction between Islam and Islamism. My research on Islamist antisemitism at the Yale Initiative for the Interdisciplinary Study of Antisemitism (YIISA), on which this study is based, revolves around this distinction.[66] This distinction in not only rejected by Islamists but unfortunately also by U.S.-based students of Islam influenced by Saidism. The Islamists do so in the context of their war of ideas against the West, which is simultaneously an act of purification or de-Westernization. In this war, the work of Qutb has a great impact.[67] His antisemitism is articulated in the language of Islamic fundamentalism,[68] which promotes the above-mentioned convergence of globalization and fragmentation.[69] Political Islam has declared a war of ideas on the United States and the Jews in order to counter their cultural impact.

Today, the tradition of Qutb is represented by the global Mufti Yusuf al-Qaradawi and his subservient followers.[70] The Islamist movement that adheres to their ideology continues the Islamization of European antisemitism based on the ideology of Qutb. The purpose of these efforts is to create an air of authenticity. Mohammed Jarisha and Yusuf al-Zaibaq, two Saudi professors who also engage in "reasoning" loyal to Qutb, state:

---

[64] See John Roth and Leonard Grob, eds., *Encountering the Stranger: A Jewish-Christian-Muslim Trialogue* (University of Washington Press, 2012), which grew from a project at the Center for Advanced Holocaust Studies, Washington, DC.

[65] On the perception of Islam under siege, see Graham Fuller and Ian Lesser, *A Sense of Siege: The Geopolitics of Islam and the West* (Boulder, CO: Westview 1995).

[66] See Tibi, *supra* note 27. For earlier contributions on this theme, see Bassam Tibi, "Between Islam and Islamism," in Tamy A. Jacoby and Brent Sasley, eds., *Redefining Security in the Middle East* (Manchester: Manchester University Press, 2002) pp. 62-82; and also Peter Demant, *Islam vs. Islamism: The Dilemma of the Muslim World* (Westpoint, CT: Praeger, 2006).

[67] The trajectory of Islamism is outlined in Qutb's most influential book: Sayyid Qutb, *Ma'alim fi al-tariq* [Signposts along the Road] (Cairo: Dar al-shuruq, 13th legal edition, 1989).

[68] On the overall context of political Islam, see Bassam Tibi, *The Challenge of Fundamentalism* (Berkeley: University of California Press, 1998, updated edition 2001) and my more recent monograph referenced in note 4.

[69] On the simultaneity of globalization and fragmentation, see Bassam Tibi, *Islam Between Culture and Politics* (New York: Palgrave, 2001, updated edition 2005) ch. 4. This concept has been further elaborated upon in Bassam Tibi, "Global Communication and Cultural Pluralism: The Place of Values in the Simultaneity of Structural Globalization and Cultural Fragmentation," in Robert Fortner, ed., *The Handbook of Global Communication* (Oxford: Blackwell, 2010).

[70] See Yusuf al-Qaradawi, *Hatimiyyat al-hall al-Islami, Vol. 1: al-Hulul al-mustawradah* [The Imported Solutions] (Cairo: Mu'ussasat al-Risalah, reprinted 1980).

> The West Waves the flag of secularism ... invades with its new values the society of Islam to replace the Islamic values.... We shall talk about Zionism, or world Jewry, in order to address the related master plan pursued by the related secret societies for the destruction of the world.[71]

The alleged master plan is then identified by these two Saudi professors as a "Jewish conspiracy." This quote resembles a textbook definition of Islamist anti-Westernism guided by antisemitism. The "Christian West," as represented by the United States, acts against Islam as a proxy for the Jews. The overall context is a universal conspiracy aimed at destroying Islam. The full equation of the terms *sahyuniyya* or "Zionism" and *al-Jahudiyya al-alamiyya* or "world Jewry," as included in the quote, not only indicates a continuation of the thinking of Qutb but also contradicts all arguments to the contrary. This equation supports the assertion that the claim that "anti-Zionism is not anti-semitism" is entirely baseless. This false claim is not only made on intellectual grounds. It is also political in that is serves to mask and legitimate real antisemitism under the cover of opposition to the injustices inflicted on Muslims by Zionism. In the narrative of the Islamists, Islam is an embattled religion, encircled by a Jewish-crusader alliance embodied by the United States. In this Islamist narrative, Islam is "under siege" and Islamism is the only appropriate response.

To summarize, the Islamization of antisemitism is a process based on the Islamist contention regarding an alliance between Judaism and crusaderism. In order to counter both "evils,'" Islamists must conduct a global Jihad in a cosmic war against the Jews. This Jihad is not to be confused with terrorism. There are peaceful Islamists, like the Turkish AKP, who also fight this Jihad and support Hamas. Then there is the Jihadist branch of political Islam. Both types of Islamists share the same worldview, as proven by John Kelsay.[72] From this Islamist perspective, Islamic civilization is viewed as the victim, besieged by an imaginary world Jewry. Qutb described the "Jew" as an "evil-doer" who pulls the strings and is therefore responsible for all the wrongdoings to which Islam has been exposed. This supposedly applies from the birth of the Islamic polity in 622 all the way up to the present. All aspects of the ideology of political Islam are rooted in the political-religious thought of Qutb, which is promoted today by Yusuf al-Qaradawi.

Building on the above analysis, I will examine the case of Hamas in the next section. Hamas demonstrates how Qutb's ideas are transformed into political action. Qutbism guides a powerful movement that is committed to the idea that the "fight between Islam and the Jews is permanent due to the uncompromising will of the Jews to destroy Islam."[73] Hamas not only espouses Islamized antisemitism but also pursues a religionized political ideology. Hamas claims to preempt the Jewish agenda by turning the tables on the Jews. The perpetrators are threatened with an imagined Holocaust. This murderous Islamist antisemitism is in many ways different from the earlier secular antisemitism of the pan-Arab nationalists. Those who claim to see a similarity, or even continuity, are wrong. There is a clear distinction

---

[71] Jarisha and Zaibaq, *supra* note 31, at pp. 3-4.

[72] John Kelsay, *Arguing for a Just War in Islam* (Cambridge, MA: Harvard University Press, 2007) p. 165 ff.

[73] Qutb, *supra* note 50, at p. 36. See also the chapter by Marc Lynch in Katzenstein and Keohane, *supra* note 30, at p. 207.

between the three anti-Jewish phenomena in the world of Islam's core in the Middle East: (1) traditional Judeophobia; (2) secular pan-Arab antisemitism; and, most recently, (3) Islamized antisemitism as established by Sayyid Qutb.

V. FROM ISLAMIST IDEOLOGY TO JIHADIST ACTION: SAYYID QUTB'S EXECUTIONERS—HAMAS

Those who regard the movement of the Muslim Brothers, which is the foundational manifestation of political Islam, as a moderate representation of Islamism overlook the facts on the ground. Former U.S. President George W. Bush, who was not the first to talk about the evils of Islamism, was also characterized by the same obsession. Islamism has revived the dichotomy between pre-Islamic ignorance, known as *jahiliyya*, and the revelation of Islam that claims to be the absolute truth. For Qutb, modernity represents a setback and a return to *jahiliyya* in a modern form. This neo-*jahiliyya* is what is evil. It is embodied by the Jews. As Marc Lynch observes, Qutb regards the confrontation between Islam and evil as a zero-sum game. However, he shies away from identifying the "evil" in question. For Qutb, these are—as shown above—the Jews and the crusaders. As already stated, the heir of Qutb is al-Qaradawi, who is not "moderate," as wrongly stated in the aforementioned Cornell/Princeton study. In fact, al-Qaradawi condones global Jihad against the United States and the Jews, who supposedly rule the United States indirectly.

A proper understanding of the Islamist movement of Hamas requires an understanding of its roots in the ideology of the Muslim Brotherhood. Hamas subscribes to this ideology and acknowledges being its offspring. One also needs to understand the overall context of the return of the sacred.[74] In this context, religion becomes a component of world politics while maintaining regional variations. 9/11 represents a watershed in this process. The global religionization of conflict adopts a different regional shape in the Middle East and elsewhere in the Islamic world (e.g. South and Southeast Asia). This religionization becomes a source of tension.[75] At issue is a general phenomenon that materializes in regional and local conflicts and makes such conflicts intractable. This insight is very important for understanding how "Islam's civil war" has turned into a "geo-civil war."[76] The Middle East conflict is deeply affected by this global development. In particular, the Arab-Israeli conflict and its Palestinian component are affected. Political Islam is replacing pan-Arab nationalism.[77] In this environment of religionized politics, one can also observe an Islamiza-

---

[74] On the debate of the "return of the sacred," a formula coined by the Harvard sociologist Daniel Bell, see the new chapter 11 completed for the 2005 edition of Bassam Tibi, *Islam Between Culture and Politics, supra* note 36, at pp. 232-272. Both editions were published in association with Harvard's CFIA.

[75] On this religionization as a source of tension, see Bassam Tibi, "Islam: Between Religious-Cultural Practice and Identity Politics," in Y. Raj Isar and Helmut Anheier, eds., *Tensions and Conflict: The Culture of Globalization Series*, Vol. 1 (New York: Sage, 2007) pp. 221-231.

[76] John Brenkman, *The Cultural Contradictions of Democracy* (Princeton, NJ: Princeton University Press, 2007) pp. 165-69, also p. 158.

[77] On Islam in the Middle East conflict, see Rifaat S. Ahmed, *al-Islam wa qadaya al-sira'al-Arabi al-Israeli* [Islam and Conflict: Studies on Islam and the Arab-Israeli Conflict] (Cairo: Dar al-Sharqiyya, 1989), see also Beverly Milton-Edwards, *Islamic Politics in Palestine* (London: Tauris, 1996 and 1999).

tion of Palestinian politics. Hamas is not a nationalist movement and dissociates itself from Palestinian secular nationalism. This has given rise to an intra-Palestinian struggle between Islamists and secular Palestinian nationalists.[78]

Against this background, Hamas acts in the context of transnational religion. Palestinian Islamist Muhsin al-Antabawi explains this concept in a pamphlet entitled: *Why Do We Reject Any Peace with the Jews*.[79] This is a publication, written on behalf of the Islamic Association of Palestinian Students in Kuwait, that articulates how a religionized conflict becomes intractable. In the specific Palestinian context, one encounters Qutb's earlier general contention that "there can be no peace between Muslims and Jews." This view, which is also held by Hamas, is applied to the conflict between Israel and Palestine. Hamas therefore cannot be appeased, nor can Iran, the regional promoter of this Islamist movement. As a result of the U.S.-Iraq war, Iran has become a regional power in the Middle East.

What matters here is Hamas' commitment to an Islamized form of antisemitism. The *al-Yahud* or "the Jews" are clearly indicated in an antisemitic manner by the term *al-sahyuniyun* or the "Zionists." Unlike Iranian President Mohammed Ahmadinejad, who was at pains to disguise his antisemitism as anti-Zionism in his well-known speech of 2007, the Palestinian al-Antabawi does not employ such camouflage. Al-Antabawi regards all Jews as part of the anti-Islamic Zionist entity. For him, all Jews are permanently conspiring in a cosmic war against Islam. His first conclusion is therefore that the Jews can never be appeased. His second conclusion is that "the solution for Palestine can only be brought by a generation mobilized against the Jews on the grounds of a combination of the Qur'an with the gun."[80] The outcome of this mobilization would appear to be the aforementioned imagined Holocaust, since there appears to be no middle way. This is the ideology of Hamas.

Clearly, Hamas represents the Palestinian variety of Islamism, which is not a religious form of nationalism as some observers argue. Instead, the movement is embedded in transnational religion. Its roots are also in the transnational Movement of the Muslim Brotherhood, and its discourse is based on the ideas of Sayyid Qutb as outlined above. To reiterate, in his pamphlet *Ma'arakatuna ma'a al-Yahud* (Our Battle Against the Jews), Qutb laid the foundations for a new pattern of Jew-hatred in political Islam, which is the origin of the Islamization of antisemitism. It is worth quoting Qutb's claim that "the Jews continue to be perfidious and sneaky, and try to mislead the Islamic *umma* in diverting it away from its religion" in order to illustrate his belief that all the tragedies that befall the Muslim *umma* stem from "Jewish conspiracies." Qutb uses this hatred of the Jews to justify a cosmic war against the

---

[78] On Palestinian nationalism, see Muhammed Mulish, *The Origins of Palestinian Nationalism* (New York: Columbia University Press, 1988). On the fight between Palestinian secularists and Islamists, see Loren Lybarger, *Identity Politics and Religion in Palestine: The Struggle between Islamism and Secularism* (Princeton, NJ: Princeton University Press, 2007); and Amal Jamal, *The Palestinian National Movement: The Politics of Contention* (Bloomington, IN: Indiana University Press, 2005).

[79] Mushin al-Antabawi, *Limatha narud al-Salam ma'a al-Yahud* [Why Do We Reject Peace with the Jews] (Cairo: Kitab al-Mukhtar, n.d.). This publication was completed at the order of the Islamic Association of Palestinian Students at the University of Kuwait, as stated in the pamphlet.

[80] Id.

Jews. This war is also being fought by Hamas, which promotes Islamist tradition and transfers its views into a political agenda. European politicians and opinion makers who want to accommodate Hamas in an inclusive approach seem to know nothing about Hamas' political agenda or Islamist antisemitism, which has been analyzed by Matthias Küntzel in a superb study.[81]

Hamas' Palestinian variety of Islamism reflects the Jew-hatred of political Islam, since it shares the Islamist belief in a conspiracy against Islam that was initiated by the Jews and continued by the crusaders. The secular PLO is still in place, but it has been virtually replaced by Hamas, which not only rules Gaza but is also very popular in the West Bank. In an important contribution to the study of Islamist antisemitism, German political scientist Matthias Küntzel notes about the Hamas Charter: "In every respect, Hamas' new document put the 1968 PLO Charter in the shade. … The Hamas Charter probably ranks as one of contemporary Islamism's most important programmatic document and its significance goes far beyond the Palestine conflict."[82] For this reason, the Hamas Charter deserves closer analysis as a prominent example of Islamized antisemitism. Even in the West, Hamas has received a certain amount of respect and attention. In Europe, Hamas is perceived positively by the liberal left as a liberation movement acting against "oppressors." However, the movement's success in the elections of January 2006 has been tainted by its terrorist actions in 2007. It continues to be an anti-American and antisemitic organization, as characterized by Andrew Levitt.[83]

The Hamas Charter clearly indicates the transnational character of the movement. Article 2 acknowledges that Hamas is rooted in the Movement of the Muslim Brotherhood.[84] This movement currently represents one of the four major branches of internationalist Islamism. In its first pronouncement on December 14, 1988, Hamas announced itself as "the armed hand of the Muslim Brotherhood." Article 32 of the Charter identifies "world Zionism" as the enemy; there is no mention of Israel. This shows that Islamism regards the conflict over Palestine as part of a cosmic war against what Qutb described as "world Jewry." Hamas perceives itself as a *ra's hurbah* or "spearhead" in this cosmic war against "world Zionism." All Muslims who fail to share this view are vilified.

There are two references in the Hamas Charter that are clearly indicative of the religionization of the conflict. The first refers to the "secret plans" in *The Protocols of the Elders of Zion* in order to unveil the "wickedness of the Jews," while the second relates to the allegation that the "Zionist master plan or conspiracy" knows no boundaries: "today Palestine, tomorrow more expansion." On these religious grounds, the Charter forbids all Muslims from engaging in any political activity aimed at achieving a peaceful solution. This rejection includes the Oslo Accords as well as the Camp David Accords. Muslims who engage in peace negotiations with Israel are

---

[81] Küntzel, *supra* note 47, at p. 109.
[82] Id., at p. 109.
[83] Levitt, *supra* note 7.
[84] In the following and throughout this section, the Hamas Charter is quoted from the original Arabic text. The quotes are translated by the author. The document appears in Ahmed Izzuldin, *Harakat al-Mqawama al-Islamiyya Hamas* [The Islamic Resistance Movement Hamas] (Cairo: Dar al-Tawzi' al-Islamiyya, 1998) pp. 43-82.

accused of committing *khiyana uzma* or "great treason." A comparison of the Charter's text with the Qutb's aforementioned polemical pamphlet against the Jews reveals a large amount of borrowing. There is also a resemblance in terms of the similarity of the argumentation. The Charter makes no distinction between Jews and Zionists—they are simply the enemy. In an obviously antisemitic manner, Article 22 vilifies Jews as the source of all evil. It is instructive to compare the following quotation from the Hamas Charter with Qutb's quotation in the previous section of this study:

> ... stood behind the French and the communist revolutions ... in the pursuit of the interests of Zionism ... they were behind the First World War that led to the abolition of the caliphate ... to get the Balfour Declaration ... Then they established The League of Nations to rule through it the world and hereafter they pulled the strings for the Second World War ... to establish the State of Israel and to replace the League of Nations by the UN and its Security Council. They rule the world ... There is no single war without the hidden hand of the Jews acting behind it....

Islamists ask what one can do to contain this "hidden hand," and they obviously imagine a new Holocaust. If the pronouncement quoted is not an expression of antisemitism, what is it then? Those Europeans who support Hamas are challenged to answer! Article 22 of the Hamas Charter demonstrates the great impact of Qutb, which is apparent throughout the Charter.

The religionization of the conflict is illustrated by the shift from the secular Palestinian nationalism of the PLO to the Islamism of Hamas. Article 27 of the Hamas Charter addresses the boundary between the secular and the religious: "Secular thought contradicts fully the religious idea.... We refuse the belittling of the place of religion in the Arab-Israeli conflict and insist instead on the *Islamiyya* or Islamicity of Palestine. We cannot replace these claims by secular thoughts. The Islamicity of Palestine is part and parcel of our religion." The outcome is a religionized conflict that does not leave room for negotiation or compromise. The main implication of this unwavering religionization is the introduction of a politicized form of religion that includes a regionalized, religionized form of antisemitism combined with a firm belief that "the Jews" control U.S. foreign policy.

Islamism is not scriptural traditionalism. Nonetheless, the Hamas Charter starts with a reference to the Qur'anic verse from Al Umran that describes Muslims as *khair umma* or "chosen people." This reference is followed by a quote from Hasan al-Banna, the founder of the Muslim Brotherhood, which reads as follows: "Israel stands and shall continue to stand until Islam eradicates it, as it did undo earlier similar entities." According to Article 6, the goal is to "wave the flag of Allah over every inch of Palestine." Next, Article 7 quotes the highly disputed *hadith* alleged to have been transmitted from the Prophet by Buchari. This *hadith* states that the day of resurrection comes with a fight against the Jews. It ends symbolically with the hiding of the Jew behind a tree and a stone. The stone and the tree shout: "Oh Muslim, oh server of Allah, a Jew is hidden behind me, come and kill him." The alleged Buchari *hadith* states that only "the *gharqad* tree fails to betray the hiding Jew, because it is Jewish." The reference to this *hadith* is telling, since it prescribes the "killing of the Jew" as "a religious obligation" and thus demonstrates the most perilous implication of the religionization of antisemitism. Applied to Israel, it becomes a call for the eradication of the Jewish state, which gives rise to fears of another Holocaust.

The deep impact of the political-religious thoughts of Qutb on the Charter of Hamas is clear. In this line it pronounces "a cosmic war" against the Jews viewed as a zero-sum game. The contemporary crusaders, who do not exist in reality, are, in the Islamist imagery, the Americans. In the realities of the 20th century, the U.S. embodies the crusaders that political Islam imagines.

The Palestinian politician, opinion leader, and writer al-Antabawi rules out "peace with the Jews" on the grounds that "this violates shari'a."[85] Given that Islamism views the United States as the executioner of the "Jewish conspiracy," this sentiment also extends to the United States. The Hamas Charter is full of this antisemitism and describes Palestine in Article 11 as *waqf* or "divine property." It acknowledges that, prior to the Islamic *futuhat* wars, Jerusalem was not an Islamic place. However, the Charter adds: "The shari'a rules that every land conquered by Muslims is their property until the 'day of resurrection' or *qiyama*." Article 13 goes on to state: "Peaceful solutions contradict the commitment of Hamas to Islam. The abandonment of any piece of Palestine is an abandonment of the religion itself." Finally, it concludes: "There is no real solution to the conflict over Palestine other than Jihad ... anything else is a waste of time." This is strong evidence for the claim that Hamas cannot be appeased.

Those Europeans who perceive Hamas positively and simultaneously criticize Israel think that the problem is the fault of "the Jews." In European polls, Israel is often described as the "foremost danger to world peace." One explanation for these attitudes is that Europe is also home to a combination of antisemitism and anti-Americanism. In an excellent study,[86] Andrei Markovits explains how the appeal of the Islamization of antisemitism, as included in the Hamas Charter, also extends to Europeans who are critical of Israel and sympathetic to Islamism.

As demonstrated in the Gaza War of 2008-2009, the war of ideas is of great importance to the Islamists of Hamas. The ideology of *ghazu fikri* or "intellectual invasion" of the Islamic world appears in the Hamas Charter. According to Article 15 of the Charter, this invasion is to be countered by means of an "armed Jihad" carried out in parallel with the war of ideas. More specifically, Article 35 states: "The lesson to learn is that the contemporary Zionist *ghazu* or invasion was preceded by the crusaders of the West.... As Muslims defeated the earlier invasion they shall also manage similarly with the new one.... Muslims learn from the past, and purify themselves from any intellectual invasion." This quotation evokes the major Islamist theme of purification. In the contemporary writings of political Islam, the search for authenticity in terms of purity assumes the shape of antisemitism. This is not merely Jew-hatred but also an exclusionary mindset. It is one of the basic features of Islamism, which not only precludes Jews and Muslims living together in peace but also alienates Muslims from the rest of humanity.[87]

---

[85] al-Antabawi, *supra* note 79, at p. 49.

[86] Andrei S. Markovits, *Uncouth Nation: Why Europe Dislikes America* (Princeton, NJ: Princeton University Press, 2007).

[87] Tibi, *supra* note 27, at ch. 3.

VI. CONCLUSION

This study has provided a source-based analysis of the Islamization of antisemitism. At issue is a phenomenon rooted in political Islam and ideologically based on the ideas of Sayyid Qutb. Hamas has been presented as the practical Palestinian variety of Islamism. Hamas-Islamists hold the misconception that the Jews are instigators of a conspiracy against Islam that is being carried on their behalf by "Western crusaders." If there were a lesson to be learnt from the history of the crusades and the Islamic *futuhat* wars,[88] it would be that religionized war is disastrous for humanity. The present analysis has dealt with the religionization of the Israeli-Palestinian conflict in the course of the Islamization of antisemitism and has revealed how it is combined with anti-Americanism. A key insight provided by this analysis is that religionized conflicts become intractable. In the past, Israel was able to negotiate with the secular PLO and even conclude the Oslo Accords,[89] which unfortunately failed to produce a permanent solution to the conflict. Nothing like this could ever be repeated with the Hamas-Islamists, because the issues in question are simply non-negotiable to them because they are divine.

In the West, many academics subscribe to the apologetic view that what is at work here is a theology of liberation. In fact, Islamist antisemitism is a right-wing ideology. What is described as "anti-crusaderism" is actually a total anti-Western ideology. It is not a protest movement against capitalism or globalization. It is important to take a fresh look at the issue based on solid, factual information. One can and should criticize U.S. and Western policies in the Islamic world, especially in the Middle East, as well as Israel's ongoing occupation of Palestine, but one should beware of endorsing Islamist antisemitism, as often happens in contemporary Western debates.

It is perplexing to see that antisemitism is not prohibited but rather that those who criticize it are accused of bashing Islam and charged with Islamophobia. U.S. university presses publish books that promote Islamists[90] and sometimes even vilify Muslim critics of Islamism, while Islamist movements, and even Iran, are praised.[91]

---

[88] On the history of crusades, see Steven Runciman, *History of the Crusades* (Cambridge: Cambridge University Press, 1954). On Jihad wars of Islamic expansion, see Bassam Tibi, *Kreuzzug und Djihad* (Munich: Bertelsmann, 1999); *contra* Efraim Karsh, *Islamic Imperialism* (New Haven, CT: Yale University Press, 2006).

[89] See David Makovsky, *Making Peace with the PLO: The Rabin-Government's Road to the Oslo Accord* (Boulder, CO: Westview, 1996). This peace process is presented from a Palestinian perspective by Mahmoud Abbas (Abu Mazen), *Through Secret Channels: The Road to Oslo* (Reading, UK: Garnet Publishers, 1995); and from an Israeli perspective by Uri Savir, *The Oslo Process: 1.100 Days That Changed the Middle East* (New York: Vintage Books, 1998).

[90] In 2003, Harvard University Press published Raymond Baker, *Islam Without Fear, Egypt and the New Islamists*. In 2008, Princeton University Press published Bruce Rutherford, *Egypt after Mubarak*. Both books provide a positive assessment of the Muslim Brothers. The most outrageous publication is Emran Qureshi and Michael Sells, eds., *The New Crusaders* (Columbia University Press, 2003). Oxford University Press publishes Tariq Ramadan and appears to take his claim to provide "Radical Reform" (the title of his 2009 book) at face value. However, based on a close reading I fail to see any reform, let alone a modest one!

[91] This is done in the book by Ahmed S. Moussali, *U.S. Foreign Policy and Islamist Politics* (Miami FL, Florida University Press, 2008). See my review article in *The International History Review* 31(1) (March 2009) pp. 204-206.

Against these views—and against all odds—the analysis provided in the present study demonstrates that antisemitic Islamism is no partner in the peace process. Islamism closes the door to all efforts toward a peaceful resolution of the Middle East conflict. The much-needed peace process requires an acknowledgment of the nationhood of the other as an equal. Islamism rebuffs this requirement most vehemently and insists on dehumanizing the Jews as part of its Islamization of anti-semitism.

In the tradition of Karl Popper and his defense of the "open society," I view Islamism as a major contemporary enemy of "open society." Also, in the tradition of my Jewish teacher Max Horkheimer, who survived the Holocaust, I, as a liberal Muslim, have chosen to join forces against "all totalitarianisms." While studying Islamism over the past several decades, I have come to the conclusion that it is the "new totalitarianism."[92] In this context, one is also reminded of Hannah Arendt's view that antisemitism is a major feature of all forms of totalitarianism.

---

[92] Bassam Tibi, *Der neue Totalitarismus* (Darmstadt: Primus, 2004); and Bassam Tibi, "The Political Legacy of Max Horkheimer and Islamist Totalitarianism," *Telos* (Fall 2009) pp. 7-15.

BIBLIOGRAPHY

Abbas, Mahmoud (Abu Mazen), *Through Secret Channels: The Road to Oslo* (Reading, UK: Garnet Publishers, 1995).

Abrahamian, Ervand, *Khomeinism* (Berkeley: University of California Press, 1993).

Ahmed, Rifaat S., *al-Islam wa qadaya al-sira'al-Arabi al-Israeli* [Islam and Conflict: Studies on Islam and the Arab-Israeli Conflict] (Cairo: Dar al-Sharqiyya, 1989).

Ajami, Fouad, *The Arab Predicament* (New York: Cambridge University Press, 1981).

Akbarzadeh, Shahram, ed., *Islam and Globalization: Critical Concepts in Islamic Studies*, Vol. 1 (New York: Routledge, 2006).

al-Antabawi, Mushin, *Limatha narfud al-Salam ma'a al-Yehud* [Why Do We Reject Peace with the Jews] (Cairo: Kitab al-Mukhtar, n.d.).

Arendt, Hannah, *The Origins of Totalitarianism* (New York: Harcourt Inc., 1951, reprinted 1976).

Baker, Raymond, *Islam Without Fear: Egypt and the New Islamists* (Cambridge, MA: Harvard University Press, 2003).

Bale, Jeffrey, "Political Paranoia vs. Political Realism: On Distinguishing Between Bogus Conspiracy Theories and Genuine Conspiratorial Politics," *Patterns of Prejudice* 41(1) (2007) pp. 45-60.

al-Banna, Hassan, *Majmu'at Rasail al-Imam al-Shahid* [Collected Writings of the Martyr Imam] (Cairo: Dar al-Da'wa, legal edition, 1990).

Baran, Zeyno, "Fighting the War of Ideas," *Foreign Affairs* (November/December 2005) pp. 68-78.

—— "The Muslim Brotherhood's U.S. Network," in *Current Trends in Islamist Ideology*, Vol. 6 (Washington, DC: The Hudson Institute, 2008) pp. 95-122.

Bostom, Andrew, ed., *The Legacy of Islamic Antisemitism* (Amherst, NY: Prometheus, 2008).

Brenkman, John, *The Cultural Contradictions of Democracy* (Princeton, NJ: Princeton University Press, 2007).

Brickerton, Ian and Carla Klausner, *Concise History of the Arab-Israeli Conflict* (Upper Saddle River, NJ: Prentice Hall, 1995).

Cabban, Helena, *The Palestinian Liberation Organization: People, Power, and Politics* (New York: Cambridge University Press, 1987).

Chubin, Shahram, *Iran's Nuclear Ambitions* (Washington, DC: Carnegie Endowment for International Peace, 2006).

Cook, David, *Understanding Jihad* (Berkeley: University of California Press, 2004).

Demant, Peter, *Islam vs. Islamism: The Dilemma of the Muslim World* (Westpoint, CT: Praeger, 2006).

Euben, Roxanne, *The Enemy in the Mirror: Islamic Fundamentalism and the Limits of Modern Rationalism* (Princeton, NJ: Princeton University Press, 1999).

Fortner, Robert, ed., *The Handbook of Global Communication* (Oxford: Blackwell, 2010).

Fuller, Graham, *The Center of the Universe: The Geopolitics of Iran* (Boulder, CO: Westview, 1991).

—— *A Sense of Siege: The Geopolitics of Islam and the West* (Boulder, CO: Westview, 1995).

Gerner, Deborah J., *One Land, Two Peoples: The Conflict over Palestine* (Boulder, CO: Westview, 1991).

Harel, Arnas and Avi Issacharoff, *34 Days: Israel, Hezbollah, and the War in Lebanon* (New York: Palgrave, 2008).
Heller, Mark, "Don't Strengthen Hamas," *International Herald Tribune*, January 30, 2009, p. 9.
Herf, Jeffrey, ed., *Antisemitism and Anti-Zionism in Historical Perspective* (New York: Routledge, 2007).
Isar, Y. Raj and Helmut Anheier, eds., *Tensions and Conflict*, Culture and Globalization Series, Vol. 1 (New York: Sage, 2007).
Izzuldin, Ahmed, *Harakat al-Mqawama al-Islamiyya Hamas* [The Islamic Resistance Movement Hamas] (Cairo: Dar al-Tawzi'al-Islmiyya, 1998).
Jacoby, Tamy A. and Brent Sasley, eds., *Redefining Security in the Middle East* (Manchester University Press, 2002).
Jafarzadeh, Mohammed and Yusuf al-Zaibaq, *Asalib al-Ghazu al-fikri lil-alam al-Islami* [Methods of the Intellectual Invasion of the World of Islam] (Cairo: Dar al-I'tisam, second printing, 1978).
Karsh, Efraim, *Islamic Imperialism* (New Haven, CT: Yale University Press, 2006).
Katzenstein, Peter and Robert Keohane, eds., *Anti-Americanisms in World Politics* (Ithaca, NY: Cornell University Press, 2007).
Kelsay, John, *Arguing the Just War in Islam* (Cambridge, MA: Harvard University Press, 2007).
al-Khalidi, Salah A., *Amerika min al-dakhil bi minzar Sayyid Qutb* [America Viewed from Inside Through the Lenses of Sayyid Qutb] (al-Mansura (Egypt) and Jedda (Saudi Arabia): Dar al-Manara, third edition, 1987).
Küntzel, Matthias, *Jihad and Jew-Hatred: Islamism, Nazism, and the Roots of 9/11* (New York: Telos Press, 2007).
Kurzman, Charles, ed., *Liberal Islam: A Sourcebook* (New York: Oxford University Press, 1998).
Laqueur, Walter, *The Changing Face of Antisemitism* (New York: Oxford University Press, 2006).
Laurence, Jonathan and Justin Vaisse, *Integrating Islam* (Washington, DC: Brookings Institution, 2006).
Leiken, Robert and Steven Brooke, "The Moderate Muslim Brotherhood," *Foreign Affairs* (April 2007) pp. 107-121.
Levitt, Matthew, *Hamas: Politics, Charity, and Terrorism in the Service of Jihad* (New Haven. CT: Yale University Press, 2006).
Lewis, Bernard, *The Jews of Islam* (Princeton, NJ: Princeton University Press, 1984).
Lybarger, Loren, *Identity Politics and Religion in Palestine: The Struggle between Islamism and Secularism* (Princeton, NJ: Princeton University Press, 2007).
Makovsky, David, *Making Peace with the PLO: The Rabin Government's Road to the Oslo Accord* (Boulder, CO: Westview, 1996).
McGough, Paul, "The Changing Face of Hamas," *International Herald Tribune*, April 13, 2009, p. 13.
Mearshheimer, John and Stephen Walt, *The Israel Lobby and U.S. Foreign Policy* (New York: Farrer and Strauss, 2008).
Milton-Edwards, Beverly, *Islamic Politics in Palestine* (London: Tauris, 1996 and 1999).
Mitchell, Richard, *The Muslim Brothers* (London: Oxford University Press, 1969).

Moussali, Ahmed S., *U.S. Foreign Policy and Islamist Politics* (Miami, FL: Florida University Press, 2008).

Mulish, Muhammed, *The Origins of Palestinian Nationalism* (New York: Columbia University Press, 1988).

Patterson, Dan, *Inside Sudan: Political Islam, Conflict, and Catastrophe* (Boulder, CO: Westview, revised edition, 2003).

Patterson, Eric, ed., *The War of Ideas* (New York: Palgrave, 2010).

Phares, Walid, *The War of Ideas: Jihadism against Democracy* (New York: Palgrave, 2007).

Pipes, Daniel, *The Hidden Hand: Middle East Fears of Conspiracy* (New York: St. Martin's Press, 1996).

al-Qaradawi, Yusuf, *Hatimiyyat al-hall al-Islami, Vol. 1: al-Hulul al-mustawradah* [The Imported Solutions] (Cairo: Mu'ssasat al-Risalah, reprinted 1980).

Qureshi, Emran and Michael Sells, eds., *The New Crusaders* (New York: Columbia University Press, 2003).

Qutb, Sayyid, *Ma'alim fi al-tariq* [Signposts along the Road] (Cairo: Dar al-Shuruq, 13th legal edition, 1989).

―― *Ma'rakatuna ma'a al-Yahud* [Our Battle with the Jews] (Cairo: Dar al-Shuruq, 10th legal edition, 1989).

―― *al-Salam al-alami wa al-Islam* [World Peace and Islam] (Cairo: Dar al-Shuruq, 10th legal edition, 1992).

Ramadan, Tariq, *Radical Reform* (New York: Oxford University Press, 2009).

Rosefsky Wickham, Carrie, *Mobilizing Islam: Religion, Activism and Political Change in Egypt* (New York: Columbia University Press, 2009).

Roth, John and Leonard Grob, eds., *Encountering the Stranger: A Jewish-Christian-Muslim Trialogue* (University of Washington Press, 2012).

Runciman, Steven, *History of the Crusades* (Cambridge: Cambridge University Press, 1954).

Rutherford, Bruce, *Egypt after Mubarak* (Princeton, NJ: Princeton University Press, 2008).

Savir, Uri, *The Oslo Process: 1,100 Days That Changed the Middle East* (New York: Vintage Books, 1998).

Sivan, Emmanuel, *Radical Islam: Medieval Theology and Modern Politics* (New Haven: Yale University Press, 1985).

Tibi, Bassam, *Die Verschwörung. Das Trauma arabischer Politik* (Hamburg: Hoffman & Campe, 1993; expanded second edition 1994).

―― *Krieg der Zivilisationen* (Hamburg: Hoffmann und Campe, 1995).

―― *Arab Nationalism: Between Islam and the Nation-State* (New York: Macmillan, 3rd edition, 1997).

―― *Conflict and War in the Middle East: From Inter-State War to New Security* (New York: St. Martin's Press, 2nd edition, 1998).

―― *Kreuzzug und Djihad* (Munich: Bertelsmann, 1999).

―― *The Challenge of Fundamentalism* (Berkeley: University of California Press, 1998, 2002).

―― *Islam between Culture and Politics* (New York: Palgrave, 2001, updated edition 2005).

―――― "Between Islam and Islamism," in Tamy A. Jacoby and Brent Sasley, eds., *Redefining Security in the Middle East* (Manchester: Manchester University Press, 2002) pp. 62-82.

―――― *Der neue Totalitarismus* (Darmstadt: Primu, 2004).

―――― "The Totalitarianism of Jihadist Islamism," *Totalitarian Movements and Political Religions* 8(1) (2007) pp. 35-54.

―――― "Islam: Between Religious-Cultural Practice and Identity Politics," in Y. Raj Issar and Helmut Anheier, eds., *Tensions and Conflict: The Culture of Globalization Series*, Vol. 1 (New York: Sage, 2007) pp. 221-231.

―――― *Political Islam, World Politics and Europe: Democratic Peace and Euro-Islam versus Global Jihad* (New York: Routledge, 2008).

―――― "Islamic Parties: Why Can't They Be Democratic?" *Journal of Democracy* 91(3) (2008) pp. 43-48.

―――― "Public Policy and the Combination of Anti-Americanism and Antisemitism in Contemporary Islamist Ideology," *The Current* 12(1) (Fall 2008) pp. 123-146.

―――― "Islam and Modern European Ideologies," in Shahram Akbarzadeh, ed., *Islam and Globalization: Critical Concepts in Islamic Studies*, Vol. 1 (New York: Routledge, 2006) pp. 206-222.

―――― *Islam's Predicament with Modernity* (New York: Routledge, 2009).

―――― "Turkey's Islamist Danger: Islamists Approach Europe." *Middle East Quarterly* 16(1) (Winter 2009) pp. 47-54.

―――― "Review of Ahmed S. Moussali, *U.S. Foreign Policy and Islamist Politics*," *The International History Review* 31(1) (2009) pp. 204-206.

―――― *Islamism and Islam: A Study of a Significant Distinction* (New Haven: Yale University Press, 2010).

―――― "Global Communication and Cultural Pluralism: The Place of Values in the Simultaneity of Structural Globalization and Cultural Fragmentation," in Robert Fortner, ed., *The Handbook of Global Communication* (Oxford: Blackwell, 2010).

Israel, Jordan, and Palestine:
One State, Two States, or Three?

Asher Susser*

I. The Historical Setting

The areas of today's Middle East that form Jordan, the West Bank and Israel have been linked together by geography, demography, history, and politics since time immemorial. The political destinies of Jordan, Israel, and Palestine, as modern political entities, have been inextricably linked since the very day of their creation.

Jordan and Israel have been intimately tied together through the Palestinian problem to the extent that it is virtually impossible to discuss Jordanian-Israeli relations in isolation from the Palestinian context; one cannot fully comprehend the Israeli-Palestinian interaction if one ignores the Jordanian component, and likewise Jordanian-Palestinian relations are inexplicable if detached from the Israeli input. Both recent and more distant history and present-day demographic realities link these three protagonists together, perhaps considerably more than they would really like. Jordan is home to a Palestinian population that quite possibly constitutes more than half of the Kingdom's total population of some six million. Moreover, the special ties linking the Arab populations on both banks of the Jordan river are anything but new, nor are they solely a consequence of the Arab-Israeli conflict and the birth of the Palestinian refugee problem.

The lay of the land has contributed to the merger of the peoples on both banks of the river since the earliest of times. Three rivers flow from east to west on the East Bank of the Jordan into the Jordan Valley, carving the East Bank into three distinct geographical segments: the Yarmuk in the north, on what today forms the border between the states of Syria and Jordan; the Zarqa in the center, flowing from its source near Amman into the Jordan Valley; and the Mujib in the south, which flows into the Dead Sea. In their flow westward, these rivers cut through the hilly terrain of the East Bank creating deep ravines and gorges, more difficult to cross than the Jordan river itself, which is easily traversed during most times of the year. Historically it was far less challenging for people and goods to travel along the east-west axis across the Jordan than along the more daunting routes on the north-south axis.

It followed naturally that political, administrative, economic, social, and family ties developed more intensively between the East and West Banks of the Jordan than between the northern and southern parts of the East Bank. Towns like Salt and

---

* Senior Fellow, Moshe Dayan Center for Middle Eastern and African Studies, Tel Aviv University; Senior Visiting Fellow, Crown Center for Middle East Studies, Brandeis University.

Karak on the East Bank, which are part of the present-day Hashemite Kingdom of Jordan, were more intimately connected through a web of historical family and commercial ties to their sister towns on the Palestinian West Bank, Nablus and Hebron respectively, than they were to each other. In the administrative divisions of both banks of the Jordan River in biblical times, then again during the Roman era, at the time of the Arab conquest, thereafter under the Ottomans, and finally with the initial formation of the British Mandate for Palestine, large areas on both banks of the river were united in the same provinces.

II. The Evolution of Polities and Collective Identities

It is frequently noted that the Middle East state order that came into being on the ruins of the Ottoman empire was an artificial imperial creation, designed to serve the immediate interests of Great Britain and France. While that is true, in the century that has passed, new authentic territorial identities have been forged in these imperial creations. This is definitely the case in the triangle consisting of Israel, Jordan, and Palestine. Despite the strong historical ties between the East and West Banks and even though the British Mandate for Palestine originally spanned both banks of the Jordan river, separate Jordanian and Palestinian identities were soon to develop. In 1922, the East Bank was formally separated from Western Palestine, as the Emirate of Transjordan was designated to become an Arab state where there would be no Zionist settlement or presence. This was seen at the time as a British concession to Arab nationalism in the form of a limitation on the Zionist enterprise.

As Zionist settlement was henceforth contained to Palestine west of the Jordan river, the conflict between Jews and Arabs was initially limited to this territory, where an indigenous nationalist movement began to develop as an outgrowth of the conflict with the Jews. However, up until 1948, the Arab nationalist movement in Palestine saw itself, in the main, as an extension of the general movement of Arab nationalism in the Middle East, of which the Palestinians were an integral part.

In the aftermath of the 1948 War, the major rump of Palestine that remained under Arab control, the West Bank, was annexed by Jordan with Israeli acquiescence. (The Gaza Strip came under Egyptian military government.) Neither Jordan nor Israel was interested in the creation of a separate Palestinian state or collective identity that might challenge either one or both of them. Jordan conducted a policy of "Jordanization," an effort to assimilate the Palestinians into the Jordanian state, in the name of Arab unity.

Following the defeat of the Arab armies in 1948, the Palestinians generally adopted an Arab nationalist stance, but instead of standing behind the King of Jordan they tended to be enthusiastic supporters of Egypt's Nasser, in the belief that his more radical anti-Western form of Arab unity, coupled with an alliance with the Soviet Union, would eventually deliver Palestine. It was they who were the most ardent proponents of the dominant Arab nationalist discourse in the mid-1950s and early 1960s.[1]

---

[1] Musa Budeiri, "The Palestinians: Tensions Between Nationalist and Religious Identities," in *Rethinking Nationalism in the Arab Middle East*, ed. James Jankowski and Israel Gershoni (New York: Columbia University Press, 1997), pp. 196, 199.

After a decade of Palestinian nationalist decline and devotion to pan-Arabism in the wake of the disaster (*nakba*) of 1948, it was the identification with the *nakba* itself, as a formative and traumatic collective experience, that was to become the core of a reconstructed Palestinian national consciousness. In the late 1950s the "revival of the Palestinian entity" stemmed from two sources. One was within the Arab League, as the Arab states, led by Egypt (then still the United Arab Republic or UAR) and Iraq, pressed for the creation of a representative Palestinian political framework. These efforts eventually culminated in the establishment of the PLO in 1964, in accordance with an Arab Summit resolution, as the organizational incarnation of Palestinian nationalism. The second source of Palestinian national revival was the initially clandestine formation of a variety of organizations devoted to the idea of independent Palestinian armed struggle. Of these, Fatah turned out to be the most important and long-lasting.

After the Six-Day War of 1967, when Jordan lost the West Bank to Israel, the policy of "Jordanization" of the Palestinians came to an abrupt end. The war was also a catastrophic defeat for pan-Arabism, which gave way in its declining appeal to two competing forces: narrowly based territorial nationalism and Islamic politics. In the Palestinian domain, this was translated into the takeover of the PLO by the formerly clandestine Palestinian fighting organizations lead by Fatah. The newly constructed PLO promoted a particular independent form of Palestinianness that sought to mobilize the masses under the banner of armed struggle against Israel, which in the late 1960s was waged mainly from Jordanian territory. This soon led to Israeli retaliation against Jordan and to an eventual decision by the Jordanians to oust the PLO from their territory in September 1970.

The civil war of 1970 was a traumatic and formative experience for the Jordanians. The policy of assimilation of the Palestinians had obviously failed. The Palestinians in Jordan were henceforth increasingly seen by the Jordanian political elite as a potential threat. From the 1970s onward, Jordan has consequently undergone an intensive process of "Jordanization," which now meant the almost total exclusion of Palestinians from positions of influence in the bureaucracy and the military and the calculated promotion of a sense of Jordanianness. Thus, from the top down, by the regime, and from the bottom up, by segments of the East Bank population, an exclusive Jordanianism was fostered, defined implicitly and at times explicitly against the Palestinian "other," with occasionally vicious anti-Palestinian overtones.

Jordan has weathered many storms, regional and domestic, and has undeniably acquired a Jordanian collective identity and stateness of its own. The Bedouin tribes in Jordan were well integrated into the state and gradually emerged as the key standard bearers of this newly articulated Jordanianness.

Thus, since the early days of the British Mandate, that is to say, over a period of nearly a century, the conflict between Zionists and Arabs has produced modern, vibrant, and authentic collective identities among nationalist Israeli Jews and equally among nationalist Jordanians and Palestinians. These have resulted in conflict not between rival tribes, sects, or ethnic groups within one single state but rather between new, competing national movements and polities that have culminated in the formation of two states, Jordan and Israel, and one in the making, sandwiched between them, namely Palestine. Some people, some of the time, in each one of these three national polities, may wish for one or both of the other two to evaporate into thin air, but that is not about to happen. These three identities and polities are here to stay, albeit with alternating measures of collaboration, competition, or conflict between them.

III. HISTORICAL FAULT-LINES: ISRAEL—PALESTINE AND THE CONFLICTING NARRATIVES

An unbridgeable abyss separates the Arab Palestinian and Zionist historical narratives. Zionism, in the widely held Jewish perspective, is a heroic project of national revival, restored dignity, and self-respect. The rise of Israel as an act of defiance against the miserable predicament of the European Jewish Diaspora is deeply imbedded in the Jewish collective memory and self-image. This sentiment has been cultivated for decades by the scathing critique of Jewish hopelessness and helplessness that has become an integral part of the collective consciousness. This pathetic manifestation of Jewish indignity and powerlessness was only the precursor to the culmination of all horror in the catastrophic destruction of the Jews in the Holocaust. Jewish national liberation, statehood, and sovereignty was therefore the literal rising from the ashes, in self-defense against the Jewish historical fate, to finally attain political independence and historical justice for the most oppressed of all peoples.

For the Palestinians, needless to say, the complete opposite is true. Zionism, in their view, had nothing to do with self-defense or justice. It was the epitome of aggression from the start. The Palestinian *nakba* or catastrophic defeat, loss of homeland, and refugeedom are at the core of the Palestinian collective identity and their self-perception of victimhood. The war had ended not only in their military defeat, but in the shattering of their society and the dispersal of half of their number as refugees in other parts of Palestine and in the neighboring Arab states.

The "shared memories of the traumatic uprooting of their society and the experiences of being dispossessed, displaced, and stateless" were to "come to define 'Palestinianness.'"[2] The traumatic and formative series of events, leading up to the outbreak of war in 1948, and its tragic consequences for the Palestinians, carried with them a powerful and pervasive sense of historical injustice to the innermost depths of the Palestinian collective soul.

The Palestinians yearn, therefore, to turn back the clock of history. The question is just how far back? Is it to 1967 or to 1948? The resolution of the so-called "1967 file" relates to the outstanding issues of borders and settlements on the West Bank and to the final status of Jerusalem. As thorny as these matters may be, they do not impinge upon Israel's existence, nor do they conflict in any way with the principle of partition and a two-state solution. The "1948 file," however, relates to two existential matters: (1) the question of the return of refugees to Israel proper; and (2) the issue of the national rights of the Palestinian Arab minority in Israel itself. Both could severely undermine Israel's viability as presently constituted, namely as the state of the Jewish people, precisely because it is these issues that might irreversibly derail the inner logic of a two-state solution.

---

[2] Beshara Doumani, "Palestine Versus the Palestinians? The Iron Laws and the Ironies of a People Denied," *Journal of Palestine Studies* 36(4) (Summer 2007), p. 52.

It is the intractable nature of questions such as those in the "1948 file" that have put an "end of conflict" settlement out of reach. This was highlighted once again in the crisis between Israel and the Palestinian Authority concerning the recognition of Israel as a *Jewish* state in the run-up to the Annapolis meeting between Prime Minister Olmert and President Abbas under the auspices of US President Bush in late November 2007, and again after Prime Minister Netanyahu made a similar demand in his Bar Ilan University speech in June 2009. Israel's demand that the Palestinians issue a binding statement to that effect was firmly and flatly rebuffed by all Palestinian spokesmen from Mahmud Abbas and Saeb Erekat on down.

An article in the semi-official Palestinian daily *al-Ayyam* summed up the matter as follows: "Such demands by Olmert and others coming from Israeli politicians ... can only push the Palestinians with their backs to the wall ... [which] would prompt them to redouble their efforts to regain at least the bare minimum of their legitimate rights as enshrined in the resolutions of international legitimacy [UN resolutions], which totally contradict Olmert's recent provocative and impossible demand."[3] But, in the Jewish Israeli mind, Olmert's conditions were neither provocative nor impossible.

This was simply an attempt to obtain from the Palestinians assurances that a two-state solution would remain the foundation for the peace process, and that all outstanding questions, including the refugee issue, would be resolved in accordance with the symmetrical two-state logic. Israel was to be the homeland of the Jewish people and Palestine would be the homeland of the Palestinian people. It followed that Jews would have the right to return to Israel and not to Palestine and Palestinians would have the right to return to the state of Palestine and not to Israel. For the Israelis, it was to ensure that the turning back of the clock would end in 1967, with the undoing of the occupation, and not proceed further to 1948, to undo the very existence of the state of Israel.

IV. Historical Fault Lines: 1967 vs. 1948—Oslo and Back Again

The Oslo Accords created a new political dynamic. In accepting the Oslo Accords, the PLO leadership gained access to the West Bank and Gaza and created the Palestinian Authority (PA) in these territories, ostensibly on the way to the attainment of a final status agreement with Israel that would lead to the establishment of a Palestinian state. This lead to the formation of new, elected Palestinian institutions, including the Presidency of the PA and the Legislative Assembly. These changes were of great historical significance. The new institutions were elected solely by the people of the West Bank (including Arab East Jerusalem) and Gaza and thus represented only them, as opposed to the PLO which claimed to represent all Palestinians everywhere, including in Israel and the Palestinian Diaspora. The PLO represented the claim to all of historical Palestine, and was an organization that had functioned from the outset in the Diaspora. The PLO, therefore, had also tended to give high priority to the Diaspora constituency and its aspirations, above all the demand for the return of refugees.

The PA, on the other hand, represented the West Bank and Gaza and focused on their most immediate concern, namely liberation from Israeli occupation.

---

[3] Ali Jaradat in *al-Ayyam*, November 19, 2007.

This meant a certain downgrading, though by no means an abandonment, of the primacy of the refugee question. The issue of Palestine, or so it seemed momentarily, was actually being reduced to the West Bank and Gaza and to the 1967 questions, at the expense of the 1948 file. Israel sought to achieve finality on that basis, namely that the Palestinians would agree to end the conflict on the basis of a grand historical trade-off. Israel would concede on the 1967 questions, including Jerusalem, in exchange for closure of the 1948 file. But this was not to be. The Palestinians, and first and foremost Yasser Arafat, would not agree to an "end of conflict" unless the 1948 file, and its primary issues and grievances, were also addressed to their satisfaction.

The Camp David summit in the summer of 2000 therefore failed, and no agreement on "end of conflict" was actually reached. Instead, Israel and the Palestinians were locked in the worst round of bloodshed they had experienced since 1948, with suicide bombers ravaging Israeli towns and the Israeli military pulverizing the PA and the Palestinians in return. The weakening of the PA, the general degeneration of Palestinian governance, and the disintegration of the peace process all served to strengthen the hand of Hamas in Palestinian politics, which reached new heights of power in January 2006, when it handsomely won the elections to the Palestinian Legislative Assembly.

Hamas had never accepted the Oslo dynamic of ostensible prioritization of the 1967 file. In the years since the failure of Camp David, Hamas has made a concerted effort to reverse the Oslo dynamic and refocus the Palestinian cause on the 1948 file and the Diaspora concerns in order to ensure that no finality could possibly be obtained on the basis of a resolution of the 1967 issues. A perusal of Palestinian documentation, formulated with Hamas input in recent years, reveals a very deliberate inversion of the Oslo dynamic, from the narrowing down to the West Bank and Gaza to the broadening out again to the Diaspora constituency and to a concentration on the primacy of the refugee question.

In June 2006, in what became known as the "Prisoners' Document," Fatah and Hamas representatives, as well as representatives from other minor organizations, who were serving sentences in Israeli jails on a wide variety of security-related offences, signed a Document of National Reconciliation. The parties emphasized not only the need to defend the rights of the refugees but also to reorganize them and to "hold a popular representative conference" that would create organizations "that would demand the right of return and the abidance by it, urging the international community to implement resolution 194 [of the UN General Assembly of December 1948] stipulating the right of the refugees to return and [their right] to compensation."[4]

The policy statement of the Hamas-led national unity government, which was formed by Isma'il Haniyya in March 2007, similarly emphasized the right of return and the implementation of resolution 194, specifically noting "the right of the Palestinian refugees to return to the lands and properties that they had abandoned," that is to say, to Israel proper. The statement also specified that any agreement reached by the PLO (which formally conducted the negotiations with Israel) would have to be approved by the Palestinians in the West Bank and Gaza *and in the Diaspora*. Any such agreement would have to be brought before a new Palestine

---

[4] *Wathiqat al-wafaq al-watani,* June 28, 2006, para. 9.

National Council (the PLO's quasi-parliamentary body, which represented all Palestinians everywhere, and would now have to include a significant representation of Hamas itself) or alternatively "a general referendum [on the agreement] would be held by the Palestinian people inside [the occupied territories] and outside [in the Diaspora]."[5]

Even the Arab League summit, in its approval of the Arab Peace Initiative as passed in March 2002 and reaffirmed in March 2007, followed suit in this regard. The Arab Peace Initiative called for comprehensive peace between the Arab states and Israel on the basis of an Israeli withdrawal to the 1967 boundaries and for an agreed solution to the refugee question based on resolution 194 and upon "the rejection all forms of resettlement" of refugees outside of Palestine.[6]

In the last two decades of negotiations between Israel and the Palestinians, on the various issues of the so-called 1967 file, such as borders, settlements, and even Jerusalem, the gaps have narrowed significantly. At the same time, however, on the truly existential so-called 1948 issues, that is to say, refugees, the status of the Arab-Palestinian minority in Israel, and the designation of Israel as the nation state of the Jewish people, positions have hardened and the gaps between the parties are as wide as ever, if not even wider.

V. THE NEWLY EMPHASIZED RELIGIOUS FAULT LINES

The rise of Hamas is transforming the Israeli-Palestinian divide from a nationalist conflict, which at least in theory could one day be reduced to a conflict over boundaries, into an insoluble clash over religions and belief in the holy word of God Almighty. For Hamas, Palestine was not the land of national liberation but of the eternal struggle of the believers against the infidels (matched on the Israeli side by the extreme right-wing ultra-nationalist religious fringe that had a virtually identical world view). Palestine's sanctity, in the Hamas view, was also a function of its ostensible designation as a *waqf* (religious endowment) by the Khalifa 'Umar bin al-Khattab, who had conquered Palestine in 638.

This depiction of Palestine as a *waqf*, however, was a Hamas invention that had no legal basis in the *Shari'a*. Legally it could not be, and historically it was never all *waqf*. But that did not really matter. The designation had political value. It served as the religious foundation for the contention that not an inch of Palestine could be conceded to the Zionists. Moreover, as a *waqf*, Palestine did not belong exclusively to the Palestinians but to all Muslims. Therefore, not in this generation, nor in any future generations, did the Palestinians or the Arabs have any right to concede any territory to an alien entity in Palestine.

Since for Hamas the Palestinian cause was not a struggle between two nationalist movements but between two rival religions, Islam and Judaism, the Palestinian cause was driven by an "Islamic essence" and was part of the larger war between Islam and Western civilization.[7] Just as the PLO and Fatah had nationalized religion

---

[5] Policy Statement of Isma'il Haniyya's government, *al-Jazira*, March 17, 2007.

[6] Riyad Summit Resolutions as published in *al-Sharq al-Awsat*, March 31, 2007.

[7] Meir Litvak, "The Islamization of the Palestinian-Israeli Conflict: The Case of Hamas," *Middle Eastern Studies* 34(1) (January 1998), pp. 148-150, 153-155.

for their more secular vision, so Hamas Islamized nationalism. For Hamas, the first and second Intifadas were part of a jihad that emanated from the mosques and embodied the return of the Palestinian people to their "authentic Islamic identity and belonging,"[8] a line of argumentation that was bound to resonate positively with a sizeable constituency.

VI. THE FAYYAD PLAN AND THE ATTEMPTED RESURRECTION OF THE OSLO DYNAMIC

Following the rise of Hamas, the failure of the Oslo process, and the passage of seventeen years since the signing of the Oslo accords, the two-state solution has undoubtedly lost much if its appeal, legitimacy, and practicality in the eyes of all concerned. On the Israeli side, there has been an entrenchment of the settlements, abetted by the fecklessness of successive Israeli governments (with the surprising exception of Ariel Sharon) in contending with the challenge of the settler movement. The Palestinian side suffers from disarray, with the PA and Hamas operating at cross-purposes ever since the Hamas electoral victory in 2006 and the takeover of Gaza in 2007. Coupled with the dispirited condition and the concomitant ideological and organizational fatigue of Fatah, there is very little prospect for a successful negotiation of a two-state agreement. Those who endorse a two-state solution "must acknowledge how much of the framework supporting it has collapsed."[9]

However, the conclusion that some draw from this grim assessment, namely that a one-state solution is the viable alternative to the faltering two-state paradigm, represents a remedy that would in all likelihood be infinitely worse than the present predicament. The "moral laboratory analysts" tend to assess reality not on the grounds of what it is but on the basis of what they believe it ought to be. Theirs is a world founded on morality, justice, and legal rectitude and on the constantly disproved assumption about the rationality of political actors. It has little connection with the real world with its highly combustible mixture of power, emotion, identity politics, political culture, and ideology, which are of virtually no consequence in the overall of scheme of the "moral laboratory analysts."

As Nathan Brown has noted, the advocates of a binational state, or what he has dubbed the "one-state non-solution," generally

> fall into the trap of holding out an admirable utopian solution without analyzing what such a state would be like in practice or how entrenched adversaries could ever construct such a state. In a sense, the one-state solution resembles communism—a utopian idea many found preferable to the grim realities but that led to horrifying results in practice.[10]

---

[8] Meir Litvak, "Hamas: Palestinian Identity, Islam, and National Sovereignty," in *Challenges to the Cohesion of the Arab State*, ed. Asher Susser (Tel Aviv: Moshe Dayan Center, TAU, 2008), pp. 156-158, 167.

[9] Nathan Brown, "Sunset for the Two-State Solution," Policy Outlook, Carnegie Endowment for International Peace, May 9, 2008; Nathan Brown, "After Abu Mazin? Letting the Scales Fall from Our Eyes," Article, Carnegie Endowment for International Peace, November 10, 2009.

[10] Brown, "Sunset for the Two-State Solution."

One should have no illusions "that the final abandonment of a two-state agenda" will simply "give way to a campaign of non-violent resistance, boycotts and sanctions that will somehow succeed in bringing Israel to its knees." The real alternative to the two-state agenda is "crystal clear: increasing conflict, violence and occupation that is increasingly dominated by religious fanatics on both sides." The alternative to the two-state paradigm is not the utopian one-state paradise but catastrophe.[11]

The evolution of a one-state reality might very well be the outcome of the final demise of the two-state idea, but that is very likely to be a horrendous reality of escalating conflict between Jewish Israelis and Palestinians, not only in the occupied territories but across the Green Line, in Israel proper, too. The clashes of October 2000 in Israel between the Israeli police and Palestinian demonstrators were just the foretaste of what the impasse might eventually produce. As Abba Eban once commented, "not for a single minute in a day do the ... Palestinians and the Israelis share a common memory, sentiment, experience or aspiration."[12] Israelis and Palestinians locked together in one state, with a history of such enmity, would more likely be a recipe for endless conflict rather than harmony.

Among Palestinians in the Diaspora and within the ranks of the Palestinian Arab intelligentsia in Israel there is strong support for the one-state agenda, far more than in the West Bank and Gaza. A two-state solution would change little for the Arabs in Israel or for the Palestinian Diaspora, but it offers the people in the West Bank and Gaza freedom and independence in a state of their own. These three Palestinian constituencies, therefore, do not have identical interests. In the West Bank at present we are witnessing a desperate Palestinian effort to resurrect the fading two-state option. The Fayyad Plan for the creation of the institutions of a Palestinian state in two years was definitely part of an identifiable and coherent school of thought in the PA in the West Bank that believed in the securing of their own self-interest first. This meant ridding themselves of the occupation and creating two states. The Diaspora intellectuals and the Israeli Arabs, with their utopian one-state ideas, were secondary and could wait, as could the refugees. This was not so much conceding the refugee cause as setting priorities, and the most urgent cause was saving the two-state paradigm. The alternative was not a "one-state wonderland" but hell on earth.

VII. Fault Lines and Common Ground between Jordanians and Palestinians

Much is usually said, justifiably, about the contemporary nationalist division between East Bank Jordanians and Palestinians and their suspicions toward their Jordanian compatriots who are of Palestinian origin. The original Jordanians are obsessed by the fear of their country being taken over by the Palestinians, who represent about

---

[11] Hussein Ibish, "Against a One-State Solution," *Informed Comment*, http://www.juancole.com/2009/11/ibish-against-one-state-solution.html.

[12] Abba Eban, "Peace: The Only Alternative Left," *New Perspectives Quarterly* 10(1) (Fall 1993) and "Israel Has No Alternative to Rabin's Realism," *New Perspectives Quarterly* 13(1) (Winter 1996), as quoted in Jenab Tutunji and Kamal Khaldi, "A Binational State in Palestine: The Rational Choice for Palestinians and the Moral Choice for Israelis," *International Affairs* 73(1) (January 1997), pp. 35, 55.

half, perhaps slightly more, of Jordan's population, and have transformed it into an "alternative homeland" (*al-watan al-badil*). As of the mid-1980s, the Jordanians have therefore been ardent supporters of the creation of a Palestinian state in the West Bank and Gaza, so that it is clear to all and sundry that Jordan is Jordan, on the one side of the river, and Palestine is Palestine, on the other.

At the same time, however, not enough attention is paid to the common ground between Jordanians and Palestinians. The great majority of Jordanians and Palestinians are Sunni Muslim speakers of the Arabic language, a collective cultural and religious identity that has bound them together for centuries. In this sense, they are bound together more significantly than they are set apart by their relatively new and more shallow modern national identities, however real and authentic they may be. Marriage is a useful barometer to identify critical social fault lines. Jordanians and Palestinians marry each other as a matter of course. The decisive fault line in these matters is religion rather than national identity, thus Jordanian Muslims invariably marry their Palestinian co-religionists as do Jordanian and Palestinian Christians.

There is no similar common ground between the Jews of Israel and either the Palestinians or the Jordanians. While the Jordanians and the Palestinians have had their bouts of conflict, these pale in comparison to the virtually incessant bloodletting of Israelis and Palestinians. It is difficult to imagine Israeli Jews and Palestinians, after decades of horrific conflict and profound mutual distrust, sharing a confederation or any other form of binational state. It would be extremely difficult to imagine Israeli Jews submitting to any political order in which they would not be protected solely by their own independent military power.

Confederation between Jordan and Palestine, however, would seem to be a more realistic proposition. First of all, it is an idea that has circulated in the Jordanian and Palestinian political discourse since the early 1970s, and it has enjoyed considerable support from many if not a majority of Jordanians and Palestinians. There are, of course, various conditions that would have to be met for such a confederation to be accepted, and even then there will certainly be those in the Jordanian political elite and in certain parts of the intelligentsia who will continue to strongly reject the idea. Those in Jordan and Palestine who agree on confederation also agree that an independent Palestinian state *must be established first*. Palestinians want to guarantee their independent statehood, and Jordanians do not want to be dragged into Palestine prematurely. Jordanians do not want to undercut Palestinian independence and leave Jordan vulnerable to an overly intimate relationship with Palestine. Such intimacy, the Jordanians fear, might eventually threaten the Jordanianness of the East Bank of the River.

However, if and when Israel disengages from the West Bank, that territory, landlocked between Israel and Jordan, will become more dependent on Jordan and the Arab world beyond. There are some Jordanian nationalists who instinctively reject any close association with Palestine as a potential threat to their political patrimony, but there are others, equally nationalist, who see in confederation an opportunity to create a political order between Jordan and Palestine that will enable Palestinians in Jordan to exercise their political rights in Palestine rather than in Jordan, even though they will most probably continue to be residents of Jordan. The confederation could provide new formulas for citizenship and civil rights that would allow the Jordanians to feel more secure in their homeland on the East Bank by having Palestinians on the East Bank participate in the politics of the West Bank rather than the politics of Jordan.

VIII. Conclusions

Foreign powers would do well to come to terms with Middle Eastern realities for what they are rather than trying to engineer the peoples of the Middle East to become what they are not. Iraq and Afghanistan are good examples of what not to do and just how not to do it. One cannot cease to be amazed by the capacity of people to ignore the realities on the ground and really believe that culture does not matter and that all nations at all times are all the same. Thus, crushing Iraq at the beginning of the 21st century was expected to produce the same result that was produced by the defeat of Germany and Japan more than half a century ago, that is, to turn Iraq into a vibrant capitalist democracy and bastion of the West.

That Iraqi society is for the most part not secular but religiously sectarian to the core, in total contradistinction to Germany and Japan, was not factored into the calculations of the those who set forth to push over the first domino in the democratization of the entire Middle East. That Iraq degenerated into horrific sectarian strife, taking the lives of nearly one hundred thousand people, should not have surprised anyone, except those who chose to ignore the realities that should have been plain for all to see.

Setting timetables for the locals to start behaving themselves is as patronizing as it sounds and is not advisable either. If the negotiations have a good chance of succeeding one does not need a timetable. If the chances of success are low, no timetable is going to make any difference. The parties will not overcome their historical grievances and mutual suspicions and abide by these timetables just because they were set by someone. Nor can they be compelled to do so.

A timetable is usually a predetermined date upon which failure to keep to it will be solemnly pronounced. So why court failure? Failure is worse than not trying at all. Great power intervention sends messages of hope to the local players that their aspirations will be met. Failure by the supreme umpires of the universe leads the parties to despair and to revert to the battlefield and to more bloodshed. Israelis and Palestinians have already been there, unfortunately only too often.

All those involved should make it their business to study the limitations, constraints, desires, aspirations, and red lines of the players and make their best effort to help them get to where they would like to go. That would be a preferable course to trying to coerce the locals to do what they have no intention of doing, in accordance with a timetable set by the political exigencies of the external powers rather than the real interests of the protagonists.

There is a ubiquitous tendency to overestimate the powers of external players and to underestimate the power and resilience of local players, as well as their customs, traditions, and cultures and their sheer grit and determination to fight for what they really believe to be their existential interests. The conflict in the Middle East was driven more by considerations of history, communal identity, collective dignity, and other socio-cultural factors than by socio-economics or political economy. This was as true of the Zionists as it was of the Palestinians. Had the Zionists been driven by mainly economic considerations, they would never have been quite as obsessed as they were with matters of identity, cultural revival, and collective dignity. Their problems as individuals could have been resolved in America as many if not most of their fellow Jews did in fact believe. The same is true of the Palestinians. Had economics driven their behavior, they could have conceded to the Zionists and profited accordingly rather than resisting them with all the suffering that their struggle eventually entailed. The causes of the conflict are not economic, nor will the solutions be founded either on largesse or economic retribution.

The Israeli-Palestinian conflict has its own very specific causes and consequences. Israel-Palestine is not Northern Ireland or South Africa. False analogies obfuscate the specificity of every case and lead to misperceptions of the facts on the ground. False universalisms and the idea that one size fits all lead to the making of these misplaced analogies, which may serve the propaganda machines but make real and realistic solutions that much harder to attain.

They introduce a host of new obstacles that make peacemaking much more difficult by creating paradigms that do not relate in the slightest to the realities at hand. Most Israelis and most Palestinians in the West Bank and Gaza still prefer a two-state solution. The US and other external players would do all parties a service by assisting them to arrive, in the most realistic fashion possible, at the goal they themselves, for the most part, wish to achieve. This is, no doubt, a tall order. The alternatives are worse.

A "Paradise of Parasites":
Hannah Arendt, Antisemitism,
and the Legacies of Empire

Dorian Bell*

Scholars of European antisemitism have sometimes been loath to analogize between modern antisemitism and colonial racism, usually out of concern for maintaining the specificity of the Holocaust.[1] Other critics, most famously Hannah Arendt in *The Origins of Totalitarianism* (1951), have identified in nineteenth-century racialist imperialism a crucial step along the path to the Final Solution.[2] Whatever the relative merits of these approaches, even the latter has overlooked (or at least, as we shall see, misapprehended) the extent to which already in the nineteenth century antisemitism and empire were evolving in tandem. The analysis that follows makes a double case for the importance of better understanding this co-constitutive relation. In a brief initial excursion into the history of French antisemitism, and taking as my example the late nineteenth-century fantasmatic *topos* of the Jewish colonial conspirator, I first want to consider how imperial circumstances furnished discursive grist for the mill of an ascendant antisemitism. Ultimately, however, I will be most concerned with moving beyond the local particularities of this development to examine how its early articulation together of Jews and empire—along with a similar such articulation a few years later in Britain—has enjoyed a strange and enduring afterlife.

Neglect of that afterlife has perpetuated a conceptual blind spot in the recent spate of scholarship inspired by Arendt's suggestion in *The Origins of Totalitarianism* that imperialism in Africa set the stage for fascism in Europe (the so-called "boomerang thesis").[3] That Arendt conceived such a circulation at all owes something, I will be arguing, to antisemitism's own nineteenth-century inflection by empire, echoing and inverting as her framework does the antisemitic accusation that Jewish imperial malfeasance visited disaster on the metropole. Recognizing this nineteenth-century discursive legacy in *The Origins of Totalitarianism*—still the most important critical reflection on the relationship between antisemitism and empire—changes how we read *The Origins*, helping correct for unavowed assumptions that structure its arguments. And yet it is also precisely in this shadow content, or rather in the gaps, interstices, and inversions it leaves behind, that emerges what I will propose is a

---

* Assistant Professor of Literature, Department of Literature, University of California, Santa Cruz.

[1] See, for instance, Postone (105) and Mosse (x).

[2] Other examples include King and Stone, Moses and Stone, and Traverso.

[3] See note 2.

valuable analytic counterpoint to conventional paradigms for thinking antisemitism and empire together.

I begin with the French example. France's 1881 invasion of Tunisia, which led to that Ottoman province's *de facto* colonization as a French protectorate, quickly became the political scandal of the season in Paris. Citing the big speculative interests that stood to gain from the French guarantee of a Tunisian debt actively traded on the Parisian stock exchange, the muckraking opposition journalist Henri Rochefort cried foul and accused Prime Minister Jules Ferry and his allies of selling French foreign policy to the highest bidder.[4] Some joining the denunciatory anti-colonial chorus were quick to assume the handiwork of Jewish speculators, paving the way for a new and ubiquitous French cultural *topos*: the Jewish colonial conspirator and profiteer, who would feature prominently in one literary phenomenon (Guy de Maupassant's 1885 novel *Bel-Ami*), several lesser novels (Robert de Bonnières' *Les Monach* [*The Monachs*] (1884), Louis Noir's *La Banque juive* [*The Jewish Bank*] (1888), and Alfred Thévenin's *Un Grand banquier* [*A Great Banker*] (1889)), and any number of the antisemitic newspapers and pamphlets that proliferated in France in the 1880s and 1890s.

Among the chief architects of the vogue was the journalist and agitator Édouard Drumont. Drumont broached the Tunisian affair in his massively influential 1886 antisemitic polemic *La France juive* [*Jewish France*], one of the definitive French bestsellers of the nineteenth century and the bible of a national antisemitic movement that, with Drumont at its helm, would roil France for the remainder of the century. Drumont's hallucinatory treatise arrived in 1886 in the wake of a series of important colonial developments that contributed to the discovery by metropolitan reactionaries of North African Jewry. The 1870 Crémieux decree granting French citizenship to indigenous Jews in French colonial Algeria had instantaneously created the most visible Jewish constituency in French history. As a proportion of the population, the 34,000 Jews in Algeria far outstripped the 80,000 Jews in the much more populous metropole. Suddenly, twenty percent of the Algerian electorate was Jewish, a proportion that in some towns reached fifty percent—a sharp contrast with France, where Jews represented no more than 0.02 percent of the population (Wilson 231; Ageron 1: 585; Poliakov 296). Drumont's bugaboo, so demographically insignificant in France, had conveniently assumed much more impressive form in the colony.

Add to this the huge financial scandal surrounding the 1881 invasion of Tunisia, along with the violent antisemitic riots in Algeria in 1884, and North Africa was becoming a particularly contentious theatre of French activity. Drumont cannily exploited this theatre to maximum rhetorical effect. By sensationalizing the imagined crimes of North African Jews, and seamlessly linking this construction to existing misgivings about the role of metropolitan French Jews in the colonial project, Drumont located in the imperial frontier a potent discursive frontier for his aggressive new brand of antisemitism.

Drumont was especially adept at deploying colonial events to offer comparative "proof" that Jewish financial and political maneuvers were common to, and coordinated across, different Jewish communities sharing a same racial bond. The 1881

---

[4] See, among Rochefort's many articles on this question, "Le Secret de l'affaire tunisienne."

Tunisian invasion proved particularly useful in this racializing endeavor, as did the Crémieux decree, both of which receive substantial attention from Drumont in *La France juive*, though for the sake of time I will limit my comments here to the Tunisian invasion. Dogged by rumors it had been prompted by backroom investment schemes, the invasion had provoked outrage over tales of political and financial skullduggery by both metropolitan and Tunisian Jews. Drumont's contribution was to insist on the coordination of these two Jewries in the affair. He charged that Madame Elias Mussali, a central Tunisian figure in the scandal whom Drumont inaccurately labeled a Jew, had conspired from across the Mediterranean to harness the financial and political wherewithal of her metropolitan brethren. In this fashion Drumont could suggest that Jews were everywhere the same, regardless of geography or culture, and that what made them the same was an innate predilection for conspiracy and financial villainy.

This villainy was made handily corporeal, and by extension racial, by Drumont's newly historicized redeployment of otherwise hackneyed Orientalist descriptions, descriptions to which he affixed signification they did not yet completely possess. Of Elias Mussali, Drumont writes the following:

> You often notice, in travel books, those African Jewesses half-lolling on cushions at the back of a secluded room in their home, resting their ring-laden fingers on a vast, flabby belly. Overcome by stoutness at thirty years of age, glistening with fat, they have but one remaining passion, to watch the heavy sequin necklace grow around their bloated neck.
>
> It was with one of these Jewesses, Madame Elias Mussali, that Roustan [*the French consul in Tunisia*] decided that it was necessary to kill a certain number of our poor soldiers... (*La France juive* 1: 476).

As Drumont himself underlines with his reference to travel books, little about this venomous portrait was likely, on the surface, to strike the reader as new. The textual and iconographic inheritance of Orientalism had conditioned the French, when they were not being regaled by stories of the Oriental Jewess's incomparable beauty, to think of her as the epitome of gluttony. As several commentators have observed, however, the nineteenth-century French Orientalist tradition had typically abstracted the object of its exoticizing fantasies from the material and political realities surrounding the Occident's ever-increasing imperial penetration of North Africa and the Middle and Far East.[5] Puncturing this aestheticizing auto-referentiality, Drumont made the Oriental Jew, in the person of Elias Mussali, step menacingly from the quaint Orientalist tableau and into the actual financial and political life of the metropole.

Along the way, Drumont cleverly drafted the tenets of a certain socialist, economic antisemitism into the service of an essentializing racialism. By extending to North African Jews suspicions about metropolitan Jewish behavior long held by anti-capitalist, antisemitic thinkers on the French Left like Proudhon and Fourier, Drumont took advantage of the Tunisian affair to transfer animosity against metro-

---

[5] On writers' and artists' disappointment in and occlusion of an imperial fact disrupting to their overseas fantasies, see Behdad (13-17), Bongie (17-19), Dobie (4-5), Said (189-191), and Terdiman (227-257).

politan "Jewish" capitalism to Jews themselves, wherever they might be. Socialist antisemitic theorists like Auguste Chirac had, from the mid-nineteenth century onward, elaborated an ambiguously structural antisemitism, one often as willing to accuse a Protestant banker of "Jewish" skullduggery (*juiverie*) as a Jewish one (Chirac 35). In North Africa, however, Drumont had found what could pass for evidence that *juiverie*, before it was a matter of behavior, was a matter of birth that ineluctably manifested itself across even the geographic and cultural gulf that separated continental and North African Jewries.

That Drumont's Tunisian conspiracy theory both emerged and departed from received Orientalist practice—drawing on stock Orientalist representations of North African Jewry, yet overtly politicizing them to an unprecedented degree—poses a useful first test to established modes of thinking antisemitism and empire together. As my terminology indicates, one of the few such ready theoretical frames can be located, and has been located, in the work of Edward Said, which I want to invoke quickly less on its own terms than for what it helps reveal about an ongoing blind spot in the reception of another such theoretical frame, namely the reflection on antisemitism and empire that traverses Hannah Arendt's *The Origins of Totalitarianism*, to which I will be turning the bulk of my remaining attention. If I call Said's project a ready frame for tracing articulations between antisemitism and empire, it is in part because he himself invited that effort, going so far as to observe that, in writing the history of Orientalism, he was "writing the history of a strange, secret sharer of Western antisemitism" (27). What he is referencing, of course, is that the nineteenth-century philological racism popularized by the likes of Ernest Renan included the Jew and the Muslim in the larger taxonomic category of the sensuous, indolent, and fanatical "Semite" who had supposedly been theologically and culturally superseded by the Aryan Christian. Denunciations of Jews now increasingly drew on the same wellspring of pseudoscientific fictions that nourished Orientalizing representations of Muslims deployed in conjunction with and legitimation of imperial conquest.

Jews, to be sure, did not control the overseas lands targeted for European domination in the nineteenth century, which helps account for why Said—concerned as he was with questions of colonial empire—limited himself to describing what he called the "Islamic branch" of Orientalism (28). Scholars have since begun sketching what might correspondingly be designated as Orientalism's "Jewish branch," remaining within a Saidian paradigm to argue, notably in the case of eighteenth- and nineteenth-century Germany, that Orientalizing discourses about European Jews accompanied attempts to subject them to an "inner European colonialism" bearing an ideological kinship with colonial expansion further afield (Hess 63). Historical specifics aside, what I want to emphasize is the supposition underpinning most comparisons between internal and external colonialisms, or between discourses about Jews and Muslims. These schemas generally posit ways in which practices and discourses aimed at Jews and imperial subalterns shared a common basis. For Said, philological racism constituted one such basis, offering as it did a combined store of historical and cultural fallacies with which to tar Europe's internal, Jewish enemy and external, Muslim foe alike. Others have thought more longitudinally, for instance locating in Christianity's theological appropriation then expurgation of Judaism a proto-imperialist template for later patterns of colonial conquest and eradication (Heschel 19-22). Either way, a basic logic remains, one that equates the Jew and the colonized as dual victims of a same, insidious race-thinking.

I borrow the term "race-thinking" from Arendt's *The Origins of Totalitarianism*. Arendt, too, subscribed to a genealogical logic according to which various nineteenth-century racisms—and by this she means full-fledged ideologies like colonial racism—emerged from a European race-thinking traceable to the Enlightenment and refined in the nineteenth century by thinkers like Arthur de Gobineau. When combined with different political exigencies, Arendt argues, this race-thinking lent itself to various manifestations of focused racism: so, for instance, did colonial racism serve the requirements of empire, or antisemitism serve the requirements of political reactions fixated on the Jews. Various European racisms might function differently and target different groups, but they all proceeded from common epistemic ground.

This genealogical demonstration by Arendt carries an unspoken and overlooked corollary critical to the rest of *The Origins of Totalitarianism*: a mutual intelligibility between racisms, owing to their common epistemic source, that by implication made it easy for them to reinforce each other. Much has been made in recent years of the "boomerang thesis" developed by Arendt in *The Origins*, in which she suggests that a bureaucratically administered racism honed in the nineteenth- and early twentieth-century imperial periphery rebounded onto the European continent and achieved its purest expression in the Nazi exterminationist project. Searching, as she wrote *The Origins* in the late 1940s, to explain the totalitarian tragedy that had just engulfed Europe, Arendt seized among other factors on the European Scramble for Africa and the role she felt it had played in unleashing the hitherto latent potential for race-thinking to destroy the European body politic. Commentators have long observed that Arendt remains vague about the actual mechanisms whereby imperial sins came home to roost, and that a central premise of her boomerang thesis—the destruction of the nation-state by imperialism—has difficulty withstanding scrutiny (Benhabib 75-76; Canovan 42-44). Those intrigued by Arendt's argument have tried, with varying results, to locate tangible historical pathways through which imperial racism might have caromed back onto Europe. Indeed, this elaborating project has become a cornerstone of the burgeoning field of comparative genocide studies. But what has gone insufficiently recognized is that the genealogical dimension to Arendt's thought on racism meant that her boomerang thesis never required, for its explanatory thrust, the existence of especially concrete channels funneling bureaucratic imperial racism toward the continent. If various continental and imperial racisms shared a common origin in race-thinking, then it was expected enough that they should easily interrelate, like the separated branches of a river joining again with new torrential force.

So conceived, racisms did not need much to catalyze their interaction: thus can Arendt propose, for example, that the mere example of the race society fashioned by the Boers in South Africa bolstered Nazi confidence in the principle of a master race (*Origins* 206-207).[6] Arendt might have noted the imbrication of racist and expansionist German discourses about Central European Slavs and Jews and central African

---

[6] All other parenthetical references to Arendt in the text refer to *The Origins of Totalitarianism*, unless otherwise indicated.

blacks as far back as Kaiser Wilhelm (Traverso 51-52), but she did not need to, at least according to the parameters of her approach. Once the deep homology between racisms was established, it became somewhat redundant to parse various causeways between phenomena that already, in their very essence, lent themselves to almost inevitable reciprocity.

Arendt herself would likely object to this characterization of her thinking, teetering as it does on the brink of the historical determinism she so vocally eschewed. She made a special point to reject any linear, narrativizing account of totalitarianism as the inevitable last link in a chain of historical causalities. Responding to the political philosopher Eric Voegelin, who interpreted *The Origins* as "a gradual revelation of the essence of totalitarianism from its inchoate forms in the eighteenth century to the fully developed" (quoted in Arendt, *Essays* 405), Arendt countered that no such inchoate, originary essence had ever existed. Her intention, she continued, had been to "talk only of 'elements', which eventually crystallize into totalitarianism, some of which are traceable to the eighteenth century, some perhaps even farther back" (*Essays* 405). Arendt's point is that the "crystallization" of these elements into totalitarianism remained contingent, even if the individual elements themselves might possess genealogical precursors. But maintaining this distinction between the synchronic, contingent figure of crystallization and the more diachronic, determining figure of genealogy proved easier said than done. *The Origins* finds Arendt slipping between the two, and never more than in her disquisitions on race. For if imperial racism in Africa was for Arendt one of the elements that crystallized with continental imperial racisms (such as what she calls "pan-Germanism") to produce totalitarian racism, this crystallization together of racisms was implicitly facilitated by the close genealogical kinship the various racisms *already* shared—so much so that, as I have already observed, Arendt hardly bothers looking for any actual discursive or material nuclei around which the crystallization might have proceeded. Crystallization, in other words, here swaps much of its contingency for the necessity of genealogy.

Critics have certainly noted the tension throughout *The Origins* between what Seyla Benhabib calls Arendt's "fragmentary historiography" of crystallization and a more traditionally linear, genealogical search for origins (95). Yet there is still more specific work to be done, I think, to recognize and account for the interwoven logics of contingency and genealogy in Arendt's thesis of boomeranging racism. One might begin by asking whether the recent and increasingly numerous efforts to give Arendt's thesis a sounder evidential basis—"to follow up" on Arendt's "intuition," as a recent volume put it (King and Stone 13)—may actually fall somewhat beside the point, at least insofar as that basis seems often to consist of identifying institutional or other pathways along which the "boomerang" ostensibly traveled from Africa to Europe. If, as Arendt implicitly allows, the crystallization of African and continental imperial racisms into totalitarian racism was expedited by their common parentage in a European race-thinking, then the existence of identifiable causal pathways between the various racisms becomes less important than the far more diffuse attainment of a saturation point. Like a crystal forming spontaneously in a concentrated solution, totalitarian racism coalesced for Arendt after colonial empire massively injected the European *zeitgeist* with the applied possibilities of a race-thinking that already suffused the continent.

Charting the attainment of such a saturation point in anything but the vaguest terms represents a challenging goal indeed. But perhaps an even greater challenge to substantiating Arendt's boomerang thesis is that the heuristics of genealogy and contingency do more than just intersect; they also subtly interfere. Presuming the common genealogical origin, in race-thinking, of imperial and totalitarian racisms has the effect of equating their chief respective targets—the colonized abroad and the Jews back home—as successive victims of two outshoots of race-thinking that naturally resonated together. The notion is intuitive enough: many an observer besides Arendt has similarly conceived the relationship between antisemitism and imperial racism as that of "one racism chasing another" (Angenot 135), characterized by relations of "mutual support" (Carroll 147). One can include Said here as well, for whom antisemitism and Orientalist imperialism drew on the same philological fantasms about "Semites." The problem with such genealogical thinking is that it obscures how the rise of empire might have contributed to the rise of modern antisemitism in ways unrelated to the direct exercise of imperial racism—that is to say, in more unpredictably contingent ways not over-determined by a common genealogy of race-thinking.

Consider the phenomenon I documented earlier, which is the myth propagated by late nineteenth-century French antisemites that Jewish interests in France were instigating French colonial interventions in North Africa for their own gain. There is no doubt this successful antisemitic narrative bore some genealogical relation to the imperial racism that helped legitimate colonial expansion; after all, the *topos* of the Jewish colonial conspirator derived much of its shock value from the image of metropolitan Jews conniving with their more alien and therefore more easily racializable indigenous Jewish counterparts in colonies like Tunisia and Algeria. But the fact also remains that many of these antisemites, Drumont among them, were at first opposed to French colonial expansion, and thus that their articulation together of the imperial and Jewish questions owed as much or even more to the fact of empire itself than to its status as a racist enterprise. In other words, there is a great deal about this co-constructedness of antisemitism and empire that, as the product of historically specific and contingent circumstances, remains uncoupled from any common parentage between discourses about Jews and Muslims. This has received little attention, however, because of the genealogical reflex that conceives the relation between empire and antisemitism as the logical transfer from the colonized to the Jews—or *vice versa*—of a racial animus evolving over time.

Further reinforcing the genealogical, metonymic narrative of a European racialism fastening sequentially onto one victim after another is the massive *telos* furnished by the Holocaust. Indeed, Arendt's boomerang thesis owes much of its abiding influence to the historicizing explanation it offers for the exterminationist Nazi campaign against European Jewry. Arendt postulates a new category of "superfluous" man jarred loose by the nineteenth-century dislocations of capital and empire, a category as emergent in the superfluous European masses consigned to the imperial periphery as in the colonized masses relegated by racism to the margins of human endeavor. All of this reaches its culminating expression in the absolute superfluousness of the concentration camp victim, rendered infinitely expendable because, as Arendt puts it, he has been banished "from the human world altogether" (444). Surging forth from Europe, then gaining potency in Africa before returning to the continent with a vengeance, superfluousness offers Arendt a conceptual pivot around which to portray the Jews as the final and arguably most quintessential victims of empire.

Yet what this lasting boomerang imagery has tended to obscure is that, for Arendt, European Jews were not just the final repository of the superfluousness set in motion by empire; they were also among the very first. With the late nineteenth-century rise of colonial empire, Arendt offers, Europe's ascendant bourgeoisie saw its first opportunity to profit from state enterprise. The resultant flow of bourgeois capital into the imperial project dislodged the Jews from their traditional, privileged role as bankers to the state. Arendt's conclusion about the outcome is profound: Jewish wealth no longer explainable as the consequence of a tangible and potentially still justifiable financial service rendered to the nation-state, the Jew could now be portrayed more convincingly than ever as the social parasite *par excellence*. Arendt, in other words, credits the rise of empire with the late nineteenth-century European emergence of a modern antisemitism that, by categorizing the Jews *en masse* as socially superfluous, prefigured a twentieth-century totalitarian exterminationism radically intent on demonstrating the Jew's corresponding expendability.

In Arendt's account, then, empire twice renders the Jews superfluous: a first time when the bourgeois project of empire ended the longtime symbiosis between European nation-states and Jewish finance; and a second time when the concentration camps made Jews the final and most abject category of "superfluous" man incarnated in Africa by colonizers and the colonized. The two processes are related, with the earlier attribution to the Jews of superfluousness setting the stage for a later attempt at eradication. But a fundamental difference also remains. Arendt's thesis of a bureaucratized colonial racism coming home to roost in the Holocaust groups Jews and the colonized on the receiving end of a single, if evolving, pattern of European racist domination. Her notion of a perceived Jewish superfluousness in the initial wake of the Scramble for Africa, however, posits a more historically contingent relationship between antisemitism and empire. If the promise of overseas riches prompted bourgeois investors to displace the Jews as financiers to the state, this had little to do with imperial racism, at least as regards the Jews. The same pretext for antisemitism would ostensibly have emerged had the bourgeoisie found any other reason to overcome its traditional disinterest in state-backed commerce, or had the Jews themselves simply decided to withhold their capital from governments.

Next to Arendt's more readily visualizable narrative tracing a rebound onto Europe of imperial misdeeds, her comparatively abstract correlation of modern antisemitism with a diminishment of Jewish influence in the age of empire has generated less commentary. For one thing, it confounds the genealogical reflex that conceives European Jewry as a variety of the colonized. For another, it attends to the prehistory of the Holocaust rather than the Holocaust itself, a peripherality compounded by the difficulty of connecting Nazi exterminationism to the modern antisemitism Arendt attributes to a Scramble for Africa in which England and France played far greater roles than Germany. Yet Arendt's claim of a Jewish superfluousness born first of the imperial fact—and only later reinforced by a boomeranging imperial racism—offers important insight not only into the actual historical articulation between antisemitism and empire, but also into what I will be arguing is her own problematic indebtedness to the late nineteenth- and early twentieth-century discourses this articulation produced. I turn now to that indebtedness, and to how Arendt's uneven efforts to transcend it structure and delimit her argument in critical ways.

Charting this hidden fault line in *The Origins* begins with recognizing that Arendt was both right and wrong in her description of how imperial circumstances other than racism shaped the development of modern antisemitism. Right, because modern antisemitism and empire indeed co-evolved in ways not always reducible to their shared basis in race-thinking. Wrong, because the historical record suggests that the rise of empire hardly led to the perception that Jews had lost their privileged relationship to the state and now only exhibited, as she puts it, a parasitic "wealth without visible function" (4). On the contrary, a series of rapid-fire, unpopular colonial adventures by France and England after 1870 emboldened many in those countries to argue that Jews were more shamelessly pulling the levers of state power than ever. It does not matter that this perceived Jewish influence was obviously understood to function toward nefarious ends. What matters is that it was understood to function at all. Citing Tocqueville's contention that the French revolutionary masses most hated the aristocracy once its waning state privileges no longer seemed to justify its continued wealth—whether or not the masses had perceived those privileges as fair—Arendt argues that Jews likewise attracted "universal hatred" when empire cost them influence in a way that made their wealth seem inexplicable (15). Yet given the success with which Jews were supposedly manipulating the state imperial project to their profit, Jewish wealth had if anything become *more* explicable, though of course only spuriously. Hence could French antisemites, for example, argue with seductive specificity that France's 1881 invasion of Tunisia had been ordered by Jewish holders of Tunisian debt. British antisemites, deploying an essentially analogous tactic, would for their part argue that Jewish diamond and gold interests in the South African Rand had in 1899 embroiled Britain in the bloody Second Boer War.

Evidently, empire offered tempting fodder for a newly politicized brand of European antisemitism. And as Arendt was the first to understand, this early encounter between two great hydras of modernity produced discourses that empire—as a comprehensive political phenomenon, and not just a racist ideology—allowed to flourish about Jews. But Arendt otherwise reads the effect of empire on antisemitism against the grain. Rather than noting how imperial adventures furnished grist for accusations of Jewish collusion with governments, she proposes the opposite: namely, that empire bred antisemitism by making Jews seem superfluous to state affairs. What accounts for this oppositional choice by Arendt, one so symmetrical in its inversion of early antisemitic arguments about empire as to seem almost willful?

The answer I want to propose concerns the fact that Arendt herself partially reprised the old antisemitic canard that Jewish finance greased the wheels of European imperialism, and helps illustrate what I will be arguing is the invisible conceptual freight carried for Arendt by the theme of superfluousness that so animates *The Origins*. Arendt's multiple invocations of the celebrated British economist J.A. Hobson, author of the 1902 anti-colonialist study *Imperialism,* are telling in this regard. Like Lenin before her, Arendt accepted Hobson's central thesis that imperialism was driven by the need of "superfluous" European capital to ceaselessly "press farther afield" in the search for new markets and investments (Hobson, *Imperialism*

361). Building on Hobson's notion, as well as on Rosa Luxemburg's related critique of imperialism as the inevitable political corollary of accumulated capital, Arendt portrayed superfluousness as both the engine and self-reproducing outcome of empire. Empire channeled abroad the superfluous labor and wealth generated by capitalism; it expropriated the resources of others to produce further superfluous wealth; and, finally, having institutionalized the superfluousness of its agents and victims, it added European Jewry to the disposable ranks of superfluous man.

Driving all this for Arendt was a bourgeoisie enthralled with making "money beget money" (137)—an obsession that, in its imperial configuration as "expansion for expansion's sake," she felt had upended the principles of the nation-state and set Europe on the path to totalitarianism and exterminationist antisemitism (126).

But Arendt did not just count the Jews among the victims of a ravaging imperial superfluousness. She argued as well that they helped to unleash it. Arendt submits that it was European Jewish financiers who "opened the channels of capital export to superfluous wealth" by facilitating government investment abroad during the initial phase of imperialism in the 1870s and 1880s (136). In support of her claim she cites Hobson, whose early critiques of imperialism contained choice words about the Jewish role in colonial South Africa. Endorsing Hobson as "very reliable in observation and very honest in analysis" (135), Arendt reproduces at length a passage from a 1900 article he penned whose tenor speaks for itself. Jewish financiers, Hobson reports, went to South Africa

> for money, and those who came early and made most have commonly withdrawn their persons, leaving their economic fangs in the carcass of their prey. They fastened on the Rand ... as they are prepared to fasten upon any other spot upon the globe. (quoted in *Origins* 135)

In a passage of the article not cited by Arendt, Hobson labels these Jewish financiers the "*causa causans* of the present trouble in South Africa" because they stood to gain economically from British imperial intervention ("Capitalism and Imperialism in South Africa" 5). Hobson's impassioned book-length denunciation of the Second Boer War, *The War in South Africa: Its Causes and Effects* (1900), likewise features Jews prominently on the "causes" side of the ledger.

To the question posed by one chapter title, "For Whom Are We Fighting?," Hobson offers a familiar response: the Jewish diamond and gold magnates, who have transformed Johannesburg into "the New Jerusalem" on the helpless watch of the "slower-witted Briton" (189-190).

Arendt's queasy ventriloquizing of Hobson figures centrally in Bernard Wasserstein's controversial recent harangue against Arendt in the *Times Literary Supplement*, in which Wasserstein charges Arendt with having internalized the antisemitism of the authorities she cited (Wasserstein 14). Though the evidence is new, the polemic is not, dating as it does to the furor that greeted Arendt's contentions in *Eichmann in Jerusalem* about Jewish cooperation with the Holocaust. Whatever complexities Arendt's use of Hobson might or might not indicate about her relationship to her own Jewishness, however, I find it more analytically productive to contemplate what it reveals about Arendt's argument in *The Origins of Totalitarianism*. And what it reveals is a thinker grappling intensely with her indebtedness to a certain epistemic paradigm. Shocking as it is for Arendt blithely to recycle Hobson's tale of vampirical

Jews—or, for that matter, to borrow approvingly an account by Hobson's contemporary J.A. Froude of Jewish merchants in South Africa "gathered like eagles over their prey" (quoted in *Origins* 198)—Arendt does so with calculated intent. Her praise for Hobson's "reliability" is mostly designed to demonstrate that, if in *Imperialism* Hobson no longer blamed the Jews for the Second Boer War, it was because he had since correctly and honestly recognized that, as she writes, "their influence and role had been temporary and somewhat superficial" (135). Arendt means to illustrate that, despite an initial role as financial facilitators, Jews were eventually wholly supplanted in their imperial function by the bourgeoisie. Jews were "only the representatives, not the owners, of the superfluous capital," she writes (200). It follows that the Jews themselves were easily made superfluous by empire, something to which, as we have seen, Arendt attributes the rise of modern antisemitism.

Notice here the inversion accomplished by Arendt. Hobson at one point considered Jews responsible for the imperial developments he decried. But Arendt takes Hobson's later silence on the matter as more than just evidence that Jews had not, in fact, played a determining role in South African affairs. Rather, she reverses the terms of the equation altogether: whereas Hobson and others blamed Jewish influence for the rise of empire, Arendt locates in the rise of empire the beginning of a perilous Jewish irrelevance. In other words, Arendt maintains the old causal link between empire and the Jewish question, even if she reverses its polarity. Arendt is in many ways clearly writing against Hobson. She explicitly rebukes him for suggesting that the Rothschilds, the international Jewish banking family and eternal bugaboo of antisemites, pulled the strings of every European war (*Origins* 24-25). More subtly, her argument about the Jews' reluctance to translate economic influence in South Africa into political influence represents an implicit rebuttal to Hobson's own contention that Jewish businessmen had, in South Africa, made an exception to their usual disinterest in political matters (*Origins* 136; Hobson, "Capitalism and Imperialism in South Africa" 5-6). Yet Arendt is also unmistakably writing *within* a long discursive tradition of linking the Jewish and imperial questions—a tradition shaped by antisemites who, beginning in the late nineteenth century, saw in the passions stirred by empire a chance to stoke hatred against Jews. This tradition, I want to argue, supplied the epistemic grounds—indeed, the condition of possibility—for Arendt to think Jews and empire together. One finds it difficult to imagine that Arendt would otherwise have formulated so circumstantial an explanation for modern antisemitism as the relative non-participation by Jews in empire, given that the terms of her argument would seem inherently to militate against conceiving any relationship between Jews and empire in the first place. That her thesis so symmetrically inverts existing assumptions about Jews and empire only underscores her dependence on so improbable a conceptual forebear.

Critics have sometimes charged, rightfully I think, that Arendt's representation of black Africans in *The Origins* does not always rise above the racialist imperialism she assails.[7] So too, I would add now, does Arendt strain mightily against the antisemitic inheritance that subtly structures one of her core claims about the implications of empire for Jews. From this perspective, Arendt's unsettlingly approving

---

[7] For a recent summary of this debate, see King and Stone (9-11); see also Rothberg (33-65).

reproduction of Hobson's antisemitic invective might be considered symptomatic, a stray artifact of her reliance on and only partial reconfiguration of an existing discourse. There is of course also the matter of Arendt's ever-contentious insistence on the Jewish portion of responsibility for antisemitism, which occasioned her somewhat perverse readiness to consider antisemitic sources reliable. At least when it comes to her indulgence of Hobson's dubious remarks about Jews in South Africa, however, I would suggest that the picture is rather more complex, and that Arendt's micro-appropriation here of antisemitic language actually finds her trying to exorcise her macro-dependence on an antisemitic discourse about empire. By deploying familiar *topoi* from the antisemitic lexicon in her depiction of an imperial South Africa afflicted by gold-lust, economic predation, and financial parasitism, Arendt lays the groundwork for reapportioning blame to a variety of other imperial actors—all of whom, Arendt means clearly to suggest, behaved more "Jewishly" than the Jews themselves.

Thus, for instance, does Arendt memorably dub colonial South Africa "the first paradise of parasites" (151), because it channeled superfluous capital and labor into the *ne plus ultra* of bourgeois fantasies: directly transforming money into more money by literally mining it from the earth. Arendt's inclusion of Jews among these "parasites," though only as temporary avatars and middlemen of the real (bourgeois) owners of parasitic wealth, possesses the rhetorical advantage of acknowledging rather than eliding the historical fact of Jewish involvement in the South African gold and diamond mines. But Arendt also willfully plays up the parasitism of these Jews, the better to transfer its stigma onto their bourgeois patrons—and to rehearse, by the same token, her own substitution of the bourgeois for the Jew in the old antisemitic narrative about empire that she has only partially recast.

Thus, too, does Arendt draw unlikely correspondences between Jews and the Boers of turn-of-the-century South Africa. "Like the Jews," she remarks, the Boers "firmly believed in themselves as the chosen people" (195); and if the Boers were the most virulent in their antisemitism, it was because they identified in the Jews a competing "claim to chosenness" (202). Arendt's analogy foreshadows her later argument that supranational racist movements in Europe shared an affinity with, and even patterned themselves after, the "rootlessness" and "tribalness" of the Jews (239). Yet it serves as well, in the manner I have been describing, to offload onto others the structural role played by Jews in the antisemitic narrative about empire that Arendt inherits and reconfigures. The Boers are like Jews for Arendt because on a certain level she requires them to function *as* Jews, something that perhaps explains why, in citing the Boers' "complete lack of literature and other intellectual achievement," she echoes a classic slur directed by antisemites at the Jewish people (196).

Arendt, in short, seeks to make Jews as redundant as possible to the economy of imperial superfluousness she theorizes. What becomes, then, of those superfluous to superfluousness itself? Like the negative of a negative, they revert to a positive, at least in the South African context. Arendt reports that after having been displaced from their earlier speculative activities, South African Jews became an island of "normalcy and productivity" in the gold-distorted imperial economy by becoming manufacturers, shopkeepers, and members of the liberal professions. This only earned them more hatred from the Boers, Arendt adds, because they were now antithetical, in their very productivity, to the parasitic economy of superfluousness predicated on the racist spoliation of labor and mineral wealth (205). The irony is of course superb, and quite intentional on Arendt's part: here is a group of non-Jews become more stereotypically "Jewish" than the Jews themselves, and hating their real Jewish neighbors for *not* engaging in predatory economic activity! With this wry series of inversions, Arendt completes her transfer away from the Jews of the "Jewish" function in the old antisemitic critique of empire whose basic conceptual armature she otherwise maintains.

Arendt's correlation of Boer antisemitism with the displacement of Jews from the financial machinery of empire recalls her larger thesis about European antisemitism, which she likewise correlates with the ultimate absence of Jews from the imperial state project. Still, the mechanisms she invokes to explain the two correlations—suspicion of Jewish productivity in the South African case, and suspicion of Jewish non-productivity in the European case—prove difficult to reconcile. The fact that Arendt's core notion about the superfluousness of Jews to the project of empire survives these varied and contradictory applications bespeaks less, I think, an analytic confusion than a steady projection by Arendt into her arguments of her own conceptual preoccupation: namely, the preoccupation to render the Jews superfluous to a theory of empire problematically descended from a bygone narrative of Jewish colonial conspiracy.

The paradoxical result is that this first and most famous attempt to link antisemitism and imperialism is simultaneously at pains, in many ways, to cleave the Jew from the story of empire. That imperative exacts a price, for instance in Arendt's patently inaccurate claim that the substantial population of indigenous Jews in French colonial Algeria did not "play much of a role" in French imperial politics (50)—counter-examples to which continue to multiply.[8] Here I would cite Said as well, who as I mentioned before gestured tantalizingly toward the reciprocity of antisemitism and empire by characterizing Orientalism as the "secret sharer of Western antisemitism." Like the captain and stowaway of the Conrad story, however, Said's secret sharers ultimately part ways, cleaved into two for Said when "the Semitic myth bifurcated in the Zionist movement; one Semite went the way of Orientalism, the other, the Arab, was forced to go the way of the Oriental" (307). Said's too-neat distinction between colonizing Jews and colonized Arabs, like Arendt's reductive differentiation between bourgeois imperialists and Jewish bystanders, obscures the historical fact that, more than any other group, Jews were everywhere made to straddle the imperial divide: at once colonizer and colonized, "European" and "Arab," assimilated middleman and scapegoated pariah. The task at hand is better to appreciate how the complex dynamics of this oscillation redefined antisemitism in the era of empire.

---

[8] Most recently, see Schreier, who documents how Algerian Jews helped shape French colonial policy in Algeria.

References

Ageron, Charles-Robert. 1968. *Les Algériens musulmans et la France (1871-1919)*, 2 vols. Paris: PUF.

Angenot, Marc. 1989. *Ce que l'on dit des Juifs en 1889: antisémitisme et discours social.* Saint-Denis: Presses Universitaires de Vincennes.

Arendt, Hannah. 1994. *Essays in Understanding 1930-1954*. Edited by Jerome Kohn. New York: Harcourt Brace.

———. 1976. *The Origins of Totalitarianism*. San Diego: Harcourt.

Behdad, Ali. 1994. *Belated Travelers: Orientalism in the Age of Colonial Dissolution.* Durham: Duke UP.

Benhabib, Seyla. 2003. *The Reluctant Modernism of Hannah Arendt*, new ed. New York: Rowman and Littlefield.

Bongie, Chris. 1991. *Exotic Memories: Literature, Colonialism, and the Fin de Siècle.* Stanford: Stanford UP.

Canovan, Margaret. 1974. *The Political Thought of Hannah Arendt*. New York: Harcourt Brace Jovanovich.

Carroll, David. 2004. "Fascism, Colonialism, and 'Race': The Reality of a Fiction." In *Fascism and Neofascism: Critical Writings on the Radical Right in Europe*, edited by Angelica Fenner and Eric D. Weitz, pp. 141-157 (New York: Palgrave Macmillan).

Chirac, Auguste. 1987 [1883]. *Les Rois de la République: histoire des juiveries*. Paris: Éditions du Trident.

Dobie, Madeleine. 2001. *Foreign Bodies: Gender, Language, and Culture in French Orientalism*. Stanford: Stanford UP.

Drumont, Édouard. 1886. *La France juive: essai d'histoire contemporaine*, 2 vols. Paris: Marpon & Flammarion.

Hess, Jonathan. 2000. "Johann David Michaelis and the Colonial Imaginary: Orientalism and the Emergence of Racial Antisemitism in Eighteenth-Century Germany." *Jewish Social Studies* 6(2), pp. 56-101.

Hobson, J.A. 1900. "Capitalism and Imperialism in South Africa." *Contemporary Review* 77, pp. 1-17.

———. 2005 [1902]. *Imperialism: A Study*. Cosimo: New York.

———. 1900. *The War in South Africa: Its Causes and Effects*. London: James Nisbet & Co.

King, Richard H., and Dan Stone, ed. 2008. *Hannah Arendt and the Uses of History: Imperialism, Nation, Race, and Genocide*. New York: Berghahn.

Moses, A. Dirk, and Dan Stone, ed. 2007. *Colonialism and Genocide*. New York: Routledge.

Mosse, George L. 1985. *Toward the Final Solution: A History of European Racism*. New York: Howard.

Poliakov, Léon. 1981. *Histoire de l'antisémitisme. 2. L'âge de la science*. Paris: Calmann-Lévy.

Postone, Moishe. 1980. "Antisemitism and National Socialism: Notes on the German Reaction to 'Holocaust.'" *New German Critique* 19, pp. 97-115.

Rochefort, Henri. 1881. "Le Secret de l'affaire tunisienne." *L'Intransigeant*, September 27, p. 1.

Rothberg, Michael. 2009. *Multidirectional Memory: Remembering the Holocaust in the Age of Decolonization*. Stanford: Stanford UP.

Said, Edward. 1979. *Orientalism.* New York: Vintage.
Schreier, Joshua. 2010. *Arabs of the Jewish Faith: The Civilizing Mission in Colonial Algeria.* Rutgers: Rutgers UP.
Terdiman, Richard. 1985. *Discourse/Counter-Discourse: The Theory and Practice of Symbolic Resistance in Nineteenth-Century France.* Ithaca: Cornell UP.
Traverso, Enzo. 2003. *The Origins of Nazi Violence.* Translated by Janet Lloyd. New York: The New Press.
Wasserstein, Bernard. 2009. "Blame the Victim—Hannah Arendt Among the Nazis: The Historian and Her Sources." *Times Literary Supplement,* October 9, pp. 13-15.
Wilson, Stephen. 2007. *Ideology and Experience: Antisemitism in France at the Time of the Dreyfus Affair.* Oxford: Littman Library of Jewish Civilization.

"I Don't Know Why They Hate Us—I Don't Think We Did Anything Bad to Hurt Them"

Jewish Girls (Aged 10-12) Reflect on Their Experiences of Antisemitism

Nora Gold*

I. INTRODUCTION

Antisemitism has existed for over 2,000 years, and, since World War II, numerous scholars have sought to understand this phenomenon, including its causes and effects (e.g., Cotler 2009; Fineberg et al. 2007; Langmuir 1990; Lappin 2008; Laqueur 2006; Maccoby 2006, 1996; Millman 2009; Poliakov 1965; Wistrich 2010, 1999, 1991). One area that has not yet been empirically explored, however, is the effect of antisemitism on contemporary Jewish children. There are historical accounts and memoirs written by Jewish adults, including Holocaust survivors, that describe Jewish childhoods deeply damaged by antisemitism. However, there are no studies that use social science research methods to document and analyze the experience of contemporary Jewish children. This is a significant lacuna, given that antisemitism is (and has been for the past two decades) on the rise around the world (B'nai Brith 2010; Penslar, Marrus, and Stein 2005). This includes Canada, which has a long history of antisemitism (Abella and Troper 2000; Brym, Shaffir, and Weinfeld 1993; Davies 1992; Penslar et al. 2005; Tulchinsky 2008). In 2008, a national survey (Statistics Canada 2010) found that about two-thirds of the religiously-motivated hate crimes in Canada were committed against "the Jewish faith," that Judaism was the most commonly targeted religion, and that in 2008 the number of such crimes (165) represented an increase of 42% over the previous year. Children are not immune to the violence that surrounds them, including ethnically-related violence (Cummings et al.

---

* PhD. Associate Scholar, Centre for Women's Studies in Education, Ontario Institute for Studies in Education, University of Toronto. I wish to acknowledge with gratitude:
– the Social Sciences and Humanities Research Council of Canada for its financial support of this research;
– Paula Bourne, former Director of the Centre for Women's Studies in Education, Ontario Institute for Studies in Education, University of Toronto, for giving this project a home;
– Natalya Timoshkina, for her capable assistance with this research; and, last but not least,
– the remarkable, delightful, and fascinating girls who took part in this research, and their parents for making this possible.

2010; Maschi et al. 2010; Pachter et al. 2010), even when their parents try to protect them. It is crucial, then, to try and understand the impact of contemporary antisemitism on Jewish children, both to address this gap in theoretical knowledge and to be able to help Jewish children who are nowadays being confronted with the reality of antisemitism.

II. BACKGROUND

This research grew out of a previous project conducted by this researcher: a national study of Canadian Jewish women and their experiences of antisemitism and sexism (Gold 2004, 1998, 1997). This study, which involved focus groups in Phase One and a random sample of Jewish women from across Canada in Phase Two, demonstrated clearly the extent of the antisemitism and sexism that Canadian Jewish women encounter in their everyday lives. It also showed the different mental health implications of these two kinds of oppression: the women in this study who reported having had many antisemitic experiences in the past had significantly higher scores on the Beck Depression Inventory than the other women in the sample. However, no such relationship was found between sexism and depression (Gold 2004). Another intriguing finding from this study was that, when the women in this study were asked where their encounters with antisemitism had taken place, the second most frequent response was "at school." Given that some of these respondents were as young as eighteen, this led this researcher to wonder whether present-day public schools were sites of antisemitic encounters for Canadian Jewish girls. Consultations with colleagues involved in anti-oppression work at several Canadian school boards revealed that antisemitism was definitely a problem in at least some of the schools (e.g., Russell et al. 1993). However, a search of the literature turned up no research at all on contemporary Jewish girls' (or boys') experiences of antisemitism. This project was therefore initiated to explore this issue.

In terms of conceptual framework, this research, like the Jewish women's study, is grounded in Jewish feminist scholarship (e.g., Beck 1995; Cantor 1995; Elior 2004; Goldstein 2009; Hyman and Ofer 2006; Nadell and Sarna 2001; *Nashim* 1998-present; Pinsky 2010; Prell 2007; Siegel, Cole, and Steinberg-Oren 2000). Jewish feminist scholarship focuses on the complex ways that the lives of Jewish women and girls are shaped by the "dual oppression" of antisemitism and sexism. This Jewish feminist work is, in turn, part of the broader feminist literature on dual oppression, which analyzes the double vulnerability of being both female and part of any diverse ethnic or cultural group (i.e., sexism + racism), as well as the additional vulnerabilities (multiple oppressions) women can experience related to classism, ageism, ableism, and/or heterosexism (Crenshaw and Morgan 2003; Szymanski and Stewart 2010; Williams 2004). Since this study of Canadian Jewish girls was originally conceptualized as paralleling the Jewish women's study (i.e., studying sexism + antisemitism), only girls were included. It became clear, however, in the course of this study, that these girls, at ages ten and eleven, were not interested in discussing sexism and had little to say about it. In contrast, they were quite preoccupied with antisemitism and wanted to comment on this at length. Hence this research project became focused almost exclusively on antisemitism.

III. Method

A. Objectives and design

The overall objective of this study was to qualitatively explore the antisemitic experiences of a sample of Canadian Jewish girls, as well as the emotional or psychological impact on them of these experiences, and whether this was related to any characteristics of their families or their schools. There was also interest in examining how these girls' experiences or understanding of antisemitism changed over a three-year period, as these girls matured cognitively, emotionally, morally, and socially. In order to explore these questions, this researcher made use of qualitative methodology, since this is most appropriate for exploratory studies in areas not previously investigated (Grinnell and Unrau 2005; Merriam 2009). The research design used was a longitudinal one, which is ideal for tracking developmental changes over time (Statistics Canada 2008).

B. Sampling

The girls selected for this study were ten years old at the beginning of this research and were located through advertisements in newspapers (one Jewish and one non-Jewish, so as to reach participants with varying degrees of affiliation with the Jewish community). They were also located through more informal methods, such as putting up signs at schools and community centers, ads in synagogue bulletins, and word-of-mouth. Because this researcher found in her previous project that Canadian Jewish women's experiences of antisemitism and/or sexism were significantly related both to their socioeconomic backgrounds and the amount and kind of Jewish education they had received, half the participants in the girls' study (eight out of the initial sixteen) were drawn from Jewish day schools and eight were from public schools,[1] and the sample as a whole reflected socioeconomic diversity. With reference to geographical location, no differences were found in the Jewish women's study in the incidence of antisemitism by region of the country or by province, therefore all the participants in this study were selected from the same city, Toronto. In terms of attrition, one girl left the study after the first year, and one left after the second, so in the third year of this research, there were fourteen girls taking part. See Table 1 for a summary of some of the demographic characteristics of these girls and their families.

C. Procedure, measures, data analysis

Participants for this research were recruited as described above and contacted by phone by this researcher, who explained the study to the girls and their parents and set up appointments for interviews. The interviews, held once per year for three years, and lasting about one hour each, took place with the informed consent of both

---

[1] The Jewish schools in this study, it should be noted, included schools affiliated with three different streams of Judaism: Orthodox, Reform, and Conservative, and the public schools were not all typical public schools, even though funded by public monies. For example, one girl attended a French immersion public school which also taught mandatory Mandarin, another girl went to a prestigious, publicly-funded performing arts school, and a third attended a very small alternative school situated within a regular public school.

the girls and their parents. At the first interview only, the parents filled out a brief questionnaire that included information about the family's income, the parents' occupations, and the girl's developmental and academic history. For all three years, in the first part of each interview, each girl also filled out the Child Attribution Style Questionnaire (CASQ) (Shatte et al. 1999), which measures children's well-being and takes about ten minutes to complete. Following the completion of the CASQ, each girl was shown a poster with seven topics on it, and was asked to talk about these topics in any order she chose. These topics were: friends, family, holidays, hobbies, school, being Jewish, and being a girl. An eighth topic, the *bat mitzvah*, was added in the second and third years of the study, as at age eleven and twelve these girls were all planning or having some sort of *bat mitzvah* celebration. These eight topics were selected so as to learn as much as possible about these girls' everyday lives, which was essential to understanding the meaning and impact of the antisemitic events they experienced, since this was the context in which they occurred.

The girls in this study were not asked explicitly about antisemitism, because this is not a word that most ten to twelve-year-olds know. Instead, the girls were asked: how do you feel about being Jewish? What are some of the good things about it (if any)? What are some of the bad things about it (if any)? Has anything good or bad ever happened to you because you are Jewish? If so, what was it? And how did you feel and react at the time? If a girl mentioned an incident that seemed to her clearly antisemitic, she was asked why she thought that had happened, or why she thought things like that happen in the world. Toward the end of each interview, the girls were also asked: "If 10 is a perfect life, and 0 is a terrible life, what number would you give your life right now?" Then they were asked why they had given this numerical rating to their lives. (This question was developed in the course of the Year 1 interviews, so during that year this question was asked of only twelve out of the sixteen girls.) In addition to the individual interviews, most of the girls also participated in focus groups that occurred once per year on two out of the three years (each year there were two groups of about eight each). At these focus groups, which took place after the last of that year's individual interviews, the girls discussed the same seven or eight topics they had already discussed individually.

At the end of the three years of this study, the data from the interviews and focus groups was analyzed qualitatively, using thematic content analysis on the girls' responses to the above questions, examining the data separately for each of the three years. The girls' comments about antisemitism were analyzed with reference to the numerical ratings they gave their lives, their scores on the CASQ, the type of school they attended (public or Jewish), and the kind of Judaism with which their family identified. All of the individual interviews and focus groups were also filmed, and out of this footage, this researcher made a 13-minute documentary film, entitled "Jewish Girl Power." This film may be viewed at http://www.noragold.com.

IV. RESULTS

A. *Positive and negative aspects of being Jewish (excluding antisemitism)*

In order to put into context these girls' experiences of antisemitism, it is important to note that all of the girls, throughout the three years of this study, felt that being Jewish was overall a positive experience. They all liked the Jewish holidays (the family get-togethers, the special foods, and the presents), some of them liked going to synagogue or "believing in God," and others enjoyed learning Jewish history or Jewish languages (one girl said that having Hebrew was like having "a secret language"). Several girls felt that being Jewish was "important" to them, and that it made them feel proud. A few girls said also that they liked being Jewish because they liked "being different." Finally, a girl in Year 1 of the study, when she was ten, indicated that she liked Judaism because of monotheism (although she did not yet know this word):

> I like being Jewish because you know that there's only one person out there who controls you, you don't have to worry about praising everything ... like a god for every single thing... There's only one and I know I only have to trust one.

In terms of the negative aspects of being Jewish (other than antisemitism), participants identified four main categories:

1. Jewish dietary restrictions: having to keep kosher, fast on fast days, eat special foods on Passover, etc. (One girl admitted to "cheating," i.e., eating non-kosher food when outside her home.)
2. Other religious prohibitions: not travelling on major Jewish holidays (and therefore having to miss field trips from public school) or not being allowed to pierce one's bellybutton (because Judaism prohibits body piercing).
3. Feeling singled out because of being the only Jew, or one of the only Jews, in one's class or school.
4. Attending Hebrew school or synagogue, which are "boring."

Items #1 and 2 were issues only for the religiously traditional girls in the study, #3 pertained only to girls attending public schools, and #4 (being bored at synagogue or Hebrew school) was shared by girls from all types of schools and religious backgrounds.

B. Experiences of antisemitism

The experiences of antisemitism that the girls in this study identified can be divided into two groups: direct ones (incidents experienced personally by the girls themselves) and indirect ones (incidents occurring to these girls' relatives, friends, and acquaintances, or in the larger environment surrounding the girls).

1. Direct Experiences

In terms of direct experiences, there were two direct incidents described by these girls in each of the first two years of this study, and one incident in the third year, that these girls felt were antisemitic. All five of these incidents took place in public schools.

In Year 1 (at age 10), a girl heard a group of her classmates saying that there was a book about Hitler they had heard of and wanted to read, because Hitler was "cool." In the second incident, a girl's music teacher decided to teach the class a Jewish song for Chanukah, but an Iranian girl told the class, "I'm not allowed to do a Jewish song because Jews are my enemy."

In Year 2 (at age 11), one girl heard a boy in her class tell the rest of the class (referring to her), "I don't like her because she's Jewish." Another girl heard "offensive comments" at her school about Jews.

In Year 3 (at age 12), a girl was sitting next to a classmate who drew a swastika on his hand and showed it to her, clearly intending to upset or offend her.

2. Indirect Experiences

Regarding indirect incidents, girls in all three years reported events that they had heard about and experienced second-hand from relatives, friends, or acquaintances. They also had indirect experiences of antisemitism from the larger environment, but this sort of indirect experience was a major factor for these girls only in Year 1 of this research. During that year, there were three very dramatic antisemitic attacks in Toronto all in one weekend in March. Within three days, the windows of a synagogue were smashed, tombstones at a Jewish cemetery were destroyed, and half a street in a Jewish neighborhood had its front doors spray-painted with swastikas. The girls in this study were very affected by these events, and in the nine interviews which took place after that weekend, all of the girls brought up at least one of these incidents. Some of them also mentioned with concern the additional fallout from that weekend, for example seeing antisemitic graffiti on the outer walls of their (Jewish) schools and having to have guards posted there at the entrance doors. Two girls were very upset about the cemetery desecrations, because their grandparents were buried at the cemetery that was vandalized (two of the grandparents were "in the front row"), but fortunately none of their tombstones were broken. Two other girls knew people living on the street where the swastikas had been spray-painted on the doors (in one case it was a cousin, and in the other a school friend). The second girl, too young to be certain about the word swastika, said that her friend's house had been "Suzuki'ed." Another girl alluded to the high-profile murder two years before of an Orthodox Jewish man by a skinhead on one of the main streets of the Jewish neighborhood, and said that she was a little scared of what was happening now in Toronto. A fourth girl said she was worried about "the pushing down of the Jew."

In contrast to Year 1, in Year 2 of this study there were no such dramatic antisemitic events in Toronto, and none of the girls mentioned incidents of antisemitic vandalism in their interviews. However, two girls still did describe disturbing indirect events. In one, a girl was told an anecdote by her Hebrew school teacher. This teacher's father's car had broken down and he had to call a towing company. The man with the tow truck arrived and asked him if he wanted to stop somewhere on the way for a coffee, and the teacher's father declined, saying he wanted to just get his car fixed as soon as possible. Soon afterwards the tow truck driver's cell phone rang, and he said to his daughter, "I'm with this guy, and I asked if he wanted to stop at a coffee shop, but the Jew wouldn't buy me a coffee."

In the second Year 2 incident, a girl had a classmate, an Orthodox boy (who therefore wore a skullcap), and one day he was riding on a bus, and a woman who was sitting down kept kicking him. He said to her, "Excuse me, you're kicking me. Can you please stop?" But she did not say anything and kept on kicking him. Then the bus got to her stop, she stood up and was trying to get through the dense crowd to get off, and she gave this boy a push, and said to him, "Move away, Jew boy!"

In Year 3, also a year without unusually dramatic antisemitic events, eight girls described indirect incidents. One girl had a Hebrew school teacher who worked part-time in a synagogue. One day, this teacher answered the phone there, and it was an antisemitic hate call. A woman started screaming obscenities at her into the phone, shouting among other things, "You Jews are the fault of every death in the world." Another girl said she knew people who had been insulted that year or made fun of because they were Jewish, for instance being called a "dirty Jew." A third girl was told a joke by a Jewish boy who had had it told to him: "What's the difference between a Jew and a pizza? Pizzas don't cry in the oven."

In Year 3, some of the girls also spoke about antisemitism in the larger environment. This is consistent with the developmental changes these girls were undergoing at age 12, especially since many of them were switching that year from elementary school to middle school and were becoming more aware of, and interested in, the world around them. In Year 3, two girls brought up the antisemitic vandalism in Toronto two years before, one of them having seen a story about it on the news. Two other girls either read in the newspaper or heard from someone else about the Jews in Iran being forced to wear an identifying symbol on their clothing, "like a Jewish star." Another girl referred to how dangerous it was to be a Jew in Afghanistan nowadays, because that country is "strongly antisemitic."

C. Antisemitism, the Holocaust, and Israel

In these interviews, there were two particular themes that emerged from the girls' comments about antisemitism, and these were the Holocaust and Israel. In these girls' minds, there were clearly strong connections between antisemitism and the Holocaust, antisemitism and Israel, and the Holocaust and Israel. This was all the more striking given that in this study they were never asked about either the Holocaust or Israel; these were associations they spontaneously made themselves. This also happened more frequently as the girls grew older. In Years 1 and 2, one-third of the girls related antisemitism to the Holocaust, but in Year 3 more than half of them did this (eight out of fourteen, or 57%). Similarly, regarding Israel, in Years 1 and 2 about one-third of the girls related antisemitism to Israel, but in Year 3 this nearly doubled, with almost two-thirds of the girls making this connection (nine out of fourteen, or 64%).

1. Antisemitism and the Holocaust

Regarding the Holocaust, one girl in Year 1, after talking about the antisemitic vandalism in Toronto, said, "It's like the Holocaust again," and two other girls expressed the same idea. One of these girls went on to say that the Holocaust scares her, "because I can't believe they did that and stuff, and like I could never survive and stuff."

In Year 2, the girl who described the incident with the tow truck driver, after saying "The Jew wouldn't buy me a coffee," continued:

> Which is, sad. I was, like, sad that someone would say something like that, especially, like, after the Holocaust and, like, stuff. And also, that guy on, like, the internet denied the Holocaust. I don't know who he is, but I heard on the radio. Well, it [the incident with the tow truck] is not as bad as that, except it's still, like, that's how it all started, you know. Well, like, with people excluding Jews, or, like, saying bad things about them one by one. And then it got bigger and bigger. And then the concentration camps.

Similarly, in Year 3, the girl who related the story about the antisemitic phone call at the synagogue then began talking about an antisemitic incident that had happened not long before in France, and then she spoke about the Holocaust:

> Wow, there's people in my area doing this. That's pretty scary. Like, if this were to ever happen again, which it could. Like, did you hear about the thing in France with the guy who got tortured? Like, these things are still happening, and if, if it comes back again I don't know if we're going to able to, like, deal with it any more. So many of us are lost… Like, to think—six million. You just… Like, how could this many people be lost?

Some of these girls seem to have been encouraged to think about the Holocaust by being given books to read about it by their teachers or parents. In Year 1 of this study, only one girl mentioned reading a Holocaust book, but in Years 2 and 3 about one-third of them referred to books they were reading about the Holocaust (usually for school, but not always). In addition, in Years 2 and 3, the girls alluded to other types of Holocaust-related educational experiences they had been exposed to: one saw a movie about it, another saw a play, and one was taken to visit a Holocaust museum. These girls were very affected by these experiences. They also seemed, as a result of them, to identify strongly with what happened to Jews during the Holocaust, and in some cases to identify especially with the Jewish children in that period. For example, one girl in Year 3 spoke about pictures she saw at a Holocaust museum, including photographs of Nazis making people remove their clothes.

> If they didn't strip they'd be killed. Or they, like, they tested with little boys, like five-year-old boys, to see how long they can go without food. And then… And it's just disgusting, like, what they did. And, like, to know all these people were Jewish and they were, like, kids like me.

Because of this identification, light-hearted comments these girls sometimes heard about the Holocaust (e.g., about Hitler being cool or the joke about the pizza) were very painful to them.

In all three years, there were some girls in this study who thought that the Holocaust could never happen again. However, others felt that it definitely could, because "some people don't even believe it happened," and even among those who do, many "haven't really learned the lesson from it."

2. Antisemitism and Israel

In terms of the connection between antisemitism and Israel, Israel was very much on the minds of the girls in this study. As with the Holocaust, they repeatedly brought up the subject of Israel unsolicited. In all three years, they recognized that the conflict in Israel was a political problem, and a complex one, and different girls in this study had different political opinions (most likely reflecting their parents'). Basically, though, the girls all saw what was happening in Israel as a Jewish issue and as related to antisemitism. For instance, one girl in Year 1 said that Israel keeps getting bombed "because that's the Jewish homeland." Another one offered, as an example of antisemitism, that "A lot of people are having wars with the Jewish people… Like in Israel." Many of the girls in this study were worried about the terrorist attacks in Israel. One girl had a friend who had been quite close to a bomb that exploded there. Two other girls heard of bombs going off in places in Tel Aviv where they themselves had been visiting a week or two before. Most of the girls felt some attachment to Israel, and six of them also had close relatives, including siblings, living there. Several girls had visited Israel, some numerous times, and one girl in Year 2 was going to sleepover camp there that summer, and another girl was planning to celebrate her *bat mitzvah* there. Because of all these personal, cultural, historical, and religious connections, any attack on Israel (physical or ideological) was experienced by these girls as attacks on them as Jews, and therefore as antisemitic events. For example, in Year 2, one girl's sister, who was a university student, came home very upset because there had been an anti-Israel rally on her campus, which to this girl and her whole family was an antisemitic demonstration. Similarly, in Year 3, another girl heard from a friend of hers that one day she was strolling through a mall with another friend, and this friend was wearing a shirt with the insignia of the Israeli army on the front. Someone walking by them made a sour face and a rude gesture toward her friend's shirt, as if to say, "Yuck, disgusting." The girl in the study who heard this story was very distressed by it, and said that although she, too, has the same Israeli shirt, after this incident, she will no longer wear it when she goes to the mall, "just in case...."

In Year 3, at age 12, two girls in this study commenting on the political situation in Israel were clearly trying to view it with some objectivity and were obviously struggling with the competing claims of Jews and Palestinians for the land. For example, one girl said about the Palestinians:

> ... In their Bible they kind of think that we're on their land. Like that it's their land, given to them by their people. Which it also says in ours. They can't both be true... We think ours is right, but obviously from their point of view... they must think that theirs is right... Like, we think they're evil cause they want to steal our land from us, but they probably think that we're evil cause we have their land and we won't give it back.

Two other girls in Year 3 commented on the role played by the Canadian media in influencing the way many Canadians regard Israel. For instance, one said,

> You don't really hear about the good stuff that happens there. You only hear about the bad.

In general, the girls in this study were quite disturbed by the lack of peace in Israel. One girl in Year 1, after talking about a terrorist attack, said,

> Everything that's happening in Israel right now makes me really sad that so many people are dying and getting injured with, well, not really a reason—well, not a good reason... Because it's just not right for someone to do such a thing and people shouldn't like even think about doing stuff like that. And what my question would be is: Why were weapons invented? Like, why were guns and bombs and stuff invented in the first place? Because right now they're not coming to any good use....

This view was also echoed by several other girls over the three years of this study. And in Year 2, two girls out of fifteen gave their lives lower ratings (an 8 instead of a 9, and a 7.5-8 instead of a 9) because of the lack of peace in Israel.

3. The Holocaust and Israel

With reference to the connection between the Holocaust and Israel—and implicitly the three-way connection between antisemitism, the Holocaust, and Israel—with some of the girls it was very noticeable how they switched quite seamlessly back and forth between these topics. For example, one girl in Year 1, talking about the Holocaust, said, "I don't think [the Holocaust] would happen now—except in Israel," and then went on to talk about the bombs going off there. Another girl in Year 1 said she worries about antisemitism and what is happening to Jews around the world, because "like in Israel how there's like, when, like there's so much bombings and stuff... Well, the Holocaust is obviously worse, but this is still really bad."

A third girl referred to a Holocaust book she had read where the girl in the story had had her parents taken away, and people around her were getting shot. The girl in this study then said,

> And sometimes you hear on the news just like people who've done bad stuff to Israel, like if they want the land of Israel, they'll just go to war because they want the land, and then people just ... and then people ... like, they just war, and then people die.

Another way in which the Holocaust and Israel were connected conceptually for some of these girls was through the idea of historical antisemitism and the way Jews have often been unjustly blamed by the countries in which they have lived. One girl in Year 2 said she saw Israel as getting all the blame for the problems in that region, and then she continued:

> That's how World War II started. 'Cause Hitler, um, convinced Germany that, like, everything that's a problem, that's wrong with the world is because of the Jews. Like, the Russian president, or something like that, like, he told his country, like, he was, like, really bad. Like, he took advantage. Like, he always took the money and everything and when they would complain, he goes, 'It's all the Jews fault. Everything that's bad is the Jews.'

The associations in these girls' minds between antisemitism, Israel, and the Holocaust were very striking, and the implications of this will be discussed later in this paper.

D. *The Emotional and psychological impact of antisemitism on these girls*

The direct and indirect antisemitic incidents described above had both emotional and psychological effects on the girls in this study. In all three years, when the girls were recounting their antisemitic experiences, they also expressed feelings of fear and anxiety, and although most of them thought it unlikely that anything bad would happen to them in Canada because they were Jewish, some felt otherwise. In Year 1, for example, one girl said she could see something bad happening to her in Canada because she was Jewish. Another girl that year said that, as a result of recent antisemitic events in Canada, she is now sometimes a little afraid of people who are not Jewish. A third girl, the one who had the incident with the Iranian girl, said she was "sometimes really happy, but sometimes really sad" that she is Jewish.

In Year 2, after telling the story about the boy being kicked on the bus, this girl said that she was glad that, unlike Orthodox Jewish boys with their skullcaps, she is not identifiable as a Jew when she goes out in public. She thinks she is safer that way. That same year, another girl, talking about her (public) school, said: "I don't point out that I'm, like, a Jewish person. If somebody doesn't ask me I'm not going to go … tell everybody I'm Jewish… I don't fully make myself a contact." In Year 3, one girl, when talking about her (public) school, said, "Sometimes I'm scared to tell people there my religion cause, like, you never know, like, there could be people in the world who, like, are antisemitic."

Two other psychological effects were noted as well. One girl in Year 1 showed some evidence of internalized antisemitism. "I wonder," she said, "if I wasn't Jewish, would I make fun of Jewish people? I just wonder that." And in Year 2, several weeks after her *bat mitzvah* (which was a very positive experience for her), a girl spoke about the possibility of converting to Christianity because of the dangers of antisemitism:

> Sometimes I feel like I want to be Christian, because I always hear about, like, this stuff about, like, people killing Jews because they're Jewish… I usually hear about it in Israel, but sometimes … like, near me, like in Toronto. Like, I think once I heard about this guy, he shot someone cause he saw that he was Jewish or something. And so he shot him.

The following year, this girl repeated this idea, saying that she could see herself converting at some point in the future, but not at the moment. When asked what sort of thing in the future might persuade her to convert, this girl answered:

> Well, I know that there's been, like, some shootings or, like, in Toronto, just because people are Jewish or, like, they've, like, graffiti on some houses. That wouldn't make me convert, but it would make me, persuade me a little bit maybe. Just like, safety.

In terms of the overall emotional or psychological well-being of the girls in this study, no relationships were found between their CASQ scores, the antisemitic experiences they related, the types of schools they attended, or their families' religious affiliations. However, there was a relationship between these girls' experiences of antisemitism and the ratings they gave their lives, though only for Year 1. (In Year 3, there was no such relationship, and in Year 2 this relationship showed itself with only two girls out of the fifteen, the ones who lowered their life ratings because of the lack of peace in Israel.) In Year 1, however, out of the twelve girls who were asked to give their lives a rating, five of them rated their lives lower than they would have otherwise because of antisemitism. This appears to be related to the weekend of antisemitic vandalism in March of that year, because all five of these girls had interviews that fell after that weekend, rather than before. These five girls came from both kinds of schools and all religious backgrounds and constituted 55% (five out of nine) of the girls interviewed after that particular weekend. When asked the reason for her lowered rating, one girl, who had given her life an 8 instead of a 10, said, "Because I'm really happy with everything that's happening [to me], but people for our culture, things aren't so good." Someone else who lowered her score said: "Because of what goes on to people who are Jewish." The fact that five out of twelve ten-year-old girls in Year 1 (41%) rated the quality of their lives lower because of antisemitism strikes this researcher as disturbing.

E. These girls' conceptualizations of antisemitism

Given the well-established relationship between cognitive and emotional processes (Oatley 2004), it is important to understand how these girls not only felt about antisemitism but also how they thought about it. All the girls in this study who described antisemitic incidents were asked why they thought that that incident had occurred, or why things like that happen in the world. Below are some of their answers, according to each year of this study.

Year 1:

> People think that they [the Jews] are lesser people. That we're lesser people.

> Because they have to blame their problems on someone, so they decided on Jews.

> Because being Jewish ... there's always going to be hatred towards you.

> People are making out that being Jewish is something like that's a bad thing, but there's nothing bad ... it's just a different ... just believing different things.

> Because they hate Jews... But I don't know why they hate us—I don't think we did anything bad to hurt them.

> I don't get why people would ever do that just because of a religion. Like, I don't think we're bad or mean or anything like that.

In Year 2:

> There always is going to be [antisemitism], 'cause some people just feel that way. Like some people feel that we should not be here... They don't like us. They're followers of Hitler.

> I think they have their own problems and sometimes it's just them, like they may be sick. But sometimes it might be just, like, people who dislike Jews because of their own reasons. And I don't know what those are.

One girl in Year 2 expressed some self-doubt because of antisemitism, and perhaps some self-blame. She said that when an antisemitic incident happens, she asks herself, "Is there something wrong with us?" This researcher asked her if she believes there is. Her answer was equivocal:

> I'm not really to say because I haven't learned all the history of our past, of our present. I'm not fully in contact about what's happening in Israel, what's going on everywhere. If we've done something to those people. So I don't think I can really, like, fully answer that question.

In Year 3, the conceptualizations of antisemitism reflected these girls' increased intellectual maturity, for example in the idea of stereotypes:

> Well, sometimes they [antisemites] have their own personal problems. I don't know what their problems would be, but, pretty much all, all in all they stereotype. They think that all Jews are bad and it's like one Jewish person was mean to them. Like they usually just stereotype one bad person.

People just don't like other people to be different or they just, they stereotype and they think that, let's say, all the Jewish people are mean, or are rich, or, as I've heard, have big noses.

F. Antisemitism and other forms of oppression

In Year 3, these girls' greater intellectual maturity and sophistication was also reflected in the understanding that antisemitism is one form of hatred among many others. In the first two years of this study, two girls each year showed evidence of this understanding, but by Year 3 this was manifested in almost half the girls (6/14). This ability to see the link between antisemitism and other kinds of oppression reflected increased maturity, not only intellectually, but also in terms of these girls' moral development.

In Year 1, the two girls who connected antisemitism with racism attended the same (Orthodox Jewish) school, and there they had been shown a puppet show about Black and Hispanic children getting stereotyped. One of the girls said that in that show, "a white person told a Black person that they were, like, lesser because they were Black. It's so stupid, because it's just a pigment." Then she drew a parallel between racism and ageism: "I don't think anyone ... [should be] less treated. Well, I think that kids are less treated than adults."

In Year 2, one girl connected the historical struggles of the Jews with the struggle of Black people for their freedom, and said it makes her angry whenever people — any people — "aren't treated the same." Another girl in Year 2 talked about going with her class to see a performance by a group of people with disabilities and, in describing it, related ableism to antisemitism and racism.

In Year 3, one girl related antisemitism to racism, sexism, and homophobia:

> Discrimination ... makes me sad. Discrimination against Jewish people and against women, and against other people, like Chinese people and Black people and Native people... And the way the Nazis and some of the Germans treated the Jews was just terrible. And that makes me sad and it makes me angry that people can treat other people that way. It doesn't really matter who you are ... what you're backgrounds is. They're just people. I mean, they're, we're all people. We're all equal. I don't get how they could feel that they're higher than the gypsies and the Jews and the homosexuals.

Similarly, another girl in Year 3, speaking about the Holocaust, connected this to racism, homophobia, and ableism:

> It's not just the Jews that were affected. Like, a lot of other people were affected: Homosexuals are affected, gypsies are affected, people with special needs are affected.

At the broadest level, these girls were talking about hate. This came up explicitly in Year 3 in one of the focus groups, where a discussion took place among the girls about the hate in the world, and what they could do to fight it. One girl said that it is not possible to get rid of the hate in the world, because "even if there are just two people in a store, they will want the same item, and they'll start fighting, and sooner or later someone will say, 'I hate you.'" Another girl said that at school they were discussing *To Kill A Mockingbird,* and how good things could be "if everyone would just accept each other, and if there was not hate in the world." Someone else mentioned that at school they were reading *The Giver*, and in that book there is the idea of a pill that could make everyone love each other. In response, one girl said that to make the world perfect, someone would have to put a magic spell on everyone, "and then, everyone would become nice and no-one would hate anyone." Finally, one girl said, "We need more love in the world and less hate."

G. Similarities and differences by religious background and type of school

In this study, no differences at all were found between the girls from the various religious backgrounds. This is the case regarding the girls' antisemitic experiences, their life ratings, and their CASQ scores. This is very interesting, because there were very large differences in lifestyle and worldview between, for example, the girls from Orthodox and Reform backgrounds. However, the similarities between these girls obviously outweighed the differences.

With reference to the different types of schools attended, there were no differences between the girls on their indirect experiences of antisemitism, their CASQ scores, or their life ratings. However, it was only the girls from public schools, throughout the three years of this study, who had direct experiences of antisemitism. The girls from Jewish schools may have direct experiences of antisemitism later in life, but for the time being, from a developmental perspective, their type of school is a protective factor for them, since according to the literature, the younger one is when exposed to environmental stressors, the more vulnerable one is (Davies 2004; Webb 2006).

In terms of developmental similarities common to all the girls in this study (from both kinds of schools and from all religious backgrounds), at the beginning of this research when the girls were ten, their families acted as the main filter through which their information about, and understanding of, antisemitism was conveyed and interpreted. This parental centrality is typical for this age and developmental stage (Davies 2004). At age 11, these girls' Hebrew school teachers also began playing a role in shaping their ideas about antisemitism. By age 12, however, as these girls approached adolescence and their general awareness of the world around them increased, they were influenced as well on this topic by peers, acquaintances, current events, the media, and the internet.

Finally, one more similarity among all the girls in this study was that there was no relationship between their scores on the CASQ and the ratings they gave their own lives, or between the CASQ scores and their experiences of antisemitism. This latter point may be because the CASQ focuses on the general personality trait of optimism vs. pessimism (Shatte et al. 1999), whereas the question about life rating picked up on the girls' more transient feelings of the moment, and therefore may have been more sensitive to external events like antisemitic incidents.

V. Discussion

This research was initiated out of concern for the emotional and psychological well-being of Jewish girls in Canadian public schools, because a previous study suggested that antisemitism there may be putting them at risk. The findings of the current research indicate that to some extent this is the case. All five of the antisemitic